W9-BAW-167

THE ROUGH GUIDE TO

Croatia

There are more than one hundred and fifty Rough Guide titles
covering destinations from Amsterdam to Zimbabwe

Forthcoming titles include
Alaska • Copenhagen • Ibiza & Formentera • Iceland

Rough Guide Reference Series
Classical Music • Country Music • Drum 'n' bass • English Football
European Football • House • The Internet • Jazz • Music USA • Opera
Reggae • Rock Music • Techno • Unexplained Phenomena • World Music

Rough Guide Phrasebooks
Czech • Dutch • Egyptian Arabic • European Languages • French • German
Greek • Hindi & Urdu • Hungarian • Indonesian • Italian • Japanese
Mandarin Chinese • Mexican Spanish • Polish • Portuguese • Russian
Spanish • Swahili • Thai • Turkish • Vietnamese

Rough Guides on the Internet
www.roughguides.com

ROUGH GUIDE CREDITS

Text editor: Gavin Thomas

Series editor: Mark Ellingham

Editorial: Martin Dunford, Jonathan Buckley, Jo Mead, Kate Berens, Amanda Tomlin, Ann-Marie Shaw, Paul Gray, Helena Smith, Judith Bamber, Orla Duane, Olivia Eccleshall, Ruth Blackmore, Geoff Howard, Claire Saunders, Alexander Mark Rogers, Polly Thomas, Joe Staines, Lisa Nellis, Andrew Tomičić, Richard Lim, Duncan Clark, Peter Buckley, Sam Thorne (UK); Andrew Rosenberg, Mary Beth Maioli, Don Bapst, Stephen Timblin (US)

Production: Susanne Hillen, Andy Hilliard, Link Hall, Helen Ostick, Julia Bovis, Michelle Draycott, Katie Pringle, Robert Evers,

Mike Hancock, Robert McKinlay

Cartography: Melissa Baker, Maxine Repath, Nichola Goodliffe, Ed Wright

Picture research: Louise Boulton, Sharon Martins

Online: Kelly Cross, Anja Mutic-Blessing (US)

Finance: John Fisher, Gary Singh, Edward Downey, Mark Hall, Tim Bill

Marketing & Publicity: Richard Trillo, Niki Smith, David Wearn, Jemima Broadbridge (UK); Jean Marie Kelly, Simon Carloss, David Wechsler (US)

Administration: Tania Hummel, Demelza Dallow, Julie Sanderson

---

PUBLISHING INFORMATION

This first edition published November 2000 by Rough Guides Ltd, 62–70 Shorts Gardens, London WC2H 9AH.
Distributed by the Penguin Group:
Penguin Books Ltd, 27 Wrights Lane, London W8 5TZ
Penguin Putnam, Inc. 375 Hudson Street, NY 10014, USA
Penguin Books Australia Ltd, 487 Maroondah Highway, PO Box 257, Ringwood, Victoria 3134, Australia
Penguin Books Canada Ltd, 10 Alcorn Avenue, Toronto, Ontario, Canada M4V 1E4
Penguin Books (NZ) Ltd, 182–190 Wairau Road, Auckland 10, New Zealand
Typeset in Linotron Univers and Century Old Style to an original design by Andrew Oliver.
Printed in England by Clays Ltd, St Ives PLC
Illustrations in Part One and Part Three by Edward Briant.

Illustrations on p.1 & p.333 by Link Hall.
© Jonathan Bousfield, 2000.
No part of this book may be reproduced in any form without permission from the publisher except for the quotation of brief passages in reviews.
400pp – Includes index
A catalogue record for this book is available from the British Library
ISBN 1-85828-544-5

The publishers and authors have done their best to ensure the accuracy and currency of all the information in *The Rough Guide to Croatia*, however, they can accept no responsibility for any loss, injury, or inconvenience sustained by any traveller as a result of information or advice contained in the guide.

THE ROUGH GUIDE TO

Croatia

written and researched by

Jonathan Bousfield

ROUGH GUIDES

We set out to do something different when the first Rough Guide was published in 1982. Mark Ellingham, just out of university, was travelling in Greece. He brought along the popular guides of the day, but found they were all lacking in some way. They were either strong on ruins and museums but went on for pages without mentioning a beach or taverna. Or they were so conscious of the need to save money that they lost sight of Greece's cultural and historical significance. Also, none of the books told him anything about Greece's contemporary life – its politics, its culture, its people, and how they lived.

So with no job in prospect, Mark decided to write his own guidebook, one which aimed to provide practical information that was second to none, detailing the best beaches and the hottest clubs and restaurants, while also giving hard-hitting accounts of every sight, both famous and obscure, and providing up-to-the-minute information on contemporary culture. It was a guide that encouraged independent travellers to find the best of Greece, and was a great success, getting shortlisted for the Thomas Cook travel guide award, and encouraging Mark, along with three friends, to expand the series.

The Rough Guide list grew rapidly and the letters flooded in, indicating a much broader readership than had been anticipated, but one which uniformly appreciated the Rough Guide mix of practical detail and humour, irreverence and enthusiasm. Things haven't changed. The same four friends who began the series are still the caretakers of the Rough Guide mission today: to provide the most reliable, up-to-date and entertaining information to independent-minded travellers of all ages, on all budgets.

We now publish more than 150 titles and have offices in London and New York. The travel guides are written and researched by a dedicated team of more than 100 authors, based in Britain, Europe, the USA and Australia. We have also created a unique series of phrasebooks to accompany the travel series, along with an acclaimed series of music guides, and a best-selling pocket guide to the Internet and World Wide Web. We also publish comprehensive travel information on our web site:

www.roughguides.com

HELP US UPDATE

We've gone to a lot of effort to ensure that the first edition of *The Rough Guide to Croatia* is accurate and up-to-date. However, things change – places get "discovered", opening hours are notoriously fickle, restaurants and rooms raise prices or lower standards. If you feel we've got it wrong or left something out, we'd like to know, and if you can remember the address, the price, the time, the phone number, so much the better.

We'll credit all contributions, and send a copy of the next edition (or any other Rough Guide if you prefer) for the best letters. Please mark letters: "Rough Guide Croatia Update" and send to:

Rough Guides, 62–70 Shorts Gardens, London WC2H 9AH, or Rough Guides, 4th Floor, 345 Hudson St, New York, NY 10014.

Or send email to: mail@roughguides.co.uk
Online updates about this book can be found on Rough Guides' Web site at **www.roughguides.com**

THE AUTHOR

Jonathan Bousfield first took his bucket and spade to the Adriatic coast in 1975, and has been making regular visits to Croatia ever since. In between times he has been rock critic of the *European* newpaper, as well as being co-author of both the *Rough Guide to Bulgaria* and the *Rough Guide to Austria*. He is currently researching a new edition of the *Rough Guide to Poland*.

ACKNOWLEDGEMENTS

The author would like to thank Jasna Marić and Renata Janeković at the Croatian National Tourist Association, and the following people at Croatia's regional tourist associations: Nena Fuchs, Martina Grilec, Marin Matušić and Igor Prikaski in Zagreb, Lidija Vrečar in Zagreb County, Vinko Bakija in Brač, Nada Prodan-Mrazović in Buzet, Nivio Filipas in Cres, Mirjana Darrer in Dubrovnik, Tanja Miličić and Nikola Zaninović in Hvar, Danijela Fanjkutić in Istria County, Krešo Glavina and Andrija Pleština in Klis, Zoran Franičević in Komiža, Stanka Kraljević in Korčula, Radmila Paliska in Labin, Nataša Cibić in Lovran, Darko Kovačić in Omiš, Damir Macanić in Osijek, Krunoslav Bobić in Pašman, Radenko Sloković in Pazin, Marino Brečević and Vesna Jovičić in Pula, Anđelka Jurašin in Slunj, Zrdavko Banović in Split, Sara Salamunić in Split County, Vanja Dadić-Marotti in Šibenik, Željko Jerolimov in Ugljan, Elida Ravnić in Vodnjan, Gordana Perić in Zadar, and anyone whose names I may have forgotten.

Invaluable help was also provided by Lidija Bajuk, Ilko Čulić, Denis Derk, Davor Draganja, Srečko Favro, Jane Foster, Nikica Gilić, Vedran Gulin, Anica Holik, Dunja Knebl, Želimir Koščević, Dejan Kršić, Boris Leiner, Marcel Mars, Mojmir Novaković, Snježana Nožinić, Tamara Obrovac, Jurica Pavičić, Darko Pecotić, Toni Prug, Ivan Ramljak, Helena Sablić-Tomić, Stella Maris, Kornel Šeper, Damir Tiljak, Stjepan Većković, Zlatko Zlatunić, Pauline Clarke at the British Embassy in Zagreb, Goran Gugić in the Lonjsko Polje Nature Reserve, Nives Tomasović of the Centar za zaštitu kulturne baštine in Hvar, Grozdana Marošević and Anamarija Starčević-Štambuk at the Institute for Ethnology and Folklore in Zagreb, the staff of Sublink, and the staff of the National University Library in Zagreb.

Thanks are also due to Martin Dunford and Kate Berens for getting the project under way, Gavin Thomas for skilled and patient editing, Rob McKinlay for typesetting, Sharon Martins for pictures, Nichola Goodliffe for maps, Jennifer Speake for proofreading, Silke Kerwick for Oz Basics research and Anja Mutic-Blessing for North American Basics research and her many other valuable contributions.

CONTENTS

Introduction x

• CHAPTER 3: ISTRIA 127–156

• CHAPTER 4: THE KVARNER GULF 157–201

• CHAPTER 5: NORTHERN DALMATIA 202–238

• CHAPTER 6: SOUTHERN DALMATIA 239–304

• CHAPTER 7: DUBROVNIK AND THE SOUTH 305–332

PART THREE CONTEXTS 333

LIST OF MAPS

MAP SYMBOLS

▬▬▬	Motorway	🛡	Fortress
═══	Major road	♜	Castle
═══	Minor road	✡	Synagogue
- - - -	Footpath	✝	Church (regional maps)
⊞⊞⊞	Steps	⊠—⊠	Gates
)=====(	Tunnel	⊙	Statue
⌣	Bridge	ⓘ	Tourist information
▪▪▪▪▪	Wall	✉	Post office
━┿━	Railway	Ⓗ	Hospital
▪▪▪▪▪▪▪	Funicular	◉	Hotel
●- - - ●	Cable car	▣	Restaurant
— —	Ferry route	▮	Building
——	River	▢	Market
━ ━ ━	International boundary	⊞	Church/cathedral
—·—·—	Chapter boundary	◯	Stadium
⋏⋏	Mountain range	▨	Built-up area
▲	Mountain peak	▨	Park
⚸	Waterfall	▨	National Park
◠	Caves	▨	Beach
✈	Airport	⊡	Cemetery

INTRODUCTION

F ew countries in contemporary Europe have experienced the collapse of communism, a war of national survival and the securing of independence all within the space of half a decade – yet this is what happened to **Croatia** (Hrvatska) at the beginning of the 1990s. Much of this drama was acted out on TV screens across the world, and images of the conflict which followed the break-up of Yugoslavia still colour outside perceptions of what the country is like today. In the circumstances, it's making it all too easy to forget that Croatia was – and still is – among Europe's prime holiday destinations, boasting one of the most dramatic stretches of coastline that the continent has to offer, with almost 2000km of shoreline and over 1000 islands and although parts of the coast were damaged during the 1991–95 conflict – the period of wartime isolation has, paradoxically, made the region all the more alluring now – over-exploitation of the coast has been kept in check, and there are still enough sparsely populated islands, quiet coves and stone-built fishing villages to make you feel you're visiting one of the Mediterranean's most unspoilt areas.

The return of the tourists has been keenly awaited by the Croats, not least because they represent the country's major source of income. Visitors will be struck by the tangible sense of pride that independent statehood has brought, and the feeling of togetherness and unity that the experience of war has engendered. National culture is a far from one-dimensional affair, however, and much of Croatia's individuality is due to its geographical position straddling the point at which the sober Central European virtues of hard work and order collide with the spontaneity, vivacity and taste for the good things in life that characterizes the countries of southern Europe – a cultural blend of Mitteleuropa and Mediterranean which gives Croatia its particular flavour. Not only that, but the country also stands on one of the great faultlines of European civilization – the point at which the Catholic West meets the Orthodox and Islamic East – and though Croats traditionally see themselves as a Western people, distinct from the other South Slavs who formerly made up the state of Yugoslavia, many of the hallmarks of Balkan culture – patriarchal families, hospitality towards strangers, and a fondness for grilled food – are as common in Croatia as in any other part of southeastern Europe, suggesting that the country's relationship with its neighbours is more complex than many Croats themselves will admit.

National sensitivity about such matters has its roots in Croatia's troubled relationship with the Serbs, who arrived in southeastern Europe at around the same time. Historical circumstances later drove the two groups psychologically and culturally apart, even though they often continued to live together – the fact that so many areas of Croatia and Bosnia-Hercegovina were ethnically mixed is one reason why the break-up of Yugoslavia was such a tragically messy affair. Despite the events of recent years, however, the destinies of Croats and Serbs look set to remain intertwined: there's still a sizeable Serb minority within Croatia, and Serbs who fled the country in the wake of the Croatian army's campaigns in 1995 are (officially, at least) being encouraged to return.

Bringing life back to war-damaged areas and resettling both Croatian and Serbian refugees is just one of the problems faced by a country which continues to suffer many of the ills experienced by post-communist societies in general: the collapse of outdated industries, high unemployment, low wages for the majority, and the rise of a new entrepreneurial class which is often flamboyantly corrupt. Unlike many of her Eastern European neighbours, however, Croatia has been slow to receive aid and investment from the West, mainly thanks to the less-than-innocent role played in the conflict in Bosnia-Hercegovina by the ruling HDZ party of former President Franjo Tuđman, whose authoritarian right-wing rule left the country with increasingly few friends on the international stage as the 1990s progressed. Tuđman's death in December 1999 and the sweeping electoral defeat of the HDZ in January 2000 unleashed popular aspirations that the new EU-friendly, centre-left coalition government will find difficult to fulfil. Nevertheless, the country had passed an important test of political maturity, and entered the new millennium eager to make up for lost time. An optimistic, welcoming and, above all, safe destination for travellers, Croatia is yet to be overrun by vacationing hordes – which is why now is the ideal time to visit.

Where to go

Croatia's underrated capital **Zagreb** is a typical Central European metropolis, combining elegant nineteenth-century buildings with plenty of cultural diversions and a vibrant café life. It's also a good base for trips to the undulating hills and charming villages of the rural **Zagorje** and **Žumberak** regions to the north and west, and to the well-preserved Baroque town of **Varaždin** to the northeast.

The rest of **inland Croatia** provides plenty of opportunities for relaxed exploring. Stretching east from Zagreb, the plainlands of **Slavonia** form the agriculturally richest parts of Croatia, with seemingly endless corn and sunflower fields fanning out from handsome, Habsburg-era provincial towns such as **Osijek** and **Vukovar** – although the latter was almost totally destroyed in a notoriously bitter siege during the 1991–95 war and will take time to rebuild. Inland Croatia also offers numerous **hiking** opportunities: **Mount Medvednica**, just above Zagreb, or the **Samoborske gorice** just to the northwest of the capital are good for gentle rambling, while the mountains of the **Gorski kotar** between Zagreb and the sea offer more scope for strenuous hikes. Also lying between Zagreb and the coast, and easily visited from either, are the deservedly hyped **Plitvice Lakes**, an enchanting sequence of forest-fringed turquoise pools linked by miniature waterfalls.

Croatia's lengthy stretch of coastline, together with its islands, is big enough to swallow up any number of tourists. At the northern end, the peninsula of **Istria** contains many of the country's most developed resorts, along with old Venetian towns like **Poreč** and **Rovinj** rubbing shoulders with the raffish port of **Pula**, home to some impressive Roman remains. Inland Istria is characterized by sleepy hilltop villages, often dramatically situated, like **Motovun**, **Grožnjan**, **Roč** and **Hum** – each mixing medieval architecture with rustic tranquillity.

Immediately south of Istria, the island-scattered **Kvarner Gulf** is presided over by the city of **Rijeka**, a hard-edged industrial centre and the Adriatic's most important transport hub. Close by are a clutch of resorts that were chic high-

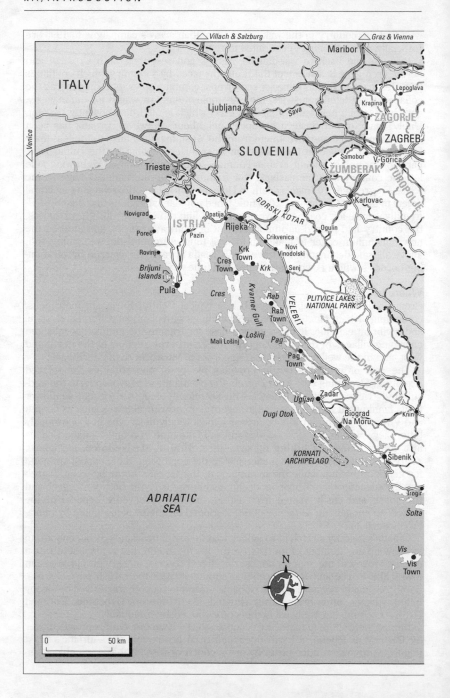

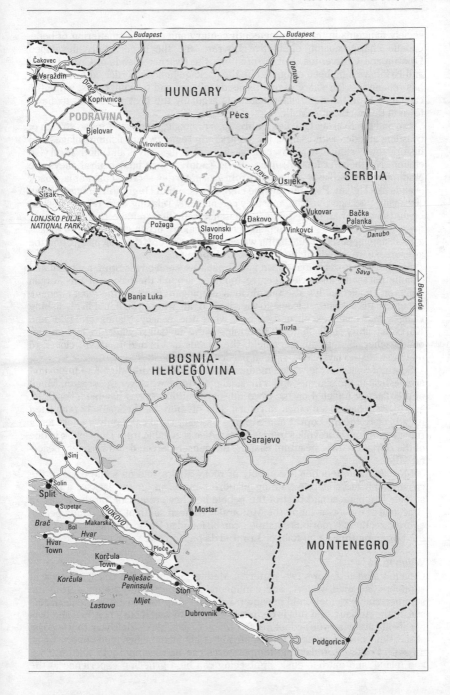

society hangouts in the late nineteenth century and retain a smattering of belle-époque charm: quaint, diminutive **Lovran**, and the larger, more developed **Opatija** and **Crikvenica**. Not far offshore, the Kvarner islands of **Cres**, **Lošinj** and **Krk** have long been colonized by the package-holiday hordes, although each has retained its fair share of quiet seaside villages and tranquil coves, while the capital of **Rab**, the next island south, is arguably the best-preserved medieval town in the northern Adriatic.

Beyond the Kvarner Gulf lies **Dalmatia**, a dramatic, mountain-fringed stretch of coastline studded with islands. It's a stark, arid region where fishing villages and historic towns cling to a narrow coastal strip rich in figs, olives and subtropical vegetation. Northern Dalmatia's main city is **Zadar**, whose busy central alleys are crammed with medieval churches. From Zadar, ferries serve a chain of laid-back islands like **Ugljan**, **Pašman** and the ruggedly beautiful **Dugi otok** – none of them see many package tourists, and they're enticingly relaxing as a result. Despite being the site of an unmissable Renaissance cathedral, middle Dalmatia's main town, **Šibenik**, is the least compelling of the region's urban centres, but it makes a good staging post en route to the waterfalls of the river **Krka**, just inland, and the awesome, bare islands of the **Kornati archipelago**.

Southern Dalmatia's main town and Croatia's second city is **Split**, a vibrant and chaotic port with an ancient centre moulded around the palace of the Roman emperor, Diocletian. It's also the obvious jumping-off point for the most enchanting of Croatia's islands. Closest to the city is **Brač**, where you'll find lively fishing villages and some excellent beaches, while the nearby islands of **Hvar** and **Korčula** feature smallish towns brimming with Venetian architecture and numerous beaches. Slightly further afield, the islands of **Vis** and **Lastovo**, closed to tourists until the late 1980s, remain particularly unspoilt.

South of Split lies the walled medieval city of **Dubrovnik**, site of an important arts festival in the summer and a magical place to be whatever the season. Much of the damage inflicted on the town during the 1991–95 war has been repaired, and tourists have been quick to return. Just offshore lie the sparsely populated islands of **Koločep**, **Lopud** and **Šipan** – oases of rural calm only a short ferry ride away from Dubrovnik's tourist bustle. Also reachable from Dubrovnik is one of the Adriatic's most beautiful islands, the densely forested and serenely peaceful **Mljet**.

Most Adriatic **beaches** are pebbly or rocky affairs, and on some parts of the coast man-made concrete bathing platforms make up for the lack of a proper strand. The biggest and best of the pebble beaches are at **Bol**, on the island of Brač, and at the towns lining the **Makarska Riviera** south of Split. Sandy beaches are rare, though glorious examples can be found at **Baška** on the island of Krk, the **Lopar peninsula** on Rab, or **Lumbarda** on Korčula.

When to go

Croatia's climate follows two patterns: Mediterranean on the coast, with warm summers and mild winters, and continental inland – slightly hotter during the summer, and extremely cold in winter. **July and August** constitute the peak season on the Adriatic, and this is definitely the time to visit if busy beaches and lively café-life are what you're looking for. Many Croats make their way to the coast at this time, and social and cultural life in the big inland cities tends to dry up as a result. Peak-season daytime temperatures can be roasting, both on the coast and inland, and dawn-to-dusk sightseeing can be a gruelling experience at the height of summer. Hotel accommodation soon fills up in the peak season, and it may be more relaxing to travel in **June and September**, when there is significantly less pressure on facilities. From October to May the coast can be very quiet indeed, and many hotels and tourist attractions may well shut up shop for the winter. **Autumn** is a good time to enjoy inland Istria, and national park areas like the Plitvice Lakes and the River Krka, when the woodland colours produced by the mixture of deciduous and evergreen trees are at their best. **Winters** are mild affairs on the Adriatic coast, and urban sightseeing in historic centres such as Zadar, Split and Dubrovnik can be enjoyable at any time of year. It's also worth bearing in mind that hotel prices on the Adriatic may be up to fifty percent cheaper in winter than they are in peak season. Winters in continental Croatia are a different kettle of fish entirely, with average daily temperatures dropping to around zero from December to February. Snow is common in inland areas over this period, and can be a picturesque backdrop to sightseeing, although transport in highland areas is frequently disrupted as a result.

CROATIA'S CLIMATE												
Average temperatures °F (°C)												
	Jan	**Feb**	**March**	**April**	**May**	**June**	**July**	**Aug**	**Sept**	**Oct**	**Nov**	**Dec**
Dubrovnik	8.3	9.1	11.2	13.9	17.8	22.2	25.6	25.0	22.3	17.8	12.9	10.2
Split	7.5	8.5	11.5	12.8	18.9	23.9	26.7	26.1	22.8	16.7	12.5	9.5
Zagreb	0	1.2	5.5	11	16	18.7	22.3	21.8	15.6	12.3	5.4	2.3

PART ONE

THE

BASICS

GETTING THERE FROM BRITAIN

Croatia is about 750 miles (1200km) from London, making the overland journey by train or car rewarding but time-consuming. Alternatively, there are frequent flights to Zagreb, and less regular services to other cities on the Adriatic coast.

FLIGHTS

It takes just over two hours to **fly direct** from London to Zagreb or Split, and about 2 hours 30 minutes to Dubrovnik. The only direct scheduled flights from the UK to Croatia are with British Airways (daily from London Gatwick to Zagreb), and Croatia Airlines (daily from London Heathrow to Zagreb; once weekly to Split). In addition, Croatia Airlines operate seasonal routes in the summer, with flights from London Gatwick to Dubrovnik (2 weekly April–Oct), London Gatwick to Split (2 weekly April–Oct) and Manchester to Dubrovnik (1 weekly April–Oct). Alternatively, you can fly to Zagreb and pick up connecting Croatia Airlines flights to Dubrovnik (2 daily), Split (2 daily), Pula (1 daily) and Zadar (1 daily).

The cheapest **fare** is an Apex return, valid for a maximum of three months, which must be booked at least two weeks in advance and include at least one Saturday night away. An Apex ticket from London to Zagreb costs around £200 in low season (Oct–April), rising to about £230–250 at peak times (mid-June to mid-Sept, plus Easter and New Year). Flights to Split and Dubrovnik – whether direct or changing at Zagreb – tend to work out £20–30 more expensive.

Discount flight agents (see box on p.4) sometimes sell seats on Croatia Airlines or British Airways for slightly less than the airlines themselves, and may have special deals on indirect flights with other carriers, such as Austrian Airlines or Swissair. **Under-26s** may get even better deals from youth and student travel firms such as USIT Campus or STA Travel (see box on p.4). The **Internet** is also an excellent source of cheap fares – www.cheapflights.co.uk and www.lastminute.co.uk are two of the largest sites – and it's also worth checking the **media** for special offers – try the Sunday papers and, in London, *Time Out* and the *Evening Standard*.

Most package-tour operators use scheduled flights to Croatia, so there are only rarely discounted tickets on **charter flights**. Cheap seats on planes from Manchester and London to Pula, Split and Dubrovnik do occasionally appear, when they'll be advertised in the press or in the windows of travel agents.

PACKAGE DEALS

The main advantage of **package holidays** is that hotel accommodation is much cheaper than if you arrange things independently, bringing mid-range hotels well within reach and making stays in even quite snazzy establishments a fraction of the price paid by walk-in guests. The season for Adriatic packages runs from May to late September; city breaks in Zagreb and Dubrovnik are available all the year round.

Low season (May & Sept) **prices** begin at about £300 for seven days, rising to £350–400 for two weeks. In high season (July & Aug) expect to pay from around £400 for a week, and from £550 for two weeks. The **resorts** most frequently offered by British companies are in Istria (Poreč and Rovinj), Dalmatia (Hvar, Korčula and Makarska) and Dubrovnik (either in Dubrovnik itself or in the Mlini-Cavtat area just to the south). Some of the hotels in Poreč and Dubrovnik are a bus ride away from their respective towns (check before you commit yourself to a particular holiday), but almost everywhere else your accommodation will be within walking distance of an attractive town or fishing port of some sort, while the frequency of public transport makes it easy to explore further.

AIRLINES, AGENTS AND TOUR OPERATORS

AIRLINES

British Airways ☎0345/222111, *www.british-airways.com*.

Croatia Airlines ☎020/8563 0022, *www.ctn.tel.hr/ctn*.

FLIGHT AGENTS

Flightbookers, 177–178 Tottenham Court Rd, London W1P 0LX (☎020/7757 2000). Low fares on an extensive offering of scheduled flights.

The London Flight Centre, 131 Earls Court Rd, London SW5 9RH (☎020/7244 6411). Long-established agent dealing in discount flights.

North South Travel, Moulsham Mill Centre, Parkway, Chelmsford, Essex CM2 7PX (☎01245/608291, fax 356612). Friendly, competitive travel agency, offering discounted fares worldwide – profits are used to support projects in the developing world, especially the promotion of sustainable tourism.

Scott's Tours, 159 Whitfield St, London W1P 5RY (☎020/7383 5353). Specialists in discount flights to Eastern Europe.

STA Travel (*www.statravel.co.uk*), 86 Old Brompton Rd, London SW7 3LH (☎020/7361 6161); 75 Deansgate, Manchester M3 2BW (☎0161/834 0668); 88 Vicar Lane, Leeds LS1 7JH (☎0113/244 9212); 78 Bold Street, Liverpool L1 4HR (☎0151/707 1123); 9 St Mary's Place, Newcastle-upon-Tyne NE1 7PG (☎0191/233 2111); 27 Forrest Road. Edinburgh (☎0131/226 7747); 184 Byres Rd, Glasgow G1 1JH (☎0141/338 6000); plus branches nationwide. Specialists in low-cost flights and tours for students and under-26s.

Trailfinders (*www.trailfinders.co.uk*), 215 Kensington High St, London W6 6BD (☎020/7937 5400); 58 Deansgate, Manchester M3 2FF (☎0161/839 6969); 254–284 Sauchiehall St, Glasgow G2 3EH (☎0141/353 2224); 22–24 The Priory Queensway, Birmingham B4 6BS (☎0121/236 1234); 48 Corn St, Bristol BS1 1HQ (☎0117/929 9000). One of the best-informed and most efficient agents for independent travellers.

The Travel Bug (*www.flynow.com*), 125 Gloucester Rd, London, SW7 4SF (☎020/7835 2000); 597 Cheetham Hill Rd, Manchester M8 5EJ (☎0161/721 4000). Large range of discounted tickets.

Travel Cuts, 295a Regent St, London W1R 7YA (☎020/7255 1944, *www.travelcuts.co.uk*). Specializes in budget, student and youth travel.

USIT Campus (national call centre ☎0870/240 1010, *www.usitcampus.co.uk*), 52 Grosvenor Gardens, London SW1W 0AG (☎020/7730 3402); 541 Bristol Rd, Selly Oak, Birmingham B29 6AU (☎0121/414 1848); 37–39 Queen's Rd, Clifton, Bristol BS8 1QE (☎0117/929 2494); 53 Forest Rd, Edinburgh EH1 2QP (☎0131/225 6111); 122 George St, Glasgow G1 1RF (☎0141/553 1818); 166 Deansgate, Manchester M3 3FE (☎0161/833 2046); plus branches nationwide. Student and youth travel specialists.

PACKAGE AND SPECIALIST TOUR OPERATORS

Balkan Holidays ☎020/7543 5555. Packages in Dubrovnik and on the Makarska Riviera. City breaks in Zagreb.

Bond Tours ☎020/8786 8511. Package operator specializing in the Dalmatian coast and islands,

with accommodation ranging from private rooms to smart hotels. City breaks in Zagreb.

Club Med ☎020/7581 1161, *www.clubmed.com*. Holiday village at Pakoštane in northern Dalmatia.

The widest range of resorts is offered by Croatia specialists like Holiday Options and Europa Skylines (see box above), who can put together customized flight-plus-accommodation deals. Almost all the travel companies connected with Croatia deal with Dubrovnik, so shop around. Europa Skylines, Bond Tours and Travelscene also offer **city breaks** to Zagreb all year round – a three-day break in Zagreb or Dubrovnik will cost

£300–£420 per person depending on which grade of hotel you choose.

A couple of operators (Leger and Skills Travel) run **coach holidays** to Croatia. These work out slightly cheaper than those involving flights, although only Istrian resorts are offered and the length of the journey can be a disadvantage – out of a nine-day holiday, you only get to spend seven nights in Croatia. Specialist operators like Dune

Dalmatian and Istrian Travel ☎020/8749 5255. Tailor-made package deals throughout Croatia, plus Jadrolinija ferry reservations.

Europa Skylines ☎020/7226 4460. Tailor-made packages using a wide choice of hotel and apartment accommodation along the Adriatic coast and to Zagreb and the Plitvice Lakes. Can also arrange fly drive deals and Adriatic cruises in motorsailers.

Holiday Options ☎01444/244499, www. holidayoptions.co.uk. Packages to a big range of destinations in Dalmatia and the islands – from the obvious (Dubrovnik) to the not so obvious (Orebić) – plus a choice of two-centre holidays, including Croatia-Slovenia combinations, and seven-day Dalmatian cruises in motorsailers.

Leger ☎01709/839039, www.leger.co.uk. Coach tours to Poreč.

Palmair ☎01202/200700. Packages to Dubrovnik, Cavtat and Korčula, and two-centre holidays combining Dubrovnik and Korčula. Direct flights from Bournemouth.

Saga ☎0800/300 500. Holidays for the older traveller in Dubrovnik and the Makarska Riviera.

Skills Travel ☎01623/421141. Coach tours to Poreč in Istria.

Solo's Holidays ☎020/8951 2000, www.solosholidays.co.uk. Singles packages in Dubrovnik and Opatija, and two centre holidays combining Opatija with a mountain resort in Slovenia.

Thomson ☎0990/502555, www.thomson -holidays.com. Packages in Rovinj and Poreč.

Travelscene ☎020/8427 4445, www. travelscene.co.uk. City breaks in Zagreb.

Travelsphere ☎01858/410818, www. travelsphere.co.uk. Packages to Rovinj.

NATURIST HOLIDAYS

Dune Leisure ☎0115/931 4110. Packages in the big Istrian resorts of Monsena (Rovinj), Koversada (Vrsar) and Solaris (Poreč).

Peng Travel ☎01708/471832. Packages in Istria.

Sunlovers Emsdale ☎01708/472715. Packages in Istria.

SAILING HOLIDAYS AND YACHT CHARTER

Activity Holidays ☎020/8232 9779. One-week sailing courses, one- and two-week flotilla sailing, and bareboat and skippered charter.

Cosmos Yachting ☎020/8547 3577, www.cosmosyachting.com. Individual yacht charter or skippered charter out of Zadar, Pula and Split.

Crestar Yachts ☎020/7730 9962. Luxury charter specialists with top-of-the-range crewed yachts and motor yachts.

Nautilus Yachting ☎01723/867445, www. nautilus-yachting.co.uk. Learn-to-sail packages based in Murter, plus bareboat yacht and motor-yacht charter.

Sailing Holidays ☎020/8459 8787. Two-week flotilla sailing holidays in mid-Dalmatia.

Setsail Holidays ☎01737/764443, www. setsail.co.uk. Yacht and motor-yacht charter out of Zadar, Primošten and Trogir; two-week flotilla sailing in Dalmatia.

Sunsail ☎023/9222 2222, www.sunsail.com. Yacht charter out of Pula and Rogoznica near Trogir; one- and two-week flotilla sailing in Dalmatia.

Templecraft Yacht Charters ☎01273/695094, www.templecraft.com. Individual yacht charter out of Pula, Zadar, Split and Dubrovnik.

Tenrag ☎01227/721874, www.tenrag.com. Yacht charter out of Pula, Zadar and Split.

Top Yacht Charter ☎0870/870 5262, www. top-yacht.com. Individual yacht charter out of Pula, Zadar and Split.

Leisure, Peng Travel and Sunlovers Emsdale offer **naturist holidays** in the self-contained mega-resorts of Istria.

SAILING AND YACHTING PACKAGES

Croatia's island-scattered littoral is the perfect place for **sailing and yachting**, and an increasing number of travel companies (see box above) offer holidays ranging from sailing courses for

beginners to boat charter for the experienced. The season usually lasts from early May to early October.

The most basic form of sailing holiday, and one which involves no previous nautical experience, is a cruise in a **motorsailer** – basically a large, engine-powered yacht with simple bunk accommodation and a crew do the work. Holiday Options and Europa Skylines both offer motorsailer cruises in Dalmatia starting at around £450 for seven days, although with Holiday Options you have to book a week's holiday in a resort as well. To learn the rudiments of sailing, you can arrange a one-week **beginner's course** with either Activity Holidays or Nautilus Yachting – prices start at about £525 per person. Those who already known the ropes might consider **flotilla sailing**, in which a group of yachts with an expertly crewed lead boat embarks on a set seven- or fourteen-day itinerary. Flotilla yachts usually range from two-berth to eight-berth, so per-person prices decrease according to the size of your group. The cheapest seven-day holiday in an eight-berth yacht is typically around £400–450 per person (rising to £550–650 in a two-berth yacht), depending on which part of the season you go in. Prices rise steeply for fancier yachts. At least one of your party will have to have sailing experience – exactly how much differs from one travel company to the next.

Yacht charter can either be "bareboat" (meaning you have to sail it yourself) or "skippered" (which means you pay for the services of a local captain). Prices are subject to many variables, the most important being the model of yacht and the number of berths. You won't get a smallish three-to four-berth bareboat yacht for much under £450 per week, while prices for larger craft can run into thousands; a skipper will cost upwards of £50 a day extra. For bareboat charter, at least one member of the party has to have about two years' sailing experience – again, precise requirements differ from company to company.

BY TRAIN

Travelling to Croatia **by train** is unlikely to save much money compared to flying, but can be a leisurely way of getting to the country if you plan to stop off in other parts of Europe on the way. The cheapest route from London to Zagreb is via Paris, Lausanne, Milan, Venice and Ljubljana, although the route via Brussels, Cologne, Salzburg and Ljubljana is equally fast and only slightly more expensive. The total journey time is around thirty hours, depending on connections – considerably longer if you cross the Channel by ferry rather than taking the Eurostar.

The cheapest **fares** require you to book fourteen days in advance and spend at least one Saturday away. Travelling from London to Zagreb via Paris on Eurostar costs a minimum of £262 (although there are sometimes reductions for

under-26s on the stretch betwen Paris and Milan). Crossing the Channel by ferry will cut about £10 off the price of the London–Paris or London–Brussels leg of the journey. Travelling from London to Zagreb via Brussels on Eurostar will cost £273 (no youth reductions). If you're making a beeline for Dalmatia, consider heading for Ancona in Italy (about 16 hours from Paris), the departure point for ferries to Zadar, Split and Dubrovnik. A London–Ancona return (travelling via Paris on Eurostar) is £234, with possible youth reductions between Paris and Milan.

Tickets are valid for two months and allow for unlimited stop-offs en route unless you travel the London–Paris or London–Brussels leg by Eurostar, in which case you'll have to commit yourself to reservations on specific services on this leg in order to qualify for the cheapest tickets. The agency which deals with continental railway travel in the UK, **Rail Europe** (179 Piccadilly, London W1V 0BA; ☎0990/848848), only sells through-tickets using Eurostar, so if you want to cross the Channel by ferry, you'll have to buy a ticket on from Paris or Brussels when you get there.

The most flexible way of getting to Croatia by train is to invest in an **InterRail** pass, which allows one month's unlimited rail travel in 29 European countries. The countries are divided into eight zones, with various passes valid for one, two, three, or all zones. As Croatia is in zone D, you'll need an all-zone pass (£349; £259 for under-26s) to get there from Britain. InterRail holders will have to pay supplements on most European express trains, although these rarely amount to more than £2–3.

BY BUS

The cheapest, though hardly the most convenient, way of getting to Croatia is by bus. **Eurolines** operate coach services from London to Zagreb (changing in Munich; 31hr) three times a week, requiring two nights on the road; and to Split (changing in Frankfurt; 36hr) daily, again requiring two nights en route. A return to Zagreb costs £132, to Split £156, with reductions of around 10 percent for under-26s and students.

BY CAR

Driving to Croatia is straightforward if motorway driving is your thing. The most direct route is to follow motorways from the Belgian coast via Brussels, Cologne, Frankfurt, Stuttgart, Munich, Salzburg and Villach as far as the Slovene capital

FERRY SERVICES TO CROATIA FROM ITALY

Ferry services from Ancona and Bari in Italy to Croatia are run by three companies: **Jadrolinija**, **SEM** and **Adriatica Navigazione**. Foot passengers can usually buy tickets on arrival in Ancona or Bari, either from the Stazione Marittima or from travel agents around town, but if you're travelling with a vehicle it's wise to book in advance, especially in July and August. Simple deck passage between the Italian and Croatian ports costs about £30/$45 (payable in local currency), but as most crossings are overnight, consider investing an additional £10/$15 for a bed in a basic cabin. Bikes cost about £15/$22, cars £35/$50. Return tickets are usually twenty percent cheaper than two singles. Jadrolinija run a couple of weeked catamaran services in summer, charging about £35/$52 each way.

If you want to **book in advance**, Serena Holidays, 40–42 Kenway Rd, London SW5 0RA (☎020/7373 8548) are agents for Adriatica Navigazione; and both Viamare, Graphic House, 2 Sumatra Rd, London NW6 1PU (☎020/7431 4560), and Dalmatian and Istrian Travel, 21 Sawley Rd, London W12 (☎020/8749 5255) are agents for Jadrolinija. If ringing from abroad, note that the country code for Croatia is ☎385, for Italy ☎39.

JADROLINIJA
(*www.tel.hr/jadrolinija*), Riva 16, Rijeka (☎51/666-111, fax 213-116); Stazione Marittima, Ancona (☎071.204.305, fax 071.200.211); c/o P. Lorusso & Co, Via Piccini, Bari (☎080.521.2840, fax 080.521.8229).

SEM
Gat Sv. Duje, Split (☎21/589-433, fax 589-215, *www.sem.hr*); c/o Agenzia Mauro, Via Loggia 6, Ancona (☎071.204.090, fax 071.202.618).

ADRIATICA NAVIGAZIONE
Zattere, 1411 Venezia (☎041.781.611, fax 041.781.894).

TIMETABLE

Jadrolinija

Ferries	Ancona–Vis–Split–Korčula (1 weekly early July to mid-Sept).
	Ancona–Split–Hvar Stari Grad (1 weekly June–Sept rising to 4 weekly July & Aug).
	Ancona–Šibenik (2 weekly June–Sept rising to 3 weekly July & Aug).
	Ancona–Split (3 weekly).
	Ancona–Zadar (3 weekly June–Sept rising to 5 weekly July & Aug).
	Bari–Dubrovnik (1 weekly rising to 4 weekly in July & Aug).
Catamarans	Ancona–Božava–Zadar (1 weekly mid-June–mid-Sept).
	Ancona–Mali Lošinj (1 weekly July & Aug)

Sem

Ferries	Ancona–Split (1 daily mid-March to Oct).
	Ancona–Hvar Stari Grad (2 weekly mid-July to Aug).
	Ancona–Vis (2 weekly mid-July to Aug).

Adriatica Navigazione

Ferries	Ancona–Split (2 weekly rising to 3 weekly in July & Aug).
	Bari–Dubrovnik (1 weekly).

Ljubljana, from where you can continue by normal road south to Rijeka on the Adriatic coast or southeast to Zagreb. An alternative approach is through France, Switzerland and Italy as far as **Ancona** on Italy's Adriatic coast, from where there are ferries to various points on the Dalmatian coast. Further down towards the heel of Italy, there are ferries from **Bari** to Dubrovnik – see box above for full details of ferry services.

If you're driving through Austria you'll have to buy a **vignette** (a windscreen sticker available at border crossings and petrol stations) to use the motorway system. The cheapest version is valid for ten days and costs öS70 (£3.50/$5).

GETTING THERE FROM IRELAND

There are no direct flights from Belfast or Dublin to Croatia. From Dublin, British Airways offer Apex returns to Zagreb via London Gatwick for around £IR500, though you'll get much cheaper fares by shopping around the discount flight agents listed in the box on p.4. These can organize deals with various European carriers – flying Dublin–Zagreb with Alitalia (via Milan) or KLM (via Amsterdam), for example, can cost as little as IR£250. From Belfast, flight agents will probably marry up a couple of operators (such as British Midland and Croatia Airlines, changing at Heathrow) to produce a combined Belfast–Zagreb return fare of about £335.

If you prefer to make your own way to London, there are numerous daily flights **from Dublin** with Ryanair, Aer Lingus and British Midland – the cheapest are with Ryanair (starting at around IR£60 return to Luton or Stansted), though the cost of the journey across London to pick up an onward flight may make the total cost greater than flying with Aer Lingus or British Midland straight to Heathrow or Gatwick. **From Belfast**, there are British Airways and British Midland flights to Heathrow for around £90 return. For the best **youth and student** deals from either city, contact USIT (see box below).

AIRLINES AND AGENTS IN IRELAND

AIRLINES

Aer Lingus (*www.aerlingus.ie*), Northern Ireland ☎0645/737747, Dublin ☎01/705 3333 or 8444 777, Cork ☎021/327155, Limerick ☎061/474239, minicom/text telephone ☎01/705 3994.
Alitalia (*www.alitalia.co.uk*), Dublin ☎01/677 5171.
British Airways (*www.british-airways.com*), Northern Ireland ☎0345/222111, Eire ☎0141/2222345.

British Midland (*www.iflybritishmidland.com*), Belfast ☎0345/554 554, Dublin ☎01/283 8833.
KLM UK (*www.klm.co.uk*), Northern Ireland ☎0990/074074, Eire ☎0345/445588.
Ryanair (*www.ryanair.com*), Dublin ☎01/609 7800.

DISCOUNT FLIGHT AGENTS

Joe Walsh Tours, 69 Upper O'Connell St, Dublin 2 (☎01/872 2555); 8–11 Baggot St, Dublin 2 (☎01/676 3053); 117 St Patrick St, Cork (☎021/277959). Discount fares agent.
Trailfinders, 4–5 Dawson St, Dublin 2 (☎01/677 7888). Competitive fares out of all Irish airports.

USIT, Fountain Centre, College St, Belfast BT1 6ET (☎028/9032 7111); 10–11 Market Parade, Patrick St, Cork (☎021/270 900); 33 Ferryquay St, Derry (☎01504/371 888); 19 Aston Quay, Dublin 2 (☎01/602 1777 or 677 8117); Victoria Place, Eyre Square, Galway (☎091/565 177); Central Buildings, O'Connell St, Limerick (☎061/415 064); 36–37 George's St, Waterford (☎051/872 601). Student and youth specialist.

GETTING THERE FROM NORTH AMERICA

There are currently no direct flights from North America to Croatia, though most major airlines offer one- or two-stop flights via major European cities. Tickets can be pretty expensive, especially during the summer, so you might get a better deal flying to Venice or Vienna, and taking a train, bus or ferry to Croatia from there.

SHOPPING FOR TICKETS

Barring special offers, the cheapest fare is usually an **Apex** ticket (maximum stay 3 months), although these have to be booked and paid for at least 21 days before departure, you have to spend at least seven days abroad, and you tend to get penalized if you change your schedule. There are also winter **Super Apex** tickets, sometimes known as "Eurosavers", which are slightly cheaper than an ordinary Apex but limit your stay to between seven and 21 days. Some airlines also issue **Special Apex** tickets to under-24s, and many airlines offer **youth** or **student fares** to under-25s.

You can normally cut costs further by going through a **specialist flight agent** – either a **consolidator**, who buys up blocks of tickets from the airlines and sells them at a discount, or a **discount agent**, who wheels and deals in blocks of tickets offloaded by the airlines, and often offers special student and youth fares and a range of other travel-related services such as travel insurance, rail passes, car rental, tours and the like. Bear in mind, though, that penalties for

changing your plans can be stiff. Some agents specialize in **charter flights**, which may be cheaper than anything available on a scheduled flight, but again departure dates are fixed and withdrawal penalties are high; check the refund policy. If you travel a lot, **discount travel clubs** are another option – the annual membership fee may be worth it for benefits such as cut-price air tickets and car rental. Full-time students and under-26s can take advantage of the excellent deals offered by discount agents specializing in **student/youth** travel, such as Council Travel and STA Travel, who often have bargain flights, even in high season, and flexible tickets valid for six months to a year with low penalties for changes or cancellations.

Don't automatically assume that tickets purchased through a travel specialist will be the cheapest: once you get a quote, check with the airlines and you may turn up an even better deal. Be advised also that the pool of travel companies is swimming with sharks – exercise caution and *never* deal with a company that demands cash up front or refuses to accept payment by credit card.

Regardless of where you buy your ticket, the **fare** will depend on the season, and will be highest from around June to September. Note also that flying on weekends ordinarily adds $50 to the round-trip fare; prices quoted below assume midweek travel.

FLIGHTS FROM THE US

There are **no direct flights** to Croatia from the US, although all the major airlines listed in the box on p.10 offer indirect flights via other major European cities, with onward connections to Zagreb, often in conjunction with Croatia Airlines, the national carrier. Apex **fares** are similar on all major airlines listed on p.10. A midweek return from New York to Zagreb in low season (Nov–Feb) starts at $550 ($750 from West Coast cities), rising to $1000 ($1200 from the West Coast) during high season (June–Sept). If you want to stay longer than a month, you'll have to buy a much more expensive one-year return ticket. You can sometimes cut the cost of high-season travel by buying a ticket from travel agents specializing in Eastern Europe, such as GeneralTurist, Atlas Travel Agency, Pino Welcome

AIRLINES, AGENTS AND TOUR OPERATORS

AIRLINES

Air Canada US ☎1-800/776-3000, Canada ☎1-800/263-0882, *www.aircanada.ca.*

Air France US ☎1-800/237-2747, Canada ☎1-800/667-2747, *www.airfrance.fr.*

American Airlines ☎1-800/624-6262, *www.americanair.com.*

Austrian Airlines ☎1-800/843-0002, *www.aua.com.*

British Airways US ☎1-800/247-9297, Canada ☎1-800/668-1059, *www.british-airways.com.*

KLM US ☎1-800/374-7747, Canada ☎1-800/361-5073, *www.klm.nl.*

Lufthansa US ☎1-800/645-3880, Canada ☎1-800/563-5954, *www.lufthansa-usa.com.*

Sabena ☎1-800/955-2000, *www.sabena-usa.com.*

Swissair US ☎1-800/221-4750, Canada ☎1-800/267-9477, *www.swissair.com.*

DISCOUNT AGENTS

Air Brokers International, 150 Post St, Suite 620, San Francisco, CA 94108 (☎1-800/883-3273, *www.airbrokers.com*). Consolidator.

Air Courier Association, 191 University Boulevard, Suite 300, Denver, CO 80206 (☎1-800/282-1202 or ☎303/278-8810, *www.aircourier.org*). Courier flight broker.

Council Travel, 205 E 42nd St, New York, NY 10017 (☎1-800/226-8624, *www.ciee.org*). Student travel organization with branches in many US cities. A sister company, Council Charter (☎1-800/223-7402), specializes in charter flights.

Educational Travel Center, 438 N Frances St, Madison, WI 53703 (☎1-800/747-5551, *www.edtrav.com*). Student/youth discount agent.

Encore Travel Club, 4501 Forbes Blvd, Lanham, MD 20706 (☎1-800/444-9800, *www.emitravel.com*). Discount travel club.

Last Minute Travel Club, 100 Sylvan Rd, Woburn, MA 01801 (☎1-800/LAST MIN). Travel club specializing in standby deals.

Now Voyager, 74 Varick St, Suite 307, New York, NY 10013 (☎212/431-1616, *www.nowvoyagertravel.com*). Courier flight broker.

Pino Welcome Travel, 501 Fifth Avenue, Suite 803, New York, NY 10017 (☎212/682-5400 or 1-800/247-6578). Discount travel agent.

STA Travel, 10 Downing St, New York, NY 10014 (☎1-800/781-4040, *www.sta-travel.com*). Worldwide specialist in independent travel with branches in other major cities nationwide.

TFI Tours International, 34 W 32nd St, New York, NY 10001 (☎1-800/745-8000). Consolidator; other offices in Las Vegas, San Francisco and Los Angeles.

Travac, 989 6th Ave, New York NY 10018 (☎1-800/872-8800, *www.travac.com*). Consolidator and charter broker.

Travel and Lotus Travel (see box on p.11) – the first two agencies are excellent sources of general advice on travelling in Croatia.

Depending on which part of Croatia you're aiming for, you may be able to save a few dollars by taking advantage of cheap fares to cities in neighbouring countries such as Venice (with Swissair or Alitalia) or Vienna (with Austrian Airlines) and travelling on from there by train, bus or ferry.

FLIGHTS FROM CANADA

All the airlines listed in the box above have one or two-stop flights **from Canada to Zagreb** via

other European cities. Apex return fares start at CDN$1150 from Toronto and CDN$1550 from Vancouver during the low season (Nov–Feb, excluding Christmas and New Year), rising to CDN$1550 and CDN$1850 during high season (June–Sept). Alternatively, it might be cheaper to travel to the US and then fly on from there (see p.9), or to fly to a European city close to Croatia, such as Venice, Vienna or Budapest, and then travel on from there.

PACKAGE TOURS

The Croatian National Tourist Office in New York (see box on p.18) will send you a list of all the

Travel Avenue, 10 S Riverside, Suite 1404, Chicago, IL 60606 (☎1-800/333-3335, *www.travelavenue.com*). Discount travel agent.

Travel Cuts, 187 College St, Toronto, ON M5T 1P7 (☎416/979-2406 or 1-800/667-2887). Canadian student travel organization with branches nationwide.

Travelers Advantage, 3033 S Parker Rd, Suite 900, Aurora, CO 80014 (☎1-800/548-1116, *www.travelersadvantage.com*). Discount travel club.

UniTravel, 11737 Administration Dr, St Louis, MO 63146 (☎1-800/325-2222; *www.unitravel.com*). Consolidator.

Worldtek Travel, 111 Water St, New Haven, CT 06511 (☎1-800/243-1723, *www.worldtek.com*). Discount travel agency.

Worldwide Discount Travel Club, 1674 Meridian Ave, Miami Beach, FL 33139 (☎305/534-2082). Discount travel club.

CROATIAN TRAVEL SPECIALISTS

Adriatic Travel, 777 W. 9th Street, San Pedro, CA 90731 (☎310/548-1446, *www.adriatic1.com*). Adriatic cruises.

Adventures Abroad, 2148–20800 Westminster Hwy, Richmond, BC V6V 2W3 (☎604/303-1099 or 1/800-665-3998, *www.adventures-abroad.com*). Eighteen-day guided tours of Croatia and Slovenia with departures from most major North American cities.

Atlas Travel Agency, 1601 18th Street NW, Suite 806, Washington DC (☎202/483-8919 or 667-7411, *www.atlas-croatia.com*). Specialist Croatian agency, with a wide range of holidays including coach tours, sailing holidays, adventure tours (such as canoeing, rafting and sea-kayaking) and programmes for senior citizens.

Forum Travel, 91 Gregory Lane, Pleasant Hill, CA (☎925/671-2900, 1-800/252-4475, *www.foruminternational.com*). Various package tours in all price ranges.

Fugazy International, 770 US-1, North Brunswick, NJ (☎1-800/828-4488). Tours to Dubrovnik, Opatija and other destinations. Also a good source of discounted plane tickets to Croatia.

General Tours, 53 Summer St, Keene, NH 03431 (☎603/357-5033 or 1/800-221-2216, *www.generaltours.com*). Various packages to Croatia and Slovenia.

GeneralTurist, 41–16 Broadway, Astoria, NY 11103 (☎718/721-6014, 1-800/726-7474, *www.generalturist.com*). One of the main Croatian specialist operators, with a wide range of packages including guided tours, city breaks, wine-tasting and culinary tours, and programmes for senior citizens.

Interpac Yachts Incorporated, 1050 Anchorage Lane, San Diego, CA 92106 (☎877/453-2628). Yacht-charter specialists.

Kompas, 2826 E Commercial Blvd, Fort Lauderdale, FL 33308 (☎1-800/233-6422). Various packages including city breaks in Dubrovnik, Split and Zagreb and customized tours.

Lotus Travel, 3108 Lincoln Way, Costa Mesa, CA 92626 (☎1-800/675-0559, *http://home.pacbell.net/european*). Useful source of information on tours to Croatia.

---

operators offering **package tours** to Croatia – the main ones are listed in the box above. The major Croatian travel agencies – in particular Atlas Travel Agency and GeneralTurist – offer an extensive selection of packages including fully guided tours (from $600 for 8 days); Adriatic cruises (from $400 for 1 week); flotilla-sailing packages (around $500 for 1 week); cycling tours ($890 for 8 days); canoeing and rafting tours ($790 for 8

days) and sea-kayaking ($945 for 8 days). There are several other North American tour operators offering escorted and independent tours to Croatia – a number of which also include Slovenia in their itinerary.

If you just want to book accommodation and transport within Croatia, contact Atlas Travel Agency, GeneralTurist or the Croatian National Tourist Board.

GETTING THERE FROM AUSTRALIA & NEW ZEALAND

The cheapest flights to Zagreb from Australia are with Malaysia Airlines via Kuala Lumpur from Sydney, Brisbane, Melbourne, Adelaide or Perth. Fares range from A$1360 in low season (Feb & Oct) to A$1900 in high season (June–Aug, Dec & Jan). Other bargain options include Lauda Air via Vienna (A$1390/1980) and Lufthansa via Frankfurt (A$1450/2020), while Qantas fly via London, Paris or Rome for A$1600/2030.

Malaysia Airlines also offer the cheapest deals to Zagreb **from New Zealand**, with flights from Auckland and fares ranging from NZ$1945 (low season) to NZ$2445 (high). Lufthansa and Air New Zealand have a joint fare from Auckland or Christchurch (from NZ$2165), while Swissair in conjunction with Qantas costs upwards of NZ$2360. British Airways fares, including a stopover in London or another European capital, start at NZ$2800.

Round-the-world fares, which usually include six stopovers, start at A$2400/NZ$3000. You can include Zagreb as one of your stops on a Qantas-British Airways "One World" ticket (from A$2500/NZ$3000 depending on season and mileage) or on the "Star Alliance" fare available from Air New Zealand and Lufthansa (from A$2700/NZ$3300). **Discount flight agents** and **specialist operators** (see box opposite) should be able to get you cheaper fares than those available from the airlines direct, while the specialist operators listed may also be able to arrange accommodation, cruises along the Dalmatian coast, sightseeing packages and rail passes.

AIRLINES

Air New Zealand Australia ☎13 2476, New Zealand ☎0800/737 000 or 09/357 3000, *www.airnz.co.nz.*

British Airways Australia ☎02/8904 8800, New Zealand ☎09/356 8690, *www.britishairways.com.au.*

Lauda Air Australia ☎1800/642 438 or 02/9251 6155, New Zealand ☎09/308 3368, *www.laudaair.com.au.*

Lufthansa Australia ☎1300/655 727 or 02/9367 3887, New Zealand ☎09/303 1529, *www.lufthansa-australia.com.*

Malaysia Airlines Australia ☎13 2627, New Zealand ☎09/373 2741, *www.malaysiaairlines.com.au.*

Qantas Australia ☎13 1313, New Zealand ☎09/357 8900 or 0800/808 767, *www.qantas.com.au.*

Swissair Australia ☎02/9232 1744 or 1800/221339, New Zealand ☎09/358 3216, *www.swissair.com.au.*

DISCOUNT AND SPECIALIST TRAVEL AGENTS

DISCOUNT TRAVEL AGENTS

Anywhere Travel, 345 Anzac Parade, Kingsford, Sydney (☎02/9663 0411, *anywhere@ozemail.com.au*).

Budget Travel, 16 Fort St, Auckland; plus other branches citywide (☎09/366 0061 or 0800/808 040).

Destinations Unlimited, 220 Queen St, Auckland (☎09/373 4033).

Flight Centre (*www.flightcentre.com.au*) Australia: 82 Elizabeth St, Sydney (☎02/9235 3522); plus branches nationwide (nearest branch ☎13 1600). New Zealand: 350 Queen St, Auckland (☎09/358 4310); plus branches nationwide.

Northern Gateway, 22 Cavenagh St, Darwin (☎08/8941 1394, *www.norgate.com.au*).

STA Travel (*www.statravel.com.au*) Australia: 855 George St, Sydney; 256 Flinders St, Melbourne, plus offices in other state capitals and major universities (nearest branch ☎13 1776, telesales ☎1300/360 960). New Zealand: 10 High St, Auckland (☎09/309 0458, telesales ☎09/366 6673); plus branches in Wellington, Christchurch, Dunedin, Palmerston North, Hamilton and at major universities.

Student Uni Travel, 92 Pitt St, Sydney (☎02/9232 8444, *sydney@backpackers.net*); plus branches in Brisbane, Cairns, Darwin, Melbourne and Perth.

Thomas Cook (*www.thomascook.com.au*) Australia: 175 Pitt St. Sydney (☎02/9231 2077), 257 Collins St, Melbourne; plus branches in other state capitals (nearest branch ☎13 1771, telesales ☎1800/801 002); New Zealand: 191 Queen St, Auckland (☎09/379 3920).

Trailfinders (*www.trailfinders.com.au*), 8 Spring St, Sydney (☎02/9247 7666); 91 Elizabeth St, Brisbane (☎07/3229 0887); Hides Corner, Shield St, Cairns (☎07/4041 1199).

Travel.com.au (*www.travel.com.au*), 76–80 Clarence St, Sydney (☎02/9249 5444 or 1800/000 447).

Usit Beyond (*www.usitbeyond.co.nz*), cnr Shortland St and Jean Batten Place, Auckland (☎09/379 4224 or ☎0800/788 336); plus branches in Christchurch, Dunedin, Palmerston North, Hamilton and Wellington.

SPECIALIST TRAVEL AGENTS

Adriatic Adventures, Shop 12, Edensor Park Plaza, Edensor Park, NSW 2176 (☎02/9823 0011).

Danube Travel, 800 Glenhuntly Rd, Caulfield, Melbourne (☎03/9530 0888).

Eastern European Travel Bureau, 5/75 King St, Sydney (☎02/9262 1144, *eetb@ozemail.com.au*); plus branches in Melbourne and Brisbane.

Eastern Eurotours, Level 9, Seabank, 12–14 Marine Parade, Southport QLD 4215 (☎07/5591 0326 and 1-800/242353).

Eurolynx, 3/20 Fort St, Auckland (☎09/379 9716).

European Travel Office, 122 Rosslyn St, West Melbourne (☎03/9329 8844); Suite 410/368, Sussex St, Sydney (☎02/9267 7714); 407 Great South Rd, Auckland (☎09/5253074).

Sky Air Services, Level 5, 379 Kent St, Sydney (☎02/9299 6388); plus branches in Adelaide, Melbourne and Perth.

RED TAPE AND VISAS

Citizens of EU countries, the US, Canada, Australia and New Zealand are allowed to enter Croatia without a visa for stays of up to ninety days. If you want to stay longer, it's easier to leave the country and re-enter again than to go through the hassle of applying for an extension at the local police station.

Visitors to Croatia are required by law to **register** with the local police within 24 hours of arrival. If you're staying in a hotel, hostel or camp site, or if you've booked a private room through a recognized agency, the job of registration will be done for you. If you're staying with friends or in a room arranged privately, your hosts are supposed to register you. In practice however, they very rarely do so. This will only become a problem if the police have reason to question you about where you're staying, which in well-touristed areas is very rare. Even if they do, official attitudes to registration are flexible: the police often turn a blind eye to tourists and hosts alike if you're merely enjoying a short holiday on the coast, but can throw you out if you've been staying in Croatia unregistered for a long period of time.

There are no **customs** restrictions on the kind of personal belongings that you need for your holiday, although you are limited to 200 cigarettes, one litre of spirits and 500g of coffee. It's a good idea to declare major items – laptop computers, boats, televisions and other electronic equipment – to ensure that you can take them out of the country when you leave. Pets are allowed in providing you have a recent vaccination certificate. You can only export 2000Kn of local currency.

CROATIAN EMBASSIES AND CONSULATES

Australia 14 Jindalee Crescent, O'Malley, Canberra ACT 2606 (☎02/6286 6988, fax 6286 3544); Consulate: Level 4, 379 Kent St, Sydney NSW 2000 (☎02/9299 8899); plus consulates in Melbourne and Perth.

Canada 229 Chapel Street, Ottawa, ON K1N 7Y6 (☎613/562-7820, fax 613/562-7821, *www.croatiaemb.net*).

Ireland No representation; contact the embassy in the UK.

New Zealand 131 Lincoln Rd, Edmonton, Auckland (☎09/836 5581, fax 836 5481).

UK 21 Conway St, London W1P 5HL (☎020/7387 1790, fax 7387 0936).

US 2343 Massachusetts Ave NW, Washington, DC 20008 (☎202/588 5899, fax 588 8936, *www.croatiaemb.org*); plus consulates in New York, Chicago and Los Angeles.

INSURANCE AND HEALTH

Though not compulsory, travel insurance including medical cover is a good idea. Many credit cards have certain levels of medical or other insurance included if you use them to pay for your trip, while some private medical schemes also cover you while abroad. If you have a good "all-risks" home insurance policy, it may well cover your possessions against loss or theft even when overseas.

Travel insurance **policies** vary a great deal: some are comprehensive, while others cover certain risks only (accidents, illnesses, delayed or lost luggage, cancelled flights and so forth).

Check exactly what is and isn't covered, and make sure the per-article limit will cover your most valuable possession. If you're planning to do any "dangerous" sports (skiing, mountaineering and the like), be sure to ask whether these activities are covered: some policies add a surcharge.

To claim **compensation** back home you'll need receipts for any medicines purchased or, in case of theft, an official police report. This isn't normally a problem, but be patient: Croatian policemen are not always the most efficient in the world when it comes to paperwork.

HEALTH

No inoculations are required for travel to Croatia, standards of public health are good, and tap water is safe everywhere. Anyone planning to spend time walking in the mountains should consider being inoculated against tick-borne encephalitis. Minor complaints can be treated at a **pharmacy** (*ljekarna*); in cities, many of the staff will speak at least some English, while even in places where the staff speak only Croatian, it should be easy enough to obtain repeat prescriptions if you bring along the empty pill container. A rota system ensures that there will be one pharmacy open at night-time and weekends – details are posted in the window of each pharmacy.

For serious complaints, head for the nearest **hospital** (*bolnica* or *klinički centar*), or call an

---

ROUGH GUIDES TRAVEL INSURANCE

Rough Guides now offer their own **travel insurance**, customized for our readers by a leading UK broker and backed by a Lloyds underwriter. It's available for anyone, of any nationality, travelling anywhere in the world, and we are convinced that this is the best-value scheme you'll find.

There are two main Rough Guide insurance plans: **Essential**, for effective, no-frills cover, starting at £10 for two weeks; and **Premier** – more expensive, but with more generous and extensive benefits. Each offers European or worldwide cover, and can be supplemented with a "Hazardous Activities Premium" if you plan to indulge in sports considered dangerous, such as skiing, scuba-diving or trekking. Unlike many policies, the Rough Guide schemes are calculated by the day, so if you're travelling for 27 days rather than a month, that's all you pay for. Alternatively, you can take out annual **multi-trip insurance**, which covers you for all your travel throughout the year (with a maximum of 60 days for any one trip).

For a **policy quote**, call the Rough Guides Insurance Line on UK freefone 0800/015 0906 or, if you're calling from outside Britain, on (+44) 1243/621046. Alternatively, get an online quote at *www.roughguides.com/insurance*.

ambulance (☎94). Hospital treatment is free to citizens of most EU countries, including the UK and Ireland; nationals of other countries should check whether their government has a reciprocal health agreement with Croatia. Conditions in Croatian hospitals are generally good, although expensive Western drugs are sometimes in short supply, and you might have to buy your own. It's not unknown for people to drive to neighbouring Slovenia or Italy in search of specific medicines.

COSTS, MONEY AND BANKS

Croatia isn't the bargain destination it was in the 1970s and 1980s, but the cost of accommodation, eating and drinking is reasonably competitive compared to Western Europe. Prices in shops are another matter, however, with food and other goods often slightly more expensive than those in EU countries.

CURRENCY

Croatia's unit of currency is the **kuna** (Kn), which is divided into 100 **lipa**. Coins come in denominations of 1, 5, 10, 20 and 50 lipa, and 1, 2 and 5 kuna; notes come in denominations of 5, 10, 20, 50, 100, 500 and 1000 kuna (the word *kuna*, meaning "marten", recalls the days in medieval Croatia when taxes were paid for in marten pelts).

At the time of writing, the **exchange rate** was about 13Kn to £1/8.5Kn to US$1 – exchange rates may be fluid, but not overly volatile. The prices of accommodation, ferry tickets, international bus tickets and tourist excursions are often quoted in Deutschmarks, although you can pay in kuna.

The kuna is not a fully convertible currency, so you can't buy it from your bank prior to leaving home; it's also hard to get rid of once you've left Croatia, although exchange offices in neighbouring countries like Slovenia and Hungary often accept it. The best advice is to spend up, or change the leftovers back to hard currency before you quit the country (some banks may ask to see your exchange receipts before doing this, so keep them safe).

COSTS

Accommodation will be your biggest single expense, with the cheapest private room weighing in at around 120–160Kn double, rising to 220Kn for a double in fashionable places like Dubrovnik. The cheapest doubles in hotels hover around the 350–450Kn mark.

As for **transport**, short journeys by ferry and bus (say from Split to one of the nearby islands) cost in the region of 20–30Kn, while moving up and down the country will naturally be more expensive (a Zagreb–Split bus ticket, for instance, costs upwards of 140Kn).

About 100Kn per person day will suffice for **food and drink** if you're shopping in markets for picnic ingredients, maybe eating out in inexpensive grill-houses and pizzerias once a day, and limiting yourself to a couple of drinks in cafés; 200–250kn a day will be sufficient for breakfast in a café, a sit-down lunch and a decent restaurant dinner followed by a couple of night-time drinks.

BANKS AND EXCHANGE

The best place to **change money** is at a bank (*banka*) or exchange bureau (*mjenjačnica*). They're generally open Monday to Friday 8am to 5pm, and Saturday 8am to 11am or noon, although summer opening hours often come into effect in the Adriatic, when an afternoon break is introduced and hours are lengthened to 8pm or even 10pm in the evenings to compensate. Banks in smaller

COSTS, MONEY AND BANKS/17

places normally close for lunch break on weekdays year round, and aren't open at all on Saturdays. Exchange bureaux are often found inside travel agencies (*putničke agencije*) and have more flexible hours, remaining open until 9–10pm seven days a week in summer if there are enough tourists around to justify it. Exchange rates in hotels usually represent extremely bad value for money, but post offices offer rates similar to those in banks (for post office opening times, see p.33).

Travellers' cheques are the safest way to carry money, and can be exchanged in almost all banks and exchange bureaux in Croatia for a one to two percent commission. American Express cheques can also be exchanged at any office of the Atlas Travel Agency. They're available for a small commission (usually one percent of the amount ordered) from any bank and some building societies in your home country, whether or not you have an account, and from branches of American Express and Thomas Cook. Another way of carrying funds is **Visa Travel Money** (*www.visa.com*), a disposable debit card prepaid with dedicated travel funds which you can access from over 457,000 Visa ATMs in 120 countries. In the UK, many Thomas Cook outlets sell the card.

Credit cards are accepted in most hotels and the more expensive restaurants and shops, and can be used to get cash advances in banks, ATMs are reasonably widespread, although those accepting MasterCard and Maestro are more common than Visa. Note also that many of the islands do not yet have ATMs.

EMERGENCIES

Wiring money is a fast but expensive way to send and receive money abroad. The money wired should be available for collection, usually in local currency, from the company's local agent within a few minutes of being sent via Western Union or Moneygram; both charge on a sliding scale, so sending larger amounts of cash is better value.

AUSTRALIA
Moneygram ☎1800/230 100
Western Union ☎1800/649 565

NEW ZEALAND
Moneygram ☎09/379 8243
Western Union ☎09/270 0050

NORTH AMERICA
Moneygram ☎1-800/543-4080
Western Union ☎1-800/325-6000

UK
Western Union ☎0800/833833
Moneygram ☎00800/0071 0971

INFORMATION AND MAPS

The best source of general information on Croatia is the **Croatian National Tourist Office** (see box below), but note that most offices prefer to deal with the public by telephone rather than admit personal callers – ring ahead and check before trying to visit them in person. The staff are generally very helpful and can usually supply brochures, accommodation details and maps of specific towns and resorts, although it's best to have a clear idea of what it is you want to find out. In the **US**, the Atlas Tourist Agency in Washington DC (see box below) is another good resource for maps, brochures and tour information. There are no Croatian tourism offices in **Ireland, Canada, Australia** or **New Zealand** – either contact your country's consulate (see box on p.14) or the tourist offices in London or Washington.

All towns and regions within Croatia have a **tourist association** (*turistička zajednica*) whose job it is to promote local tourism. Many of these maintain tourist offices (*turistički ured* or *turistički informativni centar*), although they vary a great deal in the services they offer. Some handle private rooms, but only in areas lacking a recognized accommodation agency. English is widely spoken, and staff in coastal resorts invariably speak German and Italian as well. Opening times vary according to the amount of tourist traffic. In July and August they might be open daily from 8am to 8pm or later, while in May, June and September, hours might be reduced to include an afternoon break or earlier closing times at weekends. Out of season, tourist offices on the coast tend to observe normal office hours (Mon–Fri 8am–3pm) or close altogether.

In areas without a tourist office, the local tourist association may still be prepared to send you information if you contact them by phone or fax during normal office hours.

MAPS

The best **maps** of Croatia are by Freytag & Berndt, who produce a 1:600,000 map of Slovenia, Croatia and Bosnia-Hercegovina, a 1:300,000 map of Croatia, a 1:250,000 map of Istria and northern Croatia and 1:000,000 regional maps of the Adriatic coast. Generalkarte also do a useful 1:200,000 map of the Adriatic coast.

City and town plans are more difficult to come by, although tourist offices often give away (or sell quite cheaply) serviceable maps of their town or island. In addition, Freytag & Berndt publish city plans of Zadar, Split and Dubrovnik. The best map of **Zagreb** is the 1:20,000 plan prepared by the Geodetski zavod Slovenije (Slovene Geodesic Institute), which is available in three versions: one published by a local firm in Zagreb, a second published by the Hungarian firm Cartographia and the third by the ubiquitous Freytag & Berndt.

All the above are available from shops in Croatia as well as the specialist map stockists listed in the box opposite.

MAP OUTLETS

IN AUSTRALIA

Mapland, 372 Little Bourke St, Melbourne (☎03/9670 4383).

The Map Shop, 6 Peel St, Adelaide (☎08/8231 2033).

Perth Map Centre, 1/884 Hay St, Perth (☎08/9322 5733).

Sydney Travel Bookshop, Shop 3, 175 Liverpool St, Sydney (☎02/9261 8200).

Worldwide Maps and Guides, 187 George St, Brisbane (☎07/3221 4330).

IN CANADA

Open Air Books and Maps, 25 Toronto St, Toronto, M5R 2C1 (☎416/363-0719).

Ulysses Travel Bookshop, 4176 St-Denis, Montréal (☎514/289-0993).

World Wide Books and Maps, 736A Granville St, Vancouver, V6Z 1G3 (☎604/687-3320).

IN IRELAND

Easons Bookshop, 40 O'Connell St, Dublin 1 (☎01/873 3811).

Fred Hanna's Bookshop, 27–29 Nassau St, Dublin 2 (☎01/677 1255).

Hodges Figgis Bookshop, 56–58 Dawson St, Dublin 2 (☎01/677 4754).

Waterstone's, Queens Bldg, 8 Royal Ave, Belfast BT1 1DA (☎028/9024 7355); 7 Dawson St, Dublin 2 (☎01/679 1415); 69 Patrick St, Cork (☎021/276 522).

IN NEW ZEALAND

Auckland Specialty Maps, 46 Albert St, Auckland (☎09/307 2217).

Mapworld, 173 Gloucester Street, Christchurch (☎03/374 5399, *www.mapworld.co.nz*).

IN THE UK

Daunt Books, 83 Marylebone High St, London W1M 3DE (☎020/7224 2295); 193 Haverstock Hill, London NW3 4QL (☎020/7794 4006).

John Smith and Sons, 57–61 St Vincent St, Glasgow, G2 5TB (☎0141/221 7472, fax 0141/248 4412, *www.johnsmith.co.uk*).

National Map Centre, 22–24 Caxton St, London SW1H 0QU (☎020/7222 2466, *www.mapsworld.com*).

Stanfords, 12–14 Long Acre, London WC2E 9LP (☎020/7836 1321, *sales@stanfords.co.uk*); c/o

Campus Travel, 52 Grosvenor Gardens, London SW1W 0AG (☎020/7730 1314); c/o British Airways, 156 Regent St, London W1R 5TA (☎020/7434 4744); 29 Corn Street, Bristol BS1 1HI (☎0117/929 9966).

The Travel Bookshop, 13–15 Blenheim Crescent, London W11 2EE (☎020/7229 5260, *www.thetravelbookshop.co.uk*).

Waterstone's, 91 Deansgate, Manchester, M3 2BW (☎0161/837 3000, *www.waterstones-manchester-deansgate.co.uk*).

IN THE US

British Travel Bookshop, 551 5th Ave, New York, NY 10176 (☎1-800/448-3039 or ☎212/490-6688).

The Complete Traveler Bookstore, 199 Madison Ave, New York, NY 10016 (☎212/685-9007); 3207 Fillmore St, San Francisco, CA 92123 (☎415/923-1511).

Elliot Bay Book Company, 101 South Main St, Seattle, WA 98104 (☎206/624-6600).

Rand McNally, 150 E 52nd St, New York, NY 10022 (☎212/758-7488); 444 N Michigan Ave, Chicago, IL 60611 (☎312/321-1751); 595 Market St, San Francisco, CA 94105 (☎415/777-3131); 1201 Connecticut Ave NW, Washington DC 20036 (☎202/223-6751); plus stores nationwide (nearest branch and telesales ☎1-800/333-0136, ext 2111).

Traveler's Bookstore, 22 W 52nd St, New York, NY 10019 (☎212/664-0995).

CROATIA ON THE WEB

Croatian National Tourist Board
www.htz.hr
Good source of general information on Croatia, with numerous links to regional tourist boards and more detailed sites dealing with history, culture and practical information.

Croatian media
www.kolporter.com
Links to a wide range of Croatian daily, weekly and monthly publications. One snag however; it's in Croatian.

Croatian News Agency
www.hina.hr
Daily Croatian news reports in English, but in dry style.

Dalmatia
www.dalmacija.net
Useful guide to the southern Adriatic – you can also book hotels and private rooms here online.

Dubrovnik
http://dubrovnik.laus.hr
The official site for Dubrovnik and the surrounding region. For accommodation, try *www.dubrovnikhotels.hr*, *a* listing of hotels owned by the Dubrovnik Hotels group, including many in the city itself as well as outlying resorts, with prices and on-line booking.

Football
www.hns-cff.hr
The Croatian Football Federation's site, with results, league tables and news of the national team.

Hvar Tourist Association
www.hvar.hr
Good introduction to one of Dalmatia's most popular islands.

Institute for War and Peace Reporting
www.iwpr.net
Web site of an organization founded to monitor the break-up of Yugoslavia after 1991. Much of the institute's attention is nowadays paid to other troube spots, but analyses of the Croatian political scene still crop up.

Istrian County Tourist Association
www.istra.com
Best of the regional tourist authority Web sites. Full details of accommodation throughout Istria and a useful calendar of events.

Tamburica music
www.tamburaweb.com
Run by North American fans of eastern Croatia's indigenous folk music, with contacts and festival details.

Zagreb
www.zagreb-touristinfo.hr
Offical Zagreb city home page with a variety of useful tips and city information. There's more Zagreb info at *www. zagreb-convention.hr*, run by the Zagreb Tourist Board and Convention Bureau.

GETTING AROUND

Croatia's train system covers the north and east pretty well, but is little use on the coast, where the country's extensive and reliable bus network comes into its own. Ferries offer a leisurely way of getting up and down the coast, and travelling the length of the Adriatic by boat is one of the most memorable journeys Croatia has to offer.

BY TRAIN

Croatian Railways (*Hrvatske željeznice*) run a smooth and efficient service and are slightly cheaper than buses in areas where routes overlap. Around Zagreb and in the north the network is pretty dense, and you can use trains to visit most places of interest in inland Croatia. Trains also run from Zagreb to Pula, Rijeka and Split on the Adriatic, but there are no rail lines running up and down the coast. The **InterRail** pass is valid for Croatia (which is in zone D), but **Eurail** isn't.

There are two types of train (*vlak*, plural *vlakovi*): *putnički* (slow ones which stop at every halt) and *IC* (inter-city trains which are faster and more expensive). **Tickets** (*karte*) are brought from the ticket counter at the station (*kolodvor*) before travel: those bought from the conductor on the train are subject to a surcharge unless you've joined the train at an insignificant halt which doesn't have a ticket counter. On some inter-city routes, buying a return ticket (*povratna karta*) is cheaper than buying a single ticket (*karta u jednom pravcu*) twice, although it often makes no difference. Seat reservations (*rezervacije*) are obligatory on some inter-city services. The only journey on which sleeping car (*spalnica*) accommodation is available is the overnight service between Zagreb and Split.

Timetables (*vozni red* or *red vožnje*) are usually displayed on boards in station departure halls – *polazci* or *odlasci* are departures, *dolasci* are arrivals. The timetable for the whole network is available in a compact paperback from most larger train stations (30Kn), or visit *www.tel.hr/hz/hengl.htm*.

BY BUS

Croatia's **bus** network is run by a confusing array of local companies, but services are well integrated and bus stations are generally well organized, with clearly listed departure times and efficient booking facilities. The buses (*autobusi*) themselves are usually modern coaches, and travelling big distances is rarely uncomfortable – stops of ten minutes or more are made every ninety minutes or so. There are few places in the country that you can't get to by bus, and there are usually hourly departures on the principal routes (Zagreb to the coast, and routes up and down the coast). Rural areas, however, may only be served by one or two departures a day, and maybe none at all at weekends. Out in the sticks, the bus timetable is much more likely to correspond to the needs of the locals: there'll be a flurry of departures in the early morning to get people to work, school or market, and a flurry of departures in mid-afternoon to bring them back again, but nothing in between.

If you're at a big city bus station, **tickets** must be obtained from ticket windows before boarding the bus, and will bear the departure time (*vrijeme polaska*), platform number (*peron*) and a seat number (*sjedalo*). Your ticket will also carry the name of the bus company you're travelling with: two different companies might be running services to the same place at around the same time. If you're not getting on at the start of the route, tickets might not go on sale until the bus actually arrives. If there's nowhere to buy a ticket, sit on the bus and wait for the conductor to sell you one. It's a good idea to buy tickets well in advance in summer if you can, especially for any services between Zagreb and the coast.

Fares are a little cheaper than in Western Europe, although costs differ slightly according to which company you're riding with and what part of the country you're in. Generally speaking, you get more kilometres for your money in inland

Croatia than you do on the coast. Long inter-city trips like Rijeka–Zadar or Split–Dubrovnik weigh in at around 90Kn; Split–Zagreb will cost around 140Kn. On bus journeys that involve a ferry crossing (such as Rijeka–Lošinj or Rijeka–Rab), the cost of the ferry will be included in the price. You'll be charged extra (5–6Kn for each item) for rucksacks and suitcases.

Tickets for **municipal buses** in towns and cities should usually be bought in advance from kiosks, and then cancelled by punching them in the machine on board. You can buy tickets from the driver as well in most cases, although this might be slightly more expensive and you may have to provide the correct change.

BY FERRY

A multitude of **ferry** services link the Croatian mainland with the Adriatic islands, most of which are run by Jadrolinija (see p.7), the main state ferry firm, although a few private operators are beginning to offer competition.

Short hops to islands **close to the mainland** – such as Brestova to Porozina on Cres, Jablanac to Mišnjak on Rab, or Orebić to Dominče on Korčula – are handled by simple roll-on-roll-off ferries which either operate a shuttle service or run every half-hour or so. Prices for foot passengers on such routes rarely exceed 10Kn (this will usually be incorporated into your fare if you're crossing by bus). A car will cost about 70Kn; a motorbike, 25Kn.

Departures to destinations slightly **further off-shore** will run to a more precise timetable. The ports which offer access to the most important groups of islands are Zadar (Ugljan, Dugi otok), Split (Šolta, Brač, Hvar, Vis and Lastovo) and Dubrovnik (Koločep, Lopud, Šipan and Mljet). Fares for foot passengers are low: approximate prices are Zadar to Sali (Dugi otok) 12Kn, Split to Hvar 25Kn, Split to Lastovo 35Kn, Split to Supetar (Brač) 18Kn, Split to Vis 25Kn, Dubrovnik to Mljet 30Kn. On these routes you'll pay 170–280Kn for a car, 50–80Kn for a motorbike. If you're travelling without a vehicle, look out for summer-only hydrofoils and catamarans linking Split with destinations on Šolta, Brač, Hvar and Vis. Although slightly more expensive than ferries, they'll be twice as fast.

Jadrolinija also operate a **coastal service** from Rijeka to Dubrovnik, calling at Zadar, Split, Stari Grad (Hvar) and Korčula on the way, and sometimes continuing to Bari in Italy and Igoumenitsa in Greece in the summer. This runs at least once a day in both directions in summer, twice a week in winter. Travelling from Rijeka to Dubrovnik takes twenty hours and always involves one night on the boat. Prices (often quoted in Deutschmarks but payable in kuna) vary greatly according to the level of comfort you require. The cheapest Rijeka–Dubrovnik fare (which involves spending the journey either on the open deck or in smoky bar areas) is 180Kn, while you'll pay double that for a couchette-style bunk bed, three times as much for a bed in a well-appointed cabin. Taking a car on the same journey will cost an extra 600Kn, a motorbike 180Kn; bicycles can be taken free of charge. Return tickets are twenty percent cheaper than the price of two singles, and prices fall by up to twenty percent in winter. **Tickets** are sold at offices or kiosks near the departure dock. For longer journeys, book in advance wherever possible; Jadrolinija addresses and phone numbers are given in the text where relevant.

All ferries apart from simple shuttle services will have a **buffet** where you can buy a full range of drinks, although food may consist of crisps and unappetizing sandwiches. The main coastal ferry has a restaurant with a full range of reasonably priced food; breakfast is included if you book a cabin.

DRIVING

Croatia's **road system** is comprehensive, but not always of good quality once you get beyond the main highways. There are currently five stretches of motorway (*autocesta*) in Croatia: Zagreb to Slavonski Brod, Varaždin to Goričan on the Hungarian border, Zagreb to Krapina, and Zagreb to Karlovac. All are subject to tolls – take a ticket as you come on and pay as you exit – though few extend far enough for you to amass significant tolls: Zagreb to Karlovac, for example, is 12Kn for a car or motorbike, Zagreb to Slavonski Brod is 44Kn. Elsewhere, the main routes (especially the main road down the Adriatic coast, the Magistrala) are single carriageway and tend to be clogged with traffic – especially in summer, when movement up and down the coast can be time-consuming. Off the beaten track, roads are sometimes badly maintained.

To drive, you'll need a driving licence, registration documents and a Green Card. **Speed limits** are 50kph in built-up areas, 80kph on normal

CAR RENTAL COMPANIES

AUSTRALIA
Avis ☎1800/225 533, *www.avis.com*
Budget ☎1300/362 848, *www.budget.com.au*
Dollar ☎02/9223 1444, *www.dollar.com*
Hertz ☎1800/550 067, *www.hertz.com.au*
National ☎13 1908, *www.nationalcar.com.au*
Thrifty ☎1300/367 227, *www.thrifty.com.au*

BRITAIN
Avis ☎0990/900500, *www.avis.co.uk*
Budget ☎0800/181181, *www.budget.com*
Europcar ☎0345/222525, *www.europcar.co.uk*
Hertz ☎0990/996699, *www.hertz.co.uk*

IRELAND
Avis ☎01/874 5844, *www.avis.co.uk*
Budget ☎0800/973 159, *www.budget.com*
Europcar ☎01/874 5844, *www.europcar.co.uk*
Hertz ☎01/676 7476, *www.hertz.co.uk*

NEW ZEALAND
Apex ☎1800/121 029
Avis ☎09/526 2800, *www.avis.com*
Budget ☎0800/652 227 or 09/375 2270,
   www.budget.co.nz
Hertz ☎09/309 0989 or 0800/655 955,
   www.hertz.com.au
National ☎09/537 2582, *www.nationalcar.co.nz*
Thrifty ☎09/309 0111, *www.thrifty.co.nz*

NORTH AMERICA
Auto Europe ☎1-800/223-5555
   www.autoeurope.com
Avis ☎1-800/331-1084, *www.avis.com*
Hertz US ☎1-800/654-3001; Canada ☎1-800/
   263-0600, *www.hertz.com*
Holiday Autos ☎1-800/422-7737

roads, 130kph on motorways. If you **break down**, the Croatian Automobile Club (HAK) has a 24-hour emergency service (☎987). **Petrol stations** (*benzinska stanica*) are usually open daily 7am–7pm, although there are 24-hour stations in larger towns and along major international routes. If there's anything wrong with your vehicle, petrol stations are probably the best places to ask where you can find a mechanic (*automehaničar* or *majstor*) or a shop selling spare parts (*rezervni dijelovi*). A tyre repair shop is a *vulkanizer*.

Finding **parking** spaces in big cities can be a nightmare, and illegally parked vehicles will be swiftly removed by tow-truck (known locally as the *pauk*, or "spider") and impounded until payment of a 500Kn fine. Most cities have garages where you can leave your car for a small fee.

CAR RENTAL

Car rental in Croatia is pricey, at around £200/$350 a week for a small hatchback with unlimited mileage, depending on the season. The major chains have offices in all the larger cities and at Zagreb airport; addresses are detailed in the "Listings" sections at the end of city accounts throughout the Guide. Most travel agents in Croatia will organize car rental through one of the big international firms or a local operator. It's usually cheaper if you arrange rental in advance, either through one of the agents listed in the box above or with specialist tour operators like Europa Skylines or Holiday Options (see above box on p.5).

BY AIR

The obvious attraction of flying is the time it saves: the plane journey from Zagreb to Dubrovnik takes an hour, compared to a whole day to get there overland. **Croatia Airlines** (*www.ctn.tel.hr/ctn*) operate domestic services between Zagreb and Pula (6 weekly), Split (2–4 daily), Zadar (1 daily) and Dubrovnik (up to 4 daily in summer). Between May and October there are flights (weekends only) to Bol on the island of Brač. A Zagreb–Dubrovnik return costs about 700Kn. There's not normally any point in booking internal flights from Croatia Airlines offices in your home country — they invariably work out twice as expensive unless you're buying them in conjunction with an international flight to Croatia.

ACCOMMODATION

The tourism boom of the 1960s and 1970s gave Croatia an impressive number of large beachside hotels, while small B&Bs and pensions are on the increase. For the moment, though, the inexpensive private rooms offered by landladies up and down the coast still represent the country's best-value accommodation. The Adriatic coast is well provided with campsites, but hostels, on the other hand, are a rarity.

HOTELS

Most Croatian **hotels** are multistorey affairs providing modern comforts but little atmosphere, although there are a handful of stately, turn-of-the-century establishments in major cities and in resorts (such as Opatija) which were originally patronized by the Habsburgs. Many of the hotels used by Western European package holidaymakers have been expensively renovated since the end of the 1991–95 war, bringing them up to contemporary international standards. Hotels which see more in the way of Croatian or East European guests have generally received less investment, and often still sport worn carpets and freakish 1970s wallpaper – although they're perfectly clean and comfortable in all other respects.

Many Croatian hotels are yet to be classified according to the international five-star grading system, and are still classified by the old letter-grading system. Generally speaking, C-class hotels (roughly equivalent to one-star) have rooms with shared WC and bathroom; B-class (two- to three-star) have rooms with en-suite facilities and, most probably, a television; A-class (four-star) is business class; and L-class (five-star)

are in the international luxury bracket. There are hardly any **C-class** (one-star) places left however: most have been refurbished in order to meet the standards required by international package companies, and those that do exist can't compete, value-wise, with private rooms.

In most places, lower **B-class** (or two-star) places represent the cheapest option – expect to pay 350–450Kn a double – but it's worth bearing in mind that the better categories of private room offer similar comforts for less money. For more expensive B-class rooms you'll pay anything between 400Kn and 700Kn. Any **A-class** (four-star) hotel will have plush carpets, bathtubs in the bathroom and a range of other facilities (such as gym or swimming pool) for around 700–1000Kn. There are currently only four **L-class** (five-star) hotels in Croatia: three in Zagreb and one in Dubrovnik (1000–1600Kn a double).

Hotels in inland Croatia charge the same price all year round. On the coast, however, prices drop by 10–20 percent in the shoulder season (May, June & Sept), and may be as much as 50 percent cheaper in winter. Some hotels in resort areas close between November and April, although most moderate-sized Adriatic towns will have at least one mid-range hotel open all year. Hotel prices almost invariably include **breakfast**. At its most basic, this will feature rolls with butter, jam, and some ham and cheese, although the majority of hotels hosting Western package guests now offer a buffet selection. Many of the hotels on the Adriatic also offer full-board (*pansion*) and half-board (*polupansion*) deals for a few extra kuna, but bear in mind that you'll be eating bland, internationalized food in large, institutionalized dining rooms.

There's a growing number of small **family-run hotels** aiming to conquer the mid-range market, offering the comforts and level of service of a good three-star hotel but in cosy, informal surroundings and at a fraction of the cost. Unfortunately, there's not enough of them in the heavily touristed parts of Croatia to make big inroads into the accommodation scene as yet, but we've recommended them throughout the guide whenever they exist.

In northern Croatia and inland Istria attempts are being made to encourage the development of **village homestays** under the banner of eco-

ACCOMMODATION PRICE CODES

The accommodation in this guide has been graded using the following price codes, based on the cost of each establishment's **least expensive double room** in high season (June–Sept), excluding special offers. Where single rooms exist, they usually cost 60–70 percent of the price of a double.

① Less than 200Kn   ④ 400–500Kn   ⑦ 800–1000Kn
② 200–300Kn   ⑤ 500–600Kn   ⑧ 1000–1200Kn
③ 300–400Kn   ⑥ 600–800Kn   ⑨ Over 1200Kn

tourism. The idea is to encourage people in agricultural areas to offer farmhouse-style accommodation and locally produced food and drink. This is still in its infancy however, and only a handful of places is currently up and running.

PRIVATE ROOMS AND APARTMENTS

Private **rooms** (*privatne sobe*) are available everywhere in Croatia where there are tourists. They're offered by locals eager to rent out unoccupied space in their homes – many Croats on the coast have enlarged or modernized their houses to provide extra rooms. Standards vary widely, but rooms are usually grouped into three categories by the tourist association in each area. **Category I** rooms are simple affairs furnished with a couple of beds, a wardrobe and not much else, and you'll be using your host's bathroom. **Category II** rooms have en-suite bathrooms, and **category III** rooms will probably come with TV and plusher furnishings. Prices start at around 120Kn for a category I double in a smallish resort, rising to about 260Kn in relatively expensive cities like Dubrovnik and Zagreb. Prices are subject to a thirty to fifty percent surcharge if you stay for less than three nights. Single travellers usually pay about seventy percent of the price of a double, although many prospective hosts are unwilling to take single guests during peak season.

Bookings are administered by local travel agencies; where there's no established travel agency, the local tourist office will handle the job. Agencies usually open daily 8am to 8pm in July and August, although they may take a long afternoon break on Sundays. In May, June and September opening hours will include longish afternoon breaks Monday to Friday, and shorter hours (often mornings only) at weekends.

If you can't find a tourist agency or tourist office, it's usually very easy to find a private room by asking around or looking for *sobe* or *Zimmer frei* signs posted up outside local houses. You may also be offered rooms by landladies waiting outside train, bus and ferry stations, especially in Split and Dubrovnik – be sure to establish the location of the room and agree a price before setting off. Rooms obtained in this way often work out slightly cheaper than the agency-approved ones, but bear in mind that your hosts are unlikely to register you with the police (for registration regulations, see "Visas and Red Tape", p.14) and probably won't be paying the tourist tax (*boravišna pristojba*) which is built into all official accommodation prices – therefore depriving the local tourist association of its main source of funding. However you find a room, it's acceptable to have a look at it before committing yourself.

APARTMENTS

Rented out in the same way as private rooms, **apartments** (*apartmani*) usually consist of a self-contained unit or floor of a house with its own kitchen and bathroom, maybe a small lounge, and possibly a terrace for sitting outside. If you're travelling as a family or in a group, apartments offer good value if sleeping quarters are not too cramped – check how many beds are crammed into a single bedroom before accepting. Two-person apartments cost around 300–360Kn per night; four-person apartments around 400–500Kn; and six-person apartments around 500–600Kn. The higher the price, the more likely you are to get a central location, TV and a parking space should you need it. Prices fall by ten to twenty percent in May, June and September.

HOSTELS AND STUDENT HALLS

HI-affiliated **youth hostels** run by the Croatian Hostelling Association (Hrvatski ferijalni i hostelski savez, De manova 9, 10000 Zagreb; ☎01/435-781, fax 422-953) are thin on the ground, although those that do exist (in Zagreb, Pula, Zadar, Šibenik, Dubrovnik and Punat on the island of Krk) are clean and well run. Prices vary according to season: around 60–80Kn for a bed in winter, rising to 80–100Kn July and August. Breakfast costs 20–30Kn. Half-board and full-board deals are also offered at very reasonable prices, although the food may not be particularly special. Most hostels close during the day, and you're expected to check in either in the morning (around 8–9am) or in the evening (typically 5–10pm). If you're doing a lot of hostelling, it's worth joining the hostelling organization of your home country to qualify for the member's rate, about fifteen percent cheaper.

In Zagreb, rooms in **student halls of residence** are rented out to travellers during the summer vacation – usually mid-July to the end of August. Rates include breakfast, with doubles costing 320–400Kn per night depending on whether facilities are en suite or shared.

CAMPSITES

Campsites (*autokamp*) abound on the Adriatic coast, ranging from large-scale affairs with plentiful facilities, restaurants and shops; to small family-run sites squeezed into private gardens or olive groves. Some major centres – notably Split and Dubrovnik – are currently without campsites, but almost everywhere else is catered for. Sites are generally open from May to September and charge 30–40Kn per person, plus 20–50Kn per pitch and 20–40Kn per vehicle. Electricity in the bigger sites costs a few extra kuna. Camping rough is illegal, and the rocky or pebbly nature of most Croatian beaches makes them uncomfortable to sleep on anyway.

Naturist campsites are a common feature of the northern Adriatic resorts, with big, self-contained complexes outside Rovinj, Poreč and Vrsar in Istria, and Krk, Baška and Punat on the island of Krk.

EATING AND DRINKING

There's a varied and distinctive range of food on offer in Croatia, largely because the country straddles two culinary cultures: the seafood-dominated cuisine of the Mediterranean and the filling schnitzel-and-strudel fare of central Europe. Drinking revolves around a solid cross-section of wines and some characterful, fiery spirits.

BREAKFAST AND SNACKS

Unless you're staying in a private room or a campsite, **breakfast** (*doručak* or *zajutrak*) will almost always be included in the cost of your accommodation. At its simplest it will include a couple of bread rolls, a few slices of cheese and/or salami, and some butter and jam. Mid- and top-range hotels will offer a buffet breakfast, complete with a range of cereals, scrambled eggs and bacon. Few Croatian cafés serve breakfast as such, though most offer pastry snacks that make a worthy substitute.

Basic **self-catering** and **picnic** ingredients like cheese (*sir*), vegetables (*povrće*) and fruit (*voće*) can be bought at a supermarket (*samoposluga*) or an open-air **market** (*tržnica*). Markets often open early (about 6am) and begin to pack up in the early afternoon, though in well-touristed areas they sometimes keep going until late evening. Bread (*kruh*) can be bought from either a supermarket or a **pekarnica** (bakery). Small outlets may offer a simple white loaf (*bijeli kruh*) and little else, although you'll usually be offered a wide choice of breads, ranging from French sticks through wholemeal loaves to pumpernickel-style black breads. You'll have to point at what you want though: names of different loaves differ from one place to the next. A *pekarnica* may often sell sandwiches (*sendviči*) filled, most commonly, with ham (*šunka*), cheese or *pršut*, Croatia's excellent home-cured ham.

For **snacks**, look out for *slastičarnice* (cake and pastry shops) selling *burek*, a flaky pastry filled with cheese – a light and delicious snack when fresh, although it can be stodgy and greasy if left standing for too long. For a more substantial snack, try the traditional southeast European repertoire of grilled meats: *ćevapi* (rissoles of minced beef, pork or lamb), *ražnjići* (shish kebab) or *pljeskavica* (a hamburger-like mixture of the same meats), all of which are often served in a *somun* – a flat bread cake which is rather larger than a standard Western-style burger bun. Although all but the grandest restaurants will have basic grill snacks on the menu, they're at their best in the unpretentious fast-food places you'll find clustered around markets and bus stations. For an excellent light lunch, look out for the traditional working-man's food of inland Croatia, *grah* (literally "beans"), a delicious soup of paprika-spiced haricot beans with bits of sausage or *pljeskavica* added. *Grah* isn't quite so common on the coast, although local bean soups such as *fažol* and *maneštra* are palatable substitutes.

RESTAURANTS

Main meals are eaten in a **restoran** (restaurant, sometimes also called a *restauracija*) or a **konoba** (tavern) – the latter is more likely to have folksy decor but essentially serves the same range of food. A **gostiona** (inn) is a more rough-and-ready version of a *restoran*. For Croatians the most important meal of the day is lunch (*ručak*) rather than dinner (*večera*), although restaurants are accustomed to foreigners who eat lightly at lunchtime and more expansively in the evening, and offer a full range of food throughout the day. *Jelovnik* means menu; *račun* is the bill.

Because many Croatians eat lunch relatively late in the afternoon, restaurants on the coast frequently offer a list of *marende* (brunch-snacks) between 11am and 1pm. These are usually no different to main meat and fish dishes, but come in slightly smaller portions, making an excellent low-cost midday meal. They're often chalked up on a board outside rather than written on a menu.

No Croatian town is without at least one **pizzeria**, where the price of a filling meal will be significantly cheaper than in a standard meat-and-fish Croatian restaurant. Most of these establishments serve Italian-style, thin-crust pizzas made to reasonably authentic recipes, and seafood pizzas are quite a feature on the coast. Pizzerias are often the best places to eat pasta dishes, although there are a growing number of spaghetterias which specialize in pasta and nothing else. Again, Croatian pasta dishes are normally authentic, cheap and filling. Pizzerias also tend to serve larger and more imaginative salads than the standard Croatian restaurant.

WHAT TO EAT

Any list of **starters** (*predjela*) should begin with *pršut*, a home-cured ham from Istria and Dalmatia which at its best is a real melt-in-the-mouth delicacy (see box on p.28). It's often served on a platter together with cheese: *Paški sir* from the island of Pag is the most famous, a hard, piquant cheese tasting somewhere between parmesan and mature cheddar; *sir sa vrhnjem* (cream cheese) is a milder alternative. *Kulen*, a spicy, paprika-laced sausage from Slavonia, is also worth trying. Soups (*juha*) are usually clear and light and are served with spindly noodles, unless you opt for the thicker *krem-juha* (cream soup).

One starter which is stodgy enough to serve as a main course is *štrukli*, a pastry-and-cheese dish which is common to Zagreb and the Zagorje hills to the north. It comes in two forms: *kuhani* (boiled) *štrukli* are enormous ravioli-like pockets of dough filled with cottage cheese; while for *pečeni* (baked) *štrukli* the dough and cheese are baked in an earthenware dish, resulting in a cross between cheese soufflé and lasagne.

MEAT DISHES

Main **meat dishes** normally consist of a grilled or pan-fried *kotlet* (chop) or *odrezak* (fillet or escalope). These are usually either *svinjski* (pork) or *teleški* (veal), and can be prepared in a variety of ways: a *kotlet* or *odrezak* cooked *na žaru* will be a simple grill, *bečki odrezak* (Wiener schnitzel) comes fried in breadcrumbs, *pariški odrezak* (Pariser schnitzel) is fried in batter, and *zagrebački odrezak* (Zagreb schnitzel) is stuffed with

---

PRŠUT

Traditionally, Croatian **pršut** is made by small producers in inland Istria and Dalmatia, where it's common for families to own a handful of pigs. The *pršut* served in restaurants is usually supplied by these small-scale producers, and the industrially produced, vacuum-packed *pršut* sold in supermarkets can't really compare with the village-made stuff for succulence.

The pigs are slaughtered in late autumn, and the hind legs from which *pršut* is made are meticulously washed, and rigorously salted. The meat is then flattened under rocks to encourage any remaining blood to seep out, and it may be repeatedly removed, cleaned, salted and flattened again until all traces of red juices have disappeared. The ham is then hung outside the house to be dried out by the Bura, a cold, dry wind which sweeps down to the coast from inland Croatia. After that, the ham is hung indoors to be smoked (often each village will have a smoking shed which is shared by all the local *pršut* producers), ready to be eaten the following summer.

---

cheese and ham. *Mješano meso* (mixed grill) appears on all menus and will usually consist of a pork or veal *kotlet*, a few *ćevapi*, a *pljeskavica* and maybe a spicy *kobasica* (sausage), served alongside a bright red aubergine and pepper relish known as *ajvar*.

Lamb (*jagnjetina*) is usually prepared as a spit-roast. When travelling inland from Dalmatian cities like Zadar and Split it's quite common to see roadside restaurants where a whole sheep is being roasted over an open fire in the carpark to tempt travellers inside. Stewed meats are less common than grills, although goulash (*gulaš*) is frequently employed as a sauce served with pasta. A main course associated with Dalmatia (where it's traditionally considered a special-occasion food eaten on the big holy days, although it's perfectly common in restaurants) is *pašticada* (beef and bacon cooked in vinegar, wine and sometimes prunes). The most common **poultry** dish is *purica z mlincima* (turkey with baked pasta slivers), which is indigenous to Zagreb and the Zagorje. Other meaty main courses include *punjene paprike* (peppers stuffed with rice and meat) and *sarma* (cabbage leaves filled with a similar mixture). *Arambašica* is a version of *sarma* found in the Dalmatian hinterland which contains more meat and less rice.

SEAFOOD DISHES

On the coast, you'll be regaled with every kind of **seafood**. Starters include *salata od hobotnice* (octopus salad), and the slightly more expensive *salata od jastoga* (nibble-size portions of lobster flesh seasoned with olive oil and herbs). **Fish** (*riba*) can come either *na žaru* (grilled), *u pećnici* (baked) or *lešo* (boiled). Grilling is by far the most common way of preparing freshly caught fish, which is sold by weight (the best fish start at about 200Kn per kilo in cheap and mid-range restaurants; 300Kn per kilo in top-class establishments). Waiting staff will tell you what fish they have in stock, or will show you a tray of fish from which to choose. A decent-sized fish for one person usually weighs somewhere between a third and half a kilo, although you can always order a big fish and share it between two people.

The tastiest white meat is said to come from the *kovač* (John Dory), *list* (sole), *orada* (gilthead seabream) and *škrpina* (scorpion fish), although the range of fish caught in Adriatic waters is almost limitless. *Oslić* (hake) is slightly cheaper than the others, and is often served sliced and pan-fried in batter or breadcrumbs rather than grilled – when it will be priced per portion rather than by weight. Cheaper still is so-called *plava riba* (literally "blue fish"), a category which includes *sardele* (sardines) and *skuša* (mackerel). Another budget choice is *girice*, tiny fish similar to whitebait which are deep fried and eaten whole. Inexpensive main courses which crop up almost everywhere on the coast are *brodet* (boiled fish accompanied by a hot peppery sauce), *lignje na žaru* (grilled squid) and *crni rižot* (squid risotto). Seafood delicacies which appear in more expensive or specialist establishments include *rakovica* (crab), *ostrige* (oysters), *skoljke* (mussels) and *jastog* (lobster). *Škampi* (scampi) usually come as whole prawns which must be cracked open with the fingers, rather than the sanitized, breadcrumbed variety found in the UK. They're often served with a *buzara* sauce, made from garlic and white wine.

VEGETARIANS IN CROATIA

Vegetarianism hasn't really caught on in Croatia, and the choice of dishes on restaurant menus is correspondingly meagre; even many of the dishes which look like good vegetarian choices – the various bean soups and the ratatouille-style *đuveč* – are often made with meat stock. One traditional meat-free dish is *štrukli*, although this is a north Croatian speciality which can rarely be found on the coast. Most vegetarians will be reduced to making a meal out of vegetable side dishes, or picking from the small number of meatless starters: *omlet sa gljivama*

(mushroom omelette) and *pohani sir* (cheese fried in breadcrumbs) are safe choices. Italian-influenced pizzerias and spaghetterias are perhaps the best bet: most pizzerias offer a *pizza vegeterianska* featuring a selection of seasonal vegetables, and there's usually a choice of meatless pasta dishes including, if you're lucky, a vegetarian lasagne.

Ja sam vegeterijanac (*vegeterijanka* is the female form of the noun) means "I am a vegetarian". To ask "Have you got anything which doesn't contain meat?", say *Imate li nešto bez mesa?*

SALADS, ACCOMPANIMENTS AND DESSERTS

You'll usually be offered a choice of what your main course is served with: boiled potatoes (*krumpir*), chips (*prženi krumpir* or *pomfrit*), rice (*riža*) and gnocchi (*njoki*) are the most common accompaniments. Indigenous forms of pasta include *fuži* in Istria, *šurlice* on the island of Krk, and *mlinci* in Zagreb and the Zagorje – the latter are lasagne-thin scraps of dough which are boiled then baked. Additional vegetables can be ordered as extra items from the menu. Croatians eat an enormous amount of bread (*kruh*), and you'll be expected to scoff a couple of large slices with your meal regardless of whatever else you order.

The most common **salads** are *zelena salata* (green salad) and *mješana salata* (mixed salad). Other common side-dishes are gherkins (*krastavci*) and pickled peppers (*paprike*). Fish dishes are usually accompanied by *blitva* (mangel), a spinach-like plant indigenous to Dalmatia which is served with boiled potatoes and garlic.

Typical restaurant **desserts** include *sladoled* (ice cream), *torta* (cake) and *palačinke* (pancakes), which are usually served *sa marmeladom* (with marmalade), *s čokoladom* (with chocolate sauce) or *s oresima* (with walnuts). If in Dubrovnik, try *rožata*, the locally produced version of creme caramel. Ice cream is also sold in a *slastičarnica* (patisserie), the traditional place for buying eat-in or take-away cakes and pastries including *baklava*, the syrup-coated pastry indigenous to the Balkans and Middle East.

DRINKING

Drinking takes place in a **kavana** (café), usually a roomy and comfortable place with plenty of

outdoor seating which serves the full range of alcoholic and non-alcoholic drinks, as well as pastries and ice creams; or in a **kafić** (café-bar), which is essentially a smaller version of the same thing. There's no precise distinction between the two, although a *kafić* will usually cater to a younger clientele. The word **pub** is frequently adopted by café-bars attempting to imitate British, or more often Irish, styles, and will probably have Guinness adverts on the walls and a familiar range of Irish brews on tap. Both cafés and café-bars open extraordinarily early (sometimes as early as 6am) in order to serve the first espresso to those going to work, although alcohol isn't served until 9am. Closing time is usually 11pm, although regulations are often relaxed in summer, when café-bars stay open much later. You can also drink coffee and soft drinks in a **slastičarnica** (patisserie; often the best place to find freshly made *limunada* or lemonade), although they're often less atmospheric than a *kavana* or a *kafić* and may close earlier in the evening.

Most Croatian **beer** (*pivo*) is of the light lager variety. Karlovacko and Ožujsko are two good brands to look out for; Favorit, from Buzet in Istria, is widely considered to be the worst. Domestic dark beers include Tomislav from Zagreb and the less widespread Osiječko Crno from Osijek. Certain foreign brands – Stella Artois, Tuborg and Kaltenberg – are made in Croatia under licence. Of the foreign beers you're likely to find served on tap in café-bars and pubs, Guinness and Kilkenny are the most common. Whether you're drinking beer in bottles or on tap, a *malo pivo* (small beer) usually means 30cl, a *veliko pivo* (large beer)

CROATIAN FOOD AND DRINK

BASIC FOODS

Fuži	Pasta twirls	*Ocat*	Vinegar	*Šalša*	Tomato sauce
Kruh	Bread	*Omlet*	Omelette	*Šećer*	Sugar
Jaje	Egg	*Papar*	Pepper	*Sol*	Salt
Jogurt	Yogurt	*Pašteta*	Paté	*Tjestenine*	Pasta
Maslac	Butter	*Riža*	Rice	*Umak*	Sauce
Njoki	Gnocchi	*Salata*	Salad		

BASIC TERMS

Čaša	Glass	*Na ražnju*	Spit roast	*Ručak*	Lunch
Dobar tek!	Bon appetit!	*Na roštilju*	Grilled	*Šolja*	Cup
Doručak	Breakfast	*Na žaru*	Grilled	*Tanjur*	Plate
Hrana	Food	*Nazdravje!*	Cheers!	*Večera*	Dinner
Jelovnik	Menu	*Nož*	Knife	*Viljuška*	Fork
Kuhano	Boiled	*Pečeno*	Baked	*Zajutrak*	Breakfast
Marenda	Brunch	*Pladanj*	Platter	*Živjeli!*	Cheers!
Na lešo	Boiled	*Prženo*	Fried	*Žlica*	Spoon

SOUPS (*JUHE*) AND STARTERS (*PREDJELA*)

Fažol	Bean soup from Istria	*Paški sir*	Hard piquant cheese from the island of Pag
Grah	Soup made from haricot beans	*Pršut*	Home-cured ham similar to Italian *prosciutto*
Jota	Bean-and-sauerkraut soup	*Sir iz ulja*	Hard yellow cheese with piquant rind, kept under vegetable or olive oil
Kobasica	Sausage		
Kozji sir	Goat's cheese		
Kulen	Spicy paprika-flavoured pork and beef salami from Slavonia	*Sir s vrhnjem*	Cream cheese
Maneštra	Bean-and-vegetable soup from Istria	*Škripavac*	Mild hard cheese from Lika
		Šunka	Ham
Ovčji sir	Sheep's cheese	*Vrat*	Cured pork neck

VEGETABLES (*POVRĆE*)

Ajvar	Spicy relish made from puréed aubergines and peppers	*Grašak*	Peas
		Hren	Horseradish
		Kiseli kupus	Sauerkraut
Bijeli luk	Garlic	*Krastavac*	Cucumber, gherkin
Blitva	Spinach-like leaves of the mangel-wurzel (eaten with fish)	*Krumpir*	Potato
		Kukuruz	Corn on the cob
Češnjak	Garlic	*Kupus*	Cabbage
Đuveč/Đuveđ	Ratatouille-style mixture of vegetables and rice, heavily flavoured with paprika	*Luk*	Onion
		Mrkva	Carrot
		Paprika	Pepper, paprika
		Paradajz, pomadora or *rajčica* Tomato	
Gljiva	Mushroom	*Repa*	Turnip
Grah	Beans	*Šampinjoni*	Champignon mushrooms

FISH (*RIBA*)

Bakalar	Cod (often dried)	Ostrige	Oysters
Barbun	Mullet	Pastrva	Trout
Brancin	Sea-bass	Rak	Crab
Cipal	Golden grey mullet	Ribice	Whitebait, sprats
Crni rižot	Squid risotto	Riblja salata	Literally "fish salad",
Dagnje	Mussels		usually octopus
Hobotnica	Octopus	Sardele	Anchovies
Iglica	Garfish	Sipa	Cuttlefish
Jastog	Lobster	Skuša	Mackerel
Jegulja	Eel	Som	Catfish
Kalamari	Squid	Smuđ	Pike perch
Kapica	Clam	Šaran	Carp
Kovač	John Dory	Škampi	Scampi
Lignje	Squid	Školjke	Mussels
List	Sole	Škrpan/škrpina	Groper, sea scorpion
Luhin	Sea perch	Štuka	Pike
Orada	Gilthead seabream	Trilja	Striped or red mullet
Oslić	Hake	Zubatac	Dentex

MEAT (*MESO*) AND POULTRY (*PERJAD*)

Bečki odrezak	Wiener schnitzel	Pašticada	Beef cooked in wine and
Bubrezi	Kidneys		mustard
Buncek	Pork hock	Patka	Duck
Čevapčići or ćevapi	Grilled mincemeat rissoles	Piletina	Chicken
Govedina	Beef	Pljeskavica	Hamburger-style minced-
Gulaš	Goulash		meat patty
Guska	Goose	Pulić	Donkey
Jagnjetina	Lamb	Purica	Turkey
Jetra	Liver	Ražnjići	Pieces of pork grilled on a
Koljenica	Pork knuckle		skewer
Kotlet	Cutlet, chop	Slanina	Bacon
Kunic	Rabbit	Srnetina	Venison
Lungić	Lean, boneless and tender	Svinjetina	Pork
	pork chop	Teletina	Veal
Mućkalica	Paprika-flavoured meat stew	Tuka	Turkey
Nogice	Pig's trotters	Zagrebački odrezak	Schnitzel stuffed with
Odrezak	Escalope of veal or pork		ham and cheese and
Panceta	Bacon		fried in breadcrumbs

DESSERTS (*DESERTI*)

Fritule	Deep-fried dough balls	Palačinke	Pancakes
	dusted with icing sugar	Rožata	Creme-caramel-style
Kifla	Breakfast pastry, croissant		custard from Dubrovnik
Kolač	Cake	Savijača	Strudel
Kremšnita	Cream cake or custard slice	Sladoled	Ice cream
Krofna	Doughnut	Štrudl	Strudel
Kroštule	Deep-fried twists of pastry	Uštipci	Deep-fried dough balls
Makovnjača	Poppy seed cake		dusted with icing sugar
Orehnjača	Walnut cake	Torta	Gateau

Continued over. . .

FRUIT (VOĆE)

Ananas	Pineapple	*Jagoda*	Strawberry	*Šljiva*	Plum
Banana	Banana	*Kajsija*	Apricot	*Smokva*	Fig
Breskva	Peach	*Kruška*	Pear	*Trešnja*	Cherry
Dinja	Melon	*Limun*	Lemon	*Višnja*	Sour cherry
Grožđe	Grapes	*Lubenica*	Watermelon		
Jabuka	Apple	*Naranča*	Orange		

DRINKS (PIĆA)

Bambus	Red wine mixed with cola	*Mineralna voda*	Mineral water
Bevanda	Wine mixed with water	*Mlijeko*	Milk
Bijelo vino	White wine	*Orahovača*	Walnut-flavoured brandy
Biska	Mistletoe-flavoured brandy	*Pelinkovac*	Bitter juniper-based aperitif
		Pivo	Beer
Borovnica	Bilberry juice	*Rakija*	Brandy
Čaj	Tea	*Šljivovica*	Plum brandy
Crno vino	Red wine	*Sok*	Juice
Crveno vino	Rosé wine	*Špricer*	White wine and soda
Džus or *Đus*	Juice	*Svjetlo pivo*	Light, lager-style beer
Gemišt	White wine and mineral water	*Topla čokolada*	Hot chocolate
		Travarica	Herb-based spirit similar to Italian *grappa*
Kava	Coffee		
Loza/Lozovača	Grape brandy	*Viljamovka*	Pear brandy
Medenica/Medovina	Honey-flavoured brandy	*Voda*	Water

means a half-litre. A small beer costs 6–10Kn; a large one, 10–15Kn. Bottled beers are slightly more expensive.

Croatia produces an impressive range of red and white **wines** (*vino*), few of which find their way onto Western supermarket shelves. Among the dry and medium-dry **whites**, look out for Vrbnička lahtina from Vrbnik on Krk; Vugava from Vis; Semion from Istria; and Kaštelet, Grk and Pošip from Korčula. Of the **reds**, the dark heady Dingač from the Pelješac peninsula has the best reputation and is the most expensive, although Babić from Primošten and Viški plavac from Vis are frequently as good, as is Teran, a fresh, light red from Istria. In shops and supermarkets table wine sells for about 20–30Kn for a litre bottle, while a decent Dingač will set you back about 80Kn. Popular wine-derived drinks include *bevanda* (white or red wine mixed with plain water), *gemišt* (white wine and fizzy mineral water), *špricer* (white wine and soda water) and the eternally popular summer tipple *bambus* (red wine mixed with cola).

Local **spirits** (*žestoka pića*) are commonly consumed as an aperitif before meals and are usually produced from grapes (in which case they're called *loza* or *lozovača*) or from other fruits – the most common of these being plum brandy (*šljivovica*) and pear brandy (*viljamovka*). Grape-based spirits are often given additional flavours and have health-giving properties, notably as *travarica* (herb brandy), *medovina* (honey brandy) or *orahovača* (walnut brandy). *Pelinkovac* is a juniper-based spirit, *vinjak* is locally produced cognac, and *maraskino* is a cherry liqueur from Zadar in Dalmatia. *Biska* is a mistletoe-flavoured aperitif from inland Istria. Foreign brandies and whiskies are available pretty much everywhere.

Apart from the vast urns of overstewed brown liquid served up by hotels at breakfast time, **coffee** (*kava*) is usually of a high quality. It is served as a strong black espresso unless specified otherwise – *kava sa mlijekom* comes with a drop of milk, *kava sa šlagom* comes with cream, and *bijela kava* (white coffee) is usually like a good caffe latte. Cappucino is also fairly ubiquitous.

Tea (*čaj*) is usually of the herbal variety; ask for *indijski čaj* (Indian tea) if you want the English-style brew. *Čaj sa limunom* is with a slice of lemon, *sa mlijekom* comes with milk.

In the best cafés coffee is served with an accompanying glass of water (*voda*); otherwise

feel free to ask for one. Mineral water (*mineralna voda*) and other **soft drinks** are often served in multiples of 10cl or *dec* (pronounced "dets"). If you want 20cl of mineral water ask for *dva deca*, 30cl is *tri deca*. If you want fruit juice, note that the word *đus* ("juice") usually means orange juice.

MAIL AND TELECOMMUNICATIONS

America; surface mail takes at least twice as long. Stamps (*marke*) can be bought either at the post office or at news-stands. If you're sending parcels home, don't seal the package until the post office staff have had a look at what's inside: customs duty is charged on the export of most things, although newsprint and books are exempt. **Post restante** services are available at the main post office (*glavna pošta*) in every sizeable town – mail should be addressed to poste restante, followed by the name of the town. Mail sent to puste restante in Zagreb (the official address is Poste Restante, 10 000 Zagreb), is held at the post office next to the train station, which is open round the clock. American Express customers can use the mailing addresses of any branch of the Atlas travel agency – they represent American Express in Croatia and will hold your mail for two months.

POST

Most **post offices** (*pošta* or *HPT*) are open Monday to Friday from 7 or 8am to 7 or 8pm, and Saturday 8am to 1 or 2pm. In villages and on islands, Monday to Friday 8am to 2pm is more common, though in big towns and resorts some offices open daily, sometimes staying open until 10pm.

Airmail (*zrakoplovom*) takes about three days to reach Britain, and eight to ten to reach North

TELEPHONES

Croatian **phone booths** use magnetic cards (*telekarta*), which you can pick up from post offices or newspaper kiosks. They're sold in denominations of 25, 50, 100, 200 and 500 units (*impulsa*). Generally speaking, a single unit will be enough for a local call, and the 25-unit card

---

PHONING ABROAD FROM CROATIA
Dial the following numbers + area code (minus initial "0") + subscriber number

To Australia ☎00 61
To Ireland ☎00 353
To New Zealand ☎00 64
To the UK 00 44
To US and Canada ☎00 1

PHONING CROATIA FROM ABROAD
Dial the following numbers + Croatian area code (minus initial "0") + subscriber number

From Australia ☎00 11 385
From Ireland 00 385
From New Zealand ☎00 385
From the UK 00 385
From US and Canada ☎011 385

(costing around 13Kn) will be sufficient for making a few longer-distance calls within the country. For **international calls** of any duration, it's probably easier to go to the post office, where you're assigned a cabin and given the bill afterwards – rates are cheapest Monday to Saturday 10pm to 7am, and all day Sunday. Avoid making international calls from your hotel room: charges are extortionate, and seem to rise in proportion to the star-rating of the hotel.

The network for GSM **mobile phones** in Croatia covers pretty much the whole country, apart from the inevitable blackspots in mountainous areas.

INTERNET

Cybercafés have been slow to catch on in Croatia, and at the time of writing there are established cybercafés only in Zagreb, Osijek, Rijeka and Labin. In addition, a number of hotels and travel agencies on the Adriatic coast have experimented with the idea of renting out Internet time to their customers, although they often only have a single computer which is permanently busy. Prices in cybercafés are generally reasonable: expect to pay about 10Kn for a one-off membership fee and around 20–30Kn per hour online.

THE MEDIA

Forty-five years of communism made the Croatian press into a tool of its political masters, a habit that has subsequently proved hard to shake off. The most prestigious of Croatia's daily newspapers, *Vjesnik* (*www.vjesnik.com*), has a reputation for stodgy reporting and obsequiousness to the government. The virtual mouthpiece first of the Croatian communists, then of the HDZ, its editorials and columns became more and more rabidly right wing until the HDZ's defeat in the elections of January 2000 led to a change of editor, though it's too early to say how the new *Vjesnik* will fare.

The other national daily, *Jutarnji List*, is breezy and populist in comparison, contains much more showbiz gossip, and is refreshingly independent politically. Closest to Western tabloids in style is the evening paper *Večernji List*, which nevertheless includes good cultural coverage buried among the human interest stories.

The most influential of the weeklies is Split's **Feral Tribune** (*www.feral-hr.com*), an irreverent cross between serious news magazine and counter-cultural youth rag, which began life as a humorous and satirical supplement of *Slobodna Dalmacija* (Dalmatia's leading regional newspaper) in the late 1980s. *Feral* was an important source of opposition to the HDZ during the 1990s, offering a vibrant alternative to the stuffy and uninspiring political analysis offered by other papers and frequently ridiculing Franjo Tuđman.

Tuđman took it personally and attempted a number of ruses to have *Feral* shut down: having it classified as a pornographic publication in order to qualify it for a higher tax rate, taking its editor to court for defaming the office of the president, and threatening its staff with military call-up being just three.

The arts are served by a variety of **cult titles** which somehow survive despite the relatively small size of the domestic market. Twice-weekly *Zarez* is an intellectual hothouse of debates and book reviews reminiscent of the *Times Literary Supplement* or *New York Review of Books*; *Cicero* is a glossy, big-budget fine arts quarterly which is great to look at even if you don't understand a word of the text. Catering for more underground tastes are *Nomad*, the alternative rock bible, and *Godine Nove*, which is devoted to what's new in literature and contemporary culture.

There are no **English-language newspapers** published in Croatia itself, although copies of the *Herald Tribune* and British dailies can be found in Zagreb, Split and Dubrovnik. English-language lifestyle and computer magazines are much more widespread, especially international fashion glossies. If you can read Italian, you could always try *La Voce del Popolo*, the daily newspaper of Croatia's Italian minority.

Like Croatia's newspapers, the three national **television** channels, all run by state-owned HRT (Hrvatski radio i televizija), have a history of overdeference to successive governments, although change is on the cards. Current output tends towards the didactic, with plenty of plodding documentaries about Croatian history and culture, although HRT1 produces plenty of lavish shows featuring Croatian pop stars, especially in the summer when outdoor concerts are screened.

HRT3 concentrates exclusively on sport. Croatia **Radio** (92.1MHz) has news in English every day at 00.10am, 8.03am, 10.03am, 2.03pm and 8.03pm, and the BBC World Service is available on short wave, though it's very difficult to get a good signal.

OPENING HOURS AND PUBLIC HOLIDAYS

Shops in Croatia are usually open Monday to Friday from 8am to 8pm, and on Saturdays from 8am to 2 or 3pm. City supermarkets often stay open until about 6pm on Saturdays, and open on Sunday mornings as well. On the coast, during summer, shops introduce a long afternoon break and stay open later in the evenings to compensate. Office hours are generally Monday to Friday 8am to 3 or 4pm.

Tourist offices, travel agents and tourist attractions often change their opening times as the year progresses, generally remaining open for longer during the summer season (usually June–Sept). Note, though, that summer opening times don't necessarily come into force at the beginning of June: most places change over from summer to winter times according to how many tourists are around, rather than according to a fixed schedule. For this reason, we've listed "summer" and "winter" opening times in the guide rather than trying to give specific months.

On the coast, **museums and galleries** are often open all day every day (sometimes with a long break in the afternoon) in July and August, and closed altogether in the depths of winter. At other times, things can be unpredictable, with attractions opening their doors when tourist traffic seems to justify it. In big cities and inland areas, museums and galleries are more likely to have regular opening times year round, and are often closed on Mondays.

Churches (*crkve*) in city centres and well-touristed areas usually stay open daily 7am–7pm or later, but many in smaller towns and villages may only open their doors around mass times. Churches or chapels which are known for being architecturally unique or which contain valuable frescoes may have set opening times (in which case we've mentioned them in the guide); otherwise you'll have to ask around to establish which of the locals has been nominated as holder of the key (*ključ*).

Monasteries (*samostani*) are often open from dawn to dusk to those who want to stroll around the cloister, although churches or art collections belonging to the monasteries conform to the opening patterns for museums and churches outlined above. Accessibility often depends on the number of monks in residence and the regulations governing the monastic order itself – Benedictines, for example, have strict rules governing how much of the day should be set aside for prayer, and Benedictine nuns traditionally shun contact with the outside world, thereby limiting opportunities for members of the public to visit. Many monasteries (such as the Dominican monastery in Dubrovnik) contain art collections that can outshine any art gallery, while other monastic collections are much more eccentric – oddments amassed over the centuries by generations of inquisitive hoarders – but no less entertaining.

PUBLIC HOLIDAYS

All shops and banks are closed on the following public holidays

January 1 New Year
January 6 Epiphany
Easter Monday
May 1 Labour Day
May 30 Day of Croatian Statehood
June 22 Day of the 1941 Anti-Fascist Uprising
August 5 National Thanksgiving Day
August 15 Assumption
November 1 All Saints
December 25 Christmas

FESTIVALS

FOLK AND RELIGIOUS FESTIVALS

As befits a devoutly Catholic country, the Croatian year is peppered with **feast days** and **religious holidays**, featuring church processions and celebratory masses. In addition, each town or village has its own patron saint, whose feast day becomes the excuse for a communal knees-up – a selection is included in the box opposite.

The church calendar frequently dovetails with an older pagan one, corresponding to the changing seasons and the agricultural cycle. The most important event in the early part of the year is the pre-Lenten **carnival** (*karneval*; often known as *fašnik* in inland Croatia, *pust* on the Adriatic), which actually begins before Christmas but does not reach a climax until Shrove Tuesday or the weekend immediately preceding it, when there are processions and masked revelry in towns all over Croatia. A lot of places organize parades with floats, with the disguises donned by the participants frequently satirizing local politicians or commenting on the events of the past year. Rijeka, Samobor and Nova Gorica (just south of Zagreb) host the biggest events. The amount of post-parade hedonism differs from place to place, although the recently revived carnival in Split has already earned a reputation for its relaxed party atmosphere. Carnival processions are repeated in summer in some Adriatic resorts – a fun fancy-dress affair aimed at children and tourists. Carnival practices in smaller places are still linked to pre-Christian fertility rites: in the villages near

Rijeka groups of men (called *zvončari* or "ringers") don sheepskins and ring bells to drive away evil spirits, while in many areas a doll known as *pust* (or *poklad* in Lastovo) is ritually burned in order to cleanse the coming agricultural year of bad luck.

The next big event is **Easter week**, characterized by solemn processions in many towns, especially Hvar, Korčula and Vodice. Traditionally, the beginning of the summer agricultural cycle was marked by **St George's Day** (*Jurjevo*; April 23), when a villager clad in branches and known as Green George (*Zeleni Juraj*) went from house to house accompanied by local children performing songs and dances. Green George received a gift from each household and in return presented them with a fertility charm in the form of a twig. Unfortunately you'll see references to Jurjevo in ethnographic museums more often than in real life, although it's still celebrated in the villages of the Stubica valley north of Zagreb, and at Hrašće and Donja Lomnica just south of Zagreb.

Another celebration with distinct pagan undertones is **St John's Day** (*Ivanje*; June 24), when local youths jump over bonfires (*Ivanjski krijes*) in a typical summer-solstice celebration. It's still practised in many places, especially in Karlovac. High summer is characterized by a sequence of important Christian holidays. **Our Lady of the Snows** (*Madona od snijega* or *sniga*; Aug 5) is celebrated with processions to churches associated with "miraculous" summer snowfalls, most famously at Kukljica on the island of Ugljan, where the procession takes the form of a flotilla of small boats. More important still is the **Assumption** (*Velika Gospa*; Aug 15), when churches throughout the country hold special services and large pilgrimages are made to Marian shrines such as Marija Bistrica near Zagreb, Ludbreg between Varaždin and Koprivnica and Sinj in the Dalmatian hinterland. The **Birth of the Virgin** (*Mala Gospa*; Sept 8) is only slightly less important in the Catholic calendar, and is celebrated in similar fashion.

All Saints' Day (*Svi sveti*; Nov 1) is one of the most important Catholic feasts of the autumn, when families visit graveyards to pay their respects to the departed. By the evening, many big-city cemeteries are transformed into a sea of candles. **St Martin's Day** (*Martinje*; Nov 11) is traditionally the day when the year's wine is first tasted, and is often used as an excuse for revelry in wine-producing areas. In accordance with a widespread central European tradition, St Martin's Day is also marked by the slaughter and roasting of a goose. A slaughter of a more widespread kind takes place at the end of November, when many rural families (especially in Slavonia and the Dalmatian hinterland) set aside a weekend in order to carry out the annual **pig slaughter** (*svinokolja* or *kolinja*), and begin preparation of the sausages and hams which will be consumed over the next year.

On **St Nicholas's Day** (*Sveti Nikola*; Dec 6) children leave out stockings and are rewarded with small presents if they're good. They also receive a gold- or silver-painted twig (*šiba*) – a symbol of the beating they will receive should they misbehave. Children are also threatened by visits from the monster Krampus, a kind of St Nicholas in reverse, who takes away bad children in his bag. **Christmas** (*Božić*) itself is much the

same as anywhere else in Europe, with presents laid out under the family Christmas tree. The main family meal is eaten on Christmas Eve (*Badnja večer*), and traditionally consists of fish (often carp), after which everyone attends midnight mass.

The country's main **folk festival** is the International Folklore Festival, held in Zagreb on the last weekend of July and traditionally the best place to see songs and dances from all over the country. The tradition of the Dalmatian *klapa* (male-voice choir) is preserved in numerous festivals up and down the coast, the biggest being the one held in Omiš in July. The remaining big folk events are all in Slavonia and have a more regional character, although the Brodsko Kolo Festival in Slavonski Brod (mid-June), Vinkovci Autumn (late Sept) and Đakovo Folk Festival (end Sept) are all worthwhile shindigs. Guests in Adriatic hotels will be treated to folklore shows, often over dinner, throughout the summer season. If you're

---

FEAST DAYS AND FOLKLORIC EVENTS

February 2 Kumpanjija Sword Dance, Korčula.

February 3 Feast of St Blaise, Dubrovnik.

Sunday before Shrove Tuesday Carnival Procession, Rijeka.

Shrove Tuesday Carnival Procession, Split.

Good Friday Procession of the Religious Brotherhoods, Korčula.

April 23 St George's Day.

May 7 Feast of St Domnius, Split.

May 8 Birthday of Cardinal Stepinac, Krašić.

Second weekend in May Roč Accordion Festival

Mid-June Brodsko Kolo Folklore Festival, Slavonski Brod.

June 24 St John's Day bonfires.

July Krk Folklore Festival.

July Klapa Festival, Omiš.

Mid-July Summer Carnival, Novi Vinodolski.

July 25 Feast of St Jacob. Performances of the Kumpanjija Sword Dance, Korčula.

July 27 St Christopher's Day. Crossbow Tournament, Rab.

July 29 Feast of St Theodore. Performance of the Moreška Sword Dance, Korčula.

Late July Carnival, I

Late July International Folklore Festival, Zagreb.

August 5 Feast of Our Lady of the Snows. Boat procession on Ugljan, and performance of the Kumpanjija Sword Dance, Korčula.

August 8 Feast of St Lawrence.

August 8 Sinjska Alka, Sinj.

August 15 Assumption. Large gatherings at Marija Bistrica, Trsat, Sinj and Aljmaš.

August 16 Feast of St Rock. Performance of the Moštra Sword Dance at Postrana and the Kumpanjija Sword Dance at Korčula.

August 21 Tilting at the Ring, Barban.

August 27–29 Feast of St Pelagius, Novigrad.

Late September Vinkovci Autumn Folklore Festival.

Last weekend in September Đakovo Folk Festival.

Last weekend in September Grape Harvest Festival, Pregrada, Zagorje.

October 8 Feast of St Simeon. Religious procession and opening of St Simeon's coffin, Zadar.

November 11 Feast of St Martin. Celebrations at Dugo Selo, Tar, Vrsar and Buzet.

December 6 Feast of St Nicholas. Presents are given to children and a fishing boat is burnt outside the Benedictine monastery at Komiža, Vis.

December 25 Christmas

CROATIAN ARTS FESTIVALS

Biennale of New Music (odd-numbered years only). Zagreb, late April.

Festival of One-Minute Films. Požega, May.

Contemporary Dance Week (Tjedan suvremenog plesa). Zagreb, early June.

Eurokaz Festival of Contemporary Theatre. Zagreb, late June.

Zadar Dreams (Zadar snova). Festival of alternative drama and performance art. Zadar, late June to early July.

Split Jazz Festival. Split, early July.

Dubrovnik Summer Festival (Dubrovačke ljetne igre). Dubrovnik, early July to late August.

Naive Art Fair (Sajam naive). Koprivnica, mid-July.

Osor Music Evenings (Osorske večeri). International chamber music festival. Osor, Cres, July.

Season of Concerts in the Church of St Donat. Zadar, July to early August.

Split Summer (Splitsko ljeto). Split, mid-July to mid-August.

Croatian Film Festival. Pula, August.

International Film Festival. Motovun, August.

Festival of Creative Disorder (Festival kreativnog nereda). Split, August.

Musical Summer (Glazbeno ljeto). Grožnjan, Aug.

PIF International Festival of Puppet Theatre. Zagreb, late August to early September.

Festival of New Film (Festival novog filma). Shorts, documentaries and art-house films. Split, late September to early October.

Varaždin Festival of Baroque Music. Performances in Varaždin cathedral and other city churches. Varaždin, late September to early October.

---

staying near Dubrovnik, local songs and dances are performed outside the church in Čilipi every Sunday morning.

CULTURAL FESTIVALS

Every Adriatic town organizes cultural events of some sort over the summer, usually featuring outdoor concerts of pop, classical music or folk. The most important of these is the **Dubrovnik Summer Festival**, six weeks of classical music and drama beginning in early July, much of which is performed in the squares and courtyards of the old town. Historical buildings also form the backdrop for a number of other classical music events, including the Osor Music Evenings on the island of Cres; summer concerts in the half-abandoned hill village of Lubenice, also on Cres; the Musical Summer in the Istrian hill town of Grožnjan; summer recitals in St Donat's Church in Zadar; and the Varaždin Festival of Baroque Music, which uses many of the city's fine churches. There are numerous outdoor events in Split over the summer, including the Split Jazz Festival, the varied music and drama collected together under the banner of the Split Summer, and the Eurovision-style grotesqueries of the Melodies of the Croatian Adriatic, a festival of domestic pop which usually takes place in the early summer.

Zagreb has a full roster of festival events, the most prestigious being the Biennale of New Music, a festival of cutting-edge contemporary classical work held in odd-numbered years, although challenging new work also crops up at the Contemporary Dance Week in early June; Eurokaz European Theatre Festival in late June; and PIF international puppet festival late August.

Avant-garde traditions elsewhere in the country are showcased at the Požega Festival of One-Minute Films, the Zadar Dreams festival of new theatre, the Split Festival of Creative Disorder, and Split's Festival of New Film and Video.

SPORT

Sport in Croatia occupies an important position in society, not least because sporting successes have proved consistently important in enhancing national prestige abroad – something of which three-times Wimbledon finalist Goran Ivanišević is an outstanding individual example. Participation in group activities carries a high value in a society in which solidarity and togetherness are prized – sometimes at the expense of individual self-expression. Male team sports have always been encouraged, and recent years have seen an explosion in the number of majorettes and marching bands – as if to provide girls with a parallel sphere of activity.

Croatian **football** (*nogomet*) has come a long way since it was introduced to the country in 1893 by the crew of a British frigate who took on a team of locals just outside Trogir's main town gate. Croatian footballers formed an important part of the Yugoslav sides of the 1960s and 1970s, whose reputation for skill and audacity earned them the tag of "the Brazilians of Europe", although few imagined the impression the Croats would make on the international scene in the 1990s. Resting on a backbone of talented individuals including Robert Prosinečki, Davor Šuker, Alen Bokšić, Slaven Bilić and Igor Štimac, the Croatian team finished above Italy to qualify for the European Championships of 1996, where they impressed many neutrals before going out in the quarter-finals to Germany. They fared even better in the 1998 World Cup, beating Germany 3–0 in the quarter-finals before narrowly succumbing in the semis to host nation France – they also defeated Holland in the play-off for third place, and Davor Šuker ended the tournament as top scorer. Croatia failed to qualify for the European Championships in 2000 after an excruciating 2–2 home draw with arch rivals Yugoslavia.

The domestic league is hampered by a lack of real competition. The big teams **Dinamo Zagreb** and **Hajduk Split** have more or less monopolized domestic honours since 1991, occasionally challenged by the likes of Rijeka and Osijek. Both Hajduk and Dinamo (under their previous name of Croatia Zagreb) have performed creditably in the Uefa Champions' League, although both teams are hamstrung by the fact that their best players invariably leave to play abroad as soon as they've made a name for themselves. Matches between the big two can attract big crowds, but otherwise attendances are all too often in the low thousands, with most fans content to follow the game on the HRT3 television channel.

The football season lasts from mid-August to late May, with a two-month winter break in January and February. Matches usually take place on Saturdays or Sundays, with extra games scheduled for Wednesday evenings as the season draws to a climax in April–May. The cheapest seats rarely cost more than 30Kn. Tickets for all but the biggest matches can be bought at the ground before the game. For international matches (usually played at Dinamo Zagreb's Maksimir stadium) or European ties, purchase tickets from the stadium box office as far in advance as possible.

After football the most popular sport is **basketball** (*košarka*), with teams like Split, Zadar and Cibona Zagreb enjoying large followings and a Europe-wide reputation. **Handball** (*rukomet*), **volleyball** (*odbojka*) and **waterpolo** (*vaterpolo*) all get a good deal of newspaper and television coverage. One sport which is definitely not televised – although you'll see a lot of it in Dalmatia – is a form of **bowls** known as *bočanje* (derived from the Italian *boccie*), which is played in villages on a sandy outdoor rectangle by local men on summer evenings.

OUTDOOR ACTIVITIES

Croatia is not well known as a destination for adventure tourism, but there are numerous outdoor activities on offer, whether hiking in the hills of the interior or scuba-diving in the Adriatic. Sailing is best organized before you arrive (see "Getting there from Britain and Ireland" on p.5).

HIKING

Hiking was first popularized in Croatia in the late nineteenth century, when the exploration of the great Croatian outdoors was considered a patriotic duty as well as a form of exercise. It's still a popular weekend activity, especially in spring and early summer, before the searing Mediterranean heat sends people scurrying for the beaches.

Easy rambling territory in inland Croatia is provided by wooded **Mount Medvednica** and the **Samobor Hills** (Samoborsko gorje), both close to Zagreb and criss-crossed by well-used trails. Higher altitudes and longer walks can be found in the **Gorski Kotar** region, between Karlovac and the coast: the main targets here are Risnjak in the north of the range, best reached from Rijeka; and Klek and Bijele stijene in the south. On the Adriatic coast, **Učka**, immediately above Opatija and Lovran, is one of the most easily accessible mountains, and can be safely bagged by the moderately fit hiker. Further south, the more challenging **Velebit** range stretches for some 100km along the eastern shore of the Kvarner Gulf; its main hiking areas are around the Zavižan summit near Senj, and the Paklenica National Park at Velebit's southern end. In Dalmatia, the principal peaks are **Kozjak** and **Mosor** (immediately west and east of Split respectively) and, most challenging of all the Adriatic mountains, **Biokovo**, above the Makarska Riviera.

Ranges such as Gorski Kotar and Velebit seem to invite extended expeditions, but unfortunately hut-to-hut walking in Croatia is still in its infancy, and there are no local travel agencies who organize it. Mountain refuges (*planinarski dom*) run by local hiking associations do exist, but they're usually only open at the weekend, making anything longer than a 36-hour trek unfeasible.

Detailed hiking **maps** are published by the Croatian Hiking Association, Kozarčeva 22, Zagreb (Hrvatski planinarski savez; Mon–Fri 9am–3pm), although they're only sporadically available in bookshops and you'll have to visit the association in person to inspect the full range. Tourist offices sometimes sell hiking maps of their own area (for instance the tourist information centre in Zagreb sells maps of Mount Medvednica), but don't bank on it.

RAFTING

An increasing range of **whitewater rafting** trips are being organized by the bigger travel agents. In inland Croatia, GeneralTurist, Praška 5, Zagreb (☎01/48-10-033, fax 48-10-420, *www.generalturist.com*) run weekend trips to the River Kupa near Karlovac from early July until late October. On the coast, branches of the Atlas Agency in Split, Trogir and Makarska organize trips down the Cetina River between May and September. A more sedate version of rafting – floating downriver on a raft rather than rushing over rapids in a dinghy – takes place on the River Zrmanja just east of Zadar; contact Flash Touring in Novigrad (see p.209). Prices vary according to the duration of the trip – expect to pay 220–350Kn per person for a day's excursion.

DIVING

There's a growing number of **scuba-diving** centres along the Adriatic coast offering lessons, guided expeditions and equipment rental. Most resorts will have somewhere offering one-day introductory courses for 200–300Kn, as well as a range of other courses for all abilities. If you already hold a diving certificate, you need to call at the harbourmaster's office (*lučka kapetanija*) and pay a registration fee before diving. One of the most rewarding areas for diving, with clear waters and rich marine life, is the Kornati islands in mid-Dalmatia, although its national park status means that diving can only be arranged through officially sanctioned operators like Neptun in Vodice (☎022/331-444, *www.neptun-sub.hr*) and Aquanaut in Murter (☎022/434-450 or 434-575).

For general information contact the Croatian Diving Federation at Pro Diving Croatia, Dalmatinska 12, 10000 Zagreb (☎01/48-48-765, fax 48-49-119, *www.diving.hr*).

WINDSURFING

There are only really two places to go in Croatia for serious **windsurfers**. The best is Bol on the island of Brač, which stands on the northern side of the narrow channel dividing Brač from Hvar, providing calm waters and channelling the right kind of winds. Second-best is the Kučišće-Viganj resort area just west of Orebić, which occupies a similar position on the Pelješac channel dividing the mainland from Korčula. You'll find plenty of people renting out gear and offering courses: boards can be rented for

200–250Kn per day; eight hours' tuition will cost about 600Kn.

SKIING

Croatia has two main **skiing** areas: Sljeme on Mount Medvednica just outside Zagreb, and Bjelolasica in the Gorski kotar between Zagreb and Rijeka. Although both are fun venues for occasional skiing if you're already visiting Croatia, neither is worth planning a holiday around. Altitudes (1035m and 1533m repectively) are too low to guarantee long periods of adequate snow cover, and most Croats treat skiing trips as spur-of-the-moment events if the weather is right. You can rent gear and sign up for lessons at either place. Sljeme is accessible from Zagreb via a combination of public transport and cable car.

TRAVELLERS WITH DISABILITIES

More attention has been paid to people with disabilities since the 1991–95 war, and the large number of wounded and disabled veterans it created. Many public places are wheelchair accessible, especially in larger cities, though in general, access to public transport and tourist sites still leaves a lot to be desired.

There's also a growing number of wheelchair-accessible hotels, though these tend to be in the more expensive price brackets. Some areas of the country seem slower to adapt than others – at the last visit, neither Split nor Hvar had a single hotel with wheelchair access.

Tourist offices throughout Croatia will usually find out whether there are any suitable accommodation facilities in their region if you ring in advance, but be sure to double-check the information they give you – some tourist office listings optimistically state that a place has disabled facilities, when in fact it doesn't.

PLANNING A HOLIDAY

There are organized tours and holidays specifically for people with disabilities – the contacts in the box on p.42 will be able to help with latest information. If you want to be more independent, it's important to become an authority on where you must be self-reliant and where you may expect

help, especially regarding transport and accommodation. It's also vital to be honest – with travel agencies, insurance companies and travel companions. Know your limitations and make sure others know them. If you don't use a wheelchair all the time but your walking capabilities are limited, remember that you are likely to need to cover greater distances while travelling (often over rougher terrain and in hotter temperatures) than you are used to. If you use a wheelchair, have it serviced before you go and carry a repair kit.

Read your travel insurance small print carefully to make sure that people with a pre-existing medical condition are not excluded, and use your travel agent to make your journey simpler: airline or bus companies can cope better if they are expecting you, with a wheelchair provided at airports and staff primed to help. A medical certificate of your fitness to travel, provided by your doctor, is also extremely useful; some airlines or insurance companies may insist on it. Make sure that you have extra supplies of drugs – carried with you if you fly – and a prescription including the generic name in case of emergency. Carry spares of any clothing or equipment that might be hard to find; if there's an association representing people with your disability, contact them early in the planning process.

CONTACTS FOR TRAVELLERS WITH DISABILITIES

AUSTRALIA
ACROD (Australian Council for Rehabilitation of the Disabled) ☎ 02/6282 4333 or 9743 2699. **Barrier Free Travel** ☎02/6655 1733.

CROATIA
Association of Organizations of Disabled People in Croatia (Savez Organizacija Invalida Hrvatske), Savska cesta 3, 10 000 Zagreb (☎ & fax 01/48-29-394). Publishes informative guides, though only available in Croatian, for disabled travellers to Zagreb, Pula, Varaždin and Rijeka.
ZET (Zagreb Electric Tram Company), Balokoviceva bb, Zagreb (☎01/66-00-443, fax: 01/685-179). Organizes free transport for disabled people anywhere in and around Zagreb in a specially adapted vehicle.

IRELAND
Disability Action Group ☎028/9049 1011. **Irish Wheelchair Association** ☎01/833 8241, fax 833 3873, *iwa@iol.ie*.

NEW ZEALAND
Disabled Persons Assembly ☎04/801 9100.

NORTH AMERICA
Mobility International USA ☎541/343-1284. Information and referral services, access guides, tours and exchange programmes. Annual membership $25.
Society for the Advancement of Travel for the Handicapped (SATH) ☎212/447-7284, *www.sath.org*. Non-profit travel-industry referral service that passes queries on to its members as appropriate; allow plenty of time for a response.

UK
Holiday Care ☎01293/774535, fax 784647, Minicom ☎01293/776943, *www.freespace.virgin.net/hol-care*. Free lists of accessible accommodation abroad.
RADAR (Royal Association for Disability and Rehabilitation) ☎020/7250 3222, Minicom ☎020/7250 4119, *www.radar.org.uk*. Advice on holidays and travel abroad.
Tripscope ☎08457/585641, *www.justmobility.co.uk/tripscope*. Telephone information service offering free advice on international transport for those with mobility problems.

POLICE, TROUBLE AND SEXUAL HARASSMENT

The crime rate in Croatia is low by European standards. Croatian police (*policija*) are generally helpful and polite when dealing with foreigners, but rarely speak English. Routine police checks on identity cards are common in Croatia: always carry your passport or driving licence.

Your main defence against petty theft is to exercise common sense and refrain from flaunting luxury items. Take out an insurance policy before you leave home (see p.15) and always carry a photocopy of the crucial information-bearing pages of your passport with you – this will enable your consulate to issue you swiftly with new travel documents in the event of your passport being stolen.

If you get into trouble with the authorities, wait until you can explain matters to someone in

English if at all possible. The police are not allowed to search your car or place of abode without a warrant. Should you be arrested, you can be held in a police station for 24 hours without charge. They will automatically notify your consulate of your arrest – this will usually take place within the first 24 hours.

SEXUAL HARASSMENT

Croatia is a patriarchal society in which many women find themselves holding down a full-time job while simultaneously managing the household on behalf of their menfolk. However, there are few specific situations in which female travellers might feel uncomfortable, and no real no-go areas, although some of the more down-at-heel café-bars can feel like male-only preserves. By Western standards, Croatia's streets are relatively safe at night, even in the cities.

Croatian men like to regard the annual deluge of foreign female tourists as fair game, but any display of Mediterranean machismo tends to be leavened by genuine attempts at gallantry and charm. A suitably firm response should be enough to cope with unwanted attentions. Alternatively, try to imitate the repertoire of stony silences and withering looks employed by the local girls.

THE AFTERMATH OF WAR

Almost a third of Croatia was occupied by Serb forces between 1991 and 1995, and although you shouldn't have any qualms about visiting these areas now, a few precautions should be borne in mind. Almost all frontline areas were heavily **mined** during the war, and few of these minefields have been fully cleared. Most are well marked with signs bearing the skull-and-bones symbol and the word "mine", although it would be unwise to trust this marking system 100 percent – some mined areas may not be so well labelled as others. Basically, any abandoned village or stretch of agricultural land which looks like it has been left uncultivated since 1995 is potentially dangerous. If you're travelling to eastern Slavonia

(Beli Manastir, Vukovar, Ilok), western Slavonia (Jasenovac, Novska, Pakrac), the area between Karlovac and Split (Slunj to Knin) and the Zadar hinterland, stick to roads and pavements and don't go wandering off into the countryside unsupervised.

Travellers exploring the above itineraries are likely to see **war damage** in the shape of shelled buildings and burned-out houses, but also a great deal of energetic building and reconstruction. Both Croats and Serbs are returning to areas where they once lived side by side, and outbreaks of intercommunal violence are now few and far between. However, the casual visitor will probably miss the nuances of Croat–Serb relations: tension still exists, many refugees continue to occupy houses claimed by others, and each community tends to stick to its own cafés and bars. Exercise discretion therefore before embarking on historical or political discussions with the locals.

> **EMERGENCY NUMBERS**
> Police ☎92
> Ambulance ☎94
> Fire ☎93

WORK AND STUDY

The easiest way to find work in Croatia is by enrolling in one of the organized programmes run by the state or various charitable organizations. Teaching English has traditionally been the main opportunity for work in Croatia, but with current high levels of unemployment, work is not that easy to find.

VOLUNTARY WORK

One source of voluntary work is Suncokret, a nongovernmental organization which provides help for socially needy Croatians and organizes summer programmes working with people traumatized by the recent war. There are a couple of camps around Croatia, and you are expected to pay for your own food and accommodation. For details, contact Suncokret, Sortina ulica 1c, 10 000 Zagreb, Croatia (☎01/655-1705 or 655-1710, fax 01/655-1715, *suncokret@zg.tel.hr*).

Voluntary work at the Eco-centar Beli, helping to protect the griffon vultures on the island of

Cres, has sometimes been available through Svanimir (Croatian Society for the Protection of Natural and Cultural Heritage). For more information, contact Vesna Tutis at Svanimir, Ilirski trg 9, 10 000 Zagreb (☎01/485-1322).

SUMMER COURSES

The **Croatian Heritage Foundation** (Hrvatska Matica Iseljenika) organizes summer courses on various aspects of Croatian culture and language, from folk dancing and music to "task forces" of young people, often of Croatian descent, who help in war reconstruction and participate in various archeological and ecological programmes. They also organize academic courses at the University of Zagreb in conjunction with American and Canadian universities. Full details from Hrvatska Matica Iseljenika, Odjel za školstvo, Trg Stjepana Radića 3, 10 000 Zagreb (☎01/611-5116, fax 01/611-1522).

DIRECTORY

ADDRESSES The street name always comes before the number. The Croatian word for street, *ulica*, is either abbreviated to *ul.* or omitted altogether if the meaning is clear enough without it. In some cases you'll come across the name of a street followed by the letters "bb", which simply mean *bez broja*, or "without a number" – this often refers to a newly constructed building which hasn't been fitted into the street's numbering system.

CIGARETTES Croatia produces major international brands of cigarettes under licence, as well as its own makes, which are not nearly as bad as their ersatz names (such as Ronhill and Walter Wolf) suggest. Cigarettes are sold in kiosks marked with the word *duhan* (tobacco), supermarkets, bars and restaurants and are much cheaper than in the EU: about 10Kn a packet for domestic brands, 15Kn a packet for international brands. *Zabranjeno pušenje* means "no smoking", and applies to cinemas, all buses, trams and Croatian Airlines flights. There are few no-smoking areas in Croatia's cafés and restaurants unless you go to a *slastičarnica* (cake shop), where smoking is very rare.

CINEMA Most towns of any size will have a cinema (*kino*), although many of these amount to little more than a ticket booth and the auditorium itself – if you want drinks or popcorn, buy them before you arrive. Ticket prices rarely exceed 20–30Kn, and films are shown in their original language with Croatian subtitles. The cinema

repertoire consists almost entirely of Hollywood films, with new releases arriving in the country a month or two after opening in Western Europe.

ELECTRICITY 220 volts. Round, two-pin plugs are used, so equip yourself with an adaptor before you leave home.

FILM Major brands of colour print film are widely available in Croatia, as well as instant developing facilities. Film for black-and-white prints or colour transparencies is harder to get hold of outside major resorts, and you won't be offered the range you're used to at home – best to stock up before you leave.

GAY AND LESBIAN Although homosexuality has been legal in Croatia since 1977, it remains something of an underground phenomenon, and public displays of affection between members of the same sex may provoke hostility, especially outside big cities. The younger generation is more liberal in its attitudes to homosexuality, and though there are few recognized gay hangouts, some of the more alternative clubs in Zagreb have a reputation for attracting a tolerant, mixed crowd. For the most part, however, life for gay men in Croatia still consists of cruising public parks and running the risk of being beaten up by skinheads. Zagreb has a small gay and lesbian community, with organizations such as Because Press, a lesbian activist group founded in 1977 (info at suncana@zamir.net), and Kontra, another lesbian group, with a help line for women. For more information, visit *www.gay-croatia.com* or *www.geocities.com/WestHollywood/1824/*.

LAUNDRY Self-service launderettes are hard to come by in Croatia, although most towns have a laundry (*praonica*) where you can leave a service wash.

LEFT LUGGAGE Most train stations have a left-luggage office, which has a daily charge (calculated on the size of your bags – roughly 5–10Kn) for each item deposited. Keep all the scrappy little receipts, or you'll never get your gear back. A few large stations have coin-operated luggage lockers which can store your baggage for up to 24 hours.

NATURISM Naturism (known locally by the German acronym FKK) has a long history on the Adriatic coast. There are self-contained naturist holiday villages in Istria (the biggest are just outside Poreč, Rovinj and Vrsar), and naturist campsites in Istria and the island of Krk. Throughout Croatia, you'll find isolated coves or stretches of beach at a discreet distance from the main family-oriented sections which have been set aside for naturists. Topless bathing is acceptable almost anywhere, but entering cafés or buses in your beachwear is strongly disapproved of.

STUDENT CARDS Student discount cards entitle you to reductions at hostels and campsites, free or reduced admission to museums, and significant discounts on certain international train tickets and Croatian Airlines flights. You can get international student cards (such as ISIC) in Croatia through the Croatian Youth Hostel Association (Hrvatski ferijalni i hostelski savez – HFHS). For more information write to: HFHS (Centar za međunarodnu suradnju, regionalni klub Zagreb), Dezmanova 9, 10 000 Zagreb (☎01/484-7474, fax 484-7472, *www.nncomp.com/hfhs*).

TAXES Prices often include a sales tax, known locally as PDV, of up to 22 percent. Foreign visitors can claim a VAT tax refund at the Croatian Customs Service for goods over 500Kn ($62.5), as long as they have kept all original invoices, though your refund can take up to a year to arrive.

TIME Croatia is always one hour ahead of GMT (except for one week at the end of September when the time is the same), six hours ahead of US Eastern Standard Time, nine hours ahead of Pacific Standard Time, ten hours behind Australian Eastern Standard Time, and twelve hours behind New Zealand.

TIPPING Tipping is not obligatory, but it's polite to round the bill up to a convenient figure, although waiting staff won't expect this if you've only had a cup of coffee – tipping is only really expected when you've had a round of drinks or a meal.

TOILETS Public toilets (*zahod* or *WC*) are rare outside bus and train stations, although every restaurant, café or bar will have one.

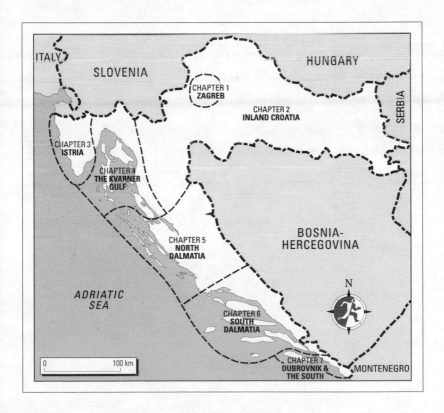

CHAPTER ONE

ZAGREB

Although it has been the capital of an independent nation for barely a decade, **ZAGREB** has served as the cultural and political focus of Croatia since the Middle Ages. Now home to almost a quarter of the country's population, the city grew out of the medieval communities of **Kaptol** and **Gradec**, although most of present-day Zagreb is the result of rapid growth in the nineteenth century, and many of the city's buildings are grand, peach-coloured monuments to the self-esteem of the Austro-Hungarian Empire. Outwardly, at least, Zagreb still shares the refined urban culture of Mitteleuropa – public transport is well organized, the streets are clean, and the parks impeccably manicured – but behind the city's Central European facade teems a complex blend of Pannonian, Mediterranean and Balkan cultures. The city's high-rise suburbs, built to accommodate families drawn to the capital by the rapid industrialization which followed World War II, continue to function as collection points for Croatia's diverse population. In recent years the city has had to make room for those displaced by war, nudging the number of inhabitants beyond the million mark. Those families which have been resident in the city for a few generations are proud to call themselves *purgeri*, a term which comes from the same Germanic root as the English word "burgher" and harks back directly to the city's Habsburg past. True purgerism in all its heel-clicking, hand-kissing extravagance may have died out, but the name lives on as an important badge of Zagreb identity. Inevitably, the *purgeri* label is used pejoratively by outsiders to describe the snobbish urban pretensions of the capital.

With most travellers to Croatia heading straight for the coast, Zagreb is rarely overrun by foreign tourists, encouraging visitors to adapt to the unhurried rhythms of local life rather than trawling from one tourist trap to another. Museums are occasionally absorbing but rarely spectacular, and Zagreb functions best as an outdoor city: downtown streets which can seem oppressively sombre during the winter suddenly become clogged with café tables as soon as

---

ACCOMMODATION PRICE CODES

The accommodation in this guide has been graded using the following price codes, based on the cost of each establishment's **least expensive double room** in high season (June–Sept), excluding special offers. Hotel room rates almost always include breakfast. Out of season, prices on the coast can fall by up to 50 percent. Where single rooms exist, they usually cost 60–70 percent of the price of a double. For more details, see p.24.

① Less than 200Kn	④ 400–500Kn	⑦ 800–1000Kn
② 200–300Kn	⑤ 500–600Kn	⑧ 1000–1200Kn
③ 300–400Kn	⑥ 600–800Kn	⑨ Over 1200Kn

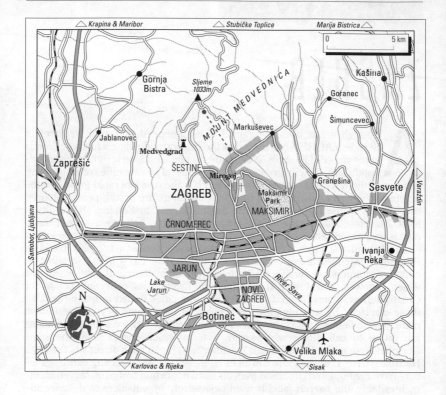

the weather improves, while popular strolling areas such as Tkalčićeva and Preradovićev trg take on a languorous Mediterranean glamour. In addition, you shouldn't leave Zagreb without exploring at least some of the city's attractive rural hinterland. To the north, the ridge of **Mount Medvednica** and its peak, **Sljeme**, provide the city with a year-round recreation area.

Some history

Despite evidence of Iron Age settlements on top of Gradec hill, the history of Zagreb doesn't really start until 1094, when Ladislas I of Hungary established a bishopric here in order to bring the northern Croatian lands under tighter Hungarian control. A large ecclesiastical community grew up around the cathedral and its girdle of episcopal buildings on **Kaptol** (which roughly translates as "cathedral chapter"), while the Hungarian crown retained a garrison opposite on **Gradec**. Both were significantly damaged during the Mongol incursions of 1240–42, prompting King Bela IV of Hungary to rebuild the settlement on Gradec and accord it the status of a royal free town in order to attract settlers and regenerate urban life. The settlements prospered from their position on the trade routes linking Hungary to the Adriatic, despite the growing Ottoman threat that began to emerge in the fifteenth century.

By the sixteenth century the name **Zagreb** (meaning, literally, "behind the hill" – a reference to the town's position at the foot of Mount Medvednica) was being used to describe both Kaptol and Gradec, although the two communities rarely got on – control of the watermills on the river dividing them was a constant source of emnity. The biggest outbreak of intercommunal fighting occurred in 1527, when the throne of Croatia was disputed by the Habsburg emperor Ferdinand II (supported by Gradec) and the Hungarian noble Ivan Zapolyai (supported by Kaptol), a conflict which culminated in the sacking of Kaptol by Habsburg troops. Gradually, however, the identities of the two settlements began to merge. Partly because of Zagreb's growing importance as a centre of political power – with the Turks in control of much of Slavonia and the Adriatic hinterland, and the Venetians pre-eminent on the coast, the Croatian lands had by the late 1500s been reduced to a northern enclave with Zagreb at its centre. The Croatian Sabor (parliament) usually met here from the sixteenth century onwards, and the Ban (governor of Croatia) resided here more or less permanently after 1621.

Much of what remained of Croatia was reorganized as the **Military Frontier** (a belt of territory running around the Habsburg Empire's border with Ottoman-controlled Bosnia), and taken away from the Sabor's control – with real political power concentrated in Vienna and Budapest, Zagreb remained very much a provincial outpost of the Habsburg Empire. The Sabor was moved to Varaždin in the mid-eighteenth century, and Zagreb may well have lost its pre-eminence in Croatian affairs permanently had Varaždin not been almost totally destroyed by fire in 1776. Even so, it wasn't until the mid-nineteenth century that the growth of Croatian national consciousness confirmed Zagreb's status as guardian of national culture. The establishment of an academy of arts and sciences (1866), a philharmonic orchestra (1871), a university (1874) and a national theatre (1890) gave Zagreb a growing sense of cultural identity, although ironically it was an Austrian, the architect Hermann Bollé (1845–1926), creator of the School of Arts and Crafts, Mirogoj Cemetery and Zagreb Cathedral, who contributed most to the city's new profile.

With the creation of Yugoslavia in 1918, political power shifted from Vienna to Belgrade – a city which most Croats considered an underdeveloped Balkan backwater. Things improved marginally after World War II, when Croatia was given the status of a socialist republic and Zagreb became the seat of its government, but the city always resented the extent to which it was overshadowed by Belgrade. Zagreb's next big period of architectural change came in the 1950s and 1960s, when visionary mayor Većeslav Holjevac presided over the city's southward expansion, and the vast concrete residential complexes of Novi Zagreb were born.

Zagreb survived the **collapse of Yugoslavia** relatively unscathed, despite the rocket attack on President Franjo Tuđman's offices on Gradec in October 1991, although there's little doubt that the long-term effects of war, economic stagnation and post-communist corruption have left their mark. Zagreb's pride has been particularly hurt by the influx of Croats from Hercegovina, who are thought to enjoy a disproportionate amount of influence in the city due to their links with the right-of-centre HDZ – the political party of the former president, Franjo Tuđman – and are only half-jokingly referred to as "white socks" due to their supposed lack of sartorial sophistication.

> The Zagreb area telephone code is ☎01

Politically, Zagreb entered the 1990s as a stronghold of the HDZ, but drifted towards the opposition (as did most of urban Croatia) as the decade wore on. A coalition of anti-Tuđman parties thought that they'd won city elections in 1997, only for Tuđman to block the appointment of a mayor until sufficient numbers of city councillors could be cajoled into voting for the HDZ candidate. With the city deprived of a convincing political life during the Tuđman era, symbols of civic pride tended to lie outside the realms of "official" culture. Prime among these were the **Bad Blue Boys**, the supporters of football team Dinamo Zagreb (see box on p.78), who began a boycott of their team's matches after the politically motivated decision to change the club's name to "Croatia Zagreb", and still enjoy the respect of people who have never followed the sport in their lives. Much the same could be said of popular local radio station **Radio 101**, whose brash style and anti-establishment stance made it a thorn in the side of successive regimes. Radio 101's moment of glory came in November 1996 when, in a clumsy attempt to extend government control over the media, the Croatian Telecommunications Council denied them a licence to broadcast. Ten thousand people staged an impromptu protest in central Zagreb that very night, and the following evening saw a 120,000-strong rally of support. The government backed down and gave Radio 101 a new lease of life, eventually awarding it another five-year franchise in November 1997.

The wave of popular grief which greeted the death of President Tuđman's in December 1999 was genuine enough: candles were laid in Markov trg and thousands of people filed past his coffin at the presidential residence in the northern suburb of Pantovaak. How Zagreb will fare in the post- Tuđman era remains to be seen.

Arrival, information and city transport

Zagreb's **airport**, situated about 10km southeast of the city, is connected with the bus station by half-hourly Croatia Airways bus (20Kn) between 7.30am and 8pm; after that time buses only run to connect with specific flights. A taxi from the airport to the centre will cost about 150–200Kn. Zagreb's central **train station** (*glavni kolodvor*) is on Tomislavov trg, on the southern edge of the city centre, ten minutes' walk from the main square, Trg bana Jelačića. The main **bus station** (*autobusni kolodvor*) is about ten minutes' walk east of the train station at the junction of Branimirova and Držićeva. Tram #6 (destination Černomerec) runs from here to Trg bana Jelačića, passing the train station on the way.

There are two main **tourist information centres** (turistibki informativni centar; TIC) in central Zagreb, one at Trg bana Jelačića 11 (summer Mon–Fri 8am–8pm, Sat & Sun 9am–6pm; winter Mon–Fri 8.30am–8pm, Sat 10am–6pm, Sun 10am–2pm; ☎278-910 or 278-855), and another a few hundred metres to the south at Zrinjevac 14 (summer Mon–Fri 8am–8pm, Sat & Sun 9am–6pm; winter Mon–Fri 9am–5pm; ☎45-52-867). Both offices have free maps, up-to-date leaflets on events and hiking maps of Mount Medvednica for sale, and can recommend accommodation options, although neither will book rooms.

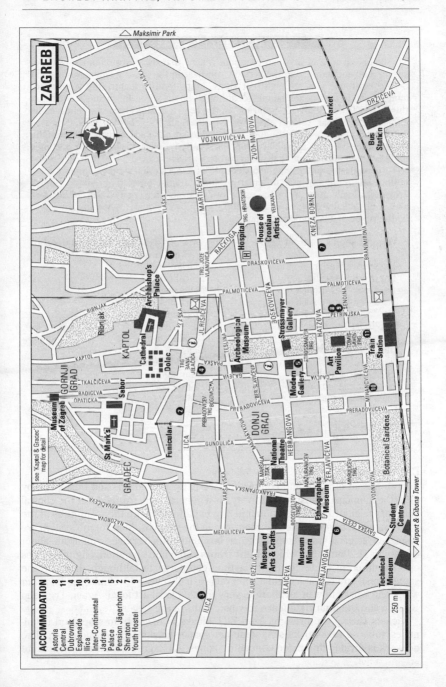

ZAGREB

△ Maksimir Park

N

ACCOMMODATION

Astoria	8
Central	11
Dubrovnik	4
Esplanade	10
Ilica	3
Inter-Continental	6
Jadran	1
Palace	5
Pension Jägerhorn	2
Sheraton	7
Youth Hostel	9

see Kaptol & Gradec map for detail

Market

Bus Station

House of Croatian Artists

Hospital

Archbishop's Palace

Cathedral

Dolac

Ribnjak

KAPTOL

GORNJI GRAD

Museum of Zagreb

St Mark's

Sabor

Funicular

Archeological Museum

Strossmayer Gallery

Modern Gallery

Art Pavilion

Train Station

DONJI GRAD

National Theatre

Ethnographic Museum

Museum of Arts & Crafts

Museum Mimara

Botanical Gardens

Student Centre

Technical Museum

GRADEC

▽ Airport & Cibona Tower

0   250 m

ZAGREB STREET NAMES

The flexible nature of Croatian grammar means that there are often two ways of saying a **street name**, and the version you hear in the spoken language may not be the same one you see on street signs. Maps tend to feature the versions of names used in the spoken language, although be prepared for inconsistencies on this score. Thus "Nikola Tesla Street" in the centre of Zagreb can be rendered as either ulica Nikole Tesle ("street of Nikola Tesla") or Teslina ulica ("Tesla's street"). The latter is more common in everyday speech and on maps, although the word *ulica* ("street") is usually dropped. Similarly, ulica Pavla Radića becomes Radićeva, and ulica Ivana Tkalčića becomes Tkalčićeva.

To complicate matters further, a couple of Zagreb's best-known squares have **colloquial names** which differ from their official ones. Trg Nikole Šubića Zrinskog usually goes under the name of Zrinjevac; and Trg Petra Preradovića is almost universally referred to as Cvjetni trg ("Flower Square"), because it used to be the venue of a large florists' market.

Version seen on street signs	Version seen on maps and used in spoken language
Trg svetog Marka	Markov trg
Trg Marka Marulića	Marulićev trg
Trg Ivana Mažuranića	Mažuranićev trg
Trg Petra Preradovića	Preradovićev trg
Trg Josipa Jurja Strossmayera	Strossmayerov trg
Trg kralja Tomislava	Tomislavov trg
Ulica kneza Branimira	Branimirova
Ulica Ljudevita Gaja	Gajeva
Ulica Grofa Draškovića	Draškovićeva
Ulica Andrije Hebranga	Hebrangova
Ulica Junije Palmotića	Palmotićeva
Ulica Pavla Radića	Radićeva
Ulica Augusta Šenoe	Šenoina
Ulica Nikole Tesle	Teslina
Ulica Ivana Tkalčića	Tkalčićeva

City transport

Zagreb has an efficient and comprehensive network of trams and buses run by ZET, the municipal transport authority. As a general rule, **trams** cover the central parts of the city (the train station and Trg bana Jelačića are the main hubs of the system), while **buses** come into their own in the suburbs. Maps of the system are displayed at each tram stop. Regular bus and tram services run from about 4.30am to 11.20pm, after which **night trams** come into operation. Night services operate different routes to their daytime counterparts (although they use the same stops), and run at irregular intervals (usually every 40–50min), so knowing when and where to wait for them is very much a local art form. Again, Trg bana Jelačića and the train station are the main hubs of the system.

Tickets (*karte*) are brought from ZET kiosks at major tram stops and terminuses, tobacco (*duhan*) kiosks, some newspaper kiosks or from the driver. The network is divided into three concentric zones. All Zagreb's tram routes operate entirely within the central zone, so you'll only enter the outer two zones if making an out-of-town excursion by suburban bus. There's a flat fare per journey: single-zone tickets are 4.50Kn from kiosks, 5Kn from the driver; two-zone tickets are 9/10Kn; three-zone tickets, 13.50/15Kn. All kiosks also sell day tickets (*dnevne karte*; 12Kn), which can be used for unlimited travel within a single zone and are valid until 4am the following morning. All tickets are validated by punching them in the machines once on board.

For **taxis**, there's an initial charge of around 10Kn, after which it's 10Kn per kilometre; prices rise by about thirty percent after midnight; they're most easily found on Trg maršala Tita, at the northern end of Gajeva, and at the bottom of Bakačeva between Trg bana Jelačića and Kaptol. There's nowhere to rent **bicycles** in central Zagreb, although open-air stalls beside Lake Jarun (see p.69) rent out bikes during the summer if you want to cycle round the lake.

Accommodation

While Zagreb is reasonably well served with medium- and top-range **hotels**, budget choices are relatively thin on the ground – so advance reservations are a good idea. There's a conveniently placed **youth hostel** at Petrinjska 77 (☎434-964, fax 434 962; closed 9am–1pm), five minutes' walk north from the train station, which has dormitory accommodation in four- or six-bed dorms for 120Kn per person, but soon fills up. Between mid-July and late September accommodation in **student halls of residence** (*studentski dom*) is often made available to tourists. Beds can be booked through the student travel office (Turistisički ured; Mon–Fri 9am–4pm; ☎619-1240) at Odrinska 8, and are located either in the Studentski Dom Cvijetno naselje, Odrinska 8 (tram #14 or #17 from Trg bana Jelačića or tram #4 from the train station to Vjesnikov nebeder – the office block where the *Vjesnik* newspaper is produced); or the Studentski Dom Stjepan Radić, Jarunska 2 (tram #17 from Trg bana Jelačića to Stjepan Radić). Rooms in Cvijetno naselje come with en-suite facilities and cost 250Kn single, 380Kn double; while those at Stjepan Radić have shared facilities and are doubles only, costing 320kn. Breakfast is included at both places. If you arrive when the tourist office is closed, try to make yourself understood to the porters, who should be able to sort you out. The nearest **campsite** is 10km southeast of town at the *Plitvice Motel* (whose motel services are currently closed pending renovation), a little-frequented spot right beside the Zagreb–Ljubljana highway – there's no public transport.

Private **rooms** can be arranged through Evistas, midway between the train and bus stations at Šenoina 28 (Mon–Fri 9am–1.30pm & 3–8pm, Sat 9.30am–5pm; ☎48-19-133, fax 431-987; ②), who will place you with a local family in the town centre or in the suburbs of Novi Zagreb (see p.70) or Jarun (see p.69). They also offer two-person apartments with bathroom and kitchenette (③), although you have to stay at least three days. Similar deals on private rooms are offered by the helpful Lacio, Trnsko 15e (9am–4pm; ☎65-52-047; ②), although their office is hidden away in the residential blocks of Novi Zagreb, a thirty-minute tram ride from likely points of arrival – from the bus station, take tram #7 (destination Savski Most) to the Trnsko stop, walk 200m south into the housing estate, then turn right.

Hotels

Unless you can afford to splash out on the handful of places which measure up to international standards, Zagreb's downtown **hotels** don't offer a great deal of choice: rooms are pretty much the same wherever you go, and few places have a distinct character. There are better deals in the suburbs, although the cheapest rooms are over 20km north of town near the Sljeme summit of Mount Medvednica (see p.70), an idyllic spot if you like woodland walks, but hardly the ideal base for urban sightseeing. All hotels include breakfast in the price unless otherwise stated.

Central Zagreb

Astoria, Petrinjska 71 (☎48-41-222, fax 48-41-212). Compact en-suite rooms with TV and phone. Furnishings are ageing fast, but rooms are generally clean. Convenient for the train and bus stations. Some triples. ④.

Central, Branimirova 3 (☎48-41-122). Small rooms with en-suite facilities and TV, diagonally opposite the train station. Rooms are smart and comfortable, if a little cramped. ⑤.

Dubrovnik, Gajeva 1 (☎48-73-555, fax 48-18-447, *hotel-dubrovnik@hotel-dubrovnik.tel.hr*). Modern glass-and-steel palace just off Trg bana Jelačića; some rooms in the older wing overlook the square. Recently renovated to international standards, offering smart en-suite rooms (doubles have baths, singles come with showers) with TV and telephone. ⑦.

Esplanade, Mihanovićeva 1 (☎45-66-666, fax 45-77-907, *www.esplanade.tel.hr/esplanade*). Luxurious outpost of Mitteleuropa next to the train station, with marble-clad Art Deco interior and opulent café and function rooms. A bit over the top for some tastes, but still the most characterful of Zagreb's hotels. ⑨.

Ilica, Ilica 102 (☎37-77-522). Friendly modern hotel with smart en-suite rooms with TV and phone, though there are only 12 of them, so ring in advance. It's on the ground floor of a low-rise office block 1500m west of Trg bana Jelačića. Take tram #6 from the bus or train station (destination Černomerec) until you see the hotel on your right. ④.

Inter-Continental, Kršnjavoga 1 (☎45-53-411, fax 444-431). Modern luxury hotel handily located close to the theatres and museums around Trg maršala Tita; it also boasts an indoor swimming pool. Staggeringly, rates do not include breakfast, which costs an additional 125Kn – the price of a slap-up meal in most Zagreb restaurants. ⑨.

Jadran, Vlaška 50 (☎45-53-777, fax 46-12-151). Modern, medium-rise hotel just east of the city centre and 15 minutes' walk from the train station. Dingy from the outside but quite pleasant inside, with modest en-suite rooms with TV and phone. Take tram #4 (destination Dubrava) from the train station or tram #8 (destination Mihaljevac) from the bus station to Draškovićeva, after which it's a short walk east along Vlaška. ④.

Palace, Strossmayerov trg 10 (☎48-14-611, fax 48-11-358). Attractive turn-of-the-century pile between the train station and Trg bana Jelačića, with very comfortable air-conditioned rooms, all with bath. ⑦.

Pension Jägerhorn, Ilica 14 (☎48-30-161). In a courtyard just off the main shopping street, and only 500m from Trg bana Jelačića. Comfortable, central and soon fills up. Take tram #6 (destination Černomerec) from the bus or train station to Trg bana Jelačića, then walk west. ⑥.

Sheraton, Kneza Borne 2 (☎45-53-535, fax 45-53-035, *www.sheraton.com*). Pretty much without equal in the comfort stakes, although it's in an uninspiring grid of streets a 10min walk east of the centre. The atmosphere in the lobby area's cafés and restaurants is rather sterile, but the hotel does boast a gym and indoor pool. ⑨.

The suburbs

Lido, Jarun (☎38-32-839). Small hotel at the eastern end of Lake Jarun, 4km southwest of the centre, featuring attractive loft rooms with en-suite facilities. Take tram #17 (destination

Jarun) from Trg bana Jelačića to the Srednjaci stop, after which it's a 10min walk down Hrgovići to the lake. ⑥.

Panorama, Trg sportova 9 (☎36-58-333 or 36-37-333, fax 30-92-657). High-rise hotel 2km east of the centre, currently being renovated floor by floor. Rooms are on the utilitarian side for the time being, though all are en suite with TV, while north-facing rooms on the higher floors come with great views of the city. Take tram #9 (destination Ljubljanica) from the train station to Trešnjevački trg, then turn right onto Trakošćanska and you'll see the hotel looming up on your left after 5min. ④.

Zagreb, Bundek bb, Novi Zagreb (☎66-37-333, fax 66-37-229). Characterless but acceptable concrete box 2.5km south of the centre offering small, minimally furnished and careworn rooms with showers. A good place from which to explore the mysterious, tree-shrouded Lake Bundek (see p.70). Plenty of parking, but no direct public transport. Take tram #6 from the train or bus station to the Sopot terminus then walk 600m north. ③.

Mount Medvednica

Hunjka, Sljemenska cesta bb (☎45-80-397, fax 46-14-355). Medium-sized hotel on the eastern shoulder of Mount Medvednica, offering simple but smart en-suite rooms with pine floors and furnishings, plus on-site restaurant. It's sited in a lovely meadow encircled by forest about 23km out of Zagreb on the road to Donja Stubica; the nearest public transport is the top station of the Sljeme cable car, a 40min walk away. ②.

Tomislavov Dom, Sljeme (☎45-55-833, fax 45-55-834). Large mountain-top hotel surrounded by woodland, with café, restaurant and small but neat en-suites with TV and telephone. Just below the summit of Sljeme, about a 5min walk from the cable car station, or 21km from the centre of Zagreb by road. ③.

The City

Central Zagreb divides into three distinct areas, joined by the main square, **Trg bana Jelačića**. Occupying the high ground north of the square are the two oldest parts of the city, **Kaptol** and **Gradec**, the former the site of the cathedral, the latter a peaceful district of ancient mansions and quiet squares. Beneath them spreads the nineteenth- and twentieth-century **Donji grad**, or "Lower Town", a bustling area of prestigious public buildings and nineteenth-century apartment blocks.

Beyond the centre, there's not much of interest among the broad boulevards and bland modern buildings which extend south to the River Sava and, beyond that, to the suburb of Novi Zagreb. Aside from the artificial lake at Jarun, southwest of the city, and the leafy park of Maksimir to the east, the most obvious target is the ramblers' paradise of nearby Mount Medvednica, served by cable car from suburban Zagreb and an easy trip out from the centre.

Trg bana Jelačića and around

A broad, flagstoned expanse flanked by cafés and hectic with the whizz of trams and hurrying pedestrians, **Trg bana Jelačića** ("Governor Jelačić Square") is as good a place as any to start exploring the city, and is within easy walking distance of more or less everything you're likely to want to see. It's also the biggest tram stop in the city, standing at the intersection of seven cross-town routes, and the place where half the city seems to meet in the evening – either beneath the tall clock on the western side of the square, or at the Znanje bookshop (colloquially known as "Krleža" after Croatia's greatest twentieth-century writer, Miroslav Krleža) on the corner of the square and Gajeva.

Originally a vast open space known as "Harmica" due to its use as a collection point for local taxes (after the Hungarian word *harmincad*, meaning a thirtieth), Trg bana Jelačića was laid out as the city's main square in the 1850s and has been Zagreb's focal point ever since. The elegant pastel blues and pinks of its surrounding buildings provide a suitable backdrop for the attention-hogging equestrian statue of the nineteenth-century Ban (governor) of Croatia, **Josip Jelačić** (see p.340), completed in 1866 by the Viennese sculptor Fernkorn just as the Habsburg authorities were beginning to erode the semi-autonomy which Jelačić had won for the nation. The square was renamed Trg republike in 1945 and the statue – considered a potential rallying point for Croatian nationalism – was concealed behind a wooden shell covered with communist propaganda slogans. Party agitators finally dismantled the statue on the night of July 25, 1947, although its constituent parts were saved from destruction by a local museum curator, who stored them in a basement of the Yugoslav (now Croatian) Academy of Arts and Sciences. In 1990 the square was renamed Trg bana Jelačića and Jelačić restored to his rightful place, although his statue now faces a different way. In the 1860s it was positioned with Jelačić's drawn sabre pointing eastwards, indicating the direction in which Croatia's then enemies – the Hungarians – were to be found. Now it points southwards, as if to emphasize the historic rupture between Croatia and her Balkan neighbours. On the eastern side of the statue is the **Manduševac**, named after a stream which used to run through the area – a small, stepped depression concealing a modest fountain, built in 1987, when the whole square was repaved in preparation for Zagreb's hosting of the World Student Games.

Occupying a large terrace overlooking Trg bana Jelačića to the north is **Dolac**, the city's main market. This feast of fruit, vegetables and meat is held every morning, but is at its liveliest on Friday mornings, when fresh fish arrives from the coast. Curving uphill immediately to the left of Dolac is **Tkalčićeva**, formerly known as "Potok" ("Stream Street") due to its position on the dried-up watercourse that once separated Kaptol from Gradec. Probably the prettiest single street in the city, Tkalčićeva preserves a neat ensemble of the one- and two-storey, steep-roofed nineteenth-century houses that have largely disappeared elsewhere. There's a smattering of boutiques and art galleries tucked into the street's low-ceilinged mansions, although most are now occupied by the youthful café-bars which have transformed Tkalčićeva into the city's prime area for drinking on warm summer evenings. Leading off to the west is **Krvavi most** ("Bloody Bridge" – a reminder of the often violent disputes between Gradec and Kaptol), a street which connects Tkalčićeva with Radićeva, offering a short cut up to Gradec.

West of Trg bana Jelačića, trams rumble along **Ilica**, the city's main shopping street, which runs below Gradec hill. South of the square is the popular modern pedestrianized area around **Gajeva**, where the glass facade of the *Dubrovnik* hotel serves as a futuristic backdrop for passing shoppers or the drinkers seated outside *Charlie Brown's*, the café where most of the city's political elite seem to gather for conspiratorial chin-wagging on Saturday and Sunday lunchtimes – even in winter, Zagreb's movers and shakers would rather freeze to death drinking coffee outside *Charlie's* than risk not being seen. A sharp right here leads into **Bogovićeva**, a promenading area full of cafés and shops which culminates in **Preradovićev trg**, a lively square known for its cinemas and pavement cafés. It's still referred to by most locals as Cvjetni trg ("Flower Square") after the flower market which used to be held here until the area was cleaned up in the 1980s – a few sanitized florists' pavilions still survive. Watching over the scene is Ivan Rendić's 1895 statue of **Petar Preradović** (1818–72), an ethnic Serb from Bjelovar in eastern Croatia who served as a general in the Austro-Hungarian army and wrote romantic poetry which, although it's no longer widely read, contributed to the development of an evolving Croatian literary language. Behind the statue rises the grey form of the **Serbian Orthodox Church** (Pravoslavna crkva), an unassuming nineteenth-century building whose icon filled interior, rich with candles and the smell of incense, is worth a quick peek.

Kaptol

Northeast of Trg bana Jelačića, the filigree spires of Zagreb's cathedral mark the edge of the district known as **KAPTOL**, home to the city's Catholic institutions and still patrolled by pious citizens and nuns of various orders. The area consists of little more than one long street – initially called Kaptol, later becoming Nova Ves in its northern reaches – and the **Cathedral** itself, at its southern end, is the district's only arresting feature. Ringed by the ivy-cloaked turrets of the eighteenth-century **Archbishop's Palace** – "a sumptuous Kremlin," fancied the archeologist Arthur Evans – the cathedral is almost wholly neo-Gothic, having been rebuilt by Viennese architects Friedrich von Schmidt and Hermann Bollé after a catastrophic earthquake in 1880. Most of the money and creative endeavour was invested in the two spires – the big architectural statement it was felt a growing city like Zagreb needed. The interior is high and bare – only four Renaissance choir stalls from the early sixteenth century and the faded remains of some medieval frescoes survive from before the earthquake. The modest main altar, bearing a copy of the statue of the Madonna and Child in the church at Maria Bistrica, stands in front of a glass casket holding an effigy of Archbishop Alojzije Stepinac (see box on p.60), head of the Croatian Church during World War II and imprisoned by the communists immediately afterwards. Stepinac's grave, near the altar on the north wall of the church, is marked by a touching relief by Ivan Meštrović in which the archbishop kneels humbly before Christ. There's another statue by Fernkorn in front of the cathedral of a richly gilded Madonna surrounded by four angels which provides a beckoning sparkle as you approach Kaptol from the south.

Descending east from the cathedral to Vlaška and turning left brings you to **Ribnjak**, a small, shady park situated on the site of a former fishpond, overshadowed on one side by the crumbling remains of Kaptol's erstwhile fortifications. One of the city's most charming open spaces, the park was reserved for Kaptol's priests until 1947, when the railings surrounding it were demolished by the same communist activists who put paid to the statue of Jelačić on Trg bana Jelačića.

Gradec

Uphill to the northwest of Trg bana Jelačića, **GRADEC** (known colloquially as "Grič") is the most ancient and atmospheric part of Zagreb, a leafy, tranquil backwater of tiny streets, small squares and Baroque palaces, whose mottled brown roofs peek out from the hill. The most leisurely approach is to take the **funicular** (*uspinjača*; daily 6.30am–9pm every 10min; 2Kn each way), which ascends from Ilica, about 200m west of Trg bana Jelačića; alternatively, wander up the gentle

ARCHBISHOP ALOJZIJE STEPINAC (1898–1960)

For many, **Alojzije Stepinac** personifies the link between the Croatian nation and the Catholic Church. Branded a quisling by the communists, but regarded by most ordinary Croats as a martyr and patriot, he has assumed immense symbolic importance since his death in 1960. It's a development which has been broadly encouraged by the Vatican: Stepinac was beatified by Pope John Paul II on his visit to Croatia in October 1998.

Born into a relatively prosperous peasant family in the village of Krašić (see p.119), 50km southwest of Zagreb, Stepinac was initially dissuaded from entering the priesthood by parents eager for him to manage the family farm. During World War I he served with the Yugoslav Legion, a body assembled by the Allies to fight for a united South-Slav state. After the war he briefly studied agronomy in Zagreb, but soon returned to Krašić, dismayed by the immoral lifestyles of his fellow students. Settling back into village life he got engaged to girl-next-door Marija Horvat, who addressed him as "my dear ice-cold betrothed" and eventually broke off the relationship, realizing that his mind was focused on more spiritual matters.

Having finally opted for the Church, Stepinac ascended through the priestly ranks at great speed, becoming Archbishop of Zagreb in 1937. Stepinac's rise was promoted by the government in Belgrade, which still viewed him as pro-Yugoslav – although Stepinac, like many Croats, had by this stage lost his faith in South Slav unity. Stepinac had little enthusiasm for Nazism, but his response to the German-imposed NDH, the "Independent State of Croatia" proclaimed in April 1941, was at best contradictory. He initially instructed Croatian priests to support the new regime, naively regarding the Nazi puppet Ante Pavelić as a patriot who would keep Croatia free from the great Catholic bugbears: communism and freemasonry. Once the true nature of the NDH became apparent, however, he began to change tack. By June 1941 he was already protesting to Pavelić about the inhuman treatment of Serbian deportees, though he initially thought the crimes committed in the name of the NDH were the work of individual hotheads rather than the regime itself – according to the memoirs of the sculptor Ivan Meštrović, the archbishop burst out crying when he finally realized that Pavelić himself was giving the orders. Stepinac consequently stepped up his criticism of the regime as the war went on, and also used his personal authority to save many individuals who would otherwise have faced execution.

As the war neared its end, Stepinac's profound hostility to the Partisans prevented him from reaching an understanding with Croatia's new masters. Eager to demoralize the anti-communist opposition, Yugoslavia's new strongman Josip Broz Tito (see box on p.90) decided to make an example of the archbishop, and had him arrested in May 1945. After a preposterous trial in which the Catholic hierarchy was accused of working in tandem with foreign intelligence services, Stepinac was found guilty of "anti-national activities" in December 1946 and sentenced to sixteen years' imprisonment.

Stepinac spent five years in Lepoglava jail (see p.92) before being allowed home to Krašić, where he occupied a modest two-room apartment in the house of the local priest. Stepinac's release was presented to the world media as an example of the communist regime's leniency, although he was effectively under house arrest until his death. Foreign journalists who tried to see the archbishop were told that a constant police guard was needed to protect Stepinac from the wrath of the working class. Made a cardinal by the pope in 1952, Stepinac was the subject of quiet admiration to those Croats who remained unconvinced by government propaganda, and his grave in Zagreb cathedral became an unofficial shrine long before the collapse of communism in 1990.

gradient of Radićeva towards the **Kamenita vrata**, or "stone gate", which originally formed the main eastern entrance to the town. Inside Kamenita vrata – actually more of a long curving tunnel than a gate – lies one of Zagreb's most popular
shrines, a simple sixteenth-century statue of the Virgin in a grille-covered niche.
Miraculous powers have been attributed to the statue, largely on account of its
surviving a fire in 1731 – a couple of benches inside the gate accommodate passing city folk eager to offer a quick prayer.

Katarinin trg and around

Just to the south of Kamenita vrata, Jezuitski trg is flanked on the left by
Klovićevi dvori, a seventeenth-century former Jesuit monastery now used for
temporary art exhibitions (Tues–Sun 10am–6pm; the admission price varies
according to what's on display), and housing a small café and courtyard that hosts
concerts during the Zagreb Summer Festival (see box on p.77). Beyond here,
where Jezuitski trg opens out onto the next square, **Katarinin trg**, is **St
Catherine's Church** (Crkva svete Katerine; daily 10am–1pm), built by the
Jesuits in the 1620s and containing one of the most delightful Baroque interiors
in Croatia, with its lacework pattern of pink and white stucco whorls which was
executed by Antonio Quadrio in the 1720s. Francesco Robba's delicate portrayal
of the Jesuit order's founder, St Ignatius of Loyola, to the right of the main altar,
is the outstanding piece of statuary.

On the north side of the square, the **Museum of Modern Art** (Muzej
suvremene umjetnosti; Tues–Sat 11am–7pm, Sun 10am–1pm; 10Kn) mounts
imaginative temporary shows from Croatia and abroad – its large collection of
contemporary work is currently in storage, awaiting the construction of a new
museum south of the centre in Novi Zagreb. On the south side of the square,
Dverce leads down to the top station of the funicular down to Ilica and to **Kula
lotršćak**, or "Burglars' Tower" (Mon–Sat 10am–6pm, Sun 10am–1pm; 10Kn),
another remnant of the upper town's fortifications, from which a bell was once
sounded every evening before the city gates were closed (to keep out burglars,
hence the name). Nowadays a small cannon is fired from the top window every
day at noon, supposedly in memory of the time when it was used to scare off
an impending attack by the Turks. The latter once succeeded in sacking
Remete (now a suburb of Zagreb) to the northeast, but never mounted a serious assault on the city itself. On either side of the tower stretches
Strossmayerovo šetalište, a promenade which follows the line of Gradec's
former south-facing fortifications. The views over the city and plains beyond
are terrific.

The Gallery of Naive Art

About fifty metres north of Katarinin trg, the **Gallery of Naive Art**, Ćirilometodska 3 (Galerija naivne umjetnosti; Tues–Fri 10am–6pm, Sat & Sun 10am–1pm;
20Kn), provides an excellent introduction to the work of Croatia's village painters.
The development of a school of painting inspired by peasant craft traditions was
largely the work of an academically trained outsider, Krsto Hegedušić, who had
been impressed by the work of untutored painters like "Le Douanier" Rousseau
while studying in Paris. Visiting family in the Slavonian village of Hlebine (see
p.99) in the 1930s, Hegedušić discovered that the paintings of local lads Ivan
Generalić and Franjo Mraz displayed much of the style and verve he had seen in
the work of other European non-academic artists, and took them under his wing,

ZAGREB: KAPTOL & GRADEC

encouraging them to exhibit more widely. The work of Generalić dominates the first of the gallery's six rooms, with his early watercolours of Croatian village life reflecting the original, socio-documentary concerns of the Hlebine painters. His pictures soon developed a more fairy-tale, symbolic style, however – his large-scale *Deer's Wedding* (1959), for instance, resembles a medieval religious painting, only with the customary saints replaced by animals and trees. Subsequent rooms deal with later generations of naive painters from across Croatia, with highlights including Ivan Lacković-Croata's scenes of villages in winter, crowded with spindly, stylized trees and snow-laden houses, and Ivan Rabuzin's meditative landscapes in which the shapes of hills and flowers are used to weave decorative patterns which verge on the abstract. The final room concentrates on Josip Generalić (son of Ivan), who painted like a comic-strip artist on acid, deserting rural themes in favour of subjects like war, actresses, and the mass suicides of cult members. His 1973 portrait of Sophia Loren is one of the most garish in the collection (note the ugly cat, which allegedly represents Loren's husband, Carlo Ponti).

Markov trg and around

It's a short walk north up Ćirilometodska to the heart of Gradec, **Markov trg**, a restrained square of golden-brown buildings which serves as the symbolic heart of Croatia. Though it's not obvious from their modest facades, the buildings on the western side of the square house the Croatian cabinet offices, while those on the east include the **Sabor** (national parliament) and the so-called **Banski dvor** (Ban's Palace), originally the seat of the Habsburg-appointed governor and now used by the Croatian president for formal receptions. Markov trg has always been an important focus of government ceremonial: rulers of Croatia were sworn in here from the mid-sixteenth century onwards, a tradition renewed by President Tuđman in the 1990s, while in 1573 peasant leader Matija Gubec (see p.86) was executed here in a parody of such ceremonies by being seated on a throne and "crowned" with a band of white-hot steel. Nowadays, however, you're unlikely to come across any signs of political activity aside from the occasional purr of a ministerial Mercedes or the furtive glances of sharp-suited security men.

The main focus of the square is the squat **St Mark's Church** (Crkva svetog Marka), a much-renovated structure whose multi-coloured tiled roof displays the coats of arms of Zagreb and Croatia to the sky – and, it would seem from opening any book on Zagreb, dozens of photographers. The emblems adorning the Croatian coat of arms (the one on the left as you face it) symbolize the three areas which originally made up the medieval kingdom: north-central Croatia is represented by the red-and-white chequerboard known as the *šahovnica* – a state symbol since the Middle Ages; Dalmatia by three lions' heads; and Slavonia by a running beast (the *kuna*, or marten, Croatia's national animal) framed by two rivers – the Sava and Drava. The church itself is a homely Gothic building, originally constructed in the fourteenth century but ravaged since by earthquake, fire and nineteenth-century restorers – though some parts, including the south portal, are original. The Baroque bell-tower was added in the seventeenth century, and the interior decorations in the 1930s by the painter Jozo Kljaković and the sculptor Ivan Meštrović. Kljaković's frescoes are imposing but rigid, portraying huge, muscle-bound Croatian kings caught in dramatic mid-gesture; Meštrović's *Crucifixion* is more sensitive, merging sympathetically with the rest of the church.

Slightly downhill to the west of Markov trg on Matoševa, the **Historical Museum of Croatia** (Hrvatski povijesni muzej; Mon–Fri 10am–5pm, Sat & Sun 10am–1pm; 10Kn), in one of the more crumbly of Gradec's Baroque mansions, houses prestigious temporary exhibitions relating to Croatian history. A few steps to the north, the **Natural History Museum** (Hrvatski prirodoslovni muzej; Tues–Fri 10am–5pm, Sat & Sun 10am–1pm; 15Kn) is much as you would expect, with a succession of cabinets displaying stuffed animals and birds. Pride of place goes to the 15-metre-long basking shark caught in the north Adriatic in 1934.

The Meštrović Atelier and the Museum of Zagreb

Just north of Markov trg, at Mletačka 8, the **Meštrović Atelier** (Mon–Fri 9am–2pm; 10Kn) occupies the house where Croatia's foremost twentieth-century sculptor, Ivan Meštrović, lived between 1924 and 1942. This is a delightful museum, and one which you don't have to be a Meštrović fan to enjoy, with an intimacy that's lacking in the artist's other former home and museum, in Split (see p.256). On display are sketches, photographs and small-scale studies for creations such as the giant *Grgur Ninski* in Split and the *Crucifixion* in St Mark's Church, along with some lovely female statuettes in the small atrium.

Beyond the Atelier, Mletačka leads into Demetrova and thence to Opatička. Turn left here to the **Museum of Zagreb** at no. 20 (Muzej grada Zagreba; Tues–Fri 10am–6pm, Sat & Sun 10am–1pm; 20Kn), undoubtedly the city's best, telling the tale of Zagreb's development from medieval times to the present day with the help of snazzy presentations and English-language texts. Approached through the courtyard of the former Convent of the Poor Clares, the museum occupies a complex of buildings tacked on to the thirteenth-century **Popov toranj**, or Priests' Tower, which was built to provide the clerics of poorly defended Kaptol with a refuge in case of attack. Alongside a modest but well-chosen selection of weaponry, furnishings and costumes, models of Zagreb through the ages reveal the changing face of the city. Sacral art taken from local churches includes an expressive seventeenth-century sculptural ensemble depicting Jesus flanked by the apostles which originally stood above the portal of Zagreb cathedral. Upstairs, political posters, photographs of political leaders and ideological slogans help to breathe life into the turbulent history of the twentieth century; a final room contains an unintentionally surreal display of the furniture destroyed by the JNA (Yugoslav People's Army) rocket attack on Gradec in October 1991, with smashed crockery and splintered furniture arranged as if part of some contemporary art exhibit.

Donji grad

South of Gradec, the modern **Donji grad** ("Lower Town") sprawls out in all its grey, grid-patterned glory. Breaking the urban uniformity is the series of interconnected garden squares, laid out from the 1870s onwards, which give the downtown area an unbroken, U-shaped succession of promenading areas and parks. Known as **Lenuci's Horseshoe** (Lenucijeva podkova) after Milan Lenuci, the city engineer responsible for its layout, this was a deliberate attempt to give Zagreb a distinctive urban identity, providing it with public spaces bordered by the set-piece institutions – galleries, museums, academies and theatres – that it was thought every modern city should have, although the horseshoe was never entirely finished and it's unlikely you'll walk round the full U-shaped itinerary intended by Lenuci. The first of the horseshoe's two main series of squares starts with Trg Niklole Šubića Zrinskog – usually referred to as **Zrinjevac** – which begins a block south of Trg bana Jelačića; to the west of Zrinjevac is the second line of squares, centred around **Trg maršala Tita**. To the south are the **Botanical Gardens**, which were intended to provide the final green link between the two arms of the horseshoe, but don't quite manage it: several characterless downtown blocks stand in the way. The set-piece buildings on and around both Zrinjevac and Trg maršala Tita wouldn't look out of place in such bastions of Mitteleuropa as Graz or Linz, giving this part of Zagreb a prosperous, dignified air, although Donji grad's other buildings are mostly offices, ministry buildings or apartments, and there's not much in the way of shopping or café life in this part of town.

Zrinjevac

Heading south from Trg bana Jelačića, the first section of Lenuci's Horseshoe, **Zrinjevac**, is a typical late nineteenth-century city park, featuring shady walks, a bandstand, and a fountain in the shape of a cake-stand topped by a mushroom designed by the ubiquitous Hermann Bollé. Until 1873, when the square was first laid out, Zrinjevac marked the southern boundary of the city, the muddy site of fairs and markets where peasants from the surrounding countryside gathered to trade cows and horses. Today's Zrinjevac is a pleasing ensemble of nineteenth-century office blocks and apartment buildings, flanked to the west by the **Archeological Museum** (Arheološki muzej; Tues–Fri 10am–1pm & 5–7pm, Sat & Sun 10am–1pm; 15Kn), with three floors of exhibits ranging from the Neolithic to the Roman eras. The most interesting of the museum's exhibits is the collection of ancient pottery decorated with zigzags and chequer patterns produced by the Vučedol culture, an upsurge in crafts and agriculture from the fourth millennium BC that takes its name from the Bronze Age settlement at Vučedol near Vukovar. Among the displays is the famous **Vučedol Pigeon** (Vučedolska golubica), the three-legged zoomorphic pouring vessel pictured on the 20Kn banknote. There are also two rooms of Egyptian mummies, mostly dating from the Ptolemaic period, one of which was found wrapped in a linen shroud (now displayed on the wall beside it) bearing ancient Etruscan writing – the longest known text in this as yet untranslated language.

Trg hrvatskih velikana

East of Zrinjevac, all roads seem ultimately to lead to **Trg hrvatskih velikana** ("Square of Great Croatians"), a large traffic roundabout which until 1990 went under the name of Trg žrtava fašizma ("Victims of Fascism Square"). Anti-fascist groups opposed to the name change traditionally gather here on May 9, although counter demonstrations by the extreme right have soured the occasion in recent years. The square is dominated by the **House of Croatian Artists** (Dom hrvatskih likovnih umjetnika; Mon 2–7pm, Tues–Sun 11am–7pm; 5Kn), an arresting circular pavilion designed as an art gallery by Meštrović in the 1930s, but converted into a mosque in August 1944 by the NDH in an attempt to cultivate Bosnian Muslim support. It's still colloquially referred to as the *džamija* ("mosque"), though its three minarets were demolished in 1947, after which it was press-ganged into use as a museum of the socialist revolution – the long, curving galleries inside are now an atmospheric venue for changing displays of contemporary painting and sculpture.

Strossmayerov trg to the train station

Back on the horseshoe just south of Zrinjevac lies **Strossmayerov trg**, and the Croatian Academy of Arts and Sciences, founded as the Yugoslav Academy of Arts and Sciences by **Bishop Juraj Strossmayer** in 1866. An accomplished linguist, art connoisseur, horse-breeder and raconteur, Strossmayer was a leading figure in the current of nineteenth-century Croatian nationalism that regarded Yugoslavism – the drawing together of all southern Slavs – as the best way of offering resistance to Croatia's traditional enemies – Hungarians, Austrians and Italians. He's still a respected figure, regardless of what may have happened in the intervening hundred years. A statue of Strossmayer by Ivan Meštrović sits among the trees in front of the building, depicted with long bony fingers and a gown spread tightly over angular knees. In the academy itself, the **Strossmayer Gallery of Old Masters** (Strossmayerova galerija starih majstora; Tues–Sun 9am–5pm; 20Kn) includes pieces by prominent Venetians, including Veronese and Tintoretto, together with a small *Mary Magdalene* by El Greco, some early Flemish canvases by Joos van Cleve and the anonymous Master of the Virgin among the Virgins, and French paintings by the likes of Fragonard and Boucher – it's currently closed for extensive renovation, but will make essential viewing when it reopens.

Across the street from the Strossmayer Gallery is the **Modern Gallery** (Moderna galerija; Tues–Sun 10am–1pm & 5–8pm; 20Kn), a vast collection of Croatian art from 1850 to World War II. Quality is largely sacrificed for quantity here, and highlights are relatively easy to pick out: Vlaho Bukovac heads the list of pre-World War I painters with his monumental *Krist na odru* ("Christ on the funeral bier") of 1905, in which ghostly angels play around the catafalque. Krsto Hegedušić (see p.100) is represented by three canvases depicting life in the village of Hlebine in the 1930s, while contemporaneous Dalmatian painters Ignjat Job and Petar Dobrović contribute animated and colourful representations of Adriatic life. Just round the corner from the Modern Gallery, the Croatian Academy's **Graphic Art Gallery** (Kabinet grafike; Mon–Sat 11am–7pm; admission prices vary depending on what on display) hosts temporary exhibitions.

At the far end of Strossmayerov trg, the early twentieth-century **Art Pavilion** (Umjetnički paviljon; Mon–Sat 11am–7pm, Sun 10am–1pm; 10Kn), resplendent in the bright yellow paint job beloved of Habsburg-era architects, hosts regular temporary art exhibitions in its gilded stucco and mock-marble interior. Beyond lie the immaculate lawns and flowerbeds of **Tomislavov trg**, its name taken from the tenth-century Croatian king, Tomislav, whose equestrian statue stands at the square's southern end, greeting travellers emerging from the Neoclassical portals of Zagreb's main train station.

Trg maršala Tita

Heading westward from Zrinjevac along either Teslina or Hebrangova, it's a five-minute walk to **Trg maršala Tita** (Marshal Tito Square), a grandiose open space dominated by the solid, peach-coloured pile of the **Croatian National Theatre**. Opened by Emperor Franz Josef in 1890 and boasting a Neoclassical portal topped by a trumpet-blowing muse, it's an ostentatious statement of late nineteenth-century Croatia's growing cultural self-confidence. In front of the theatre, in a circular concrete pit, is yet another work by Meštrović, the tenderly erotic *Well of Life* (1905), while in the southwestern corner of the square, somewhat overshadowed by a trio of pines, is a sculpture by Fernkorn, showing St George on a rearing horse laying into a snarling dragon.

On the western side of the square, a long gabled building houses the **Museum of Arts and Crafts** (Muzej za umjetnost i obrt; Tues–Fri 10am–6pm, Sat & Sun 10am–1pm; 20Kn), a rewarding collection of furniture, ceramics, clothes and textiles from the Renaissance to the present day. The interior is impressive in itself, with gilt lion heads gazing down from cast-iron balustrades above the central atrium. The first floor kicks off with a parade of furniture and porcelain through the ages, culminating in a hall of religious art with restored wooden altarpieces from churches all over northern Croatia. Most striking is the seventeenth-century altar of St Mary from the village of Remetinec, northeast of Zagreb, showing a central Madonna and Child flanked by smaller panels in which a whole panoply of saints bend in a stylized swoon of spiritual grace. Objects on the second floor reflect turn-of-the-century Zagreb's status as a prosperous outpost of Mitteleuropa, with locally produced ceramics from the Arts and Crafts School (Zagreb's school of applied art, opened in 1882), as well as imported furnishings – notably Tiffany and Gallé glassware, and a chair and plant-pot stand by doyen of the Viennese arts-and-crafts scene, Josef Hoffmann. The third floor has clocks from throughout the ages, a lot of silverware, and a collection of early twentieth-century stained glass produced by local firm Koch & Marinković. Amongst the last, look out for

Vilko Gecan's *Life of the Woodcutter (Život drvosječe)* from 1924: five idealized panels illustrating the life-cycle of the Croatian peasant.

The Mimara Museum

Lying just southwest of Trg maršala Tita on Rooseveltov trg is the most prestigious – and controversial – museum in the area, the **Mimara Museum** (Muzej Mimara; Tues–Sat 10am–5pm, Sun 10am–2pm; 25Kn). Housed in an elegant neo-Renaissance former high school, the museum is made up of the bequest of **Ante Topić Mimara** (1899–1987), a native of Dalmatia who grew rich abroad and presented his vast art collection to the nation. No one really knows how he amassed his wealth, how he came by so many prized objects, or indeed whether he was even the real Ante Topić Mimara – some maintain that he was an impostor who, in the chaos of a World War I battlefield, stole the identity tags of a fallen comrade.

Whatever the truth, Mimara's tastes were nothing if not eclectic. On the ground floor are exhibits of ancient glassware from Egypt, Greece, Syria and the Roman Empire, together with later examples of glass from Venice and the rest of Europe. Close by are Persian carpets from the seventeenth to the nineteenth centuries, Chinese vases from the Shang to the Song dynasty, and Indian, Khmer and Japanese art through the ages. European pieces include Carolingian and Gothic reliquaries, and an exquisitely carved ivory English hunting horn from the 1300s. Upstairs there's more ancient material (pre-Columbian artefacts, Etruscan sculpture) assorted European sculpture, and, what should be the crowning section of the museum, the collection of European paintings. However, doubt still shrouds the authenticity of many of the paintings on display – most of the canvases are labelled "workshop of . . ." or "school of . . ." in order to avoid outright controversy. If one believes the attributions, Raphael, Veronese and other Italian artists get a good look in, as do Rubens and Rembrandt and the Dutch and Flemish painters, as well as later artists like Manet.

From Trg braće Mažuranića to the Botanical Gardens

South of Trg maršala Tita, the horseshoe continues with Trg braće Mažuranića, an unspectacular quadrangle of administrative buildings, including the **Ethnographic Museum** (Etnografski muzej; Tues–Thurs 10am–6pm, Fri–Sun 10am–1pm; 10Kn), a dimly lit and seemingly little visited place. Its collection of costumes from every corner of Croatia is as complete as you'll get, displaying numerous examples of the embroidered aprons and tunics that are found throughout the country. Downstairs lies an engaging jumble of artefacts brought back from the South Pacific, Asia and Africa by intrepid Croatian explorers. Foremost among these were the brothers Mirko and Stjepan Seljan, who served King Menelik II of Ethiopia as provincial governors, studied indigenous cultures in Brazil and Paraguay, and built roads in Peru – where Mirko disappeared in 1912. Stjepan went on to become a mine-owner in Brazil, where he died in 1936.

Marulićev trg, the next square to the south, is named after and boasts a statue of Renaissance writer and father of Croatian literature **Marko Marulić** (1450–1524), author of *Judita*, the first narrative poem in the Croatian language. A reworking of the biblical tale of Judith, who killed the Assyrian general Holofernes, Marulić's poem was taken to be an allegory of Croatia's struggles agtainst the Turks. The square was controversially – some say tastelessly – modernized in the late 1990s, when the lawn was lowered and the statue surrounded by what look like rows of airport landing lights which illuminate the bard at night in a manner not entirely in keeping with the restrained nineteenth-century apartment houses on either side. The bottom end of Marulićev trg is occupied by the former **University Library** (Sveučilišna knjižnica; now home to the state archives), opened with much pomp in 1913 and arguably Zagreb's finest Secession-era building, mixing a staid Neoclassical facade with eccentric ornamental details, such as the globes held aloft by owls which adorn each corner of the flattened, tent-like cupola.

On the far side of the library, just across Mihanovićeva beside the railtracks, are the city's tranquil **Botanical Gardens** (Botanički vrt; Tues–Sun 9am–7pm; free), with well-tended but modest plant collections fading into wilder areas of long grass and overgrown pathways. The novelist Miroslav Krleža, who used to sit here to write his diary during World War I, compared the gardens to a "boring second-rate cemetery" – it's nowhere near that bad, of course, although it's more a place for quiet relaxation than for botanical inspiration.

The Technical Museum and beyond

South of the Mimara Museum, **Savska cesta** heads southwest towards the concrete-and-steel confections of twentieth-century Zagreb, passing the **Technical Museum** (Tehnički muzej; Tues–Fri 9am–5pm, Sat & Sun 9am–1pm; 20Kn), one of the city's more entertaining collections, at no. 18. The display begins with a jumble of wooden watermills and steam turbines designed to illustrate the harnessing of natural power sources, along with a line-up of disembodied plane engines (including a Rolls-Royce Merlin II from 1938, used to power the Spitfire aircraft) which has the abstract dignity of a sculpture gallery. A central hall holds buses, cars, trams and aeroplanes, as well as a World War II Italian submarine captured by the Partisans in 1944 and drafted into the Yugoslav navy under the name *Mališan* ("The Nipper"). Other attractions (all included in the general admission price) include a small planetarium with regular showings (Tues–Fri at 4pm, Sat & Sun at noon); a reconstruction of a mine shaft (entrance by guided tour only: Tues–Fri at 3pm, Sat & Sun at 11am); and the reconstructed laboratory of pioneering physicist Nikola Tesla (entrance by guided tour only: Tues–Fri at 3.30pm, Sat & Sun at 11.30am).

Over the road lies the **Student Centre** (Studentski centar), where a theatre and cinema occupy the pavilions of the former Zagreb Fair. A thriving cultural venue in the 1970s and 1980s, the centre was deliberately run down by HDZ appointees eager to bring student life under closer political control in the 1990s. Further south along Savska, trams rattle on towards the River Sava, passing an important symbol of Zagreb en route: the cylindrical **Cibona Tower**, an office block whose highly reflective surface exudes a silvery, futuristic haughtiness.

The suburbs

Zagreb's sightseeing potential is largely exhausted once you've covered the compact centre, although there are a few worthwhile trips into the suburbs. The parkland of **Maksimir**, **Lake Jarun** and **Mirogoj Cemetery** – all easily accessible by tram or bus – are the main places to aim for if you want a break from the downtown streets.

Western Zagreb is particularly devoid of interest, although those travelling along Ilica en route to the Černomerec tram terminal will pass one of Zagreb's more poignant sights, the **Zid boli** (Wall of Pain). Running along the pavement outside the (now empty) United Nations compound 3km west of the centre, this is a low, *ad hoc* structure, each brick of which is inscribed with the name of a casualty from the siege of Vukovar in 1991. Largely the work of refugees from Vukovar and their relatives (many of whom still come here to lay flowers or light candles), the wall is intended to act as both a memorial to the victims and a reminder of the international community's failure to take decisive action at the time.

Maksimir

Three kilometres east of the centre is Zagreb's largest and lushest open space, **Maksimir**, reached by tram #11 or #12 (direction Dubrava) from Trg bana Jelačića. Named after Archbishop Maximilian Vrhovac, who in 1774 established a small public garden in the southwestern corner of today's park, Maksimir owes much to his successors Aleksandar Alagović and Juraj Haulik, who imported the idea of the landscaped country park from England. It's perfect for aimless strolling, with the straight-as-an-arrow, tree-lined avenues at its southwestern end giving way to more densely forested areas in its northern reaches. As well as five lakes, the park is dotted with follies, including a belvedere (nowadays closed and covered in graffiti) and a mock Swiss chalet (Švicarska kuća), now a café, which gets mobbed on fine Sunday afternoons. The eastern end of the park holds the city's **zoo** (daily 9am–5pm; 20Kn) – shaded by trees and partly situated on a small island, it's a pleasant place to stroll whether or not you're taken by the animals. On the opposite side of the road to the park stands the **Maksimir football stadium**, home to both Dinamo Zagreb and the national side (see box on p.78).

Mirogoj

Ranged across a hillside just over 2km northeast of the centre, the main city cemetery of **Mirogoj** was laid out by Hermann Bollé in 1876. The main (western) entrance to the graveyard is in many ways his most impressive work: an ivy-covered, fortress-like wall topped by a row of greening cupolas. The cemetery serves all Zagreb's citizens regardless of faith, so alongside the Catholic gravestones you'll find Orthodox memorials bearing Cyrillic script, Muslim graves adorned with the crescent of Islam, and socialist-era tombstones boasting the *petokraka*, or five-pointed star. The most evocative part of this vast necropolis is the arcades running either side of the main entrance, containing work by some of Croatia's best turn-of-the-century sculptors, with rows of elegantly rendered memorials overlooked by spindly cast-iron lanterns. Heading right from the entrance, it's difficult to miss Ivan Rendić's grieving female figures atop the graves of Petar Preradović and Emanuel Priester; while slightly further on, Robert Frangeš Mihanović's extraordinary bleak relief of stooping bearded figures decorates the family tomb of the Mayer family. Head left from the entrance to find the Miletić tomb, where Rudolf Valdec's fine *Angel of Death* is framed on either side by outstretched sculpted hands into which descendants of the family still place roses.

Bus #106 heads up to Mirogoj from Kaptol every fifteen minutes or so; otherwise, take tram #14 (direction Mihaljevac) from Trg bana Jelačića to Gupčeva Zvijezda, then walk for ten minutes up to the cemetery via Mirogojska cesta.

Jarun

On sunny days city folk head out to **Jarun**, a two-kilometre-long artificial lake encircled by footpaths and cycling tracks 4km southwest of the city centre. It's an important venue for rowing competitions, with a large spectator stand at the western end, although most people come here simply to stroll or sunbathe. The best spot for the latter is **Malo jarunsko jezero** at Jarun's eastern end, a bay sheltered from the rest of the lake by a long thin island. Here you'll find a shingle beach, several outdoor cafés (which remain open well into the night), and grassy, partly shaded areas of park. This is a good place from which to clamber up onto the dyke which runs along the banks of the **River Sava**, providing a good vantage point from which to survey the cityscape of Novi Zagreb beyond.

The best way of getting to the **western end** of the lake is to catch tram #17 from Trg bana Jelačića to the Jarun terminus, a five-minute walk north of the water's edge. If you're only heading for Malo jarunsko jezero, it's probably easier to get off the tram at the Stjepan Radić stop and walk down Jarunska (10–15min), passing the high-rise blocks of Zagreb university's student village on your right.

Novi Zagreb

Spread over the plain on the southern side of the River Sava, **Novi Zagreb** (New Zagreb) is a vast grid-iron of housing projects and multi-lane highways that nowadays looks much less attractive than its utopian planners intended. Thrown up in the 1960s in order to accommodate the stream of migrants drawn by the booming economy of the big city, it's a true melting-pot of Croatia's population. The central part of Novi Zagreb is not that bad a place to live: swathes of park help to break up the architectural monotony, and each residential block has a clutch of bars and pizzerias in which to hang out. Outlying areas have far fewer facilities, however, and possess the aura of half-forgotten dormitory settlements on which the rest of Zagreb has turned its back.

Those drawn to the aesthetics of high-rise buildings and graffiti will find the area strangely compelling, but otherwise there's little to do here except visit the **Zagreb Fair Grounds** (Zagrebački velesajam) on Avenija Dubrovnik, where major trade exhibitions take place throughout the year – the Zagreb tourist office will have details of what's on. To get there, take tram #14 (destination Zapruđe) until you see the main entrance building on your left.

The only other reason to venture into this part of town is to stroll around the **Bundek**, an incongruously swampy, kidney-shaped lake surrounded by thick woods and untended meadows. Located on the northern fringes of Novi Zagreb near the banks of the Sava, it's popular with picnickers and dog-walkers eager to escape from the concrete wastelands nearby. Paths lead towards the Bundek from opposite the *Zagreb* hotel (see p.57 for directions).

Mount Medvednica

The wooded slopes of **Mount Medvednica**, or "Bear Mountain" (also known as the Zagrebačka Gora, or "Zagreb uplands"), offer the easiest escape from the city, with the range's highest peak, **Sljeme** (1035m), accessible by cable car and easily seen on a half-day trip. It's a densely forested mountain range and the views from the top are not as impressive as you might expect, but the walking is good and there's a limited amount of skiing in winter, when you can rent gear from shacks near the summit. You can drive to Sljeme by heading north out of central Zagreb along Ribnjak, and taking a well-signed right turn after about 3km. By public transport, take tram #14 from Trg bana Jelačića to the Mihaljevac terminus, followed by #15 to the Dolje terminus, from where it's a ten–minute walk via pedestrian tunnel and woodland path to the cable car station (*žičara*; daily 8am–8pm; departures on the hour; 6Kn one way, 10Kn return). From here it's a stately twenty-minute journey to the top, with expansive views of greater Zagreb opening up as you ascend. If the cable car isn't running due to mainte-nance work or bad weather, a small yellow sign reading *žičara ne vozi* is posted at the Mihaljevac tram terminus.

Once at the top, a flight of steps leads straight ahead past a couple of refresh-ment huts to the summit, capped by a TV transmission tower. Completed in 1980, the tower's top floor originally housed a restaurant and viewing terrace, but the lifts broke down after three months and it's been closed to the public ever since. Views of the low hills of the Zagorje to the north occasionally reveal themselves through gaps in the surrounding trees, a rippling green landscape broken by red-roofed villages. A left turn out of the cable car station brings you to the *Tomislavov Dom* hotel (see p.57), home to a couple of cafés and a restaurant, while a right turn leads after ten minutes to Činovnička livada, a sloping meadow popular with picnickers. The path carries on over the meadow towards the **Chapel of Our Lady of Sljeme** (Majke Božje Sljemenske; Thurs, Sat & Sun 10am–6pm), built in 1932 to commemorate the 1000th anniversary of Croatia's conversion to Christianity. Ostensibly inspired by Croatian medieval architecture, it's actually a highly idiosyncratic modern building, featuring elegantly sloping buttresses and an obliquely angled bell-tower. Paths continue east along the ridge, emerging after about twenty minutes at the Puntijarka mountain refuge, a popular refresh-ment stop whose cafeteria serves excellent *grah* (bean soup) and grilled meats. Another twenty minutes along the ridge brings you to the *Hunjka* hotel (see p.57), where there's another small restaurant and several more trails leading off into the woods which cover Medvednica's eastern flanks.

Medvedgrad

Commanding a spur of the mountain 4km southwest of Sljeme, the fortress of **Medvedgrad** was built in the mid-thirteenth century at the instigation of Pope Innocent IV in the wake of Tatar attacks, although its defensive capabilities were never really tested, and it was abandoned in 1571. Then, in the 1990s, it was decid-ed to rebuild the fortress as a monument to the Croatian nation. Walls and towers were swiftly reconstructed, and an **Altar of the Homeland** (Altar domovine) – an eternal flame surrounded by stone blocks and glass sculptures in the form of tears – was placed at the fortress's eastern rim. Conservationists were dismayed by the altar's failure to blend in with its historic surroundings, but it has quickly assumed an important role in state ceremonial, with the president of the republic and other dignitaries laying wreaths here on national holidays. You can roam the castle's south-facing ramparts, enjoying panoramic views of Zagreb and the plain beyond, and there's a restaurant in a subterranean hall serving traditional north-Croatian favourites like *grah*, *štrukli* and *štrudl*.

Unless you're walking here from Sljeme via the marked paths which slant down from the *Tomislavov Dom* hotel, Medvedgrad is best approached from the village of Šestine, 5km northwest of central Zagreb, which can be reached by bus #102 from Mihaljevac or Britanski trg (400m west of Trg bana Jelačića along Ilica). Get off when you see the bright yellow Šestine church 4km out of the centre and walk north past the church towards the *Šestinski Lagvić* restaurant (see p.73) 1km uphill. About 80m beyond the restaurant a path darts into the woods on the left;

it's initially difficult to spot – look out for the red-and-white waymarkings painted onto a nearby tree. From here it's a straightforward forty-minute ascent through oak forest to the fortress.

Eating

Whatever your budget, there's no shortage of places to eat in Zagreb, although the range of food on offer is pretty much the same wherever you go. The majority of **restaurants** concentrate on the pork- and veal-based central European dishes indigenous to northern Croatia, and there are several excellent fish restaurants which are as good as anything you'll find on the coast. Decent Italian pasta is widely available, and there's a surfeit of pizzerias around Trg bana Jelačića and Tkalčićeva. Those keen to experience more exotic cuisine, however, are unlikely to be satisfied by Zagreb's handful of Chinese and Mexican restaurants. Some of the best restaurants for traditional food are to be found in the **northern suburbs** – worth the trek out if you want to observe the local bigwigs at play.

Naturally, **prices** vary according to what you're eating: pizzas, pasta and grills are cheapest, fresh fish the most expensive, with standard Croatian meat dishes falling somewhere in between. We've graded the restaurants below according to the following ranges: **inexpensive** (30–60Kn), **moderate** (60–100Kn), and **expensive** (100–150Kn), based on the average cost of a basic meal (main course, salad and a drink). Indulging in aperitifs, bottles of wine and desserts will, of course, push the bill up considerably. Restaurants are usually open daily from around 11am until 11pm or midnight unless stated otherwise. If it's advisable to book a table in advance, we've included a telephone number.

For **snacks**, the best place to find *burek* (cheese pastry) or cheap grills is the area around Dolac market, just above Trg bana Jelačića. *Mimice*, Jurišićeva 21, is a stand-up buffet serving inexpensive portions of whitebait (*ribice*), squid (*lignje*) and other fishy snacks. *Pingvin*, inside the courtyard at Teslina 7, is a good sandwich bar open until 2am. There are also a few 24-hour **bakeries** in the city centre: *Pekarnica Dora*, at Strossmayerov trg 7; *Pekarna Grič*, Vlaška 7; and *Pekarnica Radićeva*, Radićeva 10. Picnic supplies can be purchased from the stalls of Dolac market or from either of the large **supermarkets** in the subterranean Importanne shopping centre in front of the train station: Konsum (Mon–Sat 6am–9pm, Sun 7am–4pm) or Jabuka (daily 7am–midnight). The best **ice cream** parlours are *Slastičarna Vincek*, Ilica 18, and *Central*, Jurišićeva 24.

Central Zagreb

Baltazar, Nova Ves 4. Five minutes' walk north of the cathedral along Kaptol, this is one of the best venues in the city for the standard north-Croatian repertoire of grilled meats, with a pleasant courtyard and attentive service. Closed Sun. Moderate to expensive.

Bijeli Val, Baruna Trenka 7, west off Strossmayerov trg (ring bell outside). Vegetarian restaurant serving a simple fixed menu. It's located on the first floor of an apartment building and decorated with contemporary art works – a bit like eating in someone's flat. Inexpensive.

Boban, Gajeva 3. Owned by football star Zvonimir Boban, this popular and central pasta restaurant with breezy service is in the vaulted cellar of the café of the same name. Inexpensive.

Cantinetta, Teslina 14. Good-quality, moderately priced Croatian, Italian and modern European food in relaxed surroundings, just south of Trg bana Jelačića. Closed Sun. Moderate.

Dubravkin Put, Dubravkin Put 2 (☎427-829). Pricey place in the leafy Tuškanac district (head west from Trg bana Jelačića along Ilica, turn right up Dežmanova and carry straight on for 5min), with excellent fish and shellfish, delicious roasted meats and plenty of outdoor seating. Closed Sun. Expensive.

Korčula, Teslina 17. Small, unpretentious Dalmatian restaurant serving excellent grilled fish and seafood risottos. Moderate to expensive.

Klub A.G. Matoš, Ilica 1 (☎429-544). Smart, top-quality Croatian-international restaurant above the Znanje bookshop on Trg bana Jelačića. Entrance from the arcade round the back. Expensive.

Lopud, Kaptol 10 (☎48 14-594). Renowned seafood restaurant just north of the cathedral. Fresh fish is flown in every morning from Dubrovnik, and there's also an extensive range of shellfish. Closed Sun. Expensive.

Nokturno, Skalinska 4. In a side-street just off Tkalčićeva offering serviceable pizzas, a varied choice of lasagnes and simple pasta dishes, good salads and a small outdoor terrace. Inexpensive.

Pivnica Medvedgrad, Savska 56. Large beer hall slightly off the beaten track, 1.5km southwest of the centre – take tram #17 (destination Jarun) from Trg bana Jelačića or tram #4 (destination Savski most) from the train station. Traditional Croatian meat dishes are served in large, cheap portions and the beer – brewed on the premises – is excellent. Moderate.

Pizzeria Dvojka, Nova ves 2. Five minutes' walk north of the cathedral, this bright, functional pizzeria has a solid range of pasta and pizzas, including mammoth *obiteljska* ("family-size") servings. Inexpensive.

Pizzeria Zadar, Preradovićev trg. Satisfying pizza and pasta dishes (including a good vegetarian lasagne) in brash, café-style surroundings at a prime city-centre location. Lots of outdoor seating too. Inexpensive.

Pod Gričkim Topom, Zakmardijeve stube 5 (☎430-690). Good Croatian food in a cosy restaurant on the steps leading down from Strossmayerovo Šetalište to Trg bana Jelačića. There's a nice garden terrace overlooking the lower town too. Moderate.

Rubelj, Dolac Market. Cheapest place in the centre for simple but tasty grilled-meat standards. Excellent value for a quick feed, but not the kind of place to linger over a meal. There are a couple more good grill places right next door if *Rubelj* is full. Inexpensive.

Stari Fijaker, Mesnička 6, about 300m west along Ilica from Trg bana Jelačića. Charmingly old-fashioned downtown restaurant with a pretty good line in standard Croatian meat dishes. Good place for a slap-up evening meal, although inexpensive standbys such as *punjene paprike* (stuffed peppers) are also available. Moderate to expensive.

The northern suburbs

Gušti, Markuševačka cesta 22, Markuševac (☎433-567). Folksy interior, traditional home cooking and frequent live *tamburica* (Slavonian folk) music. Take tram #14 to the Mihaljevac terminus, followed by tram #5 to the Dolje terminus, followed by a 10min walk northeast along Gračanska (subsequently Markuševačka) cesta. Expensive.

Okrugljak, Mlinovi 28 (☎277-973). Traditional Croatian food in folksy surroundings, with plenty of outdoor seating and regular live music from violin and piano. It's a popular venue for family celebrations. Take tram #14 to the Mihaljevac terminus, then it's a 10min walk north on the road to Šestine. Expensive.

Šestinski Lagvić, Šestinska cesta bb (☎426-486). Just above the village of Šestine on a shoulder of Mount Medvednica, this is a convenient stop-off en route to Medvedgrad with a (often crowded) terrace looking back down towards the city. Known for its *štruklji* and other north-Croatian favourites. Take tram #14 to the Mihaljevac terminus, then bus #102 to Šestine. Get off at the church and walk a little way uphill. Moderate to expensive.

Drinking and nightlife

There's a wealth of **café-bars** with outdoor seating in central Zagreb, especially in the pedestrianized area around Bogovićeva and Preradovićev trg. The other main strolling area is Tkalčićeva, just north of Trg bana Jelačića, which, with a watering hole every few metres, looks like one vast outdoor bar. There's little difference between individual establishments when it comes to the kind of music they play or the range of drinks on offer: it's really just a question of finding a free table from which to watch the world go by. Saturday morning is the traditional time for meeting friends and lingering over a coffee, although downtown areas remain busy day and night, seven days a week, if the weather is good enough for alfresco imbibing. Things quieten down as soon as the weather gets cold, although the more characterful café-bars retain their clientele through the winter.

The cafés and bars listed below are open daily from early in the morning until 11pm or midnight unless stated otherwise. Larger cafés may offer a range of pastries, ice creams and sandwiches, but there are no hard-and-fast rules about this. Late-night drinking takes place in clubs (see p.75) or in the rather unatmospheric café-bars of the Importanne shopping centre in front of the train station. The latter are open round the clock and function as useful pre-dawn bolt-holes if you can't face waiting for Zagreb's elusive night trams. The number of **cyber-cafés** in Zagreb is on the increase: expect to pay 10Kn for one-off membership fee plus 20–30Kn per hour online.

Cafés and bars

Atrij, Teslina 7. One of several café-bars in a courtyard one block south of Trg bana Jelačića, heaving with bright young things at the weekend.

Brazil, north bank of the River Sava, near Savski most. Small but characterful bar in a (now landlocked) boat, with an interior decorated in the style of an Amazonian thatched hut. Lively at weekends, when it's usually open past midnight. Take tram #4 from the train station to the Savski most terminus and head east along the dyke above the river. *Brazil* is the second structure down to the right.

Bulldog Pub, Bogovićeva. Not really a pub, more an elegant split-level bar and pavement café, and one of the most popular meeting places in town, especially on Saturday mornings.

Café Godot, Savska. Cosy and relaxing place somewhere between a European café and an Irish pub in feel. Convenient place for a drink after visiting the Technical Museum.

Dobar Zvuk, Gajeva 18. Popular café-bar with a slightly bohemian clientele, restrained music and adverts for Irish beer on the wall. No outdoor seating.

Dubrovnik, Trg bana Jelačića. Roomy and rather posh café attatched to the hotel of the same name, occupying classic position by the square. Good range of cakes and ice cream.

Hard Rock Caffe, Gajeva 10. Not part of the international chain, but with a similarly raucous, memorabilia-crowded ambience. In summer the *Caffe* sets out tables in the garden of the Archeological Museum just across the road – an excellent place to enjoy a coffee amidst replica Roman gravestones.

Kazališna Kavana, Trg maršala Tita. Zagreb's only surviving Viennese-style coffee house, though it's been modernized many times over the years, and the literary and artistic set who used to hang out here have moved on. A good place to recharge your batteries after a visit to the Mimara Museum.

Kolding, Berislavićeva 8, three blocks south of Trg bana Jelačića. Civilized cellar bar with vaguely turn-of-the-century furnishings. Nice place for an intimate drink, and plenty of outdoor seating in the courtyard.

K. u. K, Jurišićeva. Small but cosy city-centre café decked out with pictures of Zagreb old and new. Closed Sun.

Pivnica Medvedgrad, Savska 56. Cavernous, if not particularly atmospheric, beer hall serving ales brewed on the premises and an extensive range of traditional Croatian food (see "Restaurants", p.73).

Pizzeria Zadar, Preradovićev trg. A classic summertime people-watching venue with a prime site on a charming lower town square. Also does good food (see "Restaurants", p.73).

Praćka Pub, Dalmatinska 14, just north of Trg maršala Tita. An unprepossessing exterior hides a small basement bar decorated with rock memorabilia. Occasional live music.

Sedmica, Kačićeva 7. Laid-back, mildly arty hangout hidden inside the hallway of an apartment block about 1km west of Trg bana Jelačića just beyond Britanski trg. Serves good Viški plavac red wine from the island of Vis.

Tolkien, Vraničanijeva. Relaxed café-bar in Gradec, with pleasant leafy courtyard and Middle Earth-inspired memorabilia inside.

Cybercafés

Aquarius.net, Držislavova 4, just west of Trg hrvatskih velikana (☎46-18-873, *www.aquariusnet.hr*). Small, dark and functional. Enter via the *Plava Ptica* café next door.

Art.net café, Preradovićeva 23 (☎48-17-123, *www.haa.hr*). Roomy, very plush and rather formal in atmosphere, with occasional live music and literary evenings. Closed Sun.

Sublink, in the courtyard of Teslina 12 (☎48-11-329, *www.sublink.hr*). Croatia's first cybercafé and still a cult Zagreb meeting-point, it's friendly and relaxed, if cramped at times.

Nightlife

It's not difficult to go out partying most nights of the week if you know where to go. The emergence of a vibrant rave, techno and house scene in the mid-1990s revived the city's declining fortunes, and current nightlife centres around a modest selection of characterful and informal discos and clubs, many of which present the only real opportunities for catching live **rock** and **jazz**. Venues tend to be open from about 10pm to 4 or 5am unless stated otherwise. Admission charges for clubs and gigs range between 30 and 60Kn – more for big, one-off events,

Live gigs and themed dance events are often arranged at short notice; the only sure way of getting **information** is to check the posters plastered liberally around the city centre or pick up flyers from record shops (see "Listings", p.80).

Aquarius, Jarun. This waterfront pavilion at the eastern end of Lake Jarun, 4km southwest of the centre, is the city's main venue for electronic dance music. Expect commercial-ish house and techno at weekends, more experimental stuff on Thursdays and Sundays. Big name Croatian pop-rock stars perform on the outdoor terrace in summer. Directions as for Lake Jarun (see p.70).

The Best, Mladost Sports Centre. Run-of-the-mill disco with a slightly snooty reputation, although rave-style events have been organized here in recent times. Tram #17 (destination Jarun) from Trg bana Jelačića to the Stjepan Radić stop, then a short walk down Jarunska.

BP Club, Teslina 7. Basement bar and jazz club owned by godfather of the Croatian jazz scene, vibe-player Boško Petrović. A convivial late-night drinking haunt with frequent live music, although gets crowded on big gig nights.

Dom Sportova, Metalčeva. Cavernous sports hall-type venue for major gigs, with bad acoustics and long lines for beer, though the enthusiasm of a big Zagreb crowd usually makes up for any inherent lack of atmosphere. Take tram #3, #9 or #12 (direction Ljubljanica) to Trešnjevački trg, then turn right up Trakošćanska.

Gjuro II, Medveščak 2. Just north of Kaptol, this unpretentious cellar club has a bohemian reputation and is a traditional meeting-point for a wide-ranging crowd of gay and straight non-conformists and media professionals. Varied programme of dance music and live performances. Open Wed–Sun.

KSET, Unska 3. Small, intimate, student-run concert venue (often jazz, blues or ethno) and themed club nights. Can be difficult to find: from Savska head east along Koturaška, turn right into Unska, then go straight over the crossroads and take the first dingy alley on the left. Open until midnight, Sept–June only.

Kulušić, Hrvojeva 6, between the bus station and Trg hrvatskih velikana. One-time mecca of the Zagreb rock scene, now largely given over to mainstream commercial disco. Open Thurs–Sun.

Lapidarij, Habdelićeva 1. Attractive cellar-like space in Gradec with programmes ranging from mainstream dance music to indie rock. Traditionally popular with a tolerant, alternative crowd.

Močvara, Tvornica Jedinstvo, Trnjanski nasip bb. Unpretentious cultural centre run by independent art cooperative URK in an old factory on the northern banks of the River Sava. Live gigs (usually alternative rock) at least twice weekly, film shows or club nights on other evenings. It's unclear at the moment whether the club will stay at its current address long term: look out for the Močvara/URK label cropping up in other locations. Open until midnight.

Saloon, Tuškanac 1a. Legendary Zagreb meeting-place in a leafy corner of town 500m west of the centre, with a warren of rooms inside and large terrace outside. A moderately dressy clientele includes a sprinkling of beautiful people and showbiz personalities, but it's not dishearteningly exclusive by any means. Music is an enjoyable mish-mash of commercial disco, except on Tues, when you'll hear classic rock from the Stones onwards.

Sax, Palmotićeva 22, two blocks east of Zrinjevac. Jazz-oriented club in large basement, with live music most nights.

Sokol, Trg maršala Tita 6 (entrance opposite the Mimara Museum). Big disco with commercial dance music, domestic pop and themed party-nights. Great fun if you just want to drink, dance, and enjoy the cattle-market atmosphere.

Tvornica, Šubićeva 1, just north of the bus station. Former ballroom currently serving as venue for live rock, club nights and theatre. There's usually something on every night of the week, but check listings info or posters before setting out.

Entertainment

Zagreb offers the rich and varied diet of **entertainment** that one would expect from a metropolis of a million people, although the combined effects of war and financial belt-tightening mean that the city is still struggling to recapture the vibrancy it enjoyed in the 1980s. The events of the last decade have produced a measure of artistic isolation: international performers rarely tour here unless lured by high-profile festivals, and cultural events also tend to thin out in August, when many of Zagreb's citizens head for the coast.

Extensive entertainment **listings** appear in the free monthly English-language pamphlet *Events and Performances*, available from the Zagreb tourist office. If you can decipher the local language, there's daily listings information in the back pages of newspapers like *Jutarnji List*, *Novi List* and *Vjesnik*. The last has cinema and theatre schedules on its Web site at *www.vjesnik.hr*.

The most accessible of Zagreb's annual events is the **International Folklore Festival** (Međunarodna smotra folklora), usually held over the last weekend in July, with performances of ethnic music and dance from all over Croatia, plus a range of international guests. Performances take place on the central Trg bana Jelačića and in venues throughout the town. Advance information can be obtained from Concert Direction Zagreb, Kneza Mislava 18 (Koncertna Direkcija Zagreb; ☎46-11-797, fax 46-11-807). Taken chronologically, the city's other important festivals are the **Music Biennale** (Musičko biennale; April), a festival of resolutely modern music held every odd-numbered year; the **Contemporary Dance Week** (Tjedan suvremenog plesa; early June); the **Eurokaz Theatre Festival** (late June), which features challenging avant-garde drama; and the **Zagreb Summer Festival** (Zagrebački ljetni festival; mid-July to mid-Aug) of orchestral and chamber music, which brings together many of the international performers appearing at the Dubrovnik festival the same year. Advance information on all these events can be obtained from the Zagreb tourist office.

Classical music and drama and ballet

Zagreb offers a respectably broad menu of performing arts events. Theatre and concert tickets are usually easy to come by, and tend to be about half the price of those in Western Europe. Drama and opera are almost invariably in Croatian, unless you happen to be in town during one of the major festivals, when international groups are invited.

Croatian Musical Institute (Hrvatski glazbeni zavod), Gundulićeva 6 (☎424-533). Main city venue for chamber music.

Croatian National Theatre (Hrvatsko narodno kazalište; HNK), Trg maršala Tita 15 (box office Mon–Fri 10am–1pm & 5–7.30pm, Sat 10am–1pm & 90min before performances; Sun 30min before each performance; ☎48-28-532). Zagreb's cultural flagship, this sumptuous Neoclassical building provides the city's main venue for prestige classical drama, as well as opera and ballet.

Gavella, Frankopanska 8 (box office 10am–1pm & 2hr prior to performances; ☎48-48-552). Medium-sized venue for local and touring theatre companies, plus occasional concerts.

Kerempuh, Ilica 31 (box office Tues–Sun 10am–8pm; ☎428-839). Offers a mixture of serious theatre, satire and comedy, with frequent late-night performances beginning at 11pm.

Komedija, Kaptol 9 (box office opens 90min prior to performances; ☎48-14-566). Musicals and operettas.

Off Theatre Bagatelle, Bednjanska 13 (box office opens 4hr prior to performances; ☎61-70-423). Fringe productions, theatre workshops and cabaret.

Scena Vidra, Draškovićeva 80 (box office Tues–Sun 10am–3pm & 2hr before performances; ☎430-183). Small studio theatre housed in a former cinema.

Student Cultural Centre, Savska 25 (box office Mon–Sat 11am–1pm & 2hr prior to performance; ☎48-43-492). Home to leading contemporary theatre company &TD, with repertoire ranging from the populist to the experimental.

Vatroslav Lisinski Concert Hall (Koncertna dvorana Vatroslav Lisinski), Trg Stjepana Radića 4 (box office Mon–Fri 9am–8pm, Sat 9am–2pm; ☎61-21-166). Modern complex with two auditoriums; favoured venue for orchestral concerts and prestige drama events.

Zagreb Youth Theatre (ZeKaeM), Teslina 5 (box office opens 1hr prior to performances; ☎48-11-955). Top-quality work by leading youth-theatre groups.

Cinemas

Zagreb's **cinemas** show a wide range of recently released Western films, which are shown in the original language with Croatian subtitles. The best of the big city centre cinemas are the Zagreb, Preradovićev trg 4, and the nearby, olde-worlde Europa, Varšavska 3. Slightly further afield, Centar Kaptol, just north of Kaptol at Nova ves 14, is a plush modern cinema with excellent sound. Kinoteka, Kordunska 1, is the main venue for art-house movies and cinema classics, while Croatia, Katančićeva, is a tiny, fifty-seater cinema with a uniquely intimate feel, showing mainstream movies or matinée cartoon features made by the local Croatia film studio.

DINAMO ZAGREB AND THE BLUE BOYS

From 1990 until the turn of the century, many **Bad Blue Boys** – as the supporters of Dinamo Zagreb call themselves – claimed to be the true defenders of the honour of Zagreb. Modelling themselves on the fans of Chelsea, the Bad Blue Boys first became newsworthy on May 13, 1990, when a Dinamo home match against Red Star Belgrade ended in chaos, an event which for many symbolized the disintegration of the Yugoslav federation. The trouble started when Red Star fans began ripping up seats and throwing them on the pitch. The police (at this time widely believed to be under Serbian influence) failed to take action, and so Dinamo fans decided to invade the pitch. The police set about truncheoning the trespassers, enraging the Dinamo players, who were still on the field of play. Zvonimir Boban, the youngest-ever Dinamo captain and a byword for coolness under pressure, was so incensed that he drop-kicked a pair of policemen himself – TV pictures of which were beamed around Europe the same night. The events of the day were soon mythologized, with the Bad Blue Boys exaggeratedly claiming that they had been the first to stand up to Greater Serbian chauvinism before the breakout of all-out war the following year.

The Bad Blue Boys therefore enjoyed considerable kudos when, in 1992, the club, backed by President Tuđman, decided to drop the "Dinamo" from the club's name on the basis that it was too reminiscent of communist ideology. The team was renamed Croatia Zagreb, in the hope that it would serve as an advertisement for the country in prestige European competitions, but the Bad Blue Boys hated it and started a campaign to restore the team's original name. Many thought that the dispute would die out as soon as the fans were provided with success on the pitch (Croatia won the championship four years on the trot between 1996 and 1999), but if anything it got worse. In spring 1999, fans were roughed up by police for wearing Dinamo scarves inside the ground, and they responded with a boycott which seriously reduced attendance figures.

Because Croatia Zagreb had been earmarked as part of the country's propaganda effort, other sides in the league began to regard the team as a privileged club which they were not allowed to beat. The team's honorary president, Franjo Tuđman, also happened to be president of the country, and most of its officials were high-ranking HDZ functionaries. Even the players were encouraged to join the HDZ-Youth, and Tuđman himself came to watch every home game, making it difficult for referees to stay impartial. In these circumstances, the Bad Blue Boys' boycott came to be seen as a principled stand against a club that had gone wrong. The final match of the 1998–99 season, in which Croata clinched yet another championship, was witnessed by a home crowd of less than 2000. As soon as Tuđman went into hospital in November 1999 club officials floated the idea of a referendum on the return of the Dinamo name; then, in January 2000, came the HDZ's humiliating election defeat. Later that month, the name Dinamo Zagreb was returned.

Sport

Football remains the city's principal sporting preoccupation, with the big teams playing matches on Sunday afternoons between August and May (with a mid-season break in Jan & Feb). Tickets rarely exceed 30Kn for league matches, when they can be bought from kiosks near the turnstiles. Prices go up for European matches or internationals, when tickets are best bought in advance from the relevant stadium. **Dinamo Zagreb** and the Croatian national team play at the Stadion Maksimir, Maksimirska 128, an all-seater, 30,000-capacity stadium, currently being rebuilt stage by stage (tram #1 or #17 from Trg bana Jelačića or #9 from the train station to the Borongaj terminus). The rather basic stadium at Kranjčevićeva 4 is home to the city's other major team, **NK Zagreb**. Take tram #3, #9 or #12 (direction Ljubljanica) to the Cibona Tower, then head straight on under the railway bridge.

Few other sports attract sizeable crowds save for **basketball**, with Zagreb's top team, Cibona, playing at the Dražen Petrović Basketball centre, Savska 30 (☎48-43-333) – matches take place on Saturdays from September to late April.

The best of the city's indoor **swimming** pools is Zimsko Plivalište Mladost, Trg sportova 10 (directions as for *Hotel Panorama*, see p.57; Mon–Fri 2–7pm, Sat & Sun 8am–7pm). For an outdoor swim, you can choose between the beach at Jarun (p.69) or the more central outdoor pool at Šalata, ten minutes' walk northeast from Trg bana Jelačića at the top end of the Schlosserove stube steps (Mon–Fri 1.30–6pm, Sat & Sun 11am–7pm).

Listings

Airlines Adria, Praška 9 (☎48-10-011); Aeroflot, Varšavska 13 (☎421-825); Air France, Gajeva 12 (☎45-58-355); Austrian Airlines, Zrinjevac 6 (☎420-255); Bosna Air, Zagreb Airport (☎45-62-672); British Airways, Sheraton Hotel, Kneza Borne 2 (☎45-53-336); Croatia Airlines, Zrinjevac 17 (☎45-51-244); KLM, Hotel Esplanade, Mihanovićeva 1 (☎45-73-133); Lufthansa, Zagreb Airport (☎45-62-187) or at GeneralTurist, Zrinjevac 18 (☎425-566); Swissair, Zrinjevac 6 (☎420-255).

Airport Enquiries ☎65-25-222.

ATMs There are usefully located ATMs on the eastern side of Trg bana Jelačića; outside Zagrebačka banka on Praška; and outside Varaždinska banka on Draškovićeva.

Books A large selection of contemporary English-language paperbacks is available from Algoritam, Gajeva 1 (next to the *Dubrovnik* hotel). International magazines are sold on the ground floor; books in the basement below.

British Council, Ilica 12 (Mon, Tues & Thurs 10am–4.30pm, Wed 1.30–6.30pm, Fri 10am–1.30pm; ☎424-733). Reading room with English-language newspapers.

Bus station Enquiries ☎060/313-333.

Car rental Avis, Hotel Intercontinental, Kršnjavoga 1 (☎48-36-296); Budget, Hotel Sheraton, Kneza Borne 2 (☎45-54-936); Hertz, Kačićeva 9a (☎48-47-222).

Embassies and consulates Australia, Hotel Esplanade, Mihanovićeva 1 (☎45-77-433); Bosna-Hercegovina, Torbarova 9 (☎46-83-764); Canada, Hotel Esplanade, Mihanovićeva 1 (☎45-77-905); Netherlands, Medvešćak 56 (☎423-959); UK, Vlaška 121 (☎45-55-310); US, Hebrangova 2 (☎455-55-00); Yugoslavia, Mesićeva 19 (☎46-80-552). There are no Irish or New Zealand consulates.

Exchange There are exchange counters (*mjenjačnica*) at all banks, travel agents and post offices. Outside regular office hours, try the exchange counter at the bus station (24hr), or at the post office next to the train station at Branimirova 4 (24hr except midnight Sat to 1pm Sun).

Ferry bookings Jadrolinija, Zrinjevac 20 (☎421-777).

Hospital The main casualty department is at Draškovićeva 19.

Laundry Service washes and dry cleaning at Petecin, Kaptol 11 (Mon–Fri 8am–8pm, Sat 8am–2pm); and Predom, Draškovićeva 31 (Mon–Fri 7am–7pm, Sat 6am–noon).

Left luggage At the bus station (24hr) and train station.

Pharmacy Ilica 43 (24hr).

Photographic supplies Foto Studio Zagreb, Praška 2.

Post offices Jurišićeva 13 (Mon–Fri 7am–9pm, Sat 7am–7pm, Sun 8am–2pm); Branimirova 4 (24hr except from midnight Sat to 1pm Sun).

Record and CD shops Aquarius, Vlaška 48 and corner of Varšavska and Gundulićeva; Croatia Records, Bogovićeva; Dancing Bear, Gundulićeva 7. Secondhand records from Dobar Zvuk, Preradovićeva 24. Jazz and classical CDs from ADD Dinaton, Preradovićeva 12.

Sporting equipment Extreme Sport, Mesnička 3 (specialists in snowboarding gear); Elan, Draškovićeva 25 (for winter sports).

Telephones National and international calls can be made from the metered booths at the post offices on Jurišićeva or Branimirova.

Taxis There are taxi ranks on Trg maršala Tita and on the corner of Teslina and Gajeva. To book, call ☎682-505 or 682-558.

Train enquiries Information on ☎9830 (domestic services), ☎45-73-238 (international services).

Travel agents Croatia Express, Teslina 4 (☎48-11-842); GeneralTurist, Praška 5 (☎48-10-033); Kvarner Express, Praška 4 (☎48-10-522).

travel details

BUSES

Zagreb to: Čakovec (10 daily; 2hr 30min); Cres (2 daily; 6hr 30min); Dubrovnik (4 daily; 11hr); Karlovac (every 30min; 50min); Korčula Town (1 daily; 13hr); Osijek (6 daily; 5hr 30min); Pag Town (5 daily; 5hr); Plitvice (hourly; 2hr 30min); Poreč (7 daily; 8hr); Pula (10 daily; 6hr 30min); Rijeka (20 daily; 3–4hr); Rovinj (7 daily; 7hr 40min); Split (8 daily; 9hr); Varaždin (12 daily; 2hr); Zadar (5 daily; 5hr).

TRAINS

Zagreb to Čakovec (6 daily; 2hr 30min); Osijek (4 daily; 5hr); Rijeka (6 daily; 4hr); Split (2 daily; 9hr); Varaždin (9 daily; 2hr 30min).

International trains

Zagreb to: Berlin (1 daily; 17hr); Budapest (2 daily; 7hr); Geneva (1 daily; 16hr); Ljubljana (4 daily; 2 daily; 2hr 20min); Milan (1 daily; 11hr); Munich (2 daily; 9hr); Salzburg (2 daily; 7hr); Trieste (3 daily; 5hr 40min); Venice (2 daily; 7hr 30min); Vienna (1 daily; 6hr 30min).

CHAPTER TWO

INLAND CROATIA

The jumble of geographical regions which make up **inland Croatia** seem, on the face of it, to have little in common with one another. Historically, however, the Croats of the interior were united by a set of cultural influences very different from those which prevailed on the coast. After the collapse of the medieval Croatian kingdom in the early twelfth century, inland Croatia fell under the sway first of Hungary, then of the Habsburg Empire, increasingly adopting the culture and architecture of central Europe. All this has left its mark: sturdy, pastel-coloured farmhouses dot the countryside, while churches sport onion domes and Gothic spires, providing a sharp contrast with the pale stone houses and Venetian-inspired campaniles of the coast.

The main appeal of inland Croatia lies in its generous selection of contrasting landscapes. It's here that the mountain chains which run from the Alps down to the Adriatic meet the Pannonian plain, which stretches all the way from Zagreb to eastern Hungary. The **Zagorje** region, just north of Zagreb, resembles southern Austria with its mixture of knobbly hills, vineyards and compact, busy villages, while southeast of Zagreb are the slightly wilder uplands of the **Žumberak** and the smoother, pastoral hills of the **Lika**. Nestling amongst the latter are the **Plitvice Lakes**, a sequence of pools linked by picturesque mini-waterfalls – Croatia's most captivating, and most visited, natural attraction. The eastern provinces of **Podravina** and **Slavonia**, watered by the rivers Drava and Sava respectively, are classic corn-growing territory: broad expanses of flat, chequered farmland only partially broken up by low green hills.

There are worthwhile urban centres here too, with well-preserved Baroque towns in which something of the elegance of provincial Habsburg life has survived. The most attractive of these is **Varaždin**, northeast of Zagreb, although **Karlovac**, to the southwest, and **Požega**, to the southeast, are also worth a look. There's little in the way of big-city thrills except in **Osijek**, inland Croatia's main urban centre after Zagreb, and the most convenient place from which to explore eastern Slavonia.

ACCOMMODATION PRICE CODES

The accommodation in this guide has been graded using the following price codes, based on the cost of each establishment's **least expensive double room** in high season (June–Sept), excluding special offers. Hotel room rates almost always include breakfast. Out of season, prices on the coast can fall by up to 50 percent. Where single rooms exist, they usually cost 60–70 percent of the price of a double. For more details, see p.24.

① Less than 200Kn	④ 400–500Kn	⑦ 800–1000Kn
② 200–300Kn	⑤ 500–600Kn	⑧ 1000–1200Kn
③ 300–400Kn	⑥ 600–800Kn	⑨ Over 1200Kn

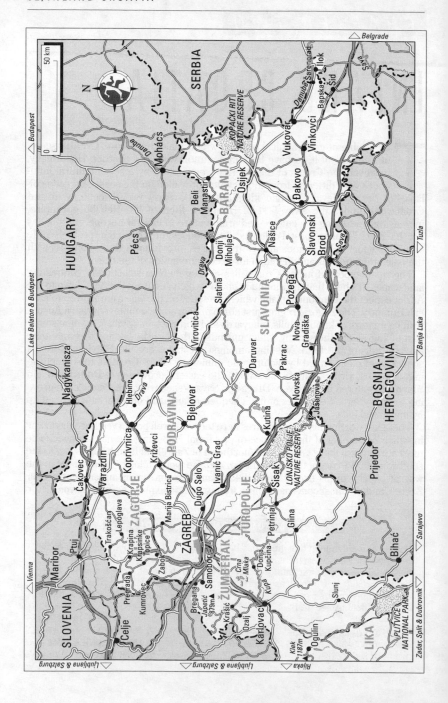

The obvious starting point for travel in the region is Zagreb, from where road and rail routes fan out in all directions: north through the Zagorje towards Slovenia, northeast via Varaždin to Hungary, and east across the Slavonian plain towards the nowadays little-used border with Serbia. Busiest of all is the route southwest towards the coast, which runs through Karlovac before splitting two ways – straight on across the Gorski kotar hills towards Rijeka, or south across the Lika towards Zadar and Split, passing the Plitvice Lakes on the way.

Some history

Croatia's long border with Bosnia and Serbia has long been ethnically mixed, a legacy of the population movements caused by Ottoman advances into the central Balkans. Christians of various creeds who had been displaced from their homes by the Turks were settled here by the Habsburgs to man the so-called **Military Frontier**, a wedge of land along the border with Ottoman-controlled territory, which was placed under direct rule from Austria and organized along military lines. Established in the sixteenth century as a belt of territories running through the north of present-day Croatia, the Military Frontier gradually moved southwards as Austrian armies threw the Ottomans back, until by the early 1700s it had stabilized into the wishbone-shaped frontier with Ottoman-controlled Bosnia which is still reflected in the modern-day border. Many of the people settled here were migrants from the southern Balkans, a mixture of Slavs and Vlach shepherds who – due to the fact that they were Orthodox Christians, and therefore subject to the Serbian patriarchate – developed a Serbian national consciousness as the centuries passed. The waning of Ottoman power in the 1700s meant that the Military Frontier lost its use as a defensive cordon, although the Habsburgs kept it as a way of maintaining a permanently armed and drilled population for use in the empire's wars in other parts of Europe . This provided the Serbs and Croats of the region with powerful national myths: both communities came to consider themselves the most war-like, noble and masculine expressions of their respective peoples, and by the early twentieth century, many Serbs regarded the Military Frontier region – or simply Krajina ("border land"), as they now called it – as the heartland of martial Serb values.

The Military Frontier was abolished in 1881, but the region's ethnically mixed character remained. After the creation of Yugoslavia in 1918, the continuing presence of a large Serbian minority in Croatia was used by successive regimes to keep Croatian autonomist leanings under control. The so-called **Independent State of Croatia** (NDH), created by Nazi Germany after the fall of Yugoslavia in 1941, tried to "cleanse" Croatia of its Serbian population by violent means – hundreds of thousands of Croatian Serbs in the border regions were either driven from their homes, forcibly converted to Catholicism, or killed. Memories of the NDH period had a profound effect on Serbian attitudes in the years leading up to the collapse of communist Yugoslavia, and with the victory of the pro-independence HDZ in the Croatian elections of April 1990, Serbian propagandists in Belgrade deliberately played on the fears of Serbs living in Croatia by suggesting that the dark days of the NDH were about to return. In an atmosphere of inter-ethnic mistrust generated in large part by the Belgrade media, Serbs living in the border regions of Croatia launched a **rebellion** from the town of Knin (see p.230) in September 1990, which later developed into all-out war following Croatia's declaration of independence in June 1991. Supported by the JNA (Yugoslav People's Army), Serbian insurgents took control of a swathe of territory stretching from

Slavonia in the east to the Knin region in the west, which they planned to detach from the nascent Croatian state. Croat settlements within these Serb-controlled areas were ethnically cleansed, while the east Slavonian town of **Vukovar**, one of the places that stood in the way of the Serbian land grab, was almost totally destroyed in the autumn of 1991. Other inland towns such as Osijek, Vinkovci, Slavonski Brod and Karlovac found themselves at the heart of Croat resistance to further Serbian expansion – although subjected to heavily shelling, all remained in Croatian hands.

By the end of 1991 large chunks of inland Croatia were under the control of the Serbs, who proceeded to organize the breakaway territory as the **Serbian Republic of the Krajina** – a nominally independent state which was in practice heavily dependent on Belgrade. The deployment of UN peacekeepers to the front line after March 1992 temporarily brought the conflict to an end, but only seemed to confirm Serb gains. Aware that international diplomacy was unlikely to secure a return of the Serb-occupied territories, the Croatian government re-equipped its armed forces and prepared to take them back by force. In May 1995 the **Blijesak** ("Flash") offensive cleared Serbian forces from western Slavonia, a pocket of land midway between Zagreb and Slavonski Brod. In August of the same year **Oluja** ("Storm") resulted in the collapse of Krajina forces around Knin. Flushed with military success, the Croats were able to negotiate a peaceful transfer of power in the one remaining area of Croatia under Serb control, eastern Slavonia. Local Serbs opted to surrender the territory without a struggle: according to the terms of the 1995 **Erdut Agreement** (Erdutski sporazum), eastern Slavonia was to be governed by the UN for two years before returning to Croatian sovereignty in January 1998. The changeover took place relatively peacefully, and despite an initial exodus of local Serbs, most chose to stay and accept the new administration.

Croats who had been forced out of Serb-controlled areas in 1991 were now free to return, although war damage and the lack of a functioning economy meant that many stayed away. The situation was complicated by the position of the local Serb population, who had fled in their thousands in the wake of Blijesak and Oluja – the right of all refugees, regardless of ethnicity, to return to their prewar homes was one of the key elements of the 1995 **Dayton Accord**, which was designed to bring a definitive end to the conflicts in Croatia and Bosnia. As a result, both Croatian and Serbian returnees are competing for an insufficient number of homes and jobs, and tensions between the two communities remain. Returning Croats are understandably suspicious of Serbian neighbours against whom they were fighting a few years before, while those Serbs who have chosen to stay feel they are being made to bear a collective guilt for the actions of a few. The question of **war crimes** remains ever-present: the graves of Croats who disappeared in 1991 are still being uncovered, while a true picture of the excesses committed by Croatian irregulars in the wake of Blijesak and Oluja is yet to be established.

Travellers making forays south or east of Zagreb will almost certainly cross parts of the former war zone, and visitors to war-affected areas will see evidence of the recent conflict in the shape of burned-out houses and large signs warning of uncleared minefields. There's no reason to be wary of travelling in the region, however: life has returned to the towns, public transport runs smoothly, and a reasonable number of hotels are back in business.

The Zagorje

Spread out between Zagreb and the Slovene border, the **Zagorje** is an area of chocolate-box enchantment: miniature wooded hills are crowned with the castles they seem designed for, and streams tumble through lush vineyards, almost all of which feature a *klet*, a small, steep-roofed structure traditionally used for storing wine, though nowadays they're more often put to use as weekend cottages. Although the area is covered with a dense patchwork of villages, human beings seem outnumbered by the chickens, geese and turkeys that scavenge between the cornfields and vegetable plots.

Denizens of the Zagorje speak *kajkavski*, a dialect named after the distinctive local word for "what?" (*"kaj?"*), and whose grammatical idiosyncrasies fall somewhere between modern Croatian and Slovene. Local delicacies include *štrukli* (pockets of dough filled with cottage cheese) and the ubiquitous *purica z mlincima*, or turkey served with *mlinci* (pasta noodles which look like scraggy bits of pastry). Look out too for *licitari*, the pepper-flavoured biscuits covered in icing which often take the form of a big red heart (*licitarsko srce*) and can sometimes assume enormous proportions – in which case they're supposed to be presented to a loved one and preserved as an ornament rather than eaten.

Most towns in the Zagorje have direct **bus** links with Zagreb, but you'll need your own transport if you want to explore the region in depth. By **car**, the road from Zagreb via Krapina to Maribor in Slovenia is the most direct route into the region, although all the interesting touring itineraries lie on the minor roads to either side. **Trains** offer a dependable, if slow, way of getting to Kumrovec (changing at Savski Marof on the Zagreb–Ljubljana line) or Krapina, Stubičke Toplice and Gornja Stubica (changing at Zabok on the Zagreb–Varaždin line).

Gornja Stubica and around

The part of the Zagorje most easily accessible from Zagreb is the gently undulating Stubica valley, spread out below the northern slopes of Mount Medvednica, which provides a lush agricultural backdrop for the long, straggling settlement of Stubica – really three villages, Stubičke Toplice, Donja Stubica and Gornja Stubica. Coming by public transport from the capital you'll have to endure the notoriously slow Zagreb–Varaždin train to Zabok, where you change for the train to Gornja Stubica. By car the most impressive approach is along the road over Mount Medvednica via Sljeme (see p.70): the views from the northern flanks of the mountain are breathtaking.

Emerging from a rustic patchwork of greens, the small spa resort of **STUBIČKE TOPLICE** is a relaxing place, although there's nothing much here apart from a cluster of sanatoriums and an open-air swimming pool complex (*kupalište*; summer daily 7am–7pm; 20Kn) behind a screen of trees in the centre. There's a **tourist office** (Mon–Fri 8am–3pm, Sat 10am–3pm; ☎049/282-727, fax 283-404) on the main street at Viktora Šipeka 24, which can provide addresses of local private **rooms** (②); and a **hotel**, the *Matija Gubec*, close by at Viktora Šipeka 27 (☎049/282-501, fax 282-403; ③), which has bland modern en-suite rooms and a large indoor swimming pool.

Six kilometres east of Stubičke Toplice, beyond the undistinguished settlement of Donja Stubica, lies **GORNJA STUBICA**, a village famous for its role as the launching place of the **Peasants' Revolt of 1573**. The inhabitants of the sixteenth-century Zagorje were overloaded with feudal obligations, while their proximity to the Habsburg–Ottoman front line landed them with the additional burden of supplying the war effort with food and manpower. To make matters worse, the Protestant leanings of local landowners offended the staunchly Catholic sensibilities of an already disgruntled peasantry. Ironically, it was the big Catholic magnates of Croatia who put the rebellion down, with the Bishop of Zagreb, Juraj Drašković, routing a badly armed peasant army at the Battle of Stubičko Polje on February 9, 1573. Drašković deliberately spread rumours that peasant leader **Matija Gubec** had been elected "king" by his co-conspirators, an accusation which served both to discredit the rebels and to provide the excuse for a fiendishly appropriate punishment – Gubec was executed in Zagreb by being "crowned" with a red-hot ring of iron.

The stirringly named **Museum of Peasant Uprisings** (Muzej seljačkih buna; daily summer 8am–7pm, winter 9am–5pm; 10Kn), in the creakily floored confines of the Orsić Palace, 2km north of the village behind Antun Augustinčić's vast hilltop statue of Gubec, has a few period weapons, but otherwise relies heavily on a didactic words-and-pictures display to tell the story of the revolt. A smaller hillock just southwest of the village is crowned by the stout lime tree known as **Gubčeva Lipa**, where the peasants supposedly met to launch the insurrection. For **food** and **drink**, the adjacent *Birtija Pod Lipom* has good local hams, cheeses and wines.

The nearest places to stay are either back in Stubičke Toplice or at *Lojzekova hiža* ("Lojzek's Cottage"; ☎049/469-325; ②), just beyond the village of Gusakovec, a well-signposted 6km drive east of town on the road to Marija Bistrica. This traditional farmhouse offers tiny but cosy en-suite attic rooms (including some with bunks for children) in a delightful spot bordered by woods on one side and livestock-filled meadows on the other.

Marija Bistrica and around

Located below the northwestern spur of Mount Medvednica, some 37km from Zagreb and 11km east of Gornja Stubica, the town of **MARIJA BISTRICA** is home to the most important Marian shrine in Croatia. It's a popular destination for pilgrims year round, though things can get particularly crowded on August 15 (Assumption) and on the Sunday preceding St Margaret's Day (July 20), when the shrine is traditionally reserved for the city folk of Zagreb.

The town itself is a small, rustic place onto which modern coach-party tourism has been rather unceremoniously grafted. It's dominated totally by the **Pilgrimage Church of St Mary of Bistrica** (Hodočasnička crkva Marije Bistričke), which perches on a hillock in the centre of town. Rebuilt on numerous occasions to accommodate ever-growing numbers of visitors, the current structure was put together by the architect of Zagreb cathedral, Hermann Bollé, between 1880 and 1884. It's a remarkably eclectic and playful building (unlike the comparatively stern cathedral) – a jumble of Baroque and Neoclassical detail crowned by a hulking black-and-red chevroned steeple flanked by castellated red-brick turrets.

The principal object of popular veneration is the **Black Madonna**, a fifteenth-century statue of the Virgin set into the main altar. According to tradition, the statue was bricked into a church wall in 1650 to prevent it from falling into the hands of marauding Turks, where it remained for 34 years until (it is said) a miraculous beam of light revealed its hiding place. News of the Madonna was spread by the then Bishop of Zagreb, Martin Borković, who was eager to promote Marija Bistrica as a spiritual centre at a time when pilgrimages in general were being encouraged throughout the Habsburg lands – popular religion was seen as a useful way of getting the masses behind the Catholic regime. The Madonna subsequently survived a fire in 1880 that destroyed almost everything else in the church, thereby adding to its aura.

The vast outdoor amphitheatre at the back of the church was built for the pope's visit here in October 1998, an occasion marked by the beatification of Archbishop Alojzije Stepinac (see box on p.60). Behind the amphitheatre, paths lead up the Calvary Hill (Kalvarija) past sculptures of the Stations of the Cross, culminating in a fine view back towards the town.

Practicalities

The road to Marija Bistrica from Zagreb crawls over the eastern shoulder of Medvednica by way of Kašina. **Buses** from Zagreb stop on the main street immediately below the church, from where the pedestrianized Zagrebačka leads up to the **tourist office** at no. 66 (Tues–Fri 7am–2pm, Sat & Sun 8am–2pm; ☎ & fax 049/468-380), which can provide the addresses of a handful of local families offering private **rooms** (②). Otherwise, accommodation in town is limited to the *Kaj* **hotel** just down the hill (☎049/469-026; ③), with acceptable but charmless en-suite rooms in a modern two-storey building. Far preferable if you have your own transport is *Lojzekova hiža*.

Lojzekova hiža is also the best place locally to **eat and drink**, although there are numerous cafés and bistros close by Marija Bistrica's church offering the usual refreshments and snacks. *Grozd*, just outside the church entrance, serves up exemplary *grah* (bean stew) and has the customary range of Croatian meat dishes. On big pilgrimage days, several establishments along the main street offer grills and spit-roasts cooked on outdoor barbecues.

North of Marija Bistrica

The road heading north out of Marija Bistrica descends towards the broad Krapina valley before rising again into the foothills of the next ridge to the north, wooded Mount Ivanščica. After 12km you hit the small market town of **ZLATAR**, unremarkable in itself, but a useful jumping-off point for the nearby village of **BELEC**, accessible by a minor road which runs northeast out of Zlatar. Standing beside Belec's main street is the **Church of Our Lady of the Snow** (Svete Marije Snježne; Sun 8–11am), deceptively ordinary from the outside, but containing a fantastic riot of frothy Baroque furniture and ornament within. Countess Elisabeth Keglević-Erdödy had the church built in 1675 after hearing that a miraculous apparition of the Virgin Mary had occurred in nearby Kostanjek. It soon became a popular pilgrimage site, especially among the Croatian nobility, who stumped up the cash for a thorough redecoration in the 1740s. Resplendent in pinks, eau de nil greens and luxurious gilt, the resulting ensemble of altars and wall-paintings (the latter executed by Ivan Ranger, a Pauline monk who worked all over northern Croatia, and also decorated the monastery church at Lepoglava) is designed to be viewed as a single work of art, although several individual details stand out. The most important of these is the wooden pulpit, carved by Josip Schokotnigg of Graz, from which statuettes of prophets seem poised to leap, above a relief of revellers dancing around the golden calf. Schokotnigg was also responsible for the altars of St Barbara and St Joseph, which stand on either side of the main altar of the Holy Trinity, a swirling mass of cherubs and gesticulating saints.

Kumrovec and around

About 30km northwest of Zagreb, close to the border with Slovenia, the village of **KUMROVEC** is renowned both as the best of Croatia's museum-villages and as the birthplace of the father of communist Yugoslavia, **Josip Broz Tito**. The simple peasant house in which Tito was born was turned into a museum during his own lifetime, while the surrounding properties were rebuilt and restored in the ensuing decades to provide an example of what a turn-of-the-century Zagorje village must have looked like. Those who remember Tito with affection still collect here every year on May 4, the anniversary of his death.

The **"Old Village" Museum** (Muzej "staro selo"; daily: summer 8am–8pm; winter 9am–5pm; 10Kn) is about twenty minutes' walk east of Kumrovec's train station, set back from the main road behind a large carpark, with a range of pastel-coloured houses and farmsteads ranged alongside a gurgling brook. Tito's birth-place is easy enough to spot: it's got a statue of the Marshal (caught in pensive mid-stride by Antun Augustinčić) in the garden. Inside, life-like recreations of the 1890s rooms contain a restrained collection of photos and mementoes, including the uniform worn by Tito while leading the Partisan struggle from the island of Vis in 1944. The other buildings are each devoted to a particular rural craft, with displays of blacksmithing, weaving and toy-making – the latter featuring dainty, brightly painted wood-carved horses and other animals. One house is given over to a series of tableaux illustrating a traditional wedding feast, with rooms crowd-ed with costumed mannequins and tables decked with imitation food.

A couple of **buses** run to Kumrovec from Zagreb daily, although **trains** (usu-ally involving a change at Savski Marof) are more frequent. There's no accom-modation in Kumrovec, but a couple of **cafés** near the museum entrance offer drinks and snacks. For something more substantial, *Zagorska klet*, within the museum complex, has local staples like cheese, sausage and *štrukli*; while *Pri Staroj Vuri*, 100m east of the museum complex in the new part of the village, has a wider choice of dishes.

Nine kilometres beyond Kumrovec, the village of **MILJANA** is overlooked by the best-preserved Renaissance palace in the Zagorje, a plain low outer wall hid-ing an asymmetrical arcaded courtyard coloured a vivacious blue and white. It was built some time in the early 1600s by the Rafkay family but fell into disuse before being bought – and painstakingly restored – by the Croatian pharmaceuti-cal magnate Franjo Kajfež in the 1970s. There are plans to open the palace and grounds to the public in the near future: the Zagorje tourist association (☎049/233-653) will have details.

The northwestern Zagorje

It's only 6km on from Miljana to the most impressive of the Zagorje castles, **Veliki Tabor** (daily 10am–6pm; 20Kn), whose imposing bastions look down on the road from a grassy hilltop. Built in the twelfth century to guard the lands of the counts of Celje (a Slovenian town 50km to the west), it acquired its present shape in the fifteenth and sixteenth centuries, when its characteristic semicircular towers were grafted onto the earlier pentagonal shell. Inside the courtyard, three tiers of galleries contain a warren of exhibition spaces filled with pikes, maces, knightly tombstones and other medieval oddments. A display of photographs and weapon-ry on the ground floor recalls Veliki Tabor's status as an important centre of resis-tance activity in World War II, when local Partisans controlled large chunks of the Zagorje between 1943 and 1945.

There are eight **buses** daily from Zagreb to the village of Desinić to the east, from where it's a three-kilometre walk to the castle. About 1km east of the cas-tle a well-signed turn-off leads up to the *Grešna Gorica* farmhouse **restaurant**, a popular venue for long weekend lunches, with a traditionally furnished din-ing room, splendid views of Veliki Tabor and a full range of Croatian cuisine together with Zagorje specialities like *štrukli*, *purica z mlincima* and *srneći gulaš* (venison goulash). The nearest **accommodation** to Veliki Tabor is the *Dvorac Bežanec* (see p.92), 12km east, or at Krapinske Toplice (see p.92), 20km southeast.

JOSIP BROZ TITO (1892–1980)

Josip Broz was born on May 7, 1892, the seventh son of peasant smallholder Franjo Broz and his Slovene wife Marija Javeršek. After training as a blacksmith and metalworker, Broz became an officer in the Austrian army in World War I, only to be captured by the Russians in 1915. Fired by the ideals of the Bolshevik Revolution, he joined the Red Army and fought in the Russian Civil War before finally heading for home in 1920.

Some believe that the man who came back to Croatia with a discernible Russian accent was a Soviet-trained impostor who had assumed the identity of the original Josip Broz – an appealing but unlikely tale. Whatever the truth, Broz found himself in a turbulent Yugoslav state in which the Communist Party was soon outlawed, and it was his success in reinvigorating demoralized party cells that ensured his rise through the ranks. He spent time in Moscow in the 1930s, somehow surviving Stalin's purges, though whether he merely kept his head down or actively betrayed party colleagues remains the subject of much conjecture.

Broz took the pseudonym **Tito** upon entering the central committee of the Yugoslav Communist Party in 1934. Nobody really knows why he chose it: the most frequently touted explanation is that the nickname was bestowed on him by colleagues amused by his bossy manner – *"ti to!"* means "you [do] that!" in Croatian – although it's equally possible that he took it from the eighteenth-century Croat writer Tito Brezovacki.

After becoming leader of the Yugoslav Communist Party in 1937, Tito's finest hour came following the German invasion of Yugoslavia in 1941, when he managed to take control of the anti-fascist uprising, even though it wasn't initially inspired by the communists. Despite repeated (and often very successful) German counter-offensives, he somehow succeeded in keeping the core of his movement alive – through a mixture of luck, bloody-mindedness and sheer charisma rather than military genius. He also possessed a firm grasp of political theatre, promoting himself to the rank of marshal and donning suitably impressive uniforms whenever Allied emissaries were parachuted into Yugoslavia to meet him. The British and Americans lent him their full support from 1943 onwards, thereby condemning all other, non-communist factions in Yugoslavia to certain political extinction after the war.

Emerging as dictator of Yugoslavia in 1945, Tito showed no signs of being anything more than a loyal Stalinist until the Soviet leader tried to get rid of him in 1948. Tito's survival – subsequently presented to the world as "Tito's historic 'no' to Stalin" – rested on his innate ability to inspire loyalty among the tightly knit circle of former Partisans who, by and large, surrounded him until his death.

Ideological innovation was never Tito's strong point, and the relaunch of Yugoslav communism as **"self-managing socialism"** (in large measure a PR

South to Krapinske Toplice

Around 6km east of Desinić, the arcade-encircled **Pilgrimage Church of St Mary** (Crkva svete Marije) squats picturesquely on a hillock at the top of the village of Vinagora. The church is relatively plain inside, but the view from here, with the rippling greens of the Zagorje hills laid out to the south, is the best in the region.

Some 4km further along the main road, the village of **PREGRADA** (served by Zagreb–Desinić buses) is dwarfed by the twin-towered **Church of the Ascension** (Crkva Uznesenja Marijinog), often called the "Zagorje Cathedral" on account of its exercise designed to win support at home and ensure financial aid from the West) was largely the work of abler theorists such as Edvard Kardelj and Milovan Đilas. Flushed with the prestige of having survived Soviet pressure in 1948, Tito concentrated on affirming Yugoslavia's position on the world stage and increasingly left the nitty-gritty of running the country to others. Forming the **non-aligned movement** with Nehru and Nasser in 1955 provided a platform which allowed him to travel the world wearing the fancy uniforms he loved so much, giving Yugoslavia an international profile which is yet to be reattained by any of its successor republics. In domestic affairs he contrived to present himself as the lofty arbiter who, far from being responsible for the frequent malfunctions of Yugoslav communism, emerged to bang heads together when things got out of control. Thus, his decision to bring an end to the Croatian Spring in 1971 was sold to the public as a Solomonic intervention to ensure social peace rather than the authoritarian exercise it really was.

Affection for Tito in Yugoslavia was widespread and genuine, if not universal. There's no doubt that Titoist communism was "softer" than its Soviet counterpart after 1948 – many areas of society were relatively free from ideological control, and from the 1950s onwards, Yugoslavs were able to travel and work abroad. However, the authority of the party – and Tito's leadership of it – was never to be questioned, and many dissenting voices ended up in prison as a result.

A vain man who loved to wear medals, dyed his hair and used a sun lamp, Tito enthusiastically acquiesced to the personality cult constructed around him. May 25 was declared his official birthday and celebrated nationwide as "Dan mladosti" (the "Day of Youth"), enhancing Tito's aura as the kindly father of a grateful people. He was also a bit of a ladies' man, marrying four times and switching partners with a speed that dismayed his more puritanical colleagues. During the war, he negotiated an exchange of prisoners with the Ustaše in order to secure the release of his second wife, Herta Hass, from a concentration camp. On her arrival at Tito's Partisan HQ, Hass was informed by bemused aides that she'd already been supplanted by wireless operator Zdenka Paunović.

For most Croats, Tito's legacy remains ambiguous. He was fortunate enough to die before Yugoslavia's economy went seriously wrong in the 1980s, and for many he remains a symbol of the good old days when economic growth (paid for by soft Western loans) led to rising living standards and a consumer boom. However, he is also seen as the man responsible for the Bleiburg massacre of 1945 (when thousands of Croatian reservists were put to death by avenging Partisans) and the crackdown on the Croatian Spring in 1971. Despite keeping Croatian national aspirations on a tight leash, however, Tito's Yugoslavia ensured Croatian territorial continuity by establishing borders which are still in existence today. For this reason alone, many streets and squares in Croatia continue to bear Tito's name.

incongruously large size. It's now home to a gargantuan organ which was intended for the cathedral in Zagreb, but was rejected on the grounds that it wasn't loud enough. Locals pour into town during the last weekend in September for the **Branje grojzdja** (grape harvest), a rural fair featuring folksongs and dances. An altogether more mysterious folk event takes place at **Kostel**, 5km north of Pregrada, on Easter Sunday, when locals gather at dawn near the church of St Emerik to fire traditional handmade pistols known as *kubure* – a stylized and solemn religious occasion rather than a sporting contest, aiming to honour God by making as loud a noise as possible.

Four kilometres southeast of Pregrada towards Krapinske Toplice, the road passes the top-notch *Dvorec Bežanec* **restaurant** and **hotel** (☎049/376-800, fax 376-810, *www.bezanec.hr*, ④), housed in a Neoclassical palace built for the Keglević family and offering spacious rooms, contemporary artworks in the corridors, and a peaceful parkland setting. The hotel can organize horse-riding (100Kn per hour) and balloon trips (from 900Kn; at least 24hr notice required).

KRAPINSKE TOPLICE itself is a tiny spa town with a renowned medical centre specializing in the treatment of cardiac complaints and serious bone and muscle injuries. It's also a great place for a **swim**, boasting four outdoor pools fed by soothing spring waters in a central park. The **tourist office** (Mon–Fri 7am–3pm, Sat 8am–10.30pm; ☎ & fax 049/232-106) in the bus station can direct you towards local private **rooms** (②); otherwise, the modern and reasonably priced *Toplice* **hotel** in the town centre (☎049/232-165, fax 232-322; ③) offers en-suite rooms with TV, together with sauna, massage and mud-treatment facilities.

From Krapinske Toplice, you can either head east to rejoin the main road just south of Krapina, or wend your way south back to Zagreb.

Krapina

Squeezed amongst the hills midway between Zagreb and Maribor, the busy little town of **KRAPINA** is famous for its connections with so-called "Krapina Man" (*krapinski čovjek*), a type of Neanderthal which lived in caves hereabouts some 30,000 years ago. The bones of several such hominids were discovered by Dragutin Gorjanović Kramberger in 1899 on Hušnjakovo hill, a short walk west of the town centre on the far side of the River Krapinica. The find is now commemorated by a **museum** just below the site (daily: summer 8am–6pm; winter 8am–3pm; 10Kn), which offers a fairly dry line-up of reconstructed skulls, together with artists' impressions of hairy men hunting bears. Outside, a pathway leads up through the woods to the exact spot where Kramberger found the bones, nowadays marked by life-size statues of a Neanderthal family.

The only other real attraction hereabouts is 2km east of town in the hillside suburb of Trški Vrh, where the arcaded **Church of St Mary of Jerusalem** (Crkva svete Marije Jeruzalemske) provides the Zagorje faithful with another important pilgrimage destination. Inside lies an exemplary riot of eighteenth-century religious fervour, although the gilded altarpieces and pink-blue frescoes work best as an integrated whole rather than as individual works of art.

Krapina's **bus** and **train stations** lie five minutes south of the town centre, where the **tourist office** at Magistratska 11 (Mon–Fri 8am–3pm, Sat 8am–noon; ☎049/371-330) can provide lots of information but no rooms. Unassuming from the outside, the *Gaj* **hotel**, Ljudevita Gaja 10 (☎049/371-580 or 370-332, fax 371-776; ③) has pristine modern en-suite rooms, some with TV. The hotel **restaurant** offers the full range of inland Croatian meat dishes in formal, starched-napkin surroundings. *Pizzeria Picikato*, Magistratska 2, has a limited range of pizzas, but comes with pleasant courtyard seating.

Lepoglava and Trakošćan

Twenty kilometres northeast of Krapina, the bland town of **LEPOGLAVA** is dominated by the dour facade of the country's largest **prison**, occupying the former buildings of a Pauline monastery. The list of those who have passed through its gates reads like a *Who's Who* of twentieth-century Croatian politics. Numerous communists, Josip Broz Tito included, languished here during the 1930s, only to turn Lepoglava to their own uses once they came to power. Archbishop Stepinac was here for five years after World War II, and subsequent internees included many who went on to play a prominent role in post-independence Croatia – President Tuđman, Dražen Budiša (leader of the Social Liberal Party), Vlado Gotovac (leader of the Liberal Party) and Ivan Zvonimir Čičak (founder of the Helsinki Committee on Human Rights) among them.

Lepoglava's only other claim to fame is the Gothic chapel of the **monastery church** (Sun 9am–noon), which stands beside the prison entrance on the main street. The lozenge-shaped gaps between the rib-vaulting were filled in with exuberantly colourful frescoes by local monk Ivan Ranger (who also worked at Belec, see p.88) in the sixteenth century, and an imposing Baroque altar installed around a much older, Byzantine-style painting of the Madonna. There are a couple of daily **buses** to Lepoglava from Zagreb, and more frequent train and bus services from Varaždin (see below), 30km to the northeast.

Trakošćan

Of all the Zagorje castles, **Trakošćan**, 11km northwest of Lepoglava, is the most visited. It's actually a bit of a fake – a fanciful nineteenth-century rebuilding of a thirteenth-century original – but the sight of its cod-medieval battlements looming above the artificial lake is one of the Zagorje's most famous. After passing through the hands of several local magnates, Trakošćan fell into the possession of the Habsburg treasury in 1566 when its then owner, Ivan Gyulay, died without heir. Twenty-two years later it was presented to the Drašković family in lieu of payment for their services in subduing the Peasants Revolt (see p.86) and fighting off the Turks. It was Count Juraj Drašković who substantially rebuilt Trakošćan in romantic, neo-Gothic style between 1853 and 1862, when the landscaped park and boating lake were also added.

The **interior** (daily: summer 9am–6pm; winter 9am–3pm; 20Kn) is a tribute to the medievalizing tastes of its nineteenth-century restorers, full of extravagantly pinnacled door frames and elaborate woodcarving. Sundry hunting trophies, suits of armour and Julija Erdödy-Drašković's idealized nineteenth-century paintings of Zagorje peasants all add to the effect. After looking round the castle, you can walk through the forest around the lake or hire pedalos from the waterside café.

There are currently no direct **buses** to Trakošćan from Zagreb, although the six daily services from Varaždin (see p.125) ensure that you can just about tackle the castle as a long day-trip from the capital. The *Coning Trakošćan* **hotel** (☎042/796-224, fax 796-205; ③), situated in meadows below the castle, has ensuite rooms with TV, along with a restaurant, bar, sauna, gym and tennis courts.

Varaždin to the Podravina

Northeast of Zagreb, road and rail lines to Budapest cross an outlying spur of the Zagorje hills before descending towards the lush farmlands bordering the River Drava, which for much of its length forms Croatia's border with Hungary. In the midst of this green, agricultural region lies **Varaždin**, mainland Croatia's best-preserved Habsburg-era town, and well worth a day-trip from Zagreb. Other settlements in the region are very much in Varaždin's shadow, although

Čakovec, half an hour to the northeast, is worth a stop-off if you're in the area. It serves as the centre of the **Međimurje**, a rustic frontier province, totally flat and traditionally isolated, which stretches out between the Mura and Drava rivers.

Southeast of Varaždin, roads run parallel to the Drava through prosperous rural **Podravina**, an area whose neat villages, orchards and maize fields exude an air of bucolic plenty. Fringed by gentle hills raked by the occasional vineyard, it's a pretty area to drive through once you get onto the country roads, although specific attractions are thin on the ground save for the village of **Hlebine**, a renowned centre of naive art just outside Podravina's main market town, **Koprivnica**. From Koprivnica, road and rail routes continue southeast through the Podravina towards the Slavonian town of Osijek (see p.107), through the dusty and uninspiring towns of Virovitica, Slatina and Našice.

Varaždin

Seventy kilometres northeast of Zagreb, **VARAŽDIN** occupied a key position on the medieval Hungarian kingdom's route to the sea and became an important military stronghold for successive Hungarian and Habsburg rulers in their struggle against Ottoman expansion. Varaždin grew fat on the profits of the Austrian–Turkish wars of the late 1600s and early 1700s, encouraging many noble families to built houses here – from 1756 to 1776 it was actually capital of Croatia, until a disastrous fire forced relocation to Zagreb. Following the fire, the town was rebuilt with opulent Baroque palaces and sturdy town houses, many of which have been returned to their original cream, ochre, pink and pale-blue colours following restoration. Most now do duty as apartment blocks, offices and banks, so there's a limit to the number of places you can actually visit, although there are a couple of museums and a generous sprinkling of churches – many of which survived the fire – all crammed within a compact and still relatively untouristed old town.

Although too far north to be directly affected by the Croat–Serb conflict, Varaždin was the site of one of the war's more unusual episodes when, in September 1991 the regional commander of the Serb-dominated JNA (Yugoslav People's Army), **Vlado Trifunović**, surrendered his garrison to the local authorities in order to avoid fighting between his troops and Croatian forces. On returning to Belgrade, Trifunović was tried for treason and sentenced to twelve years in jail. Bizarrely, he was also charged by Varaždin district court for nebulous "war crimes". Now released from prison and living in Belgrade, Trifunović continues to protest his innocence on both counts.

The Town

The heart of the old town is largely pedestrianized, with modern boutiques and cafés hidden behind the shuttered windows and carved doorways that embellish the former town houses of the nobility. From the small, triangular Trg slobode (your likely starting point if arriving from the bus or train stations), Gundulićeva leads north to **Franjevački trg** – really a broad street rather than a square – flanked by the mansions of wealthy merchants, their ostentatious arched portals surmounted by family crests and heavy stone balconies. On the square's northern side is the seventeenth-century **Franciscan Church of St John the Baptist** (Crkva svetog Ivana Krstitelja); outside is a scaled-down copy of Ivan Meštrović's *Grgur Ninski* statue, the original of which is in Split.

Franjevački trg's eastern end opens out onto **Trg kralja Tomislava**, the main town square, surrounded by balustraded palaces and overlooked by the sky-rocketing clock tower of the sixteenth-century **town hall**. Just off the main square to the east, the **Church of the Ascension** (Crkva Marijinog Uznesenja) stands on the cusp of the Baroque and Rococo eras, its plain, whitewashed interior enhanced by the gilded statuary of its high altar and side chapels. A block north, the bright orange exterior of the seventeenth-century Palača Šermage conceals the town's **Art Gallery** (Galerija starih i novih majstora; Tues–Fri 10am–4pm, Sat & Sun 10am–1pm; 10Kn), which holds a few old Dutch and French paintings by lesser masters, as well as a fair amount of obscure Croatian work.

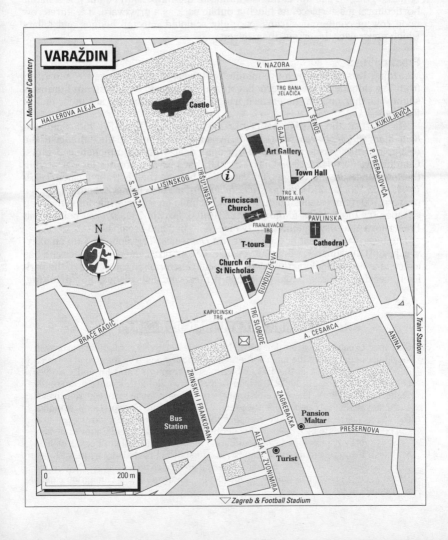

Immediately opposite, a wooden drawbridge and gatehouse marks the entrance to the **Castle** (*stari grad*), an irregular rectangle surrounded by two concentric moats divided by grassy earthworks. Dating from the mid-1500s, when Varaždin was in the front line against the advancing Turks, it was eventually transformed into a stately residence by the powerful Erdödy family, who lorded it over the region for several centuries. The courtyard, with its three tiers of balustrades, has been beautifully restored; the **museum** within (Tues–Fri 10am–5pm, Sat & Sun 10am–1pm; 10Kn) contains the usual display of weaponry and period furniture.

About 400m west of the castle, down Hallerova aleja, the **Municipal Cemetery** (*gradsko groblje*), laid out at the beginning of the nineteenth century, is a minor horticultural masterpiece. As much a public park as a graveyard, it features row upon row of coniferous shrubs, carefully sculpted into tall hedges and pillars which tower over the graves themselves.

Practicalities

Varaždin's **bus station** is a five-minute walk west of the town centre, separated from Trg slobode by the modern, flagstoned Kapucinski trg. The **train station** is slightly further out, on the eastern fringes of the town centre at the far end of Kolodvorska.

The staff at the **tourist office**, Ivana Padovca 3 (Mon–Fri 7am–9pm, Sat 8am–3pm; ☎042/210-985, fax 210-987), in an alleyway opposite the entrance to the castle, are enthusiastic and helpful but don't deal with accommodation. T-tours, Gundulićeva 2 (☎042/210-989, fax 210-990), have private **rooms** (①–②) both in the town and outlying villages. Of Varaždin's **hotels**, the centrally located *Turist* (☎042/105-105, fax 215-028, *turist@vz.tel.hr*; ④), at Aleja Kralja Zvonimira bb, is a modern 100-room establishment with comfortable en suites; while for something cheaper, try the *Pansion Maltar* (☎042/310-100, fax 211-190; ③), just behind it at Prešernova 1, a cosy and informal twelve-room bed-and-breakfast.

The best places to **eat** in the centre are *Domenico*, Trg slobode 7 (in an alleyway just off the square), which serves up excellent pizza and pasta dishes and has a nice terrace overlooking the town park; and *Gastrocom* in the centre of the park itself, serving a wider range of standard meat and fish dishes. For **drinking,**

ONWARD TRAVEL INTO HUNGARY

Crossing Croatia's long border with Hungary is relatively straightforward, with local buses connecting the main settlements on both sides. The main road between Zagreb and Budapest is the E71, which passes through Varaždin and Čakovec before crossing the border at Goričan (a motorway along this route is currently under construction). There are also road crossings at Gola (between Koprivnica and Nagyatad), Terezino Polje (between Virovitica and Barcs), Donji Miholjac (between Našice and Pécs) and Kneževo (between Osijek and Szekszárd).

The best places to pick up cross-border **buses** are Varaždin and Čakovec (3 daily to Nagykánisza), Virovitica (3 daily to Barcs) and Osijek (3 daily to Pécs, 1 daily to Mohács). If you're aiming for Budapest, the most direct route is by **train**, with two daily expresses – the *Kvarner* (Rijeka–Zagreb–Koprivnica–Budapest) and the *Drava* (Venice–Ljubljana–Čakovec–Budapest) – connecting the Hungarian capital with points in Croatia.

Kavarna Korso, Trg kralja Tomislava, is a venerable relic of Habsburg times, offering numerous varieties of coffee and a wealth of cakes. *Zlatni Lampaš*, just north of here at Trg bana Jelačića 3, is a comfortable pub-style bar in a stylish cellar.

The tourist office has details of the annual **Festival of Baroque Music** (late Sept to early Oct), which features concerts in many of the town's historic churches. Varaždin also has a first-division **football** team, Varteks (named after the textile company which sponsors them), who play in a small but spanking new stadium just south of town on the Zagreb road.

Čakovec

Northeast of Varaždin the main road to Hungary crosses the River Drava and traverses the flatlands of the Međimurje before arriving at ČAKOVEC, some 15km beyond. It's a relaxing if unspectacular provincial town, centred on a largely modern downtown area around Trg kralja Tomislava. The western end of the square features one of the finest Secession-era buildings in Croatia, the so-called **Casino**, designed by Hungarian architect Ödön Horvath in 1908 – a vivacious red-brick structure whose mushroom-shaped protuberances look like a deliberate affront to its po-faced neighbours.

Čakovec's main draw, however, is its seventeenth-century **Castle**, in a park just west of the centre, the former home of the powerful Zrinski family (see box on p.98). Beyond the moat and surviving western wall, the two-storey Baroque palace in the heart of the fortress now houses the **Museum of the Međimurje** (Tues–Fri 10am–3pm, Sat & Sun 10am–1pm; 15Kn). Objects connected with the Zrinskis, including the fine Renaissance tombstone of Nikola Šubić Zrinski, are complemented by two rooms of Iron Age finds from nearby Goričan, including several big urns decorated with geometric patterns and an enormous drinking vessel whose handle is adorned with pictures of horned beasts. The rest of the collection is a bit of a hotch-potch, featuring nineteenth-century furnishings, a reconstructed town pharmacy, and an old telescope built by the local astronomical society.

Practicalities

Čakovec's **bus station** is a block north of Trg Kralja Tomislava, while the **train station** is slightly further out to the southwest. There's a helpful **tourist office** at Ulica kralja Tomislava 18 (Mon–Fri 8am–7pm, Sat 8am–noon; ☎040/313-319 or 315-063, fax 315-106). Čakovec's proximity to the Hungarian border ensures that there are a couple of decent **accommodation** options: *Pansion kod Jape* (☎040/310-238, fax 310-243; ③), just north of the castle and a few steps west of the bus station at Zrinsko-Frankopanska bb, offers cosy and rather swish en suites in a brand new building; while the *Hotel Park* (☎040/319-255, fax 319-266; ④), a couple of hundred metres further west at Zrinsko-Frankopanska bb, is a 1960s box which conceals comfy and well-appointed en suites. Downtown **eating** options include local fish specialities at the *Riblji Restoran* and cheaper Italian fare at *Pizzeria Pipo*, both part of the same complex just off Trg kralja Tomislava at Ulica kralja Tomislava 2. *Gradska kavana*, just off Ulica kralja Tomislava at Matice Hrvatska 2, is a good place to enjoy a daytime **drink**; while *Arcus*, down from the tourist office at Strossmayerova 8, is an elegant café-bar with a youngish clientele and occasional discos in the cellar bar.

THE ZRINSKIS

From the sixteenth century onwards, eastern Croatia's status as a borderland disputed between the Habsburg and Ottoman empires led to the rise of a new breed of warrior aristocrats, whose power rested on military prowess on the battlefield and unswerving loyalty to the Habsburg dynasty. One of the most powerful Croatian families of the time was the Zrinskis, four of whom were elected BAN (governor) of Croatia between the mid-sixteenth and mid-seventeenth centuries.

The first of these was **Nikola Šubić Zrinski** (1508–66), who was awarded the castle of Čakovec by Habsburg Emperor Ferdinand I in 1546 – an acknowledgement of his financial contribution to the war against the Turks. Zrinski used Čakovec as a base from which to grow rich on the export of Međimurje livestock, although the need to ward off Turkish attacks remained a lifelong preoccupation. When Suleyman the Magnificent advanced into Habsburg territory in 1566, Zrinski led the defence of the fortress of **Szigetvár** in southern Hungary (about 100km southeast of Čakovec). Faced by overwhelmingly superior forces, Zrinski led his men on an attempted breakout from the fortress. They perished to the last man, but their heroism weakened the Ottomans sufficiently to stall their advance. Zrinski's exploits were immortalized by his great-grandson, **Nikola VII** (1620–64), whose epic Hungarian-language poem *Szigeti Veszedelem* ("Sziget in Peril") was to become a standard text for Hungarian patriots.

The Zrinskis continued to flourish as long as the Habsburg court valued their role as frontier barons, but the relationship became strained after the **Treaty of Vásvár** in 1664, which many Hungarian and Slavonian aristocrats felt made too many territorial concessions to the Turks. Feeling that loyalty to the Habsburgs had been insufficiently rewarded, a group of Hungarian nobles under **Wesselényi** conspired to establish an independent Hungary with a French or Polish monarch at its head. The conspiracy was enthusiastically supported by Nikola VII Zrinski, but Wesselényi died in 1667 and Nikola was killed by a boar during a hunt, leaving Nikola's brother **Petar Zrinski** (1621–71) and brother-in-law **Fran Krsto Frankopan** to assume leadership of the revolt. A harebrained scheme to kidnap the Emperor Leopold I in November 1667 having failed, Zrinski opened negotiations with the Turks, promising to make Hungary-Croatia a vassal state of the Ottoman Empire in return for help against the Austrians. Turkish help never materialized – indeed Turkish diplomats are thought to have provided details of the conspiracy to Leopold's court. After failing miserably to whip up any popular support, Zrinski and his allies surrendered, expecting to be treated leniently by an emperor keen to rebuild bridges with his unruly aristocratic subjects. In the end, however, Leopold had both Zrinski and Frankopan executed in Wiener Neustadt on April 30, 1671. Their bodies were returned home to be buried in Zagreb cathedral in 1919, although the fact that they'd originally been thrown into a common grave meant that the bones of innumerable other execution victims had to be collected in order to make sure that Zrinski and Frankopan were among them.

The Zrinskis and Frankopans remain important symbols of Croatia's unfulfilled destiny in central Europe. Neither were ever Croatian patriots in the modern sense: they belonged to a cosmopolitan aristocracy which invested most of its political energies in the defence of family privileges. However, the ending of both the Zrinski and Frankopan dynasties in 1671 dealt Croatian culture a serious blow; both families supported the publishing of Croatian-language books, and Fran Krsto Frankopan was himself an able poet. Once they had been replaced by nobles solidly oriented towards Vienna and Budapest, Croatia was deprived of an upper class with any real enthusiasm for national culture.

The weekend preceding Shrove Tuesday sees the traditional **Međimurje carnival** (Međimurski fašnik) parades, when villagers from the surrounding area converge on the town sporting – among other things – wild animal masks and imitation storks' heads on sticks. Details from the tourist office.

Koprivnica and Hlebine

Southeast of Varaždin and Čakovec stretches the **Podravina**, a ribbon of maize- and sunflower-covered flatlands running between the River Drava to the northeast and the low hills of the Bilogora to the south. Most routes pass through the agribusiness centre of **KOPRIVNICA**, where the rail lines from Zagreb to Osijek and Budapest part company. It's a neat and prosperous provincial town, laid out around an attractive central square with an adjoining grassy park, but there are few specific attractions and its main use is as a jumping-off point for the village of Hlebine and the nearby Hungarian border.

The **bus** and **train** stations lie next to each other ten minutes' walk west of the main square, Florijanski trg, where the **tourist office** (Mon–Fri 8am–4pm, Sat 8am–noon; ☎048/621-433, fax 623-178) can help with local information. The only accommodation is at the *Podravina* **hotel** (☎048/621-026, fax 621-178; ④), a couple of blocks south of the tourist office. For **eating**, the *Pivnica Kraluš* on the main square offers the standard Croatian culinary repertoire in beer cellar-like surroundings.

One annual festival worth looking out for is the **Naïve Art Fair** (Sajam naïve; usually on the second weekend of July), when there's a big display of local arts and crafts together with folklore performances on the main square.

Hlebine

Sixteen kilometres southeast of Koprivnica, the village of **HLEBINE** has been associated with naïve art since the 1930s, and remains home to an estimated 200 self-taught painters and sculptors. Hlebine's emergence as an art centre came about largely by accident, when the academically trained local artist Krsto Hegedušić returned home to visit his parents and discovered the drawings of the young, untutored Ivan Generalić displayed in the village shop. Hegedušić took Generalić and a couple of other promising village artists under his wing, establishing a tradition of peasant painting which subsequent Hlebine generations have continued to develop as a professional craft.

The **Hlebine Art Gallery** (Galerija Hlebine; Mon–Sat 10am–4pm; 10Kn), a modern pavilion on your left as you enter the village from the Koprivnica direction, documents the work of the Hlebine School, with changing exhibitions chosen from their extensive archive collection. There's a special room devoted to Ivan Generalić, whose personal brand of magical realism had an enormous impact on successive generations, and helped make Hlebine painters so popular with the buying public. Generalić's rather jolly, bucolic vision of peasant life is showcased here with portraits of local characters, fanciful visions (such as the *Eiffel Tower in Hlebine*), and examples of one of his favourite subjects, the crucified rooster (*raspeti petao*) – not the mock-religious image you might imagine, but the artist's revenge on the beast that used to wake him up every morning when he was a child. Ten minutes' walk further down the village's main street, the **Galerija Josip Generalić** (pre-arranged group visits only; ☎048/836-430, *www.generalic.com*) occupies the former studio of both Ivan Generalić and his son Josip

THE HLEBINE SCHOOL

The Hlebine School would never have existed without the academically trained painter, **Krsto Hegedušić** (1901–75). While studying in Paris, Hegedušić became an admirer of untutored, "naive" artists such as Henri "Le Douanier" Rousseau and the Georgian painter of Tbilisi streetlife, Pirosmani. Returning to Hlebine, he was amazed to find that village youths such as **Ivan Generalić** and **Franjo Mraz** seemed to possess the same talent for rendering the world around them in a fresh and vivid style. Hegedušić was heavily influenced by the work of great Flemish painters like Pieter Bruegel the Elder, and probably saw Generalić and Mraz as an opportunity to reinvent Bruegel in a contemporary Croatian setting – he was also a left-leaning intellectual who believed that rural life should be depicted in a non-idealized way to show people how the Croatian peasant really lived. He invited Generalić and Mraz to exhibit with Zemlja ("Earth"), a group of Zagreb artists and architects, giving naive painting a respectability which has endured ever since. Hegedušić also encouraged the young artists to adopt the traditional craft of painting in oil or tempera on glass, a technique which gave their colourful scenes of village life an added luminescence.

The early works of Generalić and Mraz were grittily documentary in conception, although for gutsy realism even they couldn't compare with the images of peasant toil being produced by **Mirko Virius** (1889–1943), a self-taught painter from Đelekovec, north of Koprivnica, who sought to present a true picture of rural povety to the urban art public. However, Zemlja was outlawed in 1935, Virius was killed in a World War II Ustaše concentration camp, and although the Hlebine School continued to diversify and develop, the social concerns of the original Hlebine painters fell into the background. Ivan Generalić entered his magic realist phase, and the second generation of Croatian village painters, such as **Ivan Rabuzin** and Ivan's son, **Josip Generalić**, increasingly used the naive style to paint the world inside their heads rather than the world outside the garden gate.

After World War II the tradition of village painting was encouraged all over Yugoslavia by a new regime eager to promote a type of people's art free of Western "decadence", although Hlebine remains the only village in Croatia where it's regarded as a legitimate local craft passed from one generation to the next. Both in communist Yugoslavia and post-independence Croatia, naive art has been hailed as an authentic expression of indigenous peasant culture, and is nowadays rather self-consciously promoted under the label "the miracle of the Croatian naive" (*Čudo hrvatske naive*). Miracle or not, most of the work produced by today's naive artists tends towards the decorative and the kitsch – largely because there's such a big market for homely rustic themes.

If you don't make it to Hlebine, the best place to view the works of Croatia's rural painters is the **Gallery of Naive Art** (Galerija naivne umjetnosti) in Zagreb (see p.61).

Generalić, and holds examples of their work, alongside paintings by Ivan's grandson Goran Generalić.

Hlebine is served by six daily **buses** from Koprivnica on weekdays, but services are few and far between at weekends, when you'll need your own transport. The only **accommodation** in the village is the lovely two-person apartment in the garden of the Galerija Josip Generalić (☎048/836-430; ②). There's a **café** and a small store where you can buy food opposite the main art gallery.

Slavonia

Stretching from Zagreb to the Danube, which forms Croatia's border with Serbia, the rich agricultural plain of **Slavonia** has an unjust reputation as the most scenically tedious region of the country. All most visitors ever see of it is the view from the Autocesta – the highway originally built to link Zagreb with Belgrade, and still the main route into the eastern corner of the country (see box below) – as it forges across unbroken flatlands. The effects of war, Serbian occupation and the painfully slow pace of reconstruction have left their mark, but the region has its attractions, not least a distinctive and often captivating rural landscape, characterized by a seemingly endless carpet of corn and sunflowers, with vineyards on the low hills to the north.

Traffic on the Autocesta thins out as it nears the little-used border with Serbia, 310km east of Zagreb, with most travellers veering north towards eastern Croatia's main urban centre, **Osijek**, a former Austrian fortress town which retains a dash of Habsburg-era elegance. The best of Slavonia's scenery lies around here, a patchwork of greens and yellows dotted with dusty, half-forgotten villages, where latticed wooden sheds groan under the weight of corn cobs and strings of red paprikas hang outside to dry in the autumn. Just north of Osijek, the **Kopački Rit** nature reserve, with its abundant birdlife, is Croatia's most intriguing wetland area, while in the far southeast the siege-scarred town of **Vukovar** – though hardly the tourist attraction it once was – is a worthwhile side-trip if you want to see the consequences of the war at first hand. Elsewhere in Slavonia there's a relative dearth of urban sights, save in the pleasant provincial towns of **Požega** and **Đakovo**.

Slavonian **culinary culture** is characterized by a rich variety of fresh fish from the Sava and Drava rivers, notably *šaran* (carp), *som* (catfish) and *štuka* (pike). A mixture of the above are stewed together to produce *fiš paprikaš*, the spicy, soupy mainstay of most restaurant menus around Osijek and in the southeast. Many Slavonian families keep a pig or two, which are traditionally slaughtered towards the end of November in the annual *kolinje*, or pig cull. Naturally enough, the main meat-based delicacy is *kulen*, a rich, paprika-flavoured sausage which is served as a snack or hors d'oeuvre.

THE AUTOCESTA

The word *autocesta* simply means "motorway", but as the Belgrade–Zagreb motorway was the first to be built in Yugoslavia, the name somehow stuck to this particular road. Planned in the aftermath of World War II both to help speed reconstruction and to embody the spirit of Yugoslav idealism, it was built in part by brigades of students who, it was hoped, would be fired by the spirit of socialism as a result of taking part – "We build the the road and the road builds us" was a popular propaganda slogan of the time. Intended to symbolize more than just a transport link between the people of Croatia and Serbia, the motorway was officially named the "Motorway of Brotherhood and Unity" (Autocesta bratstva i jedinstva). The failure of Titoist idealism is nowhere more eloquently summed up than in the fate of this road, which now leads, in effect, nowhere.

The Turopolje

Just southwest of the main route into Slavonia, the **Turopolje** (supposedly named after the tur, a now extinct, bison-like beast which once roamed the area) extends south from Zagreb for some 20–30km before coming up against the low hills of the Vukomeričke Gorice. It's not an outstandingly interesting area, but if traditional village architecture is your thing, it merits a brief trip. Several villages harbour surviving pockets of wooden Turopolje houses, characterized by the covered staircases which run up the outside of the building, usually finishing at a second-floor veranda, while several timber churches add a quaintly Ruritanian atmosphere to what is otherwise a rapidly urbanizing region.

The main road from Zagreb to Sisak passes through – or near – the main points of interest. Zagreb–Sisak commuter **trains** serve Velika Gorica and Mraclin, while **buses** from the main Zagreb bus station (the bus stands are reached by passing under the tracks through the subterranean Importanne shopping centre) to Sisak go through Buševec. In addition, bus #268 runs from Zagreb to Velika Gorica, the region's main town.

Velika Mlaka, Velika Gorica and around

Barely 5km beyond the southern boundaries of Novi Zagreb the main road (served by the #268 Velika Gorica bus) passes the village of **VELIKA MLAKA**, nowadays a prosperous dormitory suburb of Zagreb. About ten minutes' walk north of the main road, an enclosure shaded by pine trees provides the setting for **St Barbara's Church** (Crkva sveta Barbara), a timber construction covered in small wooden shingles and topped by a jaunty spire. Founded in 1642, it was substantially rebuilt in 1912, when the porch – decorated with sun symbols and squiggle patterns – was added. A few oblong wooden houses and barns still survive in the surrounding streets, although most have been demolished to make way for the kind of sturdy family houses that wouldn't look out of place anywhere between here and Hamburg.

Bus #268 finishes up in **VELIKA GORICA**, a plain, residential town situated a few kilometres beyond Zagreb airport. Velika Gorica's bus terminal is just off the main street, where the fetchingly pink-and-orange former town hall contains the **Museum of the Turopolje** (Tues–Fri 10am–6pm, Sat & Sun 10am–1pm; closed Aug; 8Kn), a small but thoughtfully presented collection of local crafts. The most striking exhibits are the traditional costumes – white, pleated skirts with vivacious crimson embroidery for the women; extravagantly wide pantaloons and black-brimmed hats for the men. Velika Gorica's only other sight is the dainty wooden **Chapel of Jesus in Wounds** (Kapela ranjenog Isusa), located in a field 3km north of the centre, a couple of hundred metres from the airport entrance. Originally raised by the widow of local nobleman Ladislav Plepelić in 1758, the chapel was substantially rebuilt in the nineteenth century. Although rarely open (Sunday mass is your best bet), it's an impressive clump of blackened timbers, dramatically floodlit at night. The #268 bus passes the airport access road on entering and leaving the town; get off here then head towards the airport until you see the chapel on your right.

Six kilometres south of Velika Gorica and just west of the main Zagreb–Sisak road, the sleepy village of **MRACLIN** (reached by bus #304 from Velika Gorica or by commuter train from Zagreb) boasts a sufficiently large number of traditional Turopolje houses to make a brief stroll through the centre worthwhile, although it won't detain you for long. Much the same might be said of **BUŠEVEC**, 5km further south, which has a small wooden church with a cone-like steeple at the southern end of the village, and several timber farmsteads nearby. Buševec is on the main Zagreb–Sisak highway, so Sisak-bound buses pass through.

The Lonjsko polje and Jasenovac

Southeast of the Turopolje lies the **Lonsko polje**, an area of wetland just east of the River Sava famous for its wooden village architecture and nesting storks. The pastures and forests of the *polje* ("field") are also home to the Posavlje horse (Posavski konj), a stocky, semi-wild breed which wanders the area, and the spotty-hided Turopolje pig (Turopoljska svinja), which lives off acorns in the forests. The other main characteristic of the *polje* are the swamplands and riverine forest which appear in spring and autumn, when the tributaries of the River Sava habitually break their banks and the area is colonized by spoonbills, herons and storks. The area between Sisak and Jasenovac was declared a nature park (*park prirode*) in 1990, although the development of tourism in the area is still in its infancy – there's nowhere to stay in the Lonsko polje, and few places to eat. Public transport is meagre, so it's best to come by car if you can.

Sisak to Krapje

The obvious northern gateway to the region is **SISAK**, a dreary, medium-sized town 22km west of the Autocesta's Popovača exit, although buses from Zagreb come via the single-lane highway which forges past Zagreb airport and Velika Gorica. Sisak is also connected to the capital by train. From Sisak you can catch a twice-daily bus to the Lonjsko polje village of Lonja (calling at Čigoč on the way) – these follow the old road from Sisak to Jasenovac, which winds along the north-east bank of the River Sava, passing through a sequence of single-street villages famous for their timber-built houses and chicken-choked yards.

The most famous of these village is **ČIGOČ**, 28km from Sisak, not least because of its importance to the local stork population, which descends on the village in ever-increasing numbers every spring (usually arriving late March/early April) ready to feast on the local fish. Most of the houses in Čigoč are traditional two-storey structures placed end-on to the road, with thatched roofs, overhanging eaves, and a main entrance on the first floor reached by a covered outside staircase known as a *ganjak* – many also have elaborately carved porches or balconies. One of these structures midway through the village houses a **park information point** (May–Sept daily 8am–4pm), which can provide a map of the area and advise on trails leading east from Čigoč and the other villages out onto the countryside, parts of which might be under water depending on the time of year. Towards the eastern end of the village, the *Stara hiža* **restaurant** offers drinks, snacks and possibly more substantial dishes, depending on what they have in stock.

Beyond lie a succession of villages similar to Čigoč but without as many storks: first is **MUŽILOVČICA**, where you'll find basic food and drink at *Seoski turizam Mužilovčica*, a beautifully preserved house housing a small private ethnographic **museum** at no. 72 on the village's only street. Six kilometres further on lies **LONJA**, another long, tumbledown village, followed after another 12km by **KRAPJE**, whose rather better-preserved wooden houses sit in a neat row, spaced at regular intervals – the orderly result of strict regulations introduced by the Habsburgs to control house-building in the settlements of the Military Frontier.

Jasenovac

Fifteen kilometres beyond Krapje and 10km south of the Novska exit of the Autocesta is **JASENOVAC**, the site of a notorious World War II concentration camp at which the Croatian Ustaše, who ran the so-called "Independent State of Croatia" on behalf of their German masters, murdered an unknown number of Serbs, Jews, gypsies and Croatian anti-fascists. Situated beside the road into town from the Novska direction, the camp was razed in 1945 and turned into

THE JASENOVAC CAMP

Croatia's wartime archbishop, Alojzije Stepinac, was so shamed by Jasenovac that he likened it to the mark of Cain, to be worn by the nation for ever. Since then, the failure of Croatian officialdom to come to terms with the enormity of Jasenovac has only served to prove the wisdom of Stepinac's words. Initially, there was a tendency among postwar Yugoslav historians to inflate the numbers of the camp's victims, and an estimated figure of 700,000 to 1,000,000 dead came to be officially accepted, despite the lack of research to back it up. Croatian historians, led by **Franjo Tuđman**, felt that the circulation of such high figures was exploited by official circles in Yugoslavia to blacken the reputation of the whole Croatian nation and render feelings of Croatian patriotism impossible for future generations. Developed over several decades, Tuđman's point of view, originally aired in the 1970s, was eventually published in his lengthy theoretical work *The Impasses of Historical Reality* in 1989, together with his assertion that only 30,000–40,000 could have died at Jasenovac. The lack of unbiased research makes all figures questionable, although outside observers nowadays consider 80,000 to be a fair estimate – the majority are likely to have been Serbs. In the dying days of Yugoslavia, Jasenovac became a political football, with the Serbian media whipping up anti-Croatian feeling by harking back to the crimes of World War II, and the Croats minimizing the importance of Jasenovac in an attempt to sweep the excesses of the Nazi period under the carpet.

Jasenovac has lost none of its power to divide opinion. Faced with the question of what to do with the memorial centre once it was returned to Croatian control, President Tuđman suggested turning Jasenovac into a memorial to all the victims of World War II by burying the remains of the fallen in one **common grave**. The idea that bones of the Ustaše might be mixed together with their victims shocked liberal opinion, as well as outraging Jewish organizations worldwide and souring Croatia's relations with Israel. Not surprisingly, the idea was swiftly dropped. Jasenovac was in the news again in May 1998, with the extradition from Argentina of one of the camp's former commanders, **Dinko Šakić**. The decision to charge Šakić with "crimes against humanity", but not with full-blown genocide, merely led to further accusations that the trial was another attempt to lessen the significance of Jasenovac rather than recognize the horrors that took place there. Šakić was found guilty and given a twenty-year sentence in October 1999.

a memorial park (*spomen-park*) two decades later, centred on a striking modern sculpture resembling a giant concrete orchid, the work of Serbian architect, sculptor and politician Bogdan Bogdanović (who, as the "liberal" mayor of Belgrade in the 1980s, was purged by Slobodan Milošević's hardliners). There's also a small museum (Mon–Fri 7am–3pm; free), although most of the archives and exhibits were removed to Belgrade during the Serbian occupation of Jasenovac in 1991–95, and only a small display of photographs remains. The memorial park itself has been de-mined, but the surrounding countryside hasn't.

The rest of Jasenovac still bears the scars of the recent war: the centre of town was cleared of Croats in 1991, and its church dynamited; the Serbs suffered a similar fate when the Croats returned in May 1995. There's little to do in town except call in at the Lonjsko Polje Nature Park administration office, housed in local government buildings opposite the (now rebuilt) church on the main square, Trg kralja Petra Svačića (Mon–Fri 8am–3pm; ☎044/672-080), where you can pick up maps and advice on exploring the park.

Požega

Some 150km east of Zagreb, at the Nova Gradiška exit, a minor road heads north from the Autocesta to **POŽEGA**, an appealing market town lying amid the small lumpish hills of the **Babja Gora**. The town was occupied by the Turks between 1536 and 1691, but today the look of the place is overwhelmingly Baroque, with its main square, Trg svetog Trojstva, surrounded by yellow, arcaded buildings, two-storey monuments to provincial contentment. On the southern side of the square, the Gothic Franciscan **Church of the Holy Spirit** (Crkva svetog Duha) was used as a mosque by the Turks and has been recently spruced up, while the older **St Lawrence's Church** (Crkva svetog Lovre) is said to contain some fine Gothic frescoes, though it's currently undergoing restoration and is inaccessible. The **Town Museum** (Gradski muzej; Mon–Fri 10am–noon & 5–7pm; 10Kn), at the east end of the main square, has a limited display of local archeological finds, and a small ethnographic section featuring some incandescent hand-woven rugs with vegetal and bird designs. Round the corner from the main square on Trg svete Terezije, opposite the dazzling white facade of the eighteenth-century **St Theresa's Church** (Crkva svete Terezije), a statue commemorates one Luka Ibrišimović Sokol, a Franciscan friar and fierce-looking warrior-priest who was instrumental in winning a famous victory over the Turks at nearby Sokolovec, liberating Požega in the process.

Požega's **tourist office**, Trg svetog Trojstva 3 (☎034/274-900, fax 274-901), can point you in the direction of a couple of **pensions** (①–②) in the suburbs. The town's only real **hotel** is the *Grgin Dol* (☎034/273-222; ④), just west of the main square at Grgin Dol 20, with smallish but smart en suites with TV. There are loads of **cafés** and simple **restaurants** tucked away in the pedestrian streets just north of the main square.

The town is also the unlikely setting for one of Croatia's strangest cultural events, the **Festival of One-Minute Films** (Revija jednominutnih filmova), which attracts largely avant-garde work from all over the world every year in May. The other cultural attraction here is the **Golden Strings of Slavonia Festival** (Zlatne žice slavonije; Sept), a celebration of tamburica music, the folk music indigenous to Slavonia (named after the *tambura*, a ferociously strummed lute-like instrument), which has come to dominate the Croatian pop mainstream in the last decade or so. Contact the tourist office for information about both festivals.

Slavonski Brod

A further 30km east along the Autocesta, **SLAVONSKI BROD** is a largely modern town whose high-rise suburbs were built to house workers drawn by the local Đuro Đaković engineering works, although a smattering of Habsburg-era buildings in the centre – including an eighteenth-century fortress – may tempt you to take a breather here before pressing on. Slavonski Brod was an important crossing point into Bosnia, which lies on the opposite bank of the Sava, until the Bosnian Serbs took control of the sister town of Bosanski Brod on the other side of the river in 1992 and blew up the bridge connecting the two settlements. Most of the erstwhile inhabitants of Bosanski Brod now live in Slavonski Brod, and are unlikely to return home given the uncertain welcome presently accorded to non-Serbs in the Serb-controlled parts of Bosnia-Hercegovina. Slavonski Brod was subjected to extensive shelling by the Serbs in 1992, and most of the riverfront buildings still bear the signs of war damage. The town hardly merits an overnight stop unless you're in town for the **Brodsko Kolo Folklore Festival** (mid-June), which features songs, dance and horse-and-trap displays from all over Slavonia. Details are available from the Slavonski Brod tourist association (π & fax 035/447-721, *tzg-sl.broda@sb.tel.hr*).

The heart of the town, **Trg I. B. Mažuranić**, faces the broad sweep of the Sava, with views of Bosanski Brod on the opposite bank. From here, Šetalište braće Radić follows the river eastwards to the eighteenth-century **Franciscan monastery** (Franjevački samostan), which features a nice colonnaded courtyard and a church rich in wooden Baroque altarpieces painted in garish green and brown hues to provide a fake marble sheen. Just north of the monastery, a modern pavilion hosting temporary exhibitions is the only currently functioning part of the **Museum of the Brod-Posavlje Region** (Muzej brodskog posavlja; Mon–Fri 9am–3pm; 10Kn), which has been forced to put the bulk of its collection into storage due to war damage. Heading back to the main square and then continuing west, you can't miss the vast earthen ramparts of **Brod Fortress** (Brodska tvrđava), built in 1715 to protect Slavonia from Ottoman-controlled Bosnia on the other side of the river. This once vast complex of barrack-buildings enclosed by star-shaped earthworks is now rather run-down, although you're free to wander round inside and scramble up onto the grassy ramparts.

Both **bus** and **train stations** are ten minutes' walk north of Trg I. B. Mažuranić. For **information**, Brod Turist, just north of the main square at Trg Pobjede 30 (Mon–Fri 8am–6pm, Sat 9am–2pm; π035/445-765), hands out leaflets and sells town maps. The *Park* **hotel**, immediately opposite (π035/231-162; ③), has functional en-suite rooms in a greying modern block. *Kavana Korso*, Trg I. B. Mažuranić, is the best place for a relaxing **drink**, although there are innumerable café-bars along Krešimirova and Starčevićeva, both of which lead east from here. For **eating**, *Pizzeria Mamma Mia*, Starčevićeva 3, has a basic range of pizzas and grills; while *Fijaker*, Krešimirova 21, offers more substantial Croatian fare.

Đakovo and Vinkovci

Beyond Slavonski Brod the Autocesta forges ever eastwards towards the frontier with Serbia some 95km distant. After 35km a secondary route breaks off north-wards towards the neat-and-tidy plains town of **ĐAKOVO**, which is served by regular buses from both Slavonski Brod and Osijek, as well as occasional trains on the Vrpolje–Osijek branch line. Whatever your point of arrival, you'll be guided into the centre by the skyline-hogging, 84-metre-high twin towers of Đakovo's neo-Gothic, red-brick **Cathedral** (daily 7am–noon & 3–7pm). This vast building, constructed between 1862 and 1882 by the Viennese Gothic Revival architect Baron Frederick Schmidt, was commissioned by Bishop Josip Juraj Strossmayer (see p.65), who used his Đakovo see as a base from which to promote a Croatian – and indeed South-Slav – cultural renaissance. Despite its initially austere appearance the cathedral is decorated with a wealth of intriguing detail, from the beehive-like cones which stand guard on either side of the entrance to the pinnacled cupola which rises above the main transept. Inside, walls and ceilings are decorated with uplifting biblical scenes by the father-and-son team of Alexander and Ljudevit Seitz, painted in the style of the Nazarenes (German contemporaries of the Pre-Raphaelites). Immediately north of the cathedral, a squat, custard-coloured building houses the **Strossmayer Museum** (Spomen-muzej Biskupa Josipa Jurja Strossmayera; Tues–Fri 8am–7pm, Sat 8am–2pm; 5Kn), with a few personal effects and copies of his writings. Beyond lies an attractive café-lined main street, at the far end of which stands one further curiosity – a dainty **parish church**, occupying the shell of a sixteenth-century mosque.

Đakovo is the scene of one of Croatia's most important **festivals** of authentic folk culture, **Đakovački vezovi** (literally "Đakovo embroidery"; last weekend in September), featuring a weekend-long series of song-and-dance performances by folkloric societies from throughout eastern Croatia and parades in local costume.

Vinkovci

Thirty kilometres due east of Đakovo, **VINKOVCI** was once the most important rail junction in the region, standing at the crossroads of lines linking Zagreb to Belgrade and Budapest to Sarajevo. With good onward connections to Osijek and Vukovar, you might find yourself changing buses or trains here, but despite a clutch of eye-catching nineteenth-century buildings in the town centre, there's nothing that merits a specific visit. **Bus** and **train stations** stand next to each other 1km north of the town centre, where there's a plush modern **hotel**, the *Slavonija* (☎032/342-777; ④).

Osijek

Tucked into the far northeastern corner of Slavonia, 30km from the Hungarian border and just 20km west of the Serbian province of Vojvodina, **OSIJEK** is the undisputed capital of the region. An easygoing, park-filled city hugging the banks of the River Drava, Osijek's relaxed spaciousness is due in large part to its being spread out across three quite separate town centres. The oldest of these, **Tvrđa**, retains the air of a living museum. Originally a Roman strongpoint, it was subsequently fortified by the Ottomans and then finally rebuilt in Baroque style by the Austrians, who kicked the Turks out in 1687. The Austrians were also responsible

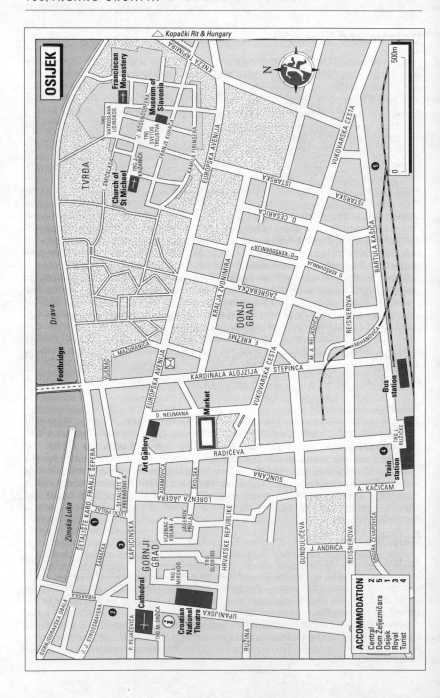

△ Kopački Rit & Hungary

OSIJEK

Franciscan Monastery

Museum of Slavonia

TVRĐA

Church of St Michael

Drava

Footbridge

Zimska Luka

GORNJI GRAD

Cathedral

Croatian National Theatre

Art Gallery

D. NEUMANA

Market

RADIĆEVA

DONJI GRAD

KARDINALA ALOJZIJA

Bus station

Train station

ACCOMMODATION	
Central	2
Dom Željezničara	5
Osijek	1
Royal	3
Turist	4

500m

for the construction of **Gornji grad** (literally "Upper Town", although it's no higher than any of the others), the nineteenth-century area which still exudes a degree of fin-de-siècle Habsburg refinement and now serves as the administrative heart of the modern city. Between the two is **Donji grad** ("Lower Town"), a residential district of little interest to visitors, which developed at around the same time as Gornji grad in order to accommodate economic migrants from the surrounding plains.

After the fall of Vukovar in November 1991, the Yugoslav People's Army and Serb irregulars laid siege to Osijek and subjected the town to a nine-month bombardment. Osijek survived, but the scars of war are still plain to see. Nowadays there's a palpable sense of isolation, brought about by Osijek's geographical position on the fringes of Croatia, pushed up against the borders of a Yugoslav state with which normal economic and cultural relations are largely frozen; the cosmopolitanism of the pre-1991 city is unlikely to re-emerge for some time.

Osijek's sights won't detain you for more than a day, but it's the obvious place from which to venture into the Kopački Rit nature reserve and it is a useful jumping-off point **to southern Hungary**, with daily buses to both Pécs (Pečuh in Croatian) and Mohács (Mohač).

The Town

The heart of modern Osijek is **Gornji grad**, centred around the neat, triangular Trg Ante Starčevića, bordered by stout nineteenth-century buildings and overlooked by the elegant spire of the town's red-brick, neo-Gothic **Cathedral**, although despite the bustle there's not much else in the way of specific attractions. Heading east along Europska avenija, just beyond the junction with Stjepana Radića, you'll pass the best group of Jugendstil buildings in Croatia, a series of town houses built for rich local German merchants, with caryatid-encrusted facades and spindly balconies.

Two kilometres along Europska avenija lies the complex of Baroque buildings known as **Trvđa** (literally "fortress"; also reachable on tram #1 from Trg Ante Starčevića or by walking along the riverside path by the Drava), a collection of military and administrative buildings thrown up by the Austrians after the destruction of the earlier Ottoman castle. Tvrđa's grid of cobbled streets zeros in on Trg svetog Trojstva, a broad expanse bearing a **plague column**, built in 1729 with funds donated by the local fortress commander's wife to give thanks for deliverance from a particularly nasty outbreak of disease, and surrounded by the faded ochre administration buildings from which Habsburg commanders organized the defence of the southern frontier. Originally built as an expression of Austro-Hungarian power, these arcaded eighteenth-century buildings today have a quietly forgotten air, now that the centre of municipal life has shifted elsewhere.

One of these buildings now houses the **Museum of Slavonia** (Muzej slavonije; Tues–Sun 10am–1pm; 6Kn), which displays sculptural fragments and gravestones recovered from Roman Mursa, Osijek's distant forerunner, and hosts temporary themed exhibitions on local history. Off the square to the west, the double onion-dome frontage of the former Jesuit **St Michael's Church** (Crkva svetog Mihovila) lords it over a knot of narrow alleys, although it's disappointingly bare inside. Much the same might be said of the **Franciscan monastery** (Franjevački samostan) church set back from the eastern side of Trg svetog Trojstva, despite the Gothic statue of the Virgin which adorns the high altar.

Alleys descend from Tvrđa towards the riverfront, where a pedestrian bridge crosses the Drava towards ritzy-sounding **Copacabana** on the opposite bank – a grassy bathing area with a waterslide and a couple of cafés. Back on the Tvrđa side of the river, a broad flagstoned path leads back towards Gornji grad, terminating at the **Zimska luka** ("winter harbour"), a dock for small pleasure craft protected by a breakwater from the strong currents of the Drava, and another popular spot for lounging around in cafés.

Practicalities

Osijek's **bus** and **train stations** are next to each other on Bartula Kašića on the south side of the town centre. From here it's a ten-minute walk first up Radićeva then left into Kapucinska to reach Trg Ante Starčevića (alternatively, travel three stops on tram #2). The helpful staff at the **tourist office**, just next to the cathedral at Županijska 2 (Mon–Fri 7am–4pm, Sat 8am–noon; ☎031/23-755, fax 23-947), can provide a free monthly events guide (*gradski vodič*), which has cultural listings.

The town's **hotels** include the plain but tolerable *Turist*, just opposite the train station at Radićeva 58 (☎031/209-622; ②); and the slightly more salubrious *Dom Željezničara*, also handy for the train and bus stations at Bartula Kašića 2a (☎031/207-640; ④). In the town centre, the slightly tatty *Royal*, Kapucinska 34 (☎031/210-105; ②), has basic rooms with shared facilities; while the *Central*, Trg Ante Starčevića 6 (☎031/126-188; ④), is a rather more characterful nineteenth-century place with comfortable en suites. The modern high-rise *Hotel Osijek*, on the waterfront at Šamačka 4 (☎031/125-333, fax 212-135; ④), is overpriced, unless you can get a room facing the river.

There are plenty of good-value **eating** possibilities on the way into town from the bus and train stations: *Mama Mia*, Radićeva 44, is probably the best of Osijek's pizzerias, while the nearby *Metro*, Radićeva 54, does a cheap and filling *fič paprikaš*. A good place to try local specialities is *Slavonska kuća* at Firingera 26 in Tvrđa, a rustic little place offering *kulen* sausage and grilled fish at reasonable prices. The more expensive *Lovački Rog*, just off Radićeva at Gundulićeva 2, is the place to eat game, top-quality schnitzels and steaks.

The cafés with outdoor seating along the Zimska luka are good places for an evening **drink**, while the string of café-bars along Radićeva attract a younger crowd; *Voodoo*, just off Radićeva at Sunčana 6, is a studenty, alternative rock-oriented meeting-place. In Tvrđa, *St Patrick's*, Trg svetog Trojstva, is a comfy Irish-style pub with a terrace facing the best of Osijek's Baroque buildings. There's a **cybercafé**, *Internet Klub Ukrik* (*www.ukrik.hr*), next to the *Voodoo* café-bar at Sunčana 8. **Clubs** go in and out of fashion fairly quickly, although you could try *Disco Bar Faust*, at Fakultetska 2 in Tvrđa, which sometimes organizes alfresco concerts in the summer, or the largely mainstream-techno *Oxygene*, opposite the tourist office at Županijska 7.

The main venue for **classical music** and **theatre** is the Croatian National Theatre (Hrvatsko narodno kazalište), Županijska 9. Osijek has two **cinemas**: the Europa, near the *Hotel Osijek* on Lučki Prilaz, and the Urania, just east at the junction of Europska and Radićeva. There's a dearth of live **rock-pop** music in Osijek, although a programme of gigs is organized during the **Summer of Youth** (Ljeto mladih) in July, with most events taking place at the Studentski centar on Istarska.

Kopački Rit and around

Beyond Osijek, the main road to Hungary forges through the pastel-coloured villages and corn-rich fields of the **Baranja**, a fertile extension of the Slavonian plain filling the triangle formed by the Drava to the west, the Danube to the east, and the low hills of southern Hungary to the north. A border region once known for its mixed population and tolerant ways (the area was 42 percent Croatian and 36 percent Serb in 1981), the Baranja spent the years from 1991 to 1998 first under Serbian occupation, then UN control. Most of the Croats fled in 1991, and are only slowly returning, kept away by poor employment prospects, painful memories, and suspicion of those local Serbs who have chosen to remain.

Eight kilometres out of Osijek the road passes through the village of **BILJE**, main gateway to the **Kopački Rit Nature Park** (Park prirode Kopački Rit). The park covers an area of marsh and partly sunken forest just north of the point where the fast-flowing River Drava pours into the Danube, forcing the slower Danube waters to back up and flood the plain. The resulting wetland is most inundated from spring through to early autumn, when fish come here to spawn and wading birds congregate to feed off them. At this time you'll see cormorants, grey herons, and, if you're lucky, black storks, which nest in the oak forests north of Bilje. Much of the park is yet to be de-mined and is for the time being only open for visits by pre-arranged groups (20Kn per person) – there's a five-person minimum; individual tourists will be admitted after mine clearance and the construction of proper entrance points has been completed. For the time being, contact the park administration, which is located in Prince Eugene of Savoy's former hunting lodge on the eastern fringes of Bilje (☎031/750-855, fax 750-755, *pp-kopacki-rit@os.tel.hr*).

The main route into the park is along the road which leads east from Bilje to **KOPAČEVO**, 3km away, a village which hosts a mixed Croatian-Hungarian population and contains some of the best traditional architecture in eastern Slavonia, with the kind of houses you'll see all over the Hungarian plain, southeastern Croatia and the Serban Vojvodina, laid end-on to the road, with long verandas facing in onto secluded courtyards. The **park entrance** is just north of Kopačevo: from here a road runs along a north-leading dyke which separates a series of commercial fishponds on the left-hand side from the magisterial sunken forest of **Lake Sakadaš** on the right, where wading birds stalk their prey among the white willows. North of here tracks continue through **Tikveš**, an area of oak forest where you stand a good chance of spotting wild pigs and deer. Josip Broz Tito used the fine villa of **Dvorac Tikveš** as a hunting lodge; it's currently semi-derelict after suffering neglect during the Serbian occupation.

Hourly Osijek–Beli Manastir **buses** pass through Bilje, from where you can walk to Kopačevo, passing the park administration office on the way. The park is in the process of opening up private **rooms** in Kopačevo (031/750-855; ②), which may well prove an excellent alternative to basing yourself in Osijek. The village is also home to the *Zelena Žaba* **restaurant**, which has excellent *kulen* salami, local fish and grilled meats.

Vukovar

Regular buses from Osijek run through the wheat- and cornfields to **VUKOVAR**, 35km to the southeast, a once beautiful town hugging the west bank of the

Danube, across which lies the Serbian province of Vojvodina. Until 1991 Vukovar was one of Yugoslavia's more prosperous towns, with a quaint Baroque centre, a successful manufacturing industry based around tyre-producing giant Borovo, and an urban culture that was lively, open and tolerant. However, proximity to the Serbian border and an ethnically mixed population (of whom 44 percent were Croat and 37 percent Serb) conspired to place Vukovar at the sharp end of the Croat–Serb conflict. The resulting **siege** and capture of Vukovar by the Yugoslav People's Army and Serbian irregulars left the centre of town in ruins and did untold emotional damage to those lucky enough to escape. Now back under Croatian control, urban life in Vukovar functions up to a point, although it will take years for true normality to return.

Inter-ethnic tension flared in April 1991, when barricades went up between the Croatian-controlled town centre and the Serb-dominated suburbs. The firing of a rocket at the Serb district of **Borovo Selo** by Croat extremists (an action in which the future Croatian defence minister Gojko Šušak was implicated) was a calculated attempt to raise the stakes. Croatian policemen patrolling Borovo Selo were shot at by Serbian snipers on May 1, and when a bus-load of their colleagues entered the same suburb the following day, they were met by an ambush in which twelve of them lost their lives. The JNA (Yugoslav People's Army) moved in, ostensibly to keep the two sides apart, digging into positions that were to serve them well with the breakout of all-out war in the autumn. On September 14, 1991 the Croatian National Guard surrounded the JNA barracks in town. Serb irregulars in the outlying areas, supported by the JNA, responded by launching an attack. Croatian refugees fled the suburbs, crowding into the centre. Aided by the fact that many of the outlying villages were ethnically Serb, the JNA swiftly encircled the town, making it all but impossible to leave (the only route out was through sniper-prone cornfields), and subjecting the population to increasingly heavy shelling. By the beginning of October the people of Vukovar were living in bomb shelters and subsisting on meagre rations of food and water, their plight worsened by the seeming inactivity of the government in Zagreb – the commander of the town's defence, Mile Dedaković Jastreb, accused President Tuđman of sacrificing Vukovar in order to win international sympathy for the Croatian cause. Vukovar finally fell on November 18, with most of the inhabitants fleeing back to the town hospital or making a run for it across the fields to the west. Of those who fell into Yugoslav hands, the women and children were usually separated from the men – many of the latter simply disappeared.

The worst atrocities took place after Yugoslav forces reached the **hospital**, which they proceeded to evacuate before the agreed arrival of Red Cross supervisors. Those captured here were bundled into trucks and driven away to be murdered, finishing up in a mass grave near the village of Ovčara, 7km southeast. About 2000 Croatian soldiers and civilians died in the defence of Vukovar; a further 2000 are still missing, although the recovery of bodies from mass graves is going on all the time. Much of the centre was turned into an uninhabitable shell, although life is gradually returning as rebuilding progresses.

In **January 1998** the town was returned to Croatia as part of the Erdut Accord, though Croats driven from Vukovar seven years earlier have been slow to return, either because their homes are still in ruins or because the local economy isn't yet strong enough to provide sufficient jobs. In 1999 there were about 12,000 Serbs and 4000 Croats – about one-third of the original population – living in the shell of a town.

The Town

Vukovar's bus station lies on the fringes of the twentieth-century town, opposite the main market. Walk through the market and turn left onto the town's main street, Moše Pijade (it's possible that this street – named after a communist ideologue – may be rechristened in the near future), to reach the **Eltz Palace** (Dvorac Eltz), an imposing aristocratic seat built for a local landowning family in the early 1700s. Badly damaged but still standing, the palace is home to the **Town Museum** (Gradski muzej; Mon–Sat 8am–4pm; 5Kn), which, although lacking a permanent display, organizes changing art exhibitions in fine, barrel-vaulted rooms.

Moše Pijade leads in the opposite direction towards the old town proper, crossing the River Vuka (which flows into the Danube a couple of hundred metres downstream) on the way. The first of the once impressive civic buildings you come across on the opposite bank is the bombed-out shell of the **Radnički Dom** ("House of the Workers"), where the Yugoslav Socialist Party met to transform itself into the Yugoslav Communist Party in June 1920, only to be banned by the government five months later. Beyond lies the town's main street, lined with late Baroque buildings with arcaded lower storeys – some of which have already been tastefully restored. On high ground to the southeast stand the remains of the eighteenth-century **Franciscan monastery** (Franjevački samostan), which once dominated the skyline and is now being painstakingly reconstructed. Beyond the monastery, the ice-cream cone shape of Vukovar's **water tower** thrusts skywards, preserved in its present shell-damaged form to serve as a symbol of the town.

Practicalities

Located near the heart of old Vukovar at the confluence of the Danube and the Vuka, the modern *Dunav* **hotel** (☎032/441-285 or 441-768, fax 441-762; ③) has neat, functional en-suite rooms, many with views towards the rivers. There are few **eating** and **drinking** opportunities aside from the hotel's own café and restaurant, the *Vukovarski povratnik* restaurant in the pockmarked office block opposite the bus station, and a few more basic places offering grills around the market.

Dunav Tours, behind the market at Moše Pijade 15 (Mon–Sat 8.30am–3pm; ☎032/441-790), may help with information, although their *raison d'être* is organizing **tours** of Vukovar for those eager to know more about the siege – they can arrange English-speaking guides if you give them a few days' notice.

Vukovar to Ilok

The main road east out of Vukovar runs parallel to the Danube, ploughing between vineyards and sunflower fields until, after about 25km, the western spur of the **Fruška Gora** hills emerges to break the monotony of the Slavonian plain. Squeezed between the hills and the riverbank, **ŠARENGRAD** is a former fishing village full of little old houses – most of them war-damaged. Six kilometres inland from Šarengrad at the end of a minor road (Vukovar–Ilok buses sometimes make the detour here), **BAPSKA** is another photogenic little place full of indigenous architecture, although heavily scarred by artillery damage and subsequent pillaging. Thirty-five kilometres out of Vukovar, **ILOK** is the last town on the Croatian stretch of the Danube, a grey, half-forgotten place built around an old Turkish fortress which stands on a bluff overlooking the river. Thanks to the vineyards carpeting the slopes of the nearby Fruška Gora, Ilok produces some excellent **wines**, although the industry was disrupted by the Serbian occupation, and harvests didn't resume until autumn 1999.

West from Zagreb: Samobor

Nestling beneath the eastern spur of the wooded Samoborske gorje (Samobor Hills) around 25km west of the Zagreb, provincial **SAMOBOR** rivalled the capital as a trade and craft centre in the Middle Ages, though it's nowadays very much a satellite of its big neighbour, attracting a smattering of day-trippers keen to explore the woods above the town or sample the local delicacy, the *samoborska kremšnita* – a wobbly mass of vanilla custard squeezed between layers of flaky pastry.

The best time to be in Samobor is immediately preceding Lent, during the **Samobor carnival** (Samoborski fašnik), one of Croatia's best-known and most authentic festivals. On the weekend before Shrove Tuesday there are parades with floats, while hedonistic locals run around town in masks creating an impromptu party atmosphere, followed by a firework display on Shrove Tuesday itself.

The Town

The town centre revolves around the long, extended triangle of **Trg kralja Tomislava**, beside which flows the Gradna – here more of an swollen brook than a river – spanned by a succession of slender bridges. Standing at the square's western end is the **Town Museum** (Gradski muzej; Tues–Fri 9am–3pm, Sat & Sun 9am–1pm; 8Kn), housed in Livadićev dvor, the nineteenth-century home of composer Ferdinand Weisner, whose enthusiasm for the liberation of the Slavs from the Habsburg yoke led him to change his name to its Slavic form, Ferdo Livadić. An important meeting place for the leaders of the Illyrian movement in the 1830s and 1840s, his home now contains a modest collection of furniture, ceramics, and fusty portraits of local burghers. More interesting is the ethnographical section in an adjacent outbuilding, where a smattering of English-language texts help to tease meaning out of the rough wooden agricultural implements on display.

From the southern side of the square, Svete Ane climbs up past the parish church and town graveyard towards **Anindol**, a wooded hillside criss-crossed by paths. After about ten minutes tracks lead off to the right towards the forest-bound chapel of St Anne (Crkvica svete Ana), from where you can choose between a steep route uphill to the chapel of St George (Crkvica sveti Jure) or a lateral path to Samobor's medieval **castle** (stari grad). Both chapels are closed except for special masses, and the castle is no more than an overgrown ruin, but the tranquillity of the surrounding woods makes a walk here worthwhile. It was on Anindol that Tito organized the founding congress of the Croatian Communist Party on August 1, 1937, in an attempt to persuade the Croats that Yugoslav communists shared their nationalist aspirations. An annual hiking festival was used as a cover: with the whole area filling up with weekend visitors, party activists could infiltrate without arousing suspicion. Only sixteen communist agents actually made it to the "congress", and Tito was reduced to scratching the resolutions of the meeting on the back of a calendar with a penknife – or so the story goes.

Practicalities

Samobor's **bus station**, five minutes' walk north of the main square, is served by buses, run by Samoborček (every 20–30min; hourly on Sun), from Zagreb's main bus station and the Černomerec tram terminal (at the end of tram lines #2, #6 and #11). The town's one **hotel**, the *Livadić*, Trg kralja Tomislava 1 (☎01/33-65-850; ⑥), is a friendly, family-run and rather plush affair, with spacious rooms furnished in nineteenth-century style offering all creature comforts. Three kilometres out of town to the northwest on the Lipovec road, *Samoborski slapovi*, Hamor 16 (☎01/33-84-059 or 33-84-061, fax 33-84-062; ④), has small, neat en-suite rooms with TV, but the real attraction is the location in a narrow wooded valley.

For **food and drink**, both the *Samoborska Pivnica*, just off the main square at Šmidhenova 3, and *Pri Staroj Vuri*, uphill southeast from the square at Giznik 2, have cheap staples like *štrukli*, as well as the full range of grilled and roasted

---

HIKING IN THE SAMOBOR HILLS

Samobor is a convenient staging post en route to the **Samobor Hills** (Samoborsko gorje), a ravine-scarred upland region which rises suddenly to the east of town, and backs directly onto the hills of the Žumberak (see p.118). An area of deep forest interspersed with sub-alpine meadows, it's perfect for gentle uphill hikes, and is correspondingly busy with local families on summer weekends. The best base for walks is **Šoićeva kuća**, a timbered cottage serving refreshments at the western end of the village of **Veliki Lipovec**, which is 9km west of Samobor along the road which passes the *Samoborski slapovi* hotel and restaurant. There's no public transport.

The most popular walk from Šoićeva kuća is the 1hr 40min ascent of wooded **Japetić**, the Samoborsko gorje's highest point. Two hundred metres southwest of Šoićeva kuća a road ascends steeply to the right, leading past cottages until asphalt gives way first to gravel track, then to footpath. After a steady climb through the woods you reach a plateau, where fairly obvious signs direct you either to Japetić's 879-metre summit, or to the Japetić mountain hut (weekends only) just to the south, which serves excellent *grah* and has good views of the Kupa valley to the southwest, with the forest-enclosed lakes of Crna Mlaka over to the left.

An alternative hike from Šoićeva kuća leads to the 607-metre peak of **Oštrc**, ninety minutes' walk to the south. Directly opposite Šoićeva kuća a marked path heads uphill into the woods, passing through the ruins of medieval Lipovec castle, continuing along a steep up-and-down path through the woods before eventually emerging onto the Preseka ridge, which runs above lush pastures. At the northeastern edge of the ridge lies Oštrc mountain hut (weekends only), which again serves good *grah* and simple cuts of meat. From here it's only 20min to the 752-metre peak of Oštrc itself, and more fine views. From Oštrc you can either return to Šoićeva kuća the way you came, or follow a marked path to Japetić via a wooded saddle known as Velika vrata (the Oštrc–Japetić leg takes 90min), although the ascent of Japetić from Velika vrata is much steeper than the direct route from Šoićeva kuća.

meats. Slightly out of town, the restaurant of the *Samoborski slapovi* is more upmarket, with excellent fish (from their own fishpond) plus an ample selection of north-Croatian dishes. The cafés on the main square are the best places to linger over coffee and cakes (*U Prolazu* is said to offer the best *samoborske kremš-nite*), while the narrow streets leading east from the square are well supplied with bars overlooking the River Gradna.

South from Zagreb to Karlovac

Croatia's busiest motorway zooms southwest from Zagreb towards the port city of Rijeka (see p.158), gateway to the northern Adriatic coast. Thirty kilometres southwest of Zagreb the road brushes the northern fringes of the **Crna Mlaka** ("Black Marsh"), an area of forested wetland rich in birdlife, notably the blue-grey heron and the elusive black stork – which, unlike the more common white variety, is extremely sensitive to human disruption and only nests in the security of isolated forests. Visitors hoping to see these creatures usually head for the vast **fish farm** in the centre of the Mlaka, a series of ponds built at the end of the nineteenth century by Austro-Hungarian developers, who also constructed a (now sadly disused) narrow-gauge railway and a (now derelict) country house known as Ribograd, or "Fishville". Unfortunately, there are few clear walking itineraries; it's best to follow the gravelly tracks which lead round the fishponds to enjoy a taste of this calm, reed-shrouded environment. There's a plainly decorated but excellent **restaurant** inside the fish farm, the *Konoba Črna Mlaka*, which serves local *šaran* (carp), *som* (catfish) and chewy, deep-fried *žablji kraci* (frogs' legs) at very reasonable prices.

Unless you're staying in Donja Zdenčina (see below), you really need your own transport to reach Crna Mlaka. Turn off the motorway at the Jastrebarsko exit and follow the road which heads left about 100m beyond the toll booths. This soon degenerates into gravel track; turn left at the sign for "IHOR Crna Mlaka". The only **accommodation** in the area is 6km east of Crna Mlaka in **DONJA ZDENČINA**, a village popular with nesting white storks, where *Seljački Turizam Šimanović*, Karla Vodopića 7 (☎01/628-8102 or 628-9096; ②; full board available by prior arrangement), offers bed-and-breakfast in a modern house with simple but comfortable rooms, some decorated with embroidered textiles made on the family loom – the owner will provide a quick weaving display if you're interested. The only drawback is that you can't actually drive from Donja Zdenčina to Crna Mlaka without taking a long roundabout route via Jastrebarsko, although you can walk there directly along forest tracks. Donja Zdenčina is easily reached using the Zagreb–Karlovac commuter trains, although drivers will find it less straightforward: despite being close to the motorway, it's not served by an exit, so you'll have to stick to the old Zagreb–Jastrebarsko–Karlovac road (stara Karlovačka cesta) and take the southbound turning to Pisarovina.

Donja Kupčina

The villages around Crna Mlaka still preserve a smattering of tumbledown wooden farmhouses, although the best examples are preserved at the village of **DONJA KUPČINA**, 15km southwest of Donja Zdenčina (head south to Jamnica, then west to Karlovac; there's no public transport to the village), in a small open-air **Folk Museum** (Zavičajni muzej; daily 9am–4pm; if the curator isn't around ask in the nearby café or ring ☎01/62-92-111). The museum has a lovely, unsanitized feel, featuring an ensemble of nineteenth-century oak farm buildings clustered around two houses in an overgrown glade. One of the houses contains implements once used in linen manufacture, a labour-intensive process in which the locally harvested flax was laboriously soaked, beaten and combed in order to produce fibres fine enough for weaving. Upstairs is a display of the garments produced, including the extravagantly embroidered dresses worn at wedding feasts – of which there were always two, one for each side of the family: the guests of bride and groom never mixed. A hundred years ago it wasn't unusual for girls in this part of Croatia to marry at the age of 12, although they slept in their mother-in-law's bed for the first few years of matrimony. The strangest exhibit in the museum is the system of winches used to raise village houses above the ground so that they could be moved on rollers to a new site – at times reaching speeds of 1km per day.

Karlovac

Less than an hour from Zagreb, **KARLOVAC** hides its provincial charms behind a screen of high-rise suburbs and light industry. The centre, however, is a minor delight: a compact grid of crumbling old houses which still preserves the street plan bequeathed to it by Habsburg planners. Initially a purely military settlement, Karlovac was built from scratch in 1579 in order to strengthen Austria's southern defences against Ottoman encroachment. It was deliberately sited between two rivers (the Kupa and the Korana) which had slightly different water levels, therefore providing a constant flow of water for the town's moat. Initially commanded by Archduke Karl of Styria – and named Karlstadt (hence the name, Karlovac) in his honour – Karlovac gradually lost its strategic importance as Habsburg forces drove the Ottomans southwards in the late 1600s, and life within the fortress walls began to develop a civilian character. The town walls were demolished in the nineteenth century, but their shape – that of a six-pointed star – is still discernible in the earthworks and moats (now drained and transformed into parks) which surround the centre.

Karlovac is an easy day-trip from Zagreb, and onward connections to Rijeka, Zadar and Split are plentiful – which is a good job seeing as there's currently no reliable source of accommodation in town. A good time to be in Karlovac is for the **St John's Day Bonfire** (Ivanjski krijes) on June 23, when the inhabitants of two riverside suburbs, Gaza and Banija, stage competing bonfire-and-firework displays on either side of the Kupa.

The Town

A good way to start exploring the town is simply to follow the course of the old fortifications, nowadays marked by an almost unbroken line of tree-lined promenades surrounding the centre. Within lies a fine ensemble of eighteenth- and nineteenth-century town houses, although damage sustained in 1991 (when the front line was only about 5km away) is still painfully visible. The main square, Trg bana Jelačića, looks particularly shell-scarred and empty, although it's worth calling in at the **Holy Trinity Church** (Crkva presvetog Trojstva) on the corner, which has an unusually low barrel-vaulted ceiling decked out with bright Baroque frescoes. A block north of here on Strossmayerov trg, a small **Town Museum** (Gradski muzej; Tues–Fri 8am–3pm, Sat & Sun 10am–noon), set in the

Baroque-style Frankopan winter palace, features scale models of old Karlovac and traditional costumes from the surrounding area. Local patriots will steer you towards the room devoted to the Karlovac-born nineteenth-century artist Vjekoslav Karas, who studied in Rome, joined the Nazarenes (a German movement roughly analogous to the British Pre-Raphaelites), and returned home to paint portraits of local worthies. Karas is as well known for his suicidal melancholy as for his paintings: he ended up drowning himself on account of an unrequited passion for local woman Irena Türk.

The main out-of-town attraction is the medieval stronghold of **Dubovac**, reached by following the banks of the Kupa to the north from central Karlovac before heading uphill to the left – a walk of about thirty minutes. Once held by the Frankopans, feudal lords of the island of Krk (see p.179) who extended their power to the Croatian mainland, it's a compact but well-preserved structure (now occupied by the *Stari Grad* restaurant) surrounding a triangular courtyard overlooked by three tiers of galleries. The grassy terrace outside affords an excellent view of Karlovac stretched out on the plain below.

Practicalities

Karlovac's **bus station** is about 500m southwest of the centre on Prilaz Vece Holjevca, the main north–south route through the town; the **train station** is about 1500m north of the centre along the same road. Tomislavova, next to the bus station, presents the most direct route into town, crossing the line of the former moat before arriving at the central square. There's a left-luggage office (*garderoba*; daily 6am–8pm) in the bus station if you're just passing through, and a helpful, if erratically open, **tourist office** (usually Mon–Fri 8am–3pm; ☎047/225-739) just west of the centre at Perivoj slobode 10.

Snack **food** is plentiful around the bus station, and *Bastion*, in the centre at Stjepana Radića 27, offers reasonable pizzas, filling sandwiches and excellent sweet and savoury pancakes. For a serious sit-down meal, try the *Stari Grad* restaurant in Dubovac castle. A generous sprinkling of central cafés caters for both daytime and night-time drinkers: *Star-F*, Mažuranićeva 6, is a relaxed place with pool tables and rock memorabilia on the walls; while *Drmeš*, Šebetićeva 3, is a brasher, altogether more raucous place extravagantly decked out in pub bric-a-brac. Regular gigs are organized by *SKUC Braće Radić*, a rough-and-ready student club on the eastern fringes of the centre on Ivan Kukuljevića.

The Žumberak

North of Karlovac, the **Žumberak** is an area of steep, vineyard-clad hills and wooded vales punctuated by small plots of pasture and corn. The region's main appeal lies in its scenery – rather like a wilder version of the Zagorje, with denser forests, faster-flowing rivers, and a higher degree of rural depopulation. Primarily given over to ageing smallholders and weekending cityfolk, the area's scattered **villages** – some of them so isolated that they're only connected to the outside world by gravel track – boast a high proportion of rickety half-timbered houses and open-sided wooden barns full of drying hay. Much of the local population is made up of so-called **Greek Catholics** (*Grkokatolici*), Orthodox Slavs who migrated to the area in the sixteenth and seventeenth centuries in the wake of Ottoman advances and were offered lands and security by the Habsburg court in return for accepting the primacy of the pope.

The main **road** into the Žumberak from Karlovac passes through the villages of **Ozalj** and **Krašić**, before working its way round the massif, close to the Slovenian border, and joining up with the other principal road into the region at Bregana, just north of Samobor. There's little **public transport** into the Žumberak proper, although Ozalj and Krašić are reachable from Karlovac by train and bus respectively. Beyond here you really need a car, and it's a delightful and rewarding region to drive through if you have a decent road map and a reasonable dose of patience – the Žumberak's minor roads provide excellent opportunities for getting lost. **Accommodation** is thin on the ground, although well worth seeking out if you're looking for a rural break: *Seoski turizam Medven* (p.120) and *Eko-selo Žumberak* (p.120) are the only current possibilities.

Ozalj

Straddling the River Kupa some 16km north of Karlovac, **OZALJ** is a small rural spot located at the point where the green limbs of the Žumberak descend to meet the plain below. Just west of the village centre, **Ozalj Castle** (Stari grad) is a Colditz-like lump of crumbling grey stone featuring temporary history exhibitions in its **museum** (Mon–Sat 7am–3pm; 10Kn). Returning to the centre of Ozalj, the main road to Krašić heads east over the Kupa, providing a fine view of the weirside **Munjara** (the "lightning factory"), a hydro-electric power station built in 1908, a charming Gothic-romantic folly whose crenellated turrets seem to echo the architecture of the castle above. Ten minutes' walk out of town to the east along the road to the village of Trg, the **Ozalj Ethno-Village** (Etno selo) comprises a couple of thatched farmsteads. You can wander freely around the small complex, although the simple peasant interiors are only sporadically open – ask at the museum in the castle.

Krašić

Ten kilometres northeast of Ozalj, the equally rustic village of **KRAŠIĆ** is fast emerging as one of Croatia's most important pilgrimage centres thanks to its status as the birthplace of **Alojzije Stepinac** (see box on p.60), archbishop of Zagreb during World War II. After being imprisoned by the communists on trumped-up charges of collaboration, Stepinac lived out the last years of his life under house arrest in Krašić, where he was cared for by a pair of nuns and accompanied by a pet sheep – a gift from a kindly local that Stepinac couldn't bear to have slaughtered. Stepinac's two-room apartment, located in the parish priest's home just behind the village church, is now preserved as a **Memorial Museum** (Spomenmuzej; open Mon–Sat whenever the priest is around; donation requested), although the ascetic Stepinac was not a great hoarder of personal effects – bedstead, writing table and church vestments being about all he left behind. The squat ochre **church** in which the ailing priest said mass was largely rebuilt in neo-Gothic style in 1913 by an architect who obviously had Jugendstil tastes – note the caryatids which peer down from the exterior walls. There's not much to see inside save for a side chapel which preserves some original chunks of medieval masonry.

There are a couple of **cafés** on the main square in front of the church, but no accommodation.

North into the Žumberak

Beyond Krašić, the road heads through a series of villages sunk deep in wooded valleys. First up is **PRIBIĆ**, an important centre of Greek Catholic culture where the splendid neo-Byzantine **Church of the Annunciation** (Crkva svetog Blagovijesta) rises up from a reedy islet at the entrance to the village. The interior is half derelict and rarely accessible, but the exterior presents a fine blend of Orthodox church architecture and Jugendstil, with fanciful eagles and gargoyles emerging from its domes.

Smothered in forest just beyond Medvenova Draga, the village of **ČUNKOVA DRAGA** is the site of the only reliable source of **accommodation** in this part of the Žumberak, *Seoski turizam Medven* (☎01/62-70-665; ③), two self-catering apartments in a converted farmhouse, idyllically situated beside an old watermill.

Ten kilometres further on, a left turn after the village of Kostanjevac leads past wooden barns and ancient, tumbledown houses to the village of **SOŠICE**, grouped around two churches standing side by side, one Catholic and one Greek Catholic – the latter is the one with the taller, rocket-like belfry. Just downhill from the churches is a small **Ethnographic Museum** (Etnografski muzej; Mon–Sat 9am–5pm; donation requested) run by local nuns, who preside over a smartly arranged collection of farm implements, antiquated looms and traditional costumes. Of the female attire on display, the rich red-and-blue-striped aprons of the local Greek Catholics contrast sharply with the simpler whites of their Catholic neighbours, demonstrating how the two communities preserved separate traditions despite centuries of coexistence.

Back on the main northbound route, the road forges an ever more lonely path through thickening forest, wheeling eastwards towards Bregana along the Croatian–Slovene frontier. Twelve kilometres before Bregana a right turn – which rapidly deteriorates into a gravel track – leads deep up a narrowing side valley, arriving after 8km at the region's most popular weekend destination, **Eko-selo Žumberak** (Žumberak Eco-Village), a bizarre cross between a Wild West homestead and a nineteenth-century Croatian village complete with riding stables, a "cowboy saloon" and an excellent **restaurant**. The Eko-selo also offers **rooms** (☎01/33-87-471; ②), some in traditional wooden houses built from recycled timbers taken from collapsing buildings throughout the region.

Returning to the Bregana route, you'll soon pass the popular recreation spot of *Divlje Vode*, a fish farm overlooked by a café-restaurant where you can eat local trout (*pastrva*) and frogs' legs (*žablji kraci*) on a shady terrace. From here it's a further 10km to Bregana and the main route south to Samobor and Zagreb.

West of Karlovac: the Gorski kotar

Road and rail routes from Karlovac to Rijeka follow an increasingly scenic route through the hills and mountains of the **Gorski kotar** (literally "wooded district") – a spectacular landscape of green river valleys and forested hillsides. It's a surprisingly untouristed area with a dearth of accommodation, although there's a nascent winter sports scene at the region's main holiday centre, **Bjelolasica**, and numerous summer hiking opportunities. The Karlovac–Rijeka road forges straight through the northern Gorski kotar, bypassing its main attractions, although the rail line initially breaks away southwards to pass through **Ogulin**, a gateway to the Bjelolasica region and a useful base from which to tackle one of the area's landmark peaks, **Klek**.

From mid-June to late September, a special **train**, the *Karlek*, runs from Zagreb to Ogulin on Saturday and Sunday mornings, returning the same evening. At Ogulin, connecting buses take *Karlek* passengers to Bjelolasica, Klek and other local beauty spots. It's possible to get to Ogulin using normal train services, but buses won't be laid on once you get there. From Ogulin there are three or four buses daily to the village of Bijelsko (see below), which is the most convenient jumping-off point for Klek.

Ogulin and around

Fifty-five kilometres southwest of Karlovac, **OGULIN** is an untidy small town built around a **castle** founded by the Frankopans in around 1500, and subsequently used as a prison. The structure still boasts an impressively turreted pair of towers, but the **museum** within (Mon–Fri 8am–2pm, Sat 9am–noon; 10Kn) is disappointing, with displays on the history of hiking in the region and a rather bare memorial cell where Josip Broz Tito was interned in 1932. Opposite the castle, a small viewing platform overlooks a canyon where the River Dobra flows into an underground passage, re-emerging several kilometres to the east before joining the River Kupa near Karlovac.

Ogulin's **train station** is ten minutes' walk from the centre (turn right outside the station and follow the main road). A new **bus station** is being built opposite the train station; in the meantime, buses stop outside the castle. The **tourist office** on the main street at B. Frankopana 2 (Mon–Fri 8am–3pm; ☎ & fax 047/525-216) can help with local hiking information and may have maps for sale. There are a few **cafés** along the main street, but no decent places to eat unless you count the *Sabljaci* restaurant, on the eastern shores of Lake Sabljak, a five-kilometre drive south of town. The nearest accommodation is in Bjelolasica.

Klek

Seven kilometres due west of Ogulin, the 1184-metre **Klek** is not the highest of the Gorski kotar mountains, but is undoubtedly one of the most dramatic. Its summit – a tall rocky cylinder rising out of a forested ridge – dominates the local landscape for miles around and, somewhat appropriately, is said to be the place where local witches and demons meet on the eve of May 1. Klek has been one of inland Croatia's most important targets for hikers ever since 1838, when the future governor of Croatia, Josip Jelačić, scaled it in the company of King Friedrich August II of Saxony, adding a dash of aristocratic glamour to a pastime then in its infancy.

You can walk to Klek and back from Ogulin by following the Bjelolasica road west of town, although it's easier to drive as far as the village of Bijelsko, 8km west of Ogulin, thereby cutting a good ninety minutes off your journey. Entering the village you'll see a house on your right with the legend "Klek: 1hr" helpfully painted on the wall. From here a well-marked trail ascends steadily through the woods, arriving at the Klek mountain hut (drinks and snacks available at weekends) after about 45 minutes. The path then coils its way round the stone barrel of Klek's upper reaches towards the summit, about another 25 minutes, although there are a couple of steep, rope-assisted sections on the way up which may deter those who lack a good head for heights. The views from Klek's broad, flat top are magnificent, although take care – there are sheer drops on almost all sides.

Bjelolasica

Seventeen kilometres beyond Bijelsko, a right turn in the village of Jasenjak leads up a narrow wooded valley to the **Bjelolasica Olympic Centre** (Olimpijski centar Bjelolasica; ☎01/61-77-707, fax 6177-708; ③) some 5km beyond. Laid out on meadows below steep, pine-covered slopes, this is a year-round tourist resort made up of several chalet-style accommodation blocks set beside a central administration and café-restaurant pavilion. As the name suggests, it's also a training camp for serious sportspeople, with numerous professional teams making use of its athletics track and indoor sports halls. Bjelolasica is Croatia's only real skiing resort, although the season is unpredictable and short (Dec–Feb, snowfalls allowing), so most winter sports fans tend to arrange *ad hoc* weekend breaks here rather than book skiing holidays in advance. Chairlifts run up the flanks of **Mount Bjelolasica**, immediately west of the resort, where there are slopes for beginners and intermediates, plus a single, 500-metre run for advanced skiers. Ski rental can also be arranged. In spring and summer Bjelolasica is a good base for medium-to-strenuous hiking, with the primary targets being the 1531-metre peak of Bjelolasica itself (3–4hr each way), or the 1335-metre **Bijele stijene**, which crowns the next ridge to the west (3–4hr each way). Basic hiking maps can be picked up at the centre.

Delnice and Risnjak National Park

Twenty kilometres northeast of Ogulin the rail line rejoins the main Karlovac–Rijeka road route near the village of Vrbovsko, after which both continue to wind their way westward through craggy, densely forested hills. Most Rijeka-bound buses and trains stop at **DELNICE**, a rather featureless town about 60km past Karlovac, from where a minor road (served by two daily buses) runs 10km northwest to the village of **CRNI LUG**, the starting point for explorations of the **Risnjak National Park** (Narodni park Risnjak), which covers a mountain group centred on the 1528-metre Veliki Risnjak.

   Food and **accommodation** are available in Crni Lug's *Nacionalni park Risnjak* motel (☎051/836-133; ③), where you can pick up hiking maps and advice before setting out for the park entrance 1km west of the village. There's a range of walking possibilities: allow about three hours each way for an assault on Veliki Risnjak itself. West of Delnice, it's not long before the green, wooded scenery changes, and you're descending through an increasingly barren karst landscape to Rijeka and the coast.

South of Karlovac: the Plitvice Lakes

Beyond Karlovac the main road to the Dalmatian coast forges due south across the upland pastures of the **Kordun** and **Lika** regions, passing through a series of villages which are slowly returning to normality after wartime occupation by the Serbs. Perched on a hilltop 35km south of Karlovac, the small town of **SLUNJ** is unremarkable save for the confluence of the Korana and Slunjčica rivers just below, with the rushing waters of the latter dropping into the Korana gorge through a series of small waterfalls and burbling rapids. In times past this natural power source led to the development of a riverside watermilling settlement known as **Rastoke**. Several traditional millers' buildings still survive: solid structures with stone lower floors and timber upper storeys. War damage has lessened

Rastoke's picturesque appeal, but it's still a delightful area for a stroll, with excellent views of the gorge from the path above the north bank of the Korana. It's all relatively easy to find: you'll glimpse Rastoke down to the right when entering the town by road from the north; buses stop 800m further uphill on Slunj's main square.

There's no other reason to hang around in Slunj, but the helpful **tourist office** just down from the square at Zagrebačka 12 (unpredictable hours, but usually Mon–Fri 8am–3pm; ☎47/777-630) can point you in the direction of private **rooms** (①) in outlying villages. There's also a functional **hotel**, the *Park* (☎047/777-524; ②), on the square, alongside a couple of cafés.

The Plitvice Lakes

Forty kilometres south of Slunj, the **PLITVICE LAKES** (Plitvička jezera) are one of the country's biggest tourist attractions, and with some justification. The eight-kilometre string of sixteen lakes, hemmed in by densely forested hills, presents some of the most eye-catching scenery in mainland Croatia, with water rushing down from the upper lakes via a sequence of waterfalls and cataracts. The lakes – a bewitching turquoise when seen from a distance – teem with fish and watersnakes, while herons frequent the shores of the quieter, northern part of the system.

Despite being occupied by Serb forces during 1991–95, the national park is still remarkably well organized: paths are easy to follow, regular shuttle buses and boats ferry visitors to major trail heads, and English-speaking staff are on hand with advice at the park's two major entry points. All this ensures that you can see a great deal in a short space of time, although keen walkers could easily spend a day or two exploring the whole area.

Around the lakes

The park (daily: summer 8am–7pm; winter dawn–dusk; 60Kn) can be entered from two points on the main Zagreb–Split road: Entrance 1 (Ulaz jedan), at the northern (lower) end of the lake system, and Entrance 2 (Ulaz dva), 2.5km further south. Both serve as convenient gateways to a range of walks.

Entrance 1, situated at the point where the lake waters flow off into the Korana gorge, is ten minutes' walk away from **Veliki slap** (literally "the big waterfall"), a high wall of water that is the park's single most dramatic feature. Paths lead to the foot of the waterfall, passing alongside the top of the smaller **Sastavci** fall, which empties into the cliff-lined Korana gorge. From Veliki Slap you can proceed south on foot towards the lower group of cataracts, where wooden walkways traverse the foaming waters. Beyond lies **Kozjak**, the largest of Plitvice's lakes. By sticking to the western side of Kozjak you'll eventually emerge at the northern terminus of the shuttle ferry service, which will take you south towards Entrance 2. Otherwise you can walk to Entrance 2 along the eastern bank of Kozjak, or take the bus from the road just above.

Entrance 2 is the best jumping-off point for the biggest group of cataracts, where waters from the highest of the Plitvice lakes, **Prošćansko**, tumble down into a succession of smaller pools and tarns before reaching Kozjak lower down. Exploring this part of the system can easily absorb at least half a day; to save time, you can take the shuttle bus to the southernmost stop (Labudovac) and take a stroll around the upper cataracts from there.

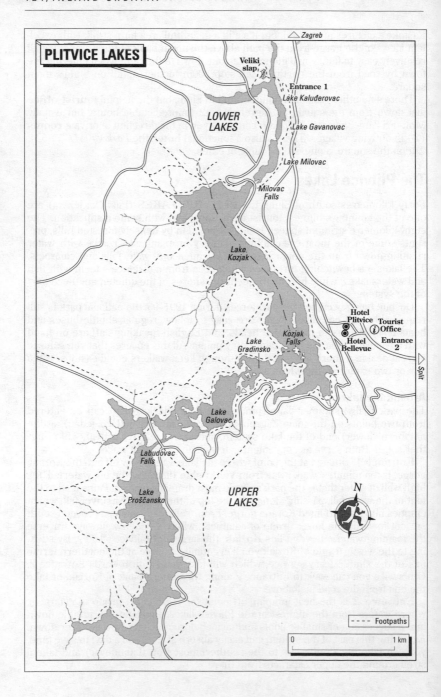

PLITVICE LAKES

△ Zagreb

Veliki slap

Entrance 1
Lake Kaluđerovac

LOWER LAKES

Lake Gavanovac

Lake Milovac

Milovac Falls

Lake Kozjak

Hotel Plitvice
Tourist Office
Hotel Bellevue
Entrance 2

Kozjak Falls

Lake Gradinsko

Lake Galovac

Labudovac Falls

Lake Proščansko

UPPER LAKES

△ Split

N

---- Footpaths

0   1 km

Practicalities

Getting to Plitvice is straightforward: most buses from Zagreb to Split and Zadar pass along the main road which fringes the park to the east, dropping passengers off at both entrances. **Moving on** can be a tricky business on summer weekends, however: buses are often full and won't pick up more passengers – in which case you'll just have to wait for the next service.

There are small **information offices** at both entrances (July & Aug 8am–8pm; April–June & Sept 9am–5pm), offering a wealth of advice but short on printed info and maps of the park. In July and August there's a kiosk at Entrance 2 offering private **rooms** (②), although most of these are in villages some way from the park and will only suit those with their own transport (at other times of the year the two information offices can give you details of available rooms, but won't make bookings for you). Both of the park's **hotels** are at Entrance 2: the *Bellevue* (☎053/751-015, fax 751-013; ④), which offers standard en-suite rooms; and the *Plitvice* (same phone number; ⑤), which has slightly plusher rooms with TV and minibar. The closest **campsite** is the *Korana*, on the main road about 7km north of Entrance 1, a large and well-organized site with bungalows (①), restaurant and supermarket, although it's too far away from the park to serve as a useful base unless you have a car.

There's a **supermarket** opposite Entrance 2, and **snack bars** offering a range of drinks and basic food at both entrances. For more substantial fare, the hotel **restaurants** at Entrance 2 are a bit bland, and it's best to head for the *Lička kuća* restaurant opposite Entrance 1, a large, touristy place decked out with folksy wooden fittings and serving traditional Lika food such as spicy sausages, *đuved* (a paprika-flavoured ratatouille with rice) and roast lamb. Look out for local women selling home-made cheese (the mild yellow *škripavac*) along the roadside. It's usually sold in large circular pieces weighing over a kilo, but you can ask for a half (*polovina*) or quarter (*četvrtina*) if you don't think you can manage a whole one.

travel details

BUSES

Đakovo to: Osijek (12 daily; 45min); Slavonski Brod (12 daily; 1hr 15min); Vinkovci (5 daily; 45min).

Karlovac to: Krašić (6 daily; 35min); Ozalj (2 daily; 25min); Plitvice (hourly; 1hr 40min); Rijecka (20 daily; 2–3hr); Split (4 daily; 8hr); Zadar (4 daily; 4hr); Zagreb (every 30min; 50min).

Koprivnica to: Hlebine (Mon–Fri 6 daily; 30min); Varaždin (12 daily; 45min).

Osijek to: Bilje/Kopački Rit (hourly; 10min); Đakovo (12 daily; 45min); Ilok (8 daily; 1hr 45min); Slavonski Brod (12 daily; 2hr); Vukovar (10 daily; 45min); Zagreb (6 daily; 5hr 30min).

Slavonski Brod to: Đakovo (12 daily; 1hr 15min); Osijek (12 daily; 2hr); Požega (5 daily; 45min); Vukovar (3 daily; 2hr); Zagreb (12 daily; 3hr).

Varaždin to: Čakovec (hourly; 30min); Koprivnica (12 daily; 45min); Trakošćan (6 daily; 50min); Zagreb (12 daily; 2hr).

Vinkovci to: Đakovo (5 daily; 45min); Ilok (5 daily; 1hr 50min); Vukovar (12 daily; 50min).

Vukovar to: Ilok (12 daily; 45min); Osijek (10 daily; 45min); Slavonski Brod (3 daily; 2hr); Vinkovci (12 daily; 50min).

Zagreb to: Čakovec (10 daily; 2hr 30min); Desinić (6 daily; 2hr); Karlovac (every 30min; 50min); Krapina (8 daily; 1hr 10min); Krapinske Toplice (12 daily; 1hr 20min); Marija Bistrica (6 daily; 1hr 15min); Osijek (6 daily; 5hr 30min); Plitvice (hourly; 2hr 30min); Požega (5 daily; 3hr); Samobor (Mon–Sat every 20–30min, Sun hourly; 40min); Sisak (hourly; 1hr 30min); Slavonski Brod (12 daily; 3hr); Varaždin (12 daily; 2hr).

TRAINS

Karlovac to: Ogulin (6 daily; 1hr); Ozalj (6 daily; 20min); Rijeka (6 daily; 3hr 20min); Split (2 daily; 7hr); Zagreb (hourly; 40min).

Savski Marof to: Kumrovec (6 daily; 55min).

Slavonski Brod to: Zagreb (8 daily; 2–3hr).

Zabok to: Gornja Stubica (8 daily; 30min); Krapina (9 daily; 25min); Stubičke Toplice (8 daily; 20min); Zagreb (14 daily; 1hr).

Zagreb to: Čakovec (6 daily; 2hr 30min–3hr); Karlovac (hourly; 40min); Koprivnica (8 daily; 1hr 30min); Ogulin (6 daily; 1hr 40min); Osijek (4 daily;

5hr); Savski Marof (20 daily; 35min); to Sisak (hourly; 1hr); Slavonski Brod (8 daily; 2–3hr); Varaždin (9 daily; 2hr–2hr 30min); Zabok (14 daily; 1hr).

INTERNATIONAL BUSES

Čakovec to: Nagykanizsa (3 daily; 2hr).

Osijek to: Mohács (1 daily; 2hr 30min); Pécs (3 daily; 3hr).

Slavonski Brod to: Tuzla (5 daily; 5hr).

Varaždin to: Maribor (4 daily; 1hr); Nagykanizsa (3 daily; 2hr 30min).

CHAPTER THREE

ISTRIA

A large, triangular peninsula pointing down into the northern Adriatic, **Istria** (in Croatian, Istra) represents Croatian tourism at its most developed. In recent decades the region's proximity to Western Europe has ensured an annual influx of sun-seeking package tourists, with Italians, Germans, Austrians and what seems like the entire population of Slovenia flocking to the mega-hotel developments that dot the coast. Istrian beaches – often rocky areas that have been concreted over to provide sunbathers with a level surface on which to sprawl – do tend to lack the charm of the out-of-the-way coves that you'll find further south in Dalmatia or the Adriatic islands, yet the modern hotel complexes and sprawling campsites have done little to detract from the region's essential charm: development has generally been kept well clear of the Italianate coastal towns, while the interior, with its hilltop towns pitched high in the mountains, is still amazingly unexplored.

Istria draws on a rich cultural legacy. A borderland where Italian, Slovene and Croatian cultures meet, Istria endured over four hundred years of Venetian rule before its incorporation first into the Austro-Hungarian Empire, then into Fascist Italy and finally the Yugoslav Federation. There's still a fair-sized Italian community, and Italian is very much the peninsula's second language. Nowhere is the region's complex identity better expressed than in its **cuisine**, where the seafood of the Adriatic meets the pasta dishes of Italy and the hearty meat-based fare of central Europe. Local delicacies include oysters (*oštrige*) from the Limski kanal, cured ham (*pršut*), wild asparagus (*šparga*) and truffles (*tartufi*) from the hills inland. Istrian meats, such as *kobasice* (big, spicy sausages) and *ombolo* (lean chops taken from a pig's back), are often cooked on the *kamin* or open hearth, or braised slowly in a *padela* or *čeripnja* – clay pots covered in embers – the ideal way to prepare diced *jarić* (kid goat) or *pulić* (donkey). One dish you won't find anywhere else is Istrian *supa*, red wine heated with sugar, olive oil and pepper then served in an earthenware jug (*bukaleta*), into which a slice of toasted bread is dipped.

ACCOMMODATION PRICE CODES

The accommodation in this guide has been graded using the following price codes, based on the cost of each establishment's **least expensive double room** in high season (June–Sept), excluding special offers. Hotel room rates almost always include breakfast. Out of season, prices on the coast can fall by up to 50 percent. Where single rooms exist, they usually cost 60–70 percent of the price of a double. For more details, see p.24.

① Less than 200Kn	④ 400–500Kn	⑦ 800–1000Kn
② 200–300Kn	⑤ 500–600Kn	⑧ 1000–1200Kn
③ 300–400Kn	⑥ 600–800Kn	⑨ Over 1200Kn

With its amphitheatre and other Roman relics, the port of **Pula**, at the southern tip of the peninsula, is Istria's largest city and a rewarding place to spend a couple of days – rooms are relatively easy to come by and many of Istria's most interesting spots are only a short bus ride away. On the western side of the Istrian peninsula are pretty resort towns like **Rovinj** and **Poreč**, with their cobbled piazzas, shuttered houses and back alleys laden with laundry. Inland Istria couldn't be more different – historic hilltop towns like **Motovun**, **Grožnjan**, **Roč** and **Hum** look like leftovers from another century, half-abandoned accretions of ancient stone poised high above rich green pastures and forests.

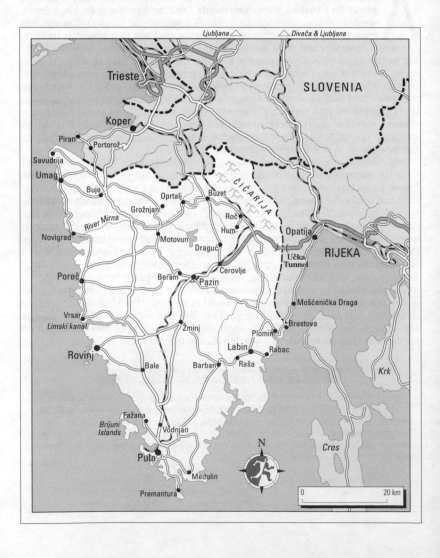

Gradec, with St Marks in background, Zagreb

Trg bana Jelačića, Zagreb

Tkalčićeva, Zagreb

War damage, Vukovar

Veliki Tabor, Zagorje

Rural scene with church, Zagorje

Plitvice Lakes National Park

Rovinj, Istria

Bale

Roman amphitheatre, Pula

Old Buzet, Istria

Trogir

St Donat's Church, Zadar

Regular **buses** connect Pula with Zagreb; otherwise, the city of Rijeka (see p.158) is the most convenient gateway to the region. There are also buses from Pula and Poreč to the Italian city of Trieste, and the Slovene resorts of Portorož and Piran on the north side of the peninsula. **Trains** from the Slovene capital Ljubljana to Pula are another way of reaching the area, while **ferries** connect Pula with Lošinj and Zadar.

Some history

Istria gets its name from the Histri, an Illyrian tribe who ruled the region before succumbing to the Romans in the second century BC. The invaders left a profound mark on Istria, building farms and villas, turning Pula into a major urban centre and creating a Romanized population which would remain Latin-speaking even under subsequent rulers. Following the disintegration of the Western Roman Empire, Istria fell under the control first of Odoacer's Ostrogoth state in the fifth century, then of Justinian's Byzantine Empire in the sixth, a period which gave the region its greatest ecclesiastical monument, the Basilica of St Euphrasius in Poreč. Slav tribes began settling the peninsula from the seventh century onwards, driving the original Romanized inhabitants of the interior into the hills, where they preserved their Latin-derived dialects for generations before finally being Slavicized from the eighteenth century onwards.

Istria became a province of the Frankish Empire in 1040, but maritime and inland Istria began to follow divergent courses as the Middle Ages progressed. Most of the interior was presented as a feudal dependency to the Patriarchate of Aquileia – a virtually independent ecclesiastical city-state owing nominal fealty to Byzantium – in the twelfth century, while the coastal towns survived as independent communes until, one by one, they adopted Venetian suzerainty from the thirteenth century onwards. The lands of the Aquileian Patriarchs subsequently came under Habsburg control, ushering in centuries of intermittent warfare between Austrians and Venetians for control of the peninsula. The fall of Venice in 1797, followed by the collapse of Napoleon's short-lived Illyrian Provinces, left the Austrians in control of the whole of Istria. They confirmed Italian as the official language of the peninsula, even though Croats outnumbered Italians by more than two to one. Istria received a degree of autonomy in 1861, with Poreč becoming the seat of a regional diet, but only the property-owning classes were allowed to vote, thereby excluding many Croats and perpetuating the Italian-speaking community's domination of Istrian politics.

Austrian rule ended in 1918, when Italy – already promised Istria by Britain and France as an inducement to enter World War I – occupied the whole peninsula. When Mussolini's Fascist Party came to power in October 1922, prospects for the Croatian majority in Istria worsened still further: the Croatian language was banished from public life, while a law of 1927 decreed that Slav surnames were henceforth to be rendered in Italian. During World War II, however, opposition to Fascism united Italians and Croats alike, and Tito's Partisan movement in Istria was a genuinely multinational affair, although this didn't prevent outbreaks of inter-ethnic violence and tit-for-tat killings. The atrocities committed against Croats during the Fascist period were avenged indiscriminately by the Partisans, and the *foibe* of Istria – limestone pits into which bodies were thrown – still evoke painful memories for Italians to this day.

After 1945, Yugoslavia's right to occupy southern Istria was more or less unquestioned by the victorious Allies, but northern Istria became the subject of bitter postwar wrangles between Yugoslavia and Italy. The Allies divided the disputed area into two zones: Zone A, controlled by Anglo-American forces, included Trieste and its hinterland; while Zone B, controlled by the Partisans, comprised Koper, Piran, Umag and Novigrad. In October 1954, a compromise designed to appease both parties saw Zone A given to the Italians, while Zone B became part of Yugoslavia. The region suffered serious depopulation as thousands of Italians fled Istria in 1945, followed by thousands more after the award of Zone B to Yugoslavia in 1954. In response, the Yugoslav government encouraged emigration to Istria from the rest of the country, and today there are a fair number of Serbs, Macedonians, Albanians and Bosnians in Istria, many of whom were attracted to the coast by the once booming tourist industry.

Geographically distant from the main flashpoints of the Serb–Croat conflict, Istria entered the twenty-first century more cosmopolitan, more prosperous and more self-confident than any other region of the country. This state of affairs was not without problems, however, with local Istrian politicians tending to regard Zagreb as the centre of a tax-hungry state which took money out of Istria without putting anything back in. Growing regionalist sentiment in the early 1990s led to the rise of the Istrian Democratic Party (Istarska demokratska stranka, or IDS), a moderate, centrist party which has remained the peninsula's most influential political force ever since. One consequence of Istria's new-found sense of identity has been a reassessment of its often traumatic relationship with Italy, and a positive new attitude towards its cultural and linguistic ties with that country.

Pula

Once the Austro-Hungarian Empire's chief naval base, **PULA** (in Italian, Pola) is an engaging combination of working port and brash Riviera town. The Romans put the city firmly on the map when they arrived in 177 BC, bequeathing it an impressive amphitheatre whose well-preserved remains are the city's single greatest attraction. Pula is also Istria's commercial heart and transport hub, possessing its sole airport, so you're unlikely to visit the region without passing through at least once. There's also an easily visited cluster of Classical and medieval sights in the city centre, while the rough-and-ready atmosphere of the crane-ringed harbour makes a refreshing contrast to the seaside towns and tourist complexes further along the coast. Central Pula can't boast much of a seafront, but there's a lengthy stretch of rocky beach about 3km south of the city centre, leading to the hotel complex on the Verudela peninsula, built in the 1980s to accommodate package-holidaying Brits.

Arrival, information and accommodation

Pula's **train station** is a ten-minute walk north of the town centre at the far end of Kolodvorska; the **bus station** is along Istarska, just south of the amphitheatre, although it's due to move to a new site northeast of the amphitheatre at Trg 1. Istarske brigade. City buses (including services to destinations just outside Pula such as Fažana and Medulin) already use the new terminal, although the central street, Giardini, is also an important hub. Tickets for city buses cost 9Kn for two journeys if bought in advance from newspaper kiosks, 14Kn if bought from the

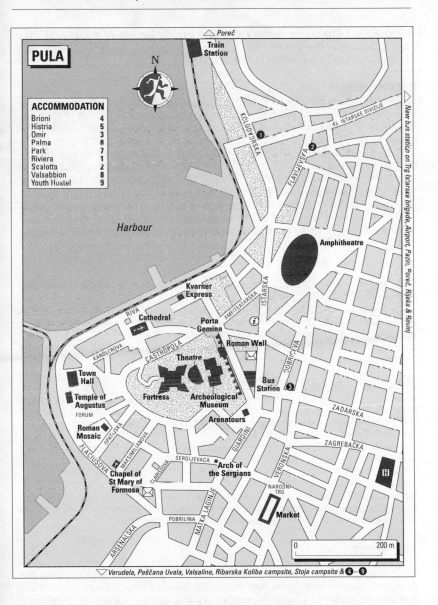

driver. Pula's **airport** is 6km northeast of the centre just off the main Rijeka road, but there's no bus link. A taxi into town will set you back 150–200Kn.

The **tourist office** (summer daily 9am–1pm & 5–8pm; winter Mon–Fri 9am–1pm; ☎052/33-557, *tz-pula@pu.tel.hr*) is currently just south of the amphitheatre at Istarska 11, although a move to the Forum is planned. The best sources of private **rooms** (①) are Arenatours, Giardini 4 (daily 7am–9pm; ☎052/34-355, fax 212-277, *marketing@arenaturist.hr*), and Kvarner Express, on the seafront at Riva 14 (Mon–Sat 9am–7pm; ☎052/22-519, fax 34-961).

Accommodation

Hotels are thin on the ground in central Pula, although there are more rooms five kilometres southeast of the centre in the upmarket bayside suburb of Pješčana uvala (bus #6 from Giardini) and at the large package-oriented hotels south of the centre on the Verudela peninsula (at the end of bus routes #3 and #7).

Pula's **youth hostel** stands on its own beach at Valsaline, 4km south of the centre (☎052/210-002 or 210-003, fax 212-394; 85Kn per bed); take bus #2 or #7 from Giardini to Vila Idola, a turn-of-the century villa which comes into view on your right as you leave suburban Pula – the hostel itself is further away to the right on the cusp of the bay. The nearest **campsites** are *Stoja*, on a rocky wooded peninsula 3km south of town (☎052/24-144, fax 24-748; bus #1 from Giardini), and *Ribarska Koliba*, down by the marina on the Verudela peninsula (☎52/22-966, fax 212-138; bus #3 or #7).

CENTRAL PULA

Omir, Dobrićeva 6 (☎052/210-614 or 218-186, fax 213-944). Small, friendly, but rather plain hotel slightly uphill from Giardini. ④.

Riviera, Splitska 1 (☎ & fax 052/211-166). Shabbily genteel hotel between the train station and the amphitheatre. Probably the finest example of Habsburg-era architecture in Istria when viewed from the outside, but the en-suite rooms are rather dowdy. ③.

Scaletta, Flavijevska 26 (☎052/541-599). One of the best family-run hotels in Croatia, with plush, pastel-coloured rooms. Needless to say, it fills up quickly. ④.

PJEŠČANA UVALA AND THE VERUDELA PENINSULA

Histria, Verudela peninsula (☎052/590-000, fax 214-175). Upmarket hotel which looks a bit like a suburban housing estate from the outside, but offers roomy en-suites with TV and bath, plus a covered pool. ⑦. There's also a self-catering apartment complex nearby (☎052/590-781, fax 22-798; ⑤, around 700Kn for 4).

Palma, Verudela peninsula (☎052/590-760, fax 214-175; ⑤), large, comfortable but bland package-oriented hotel. The nearby *Park* (☎052/34-611, fax 34-073; ④) and *Brioni* (☎052/215-585, fax 213-671; ④) are very similar. Rooms in all three can be booked through Arenatours (see above) in central Pula.

Valsabbion, Pješčana uvala IX/26 (☎052/222-991, fax 218-033, *www.valsabbion.com*;) Modern family-run place, featuring attractive rooms with warm orange-pink colour schemes, a fitness studio with small swimming pool and a superb restaurant. ⑤.

The Town

According to legend, Pula was founded by the Colchians, who pursued the Argonauts here after the latter had stolen the Golden Fleece. The prosaic truth is that Pula began life as a minor Illyrian settlement, and there's not much evidence of a significant town here until the arrival of the Romans, who transformed Pula into an important commercial centre endowed with all the imperial trimmings – temples, theatres and triumphal arches – appropriate to its status. The chief reminder of Roman times is the immense **Amphitheatre** (*amfiteatar* or *arena*; daily: summer 8am–8pm, 30Kn; winter 9am–5pm, 15Kn), just north of the centre,

JAMES JOYCE IN PULA

In October 1904 the 22-year-old James Joyce eloped to mainland Europe with his girlfriend (and future wife) Nora Barnacle. He sought work with the Berlitz English language schools in Zürich and Trieste, but the organization found him a post in Pula instead, where he was paid £2 for a sixteen-hour week teaching Austro-Hungarian naval officers (one of whom was Miklos Horthy, ruler of Hungary between the wars). Despite their straitened circumstances, the couple enjoyed this first taste of domestic life, although Joyce viewed Pula as a provincial backwater and, eager to get away at the first opportunity, accepted a job in Trieste six months later.

There are few places in Pula which boast Joycean associations: a wall plaque on an apartment block opposite the Arch of the Sergians marks the site of the language school where Joyce taught, and the building of the *Café Miramar*, where Joyce went every day to read the newspapers, survives as a furniture store – it's opposite the entrance to the Uljanik shipyard on the Riva. You can always enjoy a drink in the café-bar *Uliks* ("Ulysses" in Croatian), situated on the ground floor of the apartment block which once housed the language school, although there's a disappointing lack of Joyce memorabilia inside.

a huge grey skein of connecting arches whose silhouette dominates the city skyline. Built towards the end of the first century BC, it's the sixth largest amphitheatre in the world, with space for 22,000 spectators, although why such a capacious theatre was built in a small Roman town of only 5000 inhabitants has never been properly explained.

The outer shell is remarkably complete, although only a small part of the seating remains anything like intact, and the interior tiers and galleries were long ago quarried by locals, who used the soft limestone to build their own houses. It's lucky, in fact, that the amphitheatre survives here at all. Overcome by enthusiasm for Classical antiquities, the sixteenth-century Venetian authorities planned to dismantle the whole lot and reassemble it piece by piece in their own city, until dissuaded by one of their more enlightened patricians, Pula-born Gabriele Emo. His gallant stand is remembered by a plaque on one of the towers, the slightly hair-raising climb up which (the steps are sometimes barred to discourage suicides) gives a good sense of the vastness of the structure and a view of Pula's industrious harbour. You can also explore some of the cavernous rooms underneath, which would have been used for keeping wild animals and Christians before they met their deaths. They're now given over to piles of crusty amphorae, reconstructed olive presses and other lacklustre exhibits.

From Giardini to the Forum

South of the amphitheatre, central Pula encircles a pyramidal hill, scaled by secluded streets and topped with a star-shaped Venetian fortress. Starting from the main downtown street of **Giardini**, **Sergijevaca** (also labelled Via Sergia) heads into the older, more atmospheric parts of town, running through the **Arch of the Sergians** (also known as Zlatna vrata, or Golden Gate), a self-glorifying monument built by one Salvia Postuma Sergia in 30 BC. The far side of the arch is the more interesting, with reliefs of winged victories framing an inscription extolling the virtues of the Sergii – one of whom (probably Salvia's husband) commanded a legion at the Battle of Actium in 31 BC.

Continue west along Sergijevaca, then left down Maksimilianova towards a patch of open ground distinguished by a further two ancient monuments. The first of these, the small sixth-century Byzantine **Chapel of St Mary of Formosa** (Crkvica Marije od Trstika), is the only surviving part of a monumental basilica complex. The chapel is occasionally used as an art gallery in summer, although the mosaic fragments that once graced its interior are now displayed in the city's Archeological Museum (see below). The rear entrance of an apartment block a few steps north of the chapel is the unlikely setting for an impressively complete second-century floor **mosaic**, uncovered in the wake of Allied bombing raids in World War II. Now restored and on display behind a metal grille, it's largely made up of non-figurative designs – geometric flower-patterns and meanders – surrounding a central panel illustrating the legend of Dirce and the bull.

Sergijevaca finishes up at the ancient Roman **Forum**, nowadays the old quarter's main square. On the far side is the **Temple of Augustus**, built between 2 BC and 14 AD to celebrate the cult of the emperor and one of the finest Roman temples outside Italy, with an imposing facade of high Corinthian columns. Inside there's a permanent exhibition (summer only; irregular hours, usually daily 9am–6pm; 10Kn) of the best of Pula's Roman finds, including the sculpted torso of a Roman centurion found in the amphitheatre, and a figure of a slave kneeling at the sandalled feet (more or less all that's left) of his master. The building next door began life as a Temple of Diana before being modified and rebuilt as the **Town Hall** (Gradska vijećnica) in the thirteenth century – a Renaissance arcade was added later. Diagonally opposite the town hall, the **Cvajner Art Gallery** occupies a medieval civic building which preserves a sixteenth-century wooden ceiling and some substantial late Gothic fresco fragments – swirling floral motifs in rich red and yellow hues.

The cathedral, fortress and Archeological Museum

Heading northeast from the Forum along Kandlerova brings you to Pula's simple and spacious **Cathedral of St Mary** (Katedrala svete Marije; daily 7am–noon & 4–6pm), a compendium of styles whose dignified Renaissance facade conceals a Romanesque modification of a sixth-century basilica, itself built on the foundations of a Roman temple. Inside, the high altar consists of a third-century marble Roman sarcophagus that's said to have once contained the remains of the eleventh-century Hungarian King Solomon, though there's little else of interest.

From almost anywhere along Kandlerova you can follow streets up to the top of the hill, the site of the original Roman Capitol and now the home of a mossy seventeenth-century **fortress** (*kaštel*), built by the Venetians, which houses the sparse and uninformative **Historical Museum of Istra** (Povijesni muzej Istre; summer daily 8am–7pm; winter Mon–Fri 9am–5pm; 7Kn); the only real highlights are the scale models of vessels built in local shipyards and a cabinet of Habsburg-era souvenir mugs decorated with the whiskery visage of Emperor Franz Josef and his World War I ally Kaiser Wilhelm II of Germany.

You can follow the path all the way across the hill from here to the other side of the town centre, passing the remains of a small **Roman Theatre** en route to the **Archeological Museum** (Arheološki muzej; May–Sept Mon–Sat 9am–8pm, Sun 10am–3pm; Oct–April Mon–Fri 9am–2pm; 20Kn). The greater part of Pula's movable Roman relics have finished up in this disappointing museum, although they're unimaginatively displayed, with pillars, capitals, mosaic fragments and statues scattered haphazardly amongst ceramics, jewellery and trinkets from prehistoric to medieval times. Just by the museum is the second-century AD **Porta Gemina**, smaller and plainer than the Arch of the Sergians, whose two arches give it its name: the Twin Gate.

Pula's beaches

Immediately south of Pula the city's dusty high-rise suburbs suddenly give way to a series of peninsulas and forest-fringed inlets. The nearest is **Stoja**, an easy three-kilometre walk southeast from the city centre (or bus #1 from Giardini), a small kidney-shaped peninsula fringed by rocks. From here you can proceed on foot along Lungomare, which runs east along the coast towards the bays of **Valsaline** and **Zlatne stijene**, passing several shingle coves on the way. Further south is the wooded **Verudela peninsula** (bus #3 or #7 from Giardini), bordered to the east by the lovely Verudski kanal inlet, site of Pula's marina. The southern extremity of the peninsula, **Punta Verudela**, is home to Pula's package hotels and a couple of good shingle beaches, of which the Havajka, on the west side of the peninsula behind the *Park* hotel, and the Ambrela, northwest of the *Brioni* hotel, are the most popular. The beaches are deluged with vacationing city folk during the summer, and remain a popular strolling area throughout the year.

Eating, drinking and entertainment

For **eating**, *Jupiter*, north of the fortress at Castropola 38, is traditionally regarded as being the best of the city's pizzerias, while *Pompei*, just off Sergijevaca at Clarissova 1, has excellent pasta dishes and generous salads. *Vespasian*, south of the amphitheatre at Amfiteatarska 11, has a mainstream selection of Croatian standards; and *Delfin*, opposite the cathedral at Kandlerova 17, is good for fish. Best of the downtown restaurants, however, is *Scaletta*, Flavijevska 26, a swish, intimate place with good seafood and meat dishes – try the *istarski odrezak* (veal stuffed with *pršut* and figs).

Further afield, a good place for traditional Istrian food is *Konoba Taj*, 3km east of the centre at Škokovica 3 (turn right off the Medulin road; ☎052/211-900), where *kobasice* (sausages) and *ombolo* (pork chops) are grilled beside a traditional hearth. *Bonarena*, Verudela, is a rough-and-ready but eternally popular grill, down by the marina where most Puležani keep their small boats, offering good *ćevapi* (mincemeat rissoles) and *lignje* (squid). More upmarket, the restaurant at the *Valsabbion* hotel has a nationwide reputation for its fresh seafood and extravagant sweets, while the nearby *Vela Nera*, on a terrace overlooking the marina in Pješčana uvala (☎052/219-209), has the usual range of fish, plus Istrian specialities like *rezanci sa tartufima* (noodles with truffles), or a very rich stewed *kunić* (rabbit).

For snacks and supplies, the covered **market** and the surrounding cafés on Narodni trg, about 100m east of the Arch of the Sergians, are the best place for buying provisions or picking up sandwiches and pastries. Nearer the Forum, the Pekarna Jozef bakery, at Kandlerova 17, is a good place to stock up on bread and cakes.

Drinking and entertainment

Most downtown **drinking** takes place in the alfresco cafés around the Forum. Popular haunts elsewhere in the centre include the *Bounty Pub*, an animated place with plenty of outdoor seating two blocks east of the Arch of the Sergians at

Veronska 8, and *Monte Serpente*, Braće čeh 14, a roomy bar with occasional live music, although it's in the northeastern suburb of Monte Serpo.

Largest and most popular of the mainstream **discos** are *Tangenta*, in Pješčana uvala, and *Aquarius* (daily in summer, weekends in winter) in the town of Medulin, 10km southeast (bus #33), which subsists on a diet of commercial techno, live rock-pop bands and "erotic" shows. *Uljanik*, Dobrilina 2, is a counter-cultural club of many years' standing offering alternative music discos and regular live rock – posters in town will provide an idea of what's on. Fort Bourgignon, 3km south of central Pula in Zlatne stijene, is an old Napoleonic fort which has been used as a venue for rave-style events in recent summers, but check the latest information before heading out there specially.

Pula's main **cinema** is the Zagreb, bang in the centre at Giardini 12. The amphitheatre hosts major opera and pop performances in the summer, as well as the Pula **film festival** in August (contact the tourist office for details), when the year's crop of domestic feature-film releases are premiered.

Listings

Airlines Croatia Airlines, Corrarina 8 (Mon–Fri 8am–4pm, Sat 9am–noon; ☎052/23-322).

Airport enquiries ☎052/552-900.

Bank Zagrebačka banka, M. Laginje 1 (Mon–Fri 7.30am–7pm; Sat 7.30am–noon). There's an ATM outside.

Car rental Europcar, Giardini 13 (☎052/217-130); Herz, Pula airport (☎052/550-900); Kvarner Express, Riva 14 (☎052/22-519).

Ferry tickets Jadroagent, Riva 14 (Mon–Fri 7.30am–3.30pm; ☎052/222-568).

Hospital Gradska Bolnica, Zagrebačka 30 (☎052/214-433).

Internet and email access Computer Club Arcadi, Cankarova 4 (daily 10am–10pm), a 5min walk west from the covered market along Flanatička.

Pharmacy Ljekarna centar, Giardini 15 (open 24hr).

Police Trg republike 2 (☎052/532-111).

Post office/telephones The main post office is at Danteov Trg 4 (daily 8am–9pm), and there's a smaller branch just south of the amphitheatre at Istarska 7 (Mon–Sat 8am–3pm).

Taxis Try the rank on Giardini or call ☎052/23-228.

Travel agents Arenatours, Giardini 4, offers local excursions and accommodation reservations; GeneralTurist, Giardini 2, sells international airline tickets.

The west coast

Istria's **west coast** represents the peninsula at its most developed. In itself it's attractive enough, with fields of rich red soil and pine woods sloping gently down to the sea, but a succession of purpose-built resorts has all but swallowed up the shoreline. Inland, the coastal strip fades imperceptibly into conifer-studded heath-land and fields bounded by drystone walls and dotted with *kažuni*, the characteristic stone huts with conical roofs traditionally used by Istrian shepherds for shelter when overnighting with their flocks. North of Pula, **Rovinj** is Istria's best-preserved old Venetian port, while the crumbling towns of **Vodnjan** and **Bale**, slightly inland, are also worth a look. Further north, the large resort of **Poreč** is still relatively unspoilt, and is home to the peninsula's finest ecclesiastical attraction, the mosaic-filled Basilica of St Euphrasius. The mega-hotels nearby offer undoubted comforts, but also a lot of concrete on the side.

The Brijuni Islands

North of Pula lie the **Brijuni** (Italian, Brioni) a small archipelago of fourteen islands that became famous as the private retreat of Tito, before being accorded national park status and opened to visitors in 1983. Visitors are still only allowed on two of the islands, **Veli Brijun** and **Mali Brijun**, and travel here is strictly controlled due to the islands' continuing use as a state residence. You can visit the Brijuni on an organized day trip, in which case you'll be whisked around the island by tourist train, or book into one of the two upmarket hotels on Veli Brijun, in which case you'll have more time and freedom to stroll around the island unsupervised.

The obvious gateway to the islands is the small fishing village of **FAŽANA**, 8km northwest of Pula (reachable from the city on bus #6). The national park office on Fažana's harbourfront square sells tickets for day-trips to the biggest island and main tourist draw, Veli Brijun, as well as arranging transport to the hotels. There are about five excursions daily from Fažana in summer, one daily in winter; each lasts roughly four hours and costs around 150Kn. If you're staying in a package hotel in Istria you'll probably be paying around 220Kn for a Brijuni excursion, with

---

THE PRESIDENTIAL PLAYGROUND

Although the islands were a popular rural retreat among wealthy Romans, the Brijunis' history as an offshore paradise really began in 1893, when they were bought by Austrian industrialist **Paul Kupelweiser**, owner of a steel mill in the Czech town of Vitkovice. Kupelweiser's aim was to turn the islands into a luxury resort patronized by the cream of Europe's aristocracy, and he brought in Nobel Prize-winning bacteriologist Robert Koch, who rid the islands of malaria by pouring petroleum on the swamps. Smart hotels and villas were built on Veli Brijun, and the Mediterranean scrub cleared to make way for landscaped parks and a golf course. Brijuni's heyday was in the period immediately before World War I: Archduke Franz Ferdinand, Kaiser Wilhelm II and Thomas Mann all stayed on the islands, and struggling English-language teacher James Joyce came here to celebrate his 23rd birthday on February 2, 1905.

Following World War I, however, the islands lost their high-society allure, and Paul Kupelweiser's son and heir, Karl, committed suicide here in 1930 after being bankrupted by the cost of their upkeep. After World War II, **Tito** decided to make Veli Brijun one of his official bases, planting much of the island's subtropical vegetation and commissioning a residence – the White Villa (Bijela Vila) – in which he was able to entertain visiting heads of state in the style to which they were accustomed. It was here that Tito, Nehru and Nasser signed the Brioni Declaration in 1956, which paved the way for the creation of the Non-Aligned Movement. Tito himself contrived to spend as much time on the Brijuni as possible, conducting government business from here when not busy hunting in his private game reserve or pottering in his gardens and orchards – tangerines from which were traditionally sent to children's homes throughout Yugoslavia as a new year's gift. After Tito's death in 1980 the islands were retained as an official residence, becoming the favoured summer destination of President Tuđman.

transport to Fažana – and possibly lunch – thrown in. Trips to Brijuni are also offered by boats in Pula harbour (from around 160Kn per person), although these tend not to stop at Veli Brijun, heading instead for a bay on Mali Brijun for swimming and a fish picnic.

If you do want to stay on the islands, there's little to choose between Veli Brijun's two hotels, the *Neptun* (☎052/525-100; ⑨) and the *Karmen* (☎052/525-400; ⑨), both of which have comfy en-suites with TV; they're next door to each other on Veli Brijun's main bay.

Veli Brijun

After a fifteen-minute crossing of the Brijuni Channel, excursion craft from Fažana arrive at Kupelweiser's hotel complex on **Veli Brijun**'s eastern shore. From here a miniature train with English-speaking guide heads north through parklands to a **safari park** at the northern tip of the island. This was originally stocked with beasts given to Tito as presents by visiting dignitaries – the two elephants presented by Indira Gandhi are still here, alongside zebras, antelopes and camels. The train continues along the western side of island to the **White Villa** and other official residences, including the Villa Jadran, where guests have included Queen Elizabeth II and Gina Lollobrigida, all watched over discreetly by liveried guards (Tito's personal quarters – together with his famous tangerine groves – were on the island of Krasnica, a few hundred metres off Veli Brijun's west coast). The train stops to allow exploration of a ruined **Byzantine fortress** at the southwestern corner of the island, its stark grey fortifications in bleak contrast to the green paradise it was built to defend.

The train then returns to the hotel complex via the scant remains of a first-century BC Roman villa at Veriga Bay. Beside the hotel complex an exhibition entitled **Tito on Brijuni** (Tito na Brijunima; open whenever excursions from Fažana arrive; free with excursion ticket), starts, on the ground floor, with a display of the animals given to Tito as presents and stuffed after their death, including four 7-week-old giraffes which contracted a virus soon after their arrival from Africa. Upstairs is a fascinating exhibition of photos documenting Tito's various personae: one moment a man of the people talking to Fažana fisherfolk; the next, sharing jokes with jet-setting house guests such as Sophia Loren, Elizabeth Taylor and Richard Burton, who played the part of Tito in the epic war film *Sutjeska* in 1970. Look out too for a photograph of Tito taking Ho Chi Minh for a spin in a motorboat, with both men sporting raffish panama hats – an experience, judging from the picture, which the Vietnamese leader appears to be enjoying somewhat less than the Marshal.

Vodnjan and Bale

Heading up the west coast, the main road runs inland through the historic town of **VODNJAN** (Dignano), 11km north of Pula, with its warren of weatherbeaten alleys gathered tightly around a time-worn main square. Vodnjan is famous for two things: the enduring presence of a large Italian-speaking community, and the well-preserved **Vodnjan mummies** – the dessicated bodies of various saints which are stored in the local **St Blaise's Church** (Crkva svetog Blaža; summer daily 9am–7pm; winter, open when the priest is around), an eighteenth-century structure, built in imitation of Palladio's San Pietro in Castello, Venice, whose soaring campanile is the highest in Istria. Inside, the "mummies" are kept behind a burgundy-coloured curtain to the rear of the main altar. Originally stored in the church of San Lorenzo in Venice, they were brought to Vodnjan in 1818 for safe-keeping after the monastic order that originally looked after them had been dissolved. Three complete and well-preserved bodies are laid out in glass cases, above which are stacked a range of smaller relics in a series of containers – one of which holds a twisted brown form reputed to be the torso and arm of St Sebastian. The most revered of the bodies is that of Leon Bembo the Blessed, a twelfth-century Venetian cleric and diplomat who gave up worldly pleasures for the monastic life, developing a reputation as a faith-healer and sage. Beside him lie St Nikoloza of Koper (with a still fresh-looking garland of flowers round her head) and St Ivan Olini of Venice, both renowned medieval healers – popular belief maintains that there's a link between the saints' healing powers and the subsequent failure of their bodies to decompose.

The **Collection of Sacral Art** (Zbirka sakralne umjetnosti; 10Kn) in the sacristy has innumerable smaller relics, including one glass jar which it's claimed contains the lower jaw and tongue of St Mary of Egypt, a sixth-century Alexandrian courtesan who converted to Christianity and thereafter opted for a life of asceticism in the desert. The star exhibit, however, is Paolo Veneziano's early fourteenth-century polyptych of St Bembo the Blessed, a wooden board which originally served as the lid of Bembo's coffin. A series of scenes show Bembo exercising his healing powers; mighty bishops and nobles visiting Bembo's deathbed; and pilgrims paying homage to Bembo's miraculously preserved body.

Buses from Pula to Pazin, Rovinj and Poreč all pick up and drop off on the western edge of town, a short walk from the main square, where you'll find Vodnjan's **tourist office** at Narodni trg 3 (summer Mon–Sat 8.30am–3pm; winter Mon–Fri 8.30am–3pm; ☎ & fax 052/511-700). The cosiest place **to stay** in town is the *Pansion San Rocco*, Sveti Roko 41 (☎052/511-611; ③), which has small but crisply furnished rooms with TV; the Wart agency on the opposite side of the road (same phone number) has **rooms** (②).

Bale

Ten kilometres beyond Vodnjan, **BALE** (Valle) occupies a hilltop site typical of the peninsula, with houses built in a defensive circle. Smaller and more deserted than Vodnjan, it's a good example of a town abandoned by its Italian population after 1945 and never properly lived in since. The most arresting edifice here, though needing renovation, is the **Soardo-Bembo Palace**, a fifteenth-century Venetian Gothic building with an elegant balcony built into its towered facade. Beside the palace, an arch topped by a clumsy-looking Venetian lion leads through into the core of the old town, which really amounts to a circular alleyway spanned by little arches, with rough stone buildings on either side. Follow this round in either direction to reach **St Elizabeth's Church** (Crkva svete Elizabete) in the central square, a largely nineteenth-century neo-Baroque building, although it preserves a Romanesque campanile and fragments from earlier sixth-and eighth-century churches in the crypt. Just outside the old town beside the road to Rovinj, the smaller, simpler, fifteenth-century **Church of the Holy Spirit** (Crkva svetog Duha) contains late Gothic frescoes and is sporadically open as a gallery in the summer months.

Pula–Rovinj buses stop on the main road just below the entrance to the old town, Trg palih boraca, where there's a small seasonal **tourist office** (summer daily 8am–8pm; ☎052/824-270), although there's nowhere in town to stay. About a kilometre northwest of town, just off the Rovinj road and worth a stop-off, the *Sweet Bar* café is renowned for its excellent cakes and pastries.

Rovinj

There are few more pleasant towns in Istria than **ROVINJ** (Rovigno). Delicately poised between medieval port and modern tourist resort, it has managed better than anywhere else along the peninsula's west coast to preserve its character by keeping major development well away from its historic centre. Its harbour is a likeable mix of fishing boats and swanky yachts, its quaysides a blend of sun-shaded café tables and fishermen's nets. Spacious Venetian-style houses and elegant piazzas lend an overridingly Italian air to the town, and the festive mood the tourists bring only adds to the atmosphere. Rovinj is also the most Italian town on this coast: there's an Italian high school, the language is widely spoken, and street signs are bilingual.

Rovinj's urban core is situated on what was formerly an island. The strait separating it from the coast was filled in during the mid-eighteenth century, after which the town expanded onto the mainland, until then the site of a quite separate settlement of Croat farmers. Initially, the urban Italian culture of Rovigno assimilated that of the mainland Slavs, until industrial development in the late nineteenth century encouraged a wave of economic migrants, tipping the demographic scales in the Croats' favour. Playing a leading role in this was the Rovinj tobacco factory, founded in 1872, which still produces the bulk of Croatia's cigarettes. Rovinj's other claim to fame is as the "Montmartre of Istria" – a tag which stems from the painters and other artists who have gravitated here since the 1950s and whose studios fill the streets of the old town. Every August, the main street, Grisia, is taken over by an open-air display of works in which all the town's artists have the right to exhibit, if they so wish.

Arrival and accommodation

It's five minutes' walk from Rovinj's **bus station** along pedestrianized Via Carrera to the main Trg maršala Tita, which marks the junction of the old island and the mainland. The **tourist office**, just off the square at Obala P. Budičin 12 (mid-June to mid-Sept daily 8am–9pm; mid-Sept to mid-June Mon–Sat 8am–3pm; ☎052/811-566, fax 816-007), should be able to provide a free map and English-language information booklet.

There's a smattering of private **rooms** (①–②) in the old town, although most are in the more modern areas. They can be booked through numerous agencies around town (usually open daily 8am–10pm in summer); try Natale, opposite the bus station at Carducci 4 (☎052/813-365, fax 811-620), or one of the group of agencies on and around the main square, such as Kvarner Express, N. Quarantotto 1 (☎052/811-155, fax 815-046), or Kompas-Istra, Trg maršala Tita (☎052/813-211). With so many private rooms, **hotels** are not worth the price unless you go slightly upmarket: the *Adriatic*, by the port on the corner of Trg maršala Tita and P. Budičin (☎052/815-088, fax 813-573; ⑥), is a venerable establishment offering comfortable en-suites with phone and TV; the more modern *Eden*, 1km south of town at L. Adamovića (☎052/800-400, fax 811-349; ⑦), is a vast modern complex surrounded by forest, with outdoor pool and generous buffet breakfast. Rovinj's two offshore islands boast a couple of modern concrete, but comfortable, hotels linked to town by regular taxi-boat: the *Katarina* on Sveta

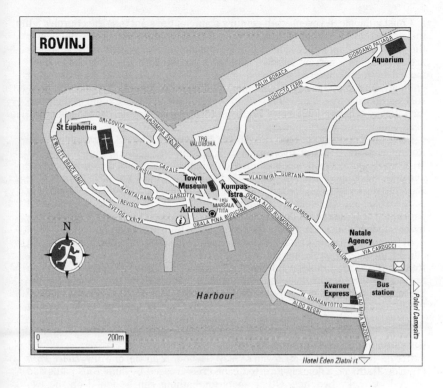

Katarina (☎052/811-233; ⑤) and the rather grander *Sol Club Istra* on Crveni otok (☎052/802-500, fax 813-484; ⑦). The nearest **campsite** is the *Polari* (☎052/801-501, fax 811-395), occupying a rocky cove 3km south of town and reached by regular bus, with a naturist section.

The Town

Heading northwest from the main square, **Trg maršala Tita**, Grisia passes through a cute – if relatively unspectacular – Baroque archway, built by the Balbi family, before climbing steeply through the heart of the old town to **St Euphemia's Church** (Crkva svete Eufemije; daily 10am–noon & 4–7pm), which dominates Rovinj from the top of its stumpy peninsula. This eighteenth-century Baroque church is home to the sixth-century sarcophagus of St Euphemia, a Christian from Chalcedon in Asia Minor who was martyred during the reign of Diocletian – she was supposedly thrown to the lions in the Constantinople hippodrome after having survived various tortures, symbolized by the wheel which leans against her flanks. The church itself is a roomy three-aisled basilica with a Baroque altarpiece at the end of each. The altar of St Euphemia is the one furthest to the right, behind which is a small sanctuary containing Euphemia's sarcophagus – a bare stone box brought to Rovinj in 800 AD to keep it safe from the Iconoclasts, who were in the process of smashing up all the relics they could find in Constantinople. A seventeenth-century statue of the saint tops the church's 58-metre-high tower, said to be modelled on that of St Mark's in Venice. It's below the church, and on either side of Grisia, that Rovinj's most atmospheric streets are to be found – narrow, cobbled alleyways packed with tiny craft shops, overlooked by high shuttered windows, spindly TV aerials and the thin, thrusting chimneys that have become something of a Rovinj trademark. It's said that pressure on housing forced married sons to set up home in a spare room of their parents' house – before long every house in town accommodated several families, each with its own hearth and chimney.

Back on Trg maršala Tita, the **Town Museum** at no. 11 (Zavičajni muzej Rovinj; summer Tues–Sat 10.30am–2pm & 6–8pm, Sun 7–10pm; winter Tues–Sat 10.30am–1.30pm; 10Kn) has various archeological oddments, antique furniture and fine art. Among the numerous Madonna and Childs are several imposing Baroque works by anonymous Venetian artists, including a dignified *Deposition of St Sebastian*, and some older, Byzantine-influenced works including the colourful pageantry of Bonifazio de Pirati's *Adoration of the Magi* (1430) and Pietro Mera's more subdued *Christ Crowned with Thorns* from the early 1500s.

At its northern end, Trg maršala Tita opens out onto **Trg Valdibora**, site of a small fruit-and-vegetable market, from where a road leads east along the waterfront to the Marine Biological Institute at Obala Giordano Paliaga 5, home to an **aquarium** (Easter–Oct daily 9am–9pm; 10Kn) featuring tanks of Adriatic marine life and flora. Finally, just opposite the bus station, stands the often overlooked twelfth-century octagonal baptistry of the **Holy Trinity Church** (Crkva svetog Trojstva), a simple, functional structure that is rarely open.

Beaches and islands around Rovinj

Paths on the south side of Rovinj's busy harbour lead beyond the *Hotel Park* towards **Zlatni rt**, a densely forested cape criss-crossed by numerous paths and fringed by rocky **beaches**. Other spots for bathing can be found on the two islands just offshore from Rovinj – **Sveta Katarina**, the nearer of the two, and **Crveni otok** (Red Island), just outside Rovinj's bay, both of which can be reached on half-hourly ferries from the harbour. Neither is exactly deserted (there's a hotel on both), but the combination of pine-shaded shores and ultra-clean waters beats anything else the coast around Rovinj has to offer.

Eating and drinking

The cheapest of the harbourfront fish **restaurants** is the *Porat*, where you can get fillets of *skuša* (mackerel) or *oslić* (hake), although the plusher and more expensive *Amfora* nearby has a wider range of top-quality fish and shellfish. For a more varied menu, try *Konoba Veli Jože*, just beyond the tourist office at Sveti Križ 1, which has top-notch seafood as well as cheaper Istrian standbys such as spicy sausages (*kobasice*) and pasta with goulash (*fuži sa gulašom*). *Spaghetteria La Vela*, just off Via Carrera on Via Mazzini, has a decent range of pasta and a few inexpensive grilled fish dishes; while *da Sergio*, on the old town's main artery, Grisia, is the best place for pizza, although it fills up quickly. For cheap eating, *Vilton*, Via Carrera 86, has decent *burek*, sandwiches and hot dogs and is open 24 hours, while the *Martin* bakery on Trg maršala Tita is the best place to pick up bread and cakes. Picnic ingredients can be had at the **supermarket** (Mon–Sat 7am–8pm, Sun 7am–11pm) on Trg maršala Tita or in the open-air **market** immediately to the north on Trg Valdibora.

For daytime **drinking**, the harbour area is full of places where you can sit outside and enjoy coffee, ice cream and cakes, although the two cafés patronized by locals on the main square – *Fontana* and *Viecia Batana* – are both cheaper and more atmospheric. In the evening, head for the knot of convivial bars on and around Joakima Rakovca, just behind the seafront: rather than aiming for a specific destination here, it's really a question of seeing who's hanging out where and what kind of music is playing.

North of Rovinj: the Limski kanal and Vrsar

North of Rovinj, the main route detours inland around the **Limski kanal**, a turquoise fjord lined with thick woods rising sheer on either side, which cuts a deep green wedge into the Istrian mainland. In Roman times this marked the boundary between the Poreč and Pula regions – *Lim* is derived from *limes*, a Latin word meaning "border" or "limit"; later it became a favourite shelter of pirates, who used it as a base from which to attack the Venetians. Mussels and oysters are cultivated here – you can sample them, along with other fresh fish, in the *Viking* and *Fjord* restaurants, both expensive but highly rated by locals. If you've a car, you can get down to the northern side of the water (and the two restaurants) via the side-road which leaves the Rovinj–Poreč route near the village of Kloštar, but the best way to see the inlet is by boat. Numerous excursions, often including a fish picnic or a lunch stop en route, are advertised on the quaysides of Rovinj, Vrsar and Poreč; expect to pay around 130–150Kn for the trip.

Occupying high ground near the mouth of the Limski kanal is **VRSAR**, a hilltop village curled tightly around a campanile-topped summit. It's quieter than Rovinj and Poreč, although there's a marina and hotel on the shoreline below. A kilometre south of town on the coast is one of the world's largest nudist colonies: **Koversada**. Established in 1960, this was the first of the Adriatic's naturist communities, and is nowadays a self-contained mini-city where up to 15,000 residents can dress as nature intended on a 24-hour basis.

Stretching north of Vrsar there's a string of **campsites** on the coastal side of the main road to Poreč, beginning with *Autocamp Turist*, swiftly followed by the *Valkanela*, then *Camping Puntica*, which has a small bay to itself. Another couple of kilometres and you're in Plava Laguna, the first of Poreč's big package-hotel suburbs.

Poreč

The largest resort in Istria – and, indeed, in Croatia – **POREČ** (Parenzo) isn't nearly as bad as you might expect. There is a huge influx of tourists here every summer, occupying a total, it's claimed, of 35,000 beds in the town and around – a staggering figure when you consider that Poreč's true population is just 3000. The hotels are mainly concentrated outside the town, in vast tourist settlements like Plava Laguna and Zelena Laguna to the south, and Pical to the north. Nearly all the tourist facilities are run by two companies, Riviera and Plava Laguna, which between them are responsible for employing most of the town's population. Despite all this, central Poreč's stone houses and quiet side-streets hung with washing have retained a degree of character which the ice-cream parlours and boutiques have failed to destroy.

Arrival and accommodation

Poreč's **bus station** is just north of the town centre, behind the marina. From here, it's a five-minute walk to the **tourist office** at Zagrebačka 11 (daily 8am–10pm; ☎052/451-458, fax 451-665), whose staff can point you in the direction of agencies offering **rooms** (②); Atlas, Bože Milanovića 11 (☎052/432-273, fax 451-184), is probably the easiest to find. For **hotels**, try the friendly and central *Poreč*, just south of the bus station at Rade Končara 1 (☎052/451-811, fax 451-730; ⑥), which has small but neat en-suite doubles and a more generous breakfast buffet than the slightly more comfortable and equally convenient *Neptun*, Obala

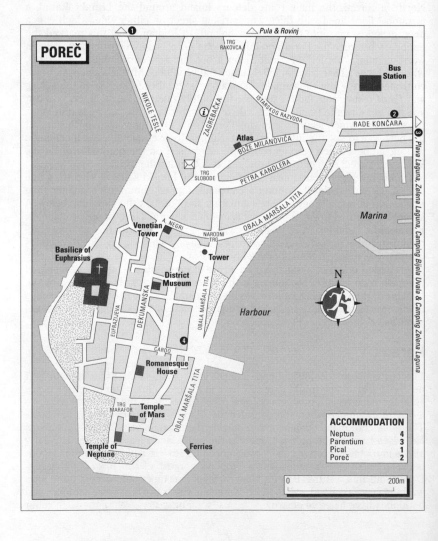

POREČ

TRG RAKOVCA

Pula & Rovinj

Bus Station

NIKOLE TESLE

ZAGREBAČKA

ISTARSKOG RAZVODA

RADE KONČARA

Plava Laguna, Zelena Laguna, Camping Bijela Uvala & Camping Zelena Laguna

Atlas

BOŽE MILANOVIĆA

TRG SLOBODE

PETRA KANDLERA

OBALA MARŠALA TITA

Marina

A. NEGRI

Venetian Tower

NARODNI TRG

Basilica of Euphrasius

Tower

District Museum

DEKUMANSKA

EURAZIJEVA

OBALA MARŠALA TITA

Harbour

N

CARDO

Romanesque House

OBALA MARŠALA TITA

TRG MARAFOR

Temple of Mars

Temple of Neptune

Ferries

ACCOMMODATION	
Neptun	4
Parentium	3
Pical	1
Poreč	2

0 — 200m

maršala Tita (☎052/400-800, fax 431-351; ⑤). The remainder of Poreč's hotels are in the big complexes north and south of town, and are virtually indistinguishable from one other apart from the two four-star places: the *Parentium* in Zelena Laguna, 5km south of town (☎411-500, fax 451-536; ⑤), and the *Pical* (☎052/407-000, fax 451-242; ⑤), 3km to the north. The hourly Plava Laguna bus runs through Zelena Laguna en route. The closest **campsites** are *Zelena Laguna* (☎052/410-541, fax 410-601), at Zelena Laguna, and, further south, *Bijela Uvala* (☎052/410-551, fax 410-600), reachable by the hourly Plava Laguna bus from the bus station.

The Basilica of Euphrasius

Poreč's star turn is the **Basilica of Euphrasius** (Eufrazijeva basilika; daily 7am–8pm; free), situated in the centre of the town just off Ljubljanska; this sixth-century Byzantine basilica has incandescent mosaics that are comparable with the celebrated examples at Ravenna. The basilica is actually the centre of a religious complex, originally created by Bishop Euphrasius between 535 and 550, which includes a bishop's palace, atrium, baptistry and campanile. Entry is through the **Atrium**, an arcaded courtyard whose walls incorporate ancient bits of masonry, although it was heavily restored in the last century. On the west side of the atrium is the octagonal **Baptistry** (Baptisterijum), bare inside save for the entrance to the campanile, which you can ascend (daily 10am–6.30pm; 10Kn) for views of Poreč's red-brown roof tiles. On the north side is the **Bishop's Palace** (daily 10am–6.30pm; 10Kn), a seventeenth-century building harbouring a further – if less captivating – selection of mosaic fragments which once adorned the basilica floor.

The basilica itself was the last of a series of churches, remains of which are still in evidence. Surviving stonework from the first, the **Oratory of St Maur** (named after the saint who is said to have lived in a house on the site), can be seen on the north side of the basilica. This was a secret place of worship when Christianity was still an underground religion, and fragments of mosaic show the sign of the fish, a clandestine Christian symbol of the time. Inside the basilica, the mosaic floor of a later, less secretive church has been carefully revealed through gaps in the existing basilica floor. The present-day basilica is a rather bare structure, everything focusing on the apse with its superb late thirteenth-century ciborium and, behind this, the **mosaics**, which have a Byzantine solemnity quite different from the geometric late Roman designs. They're studded with semi-precious gems, encrusted with mother-of-pearl and punctuated throughout by Euphrasius' personal monogram – he was, it's said, a notoriously arrogant man. The central part of the composition shows the Virgin enthroned with Child, flanked by St Maur, a worldly-looking Euphrasius holding a model of his church and, next to him, his brother. Underneath are scenes of the Annunciation and Visitation, the latter surprisingly realistic, with the imaginative addition of a doltish, eavesdropping servant.

The rest of the town

After you've seen the basilica, the rest of Poreč can seem rather a let-down, though it's a pleasant enough place to stroll around, with a handful of buildings to aim for, many of them spread along Dekumanska. At its eastern end stands a **Venetian tower** from 1448, now used as a venue for art exhibitions. Not far from the basilica at Dekumanska 9, the **District Museum** (Zavičajni muzej; summer daily 9am–noon & 4–7pm; winter Mon–Fri 9am–noon; 10Kn), housed in the Baroque Sinčić Palace, displays archeological finds (mainly Greek and Roman) from the surrounding area, including various Roman tombstones, one of which depicts a patrician standing at the base of an olive tree – local olives were famed throughout Italy during antiquity. Upstairs, rooms are decorated with portraits of the family of Rinaldi Carli – Venetian ambassador to Constantinople in the late 1600s – dressed in Ottoman garb. Walk south towards the end of the peninsula and you'll find the distinctive thirteenth-century building with an unusual projecting wooden balcony known as the **Romanesque House** (Romanička kuća) – it's now another venue for art shows. Just beyond here, **Trg Marafor** occupies the site of the Roman forum and still preserves remains of temples to Mars and Neptune. Little is known about these and they're now not much more than heaps of rubble.

The **beaches** around the old town, such as they are, are generally crowded and unpleasant and it's better to take a boat from the harbour (7am–11pm every 30min; 12Kn) to the island of **Sveti Nikola**, though this too gets busy with sunbathers from its pricey hotel. Alternatively, staying on the mainland, walk south beyond the marina, where pathways head along a rocky coastline shaded by gnarled pines to reach several rocky coves; you'll eventually end up at Zelena Laguna, where there are concreted bathing areas.

Eating and drinking

There's a decent sprinkling of places **to eat** in the old town. *Altercafé*, Zagrebačka, has reasonable croissants, sandwiches, pastries and pizza slices, while *Pizzeria Nono*, further up the same street at Zagrebačka 4, has cheap and good-quality pizza. *Amicus*, just off Dekumanska at Eufrazijeva 45, is an unpretentious but reliable source of excellent-value pasta, grilled meat and seafood, and *Sirena*, Trg Marafor, has more of the same. The best place for traditional Istrian fare is the ever-popular *Istra*, on the corner of Obala maršala Tita and Bože Milanovića, which offers top-of-the-range seafood including the local speciality *jastog sa rezancima* (lobster with pasta noodles), meaty alternatives such as *svinjski but* (roast pork in a rich sauce) as well as cheaper lunchtime favourites like *fuži* (noodles in goulash sauce) and *maneštra* (Istrian bean soup).

Central Poreč is full of **cafés** and **bars** with outdoor seating – those in front of the *Hotel Poreč* are currently the fashionable places to hang out if the weather's good; otherwise, try the Hollywood memorabilia-fixated *Ciak* on Trg narodni. The biggest **disco** in town is the *International Club* in Zelena Laguna, which doles out commercial techno accompanied by "erotic" dancers, wet T-shirt competitions and suchlike during the summer.

Novigrad, Umag and Savudrija

Once you've seen Rovinj and Poreč, the remainder of the west coast is a bit of an anticlimax. Heading north, the next town, **NOVIGRAD** (Cittanova), is another pleasant little place with a Venetian-style campanile spearing skywards from its town centre, although it's lost most of its old buildings apart from a few toothy sections of town wall. There's a big area of hotels – featuring the customary rocky and concrete beaches – just southeast of town, along with a big woodland **campsite** which is full of squirrels. For bathing, the rocky reefs north of town are more attractive and less crowded.

Fifteen kilometres north of Novigrad, **UMAG** (Umago) is typical of the settlements of Istria's west coast: a once attractive town, set on a tiny peninsula, now
almost completely given over to the holiday business with its merciless profusion
of concrete lidos, holiday chalets and autocamps. Most of the development is to
the north of town, a long string of hotels and tourist settlements connected to
Umag's centre by a regular miniature train. It's a better idea to go straight on to
SAVUDRIJA (Punta di Salvore), a small fishing village about 5km away on the
very northwestern tip of the Istrian peninsula. **Rooms** (①) can be had here
through Istratours, and there's a large **campsite** shaded by pines and with some
fair stretches of beach.

Inland Istria

You don't need to travel away from the sea for long before the hotels and flash
apartments give way to rustic villages of heavy grey-brown stone, many of them
perched high on hillsides, a legacy of the times when a settlement's defensive
position was more important than its access to cultivable land. The landscape is
varied, with fields and vineyards squeezed between pine forests and orchards of
oranges and olives. It's especially attractive in autumn, when the hillsides turn a
dappled green and auburn, and the hill villages appear to hover eerily above the
early morning mists.

Istria's hilltop settlements owe their appearance to the region's borderland status. Occupied since Neolithic times, they were fortified and refortified by successive generations, serving as strongpoints on the shifting frontier between Venice
and Hungary, or Christendom and the Ottoman Turks. They suffered serious
depopulation in the last century, first as local Italians emigrated in the 1940s and
1950s, then as the rush for jobs on the coast began in the 1960s. Empty houses in
these half-abandoned towns have been offered to painters, sculptors and musicians in an attempt to keep life going on the hilltops and stimulate tourism at the
same time – hence the reinvention of Motovun and Grožnjan in particular as cultural centres.

Istria's administrative capital, **Pazin**, is the hub of the bus network and, although
it's the least attractive of the inland towns, it's the nearest base for visiting the
fifteenth-century frescoes in the nearby village of **Beram**. Of the hill settlements,
Motovun and **Buzet** are accessible by bus from Pazin or Pula, but you'll need your
own transport to make side-trips to the likes of **Grožnjan**, **Oprtalj** and **Hum**. The
train line from Pula to Divača in Slovenia (where you change for Ljubljana or
Zagreb) can be useful, visiting Pazin before passing close to Hum, Roč and Buzet,
although a certain amount of walking is required to get to the last three.

Inland Istria's only real drawback for tourists is its lack of facilities: there are
hotels in Motovun, Istarske Toplice and Buzet, but there's still not enough of the
cosy farmhouse accommodation that the area seems to be made for. Cries of
"Istria: the new Tuscany" may therefore be premature – which is precisely why
now is the right time to come.

Pazin and Beram

Lying in a fertile bowl bang in the middle of the Istrian peninsula, unassuming
PAZIN is an unlikely regional capital. A relatively unindustrialized provincial

town, it was chosen following World War II by Yugoslavia's new rulers, who were eager to establish an Istrian administration far away from the Italianate coastal towns – the choice of Pazin was a deliberate slap in the face for cosmopolitan Pula. Although fairly bland compared to Istria's other inland towns, Pazin does boast a couple of attractions, most notably its medieval castle and the limestone gorge below. and it's also a useful base from which to visit the renowned frescoes in the nearby church at Beram.

Arriving at Pazin's **train** and **bus** stations, it's a straightforward downhill walk towards the inoffensive, largely low-rise centre, beyond which rises the **Castle**, a stern ninth-century structure, remodelled many times since, and one of the main reasons why Pazin never fell to the Venetians. Inside there's an **Ethnographic Museum** (Etnografski muzej; Mon–Sat 10am–3pm; 12Kn) with a fine collection of traditional Istrian costumes, housed in atmospheric medieval galleries, along with a wide-ranging display of rural handicrafts and a mock-up of a kitchen featuring the traditional Istrian *kamin*, or hearth: a fire laid on an open brick platform, around which the cooking pots were arranged.

The castle overhangs the gorge of the River Fojba below, where a huge abyss sucks water into an underground waterway which resurfaces towards the coast. This chasm was supposed to have prompted Dante's description of the gateway to Hell in his *Inferno*, and inspired Jules Verne to propel one of his characters – Matthias Sandorf from the eponymous book, published in 1885 – over the side of the castle and into the pit. In the book, Sandorf manages to swim along the subterranean river until he reaches the coast – a feat probably destined to remain forever in the realms of fiction. Verne himself never came to Pazin, contenting himself with the pictures of the castle posted to him by the mayor. Back in the town centre, the plain exterior of **St Nicholas's Church** (Crkva svetog Nikole) conceals a thirteenth-century core; the sanctuary vaulting is filled with late fifteenth-century frescoes showing scenes from the life of Christ in faded, hard-to-make-out panels.

Pazin's **tourist office**, just short of the castle at Stari trg 8 (summer daily 8am–6pm; winter Mon–Fri 8am–3pm; ☎ & fax 052/622-460, *tz-pazin@pu.tel.hr*), can help with town plans, information on central Istria and a useful leaflet on Beram church. **Accommodation** in Pazin is limited to the *Motel Lovac*, Šime Kurelića 4 (☎052/624-324 or 624-384; ⑤), just off the main road to Poreč at the western end of town, but within easy walking distance of the centre. The *Pizzeria Forum* on Stari trg, opposite the tourist office, is unspectacular but cheap; while the *Kaštel* restaurant in the castle offers substantial schnitzels and seafood.

Beram

Six kilometres west of Pazin, just off the road to Poreč and Motovun, **BERAM** is an unspoilt hilltop village with moss-covered stone walls and some of the finest sacred art in the region. One kilometre northeast of the village is the **Chapel of Our Lady of the Rocks** (Crkvica svete Marije na škriljinah), a diminutive Gothic church with a set of frescoes dating from 1475, signed by local artist Vincent of Kastav. The key (*ključ*) to the chapel is kept by a villager, usually at house no. 22 or no. 33 in the centre (there are no street names). If you ask in Pazin, the tourist office may ring ahead to ensure that there's someone waiting in Beram for you. It's polite to give a small sum of money to the keyholder in lieu of an entrance fee.

Of the many well-executed New Testament scenes which cover the chapel interior, two large frescoes stand out. The marvellous, eight-metre-long equestrian pageant of the *Adoration of the Kings* reveals a wealth of fine detail – distant ships, mountains, churches and wildlife – strongly reminiscent of early Flemish painting, while on the west wall a *Dance of Death* is illustrated with macabre clarity against a blood-red background: skeletons clasp scythes and blow trumpets, weaving in and out of a Chaucerian procession of citizens led by the pope. A rich merchant brings up the rear, greedily clinging to his possessions while indicating the money with which he hopes to buy his freedom.

Motovun and around

Fifteen kilometres northwest of Pazin is perhaps the most famous of the Istrian hill towns, **MOTOVUN**, an unwieldy clump of houses straddling a green wooded hill, high above a patchwork of wheatfields and vineyards. The place has a genuine medieval charm, exuding a tranquil nobility unequalled in Istria. A winding road zigzags its way up from the valley floor, eventually passing through two gates which breach the stout ramparts surrounding the old town. The first of the gates has a display of stone reliefs of Venetian lions inside the arch, while the second, 100m beyond, leads directly out onto a main square fronted by the Renaissance **St Stephen's Church** (Crkva svetog Stjepana), topped by a campanile whose crenellated top looks like a row of jagged teeth. The town's water supply used to be kept in a vast tank beneath the square, hence the medieval well in front of the church bearing a relief of Motovun's skyline with its five towers. At the far end of the square a path leads to a promenade around the town battlements made up of two concentric walls with a tiny moat (nowadays dry) in between. From here there are fantastic views over the Mirna Valley and surrounding countryside, which produces some of the finest Istrian wines – Teran and Malvasija are among the better known.

There are five **buses** daily to Motovun from Pazin, while the twice daily Pula–Buzet bus picks up and drops off at the bottom of Motovun's hill. Up on the main square, the *Kaštel* **hotel** (☎052/681-735 or 681-607, fax 681-652; ③) offers simple en-suites in a building of medieval origins, and also harbours a café and restaurant.

Oprtalj to Buje

Immediately north of Motovun the road reaches the Mirna Valley and a major crossroads: the right fork heads east towards Buzet; the left fork makes for Buje and the coast. Heading straight on, a minor road runs through the village of Livade before winding steeply and tortuously through thick forest to **OPRTALJ**, which straddles a grassy ridge high above the plain. The village is similar to Motovun but altogether more deserted: half its houses are in ruins, and tufts of grass grow from the walls of the rest. The sixteenth-century **Chapel of St Rock** (Crkvica svetog Roka) at the entrance to town has some interesting fresco fragments if you can gain access (ask for the key in the village); otherwise it's a good place for a peaceful wander and a quiet drink in the *Café Volta* near the town gate.

Eight kilometres west of the Mirna Valley crossroads, a side-road darts up towards **GROŽNJAN**, another hill village which was given a new lease of life when many of its abandoned properties were offered to artists and musicians as studios. There's also a summer school for young musicians, the Jeunesses Musicales, many of whom take part in outdoor concerts organized as part of the **Grožnjan Musical Summer** (Grožnjansko glazbeno ljeto), which takes place every August. High summer is the best time to come, when most of the artists are actually in residence and a smattering of gift shops open their doors. Outside this time, Grožnjan can be exceedingly quiet, but it's an undeniably attractive spot, with its jumble of shuttered houses made from rough-hewn, honey-brown stone, covered in creeping plants. Should you wish **to stay**, the *Ladonja* restaurant has a few rooms (☎052/776-125; ②), while the International Music School Jeunesses Musicales Croatia sometimes has rooms available in July and August (☎052/776-106; ①).

Proceeding northwest from Grožnjan towards the Slovene border you'll pass through the slightly larger town of **BUJE**, its old quarter piled up on a hill with patches of newer development below. Buje was known as the "spy of Istria" for its hilltop site, and it still commands an invigorating panorama, the cobbled streets looking out over fertile fields to the distant sea. The town ramparts, dating from the fifteenth to the seventeenth centuries, enclose a warren-like medieval centre with a lovely central square sided by a Venetian Gothic palace and loggia.

The northeast: Buzet, Roč and Hum

East of Motovun, the road to Buzet follows the course of the Mirna Valley as it gradually narrows, running between wooded crags. Roughly midway between Motovun and Buzet, the small settlement of **ISTARSKE TOPLICE** is inland Istria's most popular health resort, its sulphurous waters famous for alleviating back problems, rheumatism and skin complaints. The local **hotel**, the *Mirna* (☎052/664-300, fax 664-310; ③), has smallish rooms with bath and TV and is a good base from which to visit the nearby hill towns, although most guests are here for the indoor swimming pool, fed by spring water which emerges ready warmed from the nearby cliffs at a temperature of 35°C.

Buzet

From Istarske Toplice it's only 10km northeast to **BUZET**, the second largest town in the Istrian interior, whose original old hilltop settlement quietly decays on the heights above the River Mirna, while the bulk of the population lives in the new town below. Though it's not as pretty as Motovun or Grožnjan, Buzet has more accommodation and is a good base from which to explore the region. The town's importance as a truffle-hunting centre is celebrated by the **Grad tartufa** festival ("Truffle City"; second weekend of Sept) – the tourist office (see opposite) has details. The truffle-hunting season falls in late September and October, when locals and their specially trained dogs head off into the woods in search of the fungus. It's rare to see fresh truffles actually for sale, although most restaurants will have at least one truffle-based recipe, even if only a simple truffle-and-pasta dish or a truffle *fritaja* (omelette). Another local speciality is *biska*, a mistletoe-flavoured brandy available in local hostelries; it can also be bought direct, along with other herbal firewaters, from Eliksir (Mon–Sat 11am–2pm & 5–10pm, Sun 11am–1pm), Vidaci 25, 3km out of town on the road to Cerovlje.

Old Buzet's cobbled streets and ruined buildings seem a world away from the new quarter down on the valley floor. A **plaque** affixed to a house on one of its tiny squares commemorates Stipan Konzul Istranin, a sixteenth-century Croatian writer active in the Reformation in Germany and the first person to translate the New Testament into Croatian. The **Town Museum** nearby (Gradski muzej; Tues, Wed, Fri & Sat 10am–2pm; 5Kn) has a small collection of Roman gravestones and a display of folk costumes, particularly strong on the functional wool and hemp garments worn by the hardy villagers of the Ćićarija, the ridge to the east which separates Istria from Slovenia. There's an expansive view from what remains of Buzet's ramparts of the Mirna Valley and east over lush green hills to the imposing grey ridge of the Ćićarija.

Buses arrive on Trg fontana, a small square in the new town. About 200m east of here, the **tourist office**, on the second floor of the town hall at II Istarske brigade 2 (Mon–Fri 8am–3pm; ☎ & fax 052/662-343), has information on private rooms (②) – although most are in out-of-town farmhouses. The *Fontana* **hotel**, Trg fontana 1 (☎052/662-466, fax 662-306; ②), is a plain but comfortable three-storey place; while the smaller *Sun Sport Motel* (☎052/663-140; ③), on the corner of Sportska and Riječka just northeast of the tourist office, offers cosier, brighter en suites in a spanking new building.

For **eating**, you're limited to the *Bistro Panorama*, just off the old town's main square, which serves up grills and *fuži-* and *njoki-*based standards in a dining room with great views of the new town below. Just downhill from the *Panorama*, *Café Galerija* is the nicest place in town for a **drink**. One of nicest restaurants in Istria – indeed in the whole of Croatia – is *Toklarija*, in the hills 5km south of town at Sovinjsko Polje (☎052/663-031). It's an atmospheric, intimate place, housed in a venerable stone building with an old oil press in the main dining room. There's a range of sumptuous meat and fish standards, but the real attraction are the seasonal local products – asparagus in spring, mushrooms and truffles in autumn, all very reasonably priced. Unfortunately, you'll need your own transport to get there.

Roč

About 10km east of Buzet, framed against the backdrop of the limestone wall of the Ćićarija, the dainty village of **ROČ** sits snugly behind sixteenth-century walls so low that the place looks more like a child's toy than an erstwhile medieval strongpoint. Roč has a strong **folk music** tradition, with performing skills passed down from one generation to the next, and almost the entire population is involved in some capacity or other with the local folk music society, Istarski željezničar ("Istrian railwayman"), which has a brass section, male and female choirs and an accordion band. The best time to catch them is during the international accordion festival (Z armoniku v Roč), which takes place on the second weekend in May: the tourist office in Buzet (see above) will have details.

There's not much to do in Roč except savour the rustic atmosphere of its narrow lanes, although it's worth having a look at the small display of **Roman tombstones** inside the arch of the main gate into town, and at the Romanesque **St Anthony's Church** (Crkva svetog Antuna), an ancient, barn-like structure with a stumpy, asymmetrical bell-tower.

Buzet–Rijeka **buses** will drop you off at the Roč turn-off 500m from the village, while the **train** station (on the Pula–Divača line) is about 1500m east of the village. If you fancy staying in a local household, Drago Cerovac, Roč 58, rents out **rooms** (☎052/666-481; ②) and also has bikes for rent (100Kn per day). For **food**, *Ročka konoba* in the centre of the village is a good place for asparagus and truffles in season, as well as the regular repertoire of *ombolo*, *kobasice* and *fuži*.

Hum

Just 6km east of Roč, a minor road leads south through rolling pastures towards the minuscule settlement of Hum. The road itself is known as the **Glagolitic**

Alley (Aleja glagoljaša) after its series of open-air concrete sculptures by Želimir Janeš illustrating themes connected with Glagolitic (see box on p.183), an archaic form of Slavonic writing which was kept alive by priests in both Istria and the islands of the Kvarner Gulf before finally succumbing to Latin script in the nineteenth century. Positioned by the roadside every kilometre or so, the sculptures mostly take the form of Glagolitic characters – strange but decorative forms like a jazzed-up version of Cyrillic script.

Heaped up on a hill surrounded by grasslands and broken up by deciduous forest **HUM** is the self-proclaimed "smallest town in the world", since it's preserved all the attributes – walls, gate, church, campanile – that a town is supposed to possess, despite its population having dwindled to a current total of just seventeen. Originally fortified by the Franks in the eleventh century, Hum was a relatively prosperous place under the Aquileian Patriarchs and the Venetians and still looks quite imposing at first sight as you pass through the town gate with its monumental fifteenth-century bell-tower capped with fine, zigzagging battlements. Beyond, the oversized, neo-Baroque **Church of the Blessed Virgin Mary** (Crkva blažene djevice Marije), built in 1802 as the last gasp of urban development in a shrinking town, lords it over a settlement which now amounts to two one-metre-wide streets paved with irregular, grassed-over cobbles, and lined by chunky grey-brown farmhouses. One of the latter holds a small **museum** (daily 11am–7pm; free), which displays essays and poems written in Glagolitic by local kids and sells souvenirs – including locally made *biska* brandy. Just outside the town walls, the Romanesque cemetery **Chapel of St Hieronymous** (Crkvica svetog Jerolim; get the key from *Konoba Hum*, see below) has a number of frescoes dating back to the late twelfth century, which display a melding of Romanesque and Byzantine styles typical of the northern Adriatic in the Middle Ages. As usual, the life of Jesus provides the subject matter: there's a fine Annunciation spanning the arch above the altar, together with a Crucifixion, Pietà and Deposition – the latter bordered by unusual rosettes and floral squiggles – on the walls. Most have been damaged by ancient, Glagolitic graffiti.

It's a bit awkward to reach Hum without your own transport. No buses venture this far, and Hum train station is a minor halt 5km downhill just beyond the village of Erkovčići. There are private **rooms** in Hum (①), but you'll have to contact the tourist office in Buzet (see p.151) for details. Those with transport might consider staying at *Agroturizam Poljanice* (☎ & fax 052/684-150 or 684-367; ②), 4km south at the end of a gravel track signed off the minor road to Borut. Housed in a farmhouse situated on high ground looking towards Mount Učka, it offers simple rooms with thick stone walls and timber floors, and a full range of local food. For **eating** and **drinking** in the village, the small but charming *Konoba Hum* serves good Istrian specialities and is very popular in summer.

Draguć

The tiny village of **DRAGUĆ** is only 6km southwest of Hum as the crow flies, though getting there by car requires a detour along the minor road between Cerovlje and Buzet. Stranded among the haystacks and cornfields between the two, Draguč occupies a thin finger of highland pointing west towards the lowlands of the Mirna basin. At the end of the finger, the fourteenth-century **Chapel of St Rock** (Crkvica svetog Roka; ask for the key (*ključ*) in the village square), contains frescoes similar to those in Beram, although slightly less well preserved. There's a large Journey of the Magi on left as you enter, with an

Annunciation above it, and a Martyrdom of St Sebastian and Flight into Egypt on the right, all rendered in vivid greens and ruddy browns redolent of the surrounding countryside.

The east coast

Compared to the tourist complexes of the west, Istria's east coast is a quiet and undeveloped area with few obvious attractions. East of Pula, the main road to Rijeka heads inland, remaining at a discreet distance from the shoreline for the next 50km. Half an hour out of Pula the road passes through **BARBAN**, a grey, largely forgotten village overlooking Krapan Bay whose only claim to fame is as the home of the annual **Tilting at the Ring** (Trka na prstenac) festival, which involves locals on horseback attempting to spear a ring on the end of a lance – a sporting contest which was widespread throughout the Mediterranean in the Middle Ages, although it now survives only here and in the Dalmatian town of Sinj (see p.263).

From Barban the road descends to cross the valley of Raška Draga before entering the village of **RAŠA**, formerly the southernmost outpost of the Labin coalfields before they were finally closed in 1999. Built by the Italians in 1937, Raša still has the feel of a model industrial settlement, with its rows of identical barrack-like houses softened by trailing vines. It also boasts a fine example of Mussolini-era architecture in **St Barbara's Church** (Crkva svete Barbare – Barbara is the patron saint of miners), an austere but graceful structure which features a campanile in the shape of a pit-head and a curving facade representing an upturned coal barrow.

Labin and around

Five kilometres beyond Raša, **LABIN** is divided into two parts, with the original medieval town crowning the hill above, and a twentieth-century suburb, **Podlabin**, sprawling across the plain below. Labin was for many years Croatia's coal-mining capital, and earned itself a place in working-class history in 1921, when striking miners declared the "Labin Republic" before being pacified by the Italian authorities. There's precious little sign of mining heritage nowadays apart from the town museum and the one remaining pit-head in Podlabin, the top of which still bears the word "Tito" proudly spelt out in wrought-iron letters. Subsidence caused by mining led to Labin's old town being partially abandoned in the 1970s and 1980s, although the subsequent decline of the coal industry, coupled with a thoroughgoing restoration programme, encouraged people to return. It's now one of the more attractive of Istria's hill towns – all the more so for its proximity to the beach at Rabac, only forty minutes' walk downhill.

The Town
Pula–Rijeka buses stop in Podlabin, from where it's a twenty-minute walk up to the main square of the old town, **Titov trg**. From here, a rough cobbled path leads through the city gate into the heart of the old town, where steep alleys thread their way among a motley collection of town houses attractively decked out in ochres, oranges and pinks. Head uphill to find the **Church of the Birth of the Blessed Virgin Mary** (Crkva rođenja blažene djevice Marije), on whose facade

a fourteenth-century rose window is upstaged by a seventeenth-century Venetian lion. The burgundy Batiala-Lazarini Palace next door now holds the **Town Museum** (Gradski muzej; June–Sept daily 10am–1pm; 10Kn), with a small collection of Roman tombstones and a display of local costumes, including examples of the enormous woollen scarves which local women used to drape over their shoulders to cushion the load when carrying water or other heavy burdens. There's also a small but atmospheric recreation of life inside a coal mine, which involves donning a (totally unnecessary) hard hat and embarking on a stooping walk between pit props.

From the museum, continue up 1 Maja to reach the highest point of the hill, marking the western boundary of the old town. There's a viewing terrace here on the site of the medieval fortress, or **Fortica**, looking down towards Rabac on the coast, with the mountainous shape of Cres beyond. From here, you can descend the western flank of the old town's hill by walking down Guiseppine Martinuzzi to the eighteenth-century Franković Palace at the bottom, which now holds the **Memorial Collection of Matthias Flacius Illyricus** (Spomen-zbirka M.F. Ilirika; same times as the Town Museum, but ask there first to check they'll be someone in attendance; 10Kn), with books and manuscripts published by Matija Vlačić (1520–75), local Protestant and right-hand man to Martin Luther. One typical engraving of the time depicts the Pope with the head of an ass, the torso of a woman and the legs of a dragon – the kind of image that would have pleased Vlačić's uncle and fellow reformist Baldo Lupetina, whose refusal to renounce his beliefs resulted in him being tied in a weighted sack and thrown into the Venetian lagoon.

Practicalities

Labin's **tourist office** (mid-June to mid-Sept daily 8am–10pm; mid-Sept to mid-June Mon–Fri 8am–3pm, Sat 9am–4pm; ☎052/855-560), on the corner of Titov trg and Boža Štemberge, should be able to provide a free town map and an update on **room** agencies. At present, the Kompas office (Mon–Fri 8am–3pm; ☎052/856-599) on Zelenice, midway between the bus station and old town, is the most reliable source; otherwise, the nearest accommodation is in Rabac (see below).

Of Labin's places to **eat**, *Kvarner*, just off Titov trg below the town gate, does cheap lunches and dinners, with daily specials often chalked up on a board outside; the more expensive *Due Fratelli*, about 2km out of town on the road to Rabac at Montozi 6, offers top-notch seafood and grilled meats. For **drinking and nightlife**, there's a surfeit of café-bars either on or just off Titov trg. Down in Podlabin, the buildings around the pit-head have been transformed into a cultural centre, the Kulturni centar Lamparna, which organizes gigs, raves, theatre and art exhibitions and has a bar and Internet café.

Rabac

Buses run roughly every hour from Podlabin to the resort village of **RABAC**, squeezed into a narrow bay on the coast; alternatively, you can walk there in about forty minutes by heading along the Rabac road then taking the path which leads right into the woods just behind the Portatours tourist agency on the edge of Labin. Initially developed by the Italians in the interwar years as a workers' holiday settlement, it nowadays has an almost totally modern appearance, its hillsides covered in apartment blocks and fringed by a line of hotels. There's a reasonable shingle beach on the northern side of the bay, and the usual string of so-so bars and restaurants along the harbour. All in all it's a bit too sanitized to compete with the west coast resorts, although the *Lanterna* hotel (☎052/872-213, fax 872-068; ⑥) is one of the best on this part of the coast, and reasonably cheap **rooms** (②) are available from Kompas (June–Sept daily 8am–8pm; ☎052/872-083) on the southern side of the harbour. There's also a **campsite** right on the beach.

Northeast of Labin

Northeast of Labin, the green edges of Istria drop steep and sheer into the sea, offering few viable places to build. Twelve kilometres out of Labin, the ancient and windswept hilltop settlement of **PLOMIN** is typical of the local villages – most of its inhabitants left for Italy in 1945, leaving the fishing port below to silt up; many of its old stone houses are now boarded up. Most Pula–Rijeka buses stop for a breather at the *Vidikovac* café 4km further on, a popular viewpoint high above the rocky shore, with the grey outline of the island of Cres rising to the east. **Cres** itself is reachable by regular car ferry from the tiny port of **BRESTOVA**, to which a side-road descends a couple of kilometres further on. Beyond Brestova, the road continues to twist and turn above the shore before descending towards Mošćenička Draga, first in a string of resorts that make up the **Opatija Riviera** (see p.165).

travel details

TRAINS

Pazin to: Buzet (8 daily; 50min); Hum (8 daily; 20min); Pula (10 daily; 1hr 10min); Roč (6 daily; 35min).

Pula to: Buzet (8 daily; 2hr); Hum (8 daily; 1hr 30min); Pazin (10 daily; 1hr 10min); Roč (6 daily; 1hr 45min).

BUSES

Pazin to: Labin (2 daily; 1hr 10min); Motovun (5 daily; 45min); Poreč (6 daily; 1hr 15min); Pula (6 daily; 1hr); Rijeka (6 daily; 1hr); Rovinj (5 daily; 1hr 10min); Zagreb (7 daily; 5hr 15min).

Poreč to: Buje (7 daily; 1hr); Lanterna (summer only; 5 daily; 30min); Novigrad (8 daily; 30min); Opatija (8 daily; 3hr 30min); Pazin (5 daily; 1hr); Pula (12 daily; 1hr 30min); Rijeka (6 daily; 4hr); Rovinj (5 daily; 45min); Umag (8 daily; 45min); Visnjan (6 daily; 20min); Vižinada (8 daily;); Vrsar (12 daily; 20min); Zagreb (7 daily; 8hr).

Pula to: Buje (5 daily; 2hr 40min); Buzet (2 daily; 2hr 30min); Dubrovnik (1 daily; 16hr); Istarske Toplice (2 daily; 2hr 15min); Karlovac (10 daily; 5hr); Labin (15 daily; 1hr); Motovun (2 daily; 2hr); Novigrad (3 daily; 2hr 10min); Opatija (hourly; 2hr); Pazin (6 daily; 1hr); Poreč (12 daily; 1hr 30min); Rijeka (hourly; 2hr 30min); Rovinj (hourly; 1hr 15min); Šibenik (4 daily; 10hr); Split (4 daily; 12hr); Svetvinaenat (5 daily; 45min); Umag (4 daily; 2hr 25min); Varaždin (1 daily; 9hr); Vodnjan (10 daily; 20min); Vrsar (4 daily; 1hr 30min); Zadar (4 daily; 6hr 30min); Zagreb (10 daily; 6hr 30min); Žminj (6 daily; 50min).

Rovinj to: Buje (3 daily; 1hr 20min); Dubrovnik (1 daily; 17hr 30min); Labin (5 daily; 2hr 25min); Pazin (Mon–Sat only 4 daily; 1hr 10min); Poreč (6 daily; 1hr); Pula (hourly; 1hr 15min); Rijeka (7 daily; 4hr); Split (2 daily; 13hr 30min); Varaždin (1 daily; 10hr 30min); Vrsar (4 daily; 25min); Zagreb (7 daily; 7hr 40min).

FERRIES

Pula to: Mali Lošinj (June–Sept 6 weekly, Oct–May 1 weekly; 2hr 25min); Silba (June–Sept 6 weekly, Oct–May 1 weekly; 5hr 20min); Zadar (June–Sept 6 weekly, Oct–May 1 weekly; 7hr 45min).

INTERNATIONAL TRAINS

Pula to: Ljubljana (2 daily; 4hr).

INTERNATIONAL BUSES

Buzet to: Koper (1 daily; 1hr 30min).

Pazin to: Trieste (1 daily; 2hr 30min).

Poreč to: Koper (3 daily; 2hr); Ljubljana (1 daily; 4hr 30min); to Piran (1 daily; 2hr); to Portorož (1 daily; 1hr 50min); Trieste (3 daily; 2hr 50min).

Rovinj to: Koper (2 daily; 2hr 40min); Trieste (1 daily; 3hr 30min).

Pula to: Koper (2 daily; 3hr 30min); to Piran (1 daily; 3hr 30min); to Portorož (1 daily; 3hr 20min); to Trieste (1 daily; 4hr 20min).

CHAPTER FOUR

THE KVARNER GULF

T he **Kvarner Gulf** – the large, deep bay which separates the Istrian peninsula to the north from Dalmatia to the south – is the first view of the coast
for many visitors, as the main road from Zagreb sweeps down to the
Adriatic at Rijeka. It's a region which brings together many of the features
which make the coast so enticing: grizzled coastal hills and mountains, an archipelago of ochre-grey islands, and fishing villages with narrow alleys and gardens
groaning under the weight of subtropical plants.

Croatia's largest port and the area's economic and political centre, **Rijeka** is
more of a transit point than a destination in itself, and most people push straight
on to the islands that crowd the gulf to the south. **Krk** is the most accessible of
these, connected to the mainland by a road bridge just half an hour's drive from
Rijeka, though the islands further out – **Rab**, **Cres** and **Lošinj** – feel more
removed from the urban bustle. Each has its fair share of historic towns whose
shuttered, Italianate houses recall the long centuries of Venetian rule, along with
some gorgeous coves and beaches – especially the sandy ones at Baška on Krk
and Lopar on Rab. Although lush and green on their western flanks, the islands
are hauntingly bare when seen from the mainland, the result of deforestation during the Venetian period, when local timber was used to feed the shipyards of
Venice; the fierce northeasterly wind known as the **Bura** (see box on p.185) has
prevented anything from growing there again. This denuded landscape is particularly evident on the most southerly of the Kvarner islands, **Pag**, with its bare,
stony hills.

The coast of the mainland which flanks the gulf was traditionally known as the
Hrvatsko primorje (literally, "Croatian littoral") to distinguish it from the
Adriatic islands and Dalmatia – largely because it never fell under Venetian con-
trol. Because of its proximity to Habsburg central Europe this stretch of the
Adriatic littoral was the first to develop as a tourist destination, with **Opatija**,
Crikvenica and **Novi Vinodolski** emerging in the late nineteenth century as

---

ACCOMMODATION PRICE CODES

The accommodation in this guide has been graded using the following price codes,
based on the cost of each establishment's **least expensive double room** in high
season (June–Sept), excluding special offers. Hotel room rates almost always
include breakfast. Out of season, prices on the coast can fall by up to 50 percent.
Where single rooms exist, they usually cost 60–70 percent of the price of a double.
For more details, see p.24.

① Less than 200Kn ④ 400–500Kn ⑦ 800–1000Kn
② 200–300Kn ⑤ 500–600Kn ⑧ 1000–1200Kn
③ 300–400Kn ⑥ 600–800Kn ⑨ Over 1200Kn

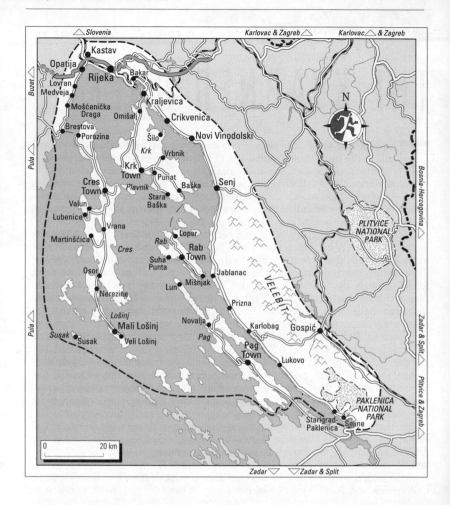

swish winter health resorts patronized by the Viennese upper crust. They're fairly bland tourist centres nowadays, although Opatija and neighbouring **Lovran** preserve something of the spirit of the *belle époque*. The southern part of the Kvarner coastline is dominated by the stark and majestic **Velebit** mountains, which can be seen at their best in the **Paklenica National Park** at the southern end of the range.

Rijeka

Rows of cumbrous cranes and rusty, sea-stained tankers front the soaring apartment blocks of Croatia's largest port, **RIJEKA** (pronounced "Ree-acre"), a down-to-earth industrial city which is the major ferry terminal along the Adriatic coast and an unavoidable transit point if you're travelling through the region by bus. Rijeka is far from beautiful, but it is the northern Adriatic's only true metropolis, mustering a reasonable number of attractions and with an appealing urban buzz, while the hilltop suburb of **Trsat**, home to a famous pilgrimage church, is particularly attractive. Accommodation in town is limited to a few run-down hotels, and if you want to stay in the area it may be better to aim for the Opatija Riviera to the west (see p.165), an area amply served by Rijeka's municipal bus network.

Some history

Although Trsat is built on an ancient hilltop site which was occupied by both Illyrians and Romans, the port below didn't really begin to develop until the thirteenth century, when it was known as **Sveti Vid na rijeci** ("St Vitus on the River"), a name subsequently shortened to the rather blunt **Rijeka** (which, like its Italian version, Fiume, simply means "river"). From 1466 the city was an Austrian possession, a prosperous port which remained under the direct control of Vienna until 1848, when Ban Jelačić (see p.340) brought it under Croatian administration. Rijeka became a bone of contention between Croatia and Hungary in the latter half of the nineteenth century, after the city was claimed by Budapest on the grounds that the Hungarian half of the Austro-Hungarian Empire should possess at least one outlet to the Adriatic. In 1868, an agreement between Croatia and Hungary – which was to have left the fate of Rijeka open to arbitration – was due to be signed by the Habsburg Emperor Franz Josef but, in a notorious piece of trickery, an additional clause presenting the port to Hungary was literally pasted in at the last moment without the Croats' knowledge.

Rijeka under the Hungarians was a booming industrial port with an expanding Croatian population. At the end of World War I the city once again came up for grabs. The 1915 **Treaty of London** had promised Dalmatia – but not Rijeka – to the Italians as a reward for joining the war on the Allied side, a promise that Britain and France were unwilling to keep come 1918. The Italians demanded Rijeka as the price for giving up their claim to territories further south. The city's inhabitants voted to join Italy in a plebiscite of October 1918 (most of Rijeka's Croatian population actually lived outside the municipal boundary in the suburb of Sušak, and so were not represented), but the Allies remained firm, garrisoning the port with an Anglo-American and French force as a prelude to handing it over to the infant state of Yugoslavia. In September 1919, however, the Italian soldier-poet **Gabriele d'Annunzio** (see box on p.160) marched into Rijeka unopposed and occupied the city, establishing a proto-fascist regime which endured until January 1921. He was eventually forced to leave by the Italian government, and February 1921's **Treaty of Rapallo** declared Rijeka a free city. Despite this, Rijeka was once again taken over by Italy following Mussolini's accession to power in 1922, an act which the Yugoslav government grudgingly accepted in the hope that it would deflect Italian territorial ambitions from the rest of the Adriatic.

Rijeka was returned to Yugoslavia after World War II, when most of the Italian population left. In the years that followed, Rijeka's traditionally strong shipbuilding industry flourished anew, and the city acquired its high-rise suburbs, though surprisingly, the economic problems of the 1980s and 1990s – when shipbuilding collapsed and the city's once strong merchant fleet was sold off vessel by vessel – don't seem to have dented Rijeka's pride. In the **post-independence** years, the city was a stronghold of centre-left values during the ten-year rule of the right-wing HDZ, imbuing it with a symbolic political importance in the new republic.

GABRIELE D'ANNUNZIO IN RIJEKA

Following World War I, Italy's failure to win Rijeka by diplomatic means was seen by many right-wing Italians as proof of the essential weakness of Italian democracy, provoking calls for an overthrow of parliamentary government in favour of some form of dictatorship. Disgruntled army officers calculated that an attack on Rijeka would be enormously popular with the Italian public, thereby preparing the ground for a coup within Italy itself. To lead the attack they chose the flamboyant poet, novelist and pilot **Gabriele d'Annunzio** (1863–1938). D'Annunzio was a compelling figure: a decadent aesthete who reinvented himself as a war hero, he volunteered for the Italian cavalry in 1915 and went on to serve with distinction in both the navy and air force, becoming a well-known nationalist in the process.

D'Annunzio marched into Rijeka on September 12, 1919 at the head of 297 volunteers – whose numbers were soon swelled by regular soldiers tacitly lent to the enterprise by their commanding officers. He immediately declared Italy's annexation of Rijeka – a declaration that the Italian government in Rome, suspicious of the radical d'Annunzio, disowned. By September 1920, d'Annunzio – who now styled himself "Il Commandante" – had established Rijeka as an independent state entitled the **Reggenza del Carnaro**, or "Regency of the Kvarner", which he hoped to use as a base from which to topple the Italian government and establish a dictatorship.

Under d'Annunzio, political life in Rijeka became an experiment in totalitarian theory from which fellow Italian nationalist Benito Mussolini was to borrow freely. D'Annunzio's main innovation was the establishment of a **corporate state**, ostensibly based on the Italian medieval guild system, in which electoral democracy was suspended and replaced by nine "corporations" – each corresponding to a different profession – by which the populace could be organized and controlled. The Regency was also a proving ground for fascism's love of spectacle, with d'Annunzio mounting bombastic parades of extravagantly uniformed followers and mass meetings (often staged to make it appear as if the public had gathered spontaneously) featuring a call-and-response style of oratory which involved carefully scripted audience participation.

Successive Italian governments failed to take action against d'Annunzio, seeing him as a wild card with which to frighten the allied powers still assembled at the Paris Peace Conference. Once Italian negotiators had received what they thought was a reasonable deal – Istria, Zadar and a couple of islands – they felt honour-bound to restore order to Rijeka, and Italian forces began a **bombardment of Rijeka** on Christmas Eve 1920. D'Annunzio surrendered four days later, finally leaving the city on January 18, thereby ending one of twentieth-century history's more bizarre episodes.

D'Annunzio's occupation of Rijeka had demonstrated to Mussolini how easy it was to mount a show of force against a dispirited liberal order, providing him with the blueprint for his own successful coup, the **March on Rome** of October 1922. Once ensconced in power, Mussolini rewarded d'Annunzio for his Rijeka escapade with a seat in the Italian senate. Despite their political similarities, however, Mussolini and d'Annunzio never really got on: both were very much theatrical personalities, and each was afraid of having his demagogic thunder stolen by the other.

Arrival, information and accommodation

Rijeka's **train station** lies a few hundred metres west of the city centre on Borisa Krešimirova; **ferries** dock by the Riva, just south of the centre. There are two **bus stations**: one on the southern fringe of the city centre, at Trg Žabica, for all long-distance buses; a second, for local buses – including Trsat, Opatija and Lovran – on the east side of the city centre, on Jelačićev trg. Municipal bus **tickets** can be bought from newspaper kiosks (valid for two journeys) or from the driver (valid for one). **Fares** are calculated according to a zonal system: most city destinations, including Sušak and Trsat, fall within zone 1 (10Kn from the driver; 13Kn from a kiosk); Opatija is in zone 3 (12Kn/17Kn); Lovran in zone 4 (14Kn/20Kn). Rijeka's **tourist office**, just off Fiumara at Užarska 14 (July & Aug daily 8am–8pm; Sept–June Mon–Fri 8am–4pm, Sat 8am–1pm; ☎051/335-882, fax 214-706, *tz-rijeka@ri.tel.hr*), has town plans and a wealth of information on the Kvarner region, including the English-language *Kvarner Info*, with listings of cultural events.

There are no private rooms in the town itself, although there are plenty along the Opatija Riviera (see p.165). Of the city's **hotels**, the colourless but comfortable *Kontinental*, just off Titov trg (☎051/372-008, fax 372-009; ③), is the only reasonable downtown hotel; the *Jadran*, 3km out of the centre on the main southbound coastal road at Šetalište XIII divizije 46 (☎051/216-600 or 216-230, fax 436-203; ③), is a plain seafront tower block which has marvellous views across the water to the island of Cres. The nearest **campsite** is *Preluk* (☎051/622-249, fax 621-913), 8km north along the road to Opatija, on the cusp of the bay as the road wheels south towards Vološko; bus #32 from Jelačićev trg passes the entrance.

The City

Much of Rijeka was rebuilt after World War II, though a fair number of nineteenth-century buildings remain, many of them in solid ranks along the **Riva**, a neglected part of town which, the odd café excepted, lacks the vibrancy of other city waterfronts along the Adriatic. Just to the north, the pedestrianized **Korzo** is Rijeka's main shopping street and the focus of most of its streetlife. The one real landmark here is the **City Tower** (Gradski toranj), a medieval gateway topped by a later Baroque structure; its position marks the old seafront before the city was extended by landfills in the eighteenth and nineteenth centuries. Known locally as "Pod uriloj" (after the Italian word for clock, *orologio*), it has a relief on its street-facing side bearing the Habsburg double-headed eagle surmounted by busts of Austrian emperors Leopold I (on the left) and Charles VI (on the right). It was the latter's decision to declare Rijeka a free port in 1717 that kickstarted the city's economic growth.

The gate beneath the clock-tower gives access to the **Old Town** (Stari grad), a rather hopeful description for an area of scruffy squares, peeling plaster and shiny, black glass-fronted department stores. Heading straight on uphill brings you out onto the sloping Trg Grivica, at the top of which stands **St Vitus' Church** (Crkva svetog Vida), surmounted by a rotunda built in 1638 in imitation of Santa Maria della Salute in Venice. Look out for the Gothic **crucifix** above the high altar. In 1296, the story goes, a gambler was losing at cards outside the church and ran inside in a rage, flinging stones at this crucifix, which began to bleed. In response to this blasphemy, the ground beneath the man's feet is said to have promptly opened up and swallowed him completely, except for one hand.

The faithful claim that one of the stones he threw is still embedded in the side of the wooden Christ.

Not far from St Vitus' – make a left turn along Žrtava fašizma – rises the late nineteenth-century Gubernatorial Palace (Guvernerova palača), whose marvellously over-the-top state rooms now provide a sumptuous setting for the **History and Maritime Museum** (Pomorski i povijesni muzej hrvatskog primorja; Tues–Sat 9am–1pm; 10Kn). It was here that d'Annunzio installed himself for his short period of power, until shelling by the Italian battleship *Andrea Doria* on Boxing Day 1920 persuaded him to leave. Its huge echoing rooms hold costumes, period portraits, weaponry and a lot of colour-coordinated drapes and furniture, while the model ships on the second floor include replicas of the huge tankers formerly made by the local 3 Maj shipyard, whose gates you'll pass when entering the town from the northwest. In the palace grounds there's a modern pavilion holding the **City Museum** (Muzej grada Rijeke; Mon–Sat 10am–1pm), which hosts changing exhibitions relating to local history.

Returning downhill towards the Korzo along F. Supila you'll pass the **University Library** (Sveučilišna knjižnica; entrance round the corner on Dolac), which is home to two exhibition spaces: the **Modern Art Gallery** (Moderna galerija), which stages occasional temporary shows, and the **Glagolitic Exhibition** (Izložba glagoljice; Tues–Fri 2–6pm; 10Kn), a worthy but less than riveting display of manuscripts written in the ecclesiastical script (see box on p.183) which was common to the Kvarner region in the Middle Ages.

Finally, opposite the bus station on Trg Žabica rises the huge, striped neo-Gothic bulk of the **Capuchin Church** (Kapucinska crkva), completed in 1908 and fronted by a large double stairway. It's said that the Capuchins – in particular a certain self-styled "Saint" Jochanza – collected money for the church with public shows of blood-sweating, making the site a minor place of pilgrimage until Jochanza was accused of charlatanry and arrested in 1913.

Trsat

East of the old centre, the thick, pea-soup-coloured River Rječina marks the edge of central Rijeka, beyond which lies the suburb of Sušak; between 1924 and 1945, walking between the city centre and here meant crossing from Italy into the Kingdom of Yugoslavia. On the north side of Titov trg, a Baroque gateway marks the start of the **Trsatske Stube**, a stairway of 538 steps, built in 1531 at the bidding of Uskok commander Petar Kružić, which leads up to the pilgrimage centre of **TRSAT** (also reachable on bus #1 or #1a from Fiumara), nowadays a suburb of Rijeka, occupying a bluff high above the modern centre. According to legend, Trsat is where the House of the Virgin Mary and Joseph rested for three years during its miraculous flight from the infidel in Nazareth to Loreto in Italy, where it was set down in December 1294. At the top, the **Church of St Mary of Loreto** (Crkva svete Marije Lauretanske) supposedly marks the spot where the house rested. The church originally dates from the fifteenth century, but was almost completely rebuilt in 1824; it's now a place of almost exclusively female pilgrimage and worship – the more devout pilgrims sometimes scale Kružić's steps on their knees. The sanctuary features an altar with an icon of the Virgin, sent here by Pope Urban V in 1367, surrounded by necklaces and other trinkets hung there by grateful pilgrims, who are required to walk round the altar three times. At the side of the church is a **Franciscan monastery** whose chapel of votive gifts (kapela zavjetnih darova) is plastered with pictures and tapestries left by those whose prayers have been answered; the numerous enthusiastic paintings depicting events such as shipwrecks and car crashes in which the Virgin is supposed to have intervened are particularly striking.

Across the road from the church, **Trsat Castle** (April–Oct Tues–Sun 9am–11pm; Feb, March, Nov & Dec Tues–Sun 9am–3pm; 10Kn) is an ivy-clad hotchpotch of turrets and towers, walkways and parapets that give views backwards up a great grey tear in the mountains and forwards to Rijeka, under its dim yellowish haze of industrial smog. Beyond is the island of Cres and, to the right, on the northwestern side of the Kvarner Gulf, the sheer mountain wall of Mount Učka. Parts of the castle date back to Roman times, when it was an important way-station on the trade routes linking the northern Adriatic with the Pannonian plain, but the fortress assumed its current shape mainly in the thirteenth century, when it became a stronghold of the Frankopans of Krk (see box on p.179). In 1826, an Austrian general of Irish descent, one Vice-marshal Laval Nugent, took the place over and restored it in Classical style, constructing the Doric temple in the middle which serves as his family's mausoleum; the castle is also used as a open-air theatre and houses a seasonal restaurant.

Eating, drinking and entertainment

Rijeka has only a meagre selection of **restaurants** – most locals head for nearby Opatija if they want a slap-up meal. The best place in town is the *Spaghetteria Moko*, just round the corner from the bus station at Riva 14, which has the finest range of pasta dishes in the region. *Slavica*, just off the Korzo on Trg republike hrvatske, serves less spectacular spaghettis, but often has cheapies like *fažol* (bean soup) advertised on the board outside, and there are plenty of sandwich joints (and a *McDonalds*) along the Korzo. If you're in Trsat, the restaurant in the castle has the standard range of schnitzels.

For daytime **drinking**, the pavement cafés lining the Korzo or those girdling the church in Trsat are the places to hang out. *Filodrammatica*, Korzo 28, has a good selection of cakes and pastries, and a rather posh inner sanctum for sit-down coffee-supping. There's a range of lively venues to choose from at night: take the steps leading uphill from the Korzo towards the Gubernatorial Palace to find the *River Pub*, F. Supila 12 (enter from the alley round the back), a welcoming, wood-panelled place with Irish ales on tap. *Celtic Café Bard*, opposite St Vitus' Church at Trg Grivica 68, also has Irish beers in a more intimate café-bar environment. *Svid Rock Café*, Riva 20, is an enormous place decorated with pop bric-a-brac and hosting frequent live music. *Palach*, hidden away on Kružna, an alleyway which dives behind the Korzo just to the rear of the Riječka banka, has a cool matt-black bar area, an **Internet café** and space for live gigs. In the old town, on the modern paved square hidden off to the side of Koblerov trg, you'll find *Saloon Club* and a cluster of similarly brash cafés, all pumping out loud techno late into the night.

For **entertainment**, big rock and pop performances take place at the Dvorana Mladost in Trsat, a modern multi-purpose auditorium located slightly uphill from the church. The Croatian National Theatre (Hrvatsko narodno kazalište), on Ivana Zajca, is the place for opera, orchestral concerts and theatre. For children, Gradsko kazalište lutaka, B. Polića 6, is a respected puppet theatre. Rijeka's two main cinemas are the Croatia, near the bus station at Krešimirova 2, and the Teatro Fenice, a venerable nineteenth-century auditorium where d'Annunzio held political rallies.

THE RIJEKA CARNIVAL

On the last Sunday before Shrove Tuesday, Rijeka plays host to the biggest carnival celebrations in Croatia, culminating in a spectacular parade. Much of the parade centres on carnival floats and fancy-dress costumes, although there is one authentic older element in the shape of the **zvončari**, young men clad in animal skins who ring enormous cow bells to drive away evil spirits. Many of the villages in the hills north of Rijeka have their own groups of *zvončari*, a tradition which has survived since pre-Christian times. The Rijeka parade, which normally culminates with a large party of *zvončari* strutting their stuff, usually kicks off at around 1pm and takes around five hours to complete. Afterwards, participants and spectators alike troop off to the Delta (the estuary of the River Rječina), where there's a funfair and an enormous marquee, in which drinking and dancing continue into the early hours.

Listings

Airlines Croatia Airlines, Trg Republike Hrvatske 9 (☎051/330-207 or 336-757, fax 331-684).

Bookshop Nova, Trpimirova 9, has a small range of English-language paperbacks.

Ferry tickets Jadrolinija, Riva 16 (Mon, Tues & Thurs–Sat 7am–6pm, Wed & Sun 7am–8pm; ☎051/211-444 or 666-100).

Hospital Krešimirova 42 (☎051/658-111), just past the train station on the right.

Left luggage There's a *garderoba* at the bus station (7am–10pm).

Market The city's main fruit and veg market is on Ivan Zajca, near the Croatian National Theatre.

Pharmacy There's a 24hr pharmacy at Jadranski trg 1.

Post office/telephones The most central post office is halfway down the Korzo (Mon–Fri 7am–9pm, Sat 7am–2pm); there's a 24hr branch beyond the train station at Krešimirova 7.

Taxi There are ranks outside the train and bus stations, or call ☎335-138.

Travel agents Croatia Express, Trg kralja Tomislava 1 (☎051/211-304); GeneralTurist, Trg Republike Hrvatske 8a (☎051/212-900); Kvarner Express, Trpimirova 2 (☎051/213-808).

The Opatija Riviera

Just to the north of Rijeka, the **Opatija Riviera** (Opatijska rivijera) is a twenty-kilometre stretch of sedate seaside resorts which lines the western side of the Kvarner Gulf. Standing at centre of the Riviera is the town of **Opatija**, whose success as a tourist resort in the latter half of the nineteenth century made it the Austro-Hungarian Empire's answer to the Côte d'Azur. Protected from strong winds by the ridge of **Mount Učka**, this stretch of coast became the favoured retreat of tubercular Viennese fleeing the icy winter temperatures of central Europe. The Habsburg ambience survives in some attractive *fin-de-siècle* architecture, the best of which is in the dainty town of **Lovran**, just southwest of Opatija. Beaches tend to be of the concrete variety, unless you head for **Medveja** just beyond Lovran, where there's a much more enticing stretch of shingle.

The main Rijeka–Pula road cuts right through the riviera. From Rijeka, **bus #32** (every 20–30min between about 4.30am and 10.30pm from Jelačićev trg) goes through Opatija and terminates in either Lovran or Mošćenička Draga. Approaching from Pula, any Rijeka-bound bus will drop you off.

Kastav

The best view of the Opatija Riviera is from the village of **KASTAV**, a worthwhile side-trip 10km north of Rijeka on the karst ridge which overlooks the gulf. A windswept knot of cobbled alleyways hemmed in by scraps of surviving fortification, Kastav is strong on atmosphere but short of real sights. Head first for **St Helena's Church** (Crkva svete Jelene), from whose terrace there's an expansive panorama of the waters below. On the other, landward side of the village, is the **Crekvina**, the stark remains of an enormous church begun by the Jesuits but never finished. Given the village as a fief by the Habsburgs, the Jesuits proved unpopular masters, greedy for taxes. One of their civilian administrators, Frano Morelli, was drowned in a well on the main square in 1666 – a crime which was committed en masse by the villagers and therefore proved unpunishable.

Kastav is easily accessible from either Rijeka (bus #18) or Opatija (bus #33). There's a **tourist office** on the main square (Mon–Fri 9am–3pm; ☎051/691-425) and a couple of good places to **eat**: *Vidikovac*, on the sea-facing side of the village, has a large outdoor terrace and simple grilled meats; the slightly grander *Kukuriku na fortici*, near the tourist office, has a wider choice of meat and fish along with Istrian-influenced standards like *njoki* (gnocchi) and *fuži* (pasta noodles). Cultural events include the **Kastav Cultural Summer** (Kastavsko kulturno ljeto), a programme of chamber music concerts in July and August; and the **White Sunday and Monday** (Bela nedeja i beli pundejak) on the first Sunday and Monday in October, when new wine is tasted and there's folk dancing in the square.

Opatija

Fifteen kilometres out of Rijeka on the main coastal road to Pula lies **OPATIJA**, the longest established of the gulf's resorts. It's a town in the best tradition of seaside magnificence, pretty in an overpowering Austro-Hungarian sort of way, a monument both to genteel early twentieth-century tourism and its subsequent decline. The Opatija of today still attracts a smattering of stylish Croats, and can be a lively place on sunny weekends throughout the year, but one can't help but feel that the town is living on past glories, offering cheap packages to elderly Europeans while true jet-setters seek their thrills elsewhere.

Arrival, information and accommodation

Trains on the Ljubljana–Rijeka line stop at Matulji, 4km uphill from Opatija (regular local buses run from here down into town), though it's more convenient to arrive by **bus**, all of which stop at a central terminal on a small square facing onto the waterfront. Turn left from here and walk for five minutes up the main street, Maršala Tita, to reach the **tourist office** at no. 101 (summer daily 8am–7pm; winter Mon–Sat 8am–3pm, Sun 8am–2pm; ☎051/271-710), which is well stocked with town maps and brochures.

Accommodation in Opatija is expensive unless you opt for the private **rooms** offered by numerous local agencies: the easiest to find is the Kompas office, just up the road from the tourist office at Maršala Tita 110. As for **hotels**, the best deals are offered by the bland modern establishments which stretch a kilometre or so southwest of the centre along Maršala Tita, such as the *Jadran* (☎051/271-100; ④) and the *Paris* (☎051/271-911; ④), both of which have smallish but smart en-suites and (sometimes compulsory) half-board arrangements. Cheapest of the Habsburg-era places is the *Palace-Bellevue*, right in the centre at Maršala Tita 200 (☎051/271-811, fax 271-964; ⑤), whose lobby and bar areas still convey a whiff of *fin-de-siècle* opulence, although the roomy en-suites boast marvellously uncoordinated 1970s colour schemes. The venerable *Kvarner* (☎051/271-233, fax 271-202; ⑥) can't be beaten for atmosphere, although the *Mozart* (☎051/271-877, fax 271-739; ⑦), centrally located at Maršala Tita 138, is currently the town's best in terms of creature comforts.

The Town

Opatija was little more than a fishing village until the arrival in 1844 of Rijeka businessman **Iginio Scarpa**, who built the opulent Villa Angiolina as a holiday home for his family and aristocratic Habsburg friends such as the Archduke

Maximilian, future Emperor of Mexico, and Maria Anna, wife of Emperor Ferdinand I. In 1882 the villa was bought by **Friedrich Schüller**, head of Austria's Southern Railways who, having supervised the completion of the line from Ljubljana to Rijeka, decided to promote Opatija as a mass holiday destination; the town's first hotels – the *Kvarner*, *Krönprinzessin Stephanie* (today's *Imperial*) and *Palace-Bellevue* – soon followed. Due to its mild climate, Opatija was originally a winter health-resort, with a season running from October to May. It soon developed a Europe-wide reputation: Franz Josef of Austria and Kaiser Wilhelm II of Germany held talks here in 1894, while playwright Anton Chekhov holidayed at the *Hotel Kvarner* in the same year.

Modern Opatija is a long, straggling resort which has lost much of its original *fin-de-siècle* character. Nowadays the town's only real attraction is the **Šetalište Franza Josefa**, a splendid tree-shaded promenade which runs along the rocky seafront all the way to the old fishing village of Volosko (2km to the north) and the sedate resort of Lovran (6km to the south), offering a far better way of exploring the town than the rather tatty and traffic-choked main street, Maršala Tita. Squeezed between the promenade and Maršala Tita, about 500m northeast of the bus station, lie the flowerbeds and lovingly clipped shrubs of the **Park Angiolina**, surrounding Scarpa's original Villa Angiolina and boasting rows of exotic palms. Just northeast of here stands the oldest and grandest of Opatija's hotels, the *Kvarner*, whose facade, complete with trumpet-blowing cherubs and bare-chested Titans, looks more like a provincial opera house than a hotel. Opatija's **beach** – a cemented-over lido opposite the bus station – is the biggest let-down in the Adriatic; it's better to head south to the shingle beach at Medveja (see p.170).

Offering a complete contrast to Opatija are the steep, narrow alleyways and shuttered houses of **VOLOSKO**, twenty minutes' walk further up the coast, past Opatija's small harbour. Again, specific attractions are thin on the ground, but it's an atmospheric place for a short wander, with its whitewashed buildings arranged into a kasbah-like maze of streets.

Eating and drinking

For **food**, there's no shortage of snack bars along the main strip. *Madonnina*, signposted just off Maršala Tita near the tourist office, is the best of the town's pizzerias; while *Pizzeria Barilla*, just above a bank at Maršala Tita 136, has a wider range of pasta dishes but no outdoor seating. For Croatian cooking, it's best to avoid the central hotel restaurants and head out: *Gusto*, at Maršala Tita 266 in the southwestern end of town, offers big grills at a reasonable price; *Villa Ariston*, nearby at Maršala Tita 243 (although its lower entrance is on the seafront promenade), is housed in an attractive turn-of-the-century villa and has top-of-the-range seafood. In the opposite direction from the town centre, *Bistro Poreč*, on the waterfront at Volosko, offers grilled meats on a vine-shaded terrace overlooking the port.

Most of the **cafés** along Maršala Tita have had all trace of the *belle époque* ripped out of them by insensitive renovators, although the one beneath the *Palace-Bellevue* hotel has a good selection of cakes and a spacious terrace on which to see and be seen. Of the evening **drinking** haunts, *Hobbiton*, on Maršala Tita near the *Mozart* hotel, is a chic, bunker-like watering hole with a wide range of mainstream and alternative music. About 1km northeast, *Café Galija*, on Opatija's harbourfront, has plenty of outdoor seating and a roomy interior, while

Vološćica, on the waterfront at Volosko, is a smaller, standing-room-only kind of place inside, although it too has an outdoor terrace.

Lovran and around

It's an easy hour's walk south along the coastal Šetalište from Opatija to **LOVRAN**, following a rocky shore punctuated by two pebbly coves at Ičići and Ika. On arrival you'll find an Italianate, green-shuttered little town with a small harbour, fringed by palatial *belle époque* villas, decorated with curly balustrades covered in green espaliers. Behind the main street, Maršala Tita, a small old quarter climbs the hill, where vine-shaded cobbled alleys converge on the fourteenth-century **St George's Church** (Crkva svetog Jurja), which has some frescoes dating from 1479 behind the main altar reminiscent in style of the wall-paintings at Beram (see p.148) and other Istrian churches. Opposite the church, the **House of St George** bears an eighteenth-century relief above the doorway of the saint slaying a dragon, which has become something of a town trademark.

Habsburg-era villas are scattered all over Lovran. Many were taken over by the state and turned into flats after World War II; sadly, none is open to the public. Some of the best are concentrated northeast of the centre along Maršala Tita, where you can hardly miss the Secessionist **Villa Gianna** at no. 23, a pink-mauve confection built in 1904 by local architect Attilio Maguolo and embellished with ornate Corinthian columns and winged dragons clutching shields inscribed with the initials IP, a reference to the original owner, Iginio Persich. Further on, beyond the *Excelsior* hotel, a further group of villas lurks in shady seaside gardens, the most famous of which is the **Villa Frappart** on Viktora Cara Emina, another Secession-inspired work built for Viennese lawyer Michel Ruault Frappart by Karl Seidl in 1890. An eclectic Byzantine Gothic building, whose colonnaded entrance gives it palatial pretensions, it's now an elite music school.

Practicalities

Buses pick up and drop off on Lovran's main street, where most of what you need is located. There's a helpful **tourist office** (daily: summer 8am–8pm; winter 9am–4pm; ☎ & fax 051/291-740) which dispenses free town plans and other bumf just off Maršala Tita, down a side-alley behind the harbour. Plentiful private **rooms** (①–②) are available from Kvarner Express, Maršala Tita 39 (☎ & fax 051/291-119), and there are a couple of good **bed-and-breakfast**-style places: *Villa Liana*, 1km southwest of Lovran along the coast road at Maršala Tita 85 (☎ & fax 051/712-742; ④), has large, old-fashioned rooms in a creaky old folly; the *Pension Štanger* has simple rooms in a centrally located house at Braidice 14 (☎051/293-266; ③). Of the three big **hotels** northeast of the centre along the Opatija road, the *Lovran*, Maršala Tita 19 (☎051/291-222, fax 292-467; ③), is the cheapest, with simple en-suites; while the *Excelsior*, Maršala Tita 15 (☎051/292-233, fax 291-989; ⑥), has spacious rooms with TV, and indoor and outdoor pools. Fully equipped **apartments** in some of Lovran's turn-of-the-century villas can be arranged through Lovranske Vile, Poljanska 27, Ičići (☎ & fax 051/704-276, *www.lovranske-vile.com*), although they don't come cheap and there's a minimum two-night stay, which will cost about 3000Kn in a four-bed apartment.

The cheapest place **to eat** is probably *Oaza*, on Maršala Tita near the Kvarner Express office, which has a range of pizza and pasta dishes, while *Knezgrad*, Trg

HIKING ON MOUNT UČKA

Dominating the skyline above Opatija and Lovran is the long, forest-covered ridge of the **Učka massif**, which divides the Kvarner region from central Istria. A tunnel under Učka's northern limbs provides a fast road link between Rijeka and the Istrian hinterland, but there's an older and more scenic route which climbs from Rijeka via the village of Veprinac over the northern shoulder of the mountain, passing a turn-off to the 1396m summit of **Vojak** before zigzagging down to join the newer main road on the other side. Rather than driving all the way to Vojak, however, the best way to enjoy Učka's wooded slopes is **to walk**. Paths are well marked, and the free *Učka* **map**, available from the Lovran tourist office, is an invaluable guide.

Lovran is the starting point for the most direct **hiking route up the mountain** – the ascent takes around 3hr 30min. A flight of rough-hewn steps leads up immediately behind Lovran's old centre, leading to the small Romanesque Chapel of St Rock on the edge of the village of Liganj. Join the road into Liganj for a couple of hundred metres before heading uphill to the right through the hamlets of Dindići and Ivulići – semi-abandoned clusters of farmhouses and moss-covered dry-stone walls. From Ivulići it's a steady two-hour ascent through oak and beech forest before you emerge onto a grassy saddle where an expansive panorama of inland Istria suddenly opens up, revealing the knobbly green and brown forms of the peninsula's central hills – the peak of Vojak is another twenty minutes' walk to the right. At the top, there's an observation tower, TV mast and splendid views of Rijeka and the spindly form of Cres beyond. If you're staying at the campsite at Medveja, there's an **alternative ascent**, taking about fifty minutes longer, which starts just behind the campsite and ascends to the village of Lovranska Draga before climbing steeply up a wooded ravine to join the main path from Lovran.

From Vojak, a path descends north to **Poklon** (1hr), where you meet up with the old Rijeka–Istria road. There's a terrace offering another view of the Kvarner Gulf here, and a mountain hut and restaurant, though they're only sporadically open. Follow the road 1km west from Poklon to reach the *Dopolavoro* restaurant, invariably packed out with day-tripping Rijeka folk at weekends who come to sample its top notch Istrian cuisine and game dishes such as pheasant and boar. From Poklon, you can work your way southeast back to Lovran (about a 2hr walk) by a downhill path which ultimately joins the main route you came up on.

On Saturdays and Sundays, **bus #34** from Opatija climbs as far as Poklon twice a day, making this a good starting point from which to tackle Vojak if time is short.

slobode, has a selection of simple meat and fish dishes, plus cheap lunches. *Grill Kvarner*, overlooking the harbour, is the best place for fresh seafood, but is correspondingly more expensive.

The Lovran area is famous for its chestnut trees, which were originally imported from Japan in the seventeenth century. They are harvested in midautumn, an event celebrated by the **Marunada Chestnut Festival** (call the tourist office for details) which takes place over three weekends in October: the first two weekends see festivities in hill villages above town, while the final weekend takes place in Lovran itself. The festival is used as an excuse for making a wide variety of cakes flavoured with chestnut purée, which are sold in all the local cafés.

Medveja and Mošćenička Draga

Three kilometres beyond Lovran, the small village of **MEDVEJA** has the area's best **beach** – a long crescent of shingle which can get crowded on summer weekends. Immediately behind the beach there's a small **tourist office** (June–Sept irregular hours, usually 8am–5pm) and the New Sound agency (☎ & fax 051/292-111), which has a few local **rooms** (①–②). There's also a well-appointed and spacious **campsite** (☎051/291-191, fax 292-471), attractively tucked into a steep-sided valley, with a supermarket and grill restaurant on site. Four kilometres further on lies **MOŠĆENIČKA DRAGA**, the Riviera's last settlement, unattractively squeezed around the monster-sized *Marina* hotel. There's another big, popular stretch of pebbly beach, a **tourist office** on Aleja Slatina (☎051/737-533) and **rooms** from the AnnaLinea agency, which has offices by the main road and near the beach (☎051/737-207 or 737-506).

Cres and Lošinj

The westernmost of the Kvarner islands, **Cres** and **Lošinj** (really a single island divided by a narrow artificial channel), together make up a narrow sliver of land which begins just south of the Istrian coast and extends most of the way across the Kvarner Gulf. Allegedly the place where Jason and the Argonauts fled with the Golden Fleece, the islands were originally known as the "Absyrtides"; according to locals, Medea killed her brother Absyrtus here as he pursued her and threw his remains into the sea, where two of his limbs became Cres and Lošinj.

Getting to the islands is relatively straightforward. **Ferries** run hourly from Brestova (see p.155), just south down the Istrian coast from Opatija, to Porozina in northern Cres, and from Valbiska on Krk to Merag on Cres. Most **buses** plying the Rijeka–Cres–Lošinj route use the Brestova ferry crossing, although at least one bus daily goes via Valbiska. If you're heading to or from either Istria or Dalmatia, there are also six ferries weekly in each direction between Pula and Zadar, which call on the way at **Mali Lošinj** – the islands' one big package resort. Smaller towns and villages on Cres, such as **Cres Town** and **Osor**, remain comparatively quiet despite their proximity to the mainland. Public transport runs up and down the main road along the island's hilly central spine, making travel between the main centres fairly easy, though to properly explore some of the smaller places on Cres – such as **Beli**, **Valun** and **Lubenice** – you'll need plenty of time and good walking shoes, or your own transport.

Cres

CRES (pronounced "Tsress") is the second largest of the Adriatic islands, only beaten in size by neighbouring Krk. It marks the transition between the lush green vegetation of northern Croatia and the bare karst of the Adriatic, with the deciduous forest and overgrown hedgerows of northern Cres – the so-called **Tramuntana** – giving way to the increasingly barren sheep-pastures of the southern part of the island. Sheep apart, there's not much agriculture on the island, and the only other economic activities are fishing and tourism.

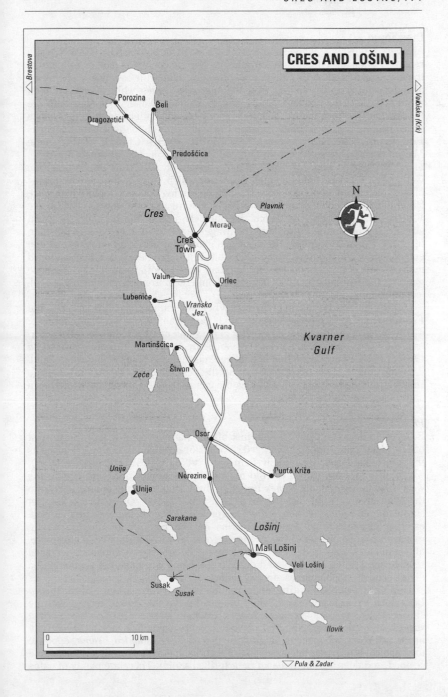

CRES AND LOŠINJ

Cres Town

An oversized fishing village strung around a small harbour, **CRES TOWN** is still relatively undisturbed by mass tourism and has the crumpled look of so many of the towns on this coast: tiny alleys lead nowhere, minuscule courtyards shelter an abundance of greenery spilling over the rails of balconies, while mauve and pink flowers sprout from cracks in walls. **Trg F. Petrića**, which opens out onto the harbour, is the town centre, flanked by a small fifteenth-century loggia and a sixteenth-century clock tower. An archway leads through to the square known as **Pod urom** ("Beneath the clock"), where **St Mary's Church** (Crkva svete Marije) boasts a fifteenth-century Gothic Renaissance portal featuring a fine relief of the Virgin and Child. Just south of here, set slightly back from the harbour, the Gothic Petris Palace holds a small **museum** which, once restored, will display piles of encrusted amphorae from the Roman trading post of Crepsa which once stood here, plus coins, manuscripts and sculpture from the town's days under Venetian and Austrian rule. From the northern end of the harbour, the main street, Creskog statuta, runs along the fringes of the town centre before finishing up at the **Porta Marcella**, a Renaissance gateway from 1595 that stands at one end of a stretch of old town wall dating from Venetian times. A couple of hundred metres south of here, past a peeling Partisan war memorial, another Renaissance gateway, the **Porta Bragadina**, leads back into the mazy centre of town via a collection of small piazzas.

Over on the southern side of town, just behind a rather ugly shipyard area, the **Franciscan monastery** (Franjevački samostan; Mon–Sat 9am–noon & 4–6.30pm; 5Kn) holds a shaded cloister and a small **museum**, in which flaky portraits of Franciscan theologians are outshone by Andrea de Murano's *Virgin and Child* of 1475, a warm depiction of a fat and mischievous Jesus with dove in hand.

Swimming in Cres takes place along the concreted Lungomare promenade which stretches west of town as far as the campsite some 1500m away; there's a naturist section on the far side.

PRACTICALITIES

Buses stop near the petrol station just off the harbour area, where the **tourist office** (daily 7am–1pm & 2–9pm; ☎051/571-535) occupies the same premises as the Cresanka Turist Biro (daily 8am–8pm; ☎051/571-161, *cresanka@ri.tel.hr*), which offers **rooms** (①) in the old town or in the suburb of Melin, 1km to the west. Also in Melin is the *Kimen* **hotel**, set back from the Lungomare 1km from the town centre (☎051/571-161 or 571-428, fax 571-163; ④), with box-like but acceptable en-suites just above the Lungomare. Rather better are the chic self-catering apartments in the ACI marina on the far side of the Franciscan monastery, which will sleep two or three people for 640–740Kn. Cres's **campsite**, fifteen minutes' walk from the centre along the Lungomare, occupying a terraced seaside site shaded by olives and other trees, has a large naturist section and a diving school (crash courses start at 190Kn).

There are plenty of **eating** opportunities around the harbour. *Slastičarnica Učka* does a reasonable *burek*; while the nearby *Pizzeria Palada* is probably the cheapest place to get a decent sit-down meal. For classier fare, *Riva* has a prime waterside position and is the best place to try top-quality fish such as *orada* (gilthead) and *škarpina* (groper). Slightly further afield, *Gostionica Belona*, opposite the Partisan war memorial on Šetalište XX aprila, has a similar range of meat and seafood, and does a good *lignje na žaru* (grilled squid). There are plenty of **cafés** along the seafront although they can sometimes get a bit windy – in which case head for the more sheltered *Café Smack* beside the church on Pod urom.

Beli

North of Cres Town, the island narrows into a long, high ridge, descending steeply towards the sea on either side. The road dives from one side of the ridge to the other, swapping views of the Istrian peninsula to the west and the mainland from Rijeka to Velebit to the east. Thirteen kilometres north of Cres Town a minor road forks right off the main road, passing through half-deserted hamlets and oak and chestnut forests en route to the village of **BELI**. Huddled atop a knobbly hill high above the channel dividing Cres from Krk, Beli is an impressive agglomeration of ancient stone houses, many of them now left uninhabited as locals move away in search of work. It's gloriously rustic and peaceful, and there's a small shingle cove below the village at the end of a steep road.

Beli is also home to the **Caput Insulae Ecology Centre** (Eko-centar Caput Insulae; daily 9–11am & 5–9pm; 10Kn), established in the mid-1980s to monitor and protect the community of **griffon vultures** (see box below) indigenous to Cres. Located at the end of a stony road to the left as you enter the village, the centre has an exhibition on the vultures, with photographs and English-language texts, and a small aviary in the back garden where sick vultures are often kept before being returned to the wild. They can also provide directions for the centre's **ecology path** (*eko-staza*), a hiking route which starts here and leads through the forest on a 7km circuit, passing through a mixed area of pasture, forest, abandoned villages and *gradine* (the small, walled-off areas of cultivable land typical to Croatia's limestone areas) on the way. The vultures themselves regularly scour the

---

THE GRIFFON VULTURES OF CRES

The white-headed **griffon vulture** formerly lived all over the Kvarner region, co-existing with a local sheep-farming economy that guaranteed the carrion-eating birds a constant supply of food. With the decline of sheep-rearing in the twentieth century, vulture numbers fell dramatically, and communities of the birds are nowadays only found on the northeast coast of Cres and in a few isolated spots on Krk and the mainland. When conservationists first came to the area in the mid-1980s there were 24 pairs of vultures on the island; that number has now risen to about seventy, not least because locals have been educated to leave dead animals for the vultures to clear up rather than removing them from the fields themselves. Fully grown griffon vultures have a wingspan of 2.5m, can weigh between 8kg and 10kg, live for up to sixty years, and can spot a sheep or donkey carcass from a distance of 6km. Their nesting area in the rocky cliffs on the eastern side of the island between Beli and Merag is now protected by law: it's forbidden to sail within 50m of the cliffs, as frightened young birds may fall out of their nests if disturbed. The vultures nest in December and produce one egg per pair, the young birds staying with their parents until August, when they begin a five-year roving period – which could take them to other vulture colonies in the Balkans or Near East – before returning to the island to breed. The main threats to the vultures are telephone wires, electricity power lines and contact with man-made poisons, such as the bait left out for vermin; the vulture population of Plavnik, an uninhabited island off the east coast of Cres, disappeared completely after the food chain had become contaminated in this way.

sparsely inhabited northern extremities of Cres in search of food – there's quite a good chance of spotting one, but don't count on it.

There are only two buses a week from Cres to Beli, and the much more regular Cres–Porozina–Rijeka buses only pass within 7km of the village. A **tourist information point** is opened in the village in season (July & Aug daily 8am–7pm; ☎051/861-089) to allocate local **rooms** (①) – at other times enquire at the tourist office in Cres Town. There's a **campsite**, the *Brajdi* (☎ & fax 051/840-522), below the village near the beach, where there's also a small grill-**restaurant**. The *Buffet Beli*, back in the village, has a wider range of meat and fish dishes and is also a good place for a drink.

Valun, Lubenice and Martinišćica

About eight buses a day leave Cres Town for Mali Lošinj (see p.176), a spectacular journey at times as the road hugs the island's central ridge before descending towards the sea at Osor. Eight kilometres south of Cres Town a minor road heads right towards the sparsely populated western side of the island. After 5km a side road descends to **VALUN**, a tiny fishing village with colourful houses crowding round its harbour, a quiet shingle beach and ultra-clear waters – it's very popular with weekending Italians, but remains more or less free from development. The **tourist office** just behind the harbour (July & Aug daily 8.30am–7pm; June & Sept Mon–Sat 8.30am–2pm, Sun 8.30am–noon; ☎051/535-050) has **rooms** (①), and there's a very attractive small **campsite** 100m east of the harbour right on the beach (☎051/535-050, fax 535-085). For **eating**, *Konoba Toš Juna* has a terrace right on the harbourfront and is a good place to try the local *škampi* (shrimps) and *creška janjetina* (Cres lamb).

Roads lead southwest from Valun to **LUBENICE**, 5km away, a windswept village occupying a ridge high above the shore. Almost medieval in appearance, it's like a more extreme version of Beli – a depopulated cluster of half-ruined stone houses. The square at the entrance to the village, from which there's an invigorating view of the rugged western coast, hosts alfresco classical music concerts every Friday evening in July and August, and there's a pair of idyllic, secluded pebbly coves far below the village, though they're only accessible by boat or via a very steep and tiring path. There are only three Cres Town–Valun–Lubenice buses a week, so you'll need a car to explore thoroughly.

Back on the main road to Lošinj, **Lake Vrana** appears below the road to the right, an emerald-green ellipse of fresh water that supplies both Cres and Lošinj – but for this lake, both islands would be utterly dry, and you can't swim here due to its importance as a source of drinking water. Shortly after passing the lake, a turn-off to the right runs down to **MARTINIŠĆICA**, a small village 9km off the main road with a long shingle beach. Modern and lacklustre in comparison to Valun or Lubenice, it nevertheless boasts a well-organized if over-large **campsite**, just west of the village on the Slatina peninsula (☎051/574-127, fax 574-167), with pitches set close to the shore between shrubs and pines.

Osor

Set beside the narrow strait which divides Cres from Lošinj, **OSOR** is an erstwhile cathedral town which has shrunk to the size of a hamlet. It's the oldest settlement on either island, a prosperous Roman city which some historians believe once had a population of 15,000, although a couple of thousand seems more realistic. Osor's regional importance survived into the medieval era, thanks in part to the reputation of eleventh-century holy man (and later saint) Gaudentius, who established the now ruined monastery of St Peter here and turned Osor into a centre of Glagolitic manuscript production. Driven out by local nobles, Gaudentius died in exile in Rome – from where his remains miraculously returned to Osor in a sea-borne wooden chest. They're now kept on the high altar of Osor's cathedral. Under Venetian rule, Osor was a typical casualty of the decline in Mediterranean trade which followed the discovery of America and the opening up of the trans-Atlantic economy. Visiting in 1771, the Italian traveller Abbé Fortis described it as the "corpse of a town, in which there are more houses than inhabitants".

Osor is nowadays a small village with a permanent population of around seventy, its streets exuding a peace that, on a hot summer's day, it seems nothing will ever disturb. The cobbled kernel of the village stands just above the **Kavuada**, the narrow channel, just eleven metres wide, which divides Cres and Lošinj. Dug either by the Romans or their Illyrian predecessors, it's now spanned by a swing bridge which opens at 9am and 5pm every day to let boats through. Presiding over a funnel-shaped main square is the **Church** (originally cathedral) **of the Assumption** (Crkva Uznesenja), completed in 1497 and boasting an elegant trefoil façade in smooth, pale stone. Opposite is the small **Archeological Museum** (Arheološki muzej; summer daily 6–10pm; 10Kn) in the Venetian town hall, which has Roman relics and a model of medieval Osor enclosed by extensive town walls, stretches of which survive in much reduced form.

On the other side of the square, a narrow street runs past the fifteenth-century **Bishop's Palace**, now a sporadically open lapidarium harbouring bits of masonry from Osor's many churches, several of which are covered with the *plutej*, a plait-like design characteristic of Croatian medieval art. The most imposing item on display is the **bishop's throne**, a composite work made from Romanesque stone fragments taken from the graveyard of St Mary's Church – the backrest is embellished with a fine carving of two birds hovering above a lion-like beast. Ten minutes north of the square, past the graveyard, lies Bijar Bay, where a small beach is overlooked by the ruins of the thirteenth-century **Franciscan monastery**, another important centre of Glagolitic culture in its day.

Rooms (①) are available from Turist Biro on the main square (☎051/237-007), and there are two **campsites**: the beautifully situated *Bijar* (☎051/237-027, fax 237-007), with a shady seafront position on the northern side of town, and *Preko Mosta* (☎051/237-350, fax 237-007), just across the bridge on the Lošinj side. For **eating**, *Konoba Livio* serves up decent pizza in a pleasant courtyard; while *Konoba Bonifačić* has a wider range of local seafood and a lovely garden. The **Osor Evenings** (Osorske večeri) festival of chamber music stages performances in the Church of the Assumption from the second weekend of July to early August – the tourist office in Lošinj (see p.176) will have details.

Lošinj

LOŠINJ is smaller and more touristed than Cres, and has a thick woolly tree cover that comes as a relief after the obdurate grey-greenness of southern Cres. Long overshadowed by its neighbour, Lošinj developed a thriving maritime trade after the demise of the Venetian Republic, with a large fleet and several shipyards, and later emerged as a holiday destination – like Opatija on the mainland it started out in the late nineteenth century as a winter health-resort for sickly Viennese.

Nowadays the island's main town, Mali Lošinj, is a magnet for package-holidaying Germans, Austrians and Croats, while its near-neighbour Veli Lošinj is smaller, quieter and relatively unspoiled.

Mali Lošinj

Straggling along either side of a deep sheltered bay, **MALI LOŠINJ** is a fast-growing resort whose outer layers of apartment and bungalow developments have happily failed to destroy the charm of its elegant core, where slender cypresses and spiky green palms poke up between tiers of peach and orange houses, covered in purple bougainvillea. Most of the hotels have been kept well out of the way on the Čikat peninsula just west of town, together with an enormous campsite and the island's most crowded beaches.

Most life in Mali Lošinj revolves around the quayside **Riva lošinjskih kapetana**, where rows of potted cacti and subtropical plants line a harbourfront overrun in summer with souvenir stalls and café tables. The Riva's southern end opens out into the triangular open space of Trg Republike Hrvatske, from where **Braće Vidulića**, the main street, runs inland, through the oldest part of town, though once you've clambered around the stepped alleys and winding streets there's not much to see save the **Art Collections** (Umjetničke zbirke; June–Sept daily 9–11am & 7–9pm; Oct–May Mon–Fri 10am–noon; 12Kn), housed in the former House of Culture just behind the harbourfront at Vladimira Gortana 35. Inside lie the combined hoards of two private collectors, beginning with that of art critic Andro Vid Mihičić, which concentrates on Croatian twentieth-century works, notably the mottled cityscapes of Paris-trained Emanuel Vidović (1870–1953). The second collection, that of Giuseppe Piperata – a Lošinj doctor who emigrated to Italy in 1945 but was prevented from taking his most valuable paintings with him – inclines more towards the Baroque. Highlights include Francesco Solimena's busy and agitated *Meeting with Rebecca*, and Il Guercino's more contemplative *Allegorical Landscape with Female Figures*, a pastoral scene of washerwomen beside a duck-filled pond.

The best place to swim is around **Čikat Bay**, 3km west of town, where a coastal path runs past a succession of concreted bathing areas, rocky beaches and a couple of stretches of pebble. It's a laidback area, good for strolling whatever the season, with Habsburg holiday villas sheltering among wind-bent tamarisks and pines, and cafés and shacks renting out snorkelling gear and surfboards along the more popular stretches.

PRACTICALITIES

Ferries from Pula and Zadar and **buses** from Rijeka and Cres stop at the northern end of Mali Lošinj's harbour, near the **tourist office** at Riva lošinjskih kapetana 29 (mid-June to mid-Sept daily 8am–10pm; mid-Sept to mid-June Mon–Fri 8am–3pm; ☎ & fax 051/231-884, *tzg-mali-losinj@ri.tel.hr*), which is well equipped with brochures and sells maps of the town. Ferry tickets for Pula and Zadar are sold by Lošinjska Plovidba on the Riva. Mountain bikes and windsurf boards (both about 50Kn per hour) can be rented on the seafront promenade in Čikat, in front of the *Bellevue* hotel.

There's a wealth of private **accommodation** in town. Numerous agencies offer private rooms (①–②) and apartments (450Kn for 4 people): Furnije, Riva lošinjskih kapetana 28 (☎ & fax 051/233-719), is the nearest to the bus stop; Lošinjska Plovidba, a few steps further down at no. 8 (☎051/231-077, fax 231-611) and

Manora, on the opposite side of harbour at Velopin 2 (☎ & fax 051/233-391), offer similar deals. If you're arriving by car, the most convenient agency is Cappelli, on the main road at the northern entrance to town at Kadin bb (☎051/231-582 or 231-178).

Of the town's **hotels**, the rather basic *Istra* (☎051/232-151; ③), Riva lošinjskih kapetana 1, isn't really worth the price compared to private rooms, and you'd do better splashing out on the smaller *Villa Anna* at Velopin 31 (☎051/233-223, fax 233-224; ⑤), on the opposite side of the bay on the way to the Čikat peninsula, which has smart rooms and a small outdoor pool. The package hotels on the Čikat peninsula are all much of a muchness, though the *Bellevue* (☎051/231-222, fax 231-268; ⑥), an enormous rectangle with garden courtyard in the middle, is preferable to the twin concrete monster-hotels *Aurora* (☎051/231-324, fax 231-542; ⑤) and *Vespera* (☎051/231-304, fax 231-402; ⑤). At the northwestern end of Čikat, a thirty-minute walk from the town centre, the vast *Autocamp Čikat* **campsite** (☎051/232-125, fax 231-708) occupies a wooded site with good access to the beaches.

The cheapest **restaurant** in town is the *Gostionica Miramare*, Vladimira Gortana 75, just behind the Riva, with a standard range of fish and grills; the sightly more expensive *Gostionica Hajduk*, Braće Vidulića 11, has a leafy terrace and good fresh fish, as does *Barracuda*, Priko 31, a friendly and popular place on the opposite side of the harbour to the Riva. For **snacks**, the Pekarnica Cole bakery, in a side street behind Trg Republike Hrvatske, is a good source of bread and pastries. There's a (not particularly cheap) fruit and veg **market** just uphill from the harbourfront on Braće Vidulića and – if you're self-catering – a fresh fish market (Mon–Sat mornings only) on Trg Republike Hrvatske. **Drinking** and **nightlife** are centred on the cafés along the Riva, a few bars on Braće Vidulića and tame euro discos in the hotels.

Veli Lošinj

Despite the name (*veli* means "big", *mali* means "little"), **VELI LOŠINJ** is actually a smaller, quieter version of Mali Lošinj, a warren of pastel-coloured houses strung tightly around a tiny natural harbour. It's about a forty-minute walk from the centre of Mali Lošinj – follow Braće Vidulića uphill, head straight over the crossroads, and take the path downhill to the left to Baldarka Bay. You can't miss the hangar-like Baroque **St Anthony's Church** (Crkva svetog Antuna), which contains a fine tempera-on-wood *Madonna with Saints* (above a side door on the left as you enter) painted by Bartolomeo Vivarini in 1475. Originally commissioned by the Venetian senate, the painting was paraded around Venice every year on the anniversary of the Battle of Lepanto to celebrate the famous naval victory over the Ottomans (October 7), until being bought by a Lošinj family shortly after the fall of the Venetian republic. Behind the town, a crenellated **Venetian tower**, built in the late sixteenth century to discourage raids by the Uskoks, peers over the waterside houses. The best place **to swim** is at the rocks beside the path from Mali Lošinj, and there are a few concreted areas near the packagey *Punta* hotel on Veli Lošinj's northwestern fringes.

Despite the presence of the *Punta*, Veli Lošinj is a much more laidback place to stay than its neighbour; the Val and Turist Biro agencies, both on the harbour, have **rooms** (①). For **eating**, head for the Rovenska harbour at the eastern end of town, where there's a trio of excellent grilled-fish restaurants by the waterside: the *Mal*, *Porat* and *Sirius*.

Susak

About 9km west of Lošinj, **Susak** is one of the most interesting of the smaller Kvarner islands. Geologically, its clay and sand composition gives it an appearance quite different from the rocky terrain of the other Adriatic islands, while its isolation has produced a distinctive way of life: islanders still speak their own dialect and have retained many traditions and customs, including an unusual method of singing directly from the throat and a local costume which consists of gaudy green-and-yellow skirts worn with even brighter pink tights. Postcards and guidebooks would have you believe you'll see this all the time, though in fact most of the island's 200 inhabitants are elderly and rarely dress up in their brightest garb, preferring a gentler version of the same costume in navy or black. The island's industry, fish-canning, has long since died out and the population rely on money sent back by relatives to supplement income from sales of, among other things, Susak's **wines** – the red *pleskunac*, and *trojiščina*, an intriguing, dry rosé. There's one village on the island, but little of historical interest, though you might want to climb up to **St Nicholas's Church** (Crkva svetog Nikole), inside which there's a large wooden twelfth-century crucifix which the locals call *Veli Buoh* – the "Great God".

The island gets its fair share of day-trippers; excursions (from around 120Kn per person including lunch) are advertised on Mali Lošinj's Riva. The Manora agency (see p.177) in Mali Lošinj can arrange private **rooms** (①) in Susak if you want to stay. For snacks and drinks there's a **café** in the village which also serves as the main local meeting place.

Krk

The largest of the Adriatic islands, **KRK** (pronounced "Kirk", with a strongly rolled *r*) is also one of its most developed, a result of its proximity to Rijeka, whose airport is situated on the island. Much of the north is industrial, and blighted by package-oriented mega-developments like those at **Omišalj** and **Malinska**; the south and east, by contrast, offer grey, furrowed mountain peaks, lustrous vineyards, olive plantations and sun-bleached villages. The main settlements are **Krk Town**, in the middle of the island, a historic little place with scraps of city wall surrounding a compact old centre; and **Baška** in the far south, a quirky fishing village with a spectacular sandy beach.

Krk was originally a Roman base called Curictum: Caesar is supposed to have had an encampment on the island, and was defeated by Pompey in a naval battle just offshore in 49 BC. Later, Krk fell under the sway of the Venetians, who in 1118 gave control of the island to the Dukes of Krk, subsequently known as the **Frankopans** (see box opposite), one of the region's most powerful feudal families. Krk returned to the Venetian fold in 1480, after which it shared in the fortunes of the rest of the Adriatic: long, slow decline, followed by a sudden economic upsurge in the late twentieth century thanks to the tourist industry. In addition, the construction of the **bridge** linking Krk to the mainland enabled many locals to take jobs in Rijeka or elsewhere without having to move away from the island, thereby saving Krk from the rural depopulation which has afflicted other parts of the region.

Its proximity to the big city hasn't stopped Krk from preserving a few peculiarities of its own. Enduring **specialities** found nowhere else include *šurlice*, long

THE FRANKOPANS

The story of the Frankopans on Krk begins with the shadowy Dujmo I, who was given control of the island by the Venetians in the twelfth century. His successors managed to turn the island into a hereditary fiefdom which came to be known as the *državina* ("statelet"), an autonomous territory only nominally under Venetian control. As the **Dukes of Krk**, Dujmo's descendants used the island as a base from which to extend their power to the mainland, grabbing a coastal strip stretching from Bakar to Novi Vinodolski in 1225 and expanding northeast into continental Croatia, establishing footholds in Ogulin and Ozalj to create an arc of family estates.

The name of **Frankopan** was officially adopted in 1430, when Duke Nikola received papal support for his claim to be descended from the ancient Roman patrician family of Frangepan – a move, it was hoped, which would accord the dynasty the prestige needed in order to compete with the other great houses of Europe. Frankopan power on Krk, however, was on the wane, and the defeat of **Duke Ivan VII** by the Hungarians in 1480 was used by the Venetians as an excuse to finally take back control of the island. On the mainland, branches of the Frankopan family remained powerful well into the seventeenth century, when the last of the male line, **Fran Krsto Frankopan**, was executed alongside his brother-in-law Petar Zrinski (see box on p.98) in 1671 after leading an anti-Habsburg rebellion.

thin tubes of pasta dough, traditionally eaten *sa gulašom* (with goulash), or *sa žgvacetom* (lamb stew), and Vrbnička Žlahtina, the excellent white wine from Vrbnik on Krk's east coast. The island also preserves an archaic musical tradition in the form of the *mijeh*, a bagpipe made out of a goat's stomach, whose shrill, atonal squalls of noise form the basis of the dances performed at the annual **Krk Folklore Festival**, which takes place at the end of July.

There are regular **buses** from Rijeka via Omišalj to Krk Town, a journey of about ninety minutes. Alternatively, **ferries** run in summer to the island from Crikvenica on the mainland to Šilo (foot passengers only; 10 daily July & Aug; though note that buses to the rest of the island from Šilo are infrequent); from Lopar on Rab to Baška (June–Sept only); and from Merag on Cres to Valbiska.

Krk Town

The island's main centre, and in the full throes of rapid expansion, modern **KRK TOWN** meanders over a series of hills in formless abandon, though at its heart there's still a small, partly walled city criss-crossed by narrow cobbled streets. The main fulcrum of the town is **Trg bana Jelačića**, a large open space just outside the town walls to the west, looking out onto a busy little harbour. An opening on the western side of the square leads through to **Vela placa**, a smaller square overlooked by the medieval guard tower, or *straža*, which sports a rare sixteenth-century 24-hour clock (noon is at the top, midnight at the bottom). Right off here down XIII Divizije, and right again down Petra Franolića, lies the town's Romanesque **Cathedral of the Assumption** (Katedrala Uznesenja; daily 9.30am–1pm), a three-aisled basilica built in 1188 on the site of a fifth-century basilica (and before that a Roman bath complex) incorporating pillars taken from a range of Roman buildings. There are two rows of ten columns fashioned in a variety of designs and materials – limestone, marble and red granite – with their capitals decorated with intricate floral patterns and scenes of birds eating fish. Among the altar paintings, look out for a sixteenth-century *Deposition* by Giovanni Antonio da Pordenone, and a largish *Battle of Lepanto* by A. Vicenti, showing the Madonna and Pope Pius V watching approvingly over victorious Venetian forces.

Built alongside the cathedral, from which it's separated by a narrow passageway, is another Romanesque structure, **St Quirinus' Church** (Crkva svetog Kvirina), whose campanile sports an onion dome topped by a trumpet-blowing angel. The campanile's upper storey is now a **Treasury** (Riznica; daily 9.30am–1pm; 5Kn) housing numerous artworks amassed by the bishops of Krk, most famously the *Madonna in Glory*, a silver-plated altarpiece made in 1477 by Venetian workshops for the last Duke of Krk, Ivan VII. It's a – literally – dazzling piece of craftsmanship, with central panels showing reliefs of the coronation of the Virgin and side panels depicting various saints. Behind the cathedral, a surviving stretch of wall incorporates the

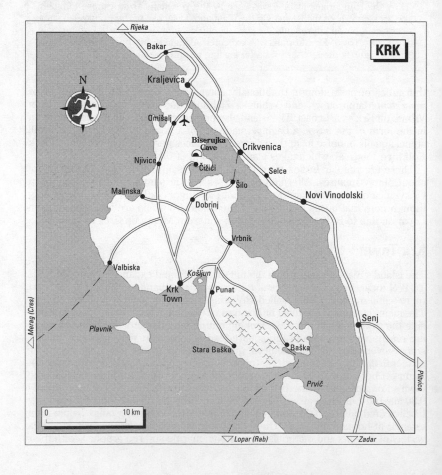

Bishop's Palace and an adjoining tower embellished with the Lion of St Mark – the symbol of Venetian sovereignty – although these sea-facing bastions were built in the fifteenth century under the Frankopans.

Krk's concreted bathing platforms aren't the most atmospheric places for swimming; the best are probably in front of the *Ježevac* campsite, west of town, and at the naturist beach about twenty minutes' walk east, by the *Politin* campsite.

Practicalities

The **tourist office** is up some steps in the northwest corner of Vela placa (daily 8am–3pm; ☎ & fax 051/221-414). **Rooms** (①) are available from three agencies: Autotrans at the bus station (☎051/221-111), 500m west of Trg bana Jelačića on the other side of the harbour; KEI, on Vela Placa (☎051/221-403, fax 221-035); or Aster, Obala hrvatske mornarice, east of Trg bana Jelačića on the waterfront. The *Marina* **hotel**, Obala hrvatske mornarice (☎051/221 128; ④), can't be beaten for convenience, offering acceptable if plain en-suites slap-bang on the seafront, while the *Koralj* (☎051/221-044, fax 221-022; ④), set amongst fragrant pine woods, is the best value of the package places east of town, with bright, modern en-suites. There's a large **campsite**, *Ježevac* (☎ & fax 051/221-081), ten minutes' walk to the right of town, and an exclusively naturist camp, *Politin* (☎051/221-351, fax 221-246), on the other side of town just beyond the *Koralj* hotel.

There are plenty of **restaurants** offering fresh seafood on the waterfront, including the restaurant of the *Murina* hotel, which also has the local staple, *šurlice*. Slightly inland, *Konoba Bacchus*, Strossmayerova 3, offers good grilled fish in a cool stone dining room. Food supplies can be picked up from the **supermarket** (Mon–Sat 7am–8pm, Sun 7am–1pm) opposite the bus station

Punat and beyond

Four kilometres east of Krk Town, the village of **PUNAT** is set on the tranquil, enclosed bay of Puntarska draga. It's a tiny place, but has still had all the trappings of tourism dumped on it – souvenir stalls, apartment blocks and a massive marina just to the right of town. There's little in the way of an old quarter, although a promising sequence of gravel beaches extends south of town, soon fading into quieter, rockier stretches of coast.

The main reason to come here is to take a taxi boat (boat owners tout for custom along the harbourfront; 20Kn return) across the bay to the **Franciscan monastery** (Franjevački samostan; Mon–Sat 9am–12.30pm & 3–6pm, Sun 10.30am–12.30pm; 10Kn) on the islet of Košljun, about 1km offshore, which was founded by monks settled here by the Frankopans in 1447. From the jetty a path leads up to the monastery church, with its lofty, wooden-beamed interior. Look out for the 1532 polyptych by Girolamo da Santacroce on the high altar, showing scenes from the life of the Virgin. In one panel, a stocky and bearded St Quirinus holds a maquette of Krk Town, accompanied by St Catherine, whose right hand rests on the wheel on which she was tortured. Stretching across the arch above the altar is a large and dignified *Last Judgement*, executed in 1654 by E. Ughetto, whose swirling panoramas of heaven, hell and purgatory provide a contrast with the simpler but no less harrowing *Stations of the Cross* by the twentieth-century Expressionist Ivo Dulčić. A side gallery holds pen-and-ink drawings by the naive painter Ivan Lacković-Croata, and there are some rather more off-the-wall exhibits in the cloister outside, like a one-eyed sheep in a glass case and a two-headed lamb in a bottle. The adjoining **museum** has an interesting mish-mash of stuff including a selection of international banknotes and coins, some ancient typewriters and gramophones and a display of local costumes. Outside, a confusing array of paths leads through the wilderness of the monastery gardens, although Košljun is so small that it's difficult to get really lost.

Krk–Baška **buses** pick up and drop off in a car park on the southeastern side of Punat. It's a short walk north along the seafront from here to the **tourist office**, housed in the same building as the post office (summer daily 7am–3pm; winter Mon–Fri 7am–3pm; ☎051/854-860, fax 854-970, *tzpunat@alf.tel.hr*), where you can collect a free town plan and the *Pastirske staze* map of local hiking routes in the green hills above town. Marina Tours, on the seafront near the tourist office (☎051/854-375, fax 854-340, *marina-punat@ri.tel.hr*), is the place to enquire about **rooms** (①). There's a simple **youth hostel**, *Ljetovalište OTC* (☎ & fax 854-037), in the centre, two blocks behind the seafront on Novi put; and the spacious *Pila* **campsite** (☎051/854-122, fax 854-101), south of town, with its own concrete beach. Four kilometres south of town on the road to Stara Baška, a side-road descends to the *Konobe* naturist campsite (☎051/854-036, fax 854-101), a self-contained resort with its own restaurants and shops.

Stara Baška

A minor road heads south out of Punat towards **STARA BAŠKA**, 12km distant, a tiny place clinging to a narrow coastal strip at the base of the sage-covered slopes of the 482-metre Veli Hlam. This would be the most beautiful spot on the island if it wasn't for the unsightly holiday homes, and there are several small stretches of shingle beach – the best of which is in Oprna Bay 2km north of the village, visible from the road as you descend from the direction of Punat.

There aren't any buses to Stara Baška, so you'll need a car – unless you want to walk here over the hills from Batomalj (see p.184), near Baška. The Zala agency in the centre of the village (☎ & fax 051/844-605) has **rooms** (①), and there's a **campsite**, the *Škrila* (☎051/844-678), on the shoreline at Stara Baška's northern end. The *Nadia* **restaurant** is the best place to eat – fresh local fish like *škarpina* (groper) and *kovač* (John Dory) are pricey but worth it – and also has rooms (☎051/844-686, fax 844-663; ③).

Baška

Lying at the island's southern end, and connected by frequent bus to Krk Town, **BAŠKA** is set in a wide bay ringed by stark mountains. At the heart of a rapidly modernizing town lies the kind of fishing village that wouldn't look out of place in Brittany or Cornwall: a tangle of crooked alleyways and colourful houses perched on a steep slope facing the sea. Baška's star attraction, however, is its two-kilometre stretch of **beach**, a mixture of sand and fine shingle that from a distance looks like a long crescent of demerara sugar. Though packed in summer, it's undoubtedly one of the best beaches in the Adriatic, and the view from here – embracing the bare offshore island of Prvić and the Velebit mountains in the background – is dramatic whatever the time of year. In season, taxi boats shuttle bathers to and from the shingle coves of Prvić, or to the succession of tiny bays east of Baška.

Twenty minutes' walk inland from Baška (back along the main road to Krk), **St Lucy's Church** (Crkva svete Lucije) in the village of **JURANDVOR** is the site of one of Croatian archeology's most important discoveries: the inscription known as the **Baška tablet** (Bašćanska ploča). The tablet, recording a gift to the church from the eleventh-century King Zvonimir, is the first mention of a Croatian king in the Croatian language and the oldest surviving text in the Glagolitic script (see box below). The original tablet is now in the Croatian Academy of Arts and Sciences in Zagreb, but there's a replica inside the church, and most places on the island seem to have sprouted copies.

THE GLAGOLITIC SCRIPT

The origins of Glagolitic go back to ninth-century monks **Cyril and Methodius**, chosen by the Byzantine emperor to convert the Slavs to Christianity. In order to translate the Gospels into the Slav tongue, Cyril and Methodius developed a new alphabet better suited to its sounds than either Latin or Greek. They began their missionary work with a trip to Moravia in 863, enjoying great success before the arrival of competing missions from Western Europe, and although their alphabet never caught on in Moravia, followers of Cyril and Methodius brought it to the Adriatic seaboard, where Croatian priests adopted it.

The script, which came to be known as **Glagolitic** (because so many manuscripts began with the words "*U ono vrijeme glagolja Isus*", "And then Jesus said"), is an extremely decorative 38-letter alphabet which borrowed some shapes from Greek, Armenian and Georgian, but which also contained much that was original. Other disciples of Cyril and Methodius made their way to Bulgaria, where they produced a modified version of the script, called **Cyrillic** in recognition of one of their mentors, versions of which are still used today in Russia, Ukraine, Bulgaria, Serbia and Macedonia.

Glagolitic took root in the areas of Croatia where Byzantine influence was at its strongest, and even with the growth of the power of the Roman Church, and Rome's use of Latin in church services, Croatian clerics stuck with the Glagolitic script and the Slav liturgy, and a succession of popes opted to tolerate Glagolitic rather than risk alienating the Adriatic clergy and driving them back into the embrace of Byzantium. The use of Glagolitic spread to the secular sphere too: the **Vinodol Codex** of 1288, drawn up by the Frankopans to delineate the rights and duties of their subjects around Novi Vinodolski, employed a flamboyant, cursive version of the script. Despite the use of the Roman alphabet elsewhere in the Catholic world, Glagolitic proved surprisingly enduring. Glagolitic prayer books were produced by clerics in Senj using the new printing technology from the 1490s onwards, and the script was still in use come the Reformation, when Croatian Protestants such as Stjepan Konzul Istranin from Buzet published Glagolitic books in Tübingen, prompting priests loyal to Rome to step up their own Glagolitic productions in response.

Ottoman advances finally brought an end to book production at Senj, and Adriatic Croatia's masters – whether Austrians or Venetians – increasingly regarded the use of Glagolitic as a sign of Slav resistance. Abbé Fortis, travelling round the Kvarner Gulf in the 1770s, noted that the Bishop of Rab was sending out Italian-speaking priests to counter the influence of local Glagolitic-using clergy. In inland Istria the script remained in use rather longer, but the Austrians prohibited its use in public documents in 1818, and the Glagolitic courses taught in Gorizia seminary were finally wound down in 1862. The growth of Croatian nationalism occasioned a Glagolitic revival in the late nineteenth century, but the universal dissemination of the Roman alphabet through secular education had by this stage already condemned Glagolitic to obscurity.

Heading west from Jurandvor, a minor road leads to the hillside village of **BATOMALJ**, 1km away, the starting point for the path across the mountains to Stara Baška. The walk takes about two and a half hours, rising steeply before skirting the 482m peak of Veli Hlam – it's reasonably well maintained and marked in either direction, although the going can be tough in wind or rain.

Practicalities

Baška's **tourist office** (daily 8am–3pm; ☎051/856-817, fax 856-544, *tz-baska @ri.tel.hr*), a short distance to the west of the town's central crossroads, has a free map showing local hiking paths. Baska's **hotels** are rotten value, apart from the swish *Corinthia* (☎051/656-111, fax 856-584, *hoteli-baska@ri.tel.hr*; ⑦), a pale, concrete behemoth behind the beach. Much better are the private **rooms** available from agencies such as Primaturist (☎051/856-971, *primaturist@ri.tel.hr*) and Guliver (☎051/586-004, fax 586-611) along the pedestrianized central street, Zvonimirova. **Camping** *Zablaće* (☎051/856-909, fax 856-604) occupies a largely shadeless site at the western end of the beach; while *Bunculuka* (☎051/856-806, fax 856-595), at the eastern side of Baška, is a nudist site with its own stretch of beach in the next bay along. A good place **to eat** is *Roberta*, on the seafront below the tourist office, with tasty seafood and grilled meats; or *Konoba Koko* on Zvonimirova, a folksy place whose interior is hung with fishing nets.

Eastern Krk: Vrbnik, Dobrinj and around

There are no major resorts on the eastern side of Krk, but a succession of attractive small settlements provide reason enough to make a brief foray into the region. East of Krk Town, a minor turning branches off the main road to Baška and climbs over a low ridge towards the fertile plain of the **Vrbničko polje**, where lush vineyards supply the wineries of **VRBNIK**, a small town perched on a fifty-metre-high sea cliff. The highly regarded local tipple, the dry white Vrbnička Žlahtina, is served in numerous local wine cellars, and the town itself – a network of narrow cobbled alleys which occasionally part to reveal views of Crikvenica and Novi Vinodolski across the water – is worth a quick amble.

The **tourist office** (☎051/857-333) on the main square has a list of private **rooms** (①); and there's a newish, medium-sized **hotel**, the *Argentum* (☎051/857-370, fax 857-352; ④), in the eastern part of town at Supec 68. *Nada*, at the sea-facing tip of the town at Glavača 22, has a good seafood **restaurant** upstairs and an evocatively fusty cellar hung with hams downstairs, where you can try the family's wine accompanied by local cheese and *pršut*. A couple of hundred metres east of the main square, *Gospoja*, at Frankopanska 1, is a larger, more modern cellar with equally excellent wines and nibbles.

Šilo, Dobrinj and the Biserujka Cave

The main harbour on the eastern side of Krk is **ŠILO**, 13km north of Vrbnik, a largely modern village with a couple of stretches of fine shingle beach and a ferry connection (foot passengers only) to Crikvenica on the mainland. The **tourist office** on the seafront at Stara cesta bb (Mon–Fri 8am–3pm; ☎ & fax 051/852-107) handles **rooms** (①) here and in Dobrinj (see opposite), and there's a big beach-side **campsite**, the *Tiha* (☎051/852-170, fax 852-362), on the peninsula on the eastern side of the bay.

Five kilometres west from Šilo, **DOBRINJ** is an inland version of Vrbnik, a hilltop village from whose church there's an expansive view north towards the sprawl of Rijeka and Mount Učka, with the resorts of Lovran and Opatija lurking at its feet. Rather like the hill towns of nearby Istria, Dobrinj seems to be reinventing itself as a cultural centre, and there's plenty to see if you're here in summer, when everything's open. On the tiny main square, the former St Anthony's Church (Crkva svetog Antuna) now houses a **gallery** which hosts varied art shows in summer, while an impossible-to-miss creamy-pink town house round the corner hosts seasonal exhibitions of contemporary painting and sculpture. Between the two, a one-room **Religious Art Collection** (Sakralna muzejska zbirka; summer daily 9am–noon & 6–9pm; 10Kn) boasts, among other trinkets, a fifteenth-century reliquary containing the head of St Ursula and a fourteenth-century altar cloth decorated with a *Coronation of the Virgin* sewn with gold thread. Just off the main square, the **Ethnological Collection** (Etnografska zbirka; summer daily 9am–noon & 6–9pm; 10Kn) contains three floors of agricultural tools, ceramics and costumes. The homely *Zora* **restaurant** on the main square is one of the best places on the island to eat *šurlice*.

Heading north of Dobrinj, it's 4km to the village of Čižići on the muddy Soline Bay, from where a well-signed road heads north to the **Biserujka Cave** (Špilja Biserujka; March–Oct daily 10.15am–4.45pm; 15Kn), a further 3km away on a coastal heath. The cavern is only about 150m long, but is well worth visiting – the stalagmite and stalactite formations are impressive, and you may also be lucky enough to catch sight of the cave's bat population.

South of Rijeka

Heading south, it's a while before you're finally free of Rijeka's industrial sprawl, which stretches way down the coast as far as the bridge to Krk. About 10km out of the city, nestling around the northern end of Bakar Bay, **BAKAR** is a case in point: a once pretty place, nowadays dominated by a vast oil refinery. It preserves its narrow streets, a derelict castle and a handful of crumbling town houses built by local mariners, but as a whole the place doesn't invite much more than a quick wander.

Ten kilometres further on, at the far end of Bakar Bay, **KRALJEVICA** is another example of an old coastal town almost entirely swallowed up by the

THE BURA

One of the Kvarner's most famous natural features is the **Bura**, a wind which is said "to be born in Senj, married in Rijeka, and die in Trieste". A cold, dry northeasterly, it blows across the central European plain and gets bottled up behind the Adriatic mountains, escaping through the passes at places like Senj, where it is claimed to be at its worst. It's said that you can tell the Bura is coming when a streak of white cloud forms atop the Velebit, the mountain ridge which stretches down the coast. At its strongest, it can overturn cars and capsize boats. When it's blowing, ferry crossings between the mainland and the islands are often suspended, and the road bridge to Krk will either be off limits to high-sided vehicles, or closed altogether.

industry of the Rijeka hinterland. It began life as the seventeenth-century strongpoint of Croatia's leading aristocratic families of the time, the Frankopans and the Zrinskis – the latter built two fortified palaces here, the Stari and Novi Grad, although they've since been much rebuilt and aren't open to the public.

Crikvenica and Novi Vinodolski

CRIKVENICA has been a tourist resort since the 1890s, when Archduke Josef, brother of Emperor Franz Josef, earmarked Crikvenica for development in a deliberate challenge to the pre-eminence of Opatija. He went so far as to name Crikvenica's first hotels – the *Erzherzog Josef* (now the *Therapia Palace*) and the *Erzherzogin Clothilde* – after himself and his wife. Following World War I, Crikvenica went on to prosper for a time as one of Yugoslavia's more modish playgrounds, though nowadays whatever charm it once possessed has been lost with the construction of the modern hotels and apartment blocks which straggle along its seafront. There really isn't anything to do but loll around on the succession of gravelly **beaches** which stretch northwest from the centre. **Strossmayerovo Šetalište** is the town's liveliest artery, leading along the waterfront from the main Trg Nikole Cara via a tangle of hotels, restaurants and tourist shops.

Crikvenica is easily reached by **bus** from Rijeka, while in July and August around ten **ferries** daily go to Šilo on Krk (see p.184). The **tourist office** (July & Aug 9am–7pm; Sept–June 9am–3pm; ☎051/241-151 or 241-051) is at Trg Sradića, a block north of the bus station; **rooms** (①–②) can be had from the Autotrans agency in the bus station, or from Kvarner Express just round the corner on Strossmayerovo Šetalište 3.

Nine kilometres south of Crikvenica, the resort town of **NOVI VINODOLSKI** ("Novi" for short) straggles along the main road for a couple of kilometres. It's actually of far greater historical significance than its rather suburban appearance might suggest, since it was here that the so-called **Vinodol Statute** (Vinodolski zakon), the oldest extant document in Croatian, was signed in 1288, recognizing the rule of the Frankopans over the surrounding district and the rights of the local citizens. Modern Novi is a dull sort of place, its waterfront lined with large hotels leading up to a scrappy harbour. Up above the main road there's a small old quarter, piled up on the hill, where you can view the austere sole remaining tower of the thirteenth-century Frankopan **castle** in a central square, another part of which holds a small **Town Museum** (Gradski muzej; Mon–Sat 9am–noon & 7–9pm, Sun 9am–noon; 10Kn), with a rather perfunctory display relating to the statute and folk costumes from the surrounding area.

There's not much beach to speak of here, merely a string of concreted platforms near the hotels. If you still want to stay, there's an enthusiastic **tourist office** on the main road, 200m south of the bus stop (daily 9am–10pm; ☎ & fax 051/244-306, *tzg-novi-vinodolski@ri-tel.hr*); Adria Tourist, in the same building, has **rooms** (①–②). There are several shoreline **campsites** along the string of attractive bays south of Novi, all of them pleasant, isolated spots to stay if you have your own transport. The first, *Povile* (☎051/793-083), is 3km south of Novi on the northern flanks of the Teplo inlet; 12km further on is *Sibinj* (☎051/796-905), followed after another 3km by *Bunica V* (☎053/616-718).

Senj

"May God preserve us from the hands of Senj." So ran a popular Venetian proverb, inspired by the warrior community known as the **Uskoks** (see box below), who in 1537 made **SENJ** their home and used it as a base from which to attack Adriatic shipping. Locals proudly claim the Uskoks as Croatian freedom fighters who helped slow the Ottoman advance, although their penchant for piracy earned the enmity of Venice and Dubrovnik, and contemporary historians tend to be more equivocal about the real nature of their activity. Modern Senj is a quiet little town of mazy alleyways, worth a brief stop-off. It also stands at the beginning of the road which heads inland over the Vratnik pass towards the Plitvice lakes (see p.123) and Karlovac (p.117) – although there's little public transport on this route and it's much easier to reach the lakes from Split or Zadar.

THE USKOKS

One result of the Ottoman Empire's steady advance into Bosnia and Croatia in the 1500s was the creation of a mass of refugees who, forced from their lands in the Balkan interior, gravitated towards the Adriatic coast, and began to organize themselves into military groups in order to repel further Ottoman encroachment. These anti-Turkish fighters were collectively known as Uskoks, although the name subsequently came to be applied to one particular group from Hercegovina, who took control of the fortress of Klis (see p.262) and defended it against Turkish forces until it finally fell in 1537.

The Uskoks subsequently withdrew to Senj, from where they mounted further resistance. Senj was under Austrian rule at the time, and the Uskoks were regarded as a useful component in the empire's defences. However, the Uskoks were consistently – perhaps deliberately – underpaid, forcing them to turn to piracy in order to survive, harassing Adriatic shipping from their fifteen-metre-long rowing boats. They considered anything Turkish a legitimate target, which in practice meant attacking the (usually Venetian) ships on which Turkish goods were transported. The Austrians turned a blind eye, regarding Uskok piracy as a convenient way of challenging Venetian dominance of the Adriatic. The Uskoks also had few qualms about attacking Christian subjects of the Ottoman sultan, especially if they were Orthodox. The Rab-born churchman Markantun Dominis (see p.192), who briefly served as Bishop of Senj, even suggested that the Uskoks would abandon piracy if they were allowed to begin taking the Orthodox Serbs and Vlachs of the Turkish-controlled interior and selling them off as slaves.

Uskok commanders were often regarded as being heroes fighting for the Catholic cause, but the lack of security for Adriatic shipping ultimately proved too much for the Venetians, who began a propaganda campaign suggesting that the Uskoks were not averse to eating and drinking the flesh and blood of their enemies, eventually provoking the so-called **Uskok War** with Austria in 1615 in an attempt to bring an end to the problem. The Uskoks gave a good account of themselves until their Austrian protectors, eager for an accommodation with Venice, withdrew their support. According to the terms of the 1617 Treaty of Madrid, the Austrians agreed to destroy the Uskok fleet and resettle the Uskoks inland. Senj was occupied by the Austrian navy, and the Uskoks left for new homes in Otočac, just to the southeast, or in the Žumberak hills north of Karlovac.

The only surviving reminder of the Uskoks in Senj nowadays is the **Nehaj Fortress** (daily: July & Aug 10am–9pm; May, June, Sept & Oct 10am–6pm; 12Kn) – the name means "fear not" or "heedless" – which looks over the town from a rubble-covered peak to the left of the harbour. It was constructed in 1558 under the auspices of Uskok commander Ivan Lenković, who obtained building materials by demolishing all the churches and monasteries which lay outside the town walls and so couldn't be defended against the Turks. Inside are three floors of exhibits illustrating the history of the Uskoks, featuring weaponry and costumes, with excellent English-language commentary. The view from the battlements justifies the climb, with the convoluted street plan of central Senj spread out immediately below, and the pale, parched flanks of Krk across the water.

The main focus of the town below is a scruffy harbourfront square, dotted with café tables, behind which lies a warren of alleyways and smaller piazzas. Face inland and go left off the square to reach the **Town Museum** (Gradski muzej; Mon–Fri 7am–3pm, Sat & Sun 10am–noon; 12Kn), which is housed in the fifteenth-century Vukasović mansion; it's a lacklustre display of archeological fragments and engravings illustrating the many literary figures to have come out of Senj over the centuries – foremost among them Pavao Ritter Vitezović (1652–1713), the poet and politician whose extravagantly titled *Kronika aliti spomen vsega i svieta vikov* ("Chronicle and Remembrance of Everything and the World from the Beginning") was one of the first history books to try to place the story of the Croats in a global framework. Just east of here, below a much-rebuilt cathedral of Romanesque origins, the rich **Religious Art Collection** (Sakralna baština; Mon–Sat mid-June to mid-Sept 9am–noon & 6–8pm; 12Kn) recalls the time when Senj was both the seat of a powerful bishopric and a major printing centre for Croatian-language religious texts. Among the Glagolitic missals, episcopal robes, paintings and silverware lie two exquisitely wrought fourteenth-century processional crosses, the biggest of which features a central relief of the Lamb of God surrounded by winged beasts symbolizing the evangelists – the lion for Mark, the bull for Luke, the eagle for John, and an angel for Matthew.

Practicalities

Buses plying the Rijeka–Zadar–Split coastal route pull up on the waterfront, close by the main square. The **tourist office**, about 400m north along the seafront at Stara cesta 2 (daily 7am–9pm; ☎053/881-068, fax 881-219), has details of the agencies which handle Senj's numerous private **rooms** (①). The best place **to eat** is the *Restaurant Martina* (which also has small but homely en-suite rooms; ☎053/881-638; ②) beside the Magistrala (coastal highway) at the northern entrance to town, offering a range of grilled meat, fish and shellfish on an outdoor terrace looking towards the sandy eastern shores of Krk. There are several pavement **cafés** on the main seafront square and numerous tiny **bars**, largely catering to the locals, in the narrow streets that wind away from here.

Rab

Less than 20km south of Krk lies **RAB**, the smallest but probably the most beautiful of the main Kvarner Gulf islands. Its eastern side is rocky and harsh, rising to a stony grey spine that supports little more than a few goats, but the western

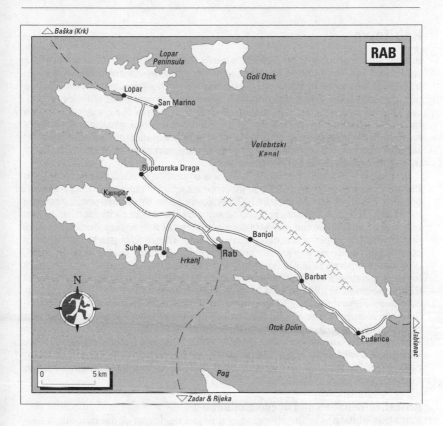

side is lush and green, with a sharply indented coast and some beautiful – if crowded – coves. Medieval **Rab Town** is the island's highlight, while the **Lopar peninsula** at the northern end of the island possesses some of the sandiest beaches in the country. The place can get crowded, especially in July and August, but not disastrously so.

Rab's main link with the rest of Croatia is the **ferry** which connects Jablanac on the mainland with Mišnjak on the island's southern tip (every 30min between 5.30am and 11pm in summer; 9 daily between 6am and 8pm in winter). The three daily Rijeka–Rab **buses** use this ferry, finishing up in Rab Town. If you miss this bus, you'll have to walk or hitch from the Magistrala to Jablanac harbour (3km) and from Mišnjak to Rab Town (8km). You can also hop over to Rab by seasonal ferry from Baška on Krk to Lopar (late May to late Sept 2–5 daily), though bear in mind that this leaves you a good 10km from Rab Town and buses don't always connect with the ferry arrivals, so you may have a wait on your hands. If travelling **on to Dalmatia** from Rab by public transport, take a Rab–Rijeka or Rab–Zagreb bus as far as the Magistrala just above Jablanac, then wait by the roadside for a southbound bus.

Rab Town

Rab's main attraction is **RAB TOWN**, a perfectly preserved late medieval Adriatic settlement squeezed onto a slender peninsula along which are dotted the city's trademark sequence of Romanesque campaniles. It's a genuinely lovely place: a tiny grey-and-ochre city, enlivened with splashes of green palm, huddles of leaning junipers and sprigs of olive-coloured cacti which push their way up between balconied palaces. The population today is only a third of what it was in Rab's fourteenth-century heyday, although it's swelled significantly by the influx of summer visitors, who create a lively holiday atmosphere without overly compromising the town's medieval character.

Starting out as a base for Roman and then Byzantine fleets, Rab Town (Arbe in Italian) grew into a prosperous, self-governing medieval commune until its incorporation into the Venetian state in 1409. Following this, the town's privileges were gradually eroded, trade was redirected towards the mother city, and, after two outbreaks of plague in the mid-1400s, urban life went into a steep decline. Things did not improve until the late nineteenth century, when Rab began to benefit from central European society's growing interest in Adriatic rest cures. In 1889, Austrian professors Leopold Schrötter and Johann Frischauf launched a strategy to develop Rab as a tourist destination, and 1897 saw the formation of the Società d'abellimento di Veglia (Society for the Beautification of Rab), a kind of embryonic tourist board. Thanks to the efforts of Austrian and Italian naturists, Rab – or, more accurately, the Frkanj peninsula just west of town – was one of the first **nudist resorts** in Europe, a status popularized by the visit of English King Edward VIII (accompanied by future wife Wallis Simpson) in the summer of 1936. Whether Edward actually got his tackle out or not remains the subject of much conjecture, but his stay on Rab provided the inspiration for a recent Croatian musical, *Kralj je gol* ("The King is Naked").

Arrival, information and accommodation

Rab's **bus station** is in the shopping centre just northeast of the harbour, a five-minute walk from Trg svetog Kristofora. The **tourist office** is behind the bus station on Mali Palit (summer daily 7am–10pm; winter Mon–Fri 8am–3pm; ☎051/771-111, fax 725-057), while most facilities are in the shopping centre behind the bus station, where you'll find a post office (Mon–Fri 7am–8pm, Sat 7am–2pm), pharmacy and a couple of supermarkets.

There are numerous agencies in town offering **rooms** (①), either in the old town or in the modern suburbs to the northeast: try Mila, by the bus station (☎ & fax 051/725-499), or Numero Uno, on the harbourfront between bus station and old town (☎ & fax 051/724-688). There are numerous acceptable package-oriented **hotels** around town: the *Istra*, on the waterfront near the bus station (☎051/724-134, fax 724-050, ⑤), is reasonable and convenient, with simple but nicely renovated en-suites; while the *Padova* (☎051/724-544, fax 724-418; ⑤), on the other side of the bay from the old town, has larger rooms with TV, plus an indoor pool. If you want to be near the coves of Frkanj, then the *Carolina* (☎051/724-133; ⑥), 5km from town at Suha Punta, is a bit of a concrete monster, but the en-suites are comfy and it's surrounded by pleasant woods. The nearest **campsite** is the *Padova III* (☎051/724-335, fax 724-539), about 2km away in the resort suburb of Banjol, though it's a largely unshaded site which can get crowded in season; simply follow the sea path on the eastern side of the harbour.

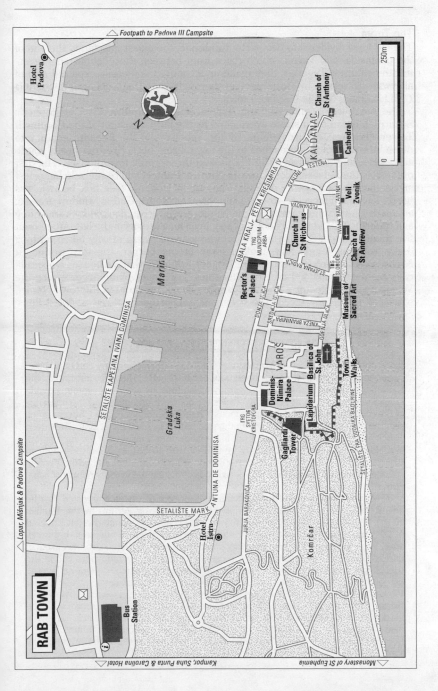

RAB TOWN

Footpath to Padova III Campsite

Hotel Padova

Marina

Gradska Luka

ŠETALIŠTE KAPETANA IVANA DOMINISA

Lopar, Mišnjak & Padova Campsite

Bus Station

Hotel Istra

ŠETALIŠTE MARK

JURJA BARAKOVIĆA

TRG SVETOG KRISTOFORA

ANTUNA DE DOMINISA

Komrčar

Kampor, Suha Punta & Carolina Hotel

Monastery of St Euphemia

ŠETALIŠTE TRA DOGGIKA BADURINE

Gagliardi Tower

Dominis Nimira Palace

Lapidarium

Basilica of St John

Town Walls

KNEZA BRANIMIRA ULICA

GORNJA ULICA

SREDNJA ULICA

DONJA ULICA

VAROS

Rector's Palace

TRG MUNICIPIUM ARBA

OBALA KRALJ - PETRA KREŠIMIRA IV

Church of St Nicholas

PLOVANOVO

STJEPANA RADIĆA

TRG SLOBODE

Museum of Sacred Art

Church of St Andrew

Veli Zvonik

IVANA RABLJANINA

SKALINE A. TESTENA

KALDANAC

Church of St Anthony

Cathedral

250m

0

The Town

The old town divides into two parts: **Kaldanac**, the oldest quarter, at the end of the peninsula, and **Varoš**, which dates from between the fifteenth and seventeenth centuries. Together they make up a compact and easily explored grid of alleyways traversed by three parallel thoroughfares: Donja ("Lower"), Srednja ("Middle") and Gornja ("Upper") ulica.

The old town is entered from **Trg svetog Kristofora** (St Christopher's Square), a broad open space overlooked by the jutting bastion of the **Gagliardi Tower** (Tvrđava Galijarda), built by the Venetians in the fifteenth century to defend the landward approaches to the town. From here, **Srednja** heads southeast, squeezing past rows of tightly packed three-storey town houses. The first of these is the Renaissance **Dominis-Nimira Palace**, where the scholar, priest and sometime archbishop of Split, Markantun Dominis (see box below), was born. The building is relatively plain save for some Gothic window frames, although a rather fine carving of the Nimira family crest, flanked by a small boy and rampant lion, adorns a doorway just down an alleyway to the left. After about five minutes' walk, Srednja opens out into a small piazza mostly taken up by a dinky Venetian loggia and, tucked away in the corner, the tiny Gothic **St Nicholas's Church** (Crkva svetog Nikole), which nowadays houses a sporadically open art gallery. Left from here lies Trg municipium Arbe, where the Venetian Gothic **Rector's Palace** (Knežev dvor) now houses the town council offices. The balcony facing the square is supported by three sculpted lions'

MARKANTUN DOMINIS (1560–1624)

Rab's most famous son was **Markantun Dominis** (Mark Anthony de Dominis), a Jesuit-educated churchman whose anti-establishment rhetoric infuriated the Catholic hierarchy of the day. After studying philosophy at Padua, Dominis quickly gained a reputation in scientific circles for his work on optics and the influence of the moon on tides, while simultaneously rising speedily through Church ranks, serving as bishop of Senj before being appointed archbishop of Split. However, Dominis's questioning of papal infallibility made him a target for the Inquisition, and after a brief sojourn in Venice he fled in 1614 to England and the Anglican Church, where he was feted as a prominent Catholic dissident and wrote his ten-volume *De Repubblica Ecclesiastica* – a vicious attack on the worldly nature of papal power.

Never wholly committed to Anglicanism, however (it's been suggested that he joined the Church of England because of the salary offered him by the English court), Dominis eventually decided to make his peace with Rome. He left England in 1622 and returned to Rome, where his hopes of fair treatment rested on his relative Pope Gregory XV. On Gregory's death in 1623, Dominis was accused of heresy and imprisoned, living out the rest of his days in a windowless cell in the Castel Sant'Angelo from where, he declared to visitors, "I can best contemplate the kingdom of heaven." Sympathy for Dominis was, nevertheless, at a low ebb. As Dr Fitzherbert, the Rector of the English College in Rome, told a visiting British aristocrat: "He was a malcontent knave when he fled from us, a railing knave while he lived with you, and a motley parti-coloured knave now he is come back." Dominis died before he could be brought to trial, and his body was burnt posthumously on Rome's Campo dei Fiori – an ignominious end for a man whose scientific and philosophical work was later to influence figures as diverse as Descartes and Newton.

heads sporting, from right to left, closed, half-open, and wide-open jaws – although they look more like overweight household pets than fearsome beasts of the savannah.

THE CHURCHES OF ST MARY AND ST ANTHONY

Southeast of Trg municipium Arbe lies the older part of town, **Kaldanac**, built on the site of the original Illyrian-Roman settlement of Arba. Kaldanac was largely abandoned after the plagues of the fifteenth century, and some of its older buildings still feature the bricked-up windows and doors which it was hoped would prevent the spread of disease. Occupying the highest part of Rab is the Romanesque **Church of St Mary the Great** (Crkva svete Marije Velike; still known locally as the "cathedral" even though the bishopric was taken away from Rab in 1828). The west front is striped pale grey and pink, with a series of blind arches cut by a Renaissance doorway that supports a harrowing Pietà of 1414. Inside are crumbling, honey-grey walls with flecks of agate-coloured marble and a set of almost gaudily carved chestnut choirstalls, dominated by the main altar and its delicate ciborium of grey marble.

A few steps away from the cathedral at the head of the peninsula, **St Anthony's Church** (Crkva svetog Antuna) preserves its original rib-vaulted apse and an imposing wooden sculpture of St Anthony (said to be twelfth-century) flanked by fifteenth-century pictures of St Christopher and St Tudor – the latter clad in Roman armour.

THE CAMPANILES AND MORE CHURCHES

Walk northwest along the ridge-top Ivana Rabljanina from the Church of St Mary and you pass the largest and most beautiful of Rab's campaniles, the perfectly symmetrical twelfth-century **Great Bell Tower** (Veli zvonik; daily 10am–1pm & 7.30–10pm; 5Kn). Topped by a balustraded pyramid, the 25-metre-high tower employs a simple architectural device: the windows on the lower storey have one arch, the windows on the second storey have two, those on the third have three, and so on. The tone of the tower's bell was mellowed – legend tells – by gold and silver dropped into the casting pot by Rab's wealthier citizens.

Rab's other three campaniles are spaced along Ivana Rabljanina and its continuation, **Gornja ulica**. The first, a smaller and more utilitarian piece of masonry from the late twelfth century, is attached to **St Andrew's Church** (Crkva svetog Andrije). The second – capped by a bulbous spire reminiscent of a bishop's mitre – is a seventeenth-century affair belonging to St Justine's Church (Crkva svete Justine), a small Renaissance structure that's now a **Museum of Sacred Art** (Muzej sakralne umjetnosti; daily: July & Aug 9am–noon & 7.30–10pm; June & Sept 7.30–9pm; 5Kn). Inside there's an assortment of manuscripts, stonework and robes, and a mid-fourteenth-century polyptych by Paolo Veneziano showing a Crucifixion flanked by saints – St Christopher is on the right, standing beside St Thecla, shown wearing a glamorous green outfit, despite the fact that she actually spent most of her life living in a cave. Pride of place goes to the reliquary holding the **skull of St Christopher**, a gold-plated casket made by a Zadar craftsman at the end of the twelfth century. Various scenes round the sides of the box depict the events surrounding the saint's martyrdom: he was beheaded by the Romans after an attempt to have him shot failed – the hand of God having turned the arrows back on his assailants. It's said that the head was brought to Rab by a local bishop in the eleventh century when the town was under attack from the Saracens

– St Christopher kindly obliged, saving the town by hurling rocks back at the besiegers.

The final campanile, a simple thirteenth-century affair similar to the one belonging to St Andrew's, stands beside the ruined **Basilica of St John the Evangelist** (Bazilika svetog Ivana Evanđeliste), which probably dates from the sixth or seventh century. The church was abandoned in the 1830s and much of its masonry taken away to mend the town's other sacred buildings, although the graceful curve of its apse can still be seen. At the top end of Gornja ulica, steps lead up to St Christopher's Church on the right, which has a small **lapidarium** (July & Aug daily 9am–1pm & 6–10pm; ask at the tourist office at other times; 5Kn) containing tombstones and other masonry. From here, more steps scale a short fifty-metre stretch of Rab's medieval town **walls**, giving fine views back over the roofs and towers. A gate through the wall leads into the fragrant **Komrčar Park**, a shady place set on the ridge from where you can walk down to the concreted bathing spots on the west side of the peninsula.

THE MONASTERY OF ST EUPHEMIA

About thirty minutes' walk northwest of town along the seaside path is the Franciscan **Monastery of St Euphemia** (Samostan svete Fumije; July & Aug Mon–Sat 10am–noon & 4–6pm; June & Sept Mon–Sat 9am–noon & 3–5pm; 5Kn). Built in 1446, this has a delicate cloister and a museum in the library above, containing illuminated manuscripts, a headless Roman figure of Diana and a fifteenth-century wooden image of St Francis. The monastery has two churches, one dedicated to St Euphemia and the larger church of St Bernardin, which has a gory late Gothic crucifix, a seventeenth-century wooden ceiling decorated with scenes from the life of St Francis and a polyptych painted by the Vivarini brothers in 1458, showing a Madonna and Child flanked by two tiers of saints.

BEACHES AND COVES

You can swim or sunbathe beside the waterside walkway on the west side of town – take the steps down beside St Justine's Church, or from Komrčar Park. There are some attractive shingle beaches east of town beyond the *Padova* hotel, but a far more popular place for bathing is the **Frkanj peninsula**, 1km west of the town as the crow flies and accessible from the harbour by taxi boat or by walking the 3km from Suha Punta (see below). The peninsula boasts numerous rocky coves backed by deep green forest; there's a large naturist area on the far side. At the northwestern end of Frkanj is **Suha Punta** (also accessible by a side-road which leaves the Rab–Kampor route just beyond the Monastery of St Euphemia), a tourist complex comprising the *Eva* and *Carolina* hotels. Beyond here lies a further sequence of bays and coves, slightly less busy than those of Frkanj and reachable by following tracks through the coastal forest.

Eating, drinking and nightlife

One of the cheapest and best places to **eat** is *Škver*, on the seaside path on the west side of the peninsula, about 200m northwest of the steps down from Komrčar Park, an unpretentious place serving no-nonsense basics like *grah* (bean stew), *lignje* (squid) and *girice* (tiny deep-fried fish) to a mixture of local fishermen and tourists. In the heart of the old town, *Paradiso Pizza*, Stjepana Radića, serves up reasonable fare in a palm-shaded courtyard. Moving up in price, *Konoba Rab*, Kneza Branimira, is a cosy split-level place with folksy touches – like dried herbs hanging from the thick stone walls – offering a good range of seafood and meat dishes including the local speciality *janjetina pod peku* (pieces of lamb cooked in an ember-covered pot). *Zlatni Rab*, Jurja Barakovića 1, and *Café Biser*, on the corner of Trg svetog Kristofora and Srednja ulica, have the best cakes and sweets, while the latter is also an eternally popular daytime spot for coffee-sipping. **Nightlife** venues go in and out of fashion from one season to the next: the **cafés** on Trg municipium Arba are classic spots for people-watching, and there's a string of small trendy **bars** along the nearby Donja ulica and Obala kralja Petra Krešimira.

The rest of the island: Kampor and the Lopar peninsula

Six kilometres northwest of Rab – and connected to it by seven buses daily – **KAMPOR** is a small, scattered village with a deep swathe of shallow sandy beach. It doesn't get too crowded even in high season, and there are a couple of small **campsites** behind the beach, as well as private **rooms** (①) available through agencies in Rab Town or by asking around. About 1km inland from Kampor, back along the road to Rab, lies the **Graveyard of the Victims of Fascism** (Groblje žrtava fašizma), a site commemorating the concentration camp established here by the Italian occupiers in 1942. It's referred to locally as the "Slovene Cemetery" due to the large numbers of Slovenes who were imprisoned and died here, although it housed a wide range of Partisans, Jews and political undesirables, rounded up in the Italian-controlled portions of Slovenia and Croatia. Most of the internees were crowded together in flimsy tents – some five thousand died in the winter of 1942–43 alone, starved of food and drink by Italian officials. After the collapse of Italy in September 1943, most of the able-bodied survivors joined Tito's Partisans, who were briefly in control of the island before the arrival of a German garrison. The site is a dignified and restful place, with long lines of graves – one for every four people who died – surrounded by well-tended lawns, trees and shrubs.

The Lopar peninsula

Another road climbs out of Rab to the north, making its way down the island's broad central valley. After passing the sprawling settlement of Supetarska Draga, the main road reaches a T-junction at the neck of the Lopar peninsula. The left turn leads to the village of **LOPAR**, a handful of houses spread around a muddy bay from where the ferry leaves for Krk. The sandy beach here isn't particularly picturesque, but is usually empty. The right turn leads to **SAN MARINO**, 1km south, a largely modern village which nevertheless lays claim to being the birthplace of St Marin, a fourth-century stonemason who fled persecution by crossing the seas to Italy, founding the town that subsequently became the republic of San Marino. Today's settlement stretches around a vast expanse of sand known as **Veli mel** (*mel* being an archaic word for "beach", although it's also referred to hereabouts as Rajska plaža – "Paradise Beach" – or simply "Copacabana"), backed by cafés and restaurants and packed with families in July and August. There's a sequence of smaller, progressively less crowded sandy beaches beyond the headlands to the north, beginning with Livačina Bay, followed by the predominantly naturist Kaštelina Bay slightly further up. Even more secluded sandy bays can be reached by heading northeast on foot from either Lopar or San Marino, where trails cross a sandy heath covered by prickly evergreens before dropping down into coves like Sahara and Stolac – the latter is reserved for naturists.

THE ADRIATIC GULAG: GRGUR AND GOLI OTOK

While lounging around on the beaches of the Lopar peninsula you're sure to catch sight of the island of **Grgur**, little more than a kilometre offshore, site of a women's prison until the 1960s and once decorated with a giant "Tito" and *petokraka* (the five-pointed communist star), both carved painstakingly out of bare rock. Immediately to the southeast is the notorious **Goli otok** ("Bare Island"), an obstinate hummock of mottled rock that was used as an island jail for communists who remained loyal to the Soviet Union after Stalin's break with Tito in 1948. Over a period of five years in the late 1940s and early 1950s a total of 15,000 *informburovci* (supporters of the Informburo, the Moscow-based organization which coordinated the work of communist parties worldwide) were "re-educated" here through forced labour in the island's quarry. Few of the inmates were guilty of seriously plotting against the regime; the majority were minor figures who had simply spoken out against Tito in private and been betrayed by a colleague or friend. On arrival, prisoners were forced to pass through a chicken-run of lined-up guards bearing sticks, before submitting to a regime of beatings and torture; recalcitrant prisoners had their heads immersed in buckets of human excrement, while those who confessed their ideological errors were recruited to torture the others. The existence of Goli otok was not publicly admitted until the 1980s, by which time Tito – on whose personal initiative the camp had been established – was already dead.

There are seven **buses** daily from Rab to Lopar, and an equal number (summer only) to the beach at San Marino. All services pass by the **tourist office** (☎051/775-508) at the T-junction between Lopar and San Marino, which shares premises with a Turist Biro office, offering private **rooms** (①). There's also a large **campsite**, the *San Marino* (☎051/775-133, fax 775-290), just behind the Veli mel beach.

Pag

Seen from the mainland, **PAG** is a stark and desolate pumice-stone of an island which looks as if it could barely support any form of life. Around eight thousand people live here, looking after three times as many sheep, who scour the stony slopes in search of the odd blade of grass. Hot afternoons always seem hotter here than anywhere else: nothing stirs, and, on the arid eastern side of the island, seemingly nothing grows except for a grey-green carpet of sage. The two main settlements are **Pag Town**, with its attractive historic centre, and **Novalja**, bland and over-commercialized, but with access to better beaches.

Pag's main claim to fame is its **cheese** (*paški sir*) – a hard, piquant sheep's cheese (with a taste somewhere between mature cheddar and parmesan) which you'll find in supermarkets all over the country. The distinctive taste is due to the method of preparation – cheeses are rubbed with a mixture of olive oil and ash before being left to mature – and the diet of the sheep, which includes many wild herbs (notably the ubiquitous sage) flavoured by salt picked up from the sea by the wind and deposited on vegetation across the island. Indeed, Pag is a salty kind of place all round: the precious stuff is the island's main industry, with saltpans stretching out along the island's central valley, and even the tap water tastes slightly brackish. Pag's other traditional industry is **lace-making**, a craft that for the moment remains refreshingly uncommercialized. Small pieces are sold from doorways by the lacemakers themselves, often wearing the dark, full-skirted local costume which seems to have endured here more than anywhere else on the Adriatic.

Approaching Pag from the north, there's a **ferry** from Prizna on the mainland, 3km below the Magistrala to Žaglav, 5km north of Novalja. The island's southern end is connected to the mainland via the **Pag Bridge** (Paški most), about 26km north of Posedarje on the Magistrala. The only public transport on the island is provided by the few Rijeka–Zadar **buses** (two daily in each direction) which pass through Novalja and Pag Town.

Pag Town

PAG TOWN originally lay about 3km south of its present site – the Pag salt industry was an attractive target for predatory neighbours and the inhabitants of Pag were able to play one aggressor off against another until the town was sacked by Zadar in 1395 and many of its leading citizens killed. The Venetians, who had taken control of the area by the 1420s, hired the architect Juraj Dalmatinac (see p.227) to build a new island capital from scratch, creating the present town with its tight grid of narrow streets along one side of a deep bay. Abbé Fortis, visiting in the late eighteenth century, called it a dismal place, adding that "I found not a single man of good sense in all that town; everybody is interested in the salt pits, and whoever talks not of salt is not regarded."

Pag is the venue of two **carnivals**: the first an authentic local event immediately before Lent; the second, in late July or early August, a re-enactment of the first for the benefit of tourists. Both feature parades and a good deal of folk music and traditional dancing, and the pre-Lenten carnival culminates with the burning of the effigy known as Marko, whose ritual death is claimed to rid the community of all the bad things which have happened over the previous year. Both carnivals traditionally featured performances of *Paška robinja* (Slave Girl of Pag), a play of Renaissance origins concerning a captive of the Turks who is purchased and freed by a good Christian knight. Made up of rhyming couplets delivered in a monotone, it's nowadays considered too boring for the average audience, and is no longer performed every year.

The Town
Flanking the town's central square, Trg kralja Petra Krešimira IV, are two of Dalmatinac's original buildings: the **Rector's Palace** (Knežev dvor), now a café and supermarket, and the **Parish Church** (Župna crkva), on the other side of the square – the rose window on the church facade echoes the patterns found in Pag lace, while a relief above the main door shows the Virgin sheltering the townspeople (some wearing traditional Pag skirts) beneath her cloak. Inside, the columns sport capitals bearing a variety of carved beasts, including griffins, and dolphins drinking from cups.

A causeway-like strip of land connects central Pag with its suburbs on the western side of Pag bay, where you'll also find the town's main, pebble, beach. Behind it lies the Lokunjica, a muddy lagoon, and the saltpans, which stretch south for 6km. Walking along the west bank of the saltpans for 2.5km brings you to **Stari grad** (Old Town), the original town which was abandoned in the 1440s. There are a few ruined buildings here, including the cloister of a Franciscan monastery, and a church dating from 1392 with a fine Gothic relief of the Virgin above the portal – it served as the model for the relief adorning the parish church in the new town. A statue of the Virgin inside the old town church is taken in procession to the new parish church on August 15 (Assumption), where it's kept until September 8 (Birth of the Virgin).

Practicalities

Rijeka–Zadar buses stop at a car park on the northern edge of town, a short walk from the **tourist office** by the bridge across the Lokunjica (summer daily 8am–9pm; winter Mon–Sat 8am–3pm; ☎ & fax 023/611-286 or 611-301). **Rooms** (①) are available from Mediteran or Suntourist behind the bus stop, or from Meridian 15, on the other side of the car park next to the *Pagus* hotel. The *Pagus* itself, Ante Starčevića 1 (☎023/611-310, fax 611-101; ④), is the least bland of the town's **hotels**, with roomy en-suites and a small stretch of private beach. The nearest **campsite** is the *Šimuni*, occupying an attractive location on the island's western shore, 8km away on the road to Novalja. The best places for traditional **food** are *Konoba Bile*, up from the parish church on Jurja Dalmatinca, and *Konoba Bodulo*, just to the north on Vangradska. There are numerous **café-bars** on the main square and along the waterfront, and a **disco**, *Peti magazin*, in one of the old salt warehouses over the bridge from the tourist office.

Novalja and around

Twenty kilometres north of Pag Town, **NOVALJA** is the island's main resort and much more developed and crowded than Pag Town. Originally a Roman settlement dating from around the first century AD, it preserves a few ancient remains, including an underground **water conduit** (*vodovod*; summer daily 9am–7pm; 5Kn), known by the locals as the "Italian Hole", a stretch of which you can walk along – it's clearly signposted just north of the seafront. There's a curving gravel beach at the south side of town, from where a stony path leads south to the much larger, pebbly **Straško beach**. Two kilometres south of town on the road to Pag Town, a side-road descends to the east-facing **Zrće beach**, a vast, gravelly expanse with a view of the pale ochre hills of eastern Pag and the greenish Velebit mountains beyond. There's a sandier beach in the next bay to the north, about ten minutes' walk, although it's more exposed to the wind.

Buses stop on the seafront, where there's a small office offering private **rooms** (①) – look for the sign saying *sobe*. The **tourist office** (Mon–Fri 8am–3pm; ☎ & fax 053/661-404, *www.novalja.hr*) is located on the first floor of the town hall, near the entrance to the conduit.

Senj to the Paklenica National Park

Back on the mainland and continuing south from Senj, the Magistrala picks its way beneath the rocky slopes of the **Velebit**, the mountain chain which follows the coast for some 100km. It's initially a forbidding sight, a stark, grey, unbroken wall, although there are patches of green pasture and forest just below its string of summits. Some of the best views of the Velebit are to be had from the eastern coasts of Rab and Pag, from where it towers over the coast like the waves of a frozen sea.

There are few coastal settlements of any size along this stretch of the Adriatic – understandably, given the steep and rocky terrain, which leaves precious little space for houses, agriculture or tourist resorts. However, there are some nice coves into which **campsites** have been attractively squeezed – *Rača* and *Žrnovica*, 10km and 13km south of Senj respectively, are two of the most pleasant. About 25km out of Senj a side-road descends to the port of **JABLANAC**, from where regular ferries cross the narrow Velebit channel to Mišnjak on the island of Rab. Most coastal buses don't make the detour to Jablanac, dropping off on the main highway 4km away instead, so if you're heading for Rab it's best to catch a direct Rijeka–Senj–Rab Town bus – Jablanac itself is small, unspectacular and not the kind of place you would want to get stuck in. Much the same could be said of **PRIZNA**, 13km south, another small harbour just off the Magistrala, from where hourly ferries leave for Žigljen on the island of Pag.

The larger but equally unrewarding town of **KARLOBAG**, another 13km south, is the starting point for a minor road which winds inland over the mountains, struggling up through the rugged terrain before arriving at **GOSPIĆ**, main town of the **Lika** region. This is another potential route up towards the Plitvice lakes (see p.123), although there's little to stop for en route other than the sheer barrenness of the landscape, though this can be oddly riveting. Travelling through the area in the 1870s, the future archeologist Arthur Evans (then Balkan correspondent for the *Manchester Guardian*) described the area as the "Croatian Siberia" – "a strange, wild land . . . with its scattered oases of fertility, its chaotic rocks, underground rivers, and mysterious caverns; a country – as everywhere else in Illyria – presenting the most startling contrasts of nakedness and cultivation."

The Paklenica National Park

The coast south from Karlobag is similarly sparse on attractions until you reach the village of **STARIGRAD-PAKLENICA**, a straggling line of modern seaside houses and apartments which constitutes the handiest base for the **PAKLENICA NATIONAL PARK**, the most accessible area for hiking in the Velebit. Designated a national park in 1949, Paklenica is the Velebit's last great flourish before the ridge trails inland to meet the Dinaric range on Croatia's border with Bosnia-Hercegovina. It contains some of the country's finest karst landscapes, featuring gorges, grizzled mountains and caves, and three quite different climates – coastal, continental and sub-alpine – which makes its weather unpredictable and, at times, extreme.

The park comprises two limestone gorges, Velika Paklenica and, 5km to the south, Mala Paklenica (literally, Big Paklenica and Small Paklenica), which run down towards the sea, towered over by 400-metre-high cliffs. **Mala Paklenica** has deliberately been left undeveloped in order to protect its status as a (relatively) untouched wilderness – paths are not maintained or marked with the same thoroughness as in Velika Paklenica, and you'll need good maps if you want to explore it.

The entrance to the **Velika Paklenica** gorge is about 2km inland from Starigrad, reached by a road which heads east just south of the *Hotel Alan*. After passing through the half-abandoned, stone village of Marasovići there's a ticket booth where you pay an entrance fee (30Kn) and receive a basic free map, if you haven't already picked one up from the national park office (see p.200). If you have your own transport you can continue to the car park 2km further on inside the park. There's no public transport from the *Hotel Alan* into the park, so without your own transport you'll have to walk the 4km to the car park.

From the car park, the gorge begins to narrow in earnest and everyone has to proceed on foot. The main path up the valley passes beneath towering cliffs and dramatic outcrops of rock, while a stream rushes down a boulder-strewn bed below. After 45 minutes of moderate ascent, a well-signposted side path heads right to **Anića kuk**, a craggy peak lying a steep climb to the south. Past here, the main path levels out for a while, passing through elm and beech forest – surprisingly lush after the arid Mediterranean scrub of the coast below. After another fifteen minutes, a second side path ascends steeply to the left. A forty-minute walk up here will bring you to **Manita peć** (open three days weekly in summer; ask at the national park office in Starigrad or at the entrance gate to the park for details), a complex of stalactite-packed caverns about 500m long. From here you can either turn back the way you came, or head on for another hour and a half (the path leads from the left of the cave as you emerge), up some fairly steep and none too easy slopes to **Vidakov kuk**, an 800-metre-high peak that gives fine views over the coast and islands.

Back on the main path, it's about twenty minutes to the *Šumarska kuća* hut, where you can get food and drink on spring and summer weekends, and a further thirty minutes to the *Borisov Dom* mountain hut, the starting point for assaults on the major peaks above. The most prominent of these is **Vaganski vrh** which, at 1757m above sea level, is the southern Velebit's highest peak. The views from the top are spectacular, but you'll need to be reasonably fit, have a good map and make an early start if you're going to attempt the walk up.

A circular walk taking in the Mala Paklenica branches off the main trail some ten minutes after the turn-off for Anića kuk. Climbing steeply across the Jurasova glava ridge, this heads south to the neck of the Mala Paklenica gorge, which leads down towards **SELINE** on the coast. The canyon is beautifully rugged, the trail not too difficult to follow, and there are some impressive rock formations en route. The whole hike takes about seven hours from entrance to exit, and you can do it in reverse from Seline if you prefer.

Practicalities

All coastal buses plying the Rijeka–Zadar route run through Starigrad, stopping in the centre near the petrol station and at the northern end of the village, where there's a small harbour. The latter stop is handiest for the **tourist office** (Mon–Fri 8am–2pm, Sat 8am–noon; ☎023/369-245 or 369-255), on the landward side of the road, although the **national park office**, 500m south (daily 8am–3pm; ☎023/369-202), is more useful if you're planning trips into the mountains – as well as having a free leaflet with a basic map of the area, they sell more detailed hiking maps, can advise on weather conditions and book rooms in Velika Paklenica's mountain hut, *Borisov Dom*.

There are plentiful private **rooms** (①) in Starigrad itself: signs for rooms (*sobe*) dangle outside most houses along the main road. The nearest **hotel** to the park entrance is the incongruously high-rise, 470-bed *Hotel Alan* (☎023/369-276, fax 369-203; ④), which also has its own stretch of private beach. *Hotel Vicko*, just north of the tourist office at Dokozina 20 (☎023/369-304; ⑤), is a smaller, cosier affair offering neat rooms with TV. There's an abundance of **campsites**, including a large, well-tended site next to the national park office and several smaller ones tucked neatly into private gardens on the access road to the entrance to Mala Paklenica. For **eating**, the *Vicko* has a good restaurant, and there's a string of inexpensive grills along the main road through Starigrad, and stores in which to stock up on provisions.

travel details

TRAINS

Rijeka to: Zagreb (6 daily; 4hr).

BUSES

Cres Town to: Beli (2 weekly; 30min); Lubenice (3 weekly; 40min); Mali Lošinj (8 daily; 1hr); Rijeka (4 daily; 2hr 30min); Valun (3 weekly; 30min); Zagreb (2 daily; 6hr 30min).

Krk Town to: Baška (8 daily; 40min); Punat (10 daily; 10min); Rijeka (12 daily; 1hr 40min).

Lovran to: Liganj (8 daily; 15min); Lovranska Draga (8 daily; 20min); Rijeka (every 30min; 45min).

Opatija to: Kastav (hourly; 20min); Lovran (every 30min; 15min); Rijeka (every 30min; 30min).

Pag Town to: Novalja (2 daily; 30min), Rijeka (2 daily; 3hr), Zagreb (5 daily; 5hr).

Rab Town to: Kampor (Mon–Sat 7 daily, Sun 1 daily; 25min); Lopar (7 daily; 30min); Rijeka (3 daily; 3hr 30min).

Rijeka to: Buzet (6 daily; 2hr); Cres (4 daily; 2hr 30min); Crikvenica (hourly; 45min); Dubrovnik (2 daily; 13hr); Karlobag (12 daily; 2hr 45min); Kastav (every 30min; 25min); Krk Town (12 daily; 1hr 40min); Lovran (every 30min; 45min); Mali Lošinj (4 daily; 3hr 30min); Novi Vinodolski (hourly; 1hr); Opatija (every 30min; 30min); Pag (2 daily; 3hr); Pazin (5 daily; 1hr); Poreč (5 daily; 3hr 30min); Pula (17 daily; 2hr–2hr 30min); Rab Town (3 daily; 3hr 30min); Rovinj (4 daily; 3hr 15min); Senj (hourly; 1hr 20min); Šibenik (11 daily; 7hr); Split (11 daily; 8hr 30min); Starigrad-Paklenica (11 daily; 3hr 35min); Umag (3 daily; 4hr 25min); Zadar (11 daily; 4hr 30min); Zagreb (20 daily; 3–4hr).

Zadar to: Pag Town (2 daily; 1hr); Rijeka (11 daily; 4hr 30min).

FERRIES

Baška to: Lopar (July & Aug 5 daily, May, June & Sept 2 daily; 50min).

Brestova to: Porozina (hourly; 30min).

Crikvenica to: Silo (10 daily July & Aug; 30min).

Jablanac to: Mišnjak (summer every 30min, winter 9 daily; 30min).

Mali Lošinj to: Pula (6 weekly; 2hr 35min); Zadar (6 weekly; 5hr 20min).

Prizna to: Žigljen (hourly; 20min).

Rijeka to: Dubrovnik (summer daily, winter 2 weekly; 22hr); Hvar (summer daily, winter 2 weekly; 12–14hr); Korčula (summer daily, winter 2 weekly; 18hr); Rab Town (summer 1 weekly; 3hr); Split (summer daily, winter 2 weekly; 10–12hr); Zadar (summer daily, winter 2 weekly; 6hr).

Valbiska to: Merag (hourly; 30min).

INTERNATIONAL TRAINS

Rijeka to: Ljubljana (2 daily; 2hr 30min).

INTERNATIONAL BUSES

Rijeka to: Basel (5 weekly); Dortmund (6 weekly); Frankfurt (daily); Ljubljana (1 daily); Medjugorje (1 daily); Munich (1 daily); Nova Gorica (1 daily); Sarajevo (5 weekly); Stuttgart (1 daily); Trieste (5 daily).

INTERNATIONAL FERRIES

Rijeka to: Bari (3 weekly in summer; 25hr); Igoumenitsa (1 weekly in summer; 38hr).

CHAPTER FIVE

NORTHERN DALMATIA

S tretching from Zadar in the north to the Bay of Kotor (now part of Montenegro) in the south, **Dalmatia** possesses one of Europe's most dramatic shorelines, as the stark, grey wall of the coastal mountains sweeps down towards a lush seaboard ribbon dotted with palm trees and olive plantations. Along the coast are beautifully preserved, Venetian-influenced medieval towns that wouldn't look out of place on the other side of the Adriatic, poised above some of the clearest waters in Europe, while further out are myriad islands adorned with ancient stone villages and enticing coves. The tourist industry mushroomed hugely in the 1970s and 1980s, before collapsing during the 1991–95 war, and though visitor numbers have been rising rapidly since the return of peace, the crowds are rarely difficult to avoid: the Adriatic islands can swallow up any number of sightseers, while tourist settlements on the mainland have been kept well away from the main towns.

The contrast between the arid maquis of Dalmatia's stony interior and the fertile seaboard is reflected in the region's dual personality: the towns on the coast and islands have long enjoyed a thriving Mediterranean civilization, while their unsettled hinterland has been much more prone to the political uncertainties and population movements of the Balkan interior. People on the coast have traditionally been able to make a living through fishing, olive-growing, wine-making or trade, whereas life in the interior – the more arid parts of which are often called *kamenjar* ("stone-field") in Croatian – has always been much harsher. Dalmatia's long history of Roman, Venetian and Italian cultural penetration has left its mark on a region where children still call adult males *barba* ("beard" – Italian slang for "uncle") and respected gents go under the name of *šjor* (the local version of *signore*), but modern Dalmatia's identity is difficult to pin down. People from northern Croatia will tell you that life is lived at a much slower pace in Dalmatia, whose inhabitants are joshingly referred to as *tovari* ("donkeys") by their compatriots, though the briefest of visits to bustling regional centres like Zadar will be enough

---

ACCOMMODATION PRICE CODES

The accommodation in this guide has been graded using the following price codes, based on the cost of each establishment's **least expensive double room** in high season (June–Sept), excluding special offers. Hotel room rates almost always include breakfast. Out of season, prices on the coast can fall by up to 50 percent. Where single rooms exist, they usually cost 60–70 percent of the price of a double. For more details, see p.24.

① Less than 200Kn	④ 400–500Kn	⑦ 800–1000Kn
② 200–300Kn	⑤ 500–600Kn	⑧ 1000–1200Kn
③ 300–400Kn	⑥ 600–800Kn	⑨ Over 1200Kn

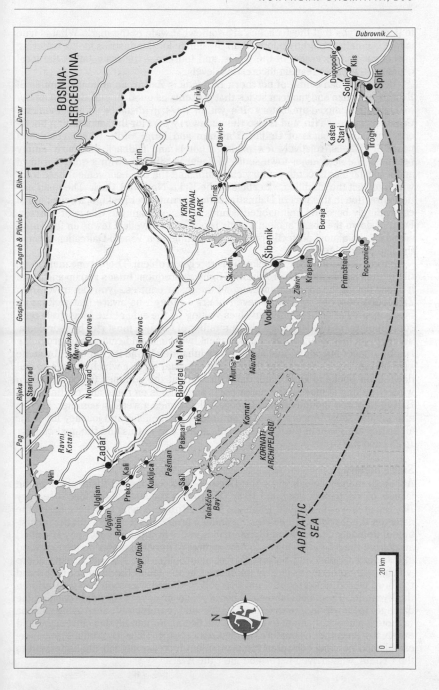

to persuade you that these clichés are somewhat wide of the mark. What is true is that Dalmatia is slightly poorer than the north: local industries took a battering in the war and recession of the 1990s, and tourism – the mainstay of the local economy – is yet to reattain its pre-1991 levels.

The main urban centre of northern Dalmatia is **Zadar**, an animated jumble of Roman, Venetian and modern styles that presents as good an introduction as any to Dalmatia's mixed-up history. It's within day-trip distance of the medieval Croatian centre of **Nin**, and is also the main ferry port for the unassuming northern Dalmatian islands of **Ugljan**, **Pašman** and **Dugi otok**, where you'll find peaceful villages, relatively few package hotels and laidback and fairly empty beaches. The next major town south of Zadar is **Šibenik**, with a quiet old town and a spectacular fifteenth-century cathedral, and the most convenient base from which to visit the tumbling waterfalls of the **Krka National Park**. The main natural attraction in this part of Dalmatia is the **Kornati archipelago**, a collection of captivatingly bare and uninhabited islands accessed from the village of **Murter**. Further down the coast, ancient **Trogir** is one of the loveliest towns on the entire seaboard, an almost perfectly preserved example of a Veneto-Dalmatian town of the late Middle Ages.

Getting around northern Dalmatia is rarely a problem. There's one main road, the Jadranska **Magistrala**, or Adriatic Highway; frequent **buses** run up and down it every day of the week, connecting all the major centres – you can travel from Zadar to Dubrovnik in around seven hours – though be aware that picking up buses in smaller centres often involves waiting by the side of the Magistrala until something turns up. There are also a number of **ferries**, most run by Jadrolinija, although an increasing number of seasonal hydrofoils and catamarans are being run by smaller operators. Just about every inhabited island is connected by some kind of regular local ferry, and there's also a coastal service which cruises up and down from Rijeka to Dubrovnik daily throughout the summer (twice a week in winter), calling at most of the major ports and islands en route and continuing to Bari in Italy and Igoumenitsa in Greece at least once a week in summer. Ferries also ply the Zadar–Ancona route in summer – frequencies and journey times for all ferries are given in the Travel Details at the end of this and the next chapter (p.237 and p.303).

Some history

Although initially colonized by the **Greeks**, who established themselves on the islands of Vis (Greek Issa) and Hvar (Pharos) at the start of the fourth century BC, the area was first called Dalmatia by the **Romans**, who may have based the name on the Illyrian word *delmat*, meaning a proud, brave man. With the imposition of Roman rule over local Illyrian tribes in the first century BC, power drifted away from the old Greek towns to new centres of imperial power on the mainland like **Jadera** (Zadar) and **Salona** (Solin, near Split). The Latinate urban culture which grew up here was largely unaffected by the fall of the Roman Empire and the brief period of Ostrogoth rule that followed, and was soon reorganized into the Byzantine Theme of Dalmatia. The Avar-Slav invasion of 614 did considerable damage to town life, weakening Zadar and completely destroying Salona (although a new settlement founded by the fleeing Roman-Illyrian citizenry would eventually become Dalmatia's largest city, Split). The Byzantines soon re-established nominal control of the region, but increasingly left the hinterland to the **Croats**, who arrived here soon after the Avars.

By the eleventh century, the Croatian state – and later its successor, the Hungaro-Croatian kingdom – was successfully challenging both Byzantium and Venice for control of the coast. Increasing numbers of Croats moved into the towns, and Croatian entrenched itself as the popular language, even if Latin was still used in writing. When Ladislas of Naples sold his rights to Dalmatia to Venice in 1409, most Dalmatian towns were given a choice – accept Venetian rule peacefully and retain a degree of autonomy, or submit by force. Contrary to Dalmatian expectations, however, the Venetians kept the towns on a short leash, muzzling traditions of municipal government by imposing on each of the cities an all-powerful rector (*knez*) responsible directly to the doge, and redirecting all import and export trade through Venice. Class divisions within Dalmatian society prevented any concerted opposition to Venetian rule, however, and rebellions were few and far between – the commoners' revolt launched by **Matija Ivanić** (see p.271) on Hvar in 1510, for instance, was as much against the local oligarchy as the occupying power.

Under the Venetians, Dalmatia was integrated into the wider Mediterranean world more than at any time since the days of the Roman Empire, opening up its cities to Renaissance culture and Italianate architecture. But however many fine loggias and campaniles the Venetians built, it would be a mistake to think that the locals had turned into good Venetians – the urban elite of fifteenth-century Dalmatia clearly saw themselves as Croats, and were keen to develop the local language as a medium fit for their patriotic aspirations. Prime movers were **Marko Marulić** of Split, whose *Judita* (Judith) of 1521 was the first ever epic tale "composed in Croatian verse", as its own title page proclaimed; and **Petar Zoranić** of Zadar, whose novel *Planine* (Mountains) of 1569 contains a scene in which the nymph Hrvatica (literally "Croatian girl") bemoans the lack of Dalmatians who show pride in their own language.

Venetian political control went largely unchallenged, however, because of the growing threat of the **Ottoman Turks**. The Venetians did their best to live in peace with the Turks in order to ensure the smooth functioning of trade, although major conflicts – notably the **Cyprus War** (1570–71) and the **Candia War** (1645–69) – occasionally brought roving armies to the Dalmatian hinterland. The Ottoman **defeat** outside Vienna in 1683 finally provided Venice with the opportunity to push the Turks back into Bosnia, but by this stage decades of conflict had changed the make-up of the Dalmatian population, as Croats from the interior had fled to the coast. Much of the hinterland itself had been devastated and repopulated with migrants from the Balkan interior, most of whom were classified as **Vlachs** (*vlah* or *vlaj* in Croatian) – a name which was sometimes applied to the nomadic tribes descended from the original Roman-Illyrian population, at others to all migrant stockbreeders from the interior. More important than the niceties of ethnic distinction, however, was the fact that the majority belonged to the Orthodox faith and, largely because they came under the jurisdiction of the Serbian Orthodox Church, came increasingly to regard themselves as Serbs.

Questions of ethnic identity are further complicated by the fact that the Venetians referred to all inlanders, regardless of who they were, as **Morlachs** (*morlacchi*), a term thought to originate in the combination of the name Vlach with the Greek word *mavro*, meaning "black" or "dark". The Morlach label came to be applied to all the inhabitants of Dalmatia who lived outside the cultured world of the coastal towns and islands, and although the hard life of the Morlachs was romanticized by foreign travellers (see box on p.206), they were shunned by

IMAGES OF DALMATIA: ALBERTO FORTIS AND THE MORLACHS

Western images of Dalmatia owe much to the writings of the Italian **Alberto Fortis**, a lapsed priest, natural scientist and tireless traveller who contributed more to the outside world's knowledge of the eastern Adriatic than anyone before or since. Fortis was particularly taken by the Morlachs (see p.205), the inhabitants of inland Dalmatia who had never been assimilated into the coast's urban Mediterranean culture. The Morlachs had already been written about by sixteenth-century humanist Palladius Fuscus of Padova, for whom they were "more like cattle than men", and the more sympathetic seventeenth-century French traveller Jacob Spon, who described them as "determined and indefatigable" people who liked nothing better than to take up arms against the Turks, but Fortis was the first to visit Morlach villages and describe how they lived. He admired their capacity for honesty, hospitality and lifelong friendship, as well as their code of honour – which allowed plenty of room for blood feuds and vengeance – thinking that the world of the Morlachs was the nearest thing that Europe still had to Homeric Greece. Fortis described the Morlachs' often abysmal living conditions, noting the tiny houses in which families slept alongside their cattle, adding that in households which actually possessed a bed, the husband slept on it while the wife was relegated to the floor. For Fortis, the Morlachs were living examples of the noble savages he had read about in Jean-Jacques Rousseau; he was particularly taken by the epic poems which Morlach bards recited to the accompaniment of the *gusla* (a droning bowed instrument), and published a translation of one of the most famous of them, *Hasanaginica* – a tale of conflict on the Christian–Ottoman border which originated in the villages somewhere inland of Makarska.

Fortis was travelling at a time when epic poems were all the rage in Western Europe, and his journeys were partly financed by Scottish laird, the Earl of Bute, whose interest in heroic folk tales had been fired after reading *Ossian*, an epic poem thought to be the work of third-century Celtic bards (although it was subsequently revealed to be a forgery cooked up by a certain James Macpherson). Both Bute and Fortis reckoned that the study of oral literature in inland Dalmatia would prove that all the valiant hero-nations of Europe had somehow been shaped by their epic poetry, and their enthusiasm soon caught on. Fortis's *Travels into*

the urban population on the coast, who were rarely aware of their existence except at fairs and markets. Until the twentieth century even educated Croats knew little about the hinterlanders, referring to them all as *morlaci, zagorci* (highlanders) or *vlaji* (a term still used as a put-down in Split, where anyone who can't see the sea from their house is a *vlaj*; see box on p.243), regardless of where they came from or what religion – Catholic or Orthodox – they professed.

For over 350 years Venice gave the Dalmatian towns peace, security and – ultimately – economic and political stagnation. The fall of the Republic in 1797 was followed by a brief Austrian interregnum until in 1808 **Napoleon** incorporated Dalmatia into his **Illyrian Provinces**, an artificial amalgam of Adriatic and west Slovene territories with its capital at Ljubljana. The reforming French played an important role in pulling Dalmatia out of its torpor, building roads, promoting trade, and opening up the region to modern scientific and educational ideas. There's little evidence that the French were popular, however: their decision to close down the monasteries deeply offended local Catholic feeling, and they also dragged Dalmatia into wars with the Austrians and the British, who occupied Vis in 1811 and shelled Zadar in 1813.

Dalmatia (1774) was an international sensation, provoking a craze for all things Morlach which lasted well into the next century. Goethe translated *Hasanaginica* into German; Sir Walter Scott performed the same service in English; while the Romantic novelist Prosper Merimée published *La guzla ou choix de poésies illyriques recueillies dans la Dalmatie, la Bosnie, la Croatia et l'Hercegovinie* (The Gusla, or a Selection of Illyrian Poetry from Dalmatia, Bosnia, Croatia and Hercegovina; 1827), which included *Hasanaginica* alongside a large number of poems by Merimée himself. As great a figure as Pushkin was entirely taken in by Merimée's book, reprinting some of the Frenchman's fraudulent epics in his *Poems of the Western Slavs*.

Nineteenth-century travel writers tended to use Fortis's work as a guidebook, uncritically repeating his comments on the Morlachs. Even Balthasar Hacquet, whose *L'Illyrie et la Dalmatie* (Illyria and Dalmatia; 1815) was in many ways better informed than Fortis about the South Slavs, still managed to include a fair share of *Arabian Nights*-style nonsense about the Morlachs, such as the assertion that "When local gendarmes capture a *haiduk* [bandit], there is no need to tie them up: it suffices to cut the waist cord of his ample trousers, which fall around his ankles and prevent him from taking flight."

What none of these travellers got to grips with was the question of who the Morlachs actually were, though the term itself became increasingly redundant as the Morlachs began to identify themselves as Serbs and Croats rather than submitting to the labels applied to them by others. Dalmatia could still be a place of dramatic contrasts, however. The sight of men in embroidered jackets and pistols stuck in their belts made a big impression on Maude Holbach, whose tellingly entitled *Dalmatia: the Land Where East meets West* (1908) gushingly informed readers that "the Dalmatians look more like stage brigands than peaceful subjects of the Austrian Empire." The Fortis effect probably reached its high water mark, however, with *Black Lamb and Grey Falcon* (1937) by Rebecca West, whose prose was always more enthusiastic when she was writing about the macho types of the Balkan hinterland rather than the civilized urbanites of the Adriatic coast. This type of response to Dalmatia is less popular now than it was, not least because the events of 1991–95 suddenly made traditional Western views of southeastern Europe appear naive and over-romanticized.

Hopes that Dalmatia would be unified with the rest of the Croatian lands after its incorporation into **Austria** in 1815 were soon dashed. Instead, Dalmatia became a separate province of the Habsburg Empire, Italian was made the official language, and German- and Italian-speaking bureaucrats were brought in to run the administration. By mid-century Dalmatia had just over 400,000 inhabitants, of whom 340,000 were Slavs and only 16,000 were Italians, and yet the first Croatian language schools didn't open until the 1860s. Many Croats living in the coastal towns still saw fluency in Italian as a mark of social and cultural superiority, and felt that they had little in common with those from inland. Things began to change in 1848, when the newly formed Croatian Sabor (Parliament) in Zagreb renewed calls for the reunification of Dalmatia with the rest of Croatia. The Viennese court quashed the idea, but could no longer prevent the growth of Croatian national consciousness in the Adriatic towns.

The creation of a Dalmatian Assembly in 1861 opened up a political arena which was dominated by the **Narodnjaci** (Nationalists), who wanted the reunion of Dalmatia with the historic heartlands of continental Croatia, and the **Autonomaši** (Autonomists), who regarded Dalmatia as a unique cultural entity populated by

"Slavo-Dalmatians" rather than Croats. The Autonomaši tended to be supported by Italians or Italianized Croats who looked to Italy – which had emerged as a unified kingdom in 1861 – rather than Austria, although the Austrian defeat of an Italian navy off the island of Vis in 1866 put paid to any immediate likelihood that the Italian Risorgimento would be repeated in Dalmatia. The importance of the Battle of Vis was not lost on the local Croats, who began to celebrate its anniversary with much pomp in order to annoy their Italian neighbours. The Narodnjaci won control of the Dalmatian Assembly in 1870, and Croatian became the official language in the Assembly in 1883, though it wasn't introduced into the civil service or the law courts until 1912.

Despite Italian claims, the whole of Dalmatia except Zadar and Lastovo fell to the Kingdom of Serbs, Croats and Slovenes (subsequently Yugoslavia) in 1918. However, the threat of **Italian irredentism** remained strong, especially after Mussolini came to power in 1922. The Italian occupation of Dalmatia between 1941 and 1943 only served to worsen relations between the two communities, and at the war's end most remaining Italians fled.

The advent of socialism in 1945 failed to staunch major **emigration** to the New World and Australasia. After World War II, the traditional olive-growing and fishing economy of the Adriatic islands and villages was neglected in favour of heavy industry, producing a degree of rural depopulation which has only partly been ameliorated by the growth of tourism. The arrival of package tourists in the 1960s brought Dalmatia hitherto unimagined prosperity (although much of the money earned from tourism went to the big Yugoslav travel companies based in Belgrade), while urban-dwellers from inland cities like Zagreb and Belgrade increasingly aspired to **vikendice** ("weekend houses") on the coast, changing the profile of the village population and turning the Adriatic into a vast recreation area serving the whole of Yugoslavia.

Many of the holiday homes owned by Serbs ended up being abandoned or sold after the **collapse of Yugoslavia**, in which Dalmatia suffered as much as anywhere else in Croatia. After securing control of the hinterland areas around Knin and Benkovac, Serbian forces never quite reached the sea – despite attempts to subdue Zadar. Coastal hotels soon filled with refugees, however, and the tourist industry wound down due to lack of custom. Slovene, Italian and German tourists have been quick to return to their former stomping grounds with the resumption of peace, and there's an increasing number of visitors from Hungary, the Czech Republic and Poland. The one big group of pre-1991 tourists yet to go back to the Adriatic is the British, as many as half a million of whom came annually to Croatia before the war. Their relative absence may be no bad thing if you're looking for peace and quiet, although the local restaurant owners are bound to disagree.

Along the coast to Nin

Approaching from the north, your first sight of Dalmatia is the lofty concrete span of the **Maslenica Bridge** (Maslenički most) as it sweeps across the **Maslenica Gorge**. The original bridge was destroyed by Serb forces in autumn 1991 in an attempt to sever Dalmatia's communications with the rest of the country, and it wasn't until January 1993 that the Croatian army regained control of Maslenica (breaking a UN-brokered ceasefire in the process). The new Maslenica Bridge, opened in 1996, is notoriously susceptible to strong winds, and if the Bura is

Makarska, Dalmatia

Krka National Park

Vineyards, Primosten

Harbour, Korčula Town

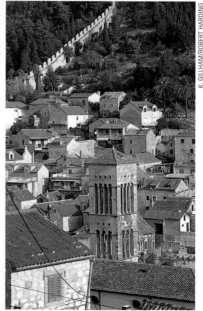

Old town, Korčula

Old town, Hvar

Sobra, Mljet

Diocletian's Palace, Split

Cathedral entrance, Split

Stradun, Dubrovnik

St Blaise's Church, Dubrovnik

Market, Dubrovnik

Old town, Dubrovnik

blowing it's often closed to high-sided vehicles, bikes and trailers – and in bad storms is shut altogether.

To the south of the Maslenica Bridge is the **Novigradsko more** ("Novigrad Sea"), a large, sheltered lagoon bordered by grey-brown hills. Just beyond the bridge, past the village of Posedarje, there's a southbound turning for the little town of **NOVIGRAD**, tucked away on the west side of the lagoon beneath a ruin-crowned hill. Novigrad has something of a history of being a front-line town: it was an important point in Venice's line of defences against the Turks, and held out successfully except for a short period in 1646–47, when Ibrahim Pasha seized the fortress. More recently it was occupied by the Serbs until won back in the Maslenica Bridge operation of 1993, although it remained so close to the front line that the locals couldn't return to their houses for another two years.

Nowadays, Novigrad is a pleasant little place, with an S-bend of solid stone houses following a quay lined with small fishing craft, and narrow streets winding uphill. The otherwise unremarkable **parish church** (župna crkva) contains a Gothic statue of the Pietà which is paraded around town on the third Sunday of September. Above the church you can pick up paths to the hilltop **castle** (fortica), where Elizabeth Kotromanić, Queen of Hungary, was murdered in 1386. The castle is now in ruins, but the climb is worth it for the views north over the Novigradsko more to the ridge of the Velebit mountains.

Buses from Zadar pull up on the Riva, where the **tourist office** (Mon–Sat 8–11am & 6–9.30pm, Sun 8–11am; ☎023/375-051) has information on local **rooms** (①). There's a nice **pension**, *Osam ferala*, on the right as you enter town (☎023/375-114 or 375-122; ②); and a **campsite**, the *Mulić*, on the eastern side of town, which has basic facilities and a pleasant pebbly **beach**.

On the eastern side of the Novigradsko more, huge rock portals announce the entrance to the narrow canyon of the **Zrmanja Gorge**, one of the most remarkable karst formations in the country, its sheer sides rising as high as 200m. The best way to see the gorge is by **boat**; the tourist office in Novigrad might be able to arrange for local fishermen to take you up the gorge if you give them 24 hours notice. This might work out cheaper than the excursions with Flash Touring, on Novigrad's Riva (☎023/375-201, fax 375-040), which organizes one-day raft trips (a gentle trip on a real raft rather than a whitewater ride) in the gorge – expect to pay around 200Kn per person including food.

Nin

To the west of the Maslenica Bridge, the Magistrala forges across the **Ravni kotari** (literally "flat districts"), a fertile expanse of farmland and one of the few places in Dalmatia where you'll see cows, sheep and pumpkins alongside more commonplace Mediterranean features such as vineyards, olive groves and maquis. About 15km beyond Posedarje, another side turning leads north to **NIN**, erstwhile ecclesiastical capital of Croatia and now a sleepy, beach-fringed town, set on a broad bay facing the southwestern extremities of the island of Pag. Initially settled by the Liburnians followed by the Romans, Nin later became a royal residence of the early Croatian kings and a major see of their bishops from 879. Like everywhere else along the coast it fell under Venetian rule in the fifteenth century, and was soon threatened by Ottoman advances, until in 1646 the Venetians evacuated the town and then shelled it from the sea, after which it slipped quietly into decay. By the time T.G. Jackson got here in 1887 Nin was no more than a large village whose inhabitants were so wan and unwholesome from malaria that his guides wouldn't let him stay there overnight.

The malaria has gone, but apart from that Nin can't have changed much since Jackson's visit, preserving a scattering of Roman ruins, crumbling walls and a clutch of quaint old churches which give evidence of Nin's former importance. Nin also boasts some decent **beaches**, with alluring sandy stretches north and east of town, and a more pebbly affair at the tourist settlement of Zaton to the west.

The Town

The town is built on a small island connected to the mainland by two bridges: Gornji most and Donji most ("upper bridge" and "lower bridge"). Buses from Zadar stop near Donji most, across which lies the main street, which leads past the plain-looking **St Anselm's Church** (Crkva svetog Anzelma), an eighteenth-century structure built on the site of Nin's former cathedral. Next door, the **treasury** (*riznica*; irregular opening hours, enquire at the tourist office; 10Kn) houses a ninth-century reliquary chest with reliefs of SS Marcela, Aselus and Ambrozius, and an ornate reliquary containing the arm of St Aselus.

Just off the main street, the small cruciform **Church of the Holy Cross** (Crkva svetog Križa) is the oldest church in the country, with an inscription on the lintel referring to Župan (Count) Godezav dated 800 AD. A simple white-washed structure with high, Romanesque windows and a solid dome, it's some-times open in summer, though it's bare inside apart from the simple stone slab which serves as an altar – ask at the tourist office or at the **Archeological Museum** at the top of the main street (Arheološki muzej; summer Mon–Sat 9am–noon & 6–9pm; winter Mon–Sat 8am–noon; 10Kn). This small but excel-lently presented museum kicks off with an ancient Liburnian *peka* (a cooking pot on top of which burning embers are piled) which looks identical to those still in use in Dalmatian kitchens today. The imported ceramics dredged up from Liburnian wrecks in Zaton harbour include a wealth of north Italian tableware and a dog-faced ornamental jug from Asia Minor. One room is devoted to two eleventh-century Croatian ships (one of which has been fully reconstructed) res-cued by marine archeologists from shallow waters nearby. Possibly sunk in front of Nin port in order to prevent attack, these easily manoeuvrable, eight-metre-long vessels could be used either for fishing or fighting, and could easily be pulled up onto land or hidden in small bays. A collection of early medieval stonework cul-minates with a large stone font sporting a clumsily engraved inscription honour-ing Višeslav, one of the first Christian rulers of the embryonic Croatian state. There's also a model of the Roman **Temple of Diana**, whose scrappy remains lie round the corner from the museum. Beyond the temple ruins lie a surviving stretch of town wall and the Gornji most, over which the austere, barn-like thirteenth-century **St Ambrose's Church** (Crkva svetog Ambroza) stands silent guard.

Entering Nin on the main road from Zadar you'll have noticed another tiny church surrounded by slender Scots pines – **St Nicholas's** (Crkva svetog Nikole), an eleventh-century structure built on an ancient burial mound and later fortified by the Turks. There's nothing much here, but the site is impressive, and there's a fine view over the blustery lowlands to the worn shape of Nin and the faint, silver-grey ridge of the Velebit mountains in the distance.

Practicalities

Buses to Nin run approximately every 45 minutes from the main Zadar bus station, dropping passengers at the western, mainland side of town, slightly uphill from the **tourist office** (summer daily 8am–8pm; winter Mon–Fri 8am–3pm; ☎023/264-280, fax 265-247, *tzg-nina@zd.tel.hr*), which has details of private **rooms** (①). Of the **campsites** north of town, the *Ninska Laguna* is a nice grassy place not too far from the beach. For **food**, there are a couple of places offering grills on the square in front of the Archeological Museum, and a wider range of meals at *Gostionica Sokol* beside the Donji most – where you'll also find a couple of cafés.

The nearest place for **swimming** is the sandy spit which curls round Nin's island to the east: head across Gornji most and bear left to get there. The other main beach area is an easy three-kilometre walk north of town – head out on the Privlaka road and turn right when you see signs to *Autocamp Nin* and *Camping Ninska Laguna*. Follow the track past the latter, before branching off on a path which leads through a purply-green, heather-like carpet of grasses and reeds before emerging onto a duney shore. The beach is genuinely sandy, and there's another fine view of the Velebit mountains across the water.

Zadar

The ancient capital of Dalmatia, **ZADAR** is a bustling town of around 100,000 people, but it preserves a relatively small-town feel, with a compact historic centre crowded onto a tapered thumb of land jutting northwest into the Adriatic. Pretty comprehensively destroyed in the last war by the Allies – it was bombed no fewer than 72 times – it lacks the perfectly preserved, museum-like quality of so many of the towns on this coast, displaying instead a pleasant muddle of architectural styles, where lone Corinthian columns stand alongside rectangular 1950s blocks, and Romanesque churches compete for space with glassy café-bars. Zadar is a major ferry port, so you'll pass through here if travelling on to the islands of the Zadar archipelago – Ugljan, Pašman, Dugi otok and a host of smaller islets. As the major urban centre between Rijeka and Split, Zadar can boast a university and a smattering of cultural distractions, but it's not near any major package destinations and tourists rarely stick around for long – leaving Zadar's café culture very much to the locals.

Long held by the Venetians (who called it Zara), Zadar was for centuries an Italian-speaking city, and you'll find the Latin influence still strong – Italian is widely understood, particularly by older people, and the place has much of the vibrancy of an Italian coastal town. It was ceded to Italy in 1921 under the terms of the Treaty of Rapallo, before becoming part of Tito's Yugoslavia in 1947, when many Italian families opted to leave. Postwar reconstruction resulted in the current patchwork of old and new architectural styles, although further damage was meted out in 1991, when a combination of Serbian irregulars and JNA (Yugoslav People's Army) forces came dangerously close to capturing the city. As the country slid towards all-out war in early autumn 1991, JNA artillery units quickly took control of the low hills around Zemunik airport east of the city, leaving Zadar open to bombardment. JNA-Serb forces reached the high-rise suburbs but never pressed on towards the centre, possibly fearing the heavy losses that would be incurred in hand-to-hand street fighting. Despite the UN-sponsored ceasefires of

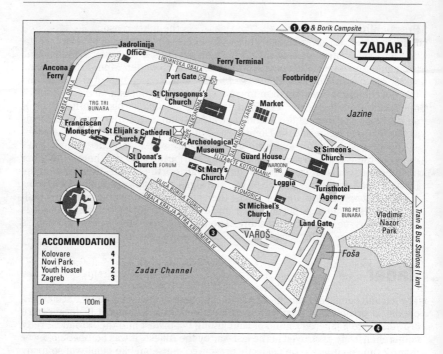

1992, Zadar remained exposed to Serbian artillery attack right up until 1995, when the Croatian Oluja offensive finally drove them back.

Arrival, information and accommodation

Ferries arrive at the quays lining Liburnska obala, from where the town centre is a five-minute walk uphill. Zadar's **train** and **bus stations** are about 1km east of the town centre, a fifteen-minute walk or a quick hop on municipal bus #5. For local bus rides, pay the driver (6Kn flat fare) or buy a ticket (8Kn) in advance, valid for two journeys, from newspaper and tobacco kiosks. Although Zadar has an active and helpful tourist association (☎023/212-412, fax 211-781, *tz-zadar @zd.tel.hr*), they don't yet have an office open to the public.

The Turisthotel agency opposite St Simeon's Church at Poljana Šime Budinića 1 (☎023/22-047, fax 313-320, *turisthotel@zd.tel.hr*) deal in private **rooms** (①–②), a few of which are in the old town, though most are in the coastal suburbs to the west, where modern low-rise houses back onto a waterfront broken up by a sequence of small marinas. Until the Habsurg-era *Hotel Zagreb* on Obala kralja Petra Krešimira IV reopens, **hotels** in central Zadar will remain in short supply. Currently the most central is the *Kolovare*, five minutes' south of the bus and train stations at Bože Peričića 14a (☎023/203-200, fax 203-300; ⑤), a smart, modern affair offering en-suite rooms with TV. Otherwise you're limited to the more careworn hotels of the Borik complex, a seafront park in Puntamika, 4km northwest of the centre (take bus #5 from the train and bus stations). Of the six bland hotels here the *Novi Park* (☎023/206-100; ④) is the most reasonable, offering comfy en-suites, albeit with paper-thin walls.

There's also a **campsite** in the Borik complex (☎023/332-074) and a mosquito-prone, HI-affiliated **youth hostel** (☎023/331-145, fax 331-190) beside Borik marina, with views of the island of Ugljan across the water.

The Town

Much of central Zadar remains a network of narrow medieval streets, surrounded by walls and barred to motor traffic. The two sides of the peninsula are quite different in feel: the **northern waterfront**, lined by a surviving section of city wall, is busy with the hustle of ferry traffic, while the **southern side**, along Obala kralja Petra Krešimira IV, seems somewhat neglected, despite its fine nineteenth-century buildings and views of offshore islands. On the eastern side of the peninsula lies the **Jazine**, the sheltered harbour beyond which lie the modern parts of town, uneventful save for a snazzy yacht club and a few marinas.

The Forum and cathedral

Zadar's main square, the **Forum**, is a messy expanse with a gravelly parking lot rubbing up against remnants of the original Roman forum, now reduced to a few hastily dumped sarcophagi and a single standing column – the only surviving pillar of a colonnade which was once the size of a football pitch. The Forum's south-western side joins up with the seafront boulevard of Obala kralja Petra Krešimira IV, where there's a fine view across the water to the hilly island of Ugljan.

Much of the original stone from the Forum found its way into the ninth-century **St Donat's Church** (Crkva svetog Donata; open sporadically in summer; enquire at the Archeological Museum opposite), next to the cathedral, a hulking cylinder of stone built – according to tradition – by St Donat himself, an Irishman who was bishop here for a time. It's an impressive example of Byzantine church architecture, resembling from the outside San Vitale in Ravenna and Charlemagne's Palatinate Chapel in Aachen. The cavernous, bare interior has a pleasing simplicity: a high-ceilinged circular space with a gallery held up by six chunky supports and two Corinthian columns. It stopped being a church in 1797, subsequently served as a shop, military store and museum, but for the moment it lies empty, used only occasionally for summer concerts.

The modern, concrete **Archeological Museum** opposite (Arheološki muzej; Mon–Sat 9am–1pm, 6–8.30pm; 10Kn) has a neatly displayed collection beginning with the Neolithic period on the top floor and moving on through Liburnian, Roman and medieval Croatian periods as you descend. There are several examples of the characteristic Liburnian gravestone or *cipus*: a tapering bollard-like affair crowned with carved leaf shapes, rather like a fat stalk of asparagus (there are several more stacked up in the yard at the back). The medieval Croatian stonework also catches the eye, particularly the fancifully rendered griffons that flank the depiction of Christ and his angels on the eleventh-century carved doorway which once adorned the portals of the (long since demolished) St Lawrence's Church.

On the same side of the square as the museum, **St Mary's Church** (Crkva svete Marije) dates from 1066 and includes some salvaged Roman and medieval pillars in the nave, though its trefoil Renaissance frontage was added in the sixteenth century, and the interior was given a thorough refurbishment in the eighteenth, when the rippling stucco balconies of the gallery were added. The Romanesque bell-tower next door was built in 1105 and is the oldest in Dalmatia. The adjacent convent is of more interest, having recently been converted to house a **Permanent Exhibition of Church Art** (Stalna izložba crkvene umjetnosti; Mon–Sat 10.30am–noon & 4.30–6pm, Sun 10am–12.30pm; 20Kn), a storehouse of Zadar's finest church treasures and very much the pride of the city. The first floor has numerous reliquaries, including a richly ornamented twelfth-century casket containing the arm of St Isidore and a thirteenth-century reliquary for the shoulder blade of St Mark, which resembles a small grand piano mounted on three clawed legs. Some very diverse iconic representations of the Madonna and Child include a Paolo Veneziano work from the 1350s, in which the rigidity of sacred painting is softened with a touch of naturalistic portraiture, with the eyes of the Virgin fixing the viewer. On the second floor there's a large fifteenth-century gang of apostles carved in wood by the Venetian Matej Moronzon in 1426, and an early six-part polyptych by Vittore Carpaccio, one panel of which features a much-reproduced picture of a youthful, tousle-haired St Martin of Tours lending his cloak to a beggar. Altogether, it's a fabulous museum, subtly arranged, beautifully lit and just small enough to be manageable in a single visit.

THE CATHEDRAL

On the northwestern side of the Forum, the twelfth- and thirteenth-century **Cathedral of St Anastasia** (Katedrala svete Stošije) is a perfect example of the late Romanesque style, with an arcaded west front reminiscent of the churches of Pisa and Tuscany. Around the door frame stretches a frieze of twisting acanthus leaves, from which various beasts emerge – look for the rodent and bird fighting over a bunch of grapes – while to either side hang figures of four apostles, engagingly primitive pieces of stonework which were probably taken from the facade of an earlier church on this site. The cathedral's **campanile** was only finished in the 1890s by the English writer and architect T.G. Jackson; if you've been to Rab you may find it familiar – he modelled it on the cathedral bell-tower there.

The **interior** is high and capacious, with the nave greedily out of proportion to the narrow aisles hidden away on each side. The lofty arcade is pretty enough, with pillars picked out in red marble, but it can't help but look a little lost in the broad expanses of flat, grey stone. At the eastern end, the Gothic ciborium of 1332 sports a series of deftly chiselled columns, each with a different geometric design, enclosing a ninth-century altar engraved with fat crosses and palms. The side altar at the end of the left-hand aisle is surmounted by a plain marble casket holding the bones of St Anastasia, made – as the workmanlike inscription records – in the time of Bishop Donat in the ninth century. Details concerning Anastasia herself are impossible to pin down: according to one legend she was a fourth-century martyr put to death in Sirmium (now Sremska Mitrovica in Serbia), although her cult probably came to Zadar from Aquileia, where she was honoured as a saintly Roman woman who performed many miracles.

From the cathedral to Narodni trg

Hidden away behind the cathedral lurks the **Orthodox Church of St Elijah** (Crkva svetog Ilije), which originally ministered to the needs of the Greek sailors in the Venetian navy before being handed over to the Serbian Church in the mid-eighteenth century, when the campanile – now with tufts of grass growing between its heavy blocks of stone – was added. Following Široka (subsequently J. Bjankinija) west from here you'll soon arrive at **Trg tri bunara**, given its name by the three wells (*tri bunara*) dating from the eighteenth century on its northern side. Turn left down A. Papavije and bear left again at the end to find the **Franciscan monastery** (Franjevački samostan), said to have been founded by St Francis himself when he visited Zadar in 1219, and purportedly the oldest Gothic church in Dalmatia, though it's actually a fairly dull renovation with a flat eighteenth-century roof. A doorway leads through to a plain but pleasing courtyard lined with the graves of Zadar nobles.

Returning to Trg tri bunara and heading north brings you to the ferry dock and a length of city wall, one of the few surviving stretches of a defensive system completed in 1570, just in time to save Zadar from a two-year Turkish siege. You can follow these fragments of wall southeast towards the Port Gate (Lučka vrata), a Roman triumphal arch which was later topped with a relief of St Chrysogonus, the city's protector, on horseback. Slightly uphill from the gate is **St Chrysogonus' Church** (Crkva svetog Krševana), a more impressive building outside than in, with a west front similar to the cathedral's and a superb colonnaded east end. To one side stands a squat, unfinished tower which never rose above the height of the church's facade, and an angular, musclebound modern statue of the Zadar-born writer **Petar Zoranić** (1508–c.1560), whose Arcadian romance *Planine* (Mountains) is often credited with being the first novel written in Croatian. On the other side of the street, the interior of the **Diokom** clothes shop incorporates elements of the medieval St Thomas's Church (Crkva svetog Tome), which once stood on this spot, with stubby remains of columns running along the sales floor and gravestones mounted on one of the walls.

Cut southeast along Krnarutića to reach the **market** (mornings only), which fills a small square hard up against the walls. Here you'll find all manner of fruit and vegetables brought in daily from the surrounding countryside, while traders in an adjacent hall sell freshly caught fish. It's a colourful scene, though no longer as exotic as it was when Maude Holbach travelled through Dalmatia in the early 1900s, remarking on the peasants who, "seated on the ground in the fashion of the East, offered their eggs and vegetables for sale in the strangest tongue that ever assailed my ears. At first glance they seemed to me more like North American Indians than any European race."

Narodni trg to St Simeon's Church

Just beyond the market, another gate leads through to the pedestrian bridge which leads across the Jazine into modern Zadar. In the other direction Jurja Barakovića heads up to **Narodni trg**, which took over from the Forum as the main focus of civic activity in the Middle Ages. It's overlooked by the sixteenth-century **Guard House** (Gradska straža), a low, single-storey building with a soaring square clock-tower, built in 1562. The niche to the left of the main entrance houses a fine bust of the Venetian governor G.G. Zane from 1608, sporting stylized furrowed brows and a square carpet of beard. Immediately opposite, the **Town Loggia** (Loža; daily 9am–1pm & 5–7pm) has been enclosed in plate glass and transformed into an art gallery.

Southeast of Narodni trg, on Trg Petra Zoranića, the Baroque **St Simeon's Church** (Crkva svetog Šimuna) was rebuilt in the seventeenth century to act as a fitting shrine for the bones of St Simeon, a minor saint who is supposed to have held the Christ Child in the Temple. The body was originally stored in the Church of St Mary the Great until its demolition to make way for the city walls in 1570. St Simeon's silver-gilt reliquary now forms the main feature of the high altar, where it's held aloft by two Baroque angels cast in bronze from captured Turkish cannons. An extravagant work of art, ordered by Queen Elizabeth of Hungary in 1377, the reliquary was fashioned from 250 kilos of silver by a team of local artisans working under the supervision of a Milanese silversmith. The story goes that Elizabeth so wanted a piece of the saint's body that she broke off a finger and hid it in her bosom, where it immediately began to decompose and fill with maggots – a process only reversed when she returned the finger to its rightful place. The creation of the reliquary was her way of atoning for the theft, though it also had a political dimension: her patronage of the cult of St Simeon increased the local popularity of her husband, King Louis of Anjou, then engaged in keeping Zadar free from the clutches of Venice. The lid of the reliquary shows the bearded saint in high relief, and, on the front, two panels dramatize the discovery of St Simeon's body in a monastery on the outskirts of Zadar and Louis of Anjou's triumphant entry into the city after relieving Zadar from an eighteen-month Venetian siege. The centre panel is a rough copy of Giotto's fresco of the Presentation in the Temple in Padua. The reliquary is opened every year on the feast of St Simeon (Oct 8).

From Trg pet bunara to the Varoš quarter

Beyond St Simeon's Church a low flight of steps leads to the five wells that give **Trg pet bunara** its name and which were the city's main source of drinking water until the late nineteenth century. Completely repaved in 1998, the square still has an antiseptic aspect which seems out of keeping with the grizzled pentagonal **Captain's Tower** (Kapetanova kula) which overlooks it from the north. Immediately southeast of here lies the entrance to the city park, laid out on a jutting, arrow-shaped bastion which once formed the landward side of Zadar's defences.

Southwest from Trg pet bunara is the **Land Gate** (Kopnena vrata), a triumphal arch topped by a row of eight cattle skulls, thought to be a death symbol intended to ward off would-be invaders, and a monumental winged lion of St Mark; tellingly, this feline symbol of Venetian power dwarfs the civic emblem – another relief of St Chrysogonus on horseback – immediately below it. On the far side of the gate lies the **Foša**, a narrow channel which once fed Zadar's moat and is now a small harbour crowded with pleasure boats. Follow this around and you're back on Zadar's southern waterfront, Obala kralja Petra Krešimira IV.

Alternatively, heading northwest from the Land Gate along Špire Brušine (subsequently Plemića Borelli, then Madijevaca) leads you back into the city centre through the charming **Varoš quarter**, whose narrow alleys are packed with little boutiques and cafés. On the corner of Špire Brušine and M. Klaića, the main portal of **St Michael's Church** (Crkva svetog Mihovila) is topped by an animated fourteenth-century relief of St Michael spearing a demon, flanked by Zadar's ubiquitous patrons, Anastasia and Chrysogonus. Peering out from the facade higher up are three fish-eyed male heads, the remains of a crudely carved late Roman gravestone. Continuing along Borelli and Madijevaca, passing the yellow brick Austrian courthouse (Sudska palača), you'll eventually emerge beside St Mary's Church on the corner of the Forum.

Eating, drinking and entertainment

You can tell that tourism in Zadar is a low-key affair from the surprisingly small number of sit-down eateries in the historical centre. There are a couple of small, family-run local **restaurants**: *Konoba Martinac*, at A. Paravije 7 (the alleyway that leads to the Franciscan monastery), offers fresh fish, excellent *lignje* (squid) and *škampi* (whole unpeeled prawns), and a small garden terrace; *Marival*, just off Narodni trg at Don Ive Prodana 3, is another cosy place with traditional Dalmatian meat and fish dishes. *Foša*, Kralja Dimitra Zvonimira 2, specializes in fish and has an outdoor terrace right on the small harbour outside the Land Gate, while the *Pet Bunara* pizzeria, just round the corner from the square of the same name on Stratico, is the place to go for an inexpensive fill-up.

Several restaurants in suburban Zadar are known for their roast lamb – the roasting meat is displayed on revolving spits outside to attract passing motorists – *Tamaris*, on the main road to Zagreb and Rijeka at Jadranska 46, is one of the longest established. For **snacks** and **picnics**, the daily market just inside the old town walls off Jurja Barakovića is the place to get fruit, veg, local cheeses and home-cured hams. There's a **supermarket**, *Zadranka* (daily 6.30am–9pm), on the corner of Široka and Dalmatinskog sabora, and a larger branch just across the footbridge over the Jazine on Josipa Jurja Strossmayera.

For **drinking**, there are several cafés along Široka and near the Forum. The roomy and snazzily decorated *Café Central* on Široka is one of the best indoor venues, attracting a broad cross-section of Zadar's population. *Kult*, on Stomorica in the Varoš quarter, has lots of outdoor seating in an attractively tatty residental courtyard, while *Rock Café Pulsations*, Rafaela Levakovića, offers a regular diet of live music from local guitar bands.

The Croatian Playhouse (Hrvatska kazališna kuća), on the corner of Široka and Dalmatinskog sabora, is the main venue for serious **drama** and **classical music**; the churches of St Donat and St Chrysogonus are also used as chamber-music venues from early July to mid-August. Zadar's **Puppet Theatre** (Kazalište lutaka), Obala kralja Tomislava, is reputed to be the best in Croatia. The most interesting of the annual arts events is **Zadar Dreams** (Zadar snova), a festival of alternative theatre held in outdoor spaces in the old town between late June and early July.

The local **basketball** team, Zadar, is one of the major forces in the Croatian game, and a source of fanatical local pride. Look out for posters advertising games: they're usually played on Saturdays from September to April at the Košarkaško igralište on the eastern fringes of the old town just off Obala kralja Tomislava. Zadar is hardly Dalmatia's greatest **beach** resort, although there are some good pebbly bathing areas in the Borik holiday complex 5km north of the centre.

Listings

Airlines Croatia Airlines, Natka Nodila 7 (☎023/314-385).

Banks Dalmatinska banka, J. Bjankinija 2 (Mon–Fri 8am–7pm, Sat 8am–noon).

Ferry tickets Jadrolinija, Liburnska obala 7 (Mon–Fri 7.30am–7.30pm, Sat 7.30am–5pm, Sun 7am–noon & 4–8pm; additional late-night opening to coincide with the arrival and departure of the coastal ferry; ☎023/212-003, fax 311-151).

Hospital Bože Peričića 5 (☎023/315-677).
Post office/telephones Just off the Forum on Šimuna Kožičića Benje (Mon–Sat 7am–9pm).
Travel agents Rimanić, A. Paravije, organizes trips to the Kornati islands (see p.223).
Taxis Try the ranks on Liburnska obala or phone ☎023/211-284.

The Zadar archipelago

The small, often bare islands of northern Dalmatia – sometimes called the **Zadar archipelago** – are of considerably less interest than those to the south, and have so far made few concessions to tourism. **Ugljan** is among the most developed, and one of the most inviting, accessible by ferry from Zadar and connected by bridge to the island of **Pašman**. Further out, the long and barren island of **Dugi otok** shelters the rest of the archipelago from the open sea before descending at its southern end to reach beautiful **Telašćica Bay**, the archipelago's most celebrated natural beauty spot.

Ugljan and Pašman

Just 5km west of Zadar, the long, thin island of **UGLJAN** is just beginning to discover the benefits of tourism, but for the moment is still largely the preserve of Croatian second-home owners. Although the most densely populated of all the Adriatic islands, it remains largely rural in feel, with a lush green covering of olive plantations which produce some of Croatia's best olive oil (the name Ugljan comes from the Croatian word for oil, *ulje*), although you're unlikely to find it on sale in the local shops – most of the island's farmers produce only a small surplus, and the whole business is surprisingly uncommercialized.

The fourteen daily **ferries** from Zadar to Ugljan drop you at the town of Preko, from where there are buses (usually coordinated to meet incoming ferries) running north to Ugljan village and Muline on the tip of Ugljan island, and south to Pašman island. Despite the presence of small colonies of package tourists (mostly Czechs and Slovaks) on Ugljan, the bulk of the tourist industry – such as it is – revolves around independent travellers, and there's plentiful private accommodation, offering ideal places to vegetate if you want to leaven the urban bustle of Zadar with a dollop of rustic peace. Beaches on both islands are modest – usually no more than concreted quays with short stretches of shingle – but they're rarely crowded.

Preko and Kali

Standing opposite Zadar, **PREKO** (literally "on the other side") is Ugljan's largest village, and feels very much like a dormitory suburb of Zadar – a quiet, unspectacular settlement, comprising a few residential streets and a small harbour. Locals swim from a concreted inlet 1km north of the harbour, or on the islet of **Galevac** (also known as Školjić, or "little island"; accessible by taxi boat in season from the quayside in Preko), 80m from the shore, where there's also a Franciscan monastery set in its own park. Once the site of a Croatian-language printing press, moved here from Zadar in 1925 to escape Italianization, there's little to see here now, although an exhibition of monastic treasures is under construction. The pleasant surrounding subtropical vegetation is like a little piece of Eden gone to seed. Overlooking the town (and looking deceptively close) is the tenth-century

Fortress of St Michael (Sveti Mihovil), an hour or so's walk along the road that heads uphill from the main island road on the western fringes of Preko. The fortress, which dates from 1203, was already largely ruined by the time the JNA – fearing it might be used as an observation post – shelled it in 1991. The views east to Zadar and west to the long, rippling form of Dugi otok – and, on a clear day, Ancona and the Italian coast – are marvellous.

Heading south, Preko runs gently into **KALI**, spread around a small hillock a kilometre or two down the coast. More immediately picturesque than Preko, Kali is also firmly committed to the local fishing industry, with trawlers crammed into the two harbours which stand on either side of its peninsula. There's little to do beyond wandering the pinched, sloping streets, although the sight of Kali's fishing boats setting sail into the evening twilight can be an evocative one – something that you won't see in the more touristy islands further south.

The Zadar ferry docks midway between Preko and Kali – turn left and walk along the seafront to get to Preko's main harbourside square, where the **tourist office** (July & Aug daily 8am–9pm; Sept–June Mon–Fri 8am–2pm; ☎023/286-108, fax 286-148) is friendly and informative, but low on brochures and maps. **Rooms** (①) in Ugljan are available from Turistička Agencija Rušev, just north of the tourist office (July & Aug daily 8am–9pm; June & Sept 8am–1pm & 5–7pm; Oct–May irregular hours but probably open mornings; ☎ & fax 023/286-085). If you want a **hotel**, the *Preko*, up some steps from the harbour (☎023/286-041; ④), has simple, sparsely furnished en-suites, some with good sea views. *Konoba Barbara*, which you'll pass when walking from the ferry dock to the village centre, is a good place **to eat** fish, and there are numerous harbourside **cafés** from which to admire the twinkling lights of suburban Zadar across the water. **Bikes** and small **boats** can be rented from the Turistička Agencija Rušev (see above) or from other ad hoc operators on the harbourfront during the season. There's a post office on Preko harbourfront and a bank with an ATM at the ferry dock.

Around the island

Ten kilometres north of Preko, and served by six daily buses from the ferry dock, **UGLJAN VILLAGE** is smaller and much more rustic, and its broad pebbly bay is an attractive spot for swimming. The *Ugljan* **hotel** (☎ & fax 023/288-024; ③) is a fairly standard concrete box, but has a lovely position on Ugljan's harbour, and offers basic but bright en-suites, some with sea-facing balconies; you can rent bikes and boats here too. There are also – at the last count – about nine **campsites**, mostly small affairs hidden away in private gardens. Also accessible from Preko by bus, the village of **MULINE**, 4km beyond Ugljan at the northern tip of the island, has three more campsites about a kilometre's walk from the bus stop, set side by side amidst picturesque woodland, together with an attractive bay with a quiet beach.

Five kilometres south of Preko on the road to Pašman lies **KUKLJICA**, a small fishing hamlet on a wide green bay. In season it's normally full of Czechs, who block-book the bungalow complex on the pine-covered eastern side of the bay, but even so things rarely get too busy. A well-signed path leads from the southern end of Kukljica's harbour to **Sabušica Bay** on the western edge of the island, where there's a quieter, concreted bathing area with naturist sections on its fringes. The **tourist office** (daily 7am–2pm; ☎023/373-876, fax 373-229), just behind the harbourside market, usually has **rooms** (①) available, and there's a smattering of cafés along the front. Most package tourists stay at the *Zelena Punta* complex (☎023/373-338, fax 373-547, *hut-kukljica@zd.tel.hr*) on the eastern side of the bay, which has cubicle-like **bungalows** (③) and swisher **apartments** (500Kn for 4 people) sheltering under pines and surrounded by concrete and stone beach areas. **Eating** in Kukljica is limited to a couple of pizzerias on the harbour, or the restaurant at the *Zelena Punta*.

Kukljica is famous for the festivities marking **Our Lady of the Snows** (Gospa od sniga) on August 5, which celebrate a "miraculous" summer fall of snow here some 400 years ago. Every year a statue of the Madonna is carried in a procession of small boats from Kukljica to a seaside chapel lurking behind the headland to the south – a regatta in which the entire village takes part. Quite why the August snowfall should have been adopted as a Catholic miracle is unclear, beside its usefulness in providing the excuse for another feast day dedicated to the Virgin.

Pašman

Immediately south of Ugljan, and linked to it by a road bridge, the island of **Pašman** is even sleepier than its neighbour, with local activity confined to a few low-key fishing villages strung out at the base of a green central ridge. About eight buses a day make the journey from Preko to **PAŠMAN VILLAGE**, 15km south of the Ždrelac strait, the first real settlement on the island, a faded little place with a pleasant shallow bay, Lučina, on its northern side. The **tourist office**, on the dusty road that passes for a seafront (July & Aug 8am–8pm; June & Sept 8am–noon; ☎ & fax 023/260-155) will direct you towards private **rooms** (①), and there are two **campsites** on Lučina Bay, the *Lučina* and *Kod Jakova*, and a **pension**, the *Ružmarin* (☎023/260-231 or 260-381; ②), also on Lucina Bay, offering small en-suite rooms and breakfast. Just round the corner from the tourist office is the *Lanterna* **restaurant**, whose terrace is a bit too exposed to southerly winds, but it has a basement where food, including all the local fish specialities, is cooked over a stone hearth.

Just beyond the next hamlet, Ugrinći, a lane to the right winds up onto Ćokovac hill, site of the **Monastery of SS Cosmas and Damian** (*Kuzma and Damjan*) (daily 4–6pm). Initially a twelfth-century Venetian fortress, it was taken over by Benedictines fleeing Biograd-na-moru in 1394, when that town was razed by the Venetians. An important centre of Glagolitic culture until it was closed down by the French in 1808, the monastery was reoccupied in the 1930s and is currently the only permanently occupied Benedictine establishment in Croatia (though Benedictine nunneries, for some reason, are more widespread). The main reasons to visit are the late fourteenth-century crucifix above the altar, and the view of modern Biograd-na-moru on the mainland.

The bus terminates in the bland settlement of **TKON**, the island's main centre, which is directly connected to Biograd-na-moru on the mainland by ten ferries daily.

Dugi otok

DUGI OTOK ("Long Island") is the largest of the islands of northern Dalmatia, 52km long though nowhere more than 5km wide. Only 1500 people live here, and parts of the island are very remote – some settlements are accessible only by sea. It's a wilder and more dramatic landscape than either Ugljan or Pašman, with sheer cliffs on its western side and a rugged, indented coastline that is justifiably popular with the yachting fraternity. Dugi otok's main attraction is **Telašćica Bay**, which is best approached from the island's main settlement, Sali, although the quiet villages and headlands of the northern part of the island are also worth a visit. It's also a possible base from which to visit the Kornati archipelago (see p.223), with boat captains in Sali offering trips, although the archipelago is more usually approached from Murter (see p.222).

There are only a couple of **ferries** daily during summer, making it impossible to visit without staying overnight, while outside summer it's difficult to get to the island at all. Sali and Brbinj are the main entry points, but there are no buses linking one to the other, so you'll need a car if you want to explore the island's single north–south road with its spectacular views of the rest of the Zadar archipelago to the east. In addition to the regular Zadar–Sali and Zadar–Brbinj services, there are weekly Ancona–Brbinj ferries in summer, plus weekly Rijeka–Brbinj and Ancona–Brbinj hydrofoils and a weekly Zadar–Božava–Ancona catamaran. There are no campsites on the island, but private **rooms** aplenty. If you're driving, note that the island's only petrol station is just north of Sali in Zaglav.

Northern Dugi otok

Despite **BRBINJ**'s importance as a ferry port there's nothing much here, and it's a good idea to catch one of the buses which head north to **BOŽAVA**, a small fishing village popular with Italian yachters – it's their first stop on the way across the Adriatic – with an attractive harbour and a path leading round the headland to the east to a rocky coast overlooked by swooning trees. **Rooms** (①) are available from the **tourist office** (☎023/377-607) at the northern end of the harbour, while the *Božava* **hotel** complex (☎023/377-618 or 377-619, fax 377-682; ①), set among pines on the west side of the harbour, offers no-frills en-suites.

Driving northwest out of Božava on the Soline road you get a good view of the north of the island as it finishes in a flourish of bays and peninsulas. Follow the road up the westernmost of these peninsulas, Veli rat, then take a left turn onto an unmarked gravel track about 3km out of Božava and proceed about 1km through fragrant forest (drivers will have to park about halfway down) until you reach one of the island's best beaches, **Sakarun**, a 500-metre-long bar of pebbles commanding a shallow bay. Carrying on up Veli rat, the road terminates beside a stumpy, ochre lighthouse, built by the Austrians and now a popular spot for bathing, with an attractively rocky coastline stretching away on both sides.

Southern Dugi otok

The island's largest village and the centre of a prosperous fishing industry, **SALI** is a quiet place, with nothing really to see or do, though the smattering of cafés round the harbour provide the requisite air of Mediterranean vivacity on warm summer nights. The **tourist office**, on the western side of the harbour (July & Aug daily 8am–8pm; Sept–May Mon–Fri 8am–3pm; ☎ & fax 023/377-094), has **rooms** (①) and **apartments** (around 315–350Kn for 4); and there's also a **hotel**, the *Sali* (☎023/377-049, fax 377-078; ④), over the hill from the harbour in the next bay to the north, Sašćica. The best time to be in Sali is the first weekend in August, when the Saljske užance **festival** takes place, with outdoor concerts, drinking and feasting, and performances of *tovareća muzika* ("donkey music" – so called because it's a tuneless racket that sounds like braying), which features the locals raucously blowing horns.

It's about 3km from Sali to the northern edge of **Telašćica Bay**, a seven-kilometre channel overlooked by smooth hills interspersed with numerous smaller bays which run down to the tangle of islands at the northern end of the Kornati archipelago (see opposite). The flora along the shoreline marks the transition from the green vegetation of the Zadar archipelago to the bare wilderness of the Kornati – banks of deep forest slope down towards the western shore of the bay, where maquis-covered offshore islands rise like grey-brown cones from the water – and the whole place has been designated a nature park. Telašćica can't quite compete with the Kornati in terms of stark beauty, but it's much more accessible. To get there, take the signposted minor road which heads west from the Sali–Božava route about 1.5km out of town. The road terminates at one of Telašćica's numerous small bay, from where a path leads southwards to the appropriately named **Uvala mir** ("Bay of Peace") about 4km beyond and a short distance from the park's main attractions. There's a bar and restaurant here, and a path which leads after five minutes' walk up a wooded hillside to a stretch of ruddy clifftop looking out towards the open sea. Five minutes south of the restaurant lies **Jezero mir**, a saltwater lake cut off from the sea by a narrow barrier of rock at the lake's southernmost end – the rock is a favourite with naturists, while the lake itself is popular swimming territory, although it's full of shrimps which nibble your legs if you stand still long enough – not as unpleasant an experience as it sounds.

Zadar to Šibenik

About 20km south of Zadar, **BIOGRAD-NA-MORU** was one of the towns developed by Croatia's medieval kings to challenge the pre-eminence of Zadar and Split. Petar Krešimir IV moved the archiepiscopate of Split here in the mid-eleventh century, and it was in Biograd that the Hungarian kings were crowned monarchs of Croatia after 1102. Biograd's period of greatness came to an end on Good Friday 1126, when the Venetians razed the town to its foundations, a catastrophe from which it never really recovered. Modern Biograd is one of the major package resorts on this part of the coast, though it's a shabby-looking place and mainly of interest for its ferry link with Tkon on the island of Pašman.

Murter and the Kornati archipelago

Around 25km south of Biograd, a side-road heads west towards the small island of **Murter**, linked to the mainland by bridge. The main settlement, **MURTER TOWN**, at the northern end of the island, is a frumpy and relatively underdeveloped little place. There's a tiny pebble beach at **Slanica** cove, twenty minutes' walk west of town – an enchanting place from which to watch the sun set over the southern Kornati – but otherwise there's not much to do apart from taking a day-trip to the Kornati archipelago.

There are eight **buses** a day from Šibenik to Murter, passing through Vodice (the place to change if you're approaching from the north) en route before pulling into Murter's main square. There's a small **tourist office** on the square (☎022/434-995 or 434-950), with info on Kornati trips; while the Kornati national park office (☎ & fax 022/434-662 or 435-058, *np-kornati@si.tel.hr*), just off the square on Hrvatskih vladara, sells maps.

Rooms (①) are available from the Coronata bureau opposite (daily 8am–1pm & 5–8pm; ☎ & fax 022/435-089), or from Atlas, just inland from the square at Hrvatskih vladara 8 (☎022/434-889 or 434-017). The marina, ten minutes' walk to the east, has a small **hotel**, the *Hramina* (☎022/434-411, fax 435-242; ②), with simple but cosy balconied en-suites overlooking the yacht berths; alternatively, the four-storey, box-like *Colentium* (☎022/431-100, fax 435-255; ④) offers comfortable, smart rooms overlooking the beach at Slanica. There's a small **campsite** at Slanica, and a string of larger ones south of town: the *Plitka Vala* (3km away), *Kosirina* (4km away on a lovely rocky bay) and *Jezera* (5km away) – Šibenik–Murter buses pick up and drop off at each of them.

There are a couple of places **to eat** on the main street, Luke. The friendly and unpretentious *Konoba Ćo* offers fresh fish as well as cheap and hearty stews like *mućkalica* (paprika-flavoured braised beef), while *Barbara* is one of the few places in Dalmatia to serve *zagorski štruklji* (the doughy envelopes of cottage cheese common to the area north of Zagreb). Moto Sport, near the petrol station on the marina side of town, is the place to rent small **boats** (200Kn a day), **scooters** (200Kn a day) and **bikes** (50Kn a day).

The Kornati archipelago

Scattered like pebbles to the south of Dugi otok lie the ninety or so islands of the **Kornati archipelago**, grouped around the 35-kilometre-long island of Kornat – the largest uninhabited landmass in the Adriatic. A national park since 1980, the Kornati archipelago comprises a distinctively harsh and bare environment, almost devoid of life. ranging in colour from stony white to pale ochre or green, sometimes mottled with patches of low shrub and hardy sage. They were once covered in forest until the people of Murter burned it down to make pasture for their sheep, who proceeded to eat everything in sight. The drystone walls used to pen them in are still visible, although the sheep themselves – save for a few wild descendants – are no more. Many of the stone cottages once used by shepherds are still inhabited for a few months in summer, either by Murterians come to fish or tend their olives, or by tourists seeking true escape.

Most people see the Kornati on a **day-trip** arranged by one of the travel agents in Murter; Atlas (see above) is one of the most reliable. Most trips weave in and out of the islands on the western side of the archipelago, stopping a couple of times so that you can stretch your legs or swim – some islands, such as Ravni žakan and Piškera, also have small restaurants and marinas. Prices start at around 100Kn per person and include the national park entrance fee, and probably lunch with wine too. If you're approaching the islands independently you'll need to buy an entrance ticket (20Kn) from the Kornati national park office in Murter, which also sells fishing permits (40Kn per day).

Staying in one of the island's stone cottages is popular with visitors who want a period of complete peace and quiet, and it's sometimes marketed by local agencies under the name "Robinson turizam" in order to lend it the requisite desert island-like appeal. You'll have to arrange accommodation with the Coronata agency in Murter (see above) well in advance, however, and commit yourself to a reasonably lengthy stay because of the logistics involved. Prices work out at about 375Kn per day for a two-person apartment, 600Kn per day for a four-person apartment, plus 500–600Kn for boat transfer there and back. Once you're there, provisions will be delivered to you by boat every two or three days – you'll be able to eat out if you've chosen one of the islands with a marina or restaurant; otherwise, you're on your own.

Vodice

The small resort town of **VODICE**, 9km south of the Murter turn-off, is, unaccountably, central Dalmatia's most successful package-holiday destination, but also one of its least atmospheric, and most of its beaches are concrete. The core of the town is likeable enough, grouped around a tiny square in the middle of the harbour, and taxi boats will take you to the offshore islets of Logorun and Tijat if you want to escape Vodice's crowded beaches. You can also use the twice-daily Vodice–Šibenik **ferry** to visit the relatively quiet islands of **Prvić** and **Zlarin**, both home to crumbling fishing villages that provide a bit more charm that Vodice, and there are local **excursions** to the Krka falls (see p.229) and the Kornati archipelago.

Most coastal buses call in at Vodice's bus station, at the eastern end of the waterfront: the **tourist office** (July & Aug daily 8am–8pm; May, June & Sept 8am–noon & 2–8pm; Oct–April Mon–Fri 8am–3pm) is five minutes' walk to the west. The package-holiday hotels represent terrible value for money in comparison to private **rooms** (①), which can be booked through the centrally located Vodičanka agency (in the same building as the tourist office; same times). If you want **hotel** comforts and are prepared to pay for them, the high-rise, three-star *Punta* (☎022/443-288, fax 443-289), just north of town, is a good choice – providing you stay in the main building (⑥) and shun the rather grisly annexes (④). For **eating**, you'll find innumerable cafés and pizzerias along the harbour, together with several restaurants offering German-language menus and slightly higher than average prices.

Šibenik and around

ŠIBENIK is one of the few towns on the Adriatic not to have a Greco-Roman heritage. Originally founded around an eleventh-century Croat fortress, it fell firmly under the control of the Venetians in the fifteenth century, becoming an important strongpoint in their struggles against the Ottomans. As the main town of middle Dalmatia, Šibenik was a thriving industrial port until the 1990s, when war and recession conspired to close down the aluminium and chrome factories, and the city entered the new century as one of Dalmatia's most economically depressed areas. It's not a resort, and there's little point in stopping if you're looking for somewhere quiet with a beach, though the mazy medieval centre is good for idle wandering and the cathedral is one of the finest architectural monuments on the coast. As a transport hub, Šibenik isn't as important as Zadar or Split, but there are ferries to a handful of offshore islands, and buses inland to the waterfalls of the **Krka National Park** and the medieval castle at **Knin**.

The Town

Clinging to the side of a hill, Šibenik's ancient centre is a steep tangle of alleys, steps and arches bisected by two main arteries, **Zagrebačka** and **Kralja Tomislava** (the latter popularly known as Kalelarga), which run between Trg Republike Hrvatske, the core of the city, and the modern square of Poljana maršala Tita. Entering the old town along Zagrebačka from Poljana maršala Tita, it's not long before you emerge into the first of Šibenik's tiny medieval

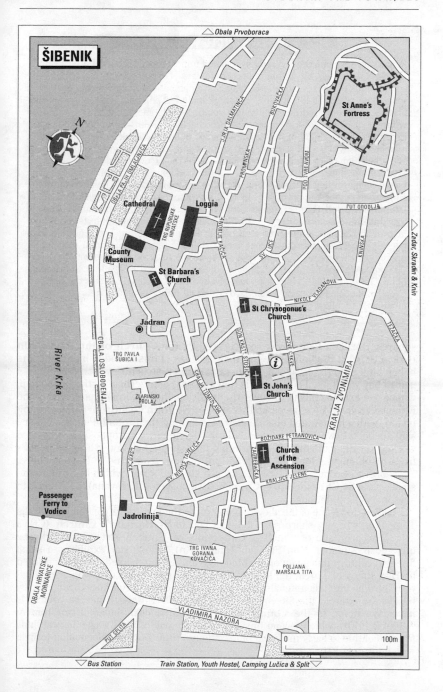

ŠIBENIK

FAUST VRANČIĆ (1551–1617)

Renaissance Šibenik produced many learned minds, most famously **Faust Vrančić** (Faustus Verantius), the author of *Machinae novae* (1615) – a book of machines and contraptions whose inventiveness rivalled the mechanical fantasies of Leonardo da Vinci. The album of 49 copper engravings included pontoon bridges, suspension bridges, wind-powered flour mills with rotating roofs and, most famously, **Homo volans** – a picture of a man jumping from a tower with a primitive parachute. Equipped with a square of sail-canvas, Vrančić opined in the accompanying text, "a man can easily descend securely and without any kind of danger from a tower or any other high place." It is not known whether Vrančić ever tried this at home.

Machinae novae was written towards the end of a busy intellectual life. The young Faust studied in Bratislava and Padua before becoming administrator of the Hungarian city of Veszprém, and in 1581 was appointed secretary to the court of **Emperor Rudolf II** in Prague – a renowned meeting place for humanists from all over Europe. He subsequently retired to become a Pauline monk in Rome, where he probably became acquainted with Leonardo's drawings, and was moved to compile his *Machinae*. Vrančić's other major (and, in terms of Croatian culture, far greater) work was his *Dictionarium quinque nobilissimarum Europae linguarum* (Dictionary of the five most noble languages of Europe, 1595), a lexicon including Latin, Greek, German, Hungarian and "Dalmatian" (Croatian). It was the first real Croatian dictionary, setting a standard which all future language reformers would be obliged to follow.

---

squares, Božidara Petranovića, overlooked by the **Church of the Ascension** (Crkva Uspenja Bogomatere). The main feature of this Baroque building is the belfry built onto the facade, a curious but elegant structure which resembles a pair of bay windows. The church is now the seat of a Serbian Orthodox bishop, whose see extends inland to cover the traditionally Serb-inhabited towns of the Kninska krajina. A few steps further on lies **St John's Church** (Crkva svetog Ivana), with a balustrated outside staircase linking the ground floor to a gallery said to be the work of sculptor Nikola Firentinac (see opposite), who also worked on the cathedral. The church's four-storey bell-tower holds Šibenik's first mechanical clock, a contraption dating from 1648. Beyond here, Zagrebačka becomes Don Krste Stošića, a stepped street which leads up to the small, plain **St Chrysogonus' Church** (Crkva svetog Krševana), now home to seasonal art exhibitions.

Heading down one of the alleys leading off to the left brings you out onto Kralja Tomislava, where a sharp right delivers you to **St Barbara's Church** (Crkva svete Barbare), site of a modest **Collection of Church Art** (Zbirka crkvene umjetnosti; summer Mon–Fri 9am–1pm; 10Kn), whose star exhibit is a small fifteenth-century polyptych of the Madonna and Child, flanked by saints, painted by Blaž Jurjev of Trogir, the leading Dalmatian artist of his day, who is credited with introducing Italian Renaissance styles to the eastern Adriatic. Down an alley beside the church, the fifteenth-century **Rector's Palace** (Kneževa palača) is nowadays home to the **County Museum** (Županijski muzej; 10am–1pm & 7–10pm; 10Kn), which has an unspectacular display of local archeological finds from Neolithic to early medieval times, though little English information to help with interpretation.

The cathedral and around

Immediately to the north of the County Museum lies Trg Republike Hrvatske and the Gothic Renaissance **St Jacob's Cathedral** (Katedrala svetog Jakova), the product of a long-running saga that stirred the imaginations and emptied the pockets of the townspeople here during the fifteenth century. Plans for a new cathedral were originally drawn up in 1402, but war, lack of funds and disputes over the site delayed the start of work until 1431, when a group of Italian architects oversaw the erection of the Gothic lower storey of the present building. In 1441, dissatisfaction with the old-fashioned Gothic design led to the appointment of a new architect, Juraj Dalmatinac (see box below), who presided over three decades of intermittent progress, interrupted by perennial cash shortages, two plagues and one catastrophic fire. The cathedral was just below roof height when he died in 1473 and his Italian apprentice Nikola Firentinac ("Nicholas of Florence" – he is thought to have been a pupil of Donatello) took over, completing the roof and the octagonal cupola, although both may have been designed by Dalmatinac. The resulting edifice is an intriguing mixture, with Venetian Gothic portals and windows at ground level and a Florentine Renaissance dome at the top.

Entry to the cathedral is by the north door, framed by arches braided with the leaves, fruit and swirling arabesques which led to Dalmatinac's style being dubbed "floral Gothic". Two lions roar companionably at each other, supporting remorseful and rather crudely carved figures of Adam and Eve. Inside, the church is a harmonious blend of Gothic and Renaissance forms; the sheer space and light of the east end draw the eye towards the soft grey Dalmatian stone of the raised sanctuary. Follow the stairs down from the southern apse to the **Baptistry**, Dalmatinac's masterpiece. It's an astonishing piece of work, a cubbyhole of Gothic carving, with

---

JURAJ DALMATINAC (C.1400–73)

Juraj Dalmatinac (George the Dalmatian) was the most prolific stonemason of the Dalmatian Renaissance, but little is known of the man save for the works he left behind. Born in Zadar some time around 1400, he learnt his trade in Venice, setting up a workshop there which made his reputation as a mason. The Šibenik town authorities engaged him to supervise completion of the cathedral in 1441, paying him 150 golden ducats a year as well as covering his family's moving expenses and providing free housing.

Work on the cathedral frequently stalled due to lack of cash, and Dalmatinac filled in his time by working on commissions elsewhere, notably in Split, where he sculpted the **sarcophagus of St Anastasius** in the cathedral (see p.252), and at Ancona, where he completed the facade of the cathedral. In 1464 he replaced Michelozzo Michelozzi as the overseer of fortification work in Dubrovnik, where he finished the finest of the system's many bastions, the **Minčeta Fortress** (p.315). Following working visits to Urbino and possibly Siena, he returned to Šibenik, where he died in 1473, the cathedral still unfinished.

Dalmatinac's great skill was to blend the intricate stoneworking techniques of the Gothic period with the realism and humanism of Renaissance sculpture. His stylistic innovations were carried over to the next generation by his pupils **Andrija Aleši** and **Nikola Firentinac**, who were involved in the completion of Šibenik cathedral before going on to produce their own masterpieces in Trogir.

four scallop-shell niches rising from each side to form a vaulted roof, beneath which cherubim scamper playfully.

Back outside the cathedral, around the exterior of the three apses, Dalmatinac carved a unique **frieze** of 71 stone heads, apparently portraits of those who refused to contribute to the cost of the cathedral and a vivid cross-section of sixteenth-century society. On the north apse, beneath two angels with a scroll, he inscribed his claim to the work with the words *hoc opus cuvarum fecit magister Georgius Mathei Dalmaticus* – "these apses have been made by Juraj Dalmatinac, son of Mate." Given the narrowness of Šibenik's central streets, it's difficult to get a reasonable view of the cathedral's barrel roof, made from a line of enormous stone slabs and considered a marvel of construction at the time, though you should be able to catch sight of the statue high up on the southeast corner; a boyish, curly-haired Archangel Michael jauntily spearing a demon.

Trg Republike Hrvatske itself is lined with historic buildings including, directly opposite the cathedral, the town hall with its sixteenth-century **loggia**, much restored after World War II bombing, part of which now houses a café. Climb the alleyways leading up to the northeast you'll eventually emerge at **St Anne's Fortress** (Tvrđava svete Ane), the nearest and most accessible of the system of fortifications constructed by the Venetians to keep Šibenik safe from the Turks. Built on the ruins of the earlier Croatian citadel, there's not much inside except for rubble, although the ramparts afford a panorama of the old town (including a clear view of the cathedral's roof), Šibenik bay beyond, and the endless green ripple of offshore islands in the background. From the castle, what remains of Šibenik's **city walls** plunge downhill to meet the sea, forming the old town's northern boundary.

Practicalities

Šibenik's **bus station** is just southeast of the city centre on Obala Hrvatske mornarice. The **train station**, for what it's worth (trains run from here only to minor inland towns), is a little further along the waterfront. The **tourist office** on Trg Ivana Pavla (summer daily 8am–8pm; winter Mon–Fri 8am–2pm; ☎022/212-075, fax 219-073) has information and maps, and can help sort out **rooms** (①). Failing that, there's a **youth hostel** 1km east of the centre at Put Luguša 1 (☎ & fax 022/216-410) – follow 29 Listopada 1918 uphill, pass under the Magistrala, and turn right when you see the the *Šubićevac* restaurant on the corner. The *Jadran* **hotel**, on the waterfront at Obala oslobođenja 52 (☎022/212-644, fax 212-480; ③), offers nondescript but perfectly comfy en-suites with TV, and is perfectly situated for the town centre. The nearest **campsite** is the *Lučica* just south of town, although it's 2km away from main road and not well served by public transport.

Visiting Šibenik is never going to be the greatest culinary experience, although a number of **eating** places offer reasonably priced schnitzels and seafood. *Pivnica Alpa*, near St Barbara's Church on Kralja Tomislava, is convenient for old-town sightseeing and has a range of snacks, pizzas and hearty meat dishes, while *Turist* on Obala oslobođenja, has outdoor seating on the waterfront and good cheap seafood dishes. The restaurant of the *Jadran* hotel is a slight step up in quality and price, and is a good place for fresh fish. If you want to buy fresh fruit and veg, there's a **market** just uphill from the bus station. For **drinking**, try the small knot of cafés on Obala oslobođenja, or the other, more youth-oriented stretch of café-bars just north of here, past the *Jadran* hotel, on Obala prvoboraca. There's a disco, the *Veslo*, at the far end of Obala prvoboraca, which sometimes has live Croatian rock-pop bands, and a **cinema** next to the hotel.

Moving on from Šibenik is relatively straightforward: all coastal **buses** heading for Split and Dubrovnik stop off here, and although the main coastal **ferry** doesn't call at Šibenik, there are four daily departures to Vodice calling at the minor islands of Zlarin and Prvić. Tickets can be bought from the Jadrolinija office on the waterfront at Obala oslobođenja 8 (☎022/213-468).

The Krka National Park

Inland from Šibenik is the River Krka, which rises just outside Knin and flows through a sequence of gorges, lakes and rapids before meeting the sea. The stretch of the Krka valley between the towns of Knin and Skradin has national park status, and it's the section of the park just east of Skradin – where the river descends via a sequence of mini-waterfalls at Skradinski buk ("Skradin Falls") before flowing through a small but picturesque canyon to Skradin – which is the most visited. There are two main entrance points to the national park: the town of Skradin itself, and Skradinski buk – with national park boats plying the stretch of water between them. There are five **buses** daily from Šibenik to Skradin, passing by the access road to Skradinski buk on the way. The entrance fee (40Kn), payable at pavilions on the access road to Skradinski buk and east of Skradin, includes travel in the national park's boats.

Twelve kilometres out of Šibenik on the north bank of the Krka, **SKRADIN** is a pleasing, one-street town of stone houses with a marina squeezed into one of the river's small inlets. There's a tourist office on the waterfront, and a couple of grill-restaurants on the harbour serving shellfish, but the main reason to come here is to catch one of the hourly national park boats up to Skradinski buk, a ten-minute journey; should you miss the boats, you can walk by following the road from Skradin along the river's right bank, taking you between steep, scrub-covered hills.

Skradinski buk itself is a bit like a smaller Plitvice (see p.123) – a 500-metre sequence of mini-cascades spilling over barriers of travertine (limestone sediment), behind which lie pools surrounded by reeds and semi-submerged forest. The main path runs along the western side of Skradinski buk, past a collection of poky stone watermills positioned directly above the rushing Krka. There's also a network of short wooden walkways which lead above the gurgling water and through the thick riverine vegetation. It's a beautiful location, and you could spend an entire day here, lolling around on the rocks beside the tumbling water.

There are more infrequent boats north from Skradinski buk to the less dramatic falls at **Roški Slapovi**, 10km further upstream. The boats stop en route at the islet of **Visovac**, where you can visit a Franciscan monastery nestling amongst a thick cluster of cypresses. The monastery has a small collection of seventeenth-century paintings and, in its valuable library, some incunabula and a beautifully illustrated fifteenth-century *Aesop's Fables*, one of only three such in the world.

Drniš and Knin

Thirty-four kilometres inland from Šibenik, the small market town of **DRNIŠ** has little to recommend it. It was occupied by Ottoman forces during the sixteenth century, when it was known as "little Sarajevo", though most of the relics of the Turkish period were obliterated when they were driven out, and the only surviving reminder is a sixteenth-century mosque, since incorporated into St John's Church (Crkva svetog Ivana). There's also a ruined tower picturesquely located above the River Čikola, and an irregularly open **Town Museum** (10Kn), which has a rather limited collection of works by local sculptor Ivan Meštrović (see box on p.257); some pieces disappeared during the Serbian occupation in 1991.

Meštrović hailed from the village of **OTAVICE**, 10km east, where he is buried in the hilltop **Meštrović Mausoleum**, a simple cube topped by a dome designed by Meštrović himself. He began the work in 1926, intending it as a family mausoleum, and was buried here after his death in the USA in 1962. Inside, an Art Nouveau-inspired sculpture of the Crucifixion is watched over by a pale, Buddha-like face, hinting at the religious syncretism towards which Meštrović leaned throughout his life. During the Serbian occupation, the bronze doors (bearing touching portraits of the Meštrović family) were stolen, reliefs were damaged, and the tombs desecrated. Restoration is in progress.

Drniš is the centre of a large area devoted to the making of *pršut* (home-cured ham), and most local families keep a few pigs. Late November's *svinokolja* or **pig slaughter** is the key event of the local agricultural year, when up to 10,000 of the beasts meet their deaths.

Knin

Some 20km inland from Drniš is the rather plain town of **KNIN**, which became notorious as the epicentre of the Serbian rebellion of 1990–95, when it was the capital of the Serbian-controlled parts of Croatia, the so-called **Republic of the Serbian Krajina** (Republika srpske krajine, or RSK). Something like ninety percent of Knin's population was Serbian by the early 1990s, making it the obvious focus for Serbian discontent in the Dalmatian hinterlands. Control of Knin was always important to Serbian military planners: the town stands on the rail line between Zagreb and Split, and to remove the town from Zagreb's control – it was argued – would seriously weaken Croatia's bargaining power should Yugoslavia ever fall apart.

Many of the key players in the ensuing Serb-Croat conflict came from Knin: Jovan Rašković, founder of the Serbian Democratic Party; Milan Babić, the RSK's first leader; Milan Martić, the Knin police chief who built up the Krajina's first armed forces; and Colonel Ratko Mladić, commander of the Knin military garrison, who practised ethnic cleansing here, forcibly ejecting Croat families from nearby villages, before becoming head of the Bosnian Serb army in 1992. The Serbian irregulars based in Knin during 1991–95 – who called themselves the *knindža*, in imitation of ninja-style comic strip heroes – melted away when the Croatian army launched the Oluja ("Storm") offensive in August 1995, and Knin's recapture on the morning of August 5, 1995 brought the war in Croatia to a rapid conclusion: Serbian resistance elsewhere in the country collapsed within two days, and pictures of President Franjo Tuđman kissing an enormous Croatian tricolour flying from Knin fortress were seen on TV across the world. Most Serb civilians fled in the wake of their defeated army in August 1995, and though many have returned, the present population is still only a fraction of what it was, the local economy is in recession, and an atmosphere of despondency prevails. The castle is worth visiting if you're passing through, but there's little else to keep you, and certainly no tourist facilities.

Knin's **train** and **bus** stations are next to one another on the main street, and it's easy to pick a route up to the **fortress** on the hill above. There's been a castle here since at least the tenth century, and it was the seat of the medieval Croatian state's last effective king, Zvonimir, towards the end of the eleventh century. The castle's fall to the Turks in 1522 hastened a change in the demographic profile of the area, with fleeing Catholics being replaced by a predominantly Orthodox population from the Balkan interior. The fortress has been impressively restored, with a central keep surrounded by concentric rings of walls, and outlying towers squatting on outcrops of rock. The battlements offer an extensive panorama of the surrounding countryside, with a view of Knin below in its bowl of brownish hills and the grey ridge of the Dinaric mountains to the northeast on the border with Bosnia-Hercegovina – the best place to enjoy it is from the terrace of the **café-restaurant** inside the fortress.

From Šibenik to Trogir

Heading south from Šibenik most traffic follows the coastal Magistrala, although there's an alternative inland route which cuts through the arid mountains before rejoining the main road at Trogir. It's worth taking if you like spit-roast lamb – the roadside restaurants in the village of **BORAJA**, 15km outside Šibenik, are famous for it.

Sticking to the Magistrala, the first place you come to is **BRODARICA**, an undistinguished village largely populated by people from **Krapanj**, a few hundred metres across the water, which has the minor distinction of being the smallest inhabited island in the Adriatic. Boats cross from Brodarica hourly, though unless you've time on your hands the trip isn't really worth it. The island isn't especially attractive and, but for the fifteenth-century **Franciscan monastery** with its couple of Renaissance paintings and a collection of sponges (diving for sponges used to be the main occupation here), there's not much to see.

The small town of **PRIMOŠTEN**, 20km south of Šibenik, is the best place on this part of the coast to rest up and do nothing for a while. Heaped up on an island that's joined to the mainland by a short causeway, it's enchanting when seen from a distance, although on closer inspection most of the houses are twentieth-century, and there's nothing of specific interest to see. There are extensive pebble and rock **beaches** lapped by ultra-clear water on the wooded promontory to the north of the town, where there are also a number of hotels.

Primošten's small **bus station** is uphill on the landward side of the causeway, a short walk from the **tourist office** (daily 7am–9pm; ☎ & fax 022/571-111) in the small square that marks the entrance to the old town. Private **rooms** (①–②), available from Turist Biro at the bus station (daily 7am–9pm), are probably a better deal than the package-style *Zora-Slava* **hotel** (☎022/570-066; ③), a typical 1960s seaside establishment with functional en-suites located on the wooded promontory north of town. The *Adriatik* **campsite**, about 3km north of town on the Magistrala, has an attractive pebble and rock beach. For **food**, the *Villa Fenč*, a little way around on the north side of the peninsula, has a large terrace and an especially wide variety of fish; and there are loads of café-pizzerias on the harbour. Wherever you eat, be sure to try the local Primošten wine, Babić – a smooth, dry red.

Trogir and around

Thirty kilometres south of Primošten, **TROGIR** is one of the most seductive towns on the Dalmatian coast, a compact brown-beige welter of palaces, jutting belfries and shambling streets fanning out from an antique central square. Founded by Greeks from Vis in the third century BC, Trogir can compare with any of the towns on the coast in terms of historic sights, and its **cathedral** is one of the finest in the Adriatic. It's also a good base for further exploration: the swarming city of Split is a short ride away on the #37 bus, and in between lies a string of attractively time-worn fishing villages known collectively as **Kaštela** after the little "castles" built here by Trogir nobles to serve as country retreats.

Arrival, information and accommodation

Trogir's old town is built on an oval-shaped island squeezed between the mainland and the larger island of Čiovo, while modern Trogir has spread onto the mainland, stretching along the coast for several kilometres. Inter-city **buses** pick up and drop off on the main street in the new town, just opposite the bridge which leads over to the old town. Also on the mainland side of the bridge is a small bus

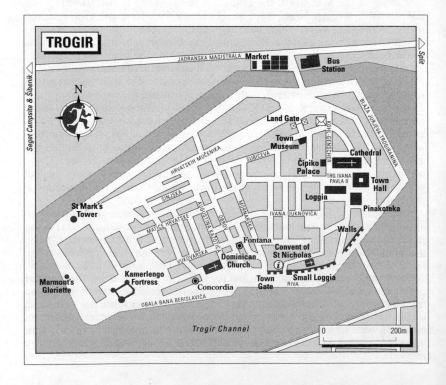

station, where the #37 bus from Split terminates. Head over the bridge and straight through the town centre to the waterfront on the opposite side to find the **tourist office** on the Riva (summer daily 8am–10pm; winter Mon–Fri 9am–3pm; ☎021/881-412 or 885-628, *tzg-trogir@st.tel.hr*), which has basic town maps.

The Čipiko agency, in the Čipiko Palace opposite the cathedral at Kohl-Genscher 41 (summer daily 8am–9pm; winter Mon–Fri 9am–1pm; ☎021/881-554), has **rooms** (①) and **apartments** (around 400Kn for 4). There are two good **hotels** in old town houses on the Riva: the *Fontana*, Obrov 1 (☎021/885-744, fax 885-755; ④), and the nearby *Concordia*, Obala bana Berislavića 22 (☎021/885-400, fax 885-401; ④) – both have friendly staff and snug en-suite rooms with TV. The nearest **campsite** is *Seget*, a thirty-minute walk northwest along the main road – coastal inter-city buses will drop off here if you're coming from the north; alternatively, local Trogir buses to Najevi, Dogradi, Viniśće, Sevid and Vranjica all go past the site if you want to save yourself the walk.

The Town

Heading across the bridge from the mainland, the old town is entered via the seventeenth-century **Land Gate** (Kopnena vrata), a simple arch topped with a statue of the town's protector, St John of Trogir (Sveti Ivan Trogirski), a miracle-working twelfth-century bishop. Straight ahead, the outwardly unassuming Garagnin palace now houses the disappointing **Town Museum** (Gradski muzej; summer daily 9am–noon & 6–9pm; winter Mon–Fri 7am–3pm, Sat 9am–noon; 10Kn), whose downstairs lapidarium boasts a few chunks of early Christian masonry and Renaissance family crests which once hung above the portals of patrician houses. Amidst the pictures and yellowing documents upstairs are proclamations issued by the Napoleonic authorities, condemning Trogir leaders to death after a failed anti-French uprising in 1807.

The cathedral

Immediately east of the museum lies Trogir's main street, Kohl-Genscher, which leads straight down to **Trg Ivana Pavla II**, a creamy-white square flanked by some of the town's most historic buildings. Dominating them all is the **Cathedral** (Mon–Sat 9am–noon & 3–7pm), a squat Romanesque structure begun in 1213 and only finished with the addition of a soaring Venetian Gothic campanile some three centuries later. A previous church on this site had been damaged by Saracen raiders in the twelfth century, but the town's control of lucrative trade routes with the Balkan interior helped pay for the construction of a new one.

The cathedral's most distinctive feature is its **west portal**, an astonishing piece of work carved in 1240 by the Slav master-mason Radovan. Radovan laid claim to his work in an immodest inscription above the door, calling himself "Most excellent in his art" – a justifiable claim given the doorway's intricate mix of orthodox iconography with scenes from ordinary life and legend, showing figures of apostles and saints, centaurs and sirens, woodcutters and leather-workers jostling for position in a chaos of twisting decoration. Roughly speaking, there is a gradual movement upwards from Old Testament figures at the bottom to New Testament scenes on the arches and lunette. Adam and Eve frame the door and stand with anxious modesty on a pair of lions. On either side, a series of receding pillars sit upon the bent backs of the undesirables of the time – Jews and Turks – while above is a weird menagerie of creatures in writhing, bucking confusion, laced together with tendrilled carvings symbolizing the months and seasons. The sequence begins with March (the year started with the Annunciation as far as the Church was concerned), symbolized by a man pruning vines, and a wild-haired youth blowing a horn (a reference to the March winds). Further on, a man killing a pig represents the autumn (pig-slaughtering and sausage-making still form an important part of the Croatian calendar), while another character in clogs cooks what look like sausages. The lunette above comprises two scenes fringed by curtains, in imitation of the two-level stages on which medieval miracle plays were often presented. The Nativity is portrayed on the upper level, and the Bathing of Christ below, with shepherds and magi crowding the wings. Above the lunette, the uppermost arch is decorated with scenes from the life of Christ.

Left of the portal, small circular windows are framed by a serpent tearing apart a half-naked libertine. Further over to the left lies the fifteenth-century **Baptistry**, a fine piece of Renaissance stonework executed by **Andrija Aleši** of Dürres, who is thought to have been an Albanian noble who fled the Turks and had to learn a trade in order to earn a living. He was apprenticed to Juraj Dalmatinac (see box on p.227) at Šibenik, and was in many ways his stylistic successor. The portal, topped by a relief of the Baptism of Christ, gives way to a coffer-ceilinged interior, where a frieze of cherubs carrying a garland leads round the walls, overlooked by a relief of St Hieronymous in the cave in smooth milky stone.

The **interior** of the cathedral is dark and gloomy, its pillars hung with paintings illustrating scenes from the life of St John of Trogir. At the head of the nave stand a Romanesque octagonal pulpit, its capitals decorated with griffins and writhing snakes, and a Baroque high altar canopied by an ornate thirteenth-century ciborium; the beautiful set of mid-fifteenth-century choirstalls were carved in Venetian Gothic style by local artist Ivan Budislavić. The north aisle of the cathedral opens up to reveal **St John's Chapel** (Kapela svetog Ivana), another spectacular example of Renaissance work, this time by Juraj Dalmatinac's other pupil, Nikola Firentinac. God the Creator is pictured at the centre of barrel-vaulted ceiling, from which a hundred angels gaze down. The space below is occupied by a ring of saintly statues, surrounded by torch-bearing cherubs who peep cheekily from behind half-closed doors, inviting the viewer to contemplate the world beyond death.

Finally, further along the north aisle from St John's Chapel lies the sacristy, which houses the **Treasury** (*riznica*; summer 9am–noon & 5–8pm; 10Kn), a mundane collection of ecclesiastical bric-a-brac. The best exhibits are the fine inlaid storage cabinets carved by Grgur Vidov in 1458, a fourteenth-century Gothic jug, scaled and moulded into snake-like form, and a silver-plated reliquary of St John of Trogir which is paraded round on his feast day.

The old town

Opposite the cathedral entrance is the **Čipiko Palace**, a well-worn fifteenth-century Venetian Gothic mansion whose balustraded triple window is said to be the work of Andrija Aleši. There's nothing inside except the Čipiko agency, though it's noteworthy for being the erstwhile home of the Čipikos, Renaissance Trogir's leading noble family. Foremost among them were Koriolan Čipiko (1425–93), author of *De bello asiatico*, an account of his wartime experiences with the Venetian fleet, and Alviz Čipiko, who commanded a galley from Trogir at the Battle of Lepanto in 1571. A giant wooden cockerel which once formed the figurehead of a Turkish ship captured by Alviz still hangs in the palace doorway. It was in the Čipiko family library that the first known manuscript of "Trimalchio's Feast", a hitherto undiscovered fragment of Petronius' *Satyricon*, was discovered in 1653, sending a frisson of excitement through literary circles all over Europe.

On the other side of the square, the **Town Loggia** (Gradska loža), with its hand-some clock-tower and classical columns, dates from the fifteenth century, though its pristine appearance is explained by a late nineteenth-century restoration. The large relief on the east wall of the loggia, showing Justice flanked by St John of Trogir and St Lawrence (the last holding the grill on which he was roasted alive), is another work by Firentinac, identifiable by the presence of his personal "sig-nature", the flower-covered pillars on either side. The relief was damaged in 1932, when a Venetian lion occupying the (now blank) space beneath the figure of Justice was dynamited – an act carried out by locals keen to erase Italian symbols from a town which was still coveted by Italian nationalists. Mussolini, eager to res-urrect territorial claims in Dalmatia, raged against "Yugoslav barbarism" and forced the Yugoslav government into a grovelling apology. The loggia's south wall has been disfigured by a surprisingly lifeless Meštrović relief of Petar Berislavić, sixteenth-century Bishop of Zagreb and Ban of Croatia, who fought a losing bat-tle against the advance of Ottoman power.

Just off the square to the southeast is the Church of St John the Baptist (Crkva svetog Ivana Krstitelja), a bare thirteenth-century structure which now holds the **Pinakoteka** (July & Aug; 8am–noon & 6–9pm; 10Kn), a display of sacred art from the best of Trogir's churches. Among a number of painted crucifixes and the like is Blaž Jurjev's polyptych showing a Madonna and Child flanked by six saints, in which the Virgin proffers an ivory breast to the infant. There are also canvases of John the Baptist and St Jerome, painted for the cathedral organ by Gentile Bellini in 1489.

South of Trg Ivana Pavla II, the ever-narrowing Kohl-Genscher leads on to the **Convent of St Nicholas** (Samostan svetog Nikole; May–Sept 9am–noon & 3–7pm; Oct–April on request at the tourist office; 10Kn), whose treasury is famous for the outstanding third-century Greek relief of Kairos, discovered in 1928. Sculpted out of orange marble, it's a dynamic fragment representing the Greek god of opportunity – once past he's impossible to seize hold of, and the back of his head is shaved just to make it even more difficult. The rest of the col-lection focuses on Byzantine-influenced sacred paintings from the sixteenth cen-tury, and the painted chests in which girls new to the convent brought their "dowries" (gifts to the convent in the form of rich textiles and ornaments) in antic-ipation of their wedding to Christ.

Along the Riva

Kohl-Genscher makes a sudden dog-leg to the right before emerging through the **Town Gate** (Gradska vrata) onto the Riva, a seafront promenade facing the island of Čiovo. Hard up against the gate stands the so-called **Small Loggia** (Mala loža), nowadays the site of a daily fish market. On either side of the gate are a few stretches of what remain of the medieval **town walls**, large chunks of which were demolished by the Napoleonic French, who hoped the fresh sea breezes would help blow away the town's endemic malaria. To the right, past a gaggle of cafés, is the campanile of the **Dominican Church** (Crkva svetog Dominika), a light, high building with a charming relief in the lunette above the main door showing a Madonna and Child flanked by Mary Magdalene, clad in nothing but her own tresses, and Augustin Kažtotić (1260–1323), Bishop of Trogir and subsequently

Zagreb. Next to Kažotić is a small praying figure representing his sister Bitkula, who commissioned the work. The main feature inside is the tomb of Šimun and Ivan Sobota, which bears a Firentinac relief of the Pietà surrounded by mourners. The coffin below is decorated with more of Firentinac's trademark flowery, pinapple-topped pillars.

Further along, the fifteenth-century **Kamerlengo Fortress** was named after the Venetian official – the "kamerling" – who ran the town's finances. An irregular quadrilateral dominated by a stout octagonal tower, it used to be one of Trogir's most popular attractions, but has unaccountably been closed to tourists for years. Beyond lies the town's football pitch, on the opposite side of which looms the tapering cylinder of **St Mark's Tower** (Kula svetog Marka), a sandcastle-style bastion built at the same time as the Kamerlengo. Finally, at the far end of the island, is **Marmont's Gloriette**, a graffiti-covered, six-pillared gazebo looking out onto Čiovo's rusting shipyard which was built for Marshal Marmont, the French governor of Napoleon's Illyrian Provinces. Just and progressive, Marmont was probably the best colonial ruler the city ever had, and the Gloriette serves as some sort of modest tribute.

Eating, drinking and entertainment

Eating out in Trogir is a joy, with dozens of restaurants tucked away in the courtyards of the centre. *Škrapa*, Augustina Kazotića, seems to undercut the prices of all the others without compromising standards, serving up *lignje na žaru* (grilled squid) and other standards on outside wooden benches, but it's often full. *Kamerlengo*, Vukovarska 2, offers top-class fish and *škampi* cooked on an outdoor charcoal grill in an L-shaped courtyard. *Konoba Fontana*, on the corner of Riva and Obrov, is pretty classy too, offering the widest range of dishes in town, excellently prepared and presented. Inland from the *Fontana*, Obrov opens out onto a flower-decked courtyard harbouring a couple of pizzerias – *Kristian*, which has a good pasta menu, and *Top Baloon*, which does a decent lasagne. Don't forget the **market** opposite the bus station, where you'll find fruit, veg, cheeses, hams and homemade wines and spirits offered by local farmers, haphazardly bottled into all kinds of containers.

Intermezzo on the Riva is the coolest place for a **drink**, although all the old town's squares are stuffed with café tables in summer, and it's really a question of picking a space that suits. The *Formula 1* **disco**, 4km east of town at the junction of the Magistrala and the Split airport road, organizes techno parties and performances by Croatian pop stars. The Trogir **Summer Festival** (early July to mid-Aug) features pop music and folklore events on various outdoor stages in the town centre.

Kaštela

East of Trogir the coastline swings around towards Split in a wide, curving bay, sheltered from the open sea by the island of Čiovo and Split's jutting peninsula. During the fifteenth and sixteenth centuries, local nobles lined this fertile sweep of coast with country houses, fortified against pirate raids to give them the appearance of castles – the settlements which have grown up in their wake go under the collective name of **KAŠTELA**. The castles were built to protect the agricultural lands to which the nobles owed their weath, but they were also rural retreats where their owners spent the summer months and received guests. Koriolan Čipiko was the first of the Trogir worthies to move out here, in 1481; his house subsequently earning the epithet Kaštel stari ("Old Castle") in order to differentiate it from those which followed, and seven summer houses survived to become the nuclei of the fishing villages that exist here now. Most of these castles were converted into flats years ago and can't be visited, but the villages look endearingly time-worn and have accessible places **to swim** if you're staying in Trogir. The #37 Trogir–Split bus links them all – the best thing to do is to hop off at, say, Kaštel Štafilić and follow the shoreline walkway south until you spot somewhere you like.

The road from Trogir passes Split airport before arriving at the first of the villages, **KAŠTEL ŠTAFILIĆ**. There's a pleasant shingle **beach** on Štafilić's western fringes, although the castle around which the village grew is now crumbling and derelict. **KAŠTEL NOVI**, immediately beyond, is perhaps most typical of the villages – an agreeable if unremarkable huddle of ancient houses with a simple, fortified tower at its centre, and not much else to speak of – save for the attractive octagonal tower of the church of St Rock (Crkva svetog Roka). **KAŠTEL STARI**, a short walk away, has a reasonable stony **beach**, but **KAŠTEL LUKŠIĆ**, just beyond, is marginally livelier, with several cafés scattered along its seafront. The castle itself is being renovated as a tourist attraction, and there's a **tourist office** (June–Sept Mon–Fri 8am–6pm, Sat 9am–1pm; Oct–May Mon–Fri 8am–3pm; ☎021/277-955) with information on the whole Kaštela region just next to it. The Ostrog Tourist Agency (Mon–Fri 8am–noon & 5–8pm), 100m further along the shore, can organize **rooms** (①) in the village. A kilometre beyond, **KAŠTEL GOMILICA** is the most picturesque of the villages, its fortress squatting impressively on a small islet joined to the mainland by a bridge. It's probably not worth covering the remaining 3km to the last outpost of Kaštela, **KAŠTEL SUĆURAC**, which is just 10km short of Split and within alarming proximity of the city's industrial installations.

travel details

TRAINS

Zadar to: Knin (2 daily; 1hr 40min).

BUSES

Brbinj to: Božava (1–2 daily; 25min).

Preko to: Kukljica (8 daily; 10min); Muline (6 daily; 25min); Pašman (8 daily; 20min); Tkon (8 daily; 30min); Ugljan (6 daily; 15min).

Šibenik to: Drniš (10 daily; 40min); Knin (10 daily; 1hr 20min); Murter (8 daily; 45min); Skradin (5 daily); Split (hourly; 2hr); Trogir (hourly; 1hr 30min); Vodice (20 daily; 15min); Zadar (hourly; 1hr 30min).

Trogir to: Šibenik (hourly; 1hr 30min); Split (every 20min; 30–50min); Zadar (hourly; 3hr).

Zadar to: Biograd (hourly; 1hr); Nin (8 daily; 45min); Novigrad (5 daily; 30min); Plitvice (5 daily; 3hr); Šibenik (hourly; 1hr 30min); Split (hourly; 3hr 30min); Trogir (hourly; 3hr); Zagreb (5 daily; 5hr).

FERRIES

Biograd to: Tkon (10 daily; 15min).

Šibenik to: Vodice (4 daily; 1hr).

Zadar to: Brbinj (2 daily; 1hr 30min); Preko (hourly; 30min); Sali (2 daily; 1hr 30min); Zaglav (2 daily; 1hr 45min).

CATAMARANS

Zadar to: Božava (mid-June to mid-Sept 1 weekly; 40min).

INTERNATIONAL FERRIES

Brbinj to: Ancona (mid-June to mid-Sept 1–2 weekly; 5hr).

Šibenik to: Ancona (July & Aug 3 weekly, June & Sept 2 weekly; 9hr).

Zadar to: Ancona (July & Aug 5 weekly, June & Sept 3 weekly; 7hr).

INTERNATIONAL CATAMARANS

Božava to: Ancona (mid-June to mid-Sept 1 weekly; 1hr 40min).

Zadar to: Ancona (mid-June to mid-Sept 1 weekly; 2hr 30min).

CHAPTER SIX

SOUTHERN DALMATIA

C roatia's second city and the undisputed capital of Dalmatia, **Split** grew out of the Roman palace of Dalmatian-born Emperor Diocletian, and successive layers of ancient, medieval and modern architecture have given the centre a unique – albeit chaotic – urban character. The most vibrant centre on the coast, it's also the transport hub around which Southern Dalmatia's ferry and bus routes revolve, so if you're heading for the southern Adriatic islands, it's almost inevitable you'll pass through. The ruins of the Roman city of **Salona**, and the medieval Croatian stronghold of **Klis**, are the main draws inland.

The coast south of Split is probably mainland Dalmatia's most enchanting stretch, with the mountains glowering over a string of long pebble beaches, although a sequence of modern tourist resorts is beginning to put the squeeze on the fishing villages. If you want to join the crowds, the resorts of the **Makarska Riviera** are justifiably popular family holiday centres, but it's the southern **islands** which are the real highlight of any trip to Dalmatia. Easiest to reach from Split is **Brač**, boasting some nice beaches at **Supetar** and a truly wonderful one at **Bol**, while lying off the southern coast of Brač is the long thin island of **Hvar**, whose capital, **Hvar Town**, rivals Dubrovnik and Trogir in the number of venerable stone buildings lining its ancient alleys. It's also a fashionable hangout for urbane Croats: chic bars rub shoulders with Gothic palaces and chapels, and water taxis convey bathers to idyllic offshore islets. Much the same can be said of the island of **Korčula**, south of Hvar, whose fascinating medieval capital, **Korčula Town**, offers a mixture of urban tourism and lazy beachcombing.

Further out, but still only a few hours by boat from Split, the islands of **Vis** and **Lastovo** were only opened up to foreign tourists in 1989, after previously serving as naval bases. Wilder and less visited, both are obligatory destinations for travellers who want a piece of the Adriatic to themselves. You can rejoin the mainland from Korčula by a short ferry-ride to the **Pelješac peninsula** – virtually an island

---

ACCOMMODATION PRICE CODES

The accommodation in this guide has been graded using the following price codes, based on the cost of each establishment's **least expensive double room** in high season (June–Sept), excluding special offers. Hotel room rates almost always include breakfast. Out of season, prices on the coast can fall by up to 50 percent. Where single rooms exist, they usually cost 60–70 percent of the price of a double. For more details, see p.24.

① Less than 200Kn   ④ 400–500Kn   ⑦ 800–1000Kn
② 200–300Kn   ⑤ 500–600Kn   ⑧ 1000–1200Kn
③ 300–400Kn   ⑥ 600–800Kn   ⑨ Over 1200Kn

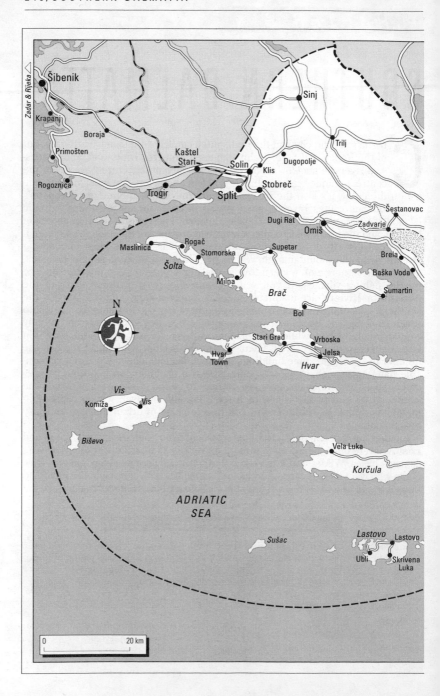

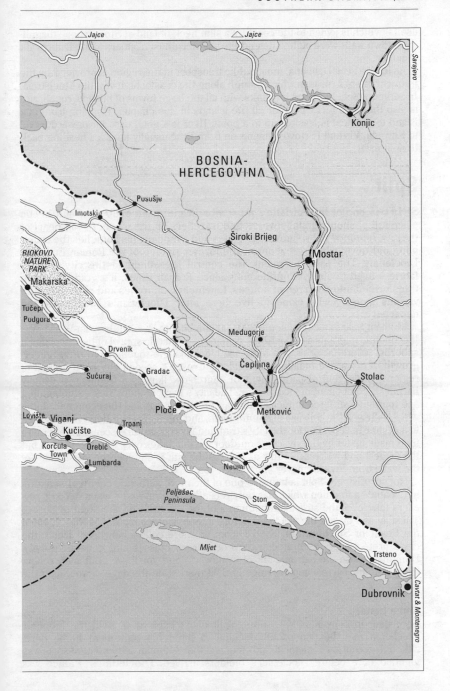

itself – which is joined to the coast by a slim neck of land at **Ston**, whose magnificent town walls were built to defend the northernmost frontiers of the Dubrovnik Republic.

As in northern Dalmatia, most public transport in the region is provided by the frequent inter-city **buses** which plough along the coastal highway, the Magistrala. In addition, Split has good bus links with all the large towns of inland Croatia, and is also the main **ferry** port for all the islands in this chapter. Hopping from one island to the next is feasible up to a point. Hvar is a good base for onward travel to Korčula, Vis and Lastovo; moving on from Brač usually involves heading back to Split first.

Split

SPLIT is one of the Adriatic's most vibrant cities: an exuberant and hectic place full of shouting stall-owners and travellers on the move. At the heart of the city, hemmed in by sprawling estates and a modern harbour, lies the crumbling old town, which grew out of the former **palace** of the Roman Emperor Diocletian. The palace remains the central ingredient in the city's urban fabric – lived in almost continuously since Roman times, it's gradually been transformed into a warren of houses, tenements, churches and chapels by the various peoples who came to live here after Diocletian's successors had departed.

Modern Split is a city of some 220,000 inhabitants, swollen by post-World War II economic migrants and post-1991 refugees – a chaotic sprawl of hastily planned suburbs, where factories and high-rise blocks jangle together out of an undergrowth of discarded building material. As Croatia's second city it's a hotbed of regional pride, and disparagement of Zagreb-dwellers is a frequent, if usually harmless, component of local banter. The city's two big industries – shipbuilding and tourism – suffered immeasurably as a result of war and the economic slump which followed the collapse of communism, and municipal belt-tightening has led to a decline in subsidies for the city's traditionally rich cultural scene. This is more than made up for by the vivacious outdoor life that takes over the streets in all but the coldest and wettest months: as long as the sun is shining, the swish cafés of the waterfront Riva are never short of custom.

Not surprisingly, Split is home to one of the more authentic **carnival seasons** in Croatia – a tradition which has only recently been revived – when masked revellers take over the streets and squares of the old town on the night of Shrove Tuesday and during the weekend before it. Split's other big day is May 7, when the **Feast of St Domnius** (Sveti Dujam or, more colloquially, Sveti Duje), the city's protector, is celebrated with processions, masses and general festivity. Domnius is also the patron saint of woodwork, and you'll see craftsmen selling chairs, tables, barrels and carvings in Split market on the days surrounding the feast.

Some history

According to conventional wisdom, Split didn't exist at all until the Emperor Diocletian (see box on p.249) decided to build his retirement home here, although recent archeological finds suggest that a Roman settlement of sorts was founded here before Diocletian's builders arrived. **Diocletian's Palace** was begun in 295 AD and finished ten years later, when the emperor came back to his native Illyria to escape the cares of empire, cure his rheumatism and grow cabbages. But this was no simple retirement, and the palace no ordinary retirement home. Diocletian maintained an elaborate court here in a building that mixed luxurious palatial apartments with the infrastructure of a Roman garrison: the northern half of the palace was occupied by servants and the garrison; to the south lay the imperial suites and public buildings. The palace as a whole measured some 200 by 240 metres, with walls two metres thick and almost twenty-five metres high, while at each corner there was a fortified keep, and four towers along each of the land walls.

The palace was home to a succession of regional despots after Diocletian's death, although by the sixth century it had fallen into disuse. In 614, it was suddenly repopulated by refugees fleeing nearby Salona, which had just been sacked by the Avars and Slavs. The newcomers salvaged living quarters out of Diocletian's neglected buildings, improvising a home in what must have been one of the most grandiose squats of all time. They built fortifications, walled in arches, boarded up windows and repelled attacks from the mainland, accepting Byzantine sovereignty in return for being allowed to preserve a measure of autonomy. The resulting city developed cultural and trading links with the embryonic Croatian state inland, and was absorbed by the Hungaro-Croatian kingdom in the eleventh century.

By the fourteenth century, Split had grown beyond the confines of the palace, with today's Narodni trg becoming the new centre of a walled city that stretched as far west as the street now known as Marmontova. **Venetian rule**, established in 1420, occasioned an upsurge in the city's economic fortunes, as the city's port

FETIVI, BODULI AND VLAJI

Although the inhabitants of Split – Splićani – may appear to be a homogenous body, they traditionally belong to three distinct groups. The old urban families – the **fetivi** – cultivate the art of talking fast with minimal lip movement. Another, more pejorative, term for a born-and-bred Splićanin is *mandril* (a "mandrill", the baboon native to West Africa): it's best not to call someone a *pravi splitski mandril* (a "real Split monkey") unless you know them well enough to get away with it.

The *fetivi* are augmented by the **boduli**, immigrants from the Adriatic islands who – according to local stereotypes – have a reputation for parsimony and keeping themselves to themselves, although they're also admired for their *bodulska furbarija*, or "islanders' cunning". In recent decades the two groups have been joined by the **vlaji** ("Vlachs"; see p.205), who migrated to the city from the Dalmatian hinterland and now throng the high-rise suburbs that stretch away from the centre. Local jokes have always condemned the *vlaji* to playing the role of rural unsophisticates, although it's often conceded that it was their hard work in the construction and shipbuilding industries that made modern-day Split what it is. The *vlaji* are born survivors – passing through the *vlaški fakultet* ("Vlach faculty") means something akin to studying at the university of life.

Nowadays the distinctions between the above groups are fast dying out, and the only real demarcation lines in Split society are between those well established in the city and the more recent arrivals from Hercegovina, who descended on Split in increasing numbers in the 1990s – either to make a fast buck or to escape the troubles in their own country.

was developed as an entrepot for Ottoman goods. Turkish power was to be an ever-constant threat, however: Ottoman armies attacked Split on numerous occasions, coming nearest to capturing it in 1657, when they occupied Marjan hill before being driven off by reinforcements hastily shipped in from Venice, Trogir and Hvar.

During the nineteenth century, **Austrian rule** brought industrialization and a railway to the city. Austrian stimulation of Adriatic shipping also helped speed the development of Split's port facilities, while the Italian seizure of Rijeka in 1919 (see box on p.160) caused the Yugoslav government to deliberately develop Split as an alternative centre of maritime trade. Split's biggest period of growth

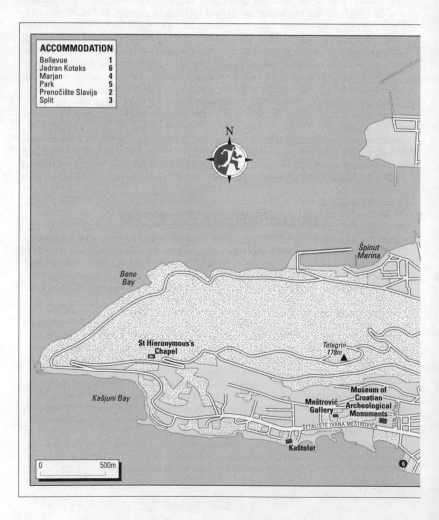

occurred after World War II, when the development of heavy industry attracted growing numbers of economic migrants from all over the country. Many of these newcomers came from the Zagora, the rural uplands stretching from the central Dalmatian coast to the Hercegovinian border, and ended up working in the enormous shipyards – colloquially known as the "Škver" – on Split's northwestern edge, providing the city with a new working-class layer. It was always said that productivity at the Škver was directly related to the on-the-pitch fortunes of **Hajduk Split** (see box on p.255), the football team which more than anything else in Split served to bind traditional inhabitants of the city with recent arrivals. Beginning with the big televised music festivals of the 1960s, Split also became

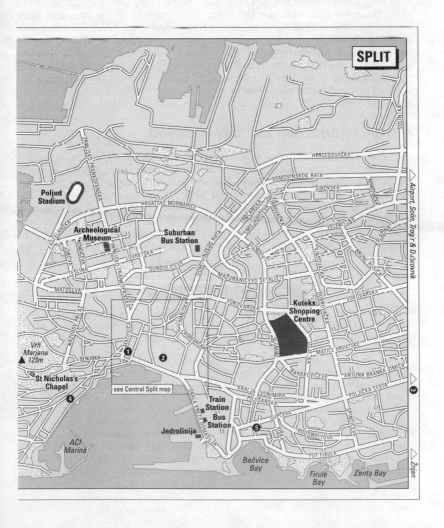

the nation's unofficial **pop music** capital, when it was promoted as a kind of Croatian San Remo, since when generations of balladeering medallion men have emerged from the city to regale the nation with their songs of mandolin-playing fishermen and dark-eyed girls in the moonlight.

The city was briefly **shelled** by the Yugoslav Navy in 1991 but was otherwise largely untouched by Serb–Croat hostilities, although refugees have added to the city's housing problems. The symptoms of late twentieth-century stagnation – decaying factories, a declining shipbuilding industry and high unemployment – are all too visible, though none of this has damaged the spirit of the Splićani themselves, who remain famous for their self-deprecating humour, best exemplified by the writings of **Miljenko Smoje** (1923–95), a native of the inner-city district of Veli Varoš. Smoje's books, written in Dalmatian dialect, document the lives of an imaginary group of local archetypes and brought the wit of the Splićani to a nationwide audience. An adaptation of his works, *Naše malo misto* (Our Little Town) was the most popular comedy programme in Croatian – and probably Yugoslav – television history. The city's tradition of irreverence lives on in the weekly newspaper and national institution **Feral Tribune**, a mixture of investigative reporting and scathing political satire which has been a thorn in the side of successive recent administrations.

Arrival, information and city transport

Both the **train** and **inter-city bus stations** are five minutes' walk southeast of the centre on the main harbourfront road, Obala kneza Domagoja, along which are ranged all the **ferry** and **hydrofoil** berths. Split's **airport** is around 20km northwest of town between Kaštela and Trogir. Croatia Airlines buses (20Kn) connect with scheduled flights, dropping passengers on the waterfront Riva, near the Croatia Airlines office; alternatively, the #37 Trogir–Split bus (13.50Kn) runs from in front of the airport to the suburban bus station on Domovinskog rata, twenty minutes' north of the centre. A taxi from the airport will cost 160–200Kn.

MOVING ON FROM SPLIT

Split is an excellent base for onward travel, with **buses** to every conceivable destination in Croatia, as well as daily services to Mostar and Sarajevo in Bosnia-Hercegovina. There are two daily **trains** to Zagreb, calling at Knin and Karlovac on the way.

Split is the Dalmatian coast's main Jadrolinija terminal, with regular **local ferries** to the islands of Brač, Vis, Lastovo, Hvar and Korčula; it's also a major stop on the summer **coastal ferry** service, which connects Split with Rijeka, Rab, Zadar and Dubrovnik. In summer, the coastal ferry carries on to Bari in Italy (1–2 weekly) and Igoumenitsa in Greece (1 weekly), while from June to September there are ferries roughly every day to Ancona in Italy. For the main coastal ferry, pre-booking is recommended. Tickets and reservations for all the above ferry services can be made through Jadrolinija in the main passenger terminal on Obala kneza Domagoja (☎021/355-399, fax 362-050). In addition, SMC run daily **hydrofoils** to Hvar and Vis (mid-May to mid-Sept), and the Italian port of Ancona (mid-March to late Oct) – there's an SMC ticket counter in the main ferry terminal (☎021/589-433, fax 589-215).

The city's tourist association (☎021/355-088) doesn't have an office open to the public, and for the time being the best source of information is the privately run **Turist Biro** on the waterfront at Riva 12. As for **city transport**, it's generally easiest to walk, though for journeys out to the Marjan peninsula and some of Split's museums you may need to take one of the city's frequent, if crowded, **buses**. These operate between 5am and midnight; tickets can be bought from the driver or conductor (5Kn) or from newspaper and tobacco kiosks (8Kn, valid for two journeys) and should be punched when you board. Tickets for Kaštela and Trogir (see p.236 and p.232) are priced according to a zonal system – pay the conductor. The principal nodal points for the municipal bus network are Trg republike, at the western end of the waterfront Riva (for the Marjan peninsula and Solin); Zagrebačka, opposite the market on the eastern side of the old town; and Domovinskog rata (for Kaštela and Trogir). There are **taxi** ranks outside the train and bus stations, and at both the eastern and western ends of the Riva.

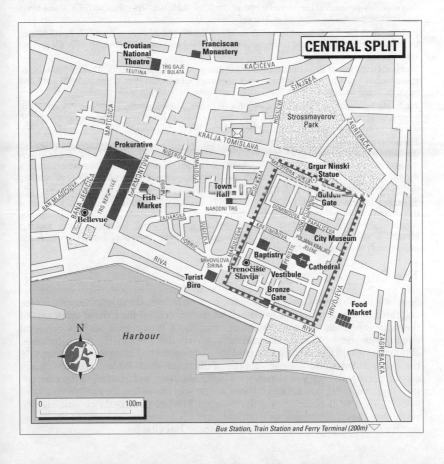

Bus Station, Train Station and Ferry Terminal (200m) ▽

Accommodation

There are plenty of private **rooms** (①–②) in Split, and it's easy to find one even in high season – contact the Turist Biro on the waterfront at Riva 12 (☎021/342-142). There are very few rooms in the old town, though the nearby residential districts of Manuš and Veli Varoš can be equally atmospheric, and the bureau also arranges accommodation in Trogir and Omiš. The unregistered rooms offered by touts at the bus station may work out cheaper, but bear in mind that there's no quality control, and many are miles out of the centre.

Some of Split's **hotels** are either still occupied by refugees or currently undergoing restoration in the wake of their departure, so there's not as much choice as you'd expect in a city of this size, and you should book ahead in July and August. All the hotels listed below include breakfast in the room price.

Hotels

Bellevue, Bana Jelačića 2 (☎021/585-701, fax 362-383). A once elegant nineteenth-century pile superbly situated at the western end of the Riva. Adequate en-suites with TV, some overlooking the flagstoned expanse of Trg republike. ④.

Jadran Koteks, Sustjepanski put 23 (☎021/361-599, fax 361-381). Smallish hotel fifteen minutes southwest of the old town, with open-air pool and smart rooms, all with TV and air con. ⑥.

Marjan, Obala kneza Branimira 8 (☎021/342-866 or 302-111, fax 342-930). Dowdy 1960s high-rise which is much nicer inside than out. Functional but comfortable rooms with TV, bath and balcony, some with views back towards the old town (a 5–10min walk away). ⑤.

Park, Hatzeov perivoj 3 (☎021/314-755, fax 314-567). Fifteen minutes' walk southeast of the centre, directly above Bačvice beach. Plain but perfectly comfortable en-suite rooms with TV. It's due to be renovated soon, so ring beforehand to check it's open. ⑤.

Prenočište Slavija, Buvinova 3 (☎021/47-053, fax 591-558). The only hotel currently open in the old town, occupying a gloomy and characterless building, although it has a couple of saving graces, notably its proximity to the sights and its fourth-floor terrace, from where there's a good view out over Split's red-tiled skyline. Plain, unadorned rooms (a mixture of singles, doubles and triples), some with shared facilities, others en suite. ②.

Split, Put Trstenika 19 (☎021/303-014 or 303-111, fax 303-011). Modern four-star 3km east of the centre, on a bluff overlooking the shore. Rooms come with TV, minibar, bath and disconcertingly bright blue-and-white 1980s decor. All have small balconies, some looking across the water to the island of Brač, and there's a small open-air pool. Bus #17, or a thirty-minute walk along the coastal path. ⑥.

The City

Split may be the largest town in Dalmatia, but nearly everything worth seeing is concentrated in the compact **old town** behind the waterfront Riva, made up in part of the various remains and conversions of Diocletian's Palace itself, and the medieval additions to the west of it. You can walk across this area in about ten minutes, although it would take a lifetime to explore all its nooks and crannies. On either side the old town fades into low-rise suburbs of utilitarian stone houses grouped tightly around narrow alleys – **Veli Varoš**, west of the old town, and **Manuš**, to the east, are the most unspoiled, and although there are no specific sights, they're worth a brief wander. West of the city centre, the wooded **Marjan peninsula** commands fine views over the coast and islands from its heights. The best of the beaches are on the north side of Marjan, or east of the ferry dock at **Bačvice**.

DIOCLETIAN

Diocletian was born in Salona, the capital of Roman Dalmatia, in 245 AD. Though the son of slaves, he proved himself quickly in the Roman military, becoming emperor in 284, at the age of 39. For 21 years he attempted to provide stability and direction to an empire under pressure – goals he achieved with some measure of success, even organizing the last triumph imperial Rome was ever to see. In the belief that the job of running the empire was too big for one man, Diocletian divided the role into four, the **Tetrarchy**, carefully parcelling out responsibility among his partners – a decision which some historians believe led directly to disintegration and civil war. Diocletian was also renowned for his persecution of Christians: those martyred during his reign included the patron saints of Split, Domnius and Anastasius, along with many other leading religious figures, Sebastian, George, Theodore and Vitus among them.

The motives for Diocletian's early **retirement** have been the subject of much speculation. The simplest reason seems to be the most accurate – he was tired of it all. What he didn't foresee was that his own creation, the Tetrarchy, would come to haunt him. The Tetrarchy had been welded together by inter-family marriage, with Diocletian's own daughter, Valeria, staying in Rome after her father's retirement as the wife of one of the Tetrarchs. Valeria became an important figure among the squabbling Tetrarchs: her husband soon died and she was passed from one to another, suffering continual mistreatment and eventually being murdered along with her son. In response to this, Diocletian appears to have poisoned himself in despair.

The Palace

Despite its importance, don't expect **Diocletian's Palace** to be an archeological "site": the shape and style of the palace have to be extrapolated from what remains, which itself is obscured by centuries of addition and alteration – the map on p.250 gives an idea of the palace's original ground plan, but doesn't show contemporary features. The palace occupies the eastern half of the old town and apart from certain set-piece buildings – notably the cathedral (originally Diocletian's mausoleum) and the baptistry (once a temple) – it has been built upon so much by successive generations that it is no longer recognizable as an ancient Roman structure. Little remains of the imperial apartments, although the medieval tenements, shops and offices which have taken their place were built in large part using stones and columns salvaged from Diocletian's original buildings.

The best place to start is on the seaward side, at Split's broad and lively waterfront, the **Riva** (officially the Obala hrvatskog naradnog preporoda, or Quay of the Croatian National Revival, although hardly anyone ever calls it that). Running along the palace's southern facade, into which shops, cafés and a warren of tiny flats have been built, the Riva is where a large part of the city's population congregates day and night to meet friends, catch up on gossip or idle away an hour or two in a café. The main approach to the palace from here is through the **Bronze Gate** (Mjedena vrata), an anonymous and functional gateway that originally gave access to the sea, which once came right up to the palace. Inside is a vaulted space which once formed the basement of Diocletian's central hall, the middle part of his residential complex, now occupied by arts and crafts stalls. On either side of here stretch the **subterranean halls** (podrum; daily: summer 8am–8pm; winter

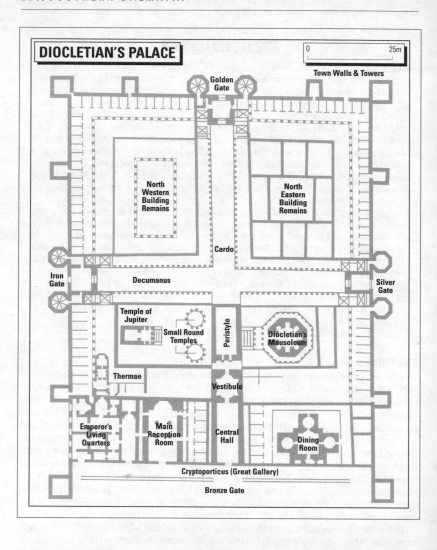

8am–noon & 4–7pm; 10Kn), built in Diocletian's time to support the apartments above – until 1956 they remained unexplored and full of centuries of debris. Parts have now been cleared out and opened to the public, and though there's nothing actually to see, they give an idea of what the palace must have once looked like, since their ground plan is an exact mirror of the imperial living quarters that formerly stood above. The long corridor which stretches east and west of the Bronze Gate corresponds to the **cryptoporticus**, or great gallery, along which the emperor would have promenaded. The large hall off the western end of the corridor stood beneath Diocletian's main reception room, while the cruciform group

ROBERT ADAM AND DIOCLETIAN'S PALACE

The rediscovery of Diocletian's Palace owes much to the eighteenth-century Scottish architect **Robert Adam**, who believed that contemporary European builders had much to learn from their Roman forebears. Adam arrived in Split in 1757 with a team of draughtsmen, spending five weeks in the city despite the hostility of the Venetian governor, who almost had them arrested as spies. The resulting book of engravings of the palace caused a sensation, offering inspiration to Neoclassical architects all over Britain and Europe. Mindful of Adam's success, Austrian Emperor Josef II commissioned Frenchman **L.F. Cassas** to supply a wider-ranging set of engravings of Dalmatia's ancient buildings, which was also published to great acclaim. A sign that attitudes towards Dalmatia were beginning to be coloured by imperial rivalries in the region came in the French edition of Cassas's book, in which Joseph Lavallée's accompanying text accused Robert Adam of having travelled "like an Englishman, that is to say with that national egoism which counts England for everything and the rest of the world for nothing". "When the English travel", Lavallée added, "the desire to appropriate precedes the desire to instruct." Whatever its original motive, Adam's work was seminal in the development of the Georgian style in England, and large chunks of London, Bath and Bristol may be claimed to owe something of their space, symmetry and grace to Diocletian's buildings in Split.

of chambers off the eastern end of the corridor stood beneath the triclinium, or dining room.

At the northern end of this basement area, imposing steps lead up and out into the **Peristyle** (Peristil), once the central courtyard of the palace complex, opening out from the point where the cardo and decumanus meet. These days it's a lively square and meeting point, crowded with café tables and surrounded by considerable remnants of the stately arches that once framed the courtyard. The Peristyle has been the site of two major cultural scandals in modern times, the first in 1968, when three students used the cover of darkness to paint the square's paving stones red – the colour both of revolutionary socialist idealism, and also of the ossified political elites in socialist states such as Yugoslavia. The action, which became known as **Red Peristyle**, has gone down in history as one of the key events in Croatian conceptual art, although the authorities were quick to condemn it as vandalism. The thirtieth anniversary of Red Peristyle was marked on the night of January 10, 1998, when Igor Grubić painted the Peristyle black (the colour of the extreme right and, by implication, the Croatia of the 1990s) – a gesture which engendered much the same official response.

At the southern end of the Peristyle, steps lead up to the **vestibule**, a round, formerly domed building that is the only part of the imperial apartment area of the palace that's anything like complete. It was here that subjects would wait before being admitted to the presence of Diocletian himself.

THE CATHEDRAL

On the east side of the Peristyle stands one of the two black granite Egyptian sphinxes, dating from around 15 BC, that originally flanked the entrance to Diocletian's mausoleum, an octagonal building surrounded by an arcade of Corinthian columns. Diocletian's body is known to have rested here for 170 years until it mysteriously disappeared – no one knows where. The building was later converted into the **Cathedral of St Domnius** (Katedrala svetog Dujma; Mon–Sat 7am–noon & 4–7pm) and a choir added.

The cathedral porch is entered through an arch guarded by two Romanesque lions with a motley collection of human figures riding on their backs, including Greek-born Maria Lascaris, wife of Hungarian King Bela IV, who briefly took refuge from the Tatars in the nearby stronghold of Klis. The walnut and oak main **doors** – carved in 1214 by local artist Andrija Buvina with an inspired comic strip-style sequence showing 28 scenes from the life of Christ – are scuffed and scraped at the bottom, but in fine condition further up. On the right looms the six-storey **campanile** (same times as cathedral; 5Kn), begun in the thirteenth century but not finished until 1908 – the climb up is worth the effort for the panoramic view over the city and beyond.

Inside, the **dome** is ringed by two levels of Corinthian columns dating from the first century BC, while a frieze depicting racing chariots, hunting scenes and, in one corner, portraits of Diocletian and his wife Priscia, runs around the base. The rest of the constricted interior is stuffed with miscellaneous artworks. Immediately to the left of the entrance, the **pulpit** is a beautifully proportioned example of Romanesque art, sitting on capitals tangled with foliage, snakes and strange beasts. Moving clockwise round the church, the next feature is the **Altar of St Domnius**, honouring the first bishop of Salona's underground Christian community, who was beheaded in 304. Built by Giovanni Morlaiter in 1767, the altar features a pair of angels holding a reliquary on which a group of celestial cherubs cavort – a symbol of man's journey to the afterlife.

Further around lies the church's finest feature, the **Altar of St Anastasius** (Staš), which preserves the bones of a Christian contemporary of Domnius who was thrown in a river with a stone tied to him on Diocletian's orders. Sheltering under an extravagant canopy, the saint's sarcophagus bears Juraj Dalmatinac's cruelly realistic relief, the *Flagellation of Christ* of 1448, showing Jesus pawed and brutalized by some peculiarly oafish persecutors, while just above is a figure of St Anastasius with a millstone round his neck. Occupying the arch which leads through to the choir, the Baroque **high altar** features a pair of delicate, gilded angels supporting what looks like a cherub-encrusted carriage clock bearing paintings on each of its faces; an ornate coffered ceiling with ten paintings on Old Testament themes by Matej Ponzoni-Pončun fills the arch above. Further around is Bonino of Milan's fifteenth-century **Altar of St Domnius**, where the saint's bones were once kept. Sheltered beneath a flowery Gothic ciborium, this uses an ancient Roman sarcophagus bearing a relief of a man with hunting dogs as a base, on which rests a larger sarcophagus etched with a reclining figure of the bishop.

Behind the high altar, the **choir** was tacked onto the mausoleum in the seventeenth century, and still feels a very different part of the church. It's worth peering closely at the latticed choir stalls, which include some particularly delicate wood-carving – the oldest in Dalmatia, dated to about 1200. To the right, a flight of steps leads up to the **treasury** (*riznica*), sporting a melange of chalices, hand-written missals, thirteenth-century Madonnas and reliquary busts of the city's three great martyrs – Domnius, Anastasius and Arnerius (Arnir), a bishop of Split who was stoned to death in 1180.

Opposite the cathedral, a narrow alley runs from a gap in the arched arcade down to the attractive **baptistry** (opening times vary, check at the cathedral), a temple built in Diocletian's time and variously attributed to the cults of Janus or Jupiter, with an elaborate ceiling and well-preserved figures of Hercules and

Apollo on the eastern portal. Later Christian additions include a skinny statue of John the Baptist by Meštrović (a late work of 1954) and, more famously, an eleventh-century baptismal font with a relief showing a Croatian king trampling on a figure thought to represent either a devil or a pagan foe. Above the two figures runs a swirling pleated pattern known as *plutej*, a design typical of the Croatian Romanesque which has subsequently been adopted as a national symbol – you'll also see it around the bands of policemen's caps.

THE REST OF THE PALACE
North of the Peristyle, Dioklecijanova follows the line of the former cardo past rows of tottering medieval houses. A right turn down Papalićeva leads to the Juraj Dalmatinac-designed **Papalić Palace**, a typical example of the sturdy Gothic town houses built by Split's fifteenth-century aristocracy. An unobtrusive gateway leads through to a secluded, ivy-covered courtyard centred on a well adorned with the star and feathers symbol of the Papalić family, with a delicate loggia at ground-floor level and an outdoor stone stairway leading to the first-floor apartments. It now houses the **City Museum** (Gradski muzej; Tues–Fri 9am–noon & 5–8pm, Sat & Sun 10am–noon; 10Kn), with well-laid-out displays of medieval weaponry, figureheads from eighteenth-century galleys and sculptural fragments – including a serene Pietà by Nikola Fiorentinac. The reconstructed Papalić dining room on the first floor contains pictures and manuscripts relating to Marko Marulić (1450–1524), author of the biblically inspired epic *Judita* and the first Dalmatian poet to abandon Latin in favour of Croatian.

Continuing north along Dioklecijanova soon brings you to the grandest and best preserved of the palace gates, the **Golden Gate** (Zlatna vrata). This was the landward – and therefore most important – entrance to the palace, and the beginning of the main road to Salona. The arched niches (now empty) originally contained statues, and the four plinths on top of the gate once supported likenesses of Diocletian and the three other tetrarchs. Built into the gate (accessible by a flight of steps inside on the left) is the twelfth-century **St Martin's Chapel**, occupying an old Roman guardhouse: home to a Black Madonna icon, it's currently undergoing long-term restoration.

Just outside the gate there's another Mestrović work, the gigantic statue of the tenth-century Bishop **Grgur Ninski**. It was completed in 1929 to mark the 1000th anniversary of the Synod of Split, at which Grgur, Bishop of Nin, fought for the right of his people to use their own language in the liturgy instead of Latin. Catching the bishop in stiff mid-gesture, it's more successful as a patriotic statement than as a piece of sculpture. This mammoth used to stand in the Peristyle before it was moved during World War II, when the Italian occupiers attempted to cleanse the town centre of anything resembling a Croatian national symbol.

Narodni trg to Marmontova
Returning to the Peristyle and heading west along the ancient decumanus, now Krešimirova – an alley lined with shops which despite its narrowness is the old town's main thoroughfare – takes you out through the Iron Gate (Željezna vrata) into **Narodni trg** ("People's Square", usually known as "Pjaca", the local version of the Italian word *piazza*), which replaced the Peristyle as the city's main square in the fourteenth century. It's overlooked to the east by a Romanesque clock-tower with the remains of a medieval sundial, behind which looms a taller, older belfry. The north side of the square is dominated by the fifteenth-century **Town**

Hall (Gradska vijećnica), with a ground-floor loggia of three large pointed arches supported by stumpy pillars – it's now home to an ethnographic museum, although this is currently closed for refurbishment.

West of the square lie the bustling narrow streets and passages of the medieval town, while to the south, Marulićeva leads down towards **Mihovilova širina**, a small square whose café-bars get packed on warm summer evenings, and the adjoining Trg braće Radića, more popularly known as **Voćni trg** (Fruit Square) because of the market that used to be held here. There's a large statue of Marko Marulić, supplied by the industrious Meštrović, in the middle, and an octagonal tower that once formed part of the fifteenth-century Venetian castle, or *kaštel* – most of which has now either disappeared or been incorporated into residential buildings. A passageway to the left of the tower brings you back out onto the Riva.

Amble east along the Riva to reach the foot of **Marmontova** – the pedestrianized thoroughfare which marks the western boundary of the medieval town. Near the southern end of Marmontova is **Trg republike**, an elogated square set back from the water and surrounded on three sides by the grandiose neo-Renaissance city council buildings known as the **Prokurative** – it's put to good use as a venue for outdoor concerts in summer. From here, Marmontova heads north, passing the animated **fish market** on Kraj svete Marije – the scene of shopping frenzy most mornings, especially Fridays – and a few remaining bastions of the star-shaped seventeenth-century fortifications which once surrounded the town, before arriving at Trg Gaje Bulata, a broad open space overlooked by the **Croatian National Theatre** (Hrvatsko narodno kazalište, or HNK), a plain brown construction much rebuilt after a fire in 1971 and unadorned save for a group of statues on the third floor representing the arts.

On the northern side of the square, the church of the **Franciscan monastery** (Franjevački samostan) is worth a peek for the large fresco behind the high altar, a flamboyantly expressionistic work by contemporary religious artist Ivan Dulčić. A central figure of Jesus hovers above the Adriatic coastline, offering salvation to the matchstick forms below, most of which are dressed in colourful Dalmatian costumes. On his left are Cyril and Methodius, inventors of Glagolitic, the script used by the medieval Croatian church, while floating in the sky are a bull, lion and eagle – symbolizing SS Luke, Mark and John the Evangelist respectively.

North of the old town

Immediately to the west of the theatre is another modern square, Ujevićeva poljana, from which Zrinsko-Frankopanska spears north towards the city's modern residential districts. Head up here for ten minutes to reach the **Archeological Museum** at no. 25 (Arheološki muzej; Tues–Sat 9am–1pm & 5–8pm, Sun 10am–noon; 20Kn), with its comprehensive displays of Illyrian, Greek, medieval and – particularly – Roman artefacts, mostly plucked from the rich excavation sites at nearby Salona. Exhibits include delicate votive figurines, amulets and jewellery embellished with tiny peep-shows of lewd love-making. Outside, the arcaded courtyard is crammed with a wonderful array of Greek, Roman and early Christian stelae, sarcophagi and decorative sculpture. There are three key exhibits. Two of these, to the left of the entrance, are Salonan sarcophagi from the third century AD: one depicts the Hippolytus and Phaedra legend and is in superb condition – the marble still glistens – while the other is of a Calydonian boar hunt,

HAJDUK SPLIT

Few football teams are as closely associated with their home city as **Hajduk Split**. Formed in February 1911 by Croatian students returning from Prague – where they had witnessed the fervour created by Czech teams Sparta and Slavia – the club is named after the Robin Hood-like brigands who opposed both Ottoman and Venetian authority from the Middle Ages onwards. Hajduk was an explicitly Croatian team at a time when Split was still part of the Austro-Hungarian Empire, and later, in World War II, the team reflected the popular mood of resistance by joining the Partisans en masse. They were also the first team in Yugoslavia to play with a *petokraka* (Communist five-pointed star) on their jerseys, and the first team to remove it when it became clear that Yugoslavia's days were numbered.

A large part of the Hajduk mystique comes from their success on the pitch: they were Yugoslav champions twice in the 1920s, three times in the 1950s, four times in the 1970s, and went on to become champions of Croatia in 1992, 1994 and 1995. They're also famous for their loyal fans, known as the **torcida** (after the Brazilian fans that Hajduk supporters had seen footage of during the 1950 World Cup). Split's version of the *torcida* launched itself in October 1950, providing the team with maximum, Rio-style support for the title-decider against Red Star Belgrade – the first time that torches, banners and massed chanting had been seen on the terraces of mainland Europe. Hajduk won the match, but football purists were shocked by the levels of popular frenzy displayed. The Yugoslav regime, which had since 1945 condescendingly regarded Hajduk as "their" club, was horrified by the idea that football supporters could organize themselves without the leadership of the Party. *Torcida* founder Vjenceslav Žuvela was given a three-year prison sentence and the captain of the team was expelled from the Communist Party. Today, Hajduk and the *torcida* remain an unavoidable part of the urban landscape, and victories over traditional enemies like Dinamo Zagreb are still celebrated with city-wide rejoicing. Some would argue that the team has become all-important to the local population as other symbols of Dalmatian identity are gradually eroded and the act of supporting Hajduk becomes one of the few communal experiences left.

Tickets for matches (20–50Kn) are sold from kiosks at the southern end of the ground. Most of the *torcida* congregate in the northern stand (*tribina sjever*), while the poshest seats are in the west stand (*tribina zapad*). Beer and popcorn are available inside, and there are numerous snack bars offering drinks and grills immediately outside. Remember to bring a sheet of newspaper to sit on; the seats are filthy. There's a **club shop** below the west stand on Poljudsko šetalište, and a **Web site** at *www.hajduk.com* (Croatian language only). The *torcida* site at *www.torcida.org* has some information in English.

which in Robert Adam's pictures stood outside Split's baptistry. The third, another sarcophagus, is much later, dating from the fourth century. Known as the "Good Shepherd", it has been the subject of much speculation on account of its mixing up of the Christian motif of the shepherd with pagan symbols of Eros and Hades on its end panels.

Carry on up the road for another five minutes and you'll catch sight of the **Poljud Stadium** over the brow of the hill. Built for the 1979 Mediterranean Games and now home to Hajduk Split football team (see box above), it's a strikingly organic structure, the curving roofs of its stands suggesting the sides of a fishing boat's hull or a gargantuan seashell.

The Marjan peninsula

Criss-crossed by footpaths and minor roads, the wooded heights of the **Marjan peninsula** offer the easiest escape from the bustle of central Split. From the old town it's an easy ten-minute walk up Senjska, which ascends westwards through the district of Veli Varoš, arriving after about ten minutes at the *Vidilica* **café** on Marjan's eastern shoulder. There's a small Jewish graveyard round the back of the café, and a terrace out front offering good views of Veli Varoš immediately below and the old town beyond. To the right of the café a stepped path climbs towards **Vrh Marjana**, where there's a wider view of the coast and islands, although there's an even better panorama from the peninsula's highest point, 175-metre-high **Telegrin**, about 1km further west.

Keeping to the left of the *Vidilica* brings you to a path which heads round the south side of the hill, arriving after about five minutes at the thirteenth-century **St Nicholas's Chapel** (Sveti Nikola), a simple structure with a sloping belfry tacked on to one side like a buttress. From here, the path continues for 2km, with wooded hillside to the right and the seaside suburbs of Marjan's south coast on the left, before arriving at **St Hieronymous's Chapel** (Sveti Jere), a simple shed-like structure pressed hard against a cliff – medieval hermits used to live in the caves which are still visible in the rock above. From here you can descend towards the road which leads round the base of the peninsula, or cross its rocky spine to reach Marjan's fragrant, pine-covered northern side. Paths emerge at sea level near **Bene** bay, where you'll find a combination of rocky and concreted bathing areas and a couple of cafés. You can also get to Bene by taking bus #12 from Trg republike.

THE MUSEUM OF CROATIAN ARCHEOLOGICAL MONUMENTS

Marjan's main cultural attractions are on its southern side, in the suburbs of Zvončac and Meje, about twenty minutes' walk from the centre or a short ride on bus #12 from Trg republike (every 30min). Heading west along Šetalište Ivana Meštrovića brings you first to the **Museum of Croatian Archeological Monuments** (Muzej hrvatskih arheoloških spomenika; Tues–Sat 9am–4pm, Sun 9am–noon; 20Kn), housed in an oversized concrete edifice with huge open-plan halls and piped-in organ muzak. The museum makes a concerted attempt to remind people of Split's medieval Croatian heritage, a phase of local history that's often forgotten in the enthusiasm for all things connected with Diocletian. Displays include a motley collection of jewellery, weapons and fragmentary reconstructions of chancel screens and ciboria (the canopies built over a church's main altar) from ninth- and tenth-century Croatian churches.

THE MEŠTROVIĆ GALLERY AND THE KAŠTELET

A couple of minutes' further along Šetalište Ivana Meštrovića at no. 39, the **Ivan Meštrović Gallery** (Galerija Ivana Meštrovića; Tues–Sun 11am–6pm; 20Kn) is housed in the ostentatious Neoclassical building that the country's most famous modern sculptor (see box opposite) planned as his home and studio. Fronted by a portentous veranda supported by Ionic columns, the house was completed in 1939 – Meštrović lived in it for just two years before fleeing to Zagreb to escape the Italian occupation in 1941.

Even if you're not mad about Meštrović, this is still an impressive collection, although the emphasis is on smooth female nudes and tender Madonnas rather than the ideological and historical subjects with which he made his reputation.

IVAN MEŠTROVIC (1883–1962)

Ivan Meštrović was born in Slavonia to a family of itinerant agricultural labourers, but his parents soon moved back to their native Dalmatia, settling in Otavice near Drniš. Meštrović was too busy tending sheep on Mount Svilaja to attend school, and had to teach himself to read and write. At the age of 16 he displayed some drawings in a local inn, prompting locals – including the mayor of Drniš – to apply to art schools on his behalf. He was turned down, but managed to land a job with a Split stonemason, thus beginning his training as a sculptor.

Awarded a place at the Viennese Acadamy in 1901 (quite a feat considering his background), he was soon exhibiting with the Art Nouveau-influenced Secession group. At the age of 22, Meštrović was already receiving big public commissions – like the Secession-influenced *Well of Life* (1905) which still stands outside the Croatian National Theatre in Zagreb. By the time he moved to Paris in 1907 a distinctive Meštrović style was beginning to emerge, blending the earthy Romanticism of Rodin with the grace of Classical sculpture and the folk motifs of southeastern Europe. This eclecticism may help explain why Meštrović – considered too daring by traditionalists but not daring enough by the moderns – never enjoyed the reputation abroad which he did at home.

Like many men of his generation, Meštrović was convinced that the Austro-Hungarian state could not survive, and that the expanding Kingdom of Serbia would provide the basis of a future Yugoslav state in which all South Slavs could live as equals – he had grown up in an area of mixed Serb-Croat settlement and was familiar with the folk epics of both communities. When the Austrian government invited Meštrović to represent them at the Rome International Exhibition of 1911, he chose to exhibit in the Serbian pavilion instead (of the 23 artists in the Serbian pavilion, incidentally, 14 were Croat).

On the outbreak of World War I Meštrović moved to Italy, until Italian designs on Dalmatia led to him moving to London, where his involvement with the Yugoslavist cause helped land him a one-man show at the Victoria and Albert Museum in 1915. The exhibition was an enormous success – to attend it was seen as a sign of support for the war effort. In 1918 Meštrović hailed the creation of Yugoslavia as the "greatest accomplishment that our people have hitherto performed", although his enthusiasm would subsequently wane. He was made Rector of the Academy of Fine Arts in Zagreb in 1923, and was in constant demand as an artist over the next two decades, working on monumental public projects such as the *Grgur Ninski* sculpture in Split (1928) and two vast, muscular Indians on horseback for Grant Park in Chicago (1928). His architectural work was in many ways more innovative than his sculptural, developing a cool, sepulchral style which found expression in the Račić mausoleum in Cavtat (1923), the Meštrović family mausoleum in Otavice (1927–31) and the Art Pavilion in Zagreb (1939).

In 1941, Meštrović was imprisoned by the Ustaše due to his history of pro-Yugoslav activity, but after four months Ante Pavelić summoned the sculptor to his office, apologized and told him he was free to emigrate. Meštrović eventually made his way to America, where he became Professor of Sculpture at the University of Notre Dame, Indiana. Much of his later work was religious, although he'd been tackling sacred subjects on and off ever since 1916, when the cycle of reliefs displayed in Split's Kaštelet was begun.

Some of the religious pieces (look out for a particularly tortured *Job* from 1946) have considerable emotional depth, although his other work can sometimes appear facile – such as the slightly daft *Joyful Youth* or the giant and ungainly

Adam and Eve. Portraits of members of his immediate family in the ground-floor drawing room are refreshingly direct, especially the honest and sensitive *My Mother* from 1909.

Meštrović's best work can be seen in the so-called **Kaštelet** ("little castle"; in theory Tues–Sun 10am–5pm, but check at the Meštrović Gallery first; admission with gallery ticket) about 200m further up the road. Built in the sixteenth century as the fortified residence of the Capogrosso family, but long used for other purposes (it was at various times a tannery and a hospital), the Kaštelet was virtually a ruin when Meštrović bought it in 1939 to house his **Life of Christ** cycle, a series of reliefs in wood that he'd been working on since 1916. Presided over by a mannered but moving *Crucifixion*, the cycle spreads like a frieze across all four walls of the church, borrowing stylistically from Assyrian bas-reliefs, Egyptian tomb paintings and Archaic Greek art. The result is an immensely powerful piece of religious sculpture, with rows of rigidly posed, hypnotically stylized figures in which the sum of Meštrović's eclecticism is for once greater than its parts. It's said that Meštrović began the cycle in response to the horrors of World War I, which may go some way to explaining its spiritual punch.

East of the centre

There's not much of interest east of the old town save for the main city beach of **Bačvice**, a few minutes' walk south past the railway station. This simple crescent of shingle can't compare with the beaches further south, but it remains a popular – and crowded – destination for Splićani of all ages. Bačvice is also the home of *picigin*, a game (only played in and around Split) rather like a netless version of volleyball played in the sea, involving a lot of acrobatic leaping around as players try to prevent a small ball from hitting the water. The front has recently been given a facelift thanks to the chic modern three-tier pavilion that curves gracefully round the beach, like a cross between an Art Deco seaside building and a high-tech metal tent. There are several cafés and a couple of swanky eateries inside (see opposite).

A coastal path leads east from Bačvice past a couple of smaller bays and a yachting marina to **Žnjan**, a large waterside expanse which was levelled so that the pope could hold a vast outdoor mass here in 1998. There are several more cafés along the way, and the whole stretch is a popular strolling area all year round.

Eating, drinking and nightlife

Suprisingly, good sit-down **restaurants** are in short supply along the well-worn tourist trail of the old town, although there are several good places a short walk away. Restaurants tend to stay open until 11pm or midnight unless stated otherwise; some have a separate menu of *marende* (cheap brunches), which is often chalked up on a board outside. For self-catering and snacks, the daily **market** at the eastern edge of the old town is an excellent place to shop for fruit, veg and local hams and cheeses; the 24-hour *Prerada* **bakery** directly opposite the market on Zagrebačka offers a dizzying array of fresh buns, cakes and strudels. *Delta*, next to *McDonalds* on Marmontova, is a good place to pick up takeaway pizza slices and pastries. The best **cakes** and sweets are from *Bobis*, who have a large café on the Riva and a smaller outlet on Marmontova.

There are plenty of **pavement cafés** along the waterfront and around the Peristyle for daytime and evening drinking. The Riva is the classic venue for hanging out and people-watching: there's not much to choose between the numerous cafés along it, although the cafés at its western end are slightly more posey and expensive than those to the east. From the Riva, evening crowds flow into the old town, where crumbling palaces and squares provide the perfect ambience for late-night supping. More café-bars can be found in the pavilion at Bačvice beach, and in the next two bays along the coastal path to the east.

There are several **discos** offering a diet of commercial techno: *Night Café Metropolis*, in the Koteks shopping centre east of the centre on Osječka; *Up & Down*, in the marina at the end of Obala kneza Branimira; and *Shakespeare*, just east of Bačvice beach at Uvala Zente 3 – the latter has a large outdoor terrace overlooking the shore. *Obojena Svjetlost*, on the beach beneath the Meštrović gallery, is an animated open-air disco-bar that stays open until the early hours in summer and often stages live Croatian rock-pop.

Restaurants

Central, Narodni trg. Excellently located on the main square, but try to get one of the outside tables – the restaurant interior is utterly unatmospheric. Straightforward, moderately priced grill menu: look out for cheaper, chalked-up daily specials such as *lešo* (fish stew), *gulaš* (goulash) and *sarme* (stuffed cabbage leaves).

Galija, Kamila Tončića 12 (on corner with Matošića). The best of the city's pizzerias – a small, unpretentious and cheap place with breezy service and wooden-bench seating on the western fringes of the old town.

Konoba kod Jože, Sredmanuska 4. Ten minutes' walk northeast of the old town in a back alley (head north along Zagrebačka and turn right into Sredmanuška after you've passed Strossmayerov park), this is one of Split's best seafood restaurants, though not too expensive. Choose between quick and cheap meals like *crni rižot* (squid risotto) or opt for the best fresh fish and lobster. Homely, intimate atmosphere with fishing nets hung from the walls.

Konoba Varoš, Ban Mladenova 7 (☎021/362-963). Handily situated just west of Trg republike – it's up an alley behind the *Hotel Bellevue* – this is a good place for reasonably priced *marende* as well as expensive slap up evening meals. Much patronized by locals and soon fills up.

Re di Mare, Špinut. In the marina on the north side of the Marjan peninsula, and handy if you're on the way back from Bene beach. Upmarket grills as well, plus a good range of reasonable pizzas as well, plus views of Mount Kozjak on other side of the bay.

Sarajevo, Domaldova 6. In the heart of the old town, this elegant place is one of Split's few old-fashioned downtown restaurants. Tuck into a full range of moderately expensive Dalmatian fish and meat dishes, including an excellent *pašticada* (beef in sweet-and-sour sauce).

Stellon, Bačvice. Chic but not overpriced pizza and pasta restaurant in the pavilion above Bačvice beach. A safe bet for vegetarians, with some satisfying main courses (try the penne with broccoli) and good salads.

Šumica, Put Firula 6 (☎021/515-911). Long-established rendezvous for the smart set just east of Bačvice beach, with a big outdoor terrace and a formal, starched-napkin interior. Excellent seafood and full range of shellfish, as well as succulent schnitzel-style meals typical of inland Croatia. Higher-than-average prices, but deservedly so.

Zlatna Ribica, Kraj svete Marije 12. No-nonsense stand-up buffet by the fish market on Marmontova offering cheap seafood snacks. Open till 8pm. Closed Sun.

Cafés and bars

Equador, Bačvice. Snazzy bar in the pavilion above Bačvice beach with deep, comfy chairs, and a range of cocktails, nibbles and salads.

Jazz III, Vuškovićeva. Crowded, dark, predominantly twenty-something, but very relaxed drinking haunt in the northwest quarter of the palace.

Pivnica Klara, Kavanjinova 5. A pub-like pair of rooms which can get packed and raucous on Fridays and Saturdays, although you can always cool off in the beer garden-style courtyard. It's a little way north of the old town: head up Zrinsko-Frankopanska and look out for Kavanjinova on the right.

Planet Jazz, Grgura Ninskog. Tightly-packed L-shaped bar with outdoor seating in a time-weathered courtyard, immediately northeast of the Peristyle, attracting a young-ish cross-section of Split society.

Song, Mihovilova Širina. Busy daytime or night-time drinking venue on a small square just behind the Riva. The place to be on warm summer weekends, if you can find a free table.

Star Rock Café, Marmontova. Brash, roomy bar decked out in rock memorabilia in *Hard Rock Café* style. A magnet for young wannabes.

Entertainment and festivals

There's top-class **drama**, **classical music** and **opera** at the prestigious Croatian National Theatre (Hrvatsko narodno kazalište, or HNK), Trg Gaje Bulata 1 (☎021/585-999). The **Split Summer Festival** (Splitsko ljeto; mid-July to mid-Aug) hosts a spate of cultural events – including a lot of classical music and at least one opera – many of which take place on an outdoor stage at the Prokurative, which is also the venue for big **pop concerts**. There's usually a **Jazz Festival** immediately preceding the Summer Festival, though its continued existence depends on sponsorship, as does the **Festival of Creative Disorder** (Festival kreativnog nereda; mid-Aug), which brings together various counter-cultural events and happenings. One older-established alternative event is the **Festival of New Film and Video** (Festival novog filma i videa; late Sept to early Oct), featuring independent short films from Croatia and full-length foreign releases. The prime venue for this is Kinoteka Zlatna Vrata **cinema**, Dioklecijanova 7, which also has a regular programme of art-house and cult films. Mainstream movies are shown at the Marjan cinema on Trg republike and the Central on Trg Gaje Bulata. Also look out for occasional gigs, events and exhibitions at the monstrous concrete **Youth Centre** (Dom omladine) on Savska, north of the Koteks shopping centre 500m east of the city centre.

The best way to find out **what's on** is to keep an eye out for posters or consult the back pages of local newspaper *Slobodna Dalmacija* – good for serious culture and cinema listings, though not so well informed about pop or alternative happenings.

Listings

Airlines Adria, Obala kneza Domagoja (☎021/581-700); Croatia Airlines, Riva 9 (☎021/362-202, fax 362-567).

Airport enquiries ☎021/203-506.

Banks Splitska banka, Riva 10.

Bookshops A small selection of English-language paperbacks can be found at Algoritam, Grgura Ninskog, or at Morpurgo, Trg republike.

Car rental Euro Rent, Obala kneza Domagoja 9 (☎021/362-700); Herz, Branimirova obala 1 (☎021/342-994).

Consulates UK, Riva 10, 3rd floor (☎021/341-464).

Ferry tickets The Jadrolinija office (☎021/355-399) is at the passenger terminal on Obala knez Domagoja. There's an SMC ticket counter for hydrofoils to Ancona, Hvar and Vis (summer only) in the main ferry terminal (☎021/589-433, fax 589-215).

Hospital Spinčićieva 1 (☎021/515-055).

Left luggage At the train station (daily 4am–10pm).

Pharmacy Ljekarna Grad, Narodni trg 16 (24hr).

Police Trg hrvatske bratske zajednice 9 (☎021/307-281).

Post office I.L. Lavčevića 9 (Mon–Fri 7am–9pm, Sat 7am–2pm); Obala kneza Domagoja (same times).

Taxis There are taxi ranks at the eastern and western ends of the Riva, or ring ☎021/343-666.

Telephones At the post office (see above).

Inland from Split

The most direct route between mid-Dalmatia, the Plitvice lakes and Zagreb heads inland from Split towards the **Zagora**, a highland area which stretches from the mountain ridge just behind the coast to the Hercegovinian border further east. A rocky, scrub-covered plateau, scattered with villages eking a living from thin and unproductive soil, the Zagora is economically poorer than the coastal strip, and many of its inhabitants (the "Vlaji" of Split lore – see box on p.243) have decamped to seek work in the big city nearby.

Most people breeze through the area en route for northern Croatia, although there's a smattering of worthwhile sights. The Roman city of **Salona** and the medieval fortress of **Klis** are only a few kilometres outside Split, and easily reached on local buses, while slightly further afield, the Marian pilgrimage centre of **Sinj** can also be visited on hourly buses from the city.

Salona

Five kilometres inland from Split, at the foot of the mountains which divide the coastal plain from the Zagora, is the sprawling dormitory suburb of Solin, a characterless modern town which has grown up beside the ruins of **SALONA**, erstwhile capital of Roman Dalmatia and probable birthplace of Diocletian. The town once boasted a population of around 60,000 and was an important centre of Christianity long before Constantine legalized the religion throughout the empire – prominent leaders of the faith (future saints Domnius and Anastasius among them) were famously put to death here by Diocletian in 304. It was later the seat of a powerful Byzantine bishopric until 614, when the town was comprehensively sacked by a combined force of Slavs and Avars, and the local population moved off to settle in what would subsequently become Split.

Located on the northwestern fringe of Solin, the **ruins of Salona** (dawn–dusk; free) stretch across a hillside just above the main road to Kaštela and Trogir. Bus #1 from Trg Gaje Bulata in central Split passes the main entrance to the ruins – en route you'll see stretches of the **aqueduct** built by Diocletian to bring fresh water to his palace from the hills to the north – numerous refurbishments later, it's still very much in use. Though extensively excavated at the end of the nineteenth century, nearly everything of interest at Salona was packed off to museums years ago, and there's relatively little left to see. The location, however, is peaceful and evocative, like an overgrown meadow scattered with weathered stones, giving views to the hazy industrial suburbs across the bay.

The part of the site closest to the entrance is **Manastirine**, an early necropolis for Christian martyrs piled high with sarcophagi around a ruined fifth-century basilica. Nearby, the former summer villa of Don Frane Bulić (the doyen of Croatian archaeology who spent the first half of the twentieth century digging here) incorporates various Roman fragments, including gravestones, in its walls. Below Manastirine, you can take the route of the old city walls as they zigzag across scrubby fields through a confusion of ruined basilicas and necropoli. Follow them as far as the second-century amphitheatre, a largely demolished structure which originally seated around 18,000 spectators and is probably the most extensive relic on the site – the grassy central space is now used to graze goats. From here you can leave Salona and walk back east along the main road past the meagre remains of a first-century theatre on the left, continuing on to central Solin where you can pick up buses back to Split.

Klis

The town of **KLIS** grew up around a strategic mountain pass on the trade routes linking the coast with the hinterland of the Zagora. The steep rock pinnacle around which the modern town huddles was first fortified by the Romans, before being taken over by the expanding medieval kingdom of the Croats; kings Mislav (835–845) and Trpimir (845–864) both based their courts here. Klis remained in Hungaro-Croatian hands until the sixteenth century, when the Turks, already in command of Bosnia, began pushing towards the coast. Commanded by Captain **Petar Kružić**, who paid for the Trsat staircase in Rijeka (see p.163), Klis withstood sieges in 1526 and 1536, but finally succumbed to Ottoman attack in 1537, when attempts to relieve the citadel ended in farce. Badly drilled reinforcements sent by the Habsburgs fled in fear from the Turks, and their attempts to re-board their boats in Solin bay caused many vessels to sink. Kružić himself – who had left the fortress to make contact with the hapless reinforcements – was captured and executed: the sight of his head on a stick was too much for Klis's remaining defenders, who gave up the fortress in return for safe passage north, where they resumed the struggle from the security of Senj (see box on p.187).

The present-day town straggles up the hillside beneath the fortress and is divided into three parts: **Klis-Varoš**, on the main road below the fortress; **Klis-Grlo**, at the top of the hill where the Drniš and Sinj roads part company; and **Klis-Megdan**, off to one side, where you'll find the main gate to the **fortress** (*tvrđava*; summer daily 9am–6pm; winter Sat–Sun 9am–5pm; if it's closed, ask in one of the nearby cafés). It's a remarkably complete structure, with three long, rectangular defensive lines surrounding a central strongpoint, the Položaj maggiore ("Grand Position", a mixed Croatian–Italian term dating from the time when Leonardo Foscolo captured the fortress for the Venetians in 1648), at the eastern, highest end of the fortress. You can't see inside many of the buildings apart for one dusty old stone chapel, but there are lots of grassy bastions to scramble around on and impressive views of the coast, with the marching tower blocks and busy arterial roads of suburban Split sprawling across the plain below, and the islands of Šolta and Brač in the distance.

Driving to Klis, take the old road which heads inland from Solin (rather than the new dual carriageway which skirts Klis to the east), go through the tunnel that separates Klis-Varoš from Klis-Grlo, and turn left when you see the sign for the *tvrđava*. **Buses** #34 and #36 go from Split to Klis-Megdan, but they're relatively infrequent, so it may be better to catch any Sinj bus, get off opposite the *Castel* café in Klis-Varoš, and walk up the hill on foot. Klis is famous for the three **restaurants** by the road junction in Klis-Grlo selling spit-roast lamb (*jagnjetina na ražnju*), each of which advertises its wares by having a carcass or two slowly revolving over open fires by the roadside. Portions are priced by the kilogram and are invariably served with spring onion (*kapulica*).

North to Sinj

From Klis, the road forges across the stony uplands of the Dalmatinska Zagora towards Sinj, 20km further on. It's a route traversed by frequent buses from Split, although you'll need your own transport to make the worthwhile side-trip to the **Vranjača Cave** (Špilja Vranjača; Easter–Oct daily 9am–5pm; ask at the nearby post office if there's no caretaker at the entrance; 15Kn), along a side-road to the east. To get there turn right about 3km beyond Klis and head through the village of **DUGOPOLJE** ("Long Field"; so named because it's in a typical *polje*, or fertile depression, common to karstic areas) towards a group of hamlets known collectively as Kotlenice. In the first of these, **VLADOVIĆI**, there's a small carpark from which a gravel track leads to the cave. Discovered by the grandfather of the cave's current caretaker and guide, the cave is explored via a steep stairway which descends some 100m down into a chamber about 150m long, filled with honey-brown stalactites and stalagmites. The 65-million-year-old formations grow at a rate of 1mm every thirty-five years and include fluted limestone curtains and forms resembling the bunched heads of cauliflowers.

Sinj and beyond

Back on the Split–Sinj route, the road crosses infertile heath before descending into **SINJ**, a provincial market centre laid out in a bowl between the hills. It's famous locally for the **Sinjska gospa** (Our Lady of Sinj), a supposedly miraculous image of the Virgin dating from around 1500 which hangs in the local parish church (on the last altar on the left-hand side as you enter). It's claimed that prayers to the Sinjska gospa saved the town on Ascension Day 1715, when the locals drove away a superior force of Ottoman Turks – it still draws pilgrims from all over Dalmatia, and is paraded through the town every year on August 15.

Victory over the Turks is also celebrated annually by the **Sinjska alka** (usually the first weekend of August) – a sort of medieval joust in which contestants attempt to thread their lances through a series of rings dangled from a rope – all at a terrific gallop. It's a riotous, boozy business, involving all the surrounding villages and taking up the whole day in a blaze of colour, costume and procession that builds up to a crescendo when the contest itself takes place. More details can be had from the small **tourist office** (Mon–Fri 9am–3pm; ☎021/826-352) next to the modern and central *Alkar* **hotel** (☎021/824-474 or 824-488, fax 824-505; ③), which has neat, recently refurbished en-suites.

Beyond Sinj, the main road heads northwest towards Knin (see p.230), while an alternative route heads southeast towards the small town of **TRILJ**, where there's an excellent **restaurant**, the *Sveti Mihovil* on the main Trg bana Jelačića, renowned for its choice of Zagora food, including *arambašići* (stuffed cabbage leaves) and *žabji kraci* (frogs' legs). Beyond Trilj you can head south towards the Cetina Gorge and Omiš (see p.296), or cross the Dinara mountain range to the east into Bosnia-Hercegovina.

Brač

The third largest of Croatia's Adriatic islands, **BRAČ** is the nearest of the major islands to Split, and is correspondingly busy in season. The south coast fishing village of **Bol**, with its spectacular beach, is the main attraction, although the beaches at **Supetar** (where ferries from Split arrive) on the north coast are no mean substitute. Away from the coast, the island's starkly beautiful interior has undoubted allure, its scrub-covered karst uplands dotted with fertile depressions containing vines, olives and orange trees, or by the great man-made piles of limestone that characterize the Dalmatian islands, built up over centuries by smallholders clearing a place in which to grow crops.

Brač is famous for its stone, and was until the development of the tourist trade dependent on the export of its milk-white **marble**, which was used in Berlin's Reichstag, the high altar of Liverpool's Catholic cathedral, the White House in Washington and, of course, Diocletian's Palace in Split. The island's other major source of wealth was the grape harvest, though the *phylloxera* (vine lice) epidemics of the late nineteenth and early twentieth centuries forced many winemakers to emigrate. Even today, the signs of this depopulation are all around in the tumbledown houses and overgrown fields of the interior.

There are seven to thirteen **ferries** a day from Split to Supetar, plus **catamarans** from Split to Bol and Split to Milna, on the western side of the island, daily between mid-June and mid-September; there's also a ferry from Makarska on the mainland to Sumartin on the eastern tip of the Brač, although there are only two or three connecting buses from here to Supetar daily. Supetar is the main hub of the island **bus** network, with frequent departures southwest to Milna, east to Pučišća, and south to Bol. **Travelling on from Brač**, some excursion operators in Bol offer trips to Hvar (they'll be chalked up on signboards in the harbour), which may be more convenient than going all the way back to Split to pick up a regular ferry.

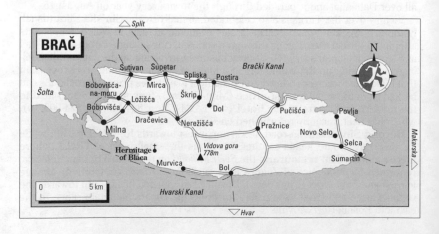

Supetar

Despite being the largest town on the island, **SUPETAR** is a sleepy place onto which package tourism has been painlessly grafted. Something of an old town survives, its mottled, rust-brown stone houses grouped around a horseshoe-shaped harbour, from where a line of modern hotels leads west along a shallow, pebble-fringed bay. The small **town museum** (Gradski muzej; daily 10am–noon & 7–11pm; 10Kn), next to the Baroque parish church, is a mundane affair, and you'd do best to head out to the **beaches** west of town, long stretches of pebble around a very shallow bay.

Standing on a peninsula screened by dark cypresses just beyond the beaches, the **town cemetery** is as much a sculpture park as a burial site, thanks in large part to **Ivan Rendić** (1849–1932), whose eclectic amalgam of Egyptian, Classical and Byzantine styles can be seen on many of the family tombs here. Rendić was one of the leading Croatian sculptors at the turn of the twentieth century and, as a native of Supetar, was repeatedly commissioned by wealthy families to design funerary monuments here, giving the cemetery a uniquely unified sculptural style. The first tomb, belonging to the Čulić family, is immediately inside the gate – a dome supported by four squat pillars and bursting with eccentric knobbly accretions which seems almost Aztec in inspiration. More tombs lie east of here in the lower part of the cemetery, where the cupola-crowned Rendić family mausoleum raises a sarcophagus to the skies on solid pillars in a manner reminiscent of Lycian tombs in southern Turkey.

Ironically, Rendić was passed over when the cemetery's grandest sepulchural monument, the **Petrinović Mausoleum**, was commissioned. Ivan Meštrović turned down the job in protest at the way in which Rendić had been snubbed, and the task eventually fell to Meštrović's contemporary **Toma Rosandić**. The resulting structure is a beautiful piece of sepulchral art: a neo-Byzantine dome pokes above the trees, topped by a kneeling angel, his long wings spearing skywards. The four external pillars carry reliefs of mourners, some playing musical instruments, others bearing flowers. Behind the mausoleum is a well-head, also by Rosandić, bearing a relief of bare-backed strongmen gripping rams by their horns.

Practicalities

Ferries from Split arrive at the modern quay just off Supetar's old harbour, roughly opposite the **bus station**. In between lies the **tourist office** at Porat 1 (July & Aug daily 8am–10pm; June & Sept daily 9am–4pm; Oct–May Mon–Fri 9am–1pm; ☎ & fax 021/630-551, *www.supetar.hr*), which is well supplied with tourist bumf. The best places to try for private **rooms** (①–②) are the Supetar Tours/Turist Biro office near the bus station (☎021/631-066, fax 630-022), Atlas (☎021/631-105, fax 631-088) and Brač Tours (☎021/631-238), both on the harbourfront. The *Palute*, at Put pašika 16 (☎021/631-541; ③), is a friendly **bed-and-breakfast** in a modern suburban street just west of the centre. The *Britanida* **hotel**, 200m east of the ferry dock at Hrvatskih velikana 26 (☎021/630-017; ⑤), is a step up in comfort, and the only hotel which remains open year round. Slightly further east, the *Barbura* **campsite** is a cramped site under vine-trellises; *Autocamp Supetar* some 1500m further along the Pučišća road, is larger and more shaded.

The best of the places **to eat** on the harbourfront is *Palute*, at Porat 4 (owned by the same family as the *Palute* bed-and-breakfast), which also has a good choice of fresh grilled fish. *Vinotoka*, just inland from the harbour at Dobova 6, has a wider menu including meat dishes and an extensive choice of local wines. Follow Vlačica uphill behind the beach to find a couple of so-so pizzerias and a **disco**. The clear waters around Supetar are perfect for **diving**. The Dive Center Kaktus (☎ & fax 021/630-421) in the *Kaktus Hotel* complex – one of the packagey places west of town – rents out gear and arranges crash courses from around 200Kn. There are several places renting out **bikes**, including M&B just outside the bus station.

West from Supetar

Fifteen minutes west of Supetar, the village of **SUTIVAN** straggles along the shore behind its rocky beach. Almost all the buildings here are made out of the local marble and, although there are no specific features of interest, it's a pretty enough little settlement of narrow alleys and ancient houses. The **tourist office**, near the bus stop (July–Sept 7am–10pm), can arrange accommodation in private rooms (①).

The road to the southwest of Sutivan heads inland through **LOŽIŠĆA**, a picturesque settlement spread across a steep ravine, with narrow, cobbled alleys hugging the hillside. Thrusting up from the valley floor is a parish church belltower, built in 1920 and sporting a fanciful, onion-domed belfry by Rendić. Beyond here the road crosses the island's empty uplands before twisting down to the sea at **MILNA**. The capital of a short-lived Russian protectorate over Brač during the Napoleonic wars, Milna is a tiny, neat and unremarkable port that curves round one of the island's many deep bays. The old village climbs uphill from the shore, a pleasant enough ensemble of narrow lanes and stone houses on either side of an eighteenth-century parish church and an adjacent ruined mansion that's curiously known as *Anglešćina* after a local myth connecting its construction with an English crusader. The harbourfront has a sprinkling of **cafés** and there's a rocky **beach** a fair walk up along the bay. The **tourist office** (Mon–Sat 8am–1pm & 3–8pm, Sun 8am–noon & 4–8pm; ☎021/636-233, fax 636-122) in the main square has plenty of **rooms** (①–②). Milna is linked to Split by a once-daily **hydrofoil** between July and September.

East from Supetar

Three buses daily make the short detour inland from Supetar to the village of **ŠKRIP**, the oldest continually inhabited settlement on Brač. Founded by the Illyrians, it's now a sleepy nest of stone houses with heavy stone roof tiles that seem in permanent danger of slipping off, while its hilltop position affords views towards the terraced ridges of the Mosor massif on the mainland. The eastern end of the village is the oldest bit, with a ruined sixteenth-century castle overlooking a smaller fortified stone residence which now serves as the **Museum of Brač** (Brački muzej; daily 10am–6pm in theory, if not always in practice; 10Kn), displaying a well-preserved Roman relief of Hercules discovered locally, and sundry nineteenth-century agricultural tools. Outside the museum lie the remains of Iron Age walls and a Roman mausoleum, which local legend says contains a wife or daughter of Diocletian.

Škrip is a restful, rustic place **to stay**: the *Konoba Herkules* hotel (☎ & fax 021/350-098; ②) offers simple but bright rooms in a modern three-storey house built in traditional Brač marble, and also has a **café-restaurant** with cypress-shaded terrace. The sea is a thirty-minute downhill walk from here – either by road to Splitska or by track to Postira, both of which have a few stretches of rocky strand. A better place to swim is **Lovrečina bay**, some 4km east of Postira, where there's a fine shingle beach overlooked by the remains of an early Christian basilica.

Bol and around

Brač's second town, **BOL** has long been the only significant settlement on the island's southern side – an isolated community stranded on the far side of the Vidova gora, the mountain ridge which overlooks this stretch of coast. In the seventh century, its isolation attracted Romans fleeing the Croat invasion; but over the following centuries Bol was attacked repeatedly by pirates, Saracens, Turks and just about anybody else who happened to be passing. Nowadays there's no denying the beauty of Bol's setting, or the charm of its old stone houses. The problem is that it's very small, and is easily swamped by tourists – an influx that grows yearly. But if you can go out of season, or are immune to crowds, it's well worth the trip.

Bol's main attraction is its beach, **Zlatni rat** (Golden Cape), which lies to the west of the centre along the wooded shoreline. Composed of fine shingle and backed by pines, the cape juts out into the sea like an extended finger, changing shape slightly from one year to the next according to the action of seasonal winds. It lies a little over 2km west of the harbour, although the walk there – along a tree-lined promenade – is part of the attraction. There are three large hotels by the promenade – the *Borak*, *Elaphusa* and *Bretanide* – and the cape can get crowded during summer, but the presence of extra beach space on the approach to the cape, and rockier coves beyond it, ensures that there's enough room for everyone.

Bol itself isn't much more than a seafront backed by a couple of rows of old houses, although newer apartment blocks are continually sprouting up on the hillside behind. The main attraction along the seafront is the **Branislav Dešković Gallery**, housed in a former Renaissance town house, which contains a good selection of twentieth-century Croatian art. Most big names get a look in – sculptor Ivan Meštrović, the religiously inspired expressionist Ivan Dulčić and contemporary painter Edo Murtić among them. Further east lies the late fifteenth-century **Dominican monastery** (Dominikanski samostan; daily 10am–noon & 5–8pm; 10Kn), dramatically located high on the promontory just beyond Bol's centre. Its **museum** holds crumbling amphorae, ancient Greek coins from Hvar and Vis, Cretan icons and an imposing Tintoretto *Madonna with Child* from 1563 among its small collection. An archway leads through the accommodation block to the superbly maintained monastery gardens overlooking the sea.

Practicalities

Buses from Supetar stop just west of Bol's harbour, at the far end of which stands the **tourist office** (June–Aug daily 8am–10pm; Sept–May Mon–Fri 8.30am–3pm; ☎021/635-122, fax 635-638, *www.bol.hr*), which has free leaflets and maps of the island – useful if you're walking to Blaca (see p.268). Private **rooms** (①–②) and **apartments** (about 475Kn for a 4-person apartment) can be obtained from Boltours, 100m west of the bus stop at Vladimira Nazora 18 (mid-April to mid-Oct daily 8.30am–9pm with possible afternoon break; ☎021/635-693 or 635-694, fax

635-695, *bol-tours@st.tel.hr*), or from Adria, 100m to the west (daily 9am–9pm; ☎021/635-966, fax 635-977). The Dominican monastery (☎021/635-533 or 635-132; ①) has simple cell-like accommodation, two-person self-catering apartments (③), and a small terrace for tents: it's all a bit spartan, but there's a cheap canteen and the garden is very nice. Of the pricey package **hotels** on the way to Zlatni rat, the *Elaphusa* (☎021/635-222 or 635-288, fax 635-150; ⑥) is reasonably good value for its comfy en-suites. The *Villa Giardino* **pension**, Novi Put 2 (☎021/635-286, fax 635-566; ④), is in a centrally located town house with, as the name suggests, a soothing garden out the back. There are several **campsites** in the new part of town uphill from the centre: *Ranč*, off Domovinskog rata (☎021/635-635), is well signed from the main road into town and is pleasantly situated in an olive grove.

Given that so many guests have half-board arrangements in their hotels, it's not surprising that central Bol has a relatively meagre roster of places **to eat**. *Konoba Gušt*, above the square at Frane Radića 14, has a wide range of fresh fish, traditional Dalmatian dishes (such as a reasonable *pašticada* – beef cooked in a sweet-and-sour sauce), and a cosy interior with agricultural implements hanging from the wall. *Spaghetteria Vidovica*, just uphill from the harbour at Rudina, does a good range of pasta dishes although portions are on the dainty side, and there are numerous places offering pizzas and grills along the waterfront.

There are several cafés and ice-cream parlours along the front, and a clutch of trendier bars just inland along Rudina: *Aquarius*, at no. 26, has a nice terrace overlooking the sea, while *Marinero*, at no. 46, has a larger tree-shaded terrace in a triangular old-town square. If you don't fancy the easy-listening crooners who seem to be on permanent duty in Bol's hotels, the best nightlife on offer is at the *Faces* **disco**, a circular concrete structure at the northern entrance to the town owned by footballer Igor Štimac. Croatian pop stars perform here over the summer.

There are a couple of **windsurfing** centres on the shore west of town, on the way to Zlatni rat, offering board rental (about 250Kn per day) and a range of courses (about 600Kn for eight hours). Big Blue (☎ & fax 021/635-614), next to the tourist office at Podan Glavice 2 and in front of the *Hotel Borak*, is one of the most reliable. Boltours (see p.267) and Big Blue also rent out **mountain bikes** (from 70Kn a day).

Around Bol

Looming over Zlatni rat to the north is the 780m peak of **Vidova gora**, the highest point on any Adriatic island. It's accessible via an asphalt road which leaves the Supetar–Bol road just south of the village of Nerežišća, and there's also a marked walking trail (2hr each way) from the centre of Bol, which heads uphill from the central parish church and crosses the main road out of town before climbing northwest onto the ridge. There's a small tavern at the summit which sometimes serves roast lamb during summer, but most people come simply to savour the view, which encompasses Zlatni rat and Bol down to the left, with the islands of Vis and Hvar visible further out.

Tucked away at the head of a valley on the western flanks of the Vidova gora is the **Hermitage of Blaca** (Pustinja Blaca; in theory Tues–Sun 8am–5pm, but check in the tourist office at Bol or Supetar as times can vary; 20Kn), about 12km out of Bol. You can walk there by following the road (which later degenerates into a track) west from Bol, passing the village of Murvica before heading inland at Blaca bay. The route is easy to follow and takes about three hours each way – a worthwhile but unshaded walk along a rugged hillside with the sea far below. You can cut out some of the effort by taking a boat trip (advertised in Bol harbour in high season) to Blaca bay and continuing from there. If you're driving, take the turn-off for Vidova gora midway between Supetar and Bol, then turn right after about 2km onto the signed gravel track for Blaca (just about passable for cars, but rough on the suspension). From the end of the track, walk along the path which heads downhill past deserted hamlets before arriving at the monastery after about forty minutes.

The hermitage was founded in 1588 by monks fleeing the Turks; the last resident – Niko Miličević, an enthusiastic astronomer who left all sorts of bits and bobs, including an assortment of old clocks and a stock of lithographs by Poussin – occupied the hermitage in the 1930s. You can also look around the ascetic living quarters and the kitchen, with its forest of blackened iron utensils surrounding an open hearth. But the principal attraction is the setting, with the simple buildings hugging the sides of a narrow, scrub-covered ravine. Islanders from all over Brač attend the **pilgrimage** to Blaca on the first Saturday after Assumption (Aug 15).

Hvar

HVAR is one of the most hyped of all the Yugoslav islands. People talk of its verdant colour, fragrant air and mild climate, and at one time local hoteliers even had enough faith in the weather to offer a money-back guarantee if the temperature ever dropped below zero. And Hvar is undeniably beautiful – a slim, green slice of land punctured by jagged inlets and a steep central ridge streaked with the long grey lines of limestone spoil heaps built up over the centuries by farmers attempting to carve out patches of cultivable land. The island's main crop is lavender, which was introduced in the 1930s and covers the island in a spongy grey-blue cloak every spring, before finding its way onto souvenir stalls across the island.

Intensively but tastefully developed as a tourist resort, the island's capital, **Hvar Town**, is one of the Adriatic's most bewitching – and best preserved – historic towns, and is a good base from which to explore the rest of the island, which is

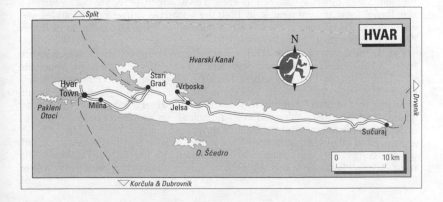

fairly low-key in comparison. Buses either take the old road across the central ridge, or speed through the recently built tunnel to reach the northern side of the island, where **Stari Grad** and **Vrboska** boast some good beaches, old stone houses and an unhurried, village feel. **Jelsa**, further east, can't quite compete with its two neighbours in terms of rustic charm, but has more accommodation than Vrboska, which is only a forty-minute walk away. East of Jelsa, the island narrows to a long, thin mountainous strip of land that extends all the way to isolated **Sućuraj**, which is linked to the mainland by regular ferries, although there's virtually no public transport between here and the rest of the island.

The daily Split–Vela Luka–Lastovo **ferry** stops at Hvar Town six days a week; on the remaining day (currently Tues), the Split–Vis ferry calls in instead (but note that only foot passengers can get off in Hvar Town). There are also **hydrofoils** to Hvar Town from Split and Vis between mid-May and mid-September, while additional ferries run between Split and Stari Grad (3–5 daily). Local buses meet the boats for onward transportation to the centre of Stari Grad, Hvar Town or Jelsa. The main **coastal ferry** (daily in summer) also stops at Stari Grad, connecting the island with Split and points to Rijeka in the north, Korčula and Dubrovnik to the south. During summer there are also ferries from **Ancona** in Italy to Stari Grad. You can also reach the island by ferry from Drvenik (see p.300) on the mainland to Sućuraj, at the eastern end of the island, four to nine times daily – though the poor bus connections mean that this approach is only really of use if you're travelling by car. Lastly, throughout the season there's a daily **catamaran** service from Jelsa to Split via Bol on Brač.

Travelling on from the island, queues for car ferries build up fast in summer, so arrive early. Advance reservations can be made at the Jadrolinija office on the quayside in Hvar Town. Tickets for hydrofoils and catamarans can be purchased on board, although local travel agents sometimes sell them in advance.

Some history

Around 385 BC, the Greeks of Paros in Asia Minor established a colony on Hvar, naming it **Pharos** (present day Stari Grad). After a period of Roman then Byzantine control, the island was thoroughly Slavicized in the eighth century, when it was overrun by the **Narentani**, a Croatian tribe from the Neretva delta. The new arrivals couldn't pronounce the name Pharos, so the place became **Hvar** instead. The early Middle Ages saw power shifting away from Stari Grad towards the settlement nowadays known as Hvar Town, which probably began life as a safe haven for mainland pirates. In 1240 the Venetians drove out the pirates and encouraged the citizens of Stari Grad to relocate to Hvar Town, due to its better defensive properties.

For the next two centuries Hvar was a self-governing commune which swore fealty to Venetian, Hungarian and Bosnian rulers at different times. The Venetians returned to stay in 1420 and ushered in a period of urban and cultural efflorescence. The aristocracy's wealth still came from the estates located on the fertile plain just east of Stari Grad, but the ascendancy of Hvar Town was confirmed by a rule stipulating that nobles had to spend at least six months of the year there in order to qualify for seats on the island's governing council.

As in most other Dalmatian towns, the nobles of Hvar had succeeded in excluding the commoners from municipal government by the fifteenth century. The most serious challenge to this oligarchical state of affairs came with the **revolt of**

1510 led by **Matija Ivanić**, a representative of the non-noble shipowners and merchants who felt that real wealth and power had been denied to them. The revolt got off to a bad start when a priest in Hvar Town claimed that the crucifix on which the plotters had sworn an oath had begun to sweat blood in a divine warning of the violence to come. The townsfolk lost their enthusiasm for the revolt but it took off elsewhere on the island, especially around Vrbanj, Vrboska and Jelsa. Ivanić himself led a raid on Hvar Town, sacking the houses of the nobles and killing many of the occupants, and Hvar's surviving aristocrats fled to the mainland and awaited Venetian intervention.

Forces sent by the republic initially calmed things down until Venetian emissary Sebastiano Giustignan proposed banishing all rebel leaders, causing another upsurge in violence. Giustignan's troops (mostly Croats from the mainland) were an unruly lot, and looted Vrboska before being driven out of the town in August 1512. An attempt to regain Jelsa was similarly defeated in September. In control of the bulk of the island for two years, Ivanić led another attack on Hvar Town in August 1514, massacring those noble families who had returned. Fearful that the revolt might spread to other Dalmatian cities, the Venetians this time reacted with swift effectiveness, defeating the rebels and hanging their leaders from the masts of their galleys. Ivanić himself escaped, dying in exile in Rome.

Despite all this, sixteenth-century Hvar went on to become one of the key centres of the Croatian Renaissance, with poets like **Hanibal Lucić** and **Petar Hektorović** (see box on p.277) cultivating intellectual links with Dubrovnik and penning works which were to have a profound influence on future generations. This golden age was interrupted in 1571, when the notorious corsair **Uluz Ali** (see box on p.273) sacked Hvar Town on behalf of the Turks and reduced it to smouldering rubble. Rebuilt from scratch, the town soon reassumed its importance as an entrepot on the east–west trade routes. Later, the movement of trade to the west and the arrival of steamships becalmed Hvar Town, which drifted into quiet obscurity until the tourists arrived in the late nineteenth century – largely due to the efforts of the Hvar Hygienic Society, founded in 1868 by locals eager to promote the island as a health retreat. The first ever guide book to the town, published in Vienna in 1903, promoted it as "Austria's Madeira", and it has been one of Dalmatia's most stylish resorts ever since.

Hvar Town

The best view of **HVAR TOWN** is from the sea, with its grainy-white and brown scatter of buildings following the contours of the bay, and the green splashes of palms and pines pushing into every crack and cranny. The harbour is alive with a constant hum of activity, whether it be the Rijeka ferry lumbering into port, hydrofoils buzzing insect-like around the bay, or tiny water taxis ferrying people to bathe on the nearby Pakleni islands. Once you're on terra firma, central Hvar reveals itself as a medieval town full of pedestrianized alleys overlooked by ancient stone houses, providing an elegant backdrop to the main leisure activity: lounging around in cafés and watching the crowds as they shuffle round the harbour. After Dubrovnik, Hvar is probably the most fashionable of the Adriatic resorts among the Croats themselves, and there's something of southern France in the chic *korzo* that engulfs the town at dusk.

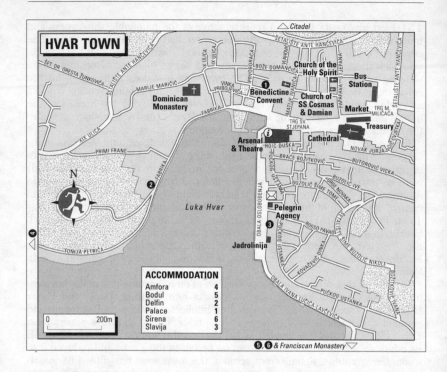

Arrival, information and accommodation

Ferries dock on the eastern side of Hvar Town's bay on Obala oslobođenja. From here, it's a couple of hundred metres to the **tourist office** (July & Aug daily 9am–10pm; June & Sept Mon–Sat 8am–1pm & 4–9pm, Sun 10am–noon & 6–8pm; Oct–May Mon–Sat 8am–1pm; ☎ & fax 021/741-059, *www.hvar.hr*), on the corner of the main square, Trg svetog Stjepana. The **bus station** is a few steps east of the main square on Trg M. Miličića. Private **rooms** (①) and **apartments** (400–475Kn for 4 people) are available from the Mengola agency on the waterfront, diagonally opposite the tourist office (Mon–Sat 9am–noon & 5–8.30pm, Sun 9–11am & 6.30–8.30pm; ☎ & fax 021/742-099), or from Pelegrin Tours, near the ferry dock (Mon–Sat 8.30am–12.30pm & 6–9pm, Sun 6–8pm; ☎ & fax 021/742-250).

Hvar Town is over-full of characterless package **hotels**, all belonging to the Sunčani Hvar conglomerate (central reservations ☎021/741-005 or 741-956, fax 742-014). None is particularly cheap unless you book as part of a package, and they fill up quickly in July and August. Least expensive are the bland but tolerable *Bodul* (④) and *Sirena* (④), both southeast of the centre along the path which leads from the ferry dock past the Franciscan monastery, while the *Delfin*, over on the western side of the harbour (☎021/741-168; ⑤), is also reasonable. Right on the ferry dock, the *Slavija* (☎021/741-820 or 741-840, fax 741-147; ④, ⑤ with sea view) is a good mid-range choice, an unassuming three-floor building with homely en-suites. Best of the bunch in terms of comfort and amenities are the monstrously proportioned, 700-bed *Amfora* (⑤), west of town on the Veneranda headland, which has an indoor pool and gym, and the more sedate *Palace* (⑥) on the harbourfront, which still preserves something of its turn-of-the-century charm. The town's **campsite** is currently closed following a forest fire; the nearest alternatives are in Stari Grad (see p.278) or Jelsa (see p.278).

Hvar's **Jadrolinija** office (daily 7am–1pm & 2–9pm) is on the ferry dock. There's an ATM just outside.

The Town

At the centre of the town is Trg svetog Stjepana, a long, rectangular main square which meets the sea at the so-called **Mandrač**, the balustraded inner harbour used for mooring small boats. Dominating the square's southwestern corner is the arcaded bulk of the seventeenth-century Venetian **Arsenal**, with an arched ground floor into which war galleys were once hauled for repairs. The upper storey of the arsenal was adapted in 1612 to house the town **Theatre** (kazalište; summer daily 9am–1pm & 8–10pm; winter daily 11am–noon; 10Kn), the oldest in Croatia and one of the first in Europe. It was built to assuage the distrust between nobles and commoners which had continued since the Ivanić rebellion, since the theatre was a civic amenity which all classes could enjoy together. The gaily painted interior, complete with two tiers of boxes, dates from the early 1800s, when locals revived and renovated the theatre after a period of neglect. The auditorium is entered through a small picture gallery (same times), which has a modest collection of twentieth-century Croatian work.

THE CATHEDRAL AND TREASURY

Towering over the eastern end of the square is the trefoil facade of **St Stephen's Cathedral** (Katedrala sveti Stjepan; no fixed opening hours – try mornings), a sixteenth-century construction whose spindly four-storey campanile employs the

---

ULUZ ALI AND THE RAID ON HVAR

Uluz Ali was born Luca Galeni in Calabria in 1508. Captured by the Ottoman Turks off Naples, he became a galley slave, until conversion to Islam won him his freedom. He made his name as a corsair, raiding Mediterranean shipping from the safety of Ottoman-controlled North Africa, was appointed *bey* (viceroy) of Algiers in 1568 and captured the city of Tunis from the Spanish the following year. In 1571, with the maritime forces of the **Holy League** (Austria, Venice and Spain) massing to take on the Ottoman navy in the eastern Mediterranean, Uluz Ali assembled a fleet of eighty ships to mount a diversionary attack on Venetian possessions in the Adriatic. After an unsuccessful raid on Korčula he arrived off Hvar Town on August 17. The population fled to the safety of their hilltop citadel and could only watch helplessly as Ali's men torched their dwellings below. The raiders meted out similar punishment to Stari Grad, Jelsa and Vrboska before withdrawing to rejoin the rest of the Ottoman fleet.

In an important postscript to the raid, the ships of the Holy League eventually caught up with the Ottomans at **Lepanto**, near Corfu, on October 7. The Turkish fleet was scattered, but it was something of a Pyrrhic victory for the Western powers. The Holy League began to fragment and the Venetians, weakened by their losses, had to give up Cyprus to the Turks in order to secure peace.

typical Venetian device of having one window on the first floor, two windows on the second, and so on up to the top. The interior is fairly unremarkable save for two notable artworks: a Venetian *Madonna and Child* (on the fourth altar on the right), a Byzantine-influenced, icon-like image painted in around 1220, which exudes a spiritual calm quite different from the tortured Baroque altarpieces nearby; and a touching fifteenth-century Pietà by Spanish artist Juan Boschetus (in the opposite – south – aisle), although its power is somewhat lessened by being framed within a larger and later work.

Immediately next door to the cathedral, the **Bishop's Treasury** (*riznica*; summer daily 9am–noon & 5–7pm; winter 10am–noon; 10Kn) houses a small but fine selection of chalices, reliquaries and embroidery. Look out for a nicely worked sixteenth-century bishop's crozier, carved into the shape of a serpent encrusted with saints and embossed with a figure of the Virgin, attended by Moses and an archangel.

NORTH TO THE CITADEL

The rest of the old town backs away north from the square in an elegant confusion of twisting lanes and alleys hiding a series of understated architectural gems. Just uphill from the cathedral, the diminutive **Church of the Holy Spirit** (Crkva svetog Duha) has a small but striking Romanesque relief of God the Creator above the portal, while just down the steps from here the **Church of SS Cosmas and Damian** (Crkva svetog Kozme i Damjana) sports a fine barrel-vaulted roof. West of here lies the main "street" in this quarter of town – actually more a flight of steps – the steep Matije Ivanića. The striking roofless **palace** at its southern end – a grey shell punctuated by delicately carved Gothic windows – is popularly ascribed to the Hektorović family, but was more likely commissioned by another noble family, the Užičić, in 1463, and never finished. Behind it, the **Leporini Palace** is identifiable by a carving of a rabbit – the family emblem – halfway up the wall. Further up Ivanića lies the **Benedictine convent** (Benediktinski samostan; usually Mon–Sat 4.30–6pm, but check at the tourist office; 10Kn), founded by the daughter-in-law of the sixteenth-century Hvar poet Hanibal Lucić, which occupies the poet's former town house. Inside there's a small display of devotional paintings, and lace made by the nuns.

Head to the top of Ivanića to find the path which zigzags its way up an agave-covered hillside to the **Citadel** (Kaštil; June–Sept 9am–7pm; 10Kn), built by the Venetians in the 1550s and strengthened by the Austrians three centuries later. There's a marine archeology collection in one of the halls, with an attractively presented display of amphorae and other sediment-encrusted Greco-Roman drinking vessels, although the real attraction is the view from the citadel's ramparts. Largely intact stretches of defensive wall plunge down the hillside towards the terracotta roofs of Hvar Town below, while beyond stretch the deep green humps of the Pakleni islands just offshore and the bulky grey form of Vis further out to the southwest.

THE DOMINICAN MONASTERY

A couple of hundred metres west of Trg svetog Stjepana, slightly set back from the shoreline, are the remains of a **Dominican monastery** (you can see its surviving bell-tower from the citadel), an important centre of religious and political life until it was expropriated by French administrators in 1811 and allowed to fall into ruin. It was here in 1525 that Friar **Vinko Pribojević** famously addressed the

Hvar nobility with his paper *De origine successibisque slavorum* (Of the Origin and History of the Slavs), a landmark text in the development of Croatian national self-consciousness. Pribojević floated the not unreasonable idea that all Slavs were ethnically related, but added the improbable hypothesis that they had their origins in Dalmatia, from where the Croatian brothers Čeh, Leh and Rus set out to found the Czech, Polish and Russian nations respectively. The tale of the three brothers is a common theme in Slavic folklore: it crops up in Poland and Russia as well as in the Croatian Zagorje town of Krapina. Pribojević's oration inspired Šime Dujmović's Art Nouveau-ish monument to Slav freedom which, dismantled by the Italians during World War II and never restored, lies around in fragments in a corner of the monastery courtyard.

The surviving apse of the monastery church now holds a small **archeology collection** (arheološka zbirka, usually open mornings in summer, but check at the tourist office; 10Kn), with exhibits ranging from prehistoric through to Roman times, including flint arrows and axe-heads from two of the island's caves – the Grapčeva and Markova – where the island's first Neolithic inhabitants holed up, and ceramics from the late Neolithic Hvar Culture, including an anthropomorphic four-legged brazier, the most arresting item in an unassuming collection.

THE FRANCISCAN MONASTERY

Occupying a headland just southeast of Hvar Town's ferry dock is the **Franciscan monastery** (Franjevački samostan; Mon–Fri 9am–noon & 4–6pm; 10Kn), founded in 1461 by a Venetian sea captain in thanks for deliverance from shipwreck. There's a small collection of paintings in the former refectory, including a melodramatic, near life-size seventeenth-century *Last Supper* by Matteo Ingoli of Ravenna, which covers almost the entire back wall, though in terms of expressive power it's outdone by the smaller and more tranquil *Mystical Wedding of St Catherine* painted by a follower of Blaž Jurjev of Trogir in around 1430.

Next door is the pleasingly simple monastic **church**, with beautifully carved choirstalls and a fanciful partition of 1583 (built to separate the commoners from the nobility), decorated with six animated scenes of the Passion by Martin Benetović, a local seventeenth-century painter, and a brace of less expressive polyptychs by Francesco da Santacroce. Look out for the extravagant dragon candle-holders that push out above the panel detail below. The floor is paved with gravestones, including that of poet and playwright Hanibal Lucić by the altar, identifiable by the fleur-de-lys and dove's wing of the family crest. In the small side-chapel, there's a moving *Christ on the Cross* by Leandro Bassano.

THE PAKLENI OTOCI

There are three kilometres of rock and concrete **beaches** east of Hvar Town in front of the big hotels, although if you want to swim it's better to head for the **Pakleni otoci** ("Islands of Hell"), a chain of eleven wooded islands just to the west of town, easily reached by water taxi from the harbour (10–20Kn each way). Only three of the islands have any facilities, and even then only a few simple bars and restaurants: **Jerolim**, a naturist island, is the nearest; the others are **Marinkovac** (with two popular beaches, Ždrilca on the northern side and U Stipanska on the south) and **Sveti Klement**, the largest of the Pakleni, with a sandy beach at Palmižana. A smaller number of water taxis serve the other islands, but you'll need to take your own food and drink.

Eating and drinking

There are dozens of places to eat in Hvar Town, none of them too expensive. For a daytime **snack**, the *Grommit* café, between the ferry dock and the tourist office on Obala oslobođenja, has the widest choice of pastries and cakes. Among the **restaurants**, the inexpensive *Creperie Alviž*, opposite the bus station, serves both savoury and sweet pancakes alongside a decent vegetarian lasagne and the usual meat and fish grills, all in a shady courtyard. The equally good-value *Devi*, just behind the Arsenal on the corner of Duška Roić and Pučkog ustanka, offers a wide range of pasta (including plenty of seafood choices) served up on long wooden tables out on the street; while *Leonardo*, on Obala oslobođenja on the harbour, is the most consistent of the pizzerias. For a slap-up seafood feast there are few places better than *Macondo*, signposted up a backstreet uphill from the main square to the north (head up Matije Ivanića and take the second right); their *škampi buzzara* (unpeeled prawns in wine sauce) is excellent.

For **drinking**, the cafés around the main square are packed from mid-morning onwards. Trade thins out for a few hours during the hottest part of the day, until the crowds return for the evening *korzo*. There are also several chic bars on the harbourside road which runs west of here for evening drinking; alternatively, try the laidback and intimate *Jazz*, on Pučkog ustanka in the tangle of streets to the south of the main square, or the brasher *Carpe Diem*, just beyond the *Hotel Slavia* on the ferry dock, a popular meeting place for the young and fashionable, which stays open late into the night. *Fortica*, in the Citadel above town, is the best of the **clubs**.

Stari Grad

Twenty kilometres east across the mountains, **STARI GRAD** is a popular and busy resort, though more laidback than Hvar Town, straggling along the side of a deep bay. The old part of Stari Grad has been pleasantly renovated, and backs onto the main street as it twists its way along the waterside. Just back from the water is Stari Grad's most famous sight, the **Tvrdalj** (June–Sept daily 9.30am–12.30pm & 4.30–7.30pm; 10Kn), the summer house and walled garden of the sixteenth-century poet and aristocrat Petar Hektorović (see box opposite). Those expecting a stately home will be disappointed: the original crenellated structure disappeared behind the present plain facade in the nineteenth century, and Hektorović's extensive gardens – which once featured clipped rows of box and medicinal herbs, as well as cypresses and oleanders sent by fellow poet Mavro Vetranović of Dubrovnik – have now been largely divided up into allotments, although a portion has been tidied up and returned to its former glories. It's still a remarkably restful location, however, built around a central cloister with a turquoise pond fed with sea water and packed with mullet. Hektorović littered the place with inscriptions (carved round the pond and on the walls of the house in Latin, Italian and Croatian) to encourage contemplation: "Neither riches nor fame, beauty nor age can save you from Death" is one characteristically cheerful effusion.

The narrow streets behind the Tvrdalj are as atmospheric as anywhere in the Adriatic: a warren of low stone houses decked in windowboxes, with alleyways suddenly opening out onto small squares. The lane to the right of the Tvrdalj as you face it leads up to the **Bianchini Palace** (Palača Biankini; June–Sept daily

PETAR HEKTOROVIĆ AND THE TVRDALJ

Renaissance poet and Hvar noble **Petar Hektorović** (1487–1572) is primarily remembered for his *Ribanje i ribarsko prigovaranje* (Fishing and Fishermen's Conversations), the first work of autobiographical realism in Croatian literature. Written in 1556, when he was already an old man, the 1680-line poem was inspired by a three-day boat trip to Brač and Šolta in the company of two local fishermen, Paskoje and Nikola, who despite being commoners are accorded a dignity which was rare for the literature of the period. Hektorović had lived through the Ivanić rebellion of the early sixteenth century, and perhaps intended *Ribanje* as a message to his fellow aristocrats – treat the lower orders with a bit of humanity, and the bonds of society will hold.

This sense of *noblesse oblige* also underpinned Hektorović's plans for the **Tvrdalj**, which he began in 1514 and carried on building for the rest of his life. As well as a place of repose for himself, it was intended to be a fortified refuge for the locals in time of attack – a self-sufficient ark which would provide food from its garden and fresh fish from the mullet pond. Hektorović's typically Renaissance fondness for order and balance was reflected in the symbolic inclusion of a pigeon loft in the main tower, to emphasize the point that the Tvrdalj was a refuge for creatures of the sky as well as the sea and earth. The house was built in simple unadorned style, both because Hektorović had a taste for rusticity and because he didn't want to provoke the locals with a display of lordly luxury. Local Venetian commanders actually sanctioned the diversion of manpower resources from Hvar Town to assist Hektorović in its construction, since it freed them from the responsibility of defending the people of Stari Grad from pirates. The Tvrdalj never fulfilled its intended purpose: it was damaged during Uluz Ali's raid of 1571, and Hektorović died the following year before finishing the thing off, though it was renovated and preserved by Hektorović's descendants until the nineteenth century, when new owners arrived and its shape was radically changed. Ironically, the one thing which most people find so memorable about the Tvrdalj – the restful arched ambulatory surrounding the fishpond – was added by the Niseteo family in 1834.

9.30am–12.30pm & 4.30–7.30pm; 10Kn), where there's a display of finds from ancient Pharos, including pottery fragments, and a *louterion* – a stone basin used for washing before a ceremony or sacrifice. To the left of the Tvrdalj a lane leads up to the **Dominican monastery**, a fifteenth-century foundation half-heartedly fortified with the addition of a single sturdy turret after Uluz Ali's attack of 1571. Rooms off the cloister house a **museum** (Mon–Fri 10am–noon; 10Kn), which houses an absorbing collection of Greek gravestones from Pharos, Creto-Venetian icons and a *Deposition* by Tintoretto. According to local tradition, the figures of Joseph of Arimathea, Mary Magdalene and the young man leaning over Christ's body in the picture are portraits of Hektorović, his granddaughter Julija, and her husband Antun Lucić – although more sober analysts have pointed out that many of the stock figures in the artist's paintings possess similar faces. There's also a small display of Hektorović's effects, including a 1532 edition of Petrarch's *Sonnets* and a copy of Polybius's *Histories*.

In the fields immediately south of the monastery, the Chapel of St Nicholas (Crkvica sveti Nikole) was the scene of an extraordinary demonstration of religiosity in 1554, when the hermit **Lukrecija of Brač** chose to be walled into a small side-room, where she lived on bread and water until her death 35 years later. Heading east from the monastery and then turning left back towards the town centre brings you past **St John's Church** (Crkva svetog Ivana), a twelfth-century Romanesque church with some sixth-century mosaics inside, and **St Stephen's Church** (Crkva svetog Stjepana), a plain, weatherbeaten example of Dalmatian Baroque with a fine Venetian campanile. Embedded in a wall opposite the church is a Roman-era gravestone relief of Winged Eros leaning nonchalantly on an upside-down torch – a classic symbol of death.

There are rock and concrete **beaches** on the northern side of the bay in front of the hotels, from where a path carries on beyond the *Arkada* mega-hotel to a much less sanitized area of rocks backed by pines.

Practicalities

Buses from the ferry terminal (4km west of town) and from Hvar Town drop you right on the harbour; walk 500m along the eastern side to reach the **tourist office** on the harbourfront (July & Aug daily 8am–10pm; Sept–June Mon–Fri 8am–2pm, Sat 10am–noon; ☎ & fax 021/765-763). The Mistral agency (Mon–Sat 9am–noon & 5–8.30pm, Sun 7–9pm; ☎021/765-281), next to the bus stop, can arrange accommodation in cheap private **rooms** (①). Stari Grad's **hotels** are grouped around the north side of the bay: the *Helios* and *St Roko* (both ☎021/765-555 or 765-565, fax 765-128; ③) are plain but comfortable; the *Arkada* (same numbers; ④) is slightly plusher, and has an indoor pool. **Autocamp** *Jurjevac* occupies a partly shaded site in what used to be the town park; it's on the south side of town beyond the tourist office.

The handiest of the town's **restaurants** are the *Pizzeria San Marino* next to the Tvrdalj; and the *Konoba Herakleia* on Vagonj, which has the customary range of Dalmatian seafood dishes.

Jelsa and Vrboska

Ten kilometres east of Stari Grad, the tiny port and fishing village of **JELSA** sits prettily by a wooded bay. Tucked away behind a nineteenth-century waterfront, the old quarter climbs up the hill, a maze of ancient alleys and lanes; the two big hotels on either side of the bay, fronted by concrete bathing platforms, seem oddly out of place. Just off the quayside is the charming octagonal sixteenth-century **Chapel of St John** (Crkva svetog Ivana), squeezed into one of the old squares and overhung by the balconies of the surrounding Renaissance buildings. Up from here is the town's fortified **parish church**, which managed to resist Uluz Ali's attack of 1571, though it's hard to make out the original design as the facade and bell-tower were added in the nineteenth century. Opening times are unpredictable – if you do manage to get in, look out for the wooden Gothic statue of the Madonna (brought here from the mainland in 1539 to keep it safe from the Ottomans) on the high altar. Avoid the crowded **beaches** by taking a taxi boat to the Glavica peninsula near Vrboska (see opposite).

Buses stop about 300m inland from the harbour, where you'll find a **tourist office** on the western side (June–Sept Mon–Sat 8.30am–12.30pm & 6.30–8.30pm, Sun 9am–noon; Oct–May Mon–Fri 9am–noon; ☎021/761-017). Virtually next door, the OSS and Atlas agencies can both arrange accommodation in private **rooms** (①). There's a **campsite**, the *Mina* (☎021/761-210, fax 761-227), on a promontory overlooking the sea at the eastern end of town.

Vrboska

The sleepy little village of **VRBOSKA** strings along the side of another of the island's deep bays, about 4km from Jelsa and easily reached by bus or water taxi, or by following the coastal path. The bus stop is on the edge of the old village, five minutes' walk along the quayside from the **tourist office** (daily 8am–1pm & 6.30–8pm, Sun 10am–noon & 6.30–8pm; ☎021/744-137), which has a small cache of **rooms** (①).

The two sides of Vrboska, on either side of the inlet, are joined by three small and picturesque bridges. Perched above the quayside is the unusual, fortified **St Mary's Church** (Crkva svete Marije; variable times, try Mon–Sat mornings), dating from 1580, which was extensively fortified to resist attacks from pirates and the Turks. The result is a high, unadorned structure with a crenellated tower on the southeast corner, and a hefty bastion on the northwest – a protruding, angular structure that looks like the prow of a beached dreadnought. The interior is partly paved with grave slabs and from the sacristy you can get onto the roof for a view of the town below. A couple of minutes away, the Baroque **St Lawrence's Church** (Crkva sveti Lovrinac) has a small collection of artworks, including a stagy-looking polyptych depicting St Lawrence flanked by John the Baptist and St Nicholas on the high altar, nowadays attributed to Paolo Veronese, although local tradition ascribes it to Titian. To the right, there's a *Madonna of the Rosary* by Leandro Bassano.

There's a series of **beaches**, including a couple of naturist ones, on the Glavica peninsula 2km northeast of town. You can find quieter spots by walking north from Vrboska, straight over Kaštilac hill (where there's a ruined tower), to the isolated bays of Hvar's north coast. From here there's a great view of the southern flanks of Brač and, away in the distance, the stark ridge of Mount Biokovo on the mainland.

Vis

A compact hump rearing dramatically out of the sea, **VIS** is situated further offshore than any of Croatia's other inhabited Adriatic islands. Closed to foreigners for military reasons until 1989, the island has never been overrun by tourists, although young Croatians have fallen in love with the place over the last decade, drawn by its wild mountainous scenery, some interesting historical relics and two good-looking small towns – **Vis Town** and **Komiža**. Komiža is the obvious base camp for trips to the islet of **Biševo**, site of one of Croatia's most famous natural wonders, the **Blue Cave**. The island is also famous for a brace of fine local wines – the white Vugava and the red Viški plavac – and the anchovy-flavoured bread bun (called *viška pogača* or *komiška pogača* depending on which town you're staying in), which is sold by local bakeries and cafés.

Vis's history has been shaped by its strategic position on the sea approaches to central Dalmatia. The **Greeks** settled here in the fourth century BC, choosing the island as a base because of its convenience as a stepping-stone between the eastern and western shores of the Adriatic and founding **Issa** on the site of present-day Vis Town. When the fall of Venice in 1797 opened up the Adriatic to the competing navies of France, Britain, Russia and Austria, Vis was again much fought over, eventually falling under the control of the **British**, who fortified the harbour and founded the

Vis Cricket Club. The British defeated Napoleon's navy off Vis in 1811, and the **Austrians** – who inherited the island from the British in 1815 – brushed aside Italian maritime ambitions in another big sea battle here in 1866. Vis's position was once more exploited during World War II (see box on p.283), when Josip Broz **Tito**'s Partisan movement was briefly based here. After the war, the island was heavily garrisoned and used for military training; not until the summer of 1989 was it finally opened up to foreigners. Militarization of the island, and the decline of traditional industries like fishing, encouraged successive waves of **emigration**: the island had 10,000 inhabitants before World War II; it now has fewer than 3000. According to local estimates, there are ten times more Komiža families living in San Pedro, California, than in the town itself.

Ferries run year round between Split and Vis Town (1–2 daily; 2hr 30min), though in winter the trip can get mighty rough. There are also seasonal ferries from Ancona in Italy (2 weekly; mid-July to late Aug) and **hydrofoils** from Split and Hvar Town (daily mid-May to mid-Sept) and Pescara in Italy (daily late June to late Sept).

Vis Town

VIS TOWN's sedate arc of grey-brown houses stretches around a deeply indented bay, above which looms a steep escarpment covered with the remains of abandoned agricultural terraces. There's not much of ancient Issa to be seen apart from a few chunks of unadorned masonry – most of which have been absorbed into the drystone walls of local gardeners – on the hills above town.

The most attractive parts of town are east of the ferry landing (to the right as you get off the boat). A five-minute walk along the front brings you to the venerable **Church of Our Lady** (Gospa od Spilica), a squat sixteenth-century structure harbouring a *Madonna and Saints* by Girolamo da Santacroce, just beyond which is the Austrian defensive bastion known as Gospina baterija (Our Lady's Battery). A barrack block at the rear of the bastion has been transformed into the **Town Museum** (Gradski muzej; Tues–Sun 9am–1pm & 5–7pm; 10Kn), a small but well-organized collection mixing Greco-Roman finds with turn-of-the-century wine presses and domestic furniture. The star exhibit is the bronze head of a Greek goddess, possibly Aphrodite, from the fourth century BC, which is claimed to be by a student of Praxiteles, although only a replica is on display – the original is locked up in the town vaults.

Another 500m east along the seafront lies the suburb of **Kut** (literally "quiet corner" or "hideaway"), a largely sixteenth-century tangle of narrow cobbled streets overlooked by the summer houses built by the nobility of Hvar. There are no specific buildings that you can visit, although the stone balconies and staircases give the place an undeniably aristocratic air. Kut's **St Cyprian's Church** (Crkva sveti Ciprijan) squats beneath a campanile adorned with unusual sun and rose motifs. There's a fine wooden ceiling inside, although it's difficult to gain access outside mass times.

Heading west around the bay from the landing stage soon brings you to a small peninsula jutting out into the bay, from which the campanile of the **Franciscan monastery** (Franjevački samostan) rises gracefully alongside a huddle of cypresses. This sixteenth-century foundation was built on the remains of a Roman theatre, and some of its interior walls follow the curving lines of the original spectator stands, although you can't get inside to have a look. The adjacent graveyard is similar to the one in Supetar (see p.265) and features some elegant nineteenth-century funerary sculpture, including a particularly fine monument by Supetar sculptor Ivan Rendić – an 1899 statue of a maiden stooping over a cross, which can be seen adorning the grave of a certain Toma Bradanović.

The town's small pebbly **beach** is just beyond the monastery, in front of the *Hotel Issa*. Continue past the hotel for twenty minutes then turn left uphill to reach **Fort Wellington**, a ruined white tower constructed by the British, which crowns a blustery ridge providing fine views back towards Vis Town to the south, or out towards the island of Hvar over to the northwest. Carry on walking to the tip of the bay to reach the now derelict **King George III** fortress, built in 1813.

Practicalities

Just to the right of the ferry dock as you step off the boat, Vis's **tourist office** (summer Mon–Sat 8am–1pm & 4–8pm, Sun 8am–1pm; winter Mon–Fri 9am–1pm; ☎ & fax 021/711-144, *www.tz-vis.hr*) is a mine of local information and can help with directions to out-of-town beaches, which might be quieter than the ones here or in Komiža. Most ferries are met by local touts offering private accommodation, although a more reliable source of **rooms** (①) is the Darlić & Darlić agency directly opposite the ferry dock at Riva svete Mikule 13 (☎ & fax 021/713-760 or 713-466).

The best of the town's **hotels** is the stately, turn-of-the-century *Tamaris*, on the waterfront at Šetalište Apolonija Zanelle 5, east of the ferry dock (☎021/711-350, fax 711-349; ④), which has cosy en-suites with TV, air con and squeaky parquet floors, as well as a handful of self-catering attic apartments for 700Kn for two or three people. The smaller, pension-like *Paula*, Petra Hektorovića 2 (☎021/711-362, *paula-hotel@st.tel.hr*; ③), offers smart modern rooms with TV amidst the picturesque alleyways of Kut. About 800m west of the ferry dock, the modern *Issa* (☎021/711-164 or 711-124, fax 711-450; ④) is owned by the same firm as the *Tamaris* and costs the same, but hasn't received the same amount of investment: the TV-less en-suite rooms are adequate but slightly tatty.

The best of the **restaurants** are in Kut: the *Paula* (see above) has top-of-the-range fish and Vis wines, served up on a walled terrace; the nearby *Val* and *Vatrica* are also worth trying for excellent seafood.

Komiža and around

Buses leave Vis harbour three times daily for the 25-minute drive to the pleasant town of **KOMIŽA**, the island's main fishing port. Compact and intimate, Komiža's curved harbourfront is lined with palm trees and fringed by sixteenth- and seventeenth-century Venetian-style houses with intricate wrought-iron balconies. Dominating the southern end of the harbour is the **Kaštel**, a stubby sixteenth-century fortress whose appearance is slightly unbalanced by the slender clock-tower which was built onto one of its corners at the end of the nineteenth century. It now holds a **Fishing Museum** (Ribarski muzej; June–Sept daily 9am–noon & 7–11pm; 10Kn), whose worthy displays of nets and knots are enlivened by the presence of a reconstructed *falkuša*, one of the traditional fishing boats with triangular sails which were common hereabouts until the early twentieth century.

At the other end of the harbour, on a tiny square known as the **Škor** (local dialect for *škver*, the part of the harbourfront onto which fishing boats were pulled up for repairs), is the mid-sixteenth-century **Palača Zanetova**, a stately but dilapidated building which was once a ducal mansion – look out for the carved Virgin and Child high up on the front wall. Among the town's churches, the most notable is the sixteenth-century **Gospa Gusarica**, set amid trees on a little beach at the northern end of town near the *Biševo* hotel, which has an eight-sided well adorned with reliefs of St Nicholas, protector of fishermen and patron of Komiža. The church's name loosely translates as "Our Lady of the Pirates" – it's said that a painting of the Virgin was stolen from the church by pirates, but that they were shipwrecked and the painting floated back into port.

About a kilometre southeast of the town on a vineyard-cloaked hillock is the seventeenth-century **Benedictine monastery** (known as "Mušter" – the local dialect word for monastery), fortified in the 1760s to provide the townsfolk with a refuge in case of attack by pirates. Surrounded by defensive bastions, it's a good vantage point from which to survey the bay of Komiža below. Most of the island's population congregate beneath the monastery every year on St Nicholas's Day (Sveti Nikola; Dec 6), when an old fishing boat is hauled here by hand and then set alight – the idea of sacrificing a boat to the patron saint of sea-farers reveals just how much pre-Christian practice is preserved in Mediterranean Catholicism.

Practicalities

Buses from Vis Town terminate about a hundred metres behind the harbour, from where it's a short walk south to the **tourist office** (summer daily 8am–1pm & 6–9pm; winter Mon–Fri 8am–1pm; ☎021/713-455), on the Riva just beyond the Kaštel. The town's only **hotel** is the *Biševo* (☎021/713-095 or 713-279, fax 713-098; ⑤), a comfortable package-tour-oriented place about five minutes' walk from the centre at the northern end of the bay. **Rooms** (①) are available from a number of agencies in the centre, such as Darlić & Darlić (daily 10am–noon & 5–7pm) on the harbourfront, and Srebrna (daily 8am–noon & 4–9pm), on Ribarska just to the north. There are a couple of pizzerias on the harbourfront, and one very good seafood **restaurant** just off Ribarska, *Bako*, which has a vine-shaded terrace right on the beach. For **drinkers**, the day begins and ends on the central Škor, which is ringed by lively and very friendly café-bars.

Mount Hum and the south coast

Rearing up above Komiža to the southeast is **Mount Hum**, at 587m Vis's highest point. You can scramble up to the top by following the tracks from behind the Benedictine monastery, although there's also a road of sorts, accessed by follow-ing the old Komiža–Vis Town route (not the new one traversed by buses), which works its way round the southern side of the island. About 6km out of Komiža, take a left to the hamlet of Žena Glava followed by a second left to Borovik, from where a deteriorating asphalt road heads uphill to the summit. There's a small chapel at the top, and a panorama of the Adriatic that reveals just why Vis was so strategically important: you can pick out the pale grey stripe of the Italian coast-line far away to the west, and the mountains of the Croatian mainland to the east. Also visible are many of the uninhabited islands of the mid-Adriatic: the hump of Svetac immediately to the west, the unearthly volcanic pyramid of Jabuka beyond it and, to the southeast, Croatia's farthest-flung Adriatic posession, Palagruža – according to legend, the last resting place of Diomedes, King of Argos and lead-ing participant in the siege of Troy.

Nearing Hum's summit by road you'll pass an overgrown concrete stairway leading to **Tito's Cave** (Titova špilja), a group of caverns from which the Marshal directed the war effort during 1944. Once a popular attraction, the caves fell into disuse after 1991, although there's talk of bringing tourists here again – the tourist office in Komiža will have up-to-date information. For the time being the caves are boarded up, so there's not much point in making a special trip to see them.

Returning to the road along the south of the island, another 5km from the Žena Glava turn-off brings you to the village of **PLISKO POLJE**, where the British constructed a speedily improvised airstrip in 1944 by linking together innumerable metal plates. It was long ago pulled up and replaced by vineyards, the fruits of which can be sampled at *Konoba Roki* in the village – a great place to sit in a

---

VIS IN 1944

The idea of establishing a British base on Vis was first aired in the autumn of 1943, when the Germans were slowly re-establishing control of the Adriatic islands after the collapse of Italy had left many of them in the hands of Tito's Partisans. Britain's principal aim was to use Vis as a forward base for the supply of the Partisans on the mainland, while at the same time harrying German garrisons elsewhere in Dalmatia. Early in 1944, British commandos, supported by a small fleet of motor torpedo boats, occupied Vis before the Germans could get there first.

The importance of the Allied presence on Vis was demonstrated in June 1944, when the island was chosen as the temporary headquarters of the Partisan high command, headed by Tito himself. Tito had narrowly escaped a German attack on his previous stronghold, Drvar (a town in western Bosnia), and was evacuated to Italy by the Allies at the end of May. Tito sailed for Vis on board the HMS *Blackmore* on June 7, entertaining the officers' mess, it is said, with a near-perfect rendition of *The Owl and the Pussycat*.

Tito immediately took up residence in a cave on the southern flanks of Mount Hum, while his staff meetings took place in another cave next door. This was the site of the first meeting between Tito and the head of the royalist Yugoslav government in exile, Ivan Šubašić, who arrived on the island June 16. Šubašić had hoped to seal an agreement by which Tito would accept the authority of both the Yugoslav government and King Petar Karađorđević, but very quickly accepted Tito's demand that the continued existence of the monarchy could only be decided after the war. It's possible that the British presence on Vis lulled Šubašić into thinking that any concessions made to Tito in 1944 could be ignored – with Allied help – once the war was over. After concluding the Tito–Šubašić Agreement, the signatories went on a motor-boat excursion to the Blue Cave on Biševo, where they indulged in skinny dipping, followed by a lunch of lobster and wine. Fitzroy Maclean, Winston Churchill's personal envoy at Partisan HQ, noted that the sea was choppy on the way back and that "several of the party were sick".

The Partisans were extremely suspicious of British intentions towards Yugoslavia, and feared that by accepting British protection on Vis they stood to lose their political independence. Tito flew to Naples in August to meet Churchill, whose jovial mood seemed to reassure him, but he still needed to assert himself with a show of disobedience. With this in mind he abandoned Vis in the dead of night on September 18, flying to join the Soviet Red Army in Romania in a Russian plane. Tito travelled on to Moscow for talks with Stalin before returning to western Romania to accompany the Red Army in its advance on the Serbian capital Belgrade. Vis's brief period in the political limelight was over.

shady courtyard trying out the local red and white wines, accompanied by *pršut* and homemade cheese. There's another eating and drinking venue, the *Konoba Senko Karuza*, about 2.5km south of Plisko Polje in Mala Travna bay, but you can only get there by walking (via the hamlet of Marine Zemlje just south of Plisko Polje) or by private boat. There's no menu: guests are served the dish of the day and then asked to pay what they think it's worth.

Biševo and the Blue Cave

Each morning small boats leave Komiža harbour for the short crossing to **Biševo**, a tiny islet just to the southwest of Vis. There's a seasonally inhabited hamlet just up from Biševo's small harbour, and a couple of attractive coves, but the main attraction here is the **Blue Cave** (Modra špilja; 25Kn) on the island's east coast, a modestly sized but entrancing grotto which can only be reached by sea. It's been a tourist attraction since the 1880s, when a minor Viennese painter Eugen von Ransonnet-Villet dynamited the entrance to the cave to widen it for boat access, and the Lloyd steamer company began advertising it as the "Austrian Capri". It probably deserves the hype: when the sun is at its height, water-filtered light shines in through a submerged side entrance to the cave to bathe everything in the cavern in an eerie shimmering blueness. Due to the narrowness of the entrance, the cave can't be entered when the sea is choppy; which can happen on all but the calmest of summer days; ask the tourist office in either Komiža or Vis Town about weather forecasts.

There are two ways to visit the cave: the easiest is to take an excursion from either Komiža or Vis Town (60–80Kn, including the cave entrance fee), although it's also possible to take a taxi boat from Komiža harbour to the island, from where you can walk to a spot near the cave entrance. Either way, you'll be transferred to a small boat and ferried into the cave. You can take a dip in the cave if you want – although be warned that the volume of tourist traffic often means that you won't be able to spend as long there as you might wish.

Korčula

Like so many islands along the coast, **KORČULA** was first settled by the Greeks, who gave it the name Korkyra Melaina, or Black Corfu, for its dark and densely wooded appearance. Even now it's one of the greenest of the Adriatic islands, and one of the most popular, thanks almost entirely to the charms of its main settlement, **Korčula Town**, whose surviving fortifications jut decorously out to sea like the bastions of an overgrown sandcastle. There are good beaches at the village of **Lumbarda** 7km away, but the rest of the island lacks any obvious highlights.

The main Rijeka–Dubrovnik **ferry** drops you right at the harbour at Korčula Town. In addition, local ferries travel daily between Split and Vela Luka at the western end of Korčula island, from where there's a connecting bus service to Korčula Town. There's also a direct bus service (1 daily) from Dubrovnik, which crosses the narrow stretch of water dividing the island from the mainland via car ferry from Orebić (see p.293), just opposite Korčula Town on the Pelješac peninsula. Orebić is the obvious gateway to Korčula if you're approaching from the south: there are 14 daily ferry sailings in summer (9 in winter) from Orebić to Dominće 3km south of Korčula Town, and a passenger-only **boat service**

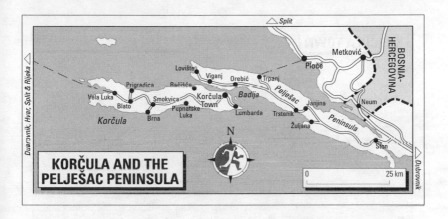

KORČULA AND THE
PELJEŠAC PENINSULA

(summer daily 6am–8pm every 1–2hr) that brings you to the centre of town. If you arrive at Dominče on one of the ferries from Orebić, you can avoid the thirty-minute walk into town by waiting for one of the Lumbarda–Korčula buses, which pass by roughly hourly in season.

Korčula Town

KORČULA TOWN sits on an oval hump of land, a medieval walled city ribbed with a series of narrow streets that branch off the main thoroughfare like the veins of a leaf – a plan designed to reduce the effects of wind and sun. Controlling access to the two-kilometre-wide channel which divides the island from the Pelješac peninsula, the town was one of the first Adriatic strongpoints to fall to the Venetians – who arrived here in the tenth century and stayed, on and off, for over eight centuries, leaving their distinctive mark on the culture and architecture of the town. Korčula's golden age lasted from the thirteenth to the fifteenth centuries, when the town acquired its present form and most of its main buildings were constructed, but a catastrophic outbreak of plague in 1529 brought an end to Korčula's expansion. Further disaster was narrowly averted in 1571 when, in the run-up to the Battle of Lepanto, Uluz Ali (see box on p.273) turned up outside the town. The Venetian garrison withdrew without a fight, leaving the locals to defend themselves under the command of local priest Antun Rožanović – they managed to repulse Ali, who went off to destroy Hvar Town instead.

With the decline of Mediterranean trade that followed the discovery of America, Korčula slipped into obscurity. The twentieth century saw the development of shipyards east of town, and the emergence of tourism. The first guests arrived in the 1920s, although it wasn't until the 1970s that mass tourism changed the face of the town, bequeathing it new hotels, cafés and a chi-chi new steel and chrome marina, now the subject of a hi-tech evening *korzo*.

Korčula's most famous event is the performance of the **Moreška** sword dance (see box on p.287), which traditionally falls on St Theodore's Day (Sept 29) – although these days it's re-enacted on a weekly basis throughout the summer for

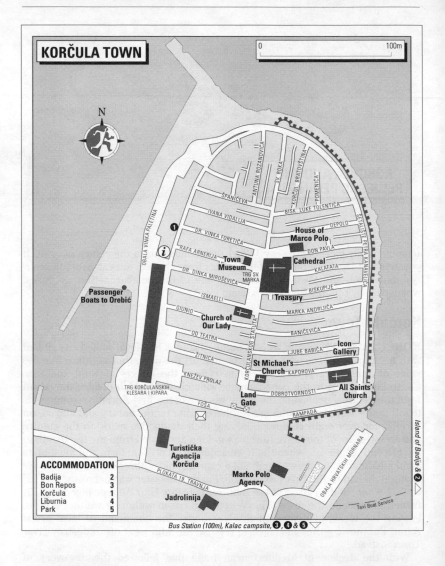

KORČULA TOWN

0   100m

N

ANTUNA ROZANOVIĆA
SV. ROKA
KORČUL BRATOVŠTINA
ŠPANIĆEVA
BISK. LUKE TOLENTIĆA
IVANA VIDALIJA
DEPOLO
DR. VINKA FORETIĆA
House of Marco Polo
RAFA ARNERIJA
DON PAVLA
OBALA VINKA PALETINA
Town Museum
Cathedral
DR. DINKA MIROŠEVIĆA
TRG SV. MARKA
KALAFATA
ISMAELLI
BISKUPIJE
Treasury
Passenger Boats to Orebić
GIUNIO
Church of Our Lady
MARKA ANDRIJIĆA
OD TEATRA
BANIČEVIĆA
ŽITNICA
LJUBE BABIĆA
Icon Gallery
KNEŽEV PROLAZ
KORČULANSKOG STATUTA
St Michael's Church
KAPOROVA
All Saints' Church
TRG KORČULANSKIH KLESARA I KIPARA
FOŠA
Land Gate
DOBROTVORNOSTI
RAMPADA
SETALIŠTE PETRA KANAVELIĆA

ACCOMMODATION

Badija	2
Bon Repos	3
Korčula	1
Liburnia	4
Park	5

Turistička Agencija Korčula
PLOKATA 19. TRAVNJA
Marko Polo Agency
Jadrolinija
OBALA HRVATSKIH MORNARA
Taxi Boat Service

Island of Badija & 2

Bus Station (100m), Kalac campsite, 3, 4 & 5

the benefit of visitors. Another good time to be in town is **Easter Week**, when the religious brotherhoods (charitable associations formed in medieval times) parade through the town with their banners – individually on the days preceding Good Friday, then all together on Good Friday itself. A comparatively recent event – but planned to become an annual feature if funds permit – is the seaborne re-enactment of the 1298 **Battle of Korčula** (Sept 7), when the Genoese under Admiral Lamba Doria defeated a numerically superior Venetian fleet, capturing Marco Polo in the process.

THE MOREŠKA AND OTHER SWORD DANCES

Korčula Town is famous for its **Moreška**, a traditional sword dance and drama that was once common throughout the Mediterranean. Judging by the name, the dance probably originated in Spain and related to the conflict between the Moors and the Christians, although in Dalmatia its rise was probably connected with the struggles against the Ottoman Turks, in particular the victory over them at the Battle of Lepanto. Whatever its origins, the Moreška has become a major tourist attraction, and its annual performance on St Theodore's Day (July 29) has been transformed into a weekly summer event, held every Thursday evening between May and September at a pitch just outside the Land Gate or – if the weather is bad – in the local cinema near the bus station. Tickets (35Kn) are available from Marko Polo Tours.

Basically the dance tells the story of a conflict between the White King and his followers (actually dressed in red) and the Black King. The heroine, Bula (literally "veiled woman"), is kidnapped by the Black King and his army, and her betrothed tries to win her back in a ritualized sword fight that takes place within a shifting circle of dancers. The adversaries circle each other and clash weapons several times before the evil king is forced to surrender, and Bula is unchained. The strangest thing about the dance is the seemingly incongruous brass band music that invariably accompanies it – a sign that the present-day Moreška falls somewhere between medieval rite and nineteenth-century reinvention.

Similar sword dances are still performed throughout the island, although once outside Korčula Town you're more likely to find them accompanied by traditional instruments such as the *mijeh* (bagpipe). The most important of these are the **Moštra**, performed in Postrana on St Rock's Day (Aug 16); and the **Kumpanjija**, which takes place in Blato on St Vincent's Day (April 28), Cara on St Jacob's Day (July 25), Smokvica on Candlemas (Feb 2), and Pupnat on Our Lady of the Snows (Aug 6). Many of these dances are performed in Korčula Town over the summer under the banner of the **Festival of Sword Dances** (Festival viteških igara), with performances at the beginning and end of the tourist season; the tourist office will have details.

In the past many of these dances would have been followed by the beheading of an ox, which was then roasted and divided among the participants. The practice was banned during the communist period, and its revival in Pupnat in 1999 was followed by lurid – and largely negative – reporting in the Croatian press. It remains to be seen whether ritual slaughter ever forms part of the dances again.

Arrival, information and accommodation

Korčula's **bus station** is 400m southeast of the old town. The **tourist office** (June–Sept Mon–Sat 8am–8pm, Sun 8am–3pm; Oct–May Mon–Sat 8am–noon & 5–8pm, Sun 8am–noon; ☎021/715-701, fax 715-866) is on the western side of the peninsula. There are two agencies dealing in private **rooms** (①), both near the entrance to the old town: the Marko Polo agency at Biline 5 (☎020/715-400, fax 715-800, *marko-polo-tours@du.tel.hr*), and the Turistička Agencija Korčula, just off Plokata 19. travnja (☎020/711-067, fax 711-710, *htp-korcula@du.tel.hr*).

The best of the town's **hotels** is the *Korčula*, on the western side of the old town (☎020/711-078, fax 711-746; ⑤), housed in the Austrian-built former town hall and boasting an elegant terrace. The cheapest option is the *Badija* (☎020/711-115, fax 711-746; ②, including compulsory full board), housed in a former Franciscan monastery on the island of Badija about 2km east of town. It's served by regular taxi boat from Korčula harbour and is well placed for some rocky offshore beaches, but the rooms are spartan and facilities are shared. Alternatively, there's a string of modern package-oriented establishments on the headland east of town: the *Park* (☎020/726-004, fax 711-746; ③), on the shore about 1km from the town centre (head east from the bus station along Šetalište Frana Kršinića), has modest en-suites, while the *Liburna* (020/726-006, fax 711-746; ③), slightly uphill, has en-suite rooms with TV and an outdoor swimming pool. Beyond the *Liburna*, past an inlet and an overgrown park, is the *Bon Repos*, on a wooded promontory 2km southeast of town (☎020/711-019, fax 711-102; ③), with simple en-suites, a small pool and a shingle beach. The Korčula–Lumbarda bus passes the hotel every hour; otherwise it's a 25-minute walk into town round the bay.

The nearest **campsite** is the *Kalac* (☎020/711-336, fax 711-746), next to the *Bon Repos* hotel, although there are quieter alternatives in the small bays west of town on the road to the village of Račišće. Four kilometres out is the *Palma*, tucked away in a private garden, while 2km further on is the *Vrbovica*, at the northern end of village of Luka Banja, on the lovely Vrbovica bay. The five daily Korčula–Račišće buses pass them both.

Bikes can be rented from the Atlas bureau in the *Park* hotel (15Kn per hour, 75Kn per day). If you're moving on from Korčula by boat, **ferry tickets** can be booked through the Jadrolinija office on Plokata 19. travnja (Mon–Fri 7.30am–8pm, Sat 7.30am–2pm, Sun 8am–1pm).

The Town

Despite recent development, Korčula Town preserves a neat beauty that has few equals on the Adriatic coast. Just up from the quay, cafés, shops and banks line the broad sweep of Plokata 19. travnja, from where an elegant nineteenth-century flight of steps sweeps up to the **Land Gate** (Kopnena vrata), the main entrance to the tiny old town. Begun in 1391, the gate was completed a century later with the addition of the **Revelin**, the hulking defensive tower that looms above it. The northern side of the gate takes the form of a triumphal arch built in 1650 to honour the military governor of Dalmatia, Leonardo Foscolo, who led Venetian forces against the Turks during the Candia War – a struggle for the control of Crete – during 1645–69.

Inside the gate lies a well-ordered grid of pale-grey stone houses, most dating from before 1800. On the far side of the gate lies Trg braće Radića, a small square bordered on one side by an elegant loggia belonging to the sixteenth-century town hall and, on the other, **St Michael's Church** (Crkva svetog Mihovila), connected to a neighbouring building by a small bridge which was used as a private entrance to the church by members of the medieval Brotherhood of St Michael – one of many such charitable brotherhoods formed during the Middle Ages throughout the Adriatic. From here, Korčulanskog statuta 1214 leads on into the town centre, passing the **Church of Our Lady** (Crkva Gospojina; daily 10am–noon & 7–11pm) on the left, a simple structure whose floor is paved with the tombstones of Korčulan nobles – it's used as a picture gallery selling works by local artists in summer. Above the high altar is a mosaic of the Virgin and Child, a dazzling confection of yellows, blues and pinks completed by Dutchman Louis Schrikkel in 1967.

THE CATHEDRAL AND TREASURY

Immediately beyond the church lies **St Mark's Cathedral** (Katedrala svetog Marka), squeezed into a diminutive space that passes for a main town square. The cathedral's facade is decorated with a gorgeous fluted rose window and a bizarre cornice frilled with strange beasts. In the centre, a matronly lady looks down with half-closed eyes: no one knows for sure who she is – suggestions have ranged from the Emperor Diocletian's wife to one of a number of Hungarian queens who helped finance the church. The main figure directly above the porch is St Mark, flanked by lions pawing smaller, more subservient animals, while the door is framed by statues of Adam and Eve.

The cathedral's **interior** is one of the loveliest on the coast, a curious mixture of styles developed over three hundred years, from the Gothic nave to the Renaissance north aisle. Local stonemason Marko Andrijić completed the elegant ciborium some time in the 1490s, topping its Corinthian columns with statuettes of Archangel Michael and the Virgin, and adding a pagoda-like roof. Beneath its canopy you can just about make out an early Tintoretto altarpiece, depicting St Mark flanked by SS Hieronymus and Bartholomew. There's a wealth of interesting clutter in the south aisle, including some of the pikes used against Uluz Ali, another Tintoretto (an *Annunciation*, with the Archangel appearing to the Virgin in a shower of sparks), and a thirteenth-century icon of the Virgin which was once kept on Badija island and is credited with offering miraculous assistance to the Venetian fleet at the Battle of Lepanto in 1571. Accompanied by a flotilla of small boats, it's taken back to Badija every year on August 2 to preside over a special thanksgiving mass. At the end of the south aisle lie the fine Renaissance tomb of Bishop Malumbra and an altar featuring a murky, time-darkened allegory of the Holy Trinity by Venetian painter Leandro Bassano.

Many of the church's treasures have been removed to the **Bishop's Treasury** (*riznica*; daily: summer 9am–1pm & 4–7pm; winter 9am–1pm; 10Kn), next door. This is one of the best small art collections in the country, with an exquisite set of paintings which takes in a striking *Portrait of a Man* by Carpaccio, a perceptive *Virgin and Child* by Bassano, a tiny *Madonna* by Dalmatian Renaissance artist Blaž Jurjev of Trogir, plus some Tiepolo studies of hands and drawings by Raphael. Oddities include an ivory statuette of Mary Queen of Scots, whose skirts open to reveal kneeling figures in doublet and hose – what it's doing in Korčula remains a mystery.

THE REST OF THE TOWN

Opposite the cathedral, a Venetian palace houses the **Town Museum** (Gradski muzej; Mon–Sat 9am–noon & 5–7pm; 10Kn), whose modest display includes a copy of a fourth-century BC Greek tablet from Lumbarda – the earliest evidence of civilization on Korčula – and, upstairs, a recreation of a typical Korčula peasant kitchen, with an open hearth surrounded by cooking pots and bed warmers.

Close by the main square, down a turning to the right, is another remnant from Venetian times, the so-called **House of Marco Polo** (Kuća Marka Pola; daily 9am–1pm & 5–7pm; 10Kn). Korčula claims to be the birthplace of Marco Polo – not as extravagant a claim as it might seem, since the Venetians recruited many sea captains from their colonies, and Polo was indeed captured by the Genoese in a sea battle off the island in 1298. Whatever the truth of the matter, it seems unlikely that he had any connection with this seventeenth-century house, which is little more than an empty shell with some terrible twentieth-century prints on the walls, although it's worth visiting if only for the outstanding view from the tower over Korčula's terracotta-coloured rooftops.

From here you can descend towards Šetalište Petra Kanavelića, the seafront walkway which leads round the outside of the peninsula. Walk south to the junction with Kaporova to find the **Icon Gallery** (Galerija ikona; Mon–Sat 9am–noon & 4–7pm), where there's a permanent display of icons in the rooms of the All Saints' Brotherhood. Most of the exhibits were looted from Cretan churches at the end of the Candia War (on the pretence of saving them from falling into infidel hands), when Venice had to hand over the Mediterranean island to the Ottoman Turks. Among the Pantokrators and Virgins emblazoned in gold leaf is a haunting fifteenth-century triptych of the Passion.

From here, a covered bridge similar to the one outside St Michael's Church takes you into **All Saints' Church** (Crkva svih svetih), with its brooding Renaissance interior and one of the most impressive Baroque altarpieces in Dalmatia – an eighteenth-century Pietà carved from walnut wood by Austrian master George Raphael Donner, enclosed by a fifteenth-century ciborium in imitation of the one in the cathedral. On the far side of the altar is another of Blaž Jurjev's fifteenth-century masterpieces, a polyptych centred on a chilling *Deposition*, below which the tiny figures of the All Saints' Brotherhood – identifiable from their trademark white robes – kneel in prayer.

BEACHES AND ISLANDS

The nearest **beaches** to the old town are on the headland around the *Hotel Marko Polo*, though they're crowded, rocky and uncomfortable. The shingle beach in front of the *Bon Repos* hotel and *Kalac* campsite is much nicer, and there's a sandy beach a short bus ride away in Lumbarda (see opposite). Alternatively, take a water taxi (10Kn) from the harbour on the eastern side of town on the way to the bus station to one of the **Skoji islands** just offshore. The largest and nearest is **Badija**, where you can either disembark at the *Hotel Badija* – from which tracks lead to secluded beaches and a couple of elementary snack bars – or continue onwards to the naturist part of the island round the corner. The long shingle beaches of Orebić (see p.293) are also only a fifteen-minute ferry ride away; boats run roughly hourly from the pier opposite the *Hotel Korčula* throughout the day.

Eating, drinking and entertainment

There are more pizzerias than you can shake a stick at in the old town, and a number of decent **restaurants** too. One longstanding tourist favourite is the excellent *Adio Mare* on Svetog Roka, just by the alleyway leading down to Marco Polo's House, which offers top-quality seafood in an atmospheric medieval house; arrive early to make sure of a table. A good second choice is the *Planjak* restaurant, just below the Land Gate on Plokata 19. travnja, which has the full range of local grill-fare and plenty of outdoor seating. At the northern end of the old town's peninsula *Konoba Morski konjić*, on Šetalište Petra Kanavelića, is a small and intimate place with good fresh fish, although the benches outside are a bit exposed to sea breezes. *Buffet Tramonto*, at the top of the stairway by the *Hotel Korčula*, has a good choice of pasta, including a couple of vegetarian options. Wherever you eat, try some of the excellent local white **wines**: Grk from Lumbarda, and Pošip and Rukatac, both from the area around the villages of Čara and Smokvica, are the best. For picnics, there's a fruit and vegetable **market** just below the Land Gate, where you'll also find a couple of supermarkets.

Drinking in Korčula is fairly low key: the cafés on Plokata 19. travnja are busy with locals and tourists alike during the daytime, while a string of bars catering for the evening crowd stretch along Šetalište Frana Kršinića, just behind the bus station. A nightlife of sorts – tame discos or warbling crooners for the most part – can be found in the hotels.

Around the island

The beauty of Korčula Town only serves to emphasize just how short on appeal the rest of the island is. The only other major attraction are the beaches just beyond the village of **LUMBARDA**, 8km south of Korčula Town and accessible by regular buses (Mon–Sat hourly; 5 daily on Sun). It takes about twenty minutes to walk to the beaches from Lumbarda. First, continue along the main road south until you reach a small chapel. From here, the track on the right leads to **Prižna bay**, a glorious 200m stretch of sand backed by a couple of cafés, while the track on the left goes to **Bilin Žal**, a far rockier strand with brief sandy stretches. There's a **tourist office** (daily 7am–9pm) in the centre of Lumbarda where the buses stop, which doles out rooms (①; full board ②).

Heading in the other direction out of Korčula Town, a single road (served by 6 buses daily) runs the length of the island west to Vela Luka, passing most of the island's major settlements en route. These are a series of largely bland villages, often connected by rough road to the nearest strip of coast, where there are usually a few holiday villas, some sort of rocky beach, a store and – sometimes – private rooms, though they're almost impossible to reach without your own transport.

Forty kilometres west of Korčula Town, **BLATO** is something of an antidote to all this, an old-fashioned country town that's easily the most agreeable of Korčula's inland settlements. First colonized by the Greeks, Blato (literally "mud" or "swamp") is at the centre of a wine growing district and is attractively bisected by a magnificent avenue of lime trees. At the western end of the island, **VELA LUKA** may be your first view of Korčula if you're arriving by ferry, but it's not really of any interest apart from a string of vivacious seafront cafés which sadly fail to overcome the town's all-round charm deficit. If you arrive late and can't get a bus out, there's a **tourist office** (Mon–Sat 8am–8pm, Sun 8am–noon; ☎020/813-619) at the rear of the triangular waterfront square which has **rooms** (①).

Lastovo

Directly south of Korčula, tiny **LASTOVO** lies at the centre of an archipelago of 45 uninhabited islets some five and a half hours from Split. Remote and virtually self-sufficient in food, Lastovo feels much more isolated that any of the other Adriatic islands, and there's a sense of pride and independence here, most obviously expressed in the annual **Poklad** festival (see box on p.292) at the beginning of Lent. Like Vis, Lastovo was closed to foreigners from 1976 until 1989 due to its importance as a military outpost, and organized tourism has never caught on, but what it lacks in hotels and amenities it more than makes up for in its extraordinary sense of isolation and in its natural, wooded beauty. The island has only one major settlement, **Lastovo Town**, where most of the remaining 1500 islanders live.

Ferries leave Split for the island's port at **UBLI** once or twice daily all year, calling at Hvar Town and Vela Luka on Korčula en route. There's a petrol station and a couple of shops opposite the ferry dock, while the incongruously chic *Lounge Lizard* café on the harbour rents out mountain bikes, but you're better off making your way directly to Lastovo Town – all ferries are met by a connecting bus.

Lastovo Town and around

Unusually for the capital of a Croatian island, **LASTOVO TOWN** faces away from the sea, spreading itself over the steep banks of a natural amphitheatre with a fertile agricultural plain below. There's a road at the top, a road at the bottom, and a maze of narrow alleys and stone stairways between. The town's buildings date mainly from the fifteenth and sixteenth centuries – although depopulation has left many empty and dilapidated – and are notable for their curious chimneys shaped like miniature minarets, although there's no record of Arab or Turkish raiders ever making it this far.

The fifteenth-century parish **Church of SS Cosmas and Damian** (Crkva svetog Kuzme i Damjana) in the centre of town is worth a look for its interior, richly adorned with sixteenth- and seventeenth-century paintings and icons, with a dainty fifteenth-century loggia opposite the entrance. Above the town lie the remains of the old French **fort**, built in 1810 above some much older fortifications and now used as a weather station – it's a stiff walk up, but worth it for the views from the top, with Lastovo on one side and the sea on the other. Heading downhill from the main square a road hairpins its way to two tiny harbours: **Lučica**, a tiny hamlet

---

THE POKLAD

Lastovo's carnival is one of the strangest in Croatia, featuring the ritual humiliation and murder of a straw puppet, the **Poklad**. After a long weekend of preparation things come to a head on Shrove Tuesday, when the Poklad is led through town on a donkey by the men of Lastovo, who dress for the occasion in a uniform of red shirts, black waistcoats and bowler hats. Following this, the Poklad is attached to a long rope and hoisted from one end of town to the other three times while fireworks are let off beneath it. Each transit is met by chanting and the drawing of swords. Finally, the Poklad is put back on the donkey and taken to the square in front of the parish church, to the accompaniment of music and dancing. At the end of the evening, the villagers dance the Lastovsko kolo, a sword dance similar to the Moreška in Korčula (see box on p.287), and the Poklad is impaled on a long stake and burnt. Drinking and dancing continues in the village hall until dawn.

Local tradition has it that the Poklad symbolizes a young messenger who was sent by Catalan pirates to demand the town's surrender, although it's more likely that the ritual actually derives from ancient fertility rites. Whatever its roots, the islanders take the occasion very seriously, and it's certainly not enacted for the benefit of outsiders. Lastovčani from all over the world return to their home village to attend the Poklad, so accommodation is at a premium. If you do want to attend, contact the tourist office well in advance.

with a mix of derelict houses and renovated holiday homes, and, a little further on, the quieter **Sveti Mihovil**.

Ask at Lastovo's tourist office whether any local boatmen are offering excursions to **Šaplun**, an uninhabited islet to the south which has a lovely fine shingle beach. Otherwise, you can walk to **ZAKLOPATICA**, a hamlet 3km away on the northern coast of the island with a yachting harbour and a couple of *konobe*; or to **Skrivena Luka** 5km south, a deep bay backed by sandy hills and cleared of vegetation by forest fires, where there are several rocky places to swim.

Practicalities

The bus from the ferry dock at Ubli stops on the main square right outside the **tourist office** (variable opening times, but always open when the bus from the boat arrives; ☎020/801-018), where you can pick up a basic map and book **rooms** (①). You'll probably be asked whether you want full board: consider this carefully, since there are precious few eating places on the island and the home-cooking you'll be offered is usually exceptionally good, and is served in enormous portions. Needless to say, fish features heavily, along with an array of the island's vegetables and wild mushrooms, washed down with local wine.

There are a couple of bars, a bank and a grocery store on the square. Hiding in the back alleys at the bottom end of the village is the town's one **restaurant**, the *Konoba Bačvara*, serving up freshly caught seafood in a snug indoor room or on a terrace hung with fishing nets. There's a **café-bar** down in Sveti Mihovil bay which often stays open until the last customer staggers home.

The Pelješac peninsula

Just across the Pelješac channel (Pelješki kanal) from Korčula is the **PELJEŠAC PENINSULA**, a slim, mountainous finger of land which stretches for some 90km from Lovište in the west to the mainland in the east. Parts of the peninsula are exceptionally beautiful, with tiny villages and sheltered coves rimmed by beaches, but although it's a reasonably popular holiday area, development remains low-key. The downside is that public transport is meagre except along the main Korčula–Orebić–Ston–Dubrovnik route, and most of the smaller places are impossible to get to without a car.

Orebić

A short ferry-hop from Korčula, the small town of **OREBIĆ** was a subsidiary trading outlet of the Dubrovnik Republic for almost 500 years, and later enjoyed a brief period of extraordinary prosperity during the nineteenth-century revival of Adriatic trade, during which the town's merchants set up a maritime society, built a huge church and constructed their own shipyards to supply an independent merchant fleet. The bubble soon burst, however, and the Society and yards were wound up in 1887, after which the town slipped back into obscurity until the emergence of mass tourism. Orebić has featured in the package brochures ever since, largely on account of its long shingle **beaches**.

Today, Orebić straggles along the seashore on either side of its jetties, an aimless but attractive mixture of the old and new. The best part of town is along the seafront, just east of the quays, where generations of sea captains built a series of comfortable country villas, set behind a luscious subtropical screen of palms and cacti. The **Maritime Museum** (Pomorski muzej; Mon–Fri 9am–noon & 6–8pm; 5Kn), at Trg Mimbeli 12, sports a few crusty amphorae and a dull collection of naval memorabilia relating to the Orebić fleet. Far better to head up to the **Franciscan monastery** (Franjevački samostan; Mon–Sat 9am–noon & 4–6pm, Sun 4–6pm; 10Kn) on a rocky spur just west of town, built in the 1480s to house a miraculous icon known as Our Lady of the Angels which was brought here by Franciscans from the Bay of Kotor, just south of Dubrovnik. The icon was thought to protect mariners from shipwreck – Orebić ship captains would sound their sirens on passing the monastery on their way into port. The picture still occupies pride of place in the church: a stylized, Byzantine-influenced Madonna and Child surrounded by an oversized frame in which gilded angels cavort in a sky full of blue-ish cotton-wool clouds. The monastery **museum** displays votive paintings commissioned by crews who were saved from pirates or storms after offering prayers to the Virgin, and models of ships once owned by Orebić magnates such as the Mimbeli brothers, whose onion-domed mausoleum can be seen in the graveyard outside. There's also a wonderful view of the Pelješac channel from the monastery's terrace.

There are even better views from the 961-metre summit of **Sveti Ilija** (St Elijah), the bare mountain which looms over Orebić to the northwest. A marked path to the summit (4hr walk each way) strikes uphill just before you get to the monastery (look out for the red-and-white paint marks on the rocks), although it's largely unshaded. The best of Orebić's **beaches** is the Trstenica, a mixture of fine shingle and sand about fifteen minutes' walk east from the ferry terminal.

West of Orebić, the road follows the coast past the untidy resorts of **KUČIŠTE** and **VIGANJ**, both of which have shingle beaches and a string of shoreside **campsites**. After 10km or so the road cuts inland and winds uphill onto the peninsula's central ridge, eventually descending into the village of **LOVIŠTE**, which rests beside a kidney-shaped bay on the peninsula's northwestern tip. The scenery is beautiful, but you really need a car to get around – there's only one bus from Orebić a day.

Practicalities

The Orebić **tourist office** (daily 8am–8pm; 020/713-718), on the main street five minutes' walk east of the landing stage, has **rooms** (①). Alternatively, there's a string of medium-rise concrete **hotels**, the *Bellevue* (④), *Rathaneum* (④) and *Orsan* (④) – all run by the same company (☎020/713-014, fax 713-193, *orebic-htp@du.tel.hr*) – spreading out west of the landing stage, looking onto a long stretch of pebble beach. Best of the bunch is the *Orsan*, with cramped but comfy rooms with TV and balcony, and a dinky outdoor pool. There are two **campsites** behind Trstenica beach, and several more in private suburban gardens further east. For **food**, the *Pelješki Dvor* restaurant, between the landing stage and tourist office, is as good a place as any for fresh seafood grills, and there are lots of other indifferent restaurants and bars along the waterfront.

East to Ston

East of Orebić, the main road twists up into the mountains before reaching, after 15km, the turning to the lazy port of **TRPANJ** (served by 4 buses daily from

Orebić), which lies at the end of a ravine on Pelješac's northern coast. It's not a bad place in which to get stuck, with a couple of cafés on the Riva, a tree-shaded pebble beach at the end of the harbour and views of the Makarska Riviera's dramatic mountain backdrop on the other side of the water. The **tourist office** (Mon–Sat 8am–2pm & 4–8pm, Sun 8am–2pm) on the front has plenty of **rooms** (①), and there are **ferries** (3–7 daily) to Ploče on the mainland proper.

Back on the main road, it's another 18km to the turn-off for **TRSTENIK**, on the peninsula's southern side, another pleasant destination set tight against the hills behind a couple of tiny beaches. A further 14km along the main road at Dubrava there's a minor road (not served by bus) down to one of the best beaches on the coast at **ŽULJANA**, 6km away – a tiny resort built round a sheltered bay at the foot of a steep rocky gorge. There's a **tourist office** with unreliable opening times right on the beach, plenty of private **rooms** (①) and a reasonable **campsite**, the *Brijezi*. For **food**, there are a couple of unpretentious bar-restaurants on the harbourfront, where you'll also see signs advertising boat trips to even more remote beaches.

Ston and Mali Ston

About 20km beyond Dubrava, the twin settlements of Ston and Mali Ston straddle the neck of land which joins Pelješac to the mainland. **STON** (sometimes called Veliki – or "Great" – Ston to differentiate it from Mali Ston), an important salt-producing town, was swallowed up by Dubrovnik in 1333, becoming the most important fortress along the republic's northern frontier. Piled up above the saltpans of its long sea inlet, the town is framed by its dramatic and unusually shaped fourteenth-century walls, whose V-shaped apex is on the hillside high above the town's narrow streets. You can walk along the stretch of walls immediately above the town, and potter around the alleyways below, amongst a mix of Renaissance- and Gothic-style houses laid out on a gridiron plan. Just west of Ston, the pre-Romanesque **St Michael's Church** (Crkva svetog Mihovila) squats atop a conical hill overlooking the saltpans and has twelfth-century frescoes inside; however, though it's only infrequently open, so ask at the tourist office before making your way up.

Fifteen minutes' walk northeast of Ston, **MALI STON** began life as the outermost stronghold of Ston's defensive system, and the line of fortifications linking Ston with Mali Ston can still be seen trailing majestically across the adjacent hillsides. It's now a sleepy little village of old stone houses pressed within its walls, looking out onto Mali Ston bay, where the village's **oyster beds** are marked out by wooden poles, hung with ropes on which the oysters are encouraged to grow prior to harvesting in May and June. The village's traditional popularity as a seafood centre has been augmented by its growing reputation as a venue for romantic weekend breaks – perhaps something to do with the oysters' aphrodisiac effect. Following the narrow lanes up from the harbour you'll soon reach a crescent-shaped fortress which formed the northeasternmost bastion of Ston's sophisticated network of defences. It's nowadays an uninhabited shell, but steps lead up to a parapet from where there are good views.

There's no **beach** in Mali Ston, but the jetties and rocks around the harbour are pleasant places to sunbathe, and the water is clean enough to swim in. Otherwise the nearest pebble beach is by the *Prapratno* campsite (see p.296) to the southwest.

Practicalities

Buses pull up on Ston's main street, where there's a **tourist office** (Mon–Fri 7am–1pm & 5–7pm, Sat 7am–1pm; ☎ & fax 020/754-452) which can fix up local **rooms** (①). There are a couple of lovely family-run **hotels** on Mali Ston's harbour: the *Villa Koruna* (☎020/754-359, fax 754-642; ③) is a six-room pension whose small but stylish rooms boast air con and TV, while the slightly grander *Ostrea* (☎020/754-555, fax 754-575, *ostrea.info@ostrea.hr*; ④) offers posher rooms with a slap-up evening meal included in the price. The nearest **campsite** is the *Prapratno*, about 4km southwest of town, down a steep side-road just off the main route to Orebić. It has its own beach, a couple of grill-restaurants and impressive views of the mountains of Mljet across the water.

Mali Ston also has several upmarket **restaurants** offering top-quality fish and shellfish: in terms of quality and service there's little to chose between the *Koruna*, the *Ostrea* (in the hotel) or the *Kapetanova Kuća*, all close to each other on the waterfront. Cheaper fare is available in Ston, where *Konoba kod Baće* on the main street has a range of inexpensive *marende* (brunches), as well as meaty grills.

The Southern Dalmatian coast

The coast south of Split is perhaps the most dramatic in the country, with some of the Adriatic's best beaches sheltering beneath the papier-mâché heights of the karst mountains, all easily accessible on the frequent coastal bus service. Most of the beaches are pebble or shingle, and all are served by at least one campsite and (usually) a stock of private rooms.

The coastline immediately south of Split is uninspiring; a twenty-kilometre stretch of modern apartments and weekend houses culminating in one of south Dalmatia's most prominent industrial white elephants, the ferro-chrome plant at **Dugi rat**. Once beyond here things improve markedly, with the historical town of **Omiš** marking the entrance to the rugged **Zrmanja gorge**, and the beaches of the **Makarska Riviera** – which runs from Brela to Gradac – perched at the base of the **Biokovo mountains**. **Ploče**, the one other big town between Makarska and Dubrovnik, is an industrial port rather than a resort, and the rest of southern Dalmatia is a relatively low on attractions until you get to **Trsteno**, just 25km north of Dubrovnik, and site of the best Renaissance gardens in Croatia.

Plentiful **buses** zoom up and down the Magistrala between Dubrovnik and Split, though Makarska and Ploče are the only places along this stretch of coast which have proper bus stations with timetable information; elsewhere, you'll just have to wait by the roadside until something turns up (during the day, it's unlikely you'll have to wait more than an hour). Makarska and Ploče are also useful **ferry** hubs: the former has links with Sumartin on Brač, the latter has regular services to Trpanj on the Pelješac peninsula.

Omiš and around

The first town of any size south of Split is **OMIŠ**, at the end of the Cetina Gorge, a defile furrowed out of the bone-grey karst by the Cetina River. For centuries, Omiš was an impregnable pirate stronghold – repeated efforts to winkle them out, including one expedition in 1221 led by the pope himself, all failed. These days the town is rather dominated by the Magistrala, which passes just south of the old quarter, a huddle of cramped alleys spread out along a pleasant central street, Knezova Kačića. Remnants of the old city walls survive, and two semi-ruined Venetian fortresses cling to the bare rocks above. The new town lies to the south, a featureless stretch of postwar buildings behind the main town **beach**, composed of hard and uninviting sand – you're better off heading for the long shingle beaches of Duće, about 2km back along the Magistrala, or for the nice shingle beach at the village of Nemira, 3km southeast.

As well as the inter-city buses plying the Magistrala, Omiš is also served by local buses from Split. The **tourist office**, just off the Magistrala on Trg kneza Miroslava (☎ & fax 021/861-350, *tz-omis@st.tel.hr*), has details of local excursions up the Cetina Gorge (see below). **Rooms** (①) are available from Active Holidays, Knezova Kačića (☎021/863-015), while the nearest **campsite** is the *Ribnjak* (☎021/862-130), just north of town and handy for the beaches of Duće. There are a couple of places to **eat** on Knezova Kačića; the atmospheric *Konoba u našeg Marina* serves up simple snacks like *pršut* and local cheese, while the nearby *Milo* has a wider range of meaty grills and seafood. The **cafés** of Trg Stjepana Radića, at the eastern end of Knezova Kačića, are lovely places to sit outside in the summer.

Omiš is famous for its festival of local **klape** – the traditional male-voice choirs of Dalmatia – which takes place on weekends throughout July, usually culminating on the last weekend of the month with open-air performances in the old town. *Klape* are an important feature of Dalmatian life, and almost every town or village has at least one of them. Songs deal with typical Dalmatian preoccupations like love, the sea and fishing, and are usually sung in local dialect. It's well worth a trip from Split; the Omiš tourist office will have details.

The Cetina Gorge

The Cetina River rises just east of Knin (see p.230) and flows down to meet the sea at Omiš, carving its way through the karst of the Zagora to produce some spectacular rock formations on the way. The most eye-catching portions are those just outside Omiš, and 23km upstream near Zadvarje, although there's no public transport along the valley so you'll need a car to see all the interesting bits. Over the summer, boat trips are advertised on Omiš's quayside, but they only go about 5km upstream before stopping at one of the riverbank restaurants. You can also **raft** down part of the gorge: excursions are arranged by the Atlas agencies in Split, Trogir and Makarska.

Heading out of Omiš, the first few kilometres are truly dramatic, with the mountains pressing in on a narrow winding valley. Further up, the valley floor widens, making room for some swampy stretches of half-sunken deciduous forest. There's a string of good waterside **restaurants** along this part of the gorge: *Kaštil Slanica*, 4km out of Omiš, specializes in freshwater fish as well as *žabji kraci* (frogs' legs) and the tasty *brudet od jegulje* (spicy eel soup), while the larger *Radmanove Mlinice* (boat trips from Omiš often end up here), about 1500m further on, is known for its *pastrva* (trout).

Soon after the *Radmanove Mlinice* the road turns inland, twisting its way up onto a plateau surrounded by dry hills streaked with scrub. The village of **ZADVARJE**, at the top of a steep sequence of hairpins, offers views of the most impressive stretch of the gorge. Follow a sign marked *Vodopad* (Waterfall) in the centre of the village to a scruffy carpark on the edge of a cliff, from where there's a view north-east towards a canyon suspended half way up a rock face, with the river plunging down via two waterfalls to a gorge deep below. The cliffs lining the canyon sprout several more minor waterfalls whenever the local hills fill up with rain.

From Zadvarje, you can either head south to rejoin the Magistrala at Dubci, or carry on northwards to Šestanovac, where a westward route breaks off towards Trilj and Sinj (see p.263).

The Makarska Riviera

South of Omiš the road twists round the headlands of the Biokovo mountains into the section of coast known as the **MAKARSKA RIVIERA**, a string of resorts boasting long pebble beaches ranging from the over-exploited to the relatively unknown. Most of the villages here were originally based a kilometre or two inland until the growth of tourism, when families abandoned their old homes and built new houses down on the coast. With a few exceptions, therefore, the shoreline resorts are predominantly modern and charmless, but if all you want is a beach and cheap beer and pizza, then the Makarska Riviera is a decent place to get them.

The town of **Makarska**, roughly in the middle of the region, has the best nightlife and is a good base from which to tackle the ascent of the Biokovo range, while **Brela**, just to the north, has managed to preserve something of its chic, coastal-village-made-good atmosphere. The south of the Riviera is quite low key in comparison, attracting tourists mainly from the former Eastern Europe and working out slightly cheaper than the north.

Brela

Surrounded by aromatic pine groves, the northernmost settlement of the Makarska Riviera, **BRELA**, sports a fine strand of beach next to a steep warren of alleyways, where a mixture of old stone houses and modern holiday homes pokes out from a blanket of subtropical vegetation. The beach, backed by a clutch of hotels, stretches for a couple of kilometres to the north of the town centre before being broken up by little rocky headlands.

The **tourist office** lies just behind a parade of shops midway along the seafront (irregular opening times; ☎ & fax 021/618-337, *tz-brela@st.tel.hr*) and has **rooms** (①–②), as do the Adria-service and Bonavija tourist agencies nearby. The best of Brela's **hotels** are the *Maestral* (☎021/603-666, fax 603-688; ⑥) and the ziggurat-like *Soline* (☎021/603-222 or 620-555, fax 620-501; ⑥), both large and comfortable package-oriented complexes with good beach access 500m north of the centre along the coastal path. Simpler but perfectly acceptable rooms can be found at the *Berulia* (☎021/603-444, fax 619-005; ⑤), which occupies a bluff overlooking another stretch of beach south of the centre.

Two **restaurants** worth eating at for their locations are the *Punta Rata*, about ten minutes' walk north of the centre along the beach, and the restaurant of the *Hotel Berulia*, which has a beautiful elevated position on the beach between Brela and Baška Voda – both have a decent range of fresh and reasonably priced seafood.

Baška Voda

BAŠKA VODA, 3km southeast along the Magistrala (though you can just as easily walk along the coastal path), is less charming and more commercialized than

Brela. The town is modern and unexciting, although the **Archeological Collection** (Arheološka zbirka; 10am–noon & 7–10pm; 3Kn) just off the Riva has a small but imaginatively presented selection of finds from Gradina, the hillock immediately west of the centre which was the site of a settlement from the Bronze Age to late Roman times. There's a recreation of a late Roman hearth, and some simply decorated storage vessels and glassware.

Some Split–Makarska buses pass right along Baška Voda's waterfront, although most coastal services pick up and drop off high above the centre on the Magistrala, from where it's a fifteen-minute walk down Put kapelice to the seafront. Here you'll find a helpful **tourist office** at Obala svetog Nikole 31 (daily 8am–7pm; ☎ & fax 021/620-713, *tzo-baska-voda@st.tel.hr*), and a string of agencies – Duga, Horizont, Bonavia and Mariva to name but four – offering **rooms** (①). Of the **hotels**, the *Slavija* (☎021/620-155, fax 620-740; ④) is a central beachfront establishment of 1930s vintage with TV in all the rooms, while the more modern *Horizont* (021/604-555, fax 620-699; ⑦), a few steps south, is one of the best hotels on the Dalmatian coast and earns its four-star rating, with spongy carpets, gleaming bathrooms and air con. There's a campsite, the *Baško Polje* (☎021/612-329), at the south end of town near the exit off the Magistrala.

Makarska

MAKARSKA, 10km south of Baška Voda, is a lively seaside town ranged round a broad bay, framed by the Biokovo massif behind and two stumpy pine-covered peninsulas on either side. There's not a lot to see here, and the real attractions are eating and lounging around on the town's two kilometres of beach. Despite 200 years of Turkish occupation, little of Ottoman vintage survives, and the Venetian and Habsburg-era buildings on the seafront coexist with modern apartment blocks thrown up after the tourism boom.

All that survives of the old town is one central square, which slants up just behind the waterfront to the Baroque St Mark's Church (Crkva sveti Marko). Outside is Ivan Rendić's statue of **Andrija Kačić-Miošić** (1704–60), the Franciscan friar whose *Razgovor ugodni naroda slovinskoga* (A Pleasant Conversation of the Slav People) was the most widely read book in the Croatian language until the twentieth century, after which its archaic style fell out of fashion. A history of the Croats written in verse, and containing material taken from folk poems recounting Slav heroism in the face of the Ottoman Turks, Kačić's work was a landmark in the creation of a modern Croatian consciousness. There's a rather pedestrian **Town Museum** (Gradski muzej; Mon–Sat 9am–2pm; 10Kn) on the Riva, featuring old nautical relics and photographs; and a **Franciscan monastery** (Franjevački samostan; Mon–Sat 9am–noon & 6–8pm; 10Kn) east of the centre, with a relaxing courtyard and a small collection of devotional paintings and church manuscripts.

The town **bus station** is on the Magistrala, a five-minute walk from the seafront, where the **tourist office** at Obala kralja Tomislava 16 (June–Sept daily 7am–9pm; Oct–May Mon–Fri 9am–3pm; ☎ & fax 021/612-002) can direct you to the innumerable central agencies offering **rooms** (①) and apartments (②, 330Kn per night for four). Of the town's **hotels**, *Biokovo*, Obala kralja Tomislava (021/615-244, fax 615-081; ④), is the most convenient, hogging a waterside position right in the centre, although it's popular with foreign tour groups and tends to fill up fast. About 1km west of town on the seafront, the *Meteor* (☎021/602-600, fax 611-419; ⑤) is a modern, pyramidal structure with a pool; a couple of hundred

MOUNT BIOKOVO

The long grey streak of the **Biokovo** ridge hovers over the Makarska Riviera for some 50km, and its highest point – 1762m **Sveti Jure** just above Makarska – is the highest point in Croatia. It takes about about four hours to climb Sveti Jure from Makarska: head uphill from St Mark's Church, cross the Magistrala and continue to the village of Makar, from where a marked path leads to the subsidiary peak of **Vošac** (1422m) and then on to Sveti Jure itself. Be warned, however, that Biokovo is not suitable for occasional hikers, and ill-prepared tourists are more likely to come to grief on its slopes than anywhere else in Croatia. The ascent is strenuous, slippery and prone to swift weather changes, so you'll need proper footwear, waterproofs, plenty to drink and an accurate weather forecast from the tourist office in Makarska. *Biokovo Aktiv*, Dalmatinska 5, Makarska (☎021/616-974), organizes guided walks up Sveti Jure and early-morning trips to watch the sunrise.

You can **drive** to the top in summer by taking the road to Vrgorac and Mostar just south of Makarska, then turning left after 7km up a steeply ascending track which works its way up to the summit from the southeast – although you'll require nerves of steel to negotiate the hairpins.

metres further on is the plainer, high-rise *Dalmacija* (☎615-777, fax 612-211; ⑤). The nearest **campsite** is the *Baško Polje* on the southeastern outskirts of Baška Voda (see p.299).

For **food**, the town centre has scores of restaurants along the Riva. *Stari Mlin*, slightly inland at Prvosvibanjska 43, is the best place for simple local food, and the slightly smarter *Peškera*, Kralja Zvonimira (also accessible from the beach west of town) is unrivalled for the choice and quality of its seafood. Simply cruise the Riva to find a place to **drink**.

The southern Makarska Riviera

The strip of coast immediately south of Makarska is one of the most intensively developed in Croatia, reminiscent of the Spanish *costas* in the number of hotels and apartment blocks that straggle along the coast. Heading south, **TUČEPI** and **PODGORA**, a few kilometres beyond Makarska, are fairly typical, with nice beaches backed by a soulless straggle of holiday homes and hotels; **DRASNIČE**, a low-key holiday spot sandwiched against the hills 5km further south, is more characterful.

The next cluster of resorts begins with the small, unremarkable port of **DRVENIK**, 15km past Drasniče. It's really two settlements separated by a small headland – Donja Vala to the north, and Gornja Vala to the south – each of which has a pebble beach. There's a **tourist office** in Donja Vala (Mon–Sat 8am–noon & 5–7pm, Sun 8am–noon) with **rooms** (①). Four kilometres further on is the quiet and charming village of **ZAOSTROG**, built around a sixteenth-century **Franciscan monastery** (Franjevački samostan), with a simple, plant-filled cloister and a small **museum** (daily 4.30–7.30pm; 10Kn) displaying church silver and traditional agricultural implements. There's a long **beach** in front of the monastery, and the path leading north out of Zaostrog back towards Drvenik leads past some attractive rocky coves. Zaostrog has two **campsites**, the slightly scruffy *Viter* at the centre of the village, and the more attractive *Uvala Borova* site occupying pine-shaded terraces about 1500m to the south.

The Makarska Riviera ends at **GRADAC**, 8km beyond Zaostrog, a frumpy but inoffensive little town with a shingle beach on each side of the central church-topped peninsula. It's got more accommodation than Zaostrog, and is the last real seaside resort before Dubrovnik. **Buses** pick up and drop off near the INA petrol station on the main highway about 1km uphill from the seafront, where you'll find a **tourist office** (daily 8am–9pm; ☎021/697-511, fax 697-375) offering **rooms** (①) and **apartments** (around 250Kn for four people). The most reasonable of the **hotels** is the *Labineca* (☎020/601-555, fax 021/697-594, *hoteli-jadran@st.tel.hr*; ③), a mammoth concrete structure with plain, balconied en-suites – it's 800m north of the centre behind a good stretch of beach.

Ploče to Dubrovnik

Eleven kilometres further south of Gradac the industrial port of **PLOČE** (which, for a brief period in the 1980s, was named Kardeljevo in honour of the bespectacled Slovene ideologist and Tito sidekick Edvard Kardelj) is one of the few genuine eyesores on the Adriatic coast. Developed to provide the cities of the Balkan interior with an outlet to the sea, Ploče lost its raison d'être with the break-up of Yugoslavia, and the town's ill-planned ensemble of tower blocks and dockside cranes slid into stagnation. It's still of marginal importance as a transport hub, however: **rail** services to the Bosnian capital Sarajevo have recently been re-established (currently summer only, but check for the latest information locally), and there's also a **ferry** to Trpanj (7 daily in summer; 3 in winter) on the Pelješac peninsula. Ploče's **bus** and **train stations** are next to each other just off the seafront, about two minutes' walk from the **ferry dock**.

From Ploče, the Magistrala cuts inland to Opužen, where the main road to Mostar and Sarajevo in Bosnia-Hercegovina (see box on p.302) breaks off to the east, passing through the small town of Metković before arriving at the border. Meanwhile, the Magistrala ploughs on across the broad, green delta of the **Neretva River**, once an expanse of marsh and malarial swamp but now – after reclamation – some of the most fertile land in the country. The area is criss-crossed by streams and irrigation channels, and it's possible to take a **boat trip** through its reedy, bird-infested waterways, although these have to be booked in advance through Atlas in Dubrovnik (see p.326) – a day-long trip including lunch will set you back upwards of 300Kn.

South of the delta the Magistrala twists down towards the nine-kilometre stretch of coast which is actually part of **Bosnia-Hercegovina** (border checks are rare, but keep passports handy just in case). This corridor was awarded to the Republic after 1945 in order to give it access to the sea, although it has no strategic or economic value at present – Bosnia-Hercegovina's trade, such as it is, still goes through Ploče. The corridor's only real settlement is the ghastly holiday village of **NEUM**. Food and cigarettes here are slightly cheaper than on the Croatian side of the border, and most Croatian inter-city buses make a pit-stop here so that passengers can do a spot of shopping. Continuing south, the lumpy mountains of the Pelješac peninsula close in against the coast until the turn-off for Ston (see p.295), where the mountains join the mainland and the dividing strip of water peters out in a chain of aquamarine salt flats.

ONWARDS TO BOSNIA-HERCEGOVINA

Bosnia-Hercegovina, or **BiH** (pronounced "bey-ha"), as it is colloquially known, is in theory a unified state comprising two "entities" – the so-called **Serbian Republic** (Republika srpska; RS), which roughly covers the east and northwest of Bosnia, and the **Muslim-Croat Federation**, which covers the rest. Within the Muslim–Croat entity, Croatian-dominated Hercegovina is virtually a state within a state, paying little heed to the government in Sarajevo. Travel between the entities is officially unrestricted, although it would still be unwise for the driver of, say, a Croatian-registered car to stray too far into Serbian areas. Most of what you are likely to want to see – dramatic, still-beautiful Sarajevo, Ottoman-influenced Mostar, and the Catholic pilgrimage centre of Međugorje – are all in the Muslim-Croat Federation.

EU, US and Canadian citizens do not need a **visa** to enter Bosnia-Hercegovina. Australians and New Zealanders need a tourist visa – you'll need to apply at the Bosnian embassy in your home country. The visa requirement is waived if you're just travelling through the Neum corridor, the nine-kilometre stretch of Adriatic coast which falls within Bosnia-Hercegovina's borders. The official **currency** of Bosnia-Hercegovina is the convertible mark (konvertabilna marka; KM), although you'll find that in Croatian-dominated Hercegovina, Deutschmarks and Croatian kuna are the only currencies accepted. **Public transport** from Croatia to the Muslim-Croat Federation is relatively straightforward. The Ploče–Mostar–Sarajevo **rail** line was reopened in 1999 to bring Bosnian holidaymakers to the Adriatic coast, but may remain a summer-only line for the time being. There are, however, numerous **buses**, with at least one departure a day from Zagreb, Split and Dubrovnik to destinations like Sarajevo, Mostar and Međugorje.

Bosnia-Hercegovina is still heavily **mined**. Stick to roads and pavements, and never go wandering off across waste ground or into the countryside.

Trsteno

Thirty kilometres south of the Ston turn-off, the straggling village of **TRSTENO** is an essential stop if you're at all interested in things horticultural. Standing by the roadside in the centre of the village is a majestic pair of 400-year-old plane trees, some fifty metres high and fifteen metres in circumference, and immediately downhill from the trees are the oldest botanical gardens in Croatia, the **Arboretum** (daily: summer 8am–9pm; winter 8am–3pm; 12Kn), founded by Dubrovnik noble Ivan Gucetić in 1502. Gucetić built his summer villa here on a terrace overlooking the sea, surrounded by decorous gardens which still exist in something approaching their original form.

Enthusiasm for out-of-town villas spread from fifteenth-century Venice to the nobles of Split, Hvar and, above all, Dubrovnik. Plants were chosen for their usefulness as much as their grace and colour, and a wide range of medicinal herbs was cultivated. The amount of land available to the Gucetićs in Trsteno also allowed for the creation of forested promenades, so that visitors could feel that they were far away from the cares of town life, although the emphasis was always on improving nature rather than allowing it to run riot. As one of the inscriptions at Trsteno has it: "Traveller, know that here lie the most obvious proofs of wild nature being perfected by art."

In front of the villa lies the oldest part of the Gucetić estate, a typical Renaissance garden in which patches of lavender, rosemary, oleander, bougainvillea, myrtle and cyclamen are divided up by lines of box hedge to form a complex geometrical design. A nearby orchard sports bushy grapefruit and mandarin trees, but once beyond here the garden has a wonderfully lush, uncontrolled feel, as pathways begin to lose themselves in a dense woodland environment comprising trees from around the world. Amidst it all, a trident-wielding statue of Neptune overlooks a pond packed with goldfish. Running northwest from the villa, an avenue of palm trees leads to yet more semi-wilderness areas, thick with cypresses and pines.

There's a **campsite** next to the gardens with an attached **café-restaurant**, and you can sunbathe on the quayside of Trsteno's tiny port, just below.

travel details

TRAINS

Split to: Zagreb (2 daily; 8hr).

BUSES

Hvar Town to: Jelsa (Mon–Sat 4 daily, Sun 1 daily; 55min); Stari Grad (Mon–Sat 4 daily, Sun 2; 35min); Sućuraj (Mon & Fri 1 daily; 1hr 10min); Vrboska (Mon–Sat 4 daily, Sun 1 daily; 45min).

Korčula Town to: Dubrovnik (1 daily; 3hr 30min); Lumbarda (Mon–Sat hourly, Sun 5 daily; 20min); Pupnat (Mon–Sat 7 daily, Sun 4 daily; 20min); Račišće (Mon–Sat 6 daily; 20min); Ston (1 daily; 2hr); Vela Luka (Mon–Sat 6 daily, Sun 4 daily; 1hr 20min); Zagreb (1 daily; 13hr).

Orebić to: Dubrovnik (2 daily, 2hr 40min); Lovište (1 daily; 35min); Ston (3 daily; 1hr 10min); Trpanj (4 daily; 45min); Zagreb (1 daily; 12hr).

Ploče to: Dubrovnik (hourly; 2hr 15min); Split (hourly; 2hr 30min).

Makarska to: Baška Voda (8 daily; 20min); Brela (8 daily; 30min); Gradac (hourly; 50min); Split (hourly; 1hr 10min); Zaostrog (hourly; 40min).

Split to: Dubrovnik (hourly; 4hr 40min); Gradac (hourly; 2hr); Klis (every 30min; 35min); Makarska (hourly; 1hr 10min); Omiš (every 30min; 40min); Plitvice (8 daily; 6hr 30min); Ploče (hourly; 2hr 30min); Rijeka (hourly; 8hr); Šibenik (hourly; 2hr); Sinj (hourly; 1hr); Trsteno (hourly; 4hr); Zadar (hourly; 4hr); Zagreb (8 daily; 9hr); Zaostrog (hourly; 1hr 50min).

Stari Grad to: Hvar Town (Mon–Sat 4 daily, Sun 2; 35min); Jelsa (Mon–Sat 10 daily, Sun 4; 20min); Sućuraj (Mon–Sat 2 daily, Sun 1; 35min); Vrboska (Mon–Sat 10 daily, Sun 4; 10min).

Ston to: Dubrovnik (3 daily; 1hr 30min); Korčula Town (1 daily; 2hr); Orebić (3 daily; 1hr 10min).

Supetar to: Bol (4 daily Mon–Sat, Sun 2; 1hr); Milna (3 daily Mon–Sat, Sun 2; 35min); Povlja (3 daily Mon–Sat, Sun 2; 1hr 10min); Škrip (3 daily; 25min); Sumartin (3 daily Mon–Sat, Sun 2; 1hr 20min).

Trsteno to: Dubrovnik (hourly; 40min).

Vela Luka to: Korčula Town (1hr 20min).

Vis Town to: Komiža (3 daily; 25min).

FERRIES

Drvenik to: Sućuraj (summer 9 daily, winter 4 daily; 20min).

Hvar Town to: Lastovo (6 weekly; 3hr); Split (1–2 daily; 1hr 50min); Vela Luka (6 weekly; 1hr 15min); Vis (weekly; 1hr 15min).

Markarska to: Sumartin (summer 5 daily, winter 3 daily; 30min).

Ploče to: Trpanj (summer 7 daily, winter 3 daily; 1hr).

Orebić to: Dominče (summer 14 daily, winter 7 daily; 15min); Korčula Town (foot passengers only; summer 8 daily; 15min).

Split to: Dubrovnik (summer 1 daily winter 2 weekly; 9hr); Hvar Town (1–2 daily; 1hr 50min); Lastovo (1 daily; 5hr); Rijeka (summer 1 daily, winter 2 weekly; 11hr); Stari Grad (3–5 daily; 2hr); Supetar (summer 13 daily, winter 7 daily; 1hr); Vela Luka (2 daily; 3hr 45min); Vis (2 daily; 2hr 30min); Zadar (summer 4 weekly, winter 2 weekly; 5hr 15min).

Stari Grad to: Dubrovnik (July to mid-Sept 1 daily; 7hr); Korčula Town (July to mid-Sept 1 daily; 3hr 30min); Rijeka (July to mid-Sept 1 daily; 11hr 30min); Split (summer 5 daily, winter 3 daily; 2hr); Zadar (July to mid-Sept 4 weekly; 6hr 45min).

Vela Luka to: Hvar Town (6 weekly; 1hr 15min); Split (2 daily; 2hr 40min–3hr 45min).

CATAMARANS

Split to: Bol (June–Sept 1 daily; 45min); Jelsa (June–Sept 1 daily; 1hr); Korčula Town (July & Aug 3 weekly; 2hr 15min); Lastovo (July & Aug 1 weekly; 2hr 45min); Vela Luka (July & Aug 1 weekly; 2hr).

HYDROFOILS

Hvar Town to: Split (mid-May to mid-Sept 2 daily; 1–2hr); Vis (mid-May to mid-Sept 2 daily; 2hr).

Split to: Hvar Town (mid-May to mid-Sept 2 daily; 1–2hr); Vis (mid-May to mid-Sept 2 daily; 1hr 40min).

Vis to: Hvar Town (mid-May to mid-Sept 2 daily; 2hr); Split (mid-May to mid-Sept 2 daily; 1hr 40min).

INTERNATIONAL FERRIES

Korčula Town to: Bari (mid-June to Sept 1–2 weekly; 11hr); Igoumenitsa (mid-June to Sept 1 weekly; 24hr).

Split to: Ancona (1 daily; 10hr); Bari (mid-June to late Sept 1–2 weekly; 15hr); Igoumenitsa (mid-June to late Sept 1 weekly; 28hr).

Stari Grad to: Ancona (July & Aug 6 weekly, June & Sept 1 weekly; 9hr); Bari (Aug 1–2 weekly; 12hr).

Vis to: Ancona (mid-July to Oct 3 weekly; 9hr).

CHAPTER SEVEN

DUBROVNIK AND THE SOUTH

DUBROVNIK's motto, *Libertas* ("liberty"), which is plastered across the sides of buses and the city's tourist literature, speaks volumes about the city's self-image and the idealized way in which it is perceived by others. For several centuries the city-state of Dubrovnik – or **Ragusa** as it was then known – managed to hang onto a modicum of independence while the rest of this coast fell under the sway of foreign powers. The Venetian Lion of St Mark is conspicuously absent, while statues of **St Blaise** (Sveti Vlaho), the symbol of Dubrovnik's independence, fill every conceivable crack and niche in the city. At its sixteenth-century height, the Ragusan Republic had the third largest merchant fleet in the world, and its galleons gave us the word "argosy", which means simply "ship of Ragusa".

An essentially medieval city reshaped by Baroque town planners after a disastrous earthquake of 1667, Dubrovnik's **historic core** seems to have been suspended in time ever since. Set-piece churches and public buildings blend seamlessly with the green-shuttered stone houses to form a perfect ensemble untouched by the twentieth-century – even modern shop signs are so strictly regulated in the old town as to be almost invisible. Outside the city walls, modern Dubrovnik is comparatively bereft of sights but exudes a Mediterranean elegance: gardens are an explosion of colourful bougainvillea and oleanders, with trees weighted down with figs, lemons, oranges and peaches.

Few visitors will notice any remaining signs of the 1991–92 **Siege of Dubrovnik**, during which over 2000 enemy shells fell on the old city. Reconstruction has been

---

ACCOMMODATION PRICE CODES

The accommodation in this guide has been graded using the following price codes, based on the cost of each establishment's **least expensive double room** in high season (June–Sept), excluding special offers. Hotel room rates almost always include breakfast. Out of season, prices on the coast can fall by up to 50 percent. Where single rooms exist, they usually cost 60–70 percent of the price of a double. For more details, see p.24.

① Less than 200Kn	④ 400–500Kn	⑦ 800–1000Kn
② 200–300Kn	⑤ 500–600Kn	⑧ 1000–1200Kn
③ 300–400Kn	⑥ 600–800Kn	⑨ Over 1200Kn

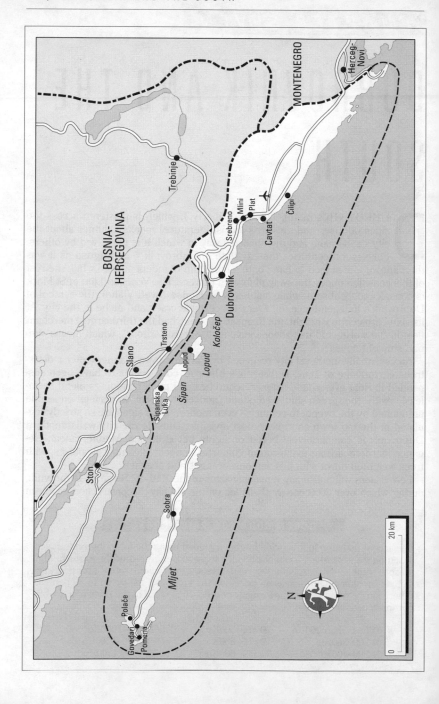

undertaken with astonishing speed, and the old town is pretty much back to its normal self. The fact that conflict took place here at all only reveals itself through subtle details: the vivacious orange-red hues of brand-new roof tiles, or the contrasting shades of grey where damaged facades have been patched up with freshly quarried stone.

Dubrovnik is worth a visit at any time of year, although late spring and summer – when life spills out onto the streets and café tables remain packed well into the night – bring out the best in the city. Croatia's cultural luminaries visit the town during the **Dubrovnik Summer Festival** in July and August, bringing an added dash of glamour to the streets, while the main event in winter is the **Feast of St Blaise** on February 3, when the patron of the city is honoured by a parade and special Mass, followed by much drinking and eating.

The main tourist resorts south of Dubrovnik, **Mlini** and **Cavtat**, are within easy reach of the city by public transport. In addition, Dubrovnik's port is the natural gateway to the southernmost **islands** of the Croatian Adriatic, with the sparsely populated, semi-wild islands of **Koločep**, **Lopud** and **Šipan** providing beach-hoppers with a wealth of out-of-town bathing opportunities. Slightly further out to sea, the green island of **Mljet** is one of the most beautiful on the entire coast, although you'll need a day or two to do it justice.

Some history

Dubrovnik was first settled in the early seventh century by Greco-Roman refugees from the nearby city of Epidaurum (now Cavtat) after it was sacked by the Slavs. The refugees took up residence in the southern part of what is now the old town, then an island known as **Laus** – which later metamorphosed into the name **Ragusa**. The Slavs, meanwhile, settled on the wooded mainland opposite, from which the name **Dubrovnik** (from *dubrava*, meaning "glade") comes. Before long the slim channel between the two was filled in and the two sides merged, producing a symbiosis of Latin and Slav cultures unique in the Mediterranean. Ethnically speaking, the city was almost wholly Slav by the fifteenth century, although leading families consistently claimed Roman lineage, and the nobility actively preserved the use of both Latin and Italian in official circles, if not always in everyday speech. They also held onto the name Ragusa, which remained in use until the early twentieth century.

Initially the city owed allegiance to **Byzantium**, but came increasingly under the influence of the **Venetians**, who gained control of the city in 1204. Protected by Venice from the expansionist Slav states of the Balkan hinterland, the city developed trade links with its inland neighbours, such as the fourteenth-century Serbian empire of Tsar Dušan. The Venetians stayed until 1358, when they were squeezed out of the southern Adriatic by Louis of Hungary. Officially, Dubrovnik became a vassal of the Hungaro-Croatian kingdom, paying an annual tribute, although it effectively became an independent city-state. The emergent **Ragusan Republic** was run by an elected senate – fear of dictatorship meant that the nominal head of state, the Rector (*knez*), was virtually a figurehead. Elected for just one month, he could only leave his palace for state occasions and, after the end of his period of duty, was ineligible for re-election for the next two years.

Civic peace was ensured by allowing the citizenry full economic freedom and the chance to grow rich through commerce. Dubrovnik's network of maritime contacts made it one of the major players in Mediterranean trade, but the key to the city's wealth was its unrivalled access to the markets of the Balkan hinterland. The Ottoman Empire, having absorbed the kingdoms of both Serbia and Bosnia,

THE SIEGE OF DUBROVNIK

Few thought that Dubrovnik would be directly affected by the **break-up of Yugoslavia**: no significant Serbian minority lived in the city, and its strategic importance was questionable. However, in October 1991 units of the JNA (Yugoslav People's Army), supported by volunteers from Montenegro and Serb-dominated eastern Hercegovina, quickly overran the tourist resorts south of Dubrovnik and occupied the high ground commanding approaches to the city. The **bombardment of Dubrovnik** began in early November and lasted until May 1992. Despite considerable damage to the town's historic core, Dubrovnik's medieval fortifications proved remarkably sturdy, with the fortresses of Revelin and St John (more familiar to tourists as the site of the aquarium) pressed into service as shelters for the civilian population.

The logic behind the attack on Dubrovnik was confused. Belgrade strategists unwisely considered it an easy conquest, the fall of which would damage Croatian morale and break the back of Croatian resistance elsewhere on the Adriatic. The attack on Dubrovnik also presented an effective way of dragging both the Montenegrins and the Serbs of eastern Hercegovina into the conflict, not least because it seemed to promise them ample opportunities for pillage.

Attacking forces employed a mixture of bad history and dubious folklore to justify their actions. Dubrovnik's links with medieval Serbia, and the fact that so many leading Ragusan families had originally come from the Balkan interior, were unconvincingly offered up as evidence that the early republic had been part of the Serbian cultural orbit. Far from treating present-day Dubrovnik as a symbol of Mediterranean civilization, opportunist Serbians painted the city as a cesspit of urban corruption that stood in decadent opposition to the pure, martial values of the patriarchal Balkan male. In a bizarre sideshow to the siege, Serbian forces in occupied Cavtat attempted to establish a quisling regime that would run the city once they captured it, declaring a new Duvrovnik Republic headed by Aleksandar Aco Apolonijo, former chief of the Dubrovnik tourist association.

Contrary to Serbian expectations, Dubrovnik's hastily arranged defences held out. In the end, the siege was broken in July 1992 by a Croatian offensive from the north, led by an elite infantry brigade known as the Tigrovi ("Tigers") under General Janko Bobetko – Croatia's first big morale-boosting victory of the war. Once Dubrovnik's land links with the rest of Croatia had been re-established, Croatian forces continued their push southwards, liberating Cavtat and Čilipi.

Direct reminders of the siege are few and far between in Dubrovnik today, but the price of reconstruction has left Dubrovnik shouldering a considerable burden of debt. Almost every hotel in the city suffered some kind of damage, whether due to enemy shelling or to the more long-term wear-and-tear involved in hosting large numbers of refugees, and the loans incurred in putting all this right will take years to pay off.

granted Dubrovnik a privileged trading position, allowing it unrestricted access to Ottoman markets in return for an annual payment of 1000 ducats, an arrangement that remained essentially unchanged until the Ragusan Republic's fall. Dubrovnik established a network of trading colonies stretching from the Adriatic to the Black Sea, from where wheat, wool, animal hides – and, for a time, slaves – could be shipped back to the mother republic before being re-exported to the West at a fat profit. As commerce grew, so did the need to protect it, and the republic extended its borders to include the whole of the coast from Konavle in the south to Pelješac (see p.293) in the north, as well as the islands of Lastovo and Mljet.

Mercantile wealth underpinned an upsurge in culture, producing a fifteenth- and sixteenth-century **golden age** when the best artists and architects in the Adriatic were drawn to the city. It was during this period that many of the urban landmarks of present-day Dubrovnik were completed: Juraj Dalmatinac and Michelozzo Michelozzi worked on the town **walls**, Paskoje Miličević drew up plans for the **Sponza Palace**, and Onofrio della Cava designed the **Rector's Palace**, as well as the two **fountains** that still bear his name. Florentine styles influenced the work of painters such as Nikola Božidarević, and successive gen- erations of writers – playwright Marin Držić and poet Ivan Gundulić among them – abandoned Latin in favour of their native tongue, breathing life into the Croatian literary Renaissance in the process.

Suzerainty over Dubrovnik had passed from the Hungaro-Croatian kingdom to the Ottoman Empire by the early sixteenth century, but shrewd diplomacy and the regular payment of tributes ensured that the city-state retained its virtual inde- pendence. Every year two envoys would visit Istanbul, hand over the agreed cash and stay for a year in fawning acquiescence until someone arrived to relieve them. In the sixteenth and seventeenth centuries Dubrovnik enjoyed the protection of both Spain (Dubrovnik ships sailed with the Armada in 1588) and the papacy, but usually avoided being dragged into explicitly anti-Turkish alliances. In fact, wars between the Ottomans and the West usually led to increased revenues for Dubrovnik, which played on its role as the only neutral port in the Adriatic.

Decline set in with the **earthquake of 1667**, which killed around 5000 people and destroyed many of the city's buildings. Bandits from the interior looted the ruins, and Kara Mustafa, Pasha of Bosnia, demanded huge tributes in return for keeping the robber bands under control. Kara Mustafa's death during the Siege of Vienna in 1683 allowed the city the chance to rebuild, producing the elegantly planned rows of Baroque town houses which characterize the centre of the city to this day. However, the Austro-Turkish conflict of 1683–1718 seriously affected Dubrovnik's inland trade, a blow from which it never really recovered. By the eighteenth century Dubrovnik's nobility was dying out, and commoners were increasingly elevated to noble rank to make up the numbers; anachronistic **feuds** between the Sorbonnesi (old patricians) and Salamanchesi (newly elevated patri- cians) – named, for some unknown reason, after the universities of Sorbonne and Salamanca – weakened the traditional social fabric still further.

The city-state was formally **dissolved by Napoleon** in 1808. The French occu- pation of the city provoked a British naval bombardment, while Russian and Montenegrin forces laid waste to surrounding territories, and the siege ended with Britain confiscating Dubrovnik's fleet. All this had disastrous consequences for the local economy: by the time British traveller W.F. Wingfield arrived in 1853, he found four out of every five suburban houses still uninhabited. In 1815 the **Congress of Vienna** awarded Dubrovnik to the Austrians, who incorporated the city into the newly formed province of Dalmatia. Political and economic activity was henceforth concentrated in towns such as Zadar and Split, leaving Dubrovnik on the fringes of Adriatic society.

The symbolic importance of Dubrovnik long outlived the republic itself. For nineteenth-century Croats the city was a Croatian Athens, a shining example of what could be achieved – both politically and culturally – by the Slav peoples. It was also increasingly a magnet for foreign travellers, who wrote about the city in glow- ing terms, save for Rebecca West, for whom it was too perfect and self-satisfied: "I do not like it," she famously wrote. "It reminds me of the worst of England."

Already a society resort in West's time, Dubrovnik enhanced its reputation for cultural chic with the inception of the **Dubrovnik Festival**, one of Europe's most prestigious, in 1949, while the construction of big hotel complexes in Lapad and Bubin Kuk to the north, and Mlini to the south, helped make Dubrovnik one of the most popular tourist destinations in Yugoslavia in the 1970s and 1980s. Much of the damage done during the **1991–92 siege** was repaired with remarkable speed, and Dubrovnik entered the new millennium fully prepared to welcome back the vacationing hordes.

Arrival, information and accommodation

The **ferry** and **bus terminals** are located about 500m apart in the port suburb of Gruž, 3km west of the old town. The main western entrance to the old town, Pile Gate, is a forty-minute slog along Ante Starčevića from Gruž, and you'd be better

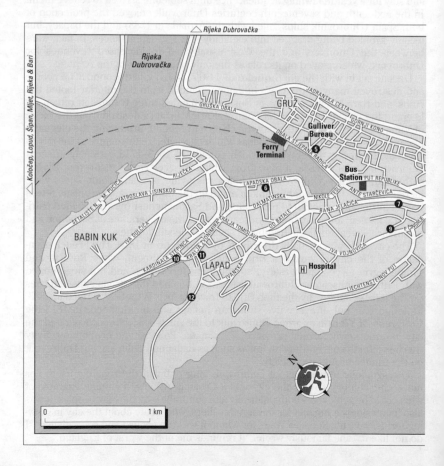

off catching a bus – #1a and #3 from the ferry terminal, #1a, #3 or #6 from behind the bus station. Flat-fare **tickets** for local buses can be bought either from the driver (6Kn; exact change only) or from newspaper kiosks (5Kn). Dubrovnik's **airport** is situated some 22km east of the city, close to the village of Čilipi (see p.332); Croatia Airlines buses meet all arrivals and run to the town bus station, returning from there ninety minutes before each departure (25min; 20Kn each way). A taxi into town will cost about 200Kn.

The privately run **tourist information centre (TIC)** in the old town, just inside the Pile Gate (summer daily 8am–10pm; winter Mon–Sat 8am–4.30pm; ☎020/426-354), makes its money by selling maps and excursions, changing money and booking private rooms, but is a good source of information. The Dubrovnik tourist association (Turistička zajednica grada Dubrovnika), C. Zuzorić 1/2, Dubrovnik (☎020/426-303 or 426-304, fax 422-480, *tzgd@du.tel.hr*), doesn't have a bureau open to the public as yet, but is happy to deal with queries by mail or phone.

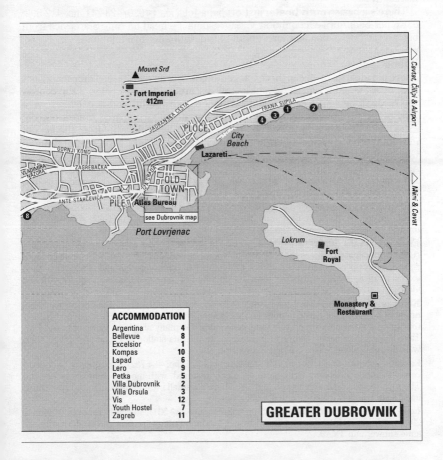

ACCOMMODATION

Argentina	4
Bellevue	8
Excelsior	1
Kompas	10
Lapad	6
Lero	9
Petka	5
Villa Dubrovnik	2
Villa Orsula	3
Vis	12
Youth Hostel	7
Zagreb	11

GREATER DUBROVNIK

Accommodation

There are numerous accommodation agencies handling private **rooms** (②). As well as the tourist information centre (see p.311), the most conveniently located ones are Gulliver, Obala Stjepana Radića 31 (summer Mon–Sat 8am–8pm, Sun 8am–noon; winter Mon–Sat 7am–7pm; ☎020/419-109), just opposite the ferry terminal, with rooms mostly in Lapad, 5km west of the old town, and Atlas, with centrally located branches at Svetog Đurđa 1 (down a flight of steps from the Pile Gate; Mon–Fri 8am–9pm, Sun 9am–1pm; ☎020/442-222, fax 411-100) and at Lučarica 1, just off Luža square in the old town (Mon–Sat 8am–7pm; ☎020/442-528, fax 420-205). Both agencies also offer a range of **apartments** (320–420Kn, depending on how well equipped they are and how many they sleep). You'll probably be approached with offers of private rooms at both the bus and ferry terminals – they're only worth considering if you arrive too late to catch one of the accommodation agencies, as there's no guarantee that they'll be anywhere near the centre.

There's a basic **youth hostel** just off bana Jelačića (☎020/423-241, fax 412-592; 85Kn per bed; April–Oct only) at V. Sagrestana 3 – head up Ante Starčevića from behind the bus station and turn uphill to the right after five minutes.

Hotels

There's a dearth of cheap **hotel** accommodation anywhere in Dubrovnik, not least near the old town. The swankiest places are in Ploče, just east of the centre, where you'll be within easy walking distance of the sights and may even have a view of the medieval walls from your balcony if you're prepared to fork out the extra cash. Elsewhere, you'll probably be a short bus ride away from the action: most of the big package hotels are on the Lapad peninsula, 5km west of the Pile Gate, where there are some pleasant, if crowded, beaches.

Argentina, Frana Supila 14 (440-555 or 426-525, fax 432-524, *www.hoteli-argentina.hr*). Large 1920s hotel a 10min walk east of the old town, with all the creature comforts including its own concrete beach and a small swimming pool. ⑥, ⑦ with sea view.

Bellevue, Pera Čingrije 7 (☎020/413-306 or 413-095, fax 414-058). Dramatically situated on a clifftop overlooking Danče Bay, some fifteen minutes' walk from Pile Gate, with standard, unfussy en-suites. Open April–Oct. ④.

Excelsior, Frana Supila 12 (☎020/414-215, fax 414-214). Just east of the old town, and recently modernized, this is the only five-star hotel on the Adriatic coast, with plush en-suite rooms, indoor pool and fitness centre. The terraces of the hotel's bar and restaurants have excellent views back towards the town, as do some of the room balconies. ⑥, ⑦ with sea view.

Kompas, Masarykov Put 9, Lapad (☎020/435-777, fax 435-877). One of the better package-oriented hotels on the Lapad peninsula, this is a well-run place used by German and British tour groups. All rooms are en suite and have cable TV; many also have views of Lapad Bay. Take bus #6 (destination Dubrava) from opposite the bus station to Lapad post office, then walk downhill along Šetalište Kralja Zvonimira. ⑥.

Lapad, Lapadska obala 37 (☎020/432-922 or 413-576, fax 424-782). Large early twentieth-century hotel overlooking Gruž harbour, nicely restored, with modern annexes tacked on. The neat rooms come with air con and TV. There's a small swimming pool in the courtyard, and Lapad beach is fifteen minutes' walk away. ④.

Lero, I. Vojnovića 14 (☎020/411-455 or 432-734, fax 432-501). Recently renovated hotel a 20min walk (or a short ride on bus #4) from Pile Gate. Rooms are neat and modern with en-suite shower and TV. ⑤.

Petka, Obala Stjepana Radića 38, Gruž (☎020/418-008, fax 418-058). Medium-rise concrete affair opposite the ferry landing. The newly refurbished rooms are small but spick and span, with shower, TV and phone, while front-facing rooms have good views of the port. ⑤.

Villa Dubrovnik, Vlaha Bukovca 6 (☎020/422-933, fax 423-465, *Villa.Dubrovnik@laus.hr*). Smallish hotel 1km east of the old town with its own gardens and concrete beach. Rooms come with all the usual comforts, plus views of the island of Lokrum. ⑦.

Villa Orsula, Frana Supila 14 (☎020/440-555 or 426-525, fax 432-524, *www. hoteli-argentina.hr*). Compact, plushly furnished rooms in a 1930s villa sandwiched between the *Argentina* and *Excelsior* hotels. Great views of the old town, a lovely terraced garden and a small concrete beach. ⑨; luxury apartments for 2 people go for 2000Kn.

Vis, Masarykov put 4, Lapad (☎020/414-166, fax 414-164). On the eastern side of Lapad Bay, this modern hotel has simple en-suites and pleasant restaurant and café terraces overlooking a generous stretch of private beach. Take bus #4 (destination *Hotel Palace*) from opposite the bus station. ④.

Zagreb, Šetalište kralja Zvonimira 31, Lapad (☎020/436-136, fax 436-006). Plain en-suite rooms in a pleasant, early twentieth-century building surrounded by stately palms, a 2min walk from Lapad beach. Directions as for *Hotel Kompas*. ③.

The Town

With a population of a little over 30,000, Dubrovnik isn't as large a city as you might think, and although it sprawls along the coast for several kilometres, its real heart is the walled and surprisingly compact **old town**. Outside the walls the city is much like any other in Croatia: the **Lapad** and **Babin Kuk peninsulas** to the northwest are home to most of the large package hotels, plus a couple of beaches, east of which is **Gruž**, the city's port and transit district.

Running above the town to the east is the bare ridge of **Mount Srđ**, 412m high and crowned by the now derelict **Fort Imperial**, built by Napoleon's occupying army in 1808. The view of the old town from the top is impressive, but the cable-car that used to run up here was ruined in the war, and you'd be quite mad to ascend Srđ on foot in the summer heat, though it's a pleasant, if steep, walk at cooler times of the year. The best place for swimming and sunbathing is the islet of **Lokrum**, a short taxi-boat ride from the old town.

The city walls

The **Pile Gate**, where buses from the ferry and bus terminals arrive, is the logical place to start exploring the old town. The northernmost of the two main entrances to the medieval city, the gate – a simple archway reached through a plain, pillbox-like bastion – is accessible by a stone bridge dating from 1471 which crosses the former moat, now a park full of fruit trees. From here, the best way to get your bearings is by making a tour of the still largely intact **City Walls** (Gradske zidine; daily: summer 9am–7.30pm; winter 10am–3pm; 10Kn), which stretch for some 2km, completely surrounding the old town. They are 25 metres high and encrusted with towers and bastions, and it's impossible not to be struck by their remarkable size and state of preservation. Some parts date back to the tenth century, but most of the original construction was undertaken in the twelfth and thirteenth centuries, with subsequent rebuildings and reinforcements carried out in the mid-fifteenth century when fear of Ottoman expansion was at its height.

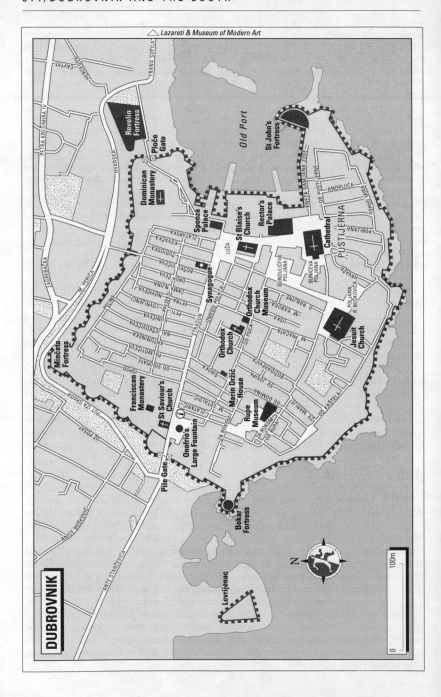

△ Lazareti & Museum of Modern Art

Old Port

DUBROVNIK

N

100m

0

Once you're on top, the views over the town are of a patchwork sea of terracotta tiles, punctuated by sculpted domes and towers and laid out in an almost uniform grid plan – the Ragusan authorities introduced strict planning regulations to take account of the city's growth as early as the 1270s, and the rebuilding programme which followed the earthquake of 1667 rationalized things still further. Heading clockwise around the walls from the Pile Gate, it's a gentle 200m climb towards the fat, concentric turrets of the **Minčeta Fortress**, which guards the old town's northern corner. It was begun in 1455 by the Florentine architect Michelozzo Michelozzi before he left and was replaced by Juraj Dalmatinac (see box on p.227), who designed the eye-catching crown of battlements that has made Minčeta such a landmark. From Minčeta it's a further 500m around the walls to the **Ploče Gate**, where you have to descend to street level for a couple of hundred metres before rejoining the walls at **St John's Fortress**, a W-shaped curve of thick stone facing out to sea. Returning towards Pile Gate along the southern, sea-facing walls, you probably get the best views of old Dubrovnik's tiled roofs and narrow, tunnel-like streets. At the northwestern corner of the old town you'll pass the **Bokar Fortress**, also by Michelozzi and Dalmatinac; a jutting bastion which once guarded sea-borne access to the moat.

Along Stradun

Back inside the Pile Gate, **Stradun** (also known as Placa), the city's main street, runs straight across the old town, following the line of the channel that originally separated the island of Ragusa from the mainland. A constant surge of tourists throngs the Stradun in summer, while the evening *korzo* is the busiest in the whole of Croatia – the street's limestone surface has been buffed to a slippery polish by the tramp of thousands of feet. The set-piece uniformity of this thoroughfare is a result of the 1667 earthquake, after which Stradun was reconstructed with the imposing, outwardly unadorned town houses you see today, displaying a civic commitment to purity and order characteristic of a city government which always had a rather disciplinarian streak, and which has been rigorously maintained by subsequent generations. All the houses have identical door and window frames, the latter flanked by uniform green shutters, and though they're nowadays full of tourist shops, laws forbidding conspicuous shop signs mean that the names of boutiques and restaurants are instead inscribed on the lanterns which hang over each doorway.

Starting at the western end of Stradun, the first thing you see is **Onofrio's Large Fountain** of 1444, a circle of water-spouting heads topped by a bulbous dome where, to guard against the plague, visitors to this hygiene-conscious city had to wash themselves before they were admitted. Built by the Italian architect Onofrio de la Cava, the fountain was the culmination of an elaborate water system that delivered water from Mount Srđ to public washing facilities right across town – though even in this relatively liberal city Jews had a separate fountain. Across the street is the small **St Saviour's Church** (Crkva sveti Spas), a simple but harmonious Renaissance structure whose facade – featuring a rose window beneath a trefoil roof line – may have influenced the cathedral at Hvar (see p.273). The church's bare interior is now used as an exhibition gallery showing contemporary work.

The Franciscan monastery and beyond

A narrow passageway leads from St Saviour's Church to the fourteenth-century **Franciscan monastery** (Franjevački samostan) complex, whose intriguing late

Romanesque cloister is decorated with rows of double arches topped by a confusion of human heads and fantastic animals. The attached **treasury** (daily: summer 9am–5pm, winter unpredictable; 5Kn) is also worth a look, with some manuscripts tracing the development of musical notation, together with relics from the apothecary's shop at the entrance to the cloister. Established in 1317, and still in business, it calls itself the oldest pharmacy in Europe. Among the Gothic reliquaries, a smooth, silver-plated fourteenth-century reliquary for St Ursula's head looks far too small and dainty to contain a human skull.

Back on the Stradun, on the right-hand side of the entrance to the monastery cloister, a small stone embellished with a **gargoyle**-like face juts out of the wall just above pavement height. For some reason, it has become a test of male endurance to stand on this stone – which is extremely difficult to balance on – facing the wall, bare chested and with arms outstretched, for as long as possible before falling off. A few steps beyond is the entrance portal to the monastery church itself, above which is a moving relief of the Pietà, carved by the Petrović brothers in 1499.

Prijeko and the Synagogue

North of the Stradun a succession of alleys filled with potted plants runs uphill towards the city walls, on the way crossing **Prijeko** (literally "across" – a reference to the time when this part of the city was divided from the rest of Dubrovnik by a channel of sea water), which runs parallel to Stradun and contains many of Dubrovnik's more touristy restaurants. Towards the eastern end of Stradun, one of these steep alleys, Žudioska ("Jews' Street"), is home to a tiny **synagogue** (Mon & Wed 10am–noon, Fri 5–7.30pm) – dating from the fifteenth century and said to be the second oldest in the Balkans. The present-day interior dates from the nineteenth century, its heavy brass lamps and candelabras hanging from a bright blue ceiling dotted with star of David motifs. Unlike other Christian powers, Dubrovnik welcomed many of the Jews expelled from Spain in 1492, although anti-Semitism was not unknown. Even before their arrival in the city, scapegoating of Jews formed part of Dubrovnik's medieval carnival, most notably in the pactice known as the *džudijata*, in which an unfortunate lunatic or criminal was dressed as a Jew before being hauled through the streets in an ox cart and made to suffer a make-believe death.

Luža Square

The Stradun's far end broadens into the pigeon-choked **Luža** square, the centre of the medieval town and even today a hub of activity, with its pavement cafés and milling tourists. Overlooking it is the fifteenth-century municipal **bell-tower** (gradski zvonik), a smooth pillar of pale stone topped by an unassuming pimple-like cupola. On the left, the **Sponza Palace** (usually open mornings and evenings if there's an exhibition on), once the city's custom house and mint, grew in storeys as Dubrovnik grew in wealth, with a facade that features broad Renaissance arches on the ground floor and florid Venetian Gothic windows on the first floor. It was designed by Paskoje Miličević in 1522, although much of the stone-carving was done by Josip Andrijić, who also worked on Korčula's cathedral (see p.289) as well as Dubrovnik's St Saviour's Church.

Inside, the majestic courtyard is given over to art exhibitions and occasional concerts in summer. A Latin inscription on the far wall refers to the public scales that once stood here, and puts God firmly on the side of trading standards: "Cheating and tampering with the weights is forbidden, and when I weigh goods God weighs me." The splay-legged, spear-wielding figures underneath (known as the *zelenci*, or "greenies", due to their weather-beaten-bronze appearance) were cast in 1578 and used to strike the bell on the nearby clocktower.

St Blaise's Church and Orlando's Column

Across the square, the Baroque **St Blaise's Church** (Crkva svetog Vlaho), completed in 1714, is in graceful counterpoint to the palace, boasting a fine facade topped by saintly statuettes which seem poised to topple down onto the square below, although the interior is relatively unspectacular. St Blaise is said to have appeared in a vision to a local priest to warn of impending Venetian attack in 791, thereby saving the city and earning himself the position of Dubrovnik's patron saint, although this story was actually invented around 1000 AD, a time of increasing anti-Venetian feeling – the latter had extended their power to the Neretva estuary and looked poised to take Dubrovnik.

Outside the church, plumb in the middle of the square, stands the carved figure of an armoured knight on top of a small column, usually referred to as **Orlando's Column**. Surprisingly for such an insignificant-looking object, this was the focal point of the city-state: erected in 1418 as a morale-boosting monument to freedom, it was here that government ordinances were promulgated and punishments carried out. Nowadays, a flag bearing the *libertas* motto flies from atop the column, and the start of the Dubrovnik Summer Festival is formally proclaimed here every July. Orlando's right arm was also the Republic's standard measurement of length (the Ragusan cubit or Dubrovački lakat, equivalent to 51.2cm); at the base of the column you can still see a line of the same length cut in the stone. The medieval cult of Orlando (or Roland) was born in the twelfth century thanks to the popularity of the epic poem, the *Song of Roland*, which told of the knight's heroic defence of a Pyrenean pass during the Arab invasion of Europe in the eighth century. The cult was a predominantly north European affair, brought to Dubrovnik at the time the city was under the protection of the Hungarian king, Sigismund of Luxemburg, who passed through the city after his defeat by the Turks at Nicopolis in 1396. The legend of Orlando was subsequently adapted to Ragusan requirements by making him the saviour of Dubrovnik in battles against the Saracens, during which he fought a duel with a pirate called Spuzente ("Smelly breath") – nobody seemed to mind that the real Saracen siege of Dubrovnik took place almost a century after Orlando's time.

The eastern side of Luža is flanked by a loggia to the right of which is **Onofrio's Little Fountain**, an altogether more dainty affair than the same sculptor's fountain at the other end of Stradun, decorated with frivolous cherub reliefs courtesy of Onofrio's contemporary, Pietro di Martina of Milan. Along from the fountain, facing the bare southern flank of St Blaise's church, the terrace of the **Gradska kavana** (literally "town café") is where Dubrovnik's more stolid burghers traditionally sit to exchange gossip and observe the ebb and flow of tourists below. The rear of the café, where another terrace looks out onto the small port on the other side of the walls, was once the city **arsenal**, into which galleys were hauled for repairs.

The Rector's Palace

From Luža you can either head northeast via the Dominican monstery and Ploče
Gate to the Revelin Fortress (see p.322), or south to the **Rector's Palace**
(Knežev dvor), the seat of the Ragusan government, in which the incumbent rector sat out his month's term of office. The palace housed all the major offices of
state, plus a dungeon and a powder store (which caused the palace to blow up
twice in the fifteenth century). The building was effectively a prison: the rector
had no real power and could only leave with the say-so of the nobles who elected
him. He could, however, have spent a month locked up in worse places. Begun in
the 1460s after the second of the powder explosions, the current palace, put
together by a loose partnership of architects (including Dalmatinac and
Michelozzi), is a masterpiece of serene proportion, fringed by an ornate arcaded
loggia held up by columns with delicately carved capitals. Furthest to the right as
you face them is the so-called **Asclepius Column**, bearing a relief of a bearded
figure – presumably the Greco-Roman god of medicine, Asclepius – sitting in a
pharmacist's laboratory. Asclepius was thought to be the patron of the ancient city
of Epidauros (modern-day Cavtat, 20km south of Dubrovnik), from which the
original population of Dubrovnik came, making him something of a distant
guardian of the Ragusan state.

The palace's Renaissance atrium is a popular venue for summer recitals. At its
centre is a bust of **Miho Pracat** (1522–1607), a rich shipowner and merchant
from the island of Lopud who left most of his wealth to the city-state on his death
– and was consequently the only citizen the republic ever honoured with a statue.
An imposing staircase leads from the atrium to the balcony, and, off here, the former state rooms, including the rooms of the city council, the Rector's study and
the quarters of the palace guard. Today these are given over to the **City Museum**
(Gradski muzej; Mon–Sat 9am–1pm; 10Kn), a badly labelled collection of dull furniture and mediocre portraiture which nevertheless contains one or two worthwhile artworks: the highlight of the first floor is the fifteenth-century polyptych,
Our Lady, a blaze of Gothic colour by Blaž Jurjev, showing a Madonna emblazoned with gold-leaf plus a panoply of red-cloaked saints. One floor up, look out
for three notable portraits of worthy Ragusans: Nikola Bunić (1635–78), the
statesman who died as a hostage in Silistra jail while trying to renegotiate the tribute paid by Dubrovnik to the Turks; an idealized picture of Cvijeta Zuzorić
(1552–1648), a poetess and legendary beauty who held contemporary men of letters – notably philosopher Nikola Gucetić, who immortalized Zuzorić in his
Dialogues – in thrall; and a kaftan-clad Marojica Kaboga (1630–92), who murdered
his father-in-law in front of the Rector's Palace but escaped from prison in the
chaos following the 1667 earthquake and, finding that there were few other capable nobles left, took charge of the defence and reconstruction of the city.

The cathedral

Across the square from the palace is Dubrovnik's **Cathedral** (Katedrala), a plain
but stately Baroque structure designed by Andrea Bufalini of Urbino in 1672 and
built under the supervision of a succession of architects imported from Italy (the
first three of whom gave up due either to illness or non-payment) before it was
finally completed by local Ilija Kalčić in 1731. According to legend the original
church – destroyed in the 1667 earthquake – was funded by a votive gift from

Richard the Lionheart, who may well have been shipwrecked (and saved) off Ragusa on his way back from the Third Crusade, though traces of the original church's foundations have revealed that it actually predated Richard's visit by a couple of decades. Inside the cathedral are a couple of Italian paintings, including Titian's polyptych of *The Assumption* behind the main altar, a work which was originally purchased by the Brotherhood of the Lazarini – a sign of how rich some of Dubrovnik's commoners' associations really were. On the west side of the nave is the icon of the Lady of Porat, a Veneto-Byzantine Madonna once carried through the streets in time of drought on account of its rain-making powers.

To the left of the altar, the **treasury** (*riznica*; daily 9am–noon & 3–6pm; 5Kn) occupies a specially built room hidden behind heavy wooden doors with three locks – the three keys were held separately by the rector, the bishop and a noble-man. Now packed with gilded shelves and small paintings, the treasury original-ly grew from two collections, one of which was attached to the now destroyed St Stephen's Church, while the other belonged to the old pre-earthquake cathedral. Stored in the Revelin Fortress after the earthquake, both were brought to their current home in a grandiose procession in 1721. One of the prime exhibits is a twelfth-century skull reliquary of St Blaise, fashioned in the shape of a Byzantine crown, studded with portraits of saints and frosted with delicate gold and enamel filigree work. Nearby are both hands and one of the legs of the same saint, the left hand having been brought here from Constantinople by merchant Tomo Vicijan. Even more eyecatching is a bizarre fifteenth-century *Allegory of the Flora and Fauna of Dubrovnik*, a jug and basin festooned with snakes, fish and lizards clam-bering over thick clumps of seaweed.

The western part of the old town

From the cathedral, it's a short walk along Kneza Damjana Jude towards the monolithic hulk of **St John's Fortress**, now refurbished to house a gloomy **aquarium** (akvarium; summer daily 10am–6pm; winter Mon–Sat 10am–1pm; 15Kn) full of Mediterranean marine life, including a pair of sad-looking sea turtles occupying pools into which visitors throw coins for good luck. Upstairs, the **Maritime Museum** (Pomorski muzej; Tues–Sun 9am–1pm; 10Kn) traces the his-tory of Ragusan sea power through a display of marine artefacts ranging from the well-stocked medicine chests of nineteenth-century ships' doctors to an excellent collection of models of Dubrovnik boats throughout the ages.

Walking back west from here along Pustijerne you'll find yourself round the back of the cathedral, south of which stretches one of the city's oldest quarters, **Pustijerna**, much of which predates the seventeenth-century earthquake and preserves a medieval feel, with crumbling, ancient houses crowding in on narrow lanes spanned here and there by arches. Dominating the northern side of Pustijerna, the **Jesuit Church** (Isusovačka crkva), Dubrovnik's largest, is mod-elled, like most Jesuit places of worship, on the enormous church of Gesù in Rome.

The steps that lead down from here also had a Roman model – the Spanish Steps – and sweep down to **Gundulićeva poljana**, the square behind the cathe-dral which is the site of the city's morning fruit and vegetable market. In the mid-dle stands Ivan Rendić's statue of Ivan Gundulić (1589–1638), whose epic poem *Osman*, describing the battles between the Turks and the Christian Slavs, was a landmark in the development of a Croatian patriotic consciousness among the

MARIN DRŽIĆ (1508–67)

In many ways Marin Držić is to Croatia what William Shakespeare is to the English-speaking world: a seminal figure who transformed the knockabout theatrical entertainments of the day into something approaching modern drama, employing an unprecedented richness of vocabulary and metaphor that helped turn the dialect of sixteenth-century Dubrovnik into a literary medium equal to the other tongues of Renaissance Europe. Držić is an important symbol of Dubrovnik's contribution to Croatian – and European – culture, and his works almost always enjoy a central role in the annual Summer Festival.

Born into a family of merchants, Držić was never a member of the aristocratic elite that ran the republic, though the city did award him a scholarship to study at the University of Siena, where his involvement with the theatre began – he was thrown out in 1542 after taking part in a banned theatrical performance. Držić returned to Dubrovnik, and in 1545 entered the service of Graf Rogendorf, an Austrian then working as a diplomat for the Ottoman Empire.

It's not known precisely how and when Držić got involved with the drama troupes active in Dubrovnik. As in other Renaissance cities, satirical, farcical and moralizing performances were put on to entertain the populace at carnival time, or were given at the private parties and wedding feasts of the wealthy. It was in this environment that Držić's bawdy, but subtly plotted, comedies appeared. His first play, the now-lost *Pomet*, was performed in Dubrovnik in 1548. *Dundo Maroje* (1551), a ribald farce set among the expatriate Dubrovnik community in Rome, is the most frequently performed work today. His only tragedy, a reworking of Euripides' *Hecuba*, was interpreted as an anti-aristocratic allegory by the city authorities.

Držić left Dubrovnik for Venice in 1562, where he became an outspoken critic of the Ragusan Republic – his final literary oeuvre took the form of five letters to Cosimo de Medici asking for Florentine help in overthrowing the Dubrovnik aristocracy. The letters went unanswered, and Držić died an embittered and lonely figure. Ragusan men of letters who had rubbished Držić's reputation while he was alive wrote glowing obituaries after his death, and he was swiftly enshrined as the literary standard against whom other Croatian writers were all measured.

educated elite. From here, Puča leads west, running parallel to Stradun, with stepped alleys branching off to meet the sea-walls. At no. 8 there's a **Orthodox Church Museum** (Muzej pravoslavne crkve; daily 9am–1pm; 10Kn), containing a display of icons packed with Virgins, Christ Pantokrators and St Georges, mostly anonymous works hailing from Crete, Greece and the Bay of Kotor in Montenegro. A couple of paces beyond is the **Orthodox Church** itself, whose simple icon screen and functional interior are not of great artistic merit, but nevertheless exude an air of peaceful harmony.

A left turn off Puča brings you to the **House of Marin Držić** at Široka 7 (Dom Marina Držića; Mon–Fri 9am–1pm, Sat 10am–noon; 10Kn), where Croatia's greatest sixteenth-century playwright (see box above) is commemorated in an imaginative audio-visual display (with English commentary) which makes a brave, if not entirely successful, stab at evoking Renaissance Dubrovnik, somewhat hampered by a lack of genuine exhibits – there's not much to actually see apart from a few facsimile manuscripts. Go south from here up Domina to reach the **Rupe Ethnographic Museum** (Etnografski muzej Rupe; Sun–Fri 9am–1pm; 5Kn), whose dull display of regional crafts isn't half as interesting as the building itself, a former municipal grain store built in 1548 and featuring fifteen huge storage pits – the *rupe* or "holes" after which the building is named – carved out of bare rock. The Dubrovnik Republic was almost wholly reliant on imported grain, and the city imposed food-carrying responsibilities on shipowners as much as twelve months in advance. On arrival, wheat was dried in the upper storeys of the building before being sent down chutes into the storage pits below.

The Dominican monastery and museum

Back on Luža, a Gothic arch leads off the northeastern corner of the square to the twisting lane which first passes the entrance to the **Old Port** (Stara luka) – nowadays given over to pleasure boats, and the ferries which run across to the island of Lokrum, just offshore (see p.323) – before reaching the **Dominican monastery**. Begun in 1301, the construction of the monastery was very much a communal endeavour: due to its position hard up against the fortifications, the city authorities provided the Dominicans with extra funds, and ordered the citizenry to contribute labour. It is approached by a grand stairway with a stone balustrade whose columns have been partly mortared in, an ugly modification carried out by the monks themselves in response to the loafers who stood at the bottom of the staircase to ogle the bare ankles of women on their way to church. At the top of the steps a doorway leads through to a fifteenth-century Gothic-Renaissance cloister, filled with palms and orange trees.

The attached **museum** (daily: summer 9am–6pm; winter 9am–5pm; 5Kn) has some outstanding examples of sixteenth-century religious art from Dubrovnik, including three canvases by **Nikola Božidarević**, the leading figure of the period, who managed to combine Byzantine solemnity with the humanism of the Italian Renaissance. Immediately on the right as you enter, Božidarević's triptych with its central Madonna and Child is famous for its depiction of Dubrovnik prior to the earthquake of 1667, when both Franciscan and Dominican monasteries sported soaring Gothic spires; on the panel to the left, St Blaise holds a model of the city, while on the right, St Dominic (accompanied by St Augustine) brandishes a model of the medieval cathedral. Nearby, Božidarević's *Annunciation* of 1513, commissioned by shipowner Marko Kolendić, contains more local detail in one of its lower panels, showing one of the donor's argosies lying off the port of Lopud. The most Italianate of Božidarević's works is the *Virgin and Child* altarpiece, also of 1513, ordered by the Đorđić family (the bearded donor kneels at the feet of St Martin in the lower right-hand corner) – note the concerted attempt at some serious landscape painting in the background.

Much more statically Byzantine in style is the largest work on display, a polyptych of 1448 in dazzling gold-leaf by Lovro Dobričević Marinov, the most illustrious of Božidarević's predecessors. It shows Christ's Baptism in the River Jordan, flanked from left to right by SS Michael, Nicholas, Blaise and Stephen – the last was put to death by stoning, hence the stylized rock shapes which the artist has rather awkwardly placed on his head and shoulders. Alongside a fine but rather statuesque *St Nicholas* (1512) by Mihajlo Hamzić, there's a smaller, much simpler, but rather more gripping *Martyrdom of St Vincent* by Frano Matkov, in which the saint is roasted on a bed of hot coals. Cabinets full of precious silver follow, including the cross of the Serbian king, Stefan Uroš II Milutin (1282–1321), inscribed with archaic Cyrillic lettering, and a reliquary which claims to contain the skull of

King Stephen I of Hungary (975–1038). The Baroque paintings in the next-door room are all fairly second-rate save for Titian's *St Blaise and St Mary Magdalene* – Blaise holds the inevitable model of Dubrovnik while sinister storm clouds gather in the background. The youth holding a fish on the right of the canvas is St Tobias, here accompanied by the donor, Ragusan noble Damjan Pucić, kneeling in prayer.

After all this fine art, the adjoining monastery **church** is a bit of a disappointment. The best artworks are a fine pastel *St Dominic*, by the nineteenth-century Cavtat artist Vlaho Bukovac, and a dramatic Veneto-Byzantine crucifix, attributed to the fourteenth-century Paolo Veneziano, which hangs over the main altar.

The Revelin Fortress to the Museum of Modern Art

Beyond the monastery, the lane emerges at the **Ploče Gate**, the main eastern entrance to the old town. It's larger than the Pile Gate, with another statue of St Blaise in the niche above (the oldest in the city) and a bridge across the moat dating from 1449. The **Revelin Fortress**, just beyond, was begun around the same time, but not finished until 1539, when fears of a coming war between the Turks and the Western powers impelled the Ragusans to hastily strengthen their defences. All other building work in the city was cancelled for four months, leaving the city's builders free to concentrate on the fortress, and leading families had to send their servants to work as labourers, or pay a fine.

Beyond Revelin is the modern suburb of **Ploče**, until the beginning of the twentieth century the scene of a large market where cattle and other goods arrived by caravan from the Balkan interior. Fear that such caravans brought disease prompted the construction in 1590 of a series of quarantine houses, or **Lazareti**, a row of brick-built accommodation blocks and courtyards which can still be seen on the left-hand side of the road. During times of pestilence, visitors entering the Dubrovnik Republic from the Ottoman Empire were obliged to stay here for forty days before proceeding any further. Ottoman traveller Evliya Çelebi, quarantined here in 1664, likened it to a comfortable and homely inn, although he regretted not being allowed out to enjoy Dubrovnik's nightlife. Sanitary concerns were still uppermost in Ragusan minds in the mid-nineteenth century, when British traveller A.A. Paton reported with satisfaction that the market here was penned in by a chest-high stone partition in order to "permit commerce and conversation without contact".

Beyond the Lazareti, Frana Supila leads gently uphill to the **Museum of Modern Art** (Umjetnička galerija; Mon–Sat 10am–1pm & 5–8pm; 10Kn) at no. 23, which hosts high-profile exhibitions on the ground floor, and showcases local painters upstairs. Of the latter, the most important is considered to be the Cavtat-born, Paris-trained Vlaho Bukovac (1855–1922), a stiff Victorian realist whose portraits of late nineteenth-century worthies are considerably less colourful than near-contemporary Marko Rešica's Post-Impressionist Adriatic landscapes, featuring wind-teased cypresses and tamarisks. A couple of post-World War II names are worth picking out: Ivo Dulčić (1916–75), whose blood-red landscape, *Crveni otok* ("Red Island"), verges on the abstract, and Antun Masle (1919–67), painter of the dreamy, Chagall-esque *Lapad*, which is one of the smallest – but best known – pieces in the entire collection.

Lokrum

Facing the suburb of Ploce is the wooded island of **LOKRUM**, 1km to the south-east. Boats leave from the old town's port (see p.321) every half-hour, and take ten minutes (May–Oct 9am–6pm; 12Kn). Reputedly the island where Richard the Lionheart was shipwrecked, it was bought in 1859 by Maximilian von Habsburg, Archduke of Austria (and subsequently Emperor of Mexico), who transformed a former Benedictine monastery here into his summer palace, created a botanical garden which he stocked with exotic plants and cacti, and wrote bad verse about the island's beauty – which his wife unwisely published after his death.

Unfortunately you can't visit the monastery – just up from the island's jetty – although you can look around the cloister (now home to a restaurant) and wander around Maximilian's **Botanical Garden** next door, where odd varieties of giant triffid-like cactus look as if they could swallow you whole. The best of the (largely rocky) **beaches** are beyond the monastery on the island's southwest side, where you'll find a small salt lake just inland, and a naturist beach at the island's southern tip. Shady paths overhung by pines run round the northern part of the island, with tracks leading uphill towards **Fort Royal**, a gun position left by the Napoleonic French whose grey, menacing ramparts rise rather suddenly from the jungle-like greenery covering the island's central ridge.

North and west of the old town

West of the old town, just outside Pile Gate, steps descend towards a small harbour overlooked by the Bokar Fortress on one side and by the monumental, wedge-shaped fortress of **Lovrijenac** (daily 9am–2pm; 10Kn) on the other. Originally built in 1050, but assuming its current shape in the sixteenth century, it was the most important component of the city's south- and west-facing defences, commanding both land and sea approaches from atop a craggy cliff. In recent times Lovrijenac has become famous as the venue for performances of Shakespeare's *Hamlet* during the Dubrovnik Summer Festival, when it becomes the perfect double for Elsinore castle.

A statue of St Lawrence brandishing a model of the fort watches over the fortress entrance, above which there's a typically proud Ragusan inscription: *Non bene pro toto libertas venditur auro* ("All the gold in the world cannot buy freedom"). There's not much to see inside the fortress, though the triangular courtyard framed by chunky arcades is impressive enough on its own, while the upper level gives a fine view of the city and its walls.

Gruž and the Rijeka Dubrovačka

Spearing westwards from the Pile Gate, Ante Starčevića heads towards the suburb of **Gruž** and Dubrovnik's main port, tucked between the mainland on the eastern side and the Lapad peninsula to the northwest. Heading inland from Gruž, the Ombla River forms a deep estuary, the **Rijeka Dubrovačka**, a four-kilometre inlet that was once a favourite resort of wealthy nobles during the period of the Dubrovnik Republic. They built many villas here, a number of which still stand – though these days the look of the place has been largely spoiled by the modern city's industrial and residential sprawl. It's an area you pass through when leaving the city for the north rather than make a special trip to see (buses

#1A and #1B run here from Pile Gate), unless you're heading for the large yachting marina near the suburb of **Komolac** at the end of the inlet, where the slightly unkempt gardens and fishponds of the **Sorkočević Palace** (the interior can't be visited) offer a distant echo of the horticultural splendours of the Ragusan Renaissance.

One kilometre beyond Komolac, on the right-hand side of the road, the river itself emerges dramatically from a limestone cliff at **MLINI**, the next settlement along, although it's a slightly scruffy area that seems to have missed out on development as a beauty spot.

Eating, drinking and nightlife

There's no shortage of **restaurants** in Dubrovnik, and culinary standards are reasonably high, although there's a lack of places with real character – the internationalizing trends of mass tourism have seen to that. Prijeko, the street running parallel to Stradun to the north, is especially stacked with eateries, although there's little to distinguish one from the other: the same range of grilled fish and schnitzel-style meats crops up almost everywhere. When Prijeko is busy, it can be a lively place to sit outside and eat, although prices here are a touch more expensive than elsewhere in the city.

For **snacks**, try the sandwich bars lining the alleys running uphill from Stradun, notably *Kaktus* on Vetranovićeva, a good place for a *pršut* sandwich. There are fruit and vegetable **markets** (Mon–Sat mornings) on Gundulićeva poljana and on the waterfront in Gruž – you can also buy fresh fish at the latter when the boat comes in. There are a couple of **supermarkets** on or near Gundulićeva poljana.

Contessa, Nikole Gucetića. Poky pizzeria uphill from Stradun which sells takeaway slices and also does a decent lasagne.

Kamenica, Gundulićeva poljana 8. Unpretentious and cheap seafood restaurant popular with locals and tourists alike. Favourites include *girice* (tiny fish deep fried and eaten whole), *kamenice* (oysters) and *mušule* (mussels).

Konoba Posat, uz Poset 1. Restaurant with a large and pleasant garden terrace just outside the city walls, slightly uphill from the Pile Gate, offering views towards Minčeta Fortress. Good for grilled meats, and not too expensive.

Marinero, Boškovićeva. Outdoor restaurant in a narrow street two blocks from Stradun, offering the usual range of meat and fresh fish dishes, including decent *lignje* (grilled or breaded squid), but at slightly cheaper prices than the establishments along Prijeko.

Moby Dick, Prijeko. Fairly representative of the eating places along Prijeko, with outdoor seating, a wide choice of fish and meat dishes, reasonably high standards and higher than average Dubrovnik prices. It's a dependable place for fresh seafood, although beware the hard sell: staff will invariably try to talk you into ordering the biggest fish caught that day.

Rozarij, corner of Prijeko and Zlatarska. Cosy and intimate restaurant, with outdoor tables crammed into a quaint corner just uphill from Luža. Good for fish and seafood, and also has a small selection of schnitzel-type meat dishes.

Drinking

Drinking in Dubrovnik is for much of the year a question of finding an outside table from which to see and be seen. The pavement cafés of Stradun are the best places for daytime and early evening drinking, with *Jadranka* and *Dubravka*, facing each other at the eastern end of Stradun, providing the classic people-watching venues. Nearby Bunićeva poljana, just behind the cathedral, becomes one vast outdoor bar on summer nights, with rows of tables spread out between the *Jazz Café Trubadour* and *Café Mirage*. You could also try the streets leading uphill from Stradun, notably Zamanjina, Kunićeva and Antuninska, where you'll find locals sitting on the steps outside tiny bars with blaring music.

The other main area for drinking is northwest of the centre, between the old town and Gruž, where a strip of flashy bars lining bana Jelačića has been dubbed "Bourbon Street" by the locals. When the weather's not good enough to sit outside it's best to head for the small number of places which have a specific character and clientele – a selection are listed below.

Classic Rock Café, Boškovićeva. Roomy first-floor bar decked out with musical instruments and band photos. Youthful atmosphere with lots of loud music – often Euro-pap rather than rock.

Hard Jazz Café Trubadour, Bunićeva poljana. Small and intimate pub-like space which explodes out onto the surrounding square as soon as the weather's warm enough for outdoor drinking. If you're a well-known face in Croatia, you have to be seen drinking here at least once in the summer. Often hosts impromptu live music (jazz, natch).

Libertina, Zlatarska. Tiny bar in a side-street next to the Sponza Palace. A good place for meeting garrulous locals.

Talir, Nalješkovićeva. Legendary post-performance hangout for actors and musicians during the festival. It's a small place, in a side-street midway down Stradun, and most people end up sitting on the steps outside.

Otok, Pobijana 8. Alternative cultural centre hidden away in a narrow alley immediately west of the cathedral, which has a popular late-night bar and occasional live music, but no outdoor seating.

Nightlife and entertainment

The best entertainment in Dubrovnik is the evening *korzo* – a spectatcle in itself. During the summer, the rich cultural diet provided by the **Summer Festival** is augmented by informal open-air pop and jazz concerts in the old town. Outside summer, look out for regular performances mounted by the town's two main cultural institutions: the **Marin Držić Theatre** (☎020/426-437), Pred Dvorom 3, which specializes in serious drama in the Croatian language; and the **Dubrovnik Symphony Orchestra**, whose concert hall is at Ante Starčevića 29 (☎020/417-101). The most central **cinema** is Kino Sloboda on Luža.

Of the **clubbing** venues, *Arsenal*, outside the Pile Gate, stages all-night commercial techno events most weekends but seems to lack either a regular clientele or a strong identity; while the slightly more upmarket *Esperanza*, near the bus station at Put Republike 30, is a popular venue for Croatian pop concerts. *Otok* (see "cafés and bars" above) organizes club evenings and **live music** (rock, ethno and jazz) at the Lazareti, an atmospheric space in the old quarantine buildings (see p.322) east of Ploče Gate. Listings information in the local press is inadequate, so you'll have to look for posters to get an idea of what's on.

Festivals

The **Dubrovnik Summer Festival** (Dubrovačke ljetne igre; July & Aug), stages classical concerts and theatre performances in Dubrovnik's courtyards, squares and bastions in the old town – sometimes offering the only chance to see inside them. The emphasis is very much on high culture: the festival usually includes two Shakespeare plays (traditionally *Hamlet* and one other), a Marin Držić play and a major opera, as well as symphonic concerts and a host of smaller chamber-music events. Seats for the most prestigious events often sell out well in advance, but it should be possible to pick up tickets for most performances at fairly short notice. The full programme is usually published in April: for further details and advance tickets contact Dubrovačke ljetne igre, Poljana Paska Miličevića 1, 20000 Dubrovnik (☎020/412-288 or 426-351, fax 427-944, *program@dubrovnik-festival.hr*). Once the festival starts, tickets (30–200Kn) can be bought from festival information points at the Pile Gate and on Stradun.

As a kind of riposte to the festival, the Otok Cultural Centre organizes the **Karantena Festival** of alternative theatre, performance art and happenings in August, with performances taking place in the Lazareti. Advance information from Otok, Pobijana 8, 2000 Dubrovnik (☎ & fax 020/423-497).

Listings

Airlines Croatia Airlines, Brsalje 9 (Mon–Fri 8am–4pm, Sat 9am–noon; ☎020/413-777).

Airport ☎020/773-377.

Banks and exchange Dubrovačka banka, Stradun (Mon–Fri 7.30am–1pm & 2–7pm, Sat 7.30am–1pm); Gospodarsko-Kreditna banka, Pile Gate (daily 8am–8pm); Zagrebačka banka, Gundulićeva poljana (Mon–Fri 8.30am–noon & 6–8pm, Sat 8.30am–noon).

Bookshop English-language paperbacks are available from Algoritam, Stradun 8.

Bus station ☎020/23-088.

Car rental Budget, Obala S. Radića 20, Gruž (☎020/411-649); Gulliver, Obala S. Radića 31, Gruž (☎020/411-088).

Ferries Tickets from Jadrolinija, Obala S. Radića 40, Gruž (☎020/418-000), and Globetour, Stradun (☎020/428-992).

Hospital At Roka Mišetića, Lapad, 4km west of the old town (☎020/431-777).

Left luggage At the bus station (daily 4.50am–9.30pm).

Pharmacy Kod Zvonika, Stradun (open 24hr).

Post office and telephones Ante Starčevića 2 (Mon–Fri 7am–8pm, Sat 7am–7pm, Sun 8am–2pm).

Taxis There are ranks outside the bus and ferry terminals and at Pile Gate, or call ☎020/24-343.

Travel agents The Atlas offices at Lučarica 1 or Svetog Đurđa 1 handle air tickets and excursions (Mon–Sat 8am–1.30pm & 2.30–7pm; ☎020/442-222).

The Elaphite Islands

The string of islands that crowd the sea between Dubrovnik and the Pelješac peninsula to the north are known as the **Elaphites** ("deer islands"), a name apparently first coined by Pliny the Elder in his 37-volume *Historia Naturalis*. The Elaphites became part of the Dubrovnik Republic from the fourteenth century, sharing in its prosperity and then its decline – by the middle of the eighteenth century many island villages lay abandoned and depopulation had become a major problem. Today, only three of the islands are inhabited – **Koločep**, **Lopud** and **Šipan** – each of which supports a modest tourist industry. Of the three,

Lopud is perhaps the most developed, although tourism everywhere is fairly low key, the absence of cars (private vehicles are not allowed on the islands) contributing to the mellow feel.

All three islands are linked to Dubrovnik by a **ferry** which runs up to Šipan and back again (up to 3 times daily in summer; 1 daily in winter), and are great places for getting away from it all – whether for a day-trip or an extended stay. As you leave Gruž harbour you'll pass the first of the Elaphiti, tiny uninhabited **Daksa** – notorious as the site of a 1945 massacre when over two hundred political opponents of the new communist regime were liquidated.

Koločep

Just half an hour from Dubrovnik by ferry, the islet of **Koločep** is a little over 2.6 square kilometres in area, and has a population of under 150 concentrated in two main hamlets: **DONJE ČELO**, on the north side of the island where the ferry docks, and **GORNJE ČELO** to the southeast. There are no special sights, but Donje Čelo is a pleasant cluster of stone houses which boasts an excellent curving sandy beach. Just uphill from the waterfront, a concreted path strikes inland towards Gornje Čelo, a huddle of vegetation-choked houses overlooking two small bays. From here you can follow innumerable paths into the dense, fragrant pine and deciduous forest that covers the southern part of the island.

Accommodation is limited to the *Hotel Ville Koločep* (☎020/757-025, fax 757-027; ⑥ with compulsory half-board), an ensemble of eight modern blocks ranged across a hillside just above Donje Čelo's beach. There's also a waterfront **café-restaurant** in Donje Čelo offering simple grills and seafood.

Lopud

In Dubrovnik's heyday, **Lopud** was the seat of one of the republic's vice-rectors and, with a population of some 4000 (today it's 400), was a favoured watering-hole of the city's nobles. A large part of Dubrovnik's merchant fleet was based here, and the ruined palaces of shipowners still occupy crumbling corners of the island's only village. Tourism here dates back to the 1920s, and the island's hotels were used by the Italians to intern Jews from Dubrovnik and Bosnia in 1942. They were shipped off to the notorious concentration camp on Rab (see p.195) the following year, though many managed to escape to join the Partisans after the collapse of Italy in 1943.

Located on the northern side of the island, the village of **LOPUD** is strung around a wide, curving bay which boasts a long, crowded and reasonably sandy **beach**. Its most prominent monument is the fortified fifteenth-century **Franciscan monastery** which overlooks the village at the head of the bay – now mostly ruined, it's due to be restored and transformed into a centre for the study of medicinal herbs. The nearby village **museum** (daily 3–4pm; guided tours Thurs at 9am) is in a better state of repair, but the exhibits are of little interest, except perhaps for the sailors' votive plates and two large paintings of the town's arms: no one's sure whether the snake is eating or regurgitating the boy.

A few paces west along the seafront from here, steps lead up to the **Đorđić-Mayner Park** (Perivoj Đorđić-Mayner), grouped around enormous pines, with the inevitable range of palms basking beneath. A few steps beyond lies the ruined palace of **Miho Pracat**, the sixteenth-century merchant and shipowner whose bust stands in the Rector's Palace in Dubrovnik (see p.318). Lopud folk tales sought to explain how Pracat came by his fabulous wealth. Somewhat improbably, he is said to have robbed Dubrovnik cathedral's treasury to pay for his business ventures, one of which involved exporting the city's cats to North Africa, where he had chanced upon a plague of rodents. An asphalted path leads south from Lopud to **Šunj Bay** (Uvala Šunj), 2km away at the opposite end of the island, a lovely shallow cove backed by a grove of pines.

Rooms (②) are available from the tourist office on the seafront (uncertain hours; if it's shut, ask around). There's also an Atlas office nearby (daily 8am–noon & 5–8pm) which books excursions and changes money. A few hundred metres west of the jetty is the *Lafodia* **hotel** (☎020/759-002 or 759-022; ④ with compulsory half-board), a modern affair whose en-suite rooms have small balconies, many with excellent views towards the harbour. The same company runs two (currently closed) seafront hotels, the *Grand* and the *Dubrava-Pracat*, both of which may be cheaper options when they reopen.

Šipan

The largest and least developed of the populated Elaphites, the island of **Šipan** is a delightful combination of craggy hills strung out around a long, fertile plain thick with olive trees and vines and dotted with the occasional hamlet. There are no special sites and there's certainly no nightlife, but if you're after some peace and quiet and gentle hikes, this is one of the best places on the coast.

Ferries terminate at the island's main settlement, **ŠIPANSKA LUKA**, a pretty little place buried at the end of a deep inlet at the island's northern end. The settlement contains the odd relic of former glories: best are the remains of the Magistrate's Palace, ten minutes along the road to Suđurađ, and the neglected villa on the harbourfront, which boasts a balcony supported by carved lions, and seems to be crying out for restoration. Šipanska Luka's main **beach** is about 500m away from the harbourfront, a tiny strip of sand pressed against a thread of rock that separates the western side of the bay from the sea. More isolated spots for bathing can be found by following the path which extends beyond the ferry jetty on the opposite side of the bay, threading its way between rocky shoreline and shady olive groves before petering out in dense undergrowth after a couple of kilometres.

Incoming ferries are often met by locals offering private **rooms** (①) – if not, just ask around. Otherwise, the harbourfront **hotel**, the *Šipan* (☎020/758-000, fax 758-004; ③; April to mid-Oct), offers standard en-suites, of which the attic rooms on the top floor are the cosiest. **Eating** and **drinking** possibilities are limited to the hotel restaurant and the couple of bars nearby.

Heading south out of Šipanska Luka, the seven-kilometre walk to **SUĐURAĐ** takes you past some lovely inland scenery. Suđurađ itself – little more than a clump of houses grouped around a bay – is overlooked by an imposing stone **tower**, all that remains of a summer palace belonging to the sixteenth-century Dubrovnik shipowner Vice Stjepović Skočibuha.

Mljet

The westernmost of the islands accessible by local ferry from Dubrovnik is **MLJET**, a thin strip of land, some 32km long and never more than 3km wide, running roughly parallel to the Pelješac peninsula (see p.293). The most visited part of the island is the green and unspoilt west, where untouched Mediterranean forest and two saltwater lakes provide the focus of the **Mljet National Park**, an area of arcadian beauty within which lie the villages of **Polače** and **Pomena**. Despite a nascent package-holiday industry in the village of Pomena, the region remains invitingly quiet and there are few shopping or nightlife opportunities. If you come here by car, be sure to fill your tank before you cross the water – there's nowhere to get petrol on the island.

According to legend, Odysseus holed up on Mljet for some time with the nymph Calypso, and the island also has fair claim to being the island of Melita, where St Paul ran aground on his way to Italy and was bitten by a viper before he set sail again (Mljet's snake problem was once so bad that a colony of mongooses had to be imported from India to get rid of them). The Romans used the island as a place of exile, and it was briefly owned by the kings of Bosnia, who sold it to the Dubrovnik in 1333. The republic sent an emissary on May 1 every year to rule the island for a year, and many of Dubrovnik's admirals built summer houses here.

Sobra to Pomena

Ferries from Dubrovnik dock 3km south of **SOBRA**, an insignificant settlement roughly halfway along the island. Sobra–Polače–Pomena buses await incoming ferries. After winding its way over to the west the road descends to **POLAČE**, little more than a row of houses stretched along a small harbour – whose waters are clean enough to swim in. The harbour is bordered to the north by the impressively lofty walls of a fourth-century AD **Roman palace**, the inner courtyard of which is now home to a couple of lemon trees and a chicken coop. A small white house on the harbour contains a **tourist office** (mid-June to mid-Sept Mon–Sat 8am–noon & 4–7pm; mid-Sept to mid-June Mon–Fri 8am–1pm; ☎020/745-125) which can point you in the direction of locals offering **rooms** (①). For **food and drink**, there are a couple of café restaurants along the front, and a small provisions store open mornings and evenings.

Sheltering in a bay at the western tip of Mljet, **POMENA** is a seaside hamlet similar to Polače – save for the presence of a large modern hotel and a harbour which is becoming increasingly popular with touring yachtspeople. The *Odisej* **hotel** (☎020/744-022; ⑥) is a prim collection of whitewashed modern blocks, although room quality varies from one part of the complex to the other – insist on a room with air con and TV. Next door, the family-run, seven-room *Pansion Pomena* (☎020/744-075; ①) presents a more down-to-earth alternative, with plain rooms and shared facilities. For **food**, the restaurant of the *Odisej* is respectable, and the *Pansion Pomena* offers excellent-value set lunches and a more elaborate range of pricey seafood in the evening. There are **exchange** facilities in the *Odisej*. Most swimmers head for the two lakes (see p.330), although there are regular taxi boats (check the lobby of the *Odisej* for details) to the naturist islet of **Pomeštak**, just offshore.

The Mljet National Park

There's no official entrance point to the **Mljet National Park** as such (and by the time you arrive in Polače or Pomena you're already well inside it), but you're expected to buy a ticket (50Kn) from one of the kiosks in Pomena, Polače or just outside Goveđari once you've settled in, and certainly before you start exploring. The kiosks also have park information and **maps** (50Kn).

The park's main attractions are its two forest-shrouded "lakes" (actually inlets connected to the sea by narrow channels), **Malo jezero** ("Small Lake") and **Veliko jezero** ("Big Lake"), which together form a stretch of water some 4km long. Both are encircled by foot- and cycle paths, and the clear, blue-green waters are perfect for bathing. Malo jezero is ten minutes' walk south of Pomena, by way of a stone-paved footpath that heads over a wooded ridge just up from the port. A ten-minute walk along the shore of Malo jezero brings you to **Mali most** ("Little Bridge"), spanning the channel feeding into Veliko jezero, which you can circumnavigate on foot in a couple of hours. If you're staying in Polače, it's possible to walk over to the lakes by road or by well-signed forest path (via the 253-metre Montokuc hill) in about 45 minutes.

Mali most is the departure point for an hourly boat service (vouchers for the trip are included with the entrance ticket) down Veliko jezero to **St Mary's Island** (Otok svete Marije), where the Benedictines established a monastery in the twelfth century. Overlooked by a sturdy defensive tower, the monastery church features unusually chunky altarpieces carved from local stone and exuberantly coloured. The central dome is enclosed in a squat quadrangular tower, whose dog-tooth-patterned exterior can be admired from the neighbouring courtyard. There's a **café-restaurant** in the monastery grounds.

Bikes are a handy way to get around the lakes: they can be rented from Mali most or in front of the *Odisej* hotel in Pomena (20Kn per hour). **Kayaks** (same price) can also be rented at Mali most.

South of Dubrovnik

Immediately south of Dubrovnik you run into what was once one of the most heavily developed parts of the coast, with a string of purpose-built resorts edging the road and obscuring all sight of the sea. The area was occupied by Serb and Montenegrin troops in the winter of 1991–92 and most of the hotels looted, although all but a small proportion have now been spruced up and put back in service. Starting with Kupari, and followed swiftly by Srebreno, Mlini, Soline and Plat, the resorts merge to form a six-kilometre line of apartment blocks, weekend villas, angular hotels and waterside cafés. The beaches here are not worth making a special visit for, and it's best to press on to **Cavtat**, 3km beyond Plat, which preserves a modicum of traditional architecture fringed by lush Mediterranean vegetation, or the village of **Čilipi**, where you can hear folk music on summer Sundays. Thirty-five kilometres south of Dubrovnik the road arrives at the border with **Montenegro** (Crna Gora in Croatian and Serbian), although you should check visa requirements in your home country before attempting to cross it.

Bus #10 runs roughly every hour from Dubrovnik to Cavtat. Beyond here, public transport is less frequent, with about three services daily to Čilipi.

Cavtat

Twenty kilometres south of Dubrovnik, and 3km off the main coastal highway, **CAVTAT** is a dainty coastal town and package resort which began life in the third century BC as Epidaurum, a colony founded by Greeks from the island of Vis. There's nothing left to see of the antique town: Epidaurum was evacuated in favour of Dubrovnik after a thorough ransacking by the Slavs in the seventh century, and the pretty fishing village of Cavtat subsequently grew up in its place. Discovered by Austro-Hungarian holidaymakers at the beginning of the twentieth century, Cavtat was a favourite haunt of the wealthy until a rash of high-rise hotel building in the 1980s changed the place's profile. Happily, the hotels are set apart from the palm-dotted seafront of the original village, which straddles the neck of a sweet-smelling wooded peninsula.

Much of Cavtat's former charm survives in the old part of town, which straddles the ridge behind the waterfront. The showpiece here is the **Račić Mausoleum** (Mon–Sat 10am–noon & 5–7pm, Sun 10am–noon; 4Kn), built on a prime spot high above the town in 1921 by Ivan Meštrović for a local shipowning family. It's one of Meštrović's more succesful stabs at architectural eclecticism: a simple, Byzantine-inspired, domed structure guarded by stern, archaic Greek angels and decorated with dog-faced gargoyles, Teutonic-looking eagles and what look like neo-Egyptian winged lambs just below the cupola.

Downhill from here on the waterfront's northern end, the rather plain-looking **Monastery of Our Lady of the Snow** (Samostan snježne Gospe) contains a couple of early Renaissance gems in its small church: the first, Vičko Lovrin's triptych of 1509 at the back of the church, shows a gold-clad Archangel Michael slaying a demon while John the Baptist and St Nicholas look on from the wings; the second, Božidar Vlatković's *Madonna and Child* (1494) on the main altar, is a small piece somewhat overpowered by its fussy Baroque frame. The modern cream-coloured building next door houses the **Vlaho Bukovac gallery** (Tues–Sat 10am–noon & 6–9pm, Sun & Mon 6–9pm), honouring the Cavtat-born painter with a selection of his stolid portraits of self-confident, early twentieth-century middle-class types.

A brace of fine shingle **beaches** lie about 1km east of the town centre in an area known as **Žal** (literally, "beach"), although the proximity of the package hotels ensures that they're usually crowded. Quieter spots, if you don't mind perching on rocks, can be found at the far end of the peninsula, ten minutes' walk north from town, or on the Sustjepan peninsula immediately to the west. The latter has a naturist section, just on the other side of the *Croatia Hotel*.

Practicalities

Ample private **rooms** (②) are available from the Astarea agency (Mon–Sat 8am–8pm, Sun 9am–noon), just by the bus stop. There's an old harbourfront **hotel** in the centre, the slightly dowdy *Supetar* (☎020/475-555, fax 478-213; ③), and a string of three more modern package-oriented hotels in the Žal area: the *Cavtat* (☎020/478-246; ④), the *Albatross* (☎020/471-333; ⑤) and the *Epidaurus* (☎020/471-444; ⑤), all owned by the same company and offering similar standards of beachfront comfort, although the *Albatross* has a large private swimming pool and plusher, air-conditioned rooms. On the other side of town, the *Croatia Hotel de Luxe* (☎020/475-555 or 478-055, fax 478-213; ⑥) is a vast multi-tiered concrete affair hogging the ridge of the Sustjepan peninsula. It's easy to get lost in its seemingly endless corridors, but it has modern air-conditioned rooms with TV, a swimming pool and a private beach facing the Cavtat waterfront.

Numerous **restaurants** line the waterfront, offering everything from cheap pizza to more expensive local specialities: the *Cavtat* is as good as any, with a repertoire ranging from simple pasta dishes to succulent fresh fish. Slightly inland, the *Konoba Kolona* offers cheap and tasty eats on a small but shady garden terrace just by the bus stop.

Buses to Dubrovnik leave roughly every hour. Privately operated **boats** (look out for boards on the waterfront or near the hotels advertising departure times) do the same trip for about 20Kn.

Čilipi

Six kilometres south of Cavtat, just beyond Dubrovnik's airport, ČILIPI is the main village of the Konavle region, a small area known for the colourful costumes of its inhabitants, characterized by the small pillbox hats donned by unmarried girls and the enormous white scarves worn by married women. They're not greatly in evidence any more, though Čilipi has become something of an excursion spot for tour operators from Dubrovnik because of the **folklore shows** which take place on the village's flagstoned central square every summer Sunday. Organized by the local folklore society, performances are held in the late morning immediately after mass, when locals and tourists alike perch on the church steps to observe a forty-minute medley of local songs and dances. Foremost among the latter is the *linđo*, which employs rigid, stylized gestures to mimic the rites of courtship, and is accompanied by the *lirica*, an archaic, droning fiddle.

Trips to Čilipi from Dubrovnik are run by the ubiquitous Atlas agency (see p.312), although you can get here independently using the three daily buses which run from Dubrovnik via Čilipi to Gruda or Molunat. There are a couple of cafés just off the main square, and a largely tourist-oriented Sunday **market** selling folksy embroidery and textiles.

travel details

BUSES

Dubrovnik to: Cavtat (hourly; 40min); Korčula (1 daily; 4hr); Orebić (2 daily; 3hr); Ploče (hourly; 2hr); Pula (1 daily; 15hr); Rijeka (3 daily; 13hr); Split (13 daily; 5hr); Šibenik (9 daily; 6hr 30min); Ston (3 daily; 1hr 30min); Trsteno (hourly; 40min); Vela Luka (1 daily; 5hr); Zagreb (4 daily; 11hr).
Sobra to: Pomena (2 daily; 1hr 10min).

FERRIES

Dubrovnik to: Koločep (1–3 daily; 30min); Lopud (1–3 daily; 50min); Rijeka (summer 1 daily, winter 4 weekly; 22hr); Sobra (1–2 daily; 2hr 15min); Sućuraj (1–3 daily; 1hr); Sipanska Luka (1–3 daily; 1hr 45min).

FLIGHTS

Dubrovnik to: Zagreb (2–3 daily; 1hr).

INTERNATIONAL BUSES

Dubrovnik to: Frankfurt (3 weekly); Mostar (2 daily); Sarajevo (2 daily); Trieste (1 daily).

INTERNATIONAL FERRIES

Dubrovnik to: Ancona (weekly; 15hr); Bari (5 weekly; 8hr); Corfu (2 weekly; 25hr).

PART THREE

THE
CONTEXTS

A BRIEF HISTORY OF CROATIA

History is a serious business in a country which has spent so much of its past under the sway of foreign powers. It's also exceedingly complicated, as the history of Croatia is interlinked, for lengthy periods, with the histories of Hungary, Austria and Venice, not to mention that of the former Yugoslavia.

CROATIA BEFORE THE CROATIANS

Our knowledge of the first humans to inhabit Croatia is patchy, although a form of Neanderthal – named **Krapina Man** after the town in which remains have been found (see p.92) – is known to have roamed the hills north of Zagreb some thirty millennia ago. By about the seventh millennium BC, Neolithic farmers had spread out along the Adriatic coast, and were increasingly using the islands as stepping stones to cross the Adriatic. Advanced Neolithic cultures certainly existed on Hvar, where 5000-year-old painted pottery offers evidence of the so-called Hvar Culture, and beside the River Danube in eastern Slavonia, where similarly rich ceramics have been unearthed at Vučedol near Vukovar.

By the first millennium BC the indigenous peoples of the region now covered by Croatia, Bosnia, Albania and Serbia had begun to co-alesce into a group of tribes subsequently known as the **Illyrians**. Although they were united by common styles of fortress-building and burial-mound construction, it's not clear whether the Illyrians ever existed as a culturally homogenous group, and they were never politically united. They did, however, produce some powerful tribal states: the Histri in Istria and the Liburnians in the Kvarner and northern Dalmatia were minor maritime powers, building towns whose names – in modified, Slavonic form – still survive, like Aenona (Nin) and Jadera (Zadar).

GREEKS, ROMANS AND BYZANTINES

Greek city-states, led by Syracuse in Sicily, began dispatching trade missions and settlers to the Adriatic coast from the fourth century BC onwards, founding colonies such as Issa (on present-day Vis) and Paros (on Hvar). The Illyrians tried unsuccessfully to drive the new colonists out, but the biggest threat to the Greeks came from King Agron and his queen and successor Teuta, whose territory stretched from present-day Zadar in the north to what is now Albania in the south.

In 229 BC the Greeks asked for Roman help against Teuta, beginning a period of **Roman expansion** that continued until 9 AD, when the eastern Adriatic and its hinterland were annexed by the future emperor Tiberius. The seaboard was reorganized into the Roman province of Dalmatia, while northern and eastern Croatia were divided between the provinces of Noricum (which covered much of present-day Austria) and Pannonia (which stretched into modern Hungary). The older Greek settlements continued to flourish, but were outshone as political and cultural centres by new Roman cities, often founded on or near sites that had previously served as power bases for the Illyrian tribes. The main Roman centres were Salona (Solin, near Split) and Jadera (Zadar), although the vast amphitheatre at Pula attests to the prosperity of Istria during this period. The Illyrians were either Romanized or absorbed by later immigrants like the Slavs.

Roman power in the Adriatic ended temporarily in 493, when the region fell to King Teodoric of the Ostrogoths, although Justinian, emperor of the eastern half of the Roman Empire, **Byzantium**, reconquered the area in 544. Inland, things were more chaotic: the **Avars**, a warlike central Asian people, briefly forged a central European empire at the beginning of the seventh century, and even reached the coast, sacking Salona and Epidaurum in 614. Refugees from these cities went on to found Split and Dubrovnik.

THE ARRIVAL OF THE CROATS

Precisely when the **Croats** – a Slav tribe who came to southeastern Europe from an area north of the Carpathians – arrived in the territories they now inhabit is a bit of a mystery, although the Byzantine Emperor Constantine Porphyrogenitus (writing 300 years after the event) stated that they were invited by the Byzantine Emperor Heraclius in the early seventh century in order to serve as a counterweight to the Avars.

One problem in tracking the movement of the Croats before their arrival in southeast Europe is that the name "Croat" (Hrvat) is thought to be of Iranian rather than Slav origin, suggesting that the Croats were subject to Iranian-speaking tribes before moving towards southeastern Europe, or even that the Croats were themselves of Iranian origin and picked up the Slav tongue from neighbours as they migrated. (The latter theory was popular among nationalist intellectuals during World War II because it seemed to lend the Croats a veneer of Aryan respectability at a time when Nazi influence was at its height, although it has now lost a good deal of its intellectual credibility.)

The Croats probably migrated to southeastern Europe at the same time as the **Serbs**, who settled in the middle of the Balkan peninsula. The fact that the groups share a common language suggests that they originated in the same area, and Serbs and Croats – along with other tribes speaking similar Slav dialects such as the Slovenes, Bulgarians and Macedonians – came to be known collectively as the **South Slavs**.

THE MEDIEVAL CROATIAN STATE

The Croats who settled along the Dalmatian seaboard established a tribal state ruled by a *knez* (prince or duke), who assumed leadership of other Slav tribes already settled in the region, as well as sundry Avars and surviving remnants of the Illyrian and Roman populations. Inland areas to the north, such as present-day Slavonia, fell under independent chieftains loosely allied to the Croats on the Adriatic. The existence of two Croatian heartlands – a southern one oriented towards the Mediterranean and a northern one looking towards central Europe – has had a profound effect on Croatian culture ever since.

Both areas maintained a tenuous independence until squeezed by powerful neighbouring empires: the Byzantines, who still held several Adriatic towns and islands, and the Carolingian Empire of the Franks, which was expanding into central Europe by the late 700s. Croat leaders boosted their legitimacy in the eyes of their more advanced western neighbours by accepting **Christianity**, and although the northern Croatian state became subject to the Franks in the 790s, the southern state played one predator off against another and prospered. Ruling from their citadel at Klis (see p.262), princes such as Mislav (835–845), Trpimir (845–864) and Domagoj (864–876) paid homage to either Byzantines or Franks as necessary, while preserving *de facto* independence and simultaneously beating off two newcomers to the Adriatic, the Venetians and the Arabs.

With the Croatian state growing stronger militarily, Branimir (879–892) threw off Byzantine vassalage once and for all, and was recognized by Pope John VIII as an independent ruler, definitively tying Croatia to the Roman rather than the Byzantine Church. His successor-but-one, **Tomislav** (910–928), pushed things further, defeating the Hungarians to gain control of northern Croatia and battling the Bulgarians to win northwestern Bosnia. Eager to secure an alliance with Tomislav, the Byzantines ceded sovereignty over Split, Trogir, Osor, Rab and Krk. Declaring himself king in 925 (previous Croatian leaders had been content to call themselves "prince"), Tomislav reorganized the Croatian Church, placing all his lands under the control of a Croatian archbishop at Split, thereby lessening papal influence without actually questioning his ultimate loyalty to the pope.

For the seventy years following Tomislav's death Croatia was financially, militarily and dynastically stable, until a succession crisis in the early eleventh century allowed both Venice and Byzantium to regain footholds on the Adriatic coast, while northern Croatia was lost to the Hungarians. **Petar Krešimir IV** (1058–75) presided over a revival of fortunes, and reunion with northern Croatia was achieved by weaning the ruler of Slavonia, **Dimitr Zvonimir**, away from Hungary and appointing him co-ruler (though Zvonimir's marriage to Princess Jelena of Hungary would later complicate the dynastic picture). Petar Krešimir died childless, and power passed to Zvonimir (1075–89), though he too died without issue, leaving the nobles to chose Stjepan II (1089–91), who also failed to produce an heir.

The kingdom began to disintegrate, leaving Zvonimir's brother-in-law, King Ladislas of Hungary, free to secure control of the north, while a group of nobles in the south regrouped under King Petar (1093–97). Independent Croatia's last monarch was defeated by a Hungarian army under Ladislas's successor Koloman at **Gvozd** (subsequently named Petrova gora or Peter's Mountain), the highland region south of Zagreb.

Hungarian control of Croatia was confirmed by the **Pacta Conventa** of 1102, according to the terms of which Croatia and Hungary remained separate states united by the same royal family. Croatia retained its own institutions – a Ban (governor) appointed by the king, and the Sabor (parliament) representing the nobility – but despite these provisions, the Hungarian crown steadily reduced the power of the Croatian aristocracy in the years that followed, speeding Croatia's demise as a united and distinct state.

CROATIA UNDER THE HUNGARIANS

Life in what became known as the **Hungaro-Croatian kingdom** was characterized by a strengthening of the feudal order, with the landed nobility growing stronger at the expense of a rural population overloaded with feudal obligations. Town life, especially in northern Croatia, underwent rapid development as Varaždin, Vukovar, Samobor and Zagreb were earmarked as centres of trade.

The Croatian lands were overrun by the **Tatars** in 1242, but King Bela IV managed to keep royal authority alive by moving from one coastal strongpoint to the next (innumerable Adriatic towns were subsequently given special privileges for assisting Bela in his flight). The material damage was enormous, however, and much medieval Croatian architecture was lost. The Hungarian monarchy was strengthened

under **Charles Robert of Anjou** (1301–42), who further weakened the remaining independence of the south Croatian nobles. Hungarian control of the Adriatic seaboard – slowly eroded by Venetian penetration during the previous century – was reasserted by Charles Robert and his son **Louis of Anjou** (1342–82), who threw the Venetians out of Dalmatia in 1358. Louis died without a male heir, and his inheritance was disputed by Sigismund of Luxembourg (Louis's son-in-law) and Charles III of Naples. The nobles of southern Croatia appointed Charles's son, **Ladislas of Naples**, king of Croatia in 1403, but his armies were no match for those of Sigismund. In 1409, Ladislas fled, selling his rights over Dalmatia to the Venetians for the sum of 100,000 ducats.

Venice was now in command of almost all of Istria and Dalmatia apart from a few Habsburg territories and **Dubrovnik**, an independent city-state owing nominal allegiance to the Hungarian crown. The Venetians were to stay for over 350 years, flooding the Adriatic seaboard with Italianate art and architecture, but taking away the traditional autonomy of the towns at the same time.

Cut off from the Adriatic, the Croatian lands in the Dalmatian hinterland and the north were also being squeezed from another direction. Croatia's immediate neighbour to the southeast was **Bosnia**, a mountainous inland region which had long been a buffer zone between Croatia, the Byzantine Empire and, more recently, Serbia, which had emerged as a unified and independent state at the end of the twelfth century. The inhabitants of Bosnia were the ethnic kin of the Serbs and Croats, and both the Croatian and Serbian churches had made inroads into the region. Large parts of Bosnia – especially the north and west – had long been in the Hungaro-Croatian sphere of influence, and from 1138 Bosnia had been a vassal of Hungary ruled by its own Ban. Powerful and resourceful rulers like Kulin (1180–1204), Stjepan II Kotromanić (1322–53) and Tvrtko I (1353–91) were nevertheless able to expand their territory at the expense of the south Croatian aristocracy, though by the fifteenth century the northward expansion of the **Ottoman Turks** had begun to threaten Bosnia, something which would have grave consequences for the Croats.

THE OTTOMAN THREAT

From their heartland in Anatolia, the Ottoman Turks had gained a foothold in southeastern Europe in the early 1300s and soon expanded their territory, fatally weakening Byzantium, swallowing Bulgaria and reducing Serbia to vassal status within a century. Staving off the Ottoman advance was a major preoccupation of Sigismund and his successors, although the mid-fifteenth-century victories of Transylvanian warlord **János Hunyadi** initially made it look as if central Europe might be saved from the Turks. However, the conquest of Bosnia by the Ottomans in the 1460s and 1470s left Croatia in an extremely vulnerable position.

In 1493, a large Hungarian-Croatian force assembled at **Krbavsko polje** (in the Lika, just south of Plitvice) was decisively beaten by the Turks, leaving the Adriatic open to Ottoman raids. In 1517, Pope Leo X called Croatia *antemurale christianitatis* ("the ramparts of Christendom") in recognition of its front-line status. To the east, the defeat of Hungary at the **Battle of Mohács** in 1526 left the Turks in command of much of Pannonia, with Slavonia and northern Croatia at their mercy.

The Hungarian King Louis II had died childless at Mohács, leaving the throne to his designated successor, the Austrian **Ferdinand I of Habsburg**. (The fact that Croatia had been absorbed into the Habsburg Empire as a constituent part of the Hungarian monarchy, rather than as an entity in its own right, was to have profound consequences for future generations, with nineteenth-century Hungarian nationalists consistently regarding Croatia as part of their own territory.) Despite the resources of his vast central European empire, Ferdinand could do little to stem the Ottoman advance. Klis, the last Croatian fortress in middle Dalmatia, fell in 1537, and by the 1540s the Turks had overrun the whole of Slavonia as far as Sisak, only 50km south of Zagreb. By the end of the century Croatia had been reduced by the Turks and Venetians to a belt of territory running from the Kvarner Gulf in the southwest to the Međimurje in the northeast, with Zagreb at its centre. The Venetians continued to hold Istria and the Dalmatian coastal strip, and the city-state of Dubrovnik further south retained its independence by paying tribute to the Ottoman Empire. The rest of Croatia was occupied by the Ottomans.

The expansion of Turkish power had also set in train a sequence of population movements, with refugees fleeing to areas that were still under the control of Christian powers. Areas depopulated by war and migration were often filled by itinerant stockbreeders, or **Vlachs**, many of whom were descended from the romanized inhabitants of ancient Illyria and still spoke a dialect of Latin akin to modern Romanian. A mixture of Catholic and Orthodox Christians, the Vlachs fell under the influence of the Croatian and Serbian churches, and were soon slavicized, coming to identify themselves as Croats or Serbs as time went on.

Vlach tribes had already served both Ottoman and Christian rulers as border guards, experience which was put to good use by the Habsburgs. The Vlachs were settled in a belt running along Croatia's borders with Ottoman territory and given lands in return for military service. This belt became known as the **Military Frontier** (Vojna Krajina), a defensive cordon ruled directly from either Graz or Vienna. It was to remain in existence until the mid-nineteenth century, by which time the Ottoman threat had long receded.

THE SEVENTEENTH AND EIGHTEENTH CENTURIES

Habsburg forces – with many Croats in their ranks – scored an important victory over the Turks at the **Battle of Sisak** in 1593, ending the myth of Ottoman invincibility and stabilizing the Habsburg–Ottoman frontier. A further Ottoman attack on Vienna in 1683 was thrown back by a combined force of Austrians, Germans and Poles. In the decades that followed, Habsburg armies led by **Prince Eugene of Savoy** gradually drove the Ottomans out of central Europe. The Venetians, who had often avoided all-out war with the Turks due to the precariousness of their position in Dalmatia, exploited Austrian gains by winning back parts of the Dalmatian hinterland. By the time of the **Peace of Passarowitz** in 1718, the Habsburgs had won back the whole of Slavonia, while the Venetians gained control of a belt of highland territory running from Knin to Imotski. Significantly, the Turks retained Bosnia and Hercegovina, and the frontiers agreed at Passarowitz are very close to those still dividing Bosnia-Hercegovina from Croatia today.

Despite the removal of immediate Turkish danger, the eighteenth century was largely one of stagnation. Because the Habsburg lands were made up of a multitude of states – its rulers were simultaneously Duke of Austria, Holy Roman Emperor and King of Hungary – political authority within the empire was often confused. In Croatia, the Military Frontier (considerably enlarged after the capture of Slavonia) was still under the direct control of Vienna, while the nobles in the rest of Croatia enjoyed a semblance of autonomy through the Croatian Sabor, which met in Zagreb and (briefly) in Varaždin. However, the Croatian aristocracy had been progressively magyarized from the late seventeenth century on (when its last great magnates, **Petar Zrinski** and **Fran Krsto Frankopan** were executed for treason; see box on p.98), and the Croatian Sabor was increasingly subordinated to the Hungarian parliament in Buda.

Agriculturally rich areas of northern Croatia and Slavonia were reasonably prosperous in the 1700s, but little was done to develop town life, trade or industry. Most official deliberations took part in either German or Latin (the official language of Hungary) rather than Croat, and few of society's leading figures took an interest in promoting indigenous culture. Venetian-controlled Dalmatia was increasingly impoverished due to a fall-off in trade, and Dubrovnik had been in slow decline since suffering a catastrophic earthquake in 1667.

THE EARLY NINETEENTH CENTURY

In 1797 the Venetian Republic was dissolved by **Napoleon**. Its possessions in Istria and Dalmatia were initially awarded to the Habsburgs in compensation for territories they had lost to the French in northern Italy, but after another bout of fighting between 1806 and 1808, Napoleon gained control of the whole of the eastern Adriatic seaboard. Stretching from Villach in Austria to the Bay of Kotor (now part of Montenegro) in southern Dalmatia, this new French protectorate was named the **Illyrian Provinces** and placed under a French governor, Marshal Marmont, who set about building roads, developing the education system and promoting Slav-language publishing, although the provinces were soon abandoned to the Austrians in 1813 following Napoleon's defeat at the hands of the Russians.

Habsburg dominance of Dalmatia was confirmed by the **Treaty of Vienna** in 1815, and the economic fortunes of the Adriatic began to revive under Austrian stewardship. The main language of the Adriatic sea trade, however, was Italian, and economic development went hand-in-hand with the italianization of maritime Croatia, disappointing many who had seen the return of Austrian power as an opportunity to renew links between the Croats of Dalmatia and the Croats of the north.

THE CROATIAN NATIONAL REVIVAL

One of Napoleon's aims in the creation of the Illyrian Provinces had been to encourage the growth of South Slav consciousness, in the hope that Croats, Slovenes and Serbs could be weaned away from other great powers that might pose as their protectors, notably Austria and Russia. For the Croatian elite, the example of Serbia itself was increasingly important. Subject to the Ottoman Empire since the fifteenth century, the Serbs had risen up against the Turks in 1804 and 1815, and the emergence of an **autonomous Serbian principality** in 1830 was greeted by many Croat intellectuals as an example of what South Slavs could achieve. Apart from an undercurrent of distrust between the Catholic and Orthodox churches, the Serbs had never been regarded as historic enemies, and the development of common links between Serbs and Croats became a popular intellectual theme.

The closeness of the Croat and Serb languages sparked a renewed interest in the orally transmitted folk poems – often speaking of heroic resistance to the Turks or some other common foe – that characterized both Serbian and Croatian popular culture, especially in mountainous areas like the Dalmatian hinterland, where the two communities lived side by side. The interest in folk poems led to a new awareness of the languages themselves: a literary form of written Serbian was established by Vuk Stefanović Karadić, whose example was followed by the Croatian writer **Ljudevit Gaj** (1809–72). Gaj set about developing a form of literary Croatian close enough to Serbian for the two to be mutually intelligible, basing it on the Štokavski dialect used by Croats in Slavonia, Hercegovina and Dubrovnik. *Danica*, the cultural supplement of his own newspaper, *Novine*

Hrvatske, changed over to the new, Štokavski-based written language in 1835.

The movement which grew out of Gaj's reforming zeal was known as **Illyrianism** (*Ilirizam*) – a name which harked back to the ancient Roman province of Illyria and therefore avoided too close an identification with any single ethnic group. Illyrianism contributed enormously to the flowering of Croatian language and culture in the mid-nineteenth century known as the **Croatian National Revival**, although the movement remained a purely Croatian affair – the infant Serbian state was much more interested in expansion than in co-operation.

Vienna initially tolerated Illyrianism as a politically useful counterweight against the boisterous nationalism of the Hungarians, but eventually took fright and came down heavily, banning any mention of the word "Illyria" in 1843. The movement lived on, however, with the formation of the Narodna stranka – the "National Party", whose members were known as the **Narodnjaci** – which from now on was to be the country's main pro-Croat, anti-Magyar force.

1848 AND AFTER

With the outbreak of **revolution in Paris** in February 1848, a wave of reforming fervour spread through Europe. In Hungary, the fiery Lajos Kossuth agitated for the introduction of a constitutional monarchy, while mobs on the streets of Vienna demanded democratic reforms. The fall of Metternich, who had been right-hand man to a succession of emperors for nearly forty years, produced a power vacuum throughout the Habsburg Empire which new organizations and personalities rushed to fill. Croatian opinion saw the 1848 revolution as a means of winning autonomy from the Hungarians and forging a new Croatian or South Slav unit within the Austrian Empire. This conflict of national interests pitched Croatian radicals against the Hungarian radicals under Kossuth who, despite their liberal credentials, continued to regard Croatia as a junior partner in a reinvigorated Hungary.

Fast losing control of a complex situation, the Habsburg court had no choice but to tolerate the emergence of Croatian autonomist sentiment, in the hope that it would serve to counterbalance the Hungarians. Vienna succumbed to popular pressure and elevated Colonel **Josip Jelačić**, a popular garrison commander in the Military Frontier and a well-known supporter of the Narodnjaci, to the position of Ban of Croatia. Jelačić immediately called elections to the Croatian Sabor in order to provide himself with a popular mandate. The Narodnjaci won a sweeping victory and, armed with the Sabor's support, Jelačić first broke off relations with the Hungarians, then declared war on them. Ultimately, however, he became a pawn in a wider game: after relying on his support to crush the revolutionaries in Hungary and Austria, reactionaries at the Viennese court gradually forgot about Croatian demands for autonomy and reintroduced centralized rule.

THE LATE NINETEENTH CENTURY

Revolution was followed by the era of **Bach's Absolutism**, named after the Austrian interior minister, Alexander Bach. Under Bach's stewardship, the Habsburg Empire, headed by archconservative **Franz Josef I** (1848–1916), attempted to reorganize itself as a centralized state in which all regionalist aspirations were suppressed in favour of loyalty to the Habsburg Empire. Bach was dispensed with in 1860, but continuing tension between Vienna and Budapest forced another reorganization of the empire in 1867. According to the terms of the **Ausgleich** ("Compromise"), the Habsburg state became the **Dual Monarchy of Austria-Hungary**. Franz Josef was to be emperor of Austria and king of Hungary simultaneously, and Vienna was to retain overall control of defence and foreign policy, but in all other respects the Austrian and Hungarian halves of the empire were to run their own affairs. While Dalmatia was to remain in the Austrian half, the bulk of Croatia found itself in a semi-independent Hungary, although these areas were allowed a measure of autonomy and the right to retain a proportion of tax revenues for domestic use.

There were two strands to Croatian nationalism in the second half of the nineteenth century: one emphasized the cultural similarities between all South Slavs, while the other had a more exclusively Croat perspective. The principal representative of the former strand was **Juraj Strossmayer** (1815–1905), Bishop of Đakovo and leader of the Narodnjaci, who thought that Croats and Serbs within the Habsburg Empire could unite to form a South

Slav state within a federal Austria-Hungary. Strossmayer also seriously considered the possibility of Austria-Hungary's collapse, concluding that an independent Yugoslav (which literally means "South Slav" in Croatian and Serbian) state, including all Croats and Serbs and supported by Russia, would be the best solution. Strossmayer used the income from his episcopal estates to fund cultural projects, founding the Yugoslav Academy of Science and Arts in Zagreb in 1867. Opposition to Strossmayer's nascent Yugoslavism was supplied by **Ante Starčević** (1823–96), who formed the **Croatian Party of Rights** (its members were called "Pravaši") in 1861. Starčević favoured the formation of an independent Croatian state under Habsburg auspices and was suspicious of any deal with the Serbs, believing that they would never treat the Croats as equals.

Party politics in Croatia after 1867 were largely manipulated by the Ban, who was responsible to the Hungarian government in Budapest. The worst offender in this regard was Ban **Károly Khuen-Héderváry** (1883–1903), who promoted Hungarian language and culture at the expense of Croatian, and indulged in electoral gerrymandering to secure a docile Sabor. Héderváry was especially adept at playing off Croats against Serbs. Austria-Hungary had occupied the Ottoman province of Bosnia-Hercegovina in 1878, thereby ending the *raison d'être* of the Military Frontier, which was abolished in 1881 and absorbed into Croatia, thereby increasing the number of Orthodox Serbs in the country. The majority of these Serbs had been living peacefully with Catholic Croats for centuries, but the existence of a youthful and expanding Serbian state to the southeast gave the Serbs of Croatia a new focus of loyalty, and they increasingly turned to political parties of their own. The Héderváry administration supported the publication of a Serb newspaper, *Srbobran*, which in 1901 ran an article which claimed that neither the Croat nation nor language really existed, and that the Serb national agenda was the only one with any future. Although by no means a reflection of what most Serbs felt, it led to anti-Serb riots in Zagreb.

Political life in **Dalmatia** after the Ausgleich was characterized by a struggle between the local branch of the Narodnjaci, who promoted Croat rights and called for the unification of Dalmatia and the rest of Croatia, and the pro-Italian Autonomaši (Autonomists), who argued that Dalmatia was not wholly Croat and had a distinct Latin–Slav identity of its own. The Serbs of the Dalmatian hinterland sided with the Autonomaši after the 1870s to prevent the Narodnjaci from gaining the upper hand, but by the end of the century fear of Italian designs on Dalmatia was beginning to unite Serbs and Croats of all political persuasions.

A wave of anti-Hungarian protests in northern Croatia in 1903 provoked the breakdown of the Héderváry regime, creating new political opportunities. The first sign of the so-called **New Course** in Croatian politics came with 1905's **Rijeka Resolution**, when Croatian deputies joined with the Hungarian opposition in calling for democratic reforms and the unification of Dalmatia with rest of Croatia. Almost immediately, Serb politicians from northern Croatia and Dalmatia followed with the **Zadar Resolution**, which promised support for the aims of the Rijeka Resolution providing that the equality of Serbs in Croatia could be guaranteed. The two sides came together to form the **Croat–Serb Coalition**, which scored a resounding success in the 1906 elections to the Croatian Sabor. Faced by a hostile Sabor, successive Bans found it difficult to form a workable government. Vienna's attempts to split the Croat–Serb Coalition by accusing 53 Croatian Serbs of working secretly for the creation of a Greater Serbia merely produced the opposite effect, and became the subject of international outrage. Croatia rapidly became ungovernable after Ban Nikola Tomašić's failed attempts to manage the elections of 1911, and the Sabor was suspended later that year by his successor, Slavko Cuvaj.

WORLD WAR I AND THE CREATION OF YUGOSLAVIA

After forty years of occupation, Austria-Hungary formally annexed Bosnia-Hercegovina in 1908, assuming responsibility for its mixed population of Catholic Croats, Orthodox Serbs and Muslim Slavs of both Serbian and Croatian stock. The annexation went down badly in Serbia, which viewed Bosnia-Hercegovina as a potential area for Serbian expansion. The ultimate goal of Serbian foreign policy – to forge a state which would include all Serbs wherever they lived, was a serious challenge to Austria-Hungary, which had a large Serbian population within its own borders. Serbian successes in the **Balkan Wars** of 1912–13, when Ottoman forces were driven out of Macedonia, increased Serbian prestige, especially among those Croats who saw Serbia as the potential nucleus of a future South Slav state.

Tension between Austria-Hungary and Serbia was therefore high when Franz Josef's nephew and heir **Archduke Franz Ferdinand** was assassinated in the Bosnian capital Sarajevo on June 28, 1914 by **Gavrilo Princip**, a young Bosnian Serb who had been supplied with weapons by Serbia's chief of military intelligence. The anti-Serbian mood in Viennese court circles had achieved critical mass, and Austria-Hungary declared war on Serbia on July 28. Germany was pulled in on the Austrian side, making a response from the Entente powers of Russia, France and Great Britain inevitable, and **World War I** was under way.

The longer the war went on, the clearer it became that Austria-Hungary might not survive. Faced by the possibility of a future without the Habsburgs, few Croatian politicians considered it practical to work for the establishment of an independent Croatia – such a state would be vulnerable to predatory Hungarian, Italian and Serbian neighbours. Instead they increasingly embraced the idea of Yugoslavia – a South Slav state which would include Serbs, Croats and Slovenes – because they knew that such a state would get the backing of the Entente powers. With Italy joining the Entente in the hope of gaining a foothold in Dalmatia, the need to promote the Yugoslav ideal was paramount.

In 1915, veteran Dalmatian politicians Frano Supilo and Ante Trumbić, joined by sculptor Ivan Meštrović and other exiles, formed the **Yugoslav Committee** in Paris in order to lobby foreign governments and make contacts with Serbian leaders. The Serbs were initially unwilling to treat the committee as an equal partner, but negotiations culminated in the signing of the **Corfu Declaration** of July 1917 in which both sides agreed that any future South Slav state would be a constitutional monarchy in which Serbs, Croats and Slovenes would enjoy equal rights, but which would be headed by Serbia's Karađorđević dynasty. In October 1918 the political leaders of the Serbs, Croats and Slovenes formed the **National Council** in Zagreb and declared their independence from Budapest and Vienna.

Austria-Hungary collapsed on November 3, and Italian troops landed in Dalmatia ready to stake a claim to the parts they coveted. The territory ruled by the National Council was in chaos: they had no army, bands of deserting soldiers were roaming the countryside, and fear of social revolution was rife. Desperate to restore order and keep the Italians out, the National Council rushed to declare union with Serbia on the basis of the Corfu Declaration, and the Serbian Prince Aleksandar Karađorđević declared the creation of the **Kingdom of Serbs, Croats and Slovenes** on December 1, 1918. The name "Yugoslavia" had been quietly dropped because Belgrade didn't think it sounded Serbian enough. The other areas incorporated into the new state were the Principality of Montenegro (Crna gora), which had strong ties to Serbia, and Macedonia, which had been conquered by Serbia during the Balkan Wars.

THE FIRST YUGOSLAVIA

Many Croats entered the new state on the assumption that it would have a federal constitution which would guarantee each of its constituent peoples a degree of autonomy. Unfortunately, the leading Serb politicians of the time had other ideas. Nikola Pašić (Serbia's wartime prime minister) and Svetozar Pribićević (leader of those Serbs who had hitherto lived in Habsburg territory) were both keen to draw Croats and Slovenes into a state controlled by Serbian politicians, arguing that because large numbers of Serbs were scattered throughout Croatia and Bosnia, only a unitary state could protect their interests.

The Croats were against the idea of a unitary state because they feared that they would always be outvoted by the numerically superior Serbs, and they gravitated towards the **Croatian Republican Peasant Party (HRSS)**, a republican movement that backed the interests of farmers against the urban bourgeoisie and which was also suspicious of Serbian centralism. When elections to the new kingdom's constituent assembly took place on November 28, 1920, the HRSS won 50 of the 93 seats allocated to Croatia. HRSS leader **Stjepan Radić** claimed that the party's victory had given him a mandate to declare Croatia an independent republic, and spoke enthusiastically of replacing the Kingdom of Serbs, Croats and Slovenes with a Balkan peasant federation comprising

Slovenia, Croatia, Serbia and Bulgaria (where a democratically elected pro-peasant government under Alexander Stamboliiski was already in power). Belgrade kept a lid on the situation by packing Radić off to prison and sending in the troops, but the HRSS's reputation as the main defender of Croat interests was secured.

Croatian deputies were unable to prevent the Constituent Assembly from passing the 1921 **Vidovdan Constitution**, which declared the now kingdom a unitary state and convinced many Croats that their new homeland was merely Greater Serbia under a different name. Radić immediately withdrew the HRSS from parliament and tried to raise support for the Croatian cause abroad, although Great Britain, France and the US were far too committed to the idea of a strong Yugoslavia to aid those hostile to the central government in Belgrade.

By the mid-1920s the complete freeze in relations between Belgrade and the Croatian political elite had persuaded Radić to change tack. He dropped the "R" for "Republican" from the party's name, ended the boycott of parliament and began working for Croatian autonomy rather than outright independence. He briefly served as a government minister before joining his old adversary, the Serbian Svetozar Pribićević, in forming a new opposition bloc, the **Peasant–Democratic Coalition**. The Radić–Pribićević alliance was a serious threat to the Belgrade establishment, and passions were already running high when Stjepan Radić was shot in the parliamentary chamber by the pro-Belgrade Montenegrin deputy Puniša Račić on June 20, 1928. Radić died two months later; his funeral in Zagreb was attended by 100,000 people. Fearful of further inter-ethnic violence, King Aleksandar suspended parliament and launched the **Sixth of January Dictatorship** at the beginning of 1929. The name of the state was changed to **Yugoslavia** later the same year, in the hope that an appeal to South Slav idealism might help paper over the country's cracks.

THE 1930S

Radić was replaced as leader of the HSS by **Vlatko Maček**, who broadened the party's appeal to make it a national movement representing all classes of Croats. Banned from political activity, the HSS sponsored various front organizations such as the Peasant Accord, which supported cultural activities in rural

areas, and the Croatian Peasant Defence Force, a paramilitary organization which was tolerated by the government because it occasionally beat up socialists.

One other organization that opposed the unitary nature of the Yugoslav state was the **Communist Party of Yugoslavia (KPJ)**, which despite being banned in 1920 continued to exert a strong influence over the intelligentsia. Initially the KPJ had envisaged Croatia as part of either a federal Yugoslavia or a wider Balkan confederation. In the mid-1920s it became communist policy to encourage the break up of Yugoslavia into independent states, but by the mid-1930s the Comintern had ordered a return to the idea of a federal Yugoslavia as a potential bulwark against the rise of Nazism. It was this concept that was inherited by **Josip Broz Tito**, whom Moscow appointed leader of the KPJ in December 1937.

Diametrically opposed to communism was the **Ustaše** – a right-wing Croatian separatist organization inspired by Italian fascism and dedicated to the violent overthrow of the Yugoslav state – which had been founded by **Ante Pavelić** in 1929. Together with the similarly inclined Internal Macedonian Revolutionary Organization (IMRO), the Ustaše orchestrated the assassination of the Yugoslav King Aleksander in Marseilles in October 1934.

Fearful that the Croat question would tear Yugoslavia apart, Prime Minister Aleksandar Stojadinović tried to reach an accommodation with the HSS, relaxing the ban on its activities. Maček, however, turned to the Serbian opposition instead, joining up with the Serbian Radical and Peasant parties to put together the **Alliance for National Agreement**, which won 37.5% of the vote in the government-manipulated elections of 1935, rising to 44.9% in 1938. New Yugoslav Prime Minister Dragiša Cvetković was charged with the task of making a deal with the Croats amidst a worsening international situation and the fear that Yugoslavia's internal weaknesses could be exploited by predatory neighbours.

The result was the Cvetković–Maček Agreement, or **Sporazum**, signed on August 26, 1939, according to which an autonomous Croatian state, the **Banovina**, was created within the borders of Yugoslavia, including all of present-day Croatia as well as those portions of western Bosnia inhabited by large numbers of

Croats. Maček became deputy prime minister in the Yugoslav government, while fellow HSS leader **Ivan Šubašić** became Ban of Croatia. Inside the Banovina the HSS became the party of government, although they were supported by the Serbian Democratic Party (SDS), which represented Serbs in Croatia.

Yugoslavia initially opted for a policy of neutrality when **World War II** broke out in September 1939, although German pressure eventually forced Cvetković to sign up to the Tripartite Pact (the alliance forged by Germany, Italy and Japan) on March 25, 1941. Pro-British officers in the Yugoslav Army launched a successful coup on March 27 and denounced the pact, but most of the leading figures in the coup were Serbs, and the new regime didn't enjoy the loyalty of Croats. When the Germans declared war on Yugoslavia on April 6, resistance quickly melted away.

WORLD WAR II

German troops entered Zagreb on April 10, 1939, and quickly established a puppet government, with Ante Pavelić's right-hand man Slavko Kvaternik announcing the formation of the **Independent State of Croatia** (**NDH**). Ustaše exiles returned home to usher in a new order on the Nazi model, with Ante Pavelić styling himself the "Poglavnik" (a Croatian rendering of "Führer") in imitation of Hitler. The rest of Yugoslavia was carved up between Germany and her allies, although a rump of Serbia was allowed to survive under German occupation. Bosnia was awarded to the NDH, although large chunks of northern and middle Dalmatia, together with the islands, were given to Italy, something for which many Croats never forgave the Ustaše. Even the NDH's own territory was split into German and Italian spheres of influence, and NDH military commanders were under the supervision of their German and Italian colleagues.

Due to the inclusion of Bosnia, the NDH now included large numbers of Serbs and Bosnian Muslims. The Muslims were regarded as allies (some Croat historians have always regarded the Bosnian Muslims as ethnic Croats who abandoned the Catholic faith in the sixteenth century), while the Serbs were regarded as a potentially traitorous element which had to be eliminated. It soon became clear that the Ustaše's attitude to Serbs was little different to

the Nazi Party's attitude to Jews. The NDH immediately embarked on three main **anti-Serbian policies**: the deportation of Croatian and Bosnian Serbs to Serbia proper, their mass conversion to Catholicism or their mass murder. It's estimated that one in six Croatian Serbs died between 1941 and 1945, many of them killed in concentration camps like Jasenovac (see p.104), where Jews, Gypsies and anti-fascist Croats were also murdered.

The sheer ferocity of the Ustaše campaign against the Serbs led to an immediate increase in guerrilla activity. The most important group early on were the **Četniks**, Serbs loyal to the Yugoslav government in exile, who often carried out vicious revenge attacks upon Croats and Muslims, but they were soon eclipsed by Tito's communist **Partisans**, who played down ethnic differences in order to forge a popular anti-fascist movement that drew support from all races and areas of society. The Partisans promised to make Yugoslavia a federal state after the war, and the collapse of Italy in September 1943 allowed them to capture weaponry and take command of large chunks of territory in Istria and Dalmatia, although they were soon chased out by the Germans. In 1944 the Partisans were recognized by the British, who withdrew all remaining support from the Četniks and persuaded the Yugoslav government in exile in London to sign an agreement recognizing Tito's authority.

The Partisans entered Zagreb on May 8, 1945. Thousands of Croatian **Domobrani** (home guardsmen), the majority of whom were no great supporters of the Ustaše, had been mobilized by Pavelić in the preceding weeks and ordered to retreat to Austria – in the hope that they could surrender to the Allies and preserve themselves as the nucleus of some future anti-communist force. The British unit that received them at the town of Bleiburg shipped them back across the border to the waiting Partisans. Some were shot immediately and thrown into mass graves; others were marched to internment camps in the deep south of Yugoslavia – a journey described as the *Križni put* or Way of the Cross in contemporary Croatian history. The total number of Croatian victims is probably around 50,000, although this figure doesn't include Slovenes and Serbs who were handed over at Bleiburg at the same time. Pavelić himself escaped to South America, then Spain, where he died in 1959.

TITO'S YUGOSLAVIA

The British had hoped that Tito's agreement with the Yugoslav government in exile would help preserve a degree of democracy in Yugoslavia after the war, but Tito acted swiftly to quash dissent. As the country moved towards democratic elections, most of the country's political parties were encouraged to join the **People's Front**, an organization dominated by the communists – those that declined were effectively prevented from campaigning. Although the ballot was nominally secret, anyone voting against the People's Front had to place their ballot papers in a separate box – sufficiently intimidating to ensure that few people took the risk. Packed with the communists and their supporters, the resulting National Assembly voted unanimously to declare Yugoslavia a republic on November 29, 1945. A new Soviet-inspired constitution was adopted, creating a federation of six national republics – Slovenia, Croatia, Bosnia-Hercegovina, Serbia, Montenegro and Macedonia. The rigid discipline of the Communist Party was to hold the whole structure together.

In Croatia, the communists' elimination of political opponents went hand in hand with an attack on the **Catholic Church**. Some members of the Church hierarchy had been enthusiastic supporters of the NDH, and it wasn't difficult to discredit the whole organization using the charge of collaboration. Archbishop Stepinac (see p.60) was offered a role in the new order if he broke off links with the Vatican – and was rewarded with a sixteen-year prison sentence when he refused.

THE BIRTH OF YUGOSLAV SOCIALISM

The Yugoslav economy was in a state of ruin in 1945, and the new government used the need for speedy reconstruction as an excuse to rush ahead with wholesale revolutionary change. Large estates were confiscated, businesses were nationalized, and a five-year plan, with the emphasis on heavy industry, was instituted. Yugoslavia's efforts to ape the USSR made it look like the model pupil, but in June 1948 Soviet leader **Josef Stalin** denounced the Yugoslav party for indulging in ideological deviations, expecting the Yugoslavs to ditch Tito and appoint a more pliant leader; with tensions rising in Europe, it's likely that Stalin wanted to enforce unity among the communist states of Eastern Europe by making an example of Tito, the only Eastern European leader who had risen to power more or less independently of the Red Army. Yugoslavia was expelled from the Cominform, the Soviet-controlled organization of European communist countries, and the Soviets made an unsuccessful appeal to Yugoslav communists to overthrow Tito.

A period of acute tension between the two countries followed, with a very real threat of Soviet invasion. Tito responded to the crisis by protesting his loyalty to the Soviet Union, while at the same time purging members of his circle whom he suspected of being Soviet agents. On the whole, however, Tito's wartime Partisan colleagues stood by their leader, and Yugoslavia's resistance to Soviet pressure won Tito new levels of popularity both at home and abroad. Party members who sided with Stalin were dubbed "Cominformists" and shipped off to endure years of harsh treatment on the infamous Goli otok, or "Bare Island" (see box on p.196).

Stalin's economic blockade, coupled with a string of bad harvests brought about by bungled attempts at collectivization, led Yugoslavia to the brink of economic collapse. Aid from the capitalist West was gratefully received, and a drastic rethink of the country's political objectives followed. The support of industrial workers was cultivated by introducing a system of **workers' self-management**, in which all enterprises would be controlled not by the state but by the people who worked in them – on the surface, a decisive move away from Stalinism. The Communist Party itself was renamed the **Yugoslav League of Communists (SKJ)**, in a (largely cosmetic) attempt to suggest that it would play a less overbearing role in the country's future. The League of Communists in each republic was allowed increasing autonomy, with the personal authority of Tito and his wartime comrades holding the whole thing together. Meanwhile, Tito joined Nehru and Nasser to form the **Non-Aligned Movement** in 1961, and although the movement itself was largely ineffective, Tito's delicate balancing act between East and West gained Yugoslavia international credibility far in excess of its size or power.

The liberalization of Yugoslav communism had its limits, however. The Montenegrin

Milovan Đilas, federal vice-president and one of Tito's closest Partisan colleagues, was forced out of office in 1954 for suggesting that the introduction of self-management should be followed by a gradual abdication of the entire communist bureaucracy. He remained Yugoslavia's most notorious dissident – whenever Tito felt the need to improve relations with the USSR, he packed Đilas off to jail as a sign of Yugoslavia's continuing communist orthodoxy.

Throughout this period Croatia was in the firm grip of Tito's trusted sidekick Vladimir Bakarić, who did his best to protect Croatian interests in the Yugoslav federation without going too far. Above all, the break with the Soviet Union removed the Stalinist straitjacket, allowing Croatia to renew its cultural links with the West. The development of **tourism** in the Adriatic kicked off in the 1960s, bringing money to economically depressed Dalmatia, although the role of Belgrade-based companies in the tourist boom was always resented.

THE CROATIAN SPRING

During the 1960s the quickening pace of economic liberalization created a rift between the conservative communists and their more reform-minded colleagues. Tito initially sided with the reformists, moving in 1966 to oust another of his wartime comrades, the Serb **Aleksandar Ranković**, the feared head of the secret police. Ranković was in favour of a unitary state in which the autonomy enjoyed by the republics would be strictly limited, and most non-Serb Yugoslavs were pleased to see him go. However, the expected democratization never really materialized, petering out in a morass of inter-republican disputes. The phenomenal economic growth of the 1960s also created tensions within the federation, with the developed northern republics of Slovenia and Croatia anxious to exploit their prosperity without the interference of central government.

In Croatia, the growing national sentiment which would lead to the so-called **Croatian Spring** first expressed itself in the cultural sphere. In 1967, 130 writers and intellectuals, supported by the country's leading cultural organization, the **Matica Hrvatska**, issued a declaration stating that Croatian was a separate language from Serbian. A group of Serbian intellectuals responded by saying that, if that was the case, then the Serbian minority in Croatia

had the right to use their own language together with the Cyrillic script. Official bodies denounced the two declarations as being provocative, and the leaders of the Matica Hrvatska were forced to resign.

By the beginning of the 1970s, the leaders of the **Croatian League of Communists** (the Yugoslav League of Communists was divided into six republican parties) were increasingly keen to play the nationalist card, hoping to gain domestic support in bargaining with central institutions for more republican autonomy. The Matica Hrvatska itself re-emerged as a mouthpiece of nationalist opinion in 1971, drawing on the support of thousands of ordinary Croats, and when nationalists won control of the Zagreb university students' union in April 1971 and the republican authorities pointedly failed to take action against them, the Croatian Spring was well under way. In November 1971 Zagreb students went on strike, calling for opponents of reform to be sacked from the party, but Tito was by this time seriously worried that things were getting out of hand, and in December accused the Croatian leadership of not taking effective steps against nationalism and chauvinism. The leaders of the Croatian League of Communists were forced to resign, and numerous student and Matica Hrvatska leaders were put on trial.

THE 1970s AND 1980s

The crackdown on the Croatian Spring sounded the death-knell for liberalization all over Yugoslavia. The silencing of reformists in Serbia soon followed, and Yugoslav socialism entered a period of ideological stagnation from which it never really recovered. Tito's personal authority kept the lid on any further outbreaks of inter-republican animosity; in Croatia itself, nationalism was once more a taboo subject, while a disproportionate number of Serbs were appointed to top posts, storing up more resentment for the future. The Croatian patriotic song *Ljepa naša domovino* ("Our Beautiful Homeland") was made the official hymn of the republic in 1972, but could only be performed in certain circumstances, and was never allowed to take precedence over the Yugoslav national anthem, *Hej slaveni*. Unofficial performances of the song were rewarded with a prison sentence of sixty days. Outside the country, Croatian exiles assassinated the Yugoslav ambassador to Sweden in 1971 and hijacked a TWA airliner in

1976, giving Western observers the impression that Croatian nationalism was a volatile and dangerous political force which was not to be encouraged. The Yugoslav secret services responded by sending hit squads abroad to silence the state's critics.

Tito died on May 4, 1980, leaving the country without an effective leader. He was replaced by an eight-man presidency in which each republic took turns to supply a head of state. The federal government was relatively weak compared to those of the individual republics, making it difficult to adopt nationwide policies capable of dealing with Yugoslavia's worsening economic problems. The economic boom of the 1960s had been financed by Western loans, but the oil-crisis-ridden 1970s had seen a drying-up of credit, leaving Yugoslavia with crippling foreign debt, galloping inflation and high unemployment.

Problems began in Kosovo, a province of southwestern Serbia which had been given autonomous status because the majority of its inhabitants were ethnic Albanians. In 1981, Albanian demonstrations in Kosovo demanding that the province be upgraded to a full republic had been put down by the army. In 1986, the Serbian Academy of Sciences issued a **Memorandum** which stated that the Serbian minority in Kosovo was under threat from Albanian nationalists, adding (without much supporting evidence) that the Serbian community in Croatia was also under pressure from Croatian cultural hegemony. Yugoslavia in the mid-1980s was a federation in which each republic felt that it was being somehow cheated by the others, and Serbia was no exception. The Memorandum was eagerly seized upon by Serbian intellectuals who argued that the constitution of Yugoslavia should be re-centralized in order to give the Serbs (numerically superior to the other nations) more power.

The Serbian League of Communists, loyal to the federalist ideal, was initially against the Memorandum. Then, on April 24, 1987, **Slobodan Milošević**, a little-known communist apparatchik, visited the town of Kosovo Polje to meet leaders of the Serbian minority in Kosovo. When local police started jostling Serb demonstrators, Milošević intervened with the now famous words "Niko ne sme da vas bije!" ("Nobody has the right to beat you!"). Propelled to national prominence as a defender of Serbian rights, Milošević realized that nationalism was

the tool with which he could remould Yugoslav communism in his own image. Using support for the Serbs in Kosovo as the issue on which all other politicians should be judged, he soon drove liberal communists out of the Serbian League of Communists, purged the Serbian media and overthrew the leadership of Vojvodina, the other province of Serbia that had been given autonomy in 1974. Many of the Serbs who joined the mass meetings in support of Milošević mistakenly thought that they were taking part in some kind of democratic revolution: in fact, they were accessories to a neo-Stalinist putsch. In March 1989 a new Serbian constitution ended the autonomy of Kosovo and Vojvodina, while shortly afterwards Milošević supporters succeeded in winning control of the leadership of another republic, Montenegro; he also found allies in the Macedonian and Bosnian parties. Milošević hoped that this growing bloc of support would be sufficient to outvote his remaining opponents in federal institutions, thereby making it possible to recast Yugoslavia in new and more centralized form.

In November 1989 the Berlin Wall came down. As the rest of Eastern Europe prepared for multi-party rule, the biggest republic in Yugoslavia was reverting to hard-line communism. The Slovenes and Croats had to assert themselves before it was too late.

THE BREAK-UP OF YUGOSLAVIA

By 1989, Slovenia, the most westernized and liberal of Yugoslavia's republics, was moving inexorably towards multi-party elections. Croatia was initially slow to follow this lead, and by the late 1980s the phrase **Hrvatska šutnja** ("Croatian silence") had been coined to describe the unwillingness of the republic's politicians to discuss the future of Yugoslavia or to champion Croatian interests. The crunch came when the Slovenes insisted in changes to the Yugoslav constitution which would guarantee the autonomy of individual republics: the Croats had to chose between supporting Slovenia or being left to the mercy of Milošević. At the last-ever congress of the Yugoslav League of Communists in January 1990, the Slovenes called for complete independence for each of the republican communist parties, a move rejected by the Serbs and their allies. The Slovene delegates walked out of the congress, followed by the Croats, who were now led by the reform-oriented **Ivica Račan**, effectively burying the Yugoslav League of Communists for good.

Democratization was moving at different speeds in different republics, however, making a smooth, pan-Yugoslav transition to non-communist rule impossible. May 1989 saw the creation of Croatia's first non-communist political organizations, among them the Croatian Democratic Union, or **HDZ**, led by former army general and dissident historian **Franjo Tuđman**. The HDZ held their first congress in February 1990, calling for Croatia's right to secede from Yugoslavia and for a reduction in the number of Serbs in Croatia's police force and state bureaucracy. striking an anti-Yugoslav tone which caught the mood of a country increasingly frustrated by the state's failure to offer any resistance to Milošević.

The HDZ easily won Croatian elections in April 1990. On May 13, a football match between Dinamo Zagreb and Red Star Belgrade was abandoned on account of a three-way fight between the two sets of fans and the Serb-dominated police, worsening relations between Croatia and Serbia still further. When the Sabor met on May 30, Tuđman was sworn in as president, and Croatian "statehood" (a potential step to full independence) was declared. The HDZ's **Stipe Mešić** became Croatia's first post-communist prime minister. The Sabor immediately began work on a new **constitution**, which contained one highly controversial passage: the Serbs who lived in Croatia were no longer to be classified as one of the constituent nations of the republic, but as a national minority – a form of words which caused great anxiety among the Serbs themselves.

THE REBELLION OF CROATIA'S SERBS

According to the 1991 census there were 580,000 Serbs in Croatia, most of whom lived in the arc of territory which ran alongside Croatia's border with Bosnia-Hercegovina. Ever since Milošević's rise to power, the Serbs of Croatia had been subjected to a Belgrade media campaign designed to make them feel endangered by their Croatian neighbours. In February 1990, the Serbian Democratic Party, or **SDS**, was formed in Knin, a town just inland from Šibenik which had an 88 percent Serbian population, and they soon assumed leadership of a community fearful of what might happen to them in a

Croatia increasingly independent of Belgrade. On June 2 the SDS organized a referendum on autonomy for Serbs living in Croatia. The Croatian authorities banned the referendum, but weren't able to prevent it. Not surprisingly, the vote was massively in favour of autonomy.

Throughout the spring and summer of 1990 the Knin Serbs had been arming themselves with the connivance of the intelligence services in Serbia proper, aided by pro-Serb officers in the Yugoslav People's Army, the **JNA**. The Croatian authorities sent a police unit to restore control of the area in June, but it was forced to back off. In July 1990 the SDS declared the autonomy of the Knin region, creating the so-called **Kninska Krajina**. Barricades went up on the roads around the town, policed by paramilitary units organized by Milan Martić, the Knin police chief. Croatian authorities sent police helicopters to restore order, but they were forced back to Zagreb by Yugoslav airforce MIGs. The Krajina declared its independence from Croatia in February 1991, seeking union with Serbia. In March, the Serb-dominated town council of Pakrac in Slavonia stated that it no longer recognized the Croatian authorities, provoking the latter to send in the police to re-establish control of the town. The JNA moved in to keep the peace. The resulting stand-off didn't produce any casualties, but Belgrade Radio reported 11 Serb deaths all the same.

THE DRIFT TO WAR

Despite the installation of democratically elected governments in Croatia and Slovenia, the state of Yugoslavia still existed at the end of 1990, and many feared that the JNA – possibly with the connivance of Milošević – would launch a military coup to prevent its break-up. Belgrade military intelligence had secretly filmed Croatia's defence minister, Martin Špegelj, negotiating the purchase of weapons from a private company in Hungary, but even when the resulting footage was broadcast on national television on January 25, 1991, the Yugoslav presidency failed to respond with the tough measures Milošević felt were needed to hold the federation together. Sensing that the break-up of Yugoslavia was now inevitable, Milošević began instead to plan for the next best thing: the creation of a Greater Serbia which would include all the parts of Croatia and Bosnia-Hercegovina where Serbs lived.

Belgrade subsequently stepped up aid and encouragement to the Knin Serbs, and in March 1990 Knin paramilitaries took control of the Plitvice National Park. Croatian police units were dispatched to arrest them, and the resulting shoot-out produced the first casualties of the Serb–Croat conflict, with two Serbs and one Croat killed. The JNA moved in, ostensibly to keep the two factions apart, but in reality sealing off the area from Croatian civilian control: a pattern to be repeated elsewhere as the spring and summer progressed. On April 29 the Croat village of Kijevo near Knin was surrounded by Serb irregulars and its inhabitants forced to leave – the first step in a campaign to **ethnically cleanse** the Serb-held parts of Croatia of any remaining Croats.

At the beginning of May, twelve Croatian policemen were massacred in Borovo Selo, a predominantly Serbian suburb of Vukovar. On May 6 a big anti-JNA demonstration in Split ended in tragedy when one soldier was killed – a conscript from Macedonia. On May 17 the head of Yugoslavia's presidency, the Serb Borislav Jović, came to the end of his one year term. The next incumbent was due to be Croatia's delegate, Stipe Mešić. Other members of the presidency were split on whether to endorse his accession: four members voted for Mešić and four against, leaving Yugoslavia without a head of state.

The Slovenes had held a referendum on full independence from Yugoslavia in December 1990; on May 19, 1991, the Croats followed suit, voting overwhelmingly in favour. Co-ordinating their actions, both Slovenia and Croatia declared their **independence** on June 26. Yugoslav Prime Minister Ante Marković, still believing that the federation could be saved, ordered the JNA to secure the country's borders, but Slovene territorial units quickly surrounded and neutralized JNA columns, and the "war" came to an end ten days later with the EU offering to mediate. The Slovenes and Croats agreed to place a three-month moratorium on independence, while the JNA withdrew from Slovenia, and the Serbs and their allies agreed to recognize Stipe Mešić as Yugoslav president. In terms of injecting new life into Yugoslavia the agreement was meaningless – Slovenia had won *de facto* independence if not outright recognition, while the fate of Croatia was left to be fought over.

THE WAR IN CROATIA

The withdrawal of the JNA from Slovenia meant that military strength could now be concentrated in the Serb-inhabited areas of Croatia, where low-level conflict – largely waged by Serbian irregulars against the Croatian police dragged on through the summer. In late August the JNA and Serb irregulars launched a major offensive to gain control of eastern Slavonia, beginning with air bombardments of Vukovar and Vinkovci. In response, the newly formed Croatian National Guard began a blockade of all JNA barracks in Croatia. Areas under firm JNA and Serb control – a chain running from Knin in the southwest through the Plitvice area, Slunj, Glina and Petrinja to the environs of Pakrac in the west – were organized into the **Republic of the Serbian Krajina (RSK)**, and Croats who lived in the region were expelled, creating almost half a million refugees. An attempt was made to cut northern Croatia off from Dalmatia by advancing towards the ports of Zadar and Šibenik, but neither city fell. In October, JNA and Montenegrin forces began the siege of **Dubrovnik**, an operation designed to weaken Croatian morale and reward Montenegro for its support of the Serbs with opportunities for territorial aggrandizement and plunder.

The Serb advance in eastern Slavonia was held up by the defenders of **Vukovar**, who displayed incredible heroism against vastly superior or odds. Many believe that Zagreb could have done more to aid Vukovar's defenders, but saw a prolonged siege as a useful way of gaining international sympathy for the Croatian cause. Vukovar fell on November 18, after which the Serb–JNA forces began the bombardment of the next big city to the north, **Osijek**.

The defence of Croatia had initially been a hastily improvised affair, but as fighting continued, the Croats gradually assembled a highly motivated military force armed with weapons captured from JNA barracks. Serb advances were halted, while a counter-offensive won back portions of western Slavonia in December. Some Croatian paramilitaries committed acts of revenge: the dynamiting of Serb-owned houses was widespread, and in Gospić, near Plitvice, civilians were allegedly murdered by members of a unit commanded by Tomislav Merčep, a populist right-wing politician who is still a public figure in Croatia.

The EU made consistent attempts to bring the two warring sides to the table, however, and agreement became possible once it became clear that the Serb–JNA offensive had been stalled by tenacious Croatian defence. The **Geneva Agreement** brokered a ceasefire: the Croats agreed to end the siege of all remaining JNA barracks, and the JNA agreed to withdraw from Croatia. At the same time, a UN peace mission headed by Cyrus Vance secured the deployment of an international peacekeeping force, UNPROFOR, to police the ceasefire line. The Serbs were happy to accept this because it froze the front line at its current position, apparently confirming their territorial gains. The peacekeepers were deployed in March 1992 and the JNA departed as agreed, but gave most of its weaponry to the forces of the RSK.

Meanwhile, Croatia was emerging from its diplomatic isolation. The Germans believed that EU recognition of Slovenia and Croatia would dissuade the JNA from further aggression, and despite initial opposition from the French and British, **Croatian statehood** was recognized by all the EU countries on January 15, 1992.

The ceasefire wasn't perfect, and shells continued to fall on Osijek, Dubrovnik and other Croatian towns. Summer 1992 saw a Croatian counter-attack break the siege of Dubrovnik, and in January 1993 the Croats recaptured the area around Maslenica in northern Dalmatia, taking the pressure off Zadar. The international community protested at Croatia's breaches of the truce, but was too preoccupied with events in neighbouring **Bosnia** to take action.

THE WAR IN BOSNIA

The ethnic balance in **Bosnia-Hercegovina** was more delicate than that of any other Yugoslav republic, with a three-way split between Serbs, Croats and Muslims. The Croats, who made up about twenty percent of the population, lived in western Hercegovina near the border with Dalmatia, where they were in the majority, and scattered among Serbs and Muslims throughout central Bosnia.

Bosnia-Hercegovina had received international recognition as an independent state at the same time as Croatia in the hope that it would discourage any attempts to partition it. In fact it had the opposite effect, and a Serbian community which wanted no part in an independent Bosnia gradually moved towards armed rebellion in spring 1992. A familiar pattern of events ensued: Serbian irregulars aided by the JNA quickly gained control of areas where Serbs lived, together with any strategic towns that potentially stood in their way, ejecting or murdering a large portion of the non-Serb population.

Initially, Bosnian Croats and Bosnian Muslims co-operated in the struggle against the Serbs, although the highly organized Bosnian–Croat army – the Croatian Defence Council or **HVO** – remained independent of the largely Muslim army of the Bosnian government in Sarajevo. With Croats and Muslims in central Bosnia increasingly squeezed by Serbian successes, the two sides started fighting each other for territory, beginning a vicious Croat–Bosnian war which began in spring 1993 and continued sporadically for a year. The conflict was disastrous for the Croats of central Bosnia, who were forced to flee towards Hercegovina or Croatia proper. It was also disastrous for the international reputation of the Croatian state, whose support for the HVO in Bosnia led to accusations that Tuđman was as cynical as Milošević in his attempts to destroy multinational Bosnia by carving it up into ethnically pure units. Indeed, Tuđman and Milošević had discussed the possibility of dividing up Bosnia between them as early as spring 1991, and it seemed that the Croatian president – in league with the hardline Croats of Hercegovina – was prepared to sacrifice the Croats of central Bosnia in order to achieve his goal. Croatian atrocities in Bosnia – the massacre of at least 104 Muslim civilians in the village of Ahmići, the internment of Muslim men in Dretelj concentration camp and the destruction of the 500-year-old Turkish bridge at Mostar – were propaganda disasters for the Croatian cause.

THE ROAD TO DAYTON

In the end the Croat–Muslim conflict was brought to an end by the US, which had adopted a harder line against the Serbs since the election of President Clinton in 1992. US sympathies were primarily with the Bosnian Muslims and their besieged capital of Sarajevo, but it was widely recognized that Croat military power would play a part in any solution. The US-sponsored **Washington Agreement** of March 1994 created a federation of Croats and

Muslims in Bosnia-Hercegovina, and an alliance between this Croat-Muslim Federation and the state of Croatia. The Croats of western Hercegovina continued to run their territory (so-called "**Herceg-Bosna**") as if it was an independent statelet, although this was overlooked in the interests of unity.

Changes on the battlefield pushed all sides nearer to a settlement in 1995. In Croatia proper, the Croats overran the remaining portions of western Slavonia in the operation known as **Blijesak** ("Flash") on May 1–2, allowing the Croatian army to liberate Serb held parts of Bosnia near the Croatian border. On August 4, the **Oluja** ("Storm") offensive was launched with an artillery bombardment of Knin, and the Serbian Krajina collapsed within three days. Fearing reprisals, the Serbian population fled through Serb-controlled Bosnian territory into Serbia proper. Oluja was followed by successful Croat-Muslim operations in Bosnia which, combined with NATO air strikes in September, persuaded both the Bosnian Serbs and their masters in Belgrade to seek a negotiated peace.

The war in Croatia had virtually ended with the Oluja campaign, although the Serbs remained in control of eastern Slavonia. According to the US-sponsored **Erdut Agreement**, eastern Slavonia would be governed by the UN for a transitional period before being returned to Croatia in January 1998. The war in Bosnia was formally brought to an end by the **Dayton Accords** of November 10, 1995, which created a unified Bosnian state including two so-called "entities": one Serbian and one Croat-Muslim. On paper, Dayton brought an end to the existence of Herceg-Bosna, but in practice it continued to lead a life quite separate from the rest of Bosnia-Hercegovina, flying Croatian flags from its public buildings and using the Croatian currency as legal tender.

CROATIA AFTER THE WAR

The HDZ which had come to power in 1990 was a broad movement which aimed to unify all Croats in the face of an outside menace. If it had any ideology it all, it was right-of-centre, preaching traditional family values, respect for the Catholic Church and national solidarity. The movement's creator, and Croatia's first president, Franjo Tuđman, was not a great admirer of Western democracy and did not want to be constrained by a strong parliament. From the start,

the advisory bodies assembled by the president had more power than the Sabor or the prime minister, and policy was usually decided by Tuđman's inner circle of confidants.

The HDZ's authoritarian streak was seen as a necessary evil while the nation was fighting for its survival in 1991, but began to look increasingly anachronistic as the years progressed, while the government's actions at home and in Bosnia helped significantly to tarnish the reputation of the new nation. Croatia dragged its feet in helping Serbs who had fled the country to return and, worse still, seemed to be providing the Croats of Hercegovina with moral support in their attempts to frustrate full implementation of the Dayton Accords, something which led the West to believe that Tuđman was still secretly working for the partition of Bosnia-Hercegovina. Croatia was threatened with UN sanctions in 1996 and again in 1999 following her refusal to extradite suspects to the Hague war crimes tribunal, while the country's unsatisfactory state of democracy – with free and fair elections rendered impossible by the fact that the state-owned TV network was a blatant government mouthpiece – ensured that Croatia was held at arm's length by the EU. Croatia was also excluded from the aid programmes made available to other former communist states, and was placed behind Romania and Bulgaria in the queue for EU membership.

Croatia's main centrist party, Dražen Budiša's **HSLS**, began to capitalize on popular dissatisfaction with the government, emerging as the principal opposition party. In early 1997 a coalition of opposition parties won a majority in Zagreb's municipal elections, but the HDZ – still the largest single party in the council chamber – refused to cede control. Tuđman himself blocked the appointment of an opposition mayor, and fringe members of the opposition coalition were gradually bought off with promises of political promotion, taking the sting out of the HDZ's defeat.

The brazen way in which the HDZ exercised power was an increasing source of resentment, and the public grew increasingly critical of the new breed of tycoons who had taken control of big enterprises with HDZ support, only to siphon off the profits and drive their companies to bankruptcy. Like the communist party before it, the HDZ began to extend its influence into all spheres of life, controlling cultural appointments and even

FRANJO TUĐMAN

Franjo Tuđman was born on May 14, 1922 to a peasant family in the Zagorje village of Veliko Trgovišće, only 15km south of Kumrovec, birthplace of Tito. His father was local leader of the Croatian Peasant Party (HSS), and Franjo involved himself in left-wing politics from an early age before joining the Partisans in 1941, rising to become a political commissar in liberated territories in eastern Croatia.

After the war, Tuđman went to the Yugoslav Defence Ministry in Belgrade, working his way through the ranks before being elevated to the rank of general in 1960 – the youngest in the army. He also began to make his name as a historian, graduating in 1957 and publishing the first of his theoretical works, *Rat protiv rata* ("War against War"). Resigning from the army in 1961 to concentrate on academic research, Tuđman was appointed to head the Institute for the History of the Workers' Movement. His thoughts were moving away from party orthodoxy, however, and while researching into Ustaše war crimes he became convinced that the numbers of their victims had been deliberately inflated by a regime eager to discredit Croatian nationalism once and for all.

Expelled from the Yugoslav League of Communists Central Committee and forced to leave the Institute on account of his work and views, Tuđman began to establish a reputation as a prominent dissident which would make him ideally placed to take advantage of the communist system's decline in the late 1980s. He was briefly imprisoned following the collapse of the Croatian Spring, and again in 1981 after giving an interview to French radio in which he spoke of Yugoslavia's need to move towards political pluralism. Tuđman's big idea was the **Promirba** (best translated as a "setting aside of old scores"), which emphasized the coming together of all strands of Croatian opinion – from Partisan to Ustaše – to build a new patriotic consensus that could stand up to Belgrade. In part this was a pragmatic move which allowed Tuđman to tap the financial resources of right-wing exiles, but it also reflected his own personal journey from left-wing idealist to social conservative. An over-readiness to accommodate the far right was a weakness of the Tuđman regime from beginning to end. At the HDZ's first congress in 1990 Tuđman announced his admiration for the NDH (the fascist puppet regime which ruled Croatia during World War II), and during the 1990 election campaign notoriously stated "Thank God my wife is neither a Serb nor a Jew", an opinion he never retracted.

Tuđman's other major hobby horse was the unviability of Bosnia-Hercegovina as an independent state. He had always regarded the division of Bosnia between himself and Milošević as a potential way of settling Serbian and Croatian differences, and even had negotiations with the Serb leader to this effect in March 1991. Many people in Croatia proper opposed Tuđman's support for the Hercegovinian Croats in the Bosnian Croat–Muslim war of 1993–94, and Croats from Hercegovina – where Croatian nationalism was traditionally purer than anywhere else – rose to positions of prominence and power under Tuđman far out of proportion with their actual numbers.

Tuđman demanded deference from his subjects, donning a red, white and blue sash whenever attending official functions, and appearing in a white uniform to receive the salute at military parades – prompting criticisms that he was becoming another Tito. In 1998, Tuđman's wife Ankica paid over 200,000DM cash (undeclared by the president when listing his assets) into a bank account – a small sum by the corrupt standards of Croatia's elite, but the family was sufficiently rattled to prosecute the bank teller who had spilled the beans.

When Tuđman died, however, thousands of ordinary Croats headed for the presidential palace to file past the coffin. He was still seen as the man who had stiffened Croatian resolve during the dark days of 1991–92, winning the country international recognition as an independent state for the first time since the Middle Ages. The final, damning verdict on the political system he had built was delivered at the general election barely one month later.

---

trying to subvert the football league. It was revealed in June 1999 that secret service operatives had been trailing referees in an attempt to ascertain which officials were the most corruptible – in the hope of securing victories for Croatia Zagreb, the president's favourite team.

In the meantime, daily life for many Croats was becoming increasingly hard. The country ended the decade with twenty percent unemployment, an average wage of around $400 a month and many companies unable to pay salaries with any regularity; 1999 saw a wave of labour unrest and a rural revolt against low grain prices.

THE END OF THE TUĐMAN ERA

News that Tuđman had stomach cancer was broken by CNN in November 1996 after the president's visit to the Walter Reed military hospital in Washington. Tuđman chose not to designate a successor, preferring to remain in sole charge until the end, and the HDZ — by now lacking any coherent political ideology — began to resemble a collection of warring factions rather than a party. The opposition had meanwhile began to unify around the need to defeat the HDZ at the next elections, which were scheduled for December 1999. A range of opposition parties banded together to form the Šestorica, or **"Six"**, in order to bargain for electoral reform, and even when this grouping split up, the HDZ was too disoriented to take advantage.

Tuđman entered hospital at the beginning of November 1999, and died on December 10. A genuine outpouring of popular grief ensued, but the HDZ had lost the one talismanic figure who could persuade Croats, out of a sense of loyalty if nothing else, to keep the party in power. The elections were put off until January 4, 2000, in the hope that the festive season would knock the wind out of the opposition's sails, with Croatian national television unleashing hitherto unseen levels of pro-HDZ bias. It was all to no avail however, as the SDP–HSLS coalition (one arm of the former Six) won a staggering 52 percent of the vote, the HDZ got 24 percent, and the other wing of the Six bloc picked up most of the rest. Three weeks later, **Stipe Mešić**, the jocular charmer who had once served as the unenthusiastic president of a dying Yugoslavia, was elected the nation's new president.

Croatia's diplomatic position began to improve almost overnight. The HDZ defeat seemed to mark the end of the Croatian government's support for the hardline nationalists of Hercegovina, and also held out the possibility of a more conciliatory attitude towards Croatia's Serbs. Mešić seemed keen to strip himself of some of the presidential trappings adopted by Tuđman, giving the Sabor and the prime minister more real power. The incoming administration was cautious about its ability to significantly improve the Croatian economy in the short term, but an anti-corruption drive promised to spell the end for many of the tycoons, and Croatia's improved standing abroad brought about a sudden increase in foreign investment.

BOOKS

There's a dearth of good books about Croatia in the English language. Many of the most entertaining accounts are by nineteenth-century travellers to the Adriatic, though sadly, their books are often only available from larger public libraries or specialist book dealers. The number of publications devoted to the break-up of the former Yugoslavia is considerable: we've listed the best of them, rather than trying to offer an exhaustive survey of the entire field.

Publishers are given in the format UK/US; where only one publisher is listed, this covers both the UK and North America; "o/p" means out of print.

TRAVEL WRITING

Abbé Alberto Fortis, *Travels into Dalmatia* (o/p). Classic eighteenth-century travelogue written by an Italian priest and containing a mine of historical anecdote and observations. Fortis's tendency to romanticize the simple and brutish lifestyles of the locals exerted a strong influence over subsequent generations of travel writers.

T.G. Jackson, *Dalmatia, the Quarnero and Istria* (o/p). First published in 1887, this is an illuminating and exhaustive three-volume guide to the architecture of the Adriatic coast, with sizeable dollops of history and reportage en route.

A.A. Paton, *Highlands and Islands of the Adriatic* (o/p). Record of a journey made in 1846–47 with the usual mixture of historical anecdote and first-hand description. Very good for local colour, and especially strong on social life in nineteenth-century Split and Dubrovnik.

Rebecca West, *Black Lamb and Grey Falcon* (Macmillan/Penguin). Classic travel book based on West's journey through Yugoslavia in the 1930s. Mixing opinionated observations with character sketches and extensive forays into history, this is definitely an acquired taste, particularly the sweeping generalizations about the Balkan Slavs, about whom West has the tendency to be over-rhapsodic. The first quarter of the book covers Croatia, after which the intrepid author moves on to Bosnia, Serbia, Macedonia and Montenegro.

HISTORY AND POLITICS

Ivo Banac, *The National Question in Yugoslavia* (Cornell University Press). Absorbing history of the competing currents of Croatian nationalism, Serbian nationalism and Yugoslavism, culminating with the Vidovdan Constitution of 1921.

Catherine Wendy Bracewell, *The Uskoks of Senj: Piracy, Banditry and Holy War in the Sixteenth-century Adriatic* (Cornell University Press). Definitive and scholarly account of the Uskoks, which lays to rest some of the more romantic myths surrounding their freebooting activities. It's also an excellent introduction to sixteenth-century Adriatic life in general.

Ivo Goldstein, *Croatia* (Hurst/McGill Queens University Press). Sober, impartial overview of Croatian history from the earliest times to the present day, written by a leading medievalist at Zagreb University.

Tim Judah, *The Serbs* (Yale University Press). Excellent analysis of the main themes in Serbian history, providing illuminating background to Serbia's central role in all the Balkan conflicts of the 1990s. The same author's *Kosovo: War and Revenge* (Yale) takes the story up to NATO's campaign against Belgrade in 1999.

Bariša Krekić, *Dubrovnik in the 14th and 15th Centuries: a City between East and West.* (University of Oklahoma Press, o/p). Probably the best English-language introduction to Dubrovnik's golden age, if you can find it.

Michael A. Ledeen, *The First Duce: D'Annunzio at Fiume* (John Hopkins University Press, o/p). This solid and entertainingly written academic history gives a definitive account of the Italian soldier-poet D'Annunzio's fifteen-month occupation of Rijeka/Fiume.

Dennison Rusinow, *The Yugoslav Experiment 1948–1974* (Hurst, o/p). Dense, scholarly account of the genesis of self-management, and the political struggles of the 1950s and 1960s, with a good account of the lead-up to the Croatian Spring of 1971.

Marcus Tanner, *Croatia: a Nation Forged in War* (Yale University Press). The best general history of Croatia currently available. Balanced, thorough, and written with enthusiasm and verve by an *Independent* journalist who observed Yugoslavia's disintegration at first hand.

THE BREAK-UP OF YUGOSLAVIA

Mark Almond, *Europe's Backyard War* (Heinemann). Well-informed if patchily written analysis of Yugoslavia's break-up written by an academic historian. It's broadly sympathetic to the Croatian cause, and Almond's most forceful prose is directed against the cynicism of Serbian policy and the hapless blundering of the Western powers.

Christopher Bennett, *Yugoslavia's Bloody Collapse* (Hurst/New York University Press). Scholarly and informed account from a journalist who was in Yugoslavia when war broke out. His central thesis – that Yugoslavia's break-up was far from inevitable until the rise of Serbian national communism under Milošević – is convincingly argued.

Misha Glenny, *The Fall of Yugoslavia* (Penguin). Vivid and often moving front-line reportage of the conflict by the BBC's former central Europe correspondent. The book is regarded by some Croat observers as being pro-Serb – a tribute to Glenny's impassioned objectivity. The same author's *The Balkans* (Granta/Penguin) is a compendious account of southeastern European history from the early nineteenth century onwards, in which Croatia plays a walk-on part. It's sometimes too wide-ranging for its own good, but Glenny's attempt to explain the history of the Balkans – and the outside world's meddling in Balkan affairs – is consistently readable and thought-provoking.

Brian Hall, *The Impossible Country* (Penguin). Hall travelled through Croatia, Serbia and other parts of Yugoslavia during the summer of 1991, just as the country was beginning to fall apart. As well as being a studiously impartial observer, he is an excellent writer, historically informed, witty and humane, and the result is one of the most compelling accounts of the last days of Yugoslavia you will find.

Branka Magaš, *The Destruction of Yugoslavia: Tracking the Break-up 1980–1992* (Verso). Collection of essays and articles written by a veteran Yugoslavia watcher. Not much on Croatia, but excellent analysis of Milošević's rise and his single-handed demolition of Yugoslav federalism.

Alec Russell, *Prejudice and Plum Brandy* (Michael Joseph). Wide-ranging Balkan reportage from the Romanian revolution to the Yugoslav break-up, including a revealing eye-witness account of the siege of Dubrovnik, observed largely from the terrace of the Hotel Argentina.

Laura Silber and Alan Little, *The Death of Yugoslavia* (Penguin; published in US as *Yugoslavia: Death of a Nation*). Combining journalistic immediacy with prodigious research, this is by far the best blow-by-blow account of the war, although it sheds little light on the long-term causes of Yugoslavia's demise. The authors had access to many of the key players in the events described, resulting in a wealth of revealing quotes.

Mark Thompson, *A Paper House* (Vintage/Pantheon). Thompson travelled throughout Yugoslavia on the eve of its break-up to produce this insightful book, part travelogue, part analysis of a fragmenting society. The same author's *Forging War: the Media in Croatia, Serbia, Bosnia and Hercegovina* (Article 19), examines the role of the Yugoslav press in stoking ethnic hatred.

CROATIAN LITERATURE

Slavenka Drakulić, *As If I Was Not There* (Abacus; published in the US as *A Novel About the Balkans*, Viking). Unflinching, often harrowing novel about a Bosnian woman's experience of life in a Serbian internment camp, written by one of Croatia's leading novelists. Drakulić's previous novel, *The Taste of a Man* (Abacus/Penguin) couldn't be more different, dealing with love and cannibalism in New York.

Earlier works *Marble Skin* and *Holograms of Fear* (both Women's Press) are short on plot, but offer powerful meditations on sensuality and mortality respectively. Drakulić's book of essays, *Café Europa* (Abacus/Penguin) eloquently captures the author's dismay at the flowering of nationalism in the former Yugoslavia.

Miljenko Jergović, *Sarajevo Marlboro* (Penguin). Jergović is a Bosnian Croat who grew up in Sarajevo and now works as a journalist in Zagreb. He's probably the best of a whole crop of Bosnian-born short-story writers to have emerged in the last few years, spinning wry tales of Balkan lives, loves and tragedies in a style which owes something to the American Robert Carver.

Miroslav Krleža, *The Return of Philip Latinowicz* (Quartet/Northwestern University Press). The best-known novel by Croatia's leading twentieth-century writer, in which a painter returns home to a provincial Slavonian town sometime in the 1920s and embarks on an affair which ends in tragedy. Intended as a dissection of Croatia's directionless upper classes in the wake of World War I, it's not as powerful as *On the Edge of Reason* (Quartet/New Directions), set in the same period, which convincingly preaches the message that bourgeois society is a form of self-deluding madness, but to rebel against it drives you insane.

Slobodan Novak, *Gold, Frankincense and Myrrh* (Forest Books, o/p). A difficult but rewarding read, this sombre, meditative study of a man looking after his sick and elderly mother one winter on the island of Rab was highly regarded in Yugoslavia when it was first published in the 1970s.

Dubravka Ugrešić, *The Museum of Unconditional Surrender* (Phoenix). Dismayed by Croatia's descent into right-wing authoritarianism, Ugrešić spent most of the 1990s living outside Croatia, and this largely autobiographical novel is a powerful meditation on memory and exile. By the same author, the heavyweight collection of essays *Culture of Lies* (Phoenix/Pennsylvania State University) is an essential read for anyone interested in the negative side of Croatian culture and nationalism in the 1990s.

CROATIAN FOLK MUSIC

Croatian folk music (*narodna glazba* or *narodna muzika*) is as diverse as you would expect from a country poised between the cultural worlds of the Mediterranean, central Europe and the Balkans. Traditional music still forms a part of everyday life in many towns and villages, with local folklore societies preserving knowledge of songs and dances long associated with weddings, feasts and seasonal merrymaking.

The state has often been an enthusiastic supporter of folk culture: communist Yugoslavia encouraged the activities of folklore groups as a way of emphasizing the shared cultural roots linking Yugoslavia's many nationalities, while post-independence Croatia (taking a slightly different view of the genre) has stressed the importance of folklore as a way of promoting Croatia's unique identity.

One of the best ways to hear folk music in Croatia is to catch one of the concerts given by the various folklore societies. **Lado**, based in Zagreb, is the state's one professional troupe, performing songs and dances from all over Croatia. All the other folklore ensembles comprise amateur enthusiasts and are likely to concentrate on a more regional repertoire. The biggest of these regional ensembles, Dubrovnik's **Lindo**, has a reputation comparable

with that of Lado, and often plays a part in the city's annual arts festival.

There's quite a range of regional festivals, (see p.36), but the biggest single folk event is Zagreb's **International Folklore Festival** (Međunarodna smotra folklora), which brings together an array of performers from all over the country alongside international guests. The cultural happenings arranged in tourist resorts throughout the summer always include at least some traditional music, and package hotels often lay on performances for their guests. Otherwise, look out for Croatian **weddings**, which usually take place on Saturdays and often involve celebrants gathering in a town park or square to be serenaded by traditional musicians.

A good deal of folk culture has filtered through into the commercial mainstream, producing a style of pop in some ways similar to country & western in the US – many of the tunes hark back to traditional melodies, but everything else is pure showbiz.

SLAVONIA AND THE TAMBURICA

The indigenous folk music of eastern Croatia, particularly Slavonia, has grown to dominate Croatian music over the last century and a half. It's characterized by the tambura – more commonly known by its diminutive form, **tamburica** – a lute-like instrument which is plucked or strummed to produce a sound not dissimilar to that of a mandolin.

Originally of Anatolian origin, the tamburica was brought to southeastern Europe by the Ottoman Turks in the fourteenth and fifteenth centuries. The instrument was gradually taken up by the local Slav population, whose frequent migrations (often between Ottoman and Habsburg lands) helped spread it still further. By the nineteenth century, the tamburica was the most common folk instrument throughout both eastern Croatia and the northern Serb province of Vojvodina.

Because the instrument was popular with both Croats and Serbs, it was championed in the mid-nineteenth century by the Illyrian movement, a Zagreb-based group of intellectuals who aimed to promote South Slav unity. As the nineteenth century progressed, the tamburica was increasingly seen as a symbol of an indigenous culture under threat from the dominant Germanic and Hungarian influences of the

Habsburg Empire. Tamburica orchestras were formed in Croatian towns and cities to play popular folk tunes, concentrating on the jolly, rhythmic melodies which often accompanied rural merrymaking. These orchestras often featured a lot of tamburica players playing in unison, creating a wall of thrumming sound which has remained a feature of tamburica music ever since; they also often provided the music for village dances at which locals perormed the *kolo* – a local variant of the circle dances found throughout southeastern Europe.

In the twentieth century the Slavonian sound increasingly came to symbolize Croatia as a whole, with the Croatian Peasant Party (the main voice for Croatian aspirations during the 1920s and 1930s) promoting the music as a way of renewing village cultural life, and it also grew in significance among the many Croatian emigrés in North America, for whom it was an important link with the homeland. Remaining popular through the Yugoslav period, tamburica music was increasingly dragged into the commercial mainstream in the 1980s, when a new generation of tamburica bands began to mix folk melodies with a modern pop sound.

Foremost among these were **Zlatni Dukati** ("The Golden Ducats"), who mixed tamburicas with electric bass and guitar and were initially popular with Serbs in Vojvodina as well as Croats throughout Croatia. By the end of the decade the band's output was beginning reflect the changing mood of Croatian society, with the release of an album entitled *Hrvatska pjesmarica* ("Croatian Songbook") featuring patriotic songs which, while not actually banned, were certainly considered subversive enough to merit scathing criticism from communist politicians. Needless to say, the album was a big hit in Croatia, and Zlatni Dukati went on to record more patriotic material during the 1991–95 war. Other tamburica-pop bands have followed in Zlatni Dukati's footsteps, most notably **Gazde** ("The Bosses"), who ditched the folksy costumes traditionally associated with the tamburica scene in favour of a leather-clad rockabilly image, and developed a similarly modified, pop-rock-influenced sound.

The need for morale-boosting popular music heavily flavoured with indigenous folk motifs led to an explosion of tamburica music during the early 1990s. The nation's radio and TV stations were quite deliberate in their attempts to replace the folk-pop music of the former Yugoslavia with something more exclusively Croatian, and the tamburica sound is nowadays an ever-present feature of the airwaves. The number of amateur and semi-professional acts is huge, although Zlatni Dukati and Gazde are probably the only tamburica groups to make a living from concert tours and album sales alone.

Tamburica music constitutes an important element in the diet of radio stations and TV show programmes. It also provides the *raison d'être* of at least one major festival, the **Zlatne Žice Slavonije** ("Golden Strings of Slavonia"), which takes place every September in the provincial town of Požega. A glitzy showbiz occasion, the festival concentrates on newly composed commercial songs rather than traditional, folkloric material.

OTHER INLAND CROATIAN MUSIC

The ubiquity of tamburica music has tended to overshadow the other musical traditions of inland Croatia, especially in Slavonia itself, where many local instruments (such as the *gajde* and *dude*, both local types of bagpipe) have almost totally died out.

The music of the **Zagreb region** and the **Zagorje** centres on the polkas and waltzes common to central Europe. There's a strong tradition of brass band music here too, although more common are the four- or five-piece string bands that you'll see playing at weddings or in restaurants, usually featuring double bass, a couple of violins and a guitar or tamburica.

The traditional sounds of the area **southwest of Zagreb** couldn't be more different, having more in common with the Balkan south than with any part of central Europe. Arid mountain regions like Lika and Hercegovina (the latter, although forming part of Bosnia-Hercegovina, is predominantly populated by Croats) are home to a harsh and dissonant form of polyphonic singing known as *ojkanje* (characterized by the ululating "oy" sound at the end of every line) or *gange*. Unaccompanied *gange* songs are traditionally performed at village festivities, and even now are rarely performed in concerts. As in Slavonia, the *kolo* is more popular in these highland areas than dancing in pairs. A form of *kolo* typical to the region is the *nijemo kolo*, or "dumb kolo", a dance performed without music, the only sound coming from the whirling and stamping of the dancers themselves. A particularly acrobatic form of this is the *Vrličko kolo* from Vrlika, a town inland from Šibenik, in which dancers hang onto each other by their belts and swing each other into the air.

The music of the **Međimurje**, in the far northeast of Croatia, has much in common with the music of neighbouring Hungary, with lilting melodies accompanied by a string band and occasionally a zither or a cimbalom. There's also a strong tradition of unaccompanied narrative songs sung by women, including many tales of unrequited love featuring, oddly enough, railway stations, at which village boys waved goodbye to their sweethearts before going off to serve with the Austro-Hungarian army. Many of these were rediscovered in the early twentieth century, when the folklorist Vinko Žganec started systematically transcribing them. The songbooks produced by Žganec were plundered by a new generation of folk singers in the 1980s and 1990s, although there's always been a question mark about their authenticity: Žganec asked local organist Florijan Andrašec to help him collect traditional tunes, paying him for every new song he came up with – it's believed Andrašec made up many songs himself to earn extra cash.

THE ADRIATIC COAST

Traditionally, the music of rural **Dalmatia** revolved around two-part songs on heroic or tragic themes, mostly sung by women. Although these still survive in some places, the tradition has been superseded in this century by the growth of the male-voice choir, or **klapa**. Today almost every town or village has a *klapa*, which usually consists of up to ten members and performs smoothly harmonized songs of a sentimental nature. Some *klape* sound like barbershop quartets; others have a raw feeling reminiscent of male polyphonic singing from Corsica or Georgia. Many Dalmatian towns hold *klapa* festivals in the summer – the most famous is at Omiš, just south of Split, in July. Further south, towards **Dubrovnik**, a three-string fiddle known as the *lirica* provides droning accompaniment to dances such as the *linđo* (an ancient courtship dance), which you'll still see performed outside Čilipi church on Sunday mornings.

Utterly different is the startling music of the **Istrian peninsula**, which uses a distinctive local scale (the *istarska ljestvica*). A lot of Istrian songs employ two-part harmonies which sound discordant to the average non-Istrian ear, and this singing style has given rise to an entire body of instruments dedicated to reproducing such harmonies. Prominent among these are the *sopila*, a large oboe which is always played in pairs; the *šurla*, which consists of two pipes with a single mouthpiece, allowing a single musician to play two parts; and the *mijeh* (also known as *meh* or *mih*), a bagpipe made from the bladder of a young goat. Istrian styles of singing and bagpipe playing are also found on the **Kvarner Gulf** islands of Cres, Krk and Rab. The most exciting exponent of Istrian music today is the *sopila* player Dario Marušić, who brings a modern-jazz sensibility to bear on a selection of raucous, uneasy-listening traditional tunes. His albums are hard to get hold of, but he does feature on the *Ethno Ambient Live: Salona 98* CD (see p.361).

NEW SOUNDS

The last decade has seen an increasing hybridization of Croatian roots music, with a string of performers attempting to breath new life into traditional forms with studio technology or new musical styles. Most of them have drawn inspiration from the fringe areas of Croatian folk (notably Međimurje and Istria), as if consciously offering an alternative to the monopoly of mainstream tamburica-pop.

First off the mark were **Vještice** (The Witches), formed in 1988 by veterans of the Zagreb New Wave scene, who created a whole new audience for traditional music by performing Međimurje folk songs in alternative rock style. This interest in the music of northeastern Croatia was picked up in the early 1990s by **Dunja Knebl**, a Zagreb woman who didn't start singing professionally until already in her mid-40s, fired by enthusiasm for the newly fashionable Međimurje songs. Around the same time, the younger Međimurje-born singer-songwriter **Lidija Bajuk** was moving in a similar direction. Both Knebl and Bajuk had grown up listening to acoustic guitar-wielding folkies from Joan Baez onwards, and their interpretations of traditional Croatian songs have an uncomplicated accessibility – without losing too much of the otherworldly strangeness of the originals.

The mid-1990s also saw the emergence of **Legen**, an ambitious techno-folk crossover act

DISCOGRAPHY

COMPILATIONS

Croatian Folksongs and Dances (Harmonia Mundi/Quintana, France). Music from Croatian communities in south Hungary in archive recordings made mostly in the 1950s and 1960s. Some really archaic songs are included, alongside excellent fiddle playing from renowned virtuoso Stipan Pavkovics and lots of good tamburica bands, notably the Pavo Yimora Baraban orchestra from Felsöszentmárton, still a centre of tamburica music today. Most of the bands have a vital raw sound, rather than showy glitz.

Croatie: Musiques d'autrefois (Ocora, France). Survey of traditional songs and instrumental music taken from Croatian radio archives between 1958 and 1993. Divided into regional areas, it begins with some Međimurje songs and includes plenty of good tamburica bands and Dalmatian *klapa* singing.

Croatie: musiques traditionelles d'aujour-d'hui (Auvidis/Unesco, France). This excellent record, compiled with the help of the Institute of Ethnology and Folklore Research in Zagreb, documents practically the whole range of Croatian music, from obscure offerings that you would be fortunate ever to hear to the sort of commercial and sentimental songs you'd be lucky to avoid. Featuring music from Istria, Međimurje, Slavonia and Dalmatia, this is undoubtedly the best place to start exploring Croatia's music, while the informative sleeve notes can point those interested in learning more in the right direction.

Village music from Yugoslavia (Elektra-Nonesuch, US). Despite the misleading subtitle "Songs and Dances from Bosnia-Hercegovina, Croatia and Macedonia", this is all Croatian music, except for one Macedonian track. Excellent songs from village performers and dance music from typical tamburica bands.

ARTISTS

Lidija Bajuk, *Kneja* (Crno Bijeli Svijet, Croatia). Traditional songs from Međimurje and eastern Croatia, alongside a couple of original numbers, all featuring guitar-heavy, contemporary-sounding arrangements. The earlier *Zora Djevojka/Dawn Maiden* (Crno Bijeli Svijet, Croatia) features a similar batch of songs delivered in simpler style – although the opening track Preko Drave ("Across the Drava"), full of lush synthesizer textures, was a Clannad-style radio hit.

Boxer, *Futura* (Carnival Tunes, Croatia). Ambient techno album which makes good use of folk motifs, weaving in samples from village recordings.

Gustafi, *Vraæamo se odmah* (Dancing Bear, Croatia; online orders at www.dancingbear.hr). Exhilarating Istrian-Mexican fiesta music held back by a couple of dull rock tracks. This 1999 album is reckoned by Croatian rock critics to be the band's best, although previous release *Sentimiento muto* (Adam Records, Croatia) is worth checking out too.

Dunja Knebl, *Iz globline srca/From the Heart of Hearts* (Dancing Bear, Croatia; online orders at www.dancingbear.hr). Haunting, mysterious folk songs from Međimurje performed by the angelic-sounding Knebl to mostly simple acoustic-guitar backing. Decent English-Croatian sleevenotes too. Knebl's earlier . . . *jer bez tebe nema mene* (Orfej, Croatia) has a much jazzier, experimental

feel, courtesy of impressionistic pianist Teo Martinović, but is difficult to find.

Legen, *Paunov Ples* (Crno Bijeli Svijet, Croatia). Traditional Croatian songs dramatically delivered by stentorian-voiced Mojmir Novaković, and backed by an array of burbling synthesizer sounds. An intriguing hybrid which succeeds in preserving the enigmatic beauty of the original songs.

Tamara Obrovac Quartet, *Ulika* (Crno Bijeli Svijet, Croatia). A collection of songs written and performed by the Pula-based Obrovac, blending jazzy textures with the folk music of the Istrian interior. Playing in Obrovac's backing band are some of the best jazz musicians in central Europe – pianist Matija Dedić, drummer Kruno Levačić and Slovene bass player Žiga Golob.

Various, *Ethno Ambient Live: Salona 98* (Crno Bijeli Svijet, Croatia). Not the exercise in folk-electronic crossover that the title might suggest, but a sparkling collection of acoustic performances recorded live at an outdoor concert in the ruins of Roman Salona, just outside Split. Legen, Lidija Bajuk, Dario Marušić, Tamara Obrovac and local Dalmatian village performers collaborate on a collection that represents all areas of Croatia. The one previous Ethno-Ambient Live album (Crno Bijeli Svijet, Croatia), featuring Legen, Bajuk and Dunja Knebl, is nowadays hard to find, but was an important landmark for the artists featured.

using synthesizers and samples to soup up folk in the manner of Transglobal Underground or Loop Guru, though with less danceable results. Legen tried to put the mystery back into Croatian folk, building their repertoire around songs celebrating seasonal rites with pagan undertones – such as St George's Day fertility rituals, or the St John's Day bonfires which still take place in many parts of the country. Knebl and Bajuk collaborated with Legen on the 1995 album **Ethno-Ambient Live**, an outstanding recording of (largely acoustic rather than synth-driven) performances in Zagreb's *Gjuro II* nightclub, which helped bring their work to a hip young audience. A second album, **Ethno-Ambient Live: Salona 98**, came out in 1999, using a wider pool of sounds and performers, notably Dalmatian *klapa* singers.

One not-so-traditional vocalist who found her way onto *Ethno-Ambient Live: Salona 98* was jazz siren **Tamara Obrovac**, who draws inspiration from Istrian melodies – lullabies and harvest-time songs rather than the ear-bending

stuff – to produce an intriguing folk-jazz hybrid, featuring rolling, part-improvised songs sung in Istrian dialect. As far as dance culture is concerned, DJ **Boxer** has gone further down the ethno-techno road pioneered by Legen, although for him folk songs are useful ingredients in a wider sound collage rather than an end in themselves.

One of Croatia's more maverick groups is Pula-based **Gustafi**, who began as a new-wave rock band before metamorphosing into an accordion-driven Mexican-Istrian crossover act that defies categorization. Their irreverent, eclectic approach seems to have rubbed off on other acts such as the Zagreb group **Cinkuši**, who perform traditional north Croatian songs with a wilfully non-traditional choice of instruments, including Mediterranean mandolin and African *djembe* drums. Among the many Irish-influenced bands in Croatia, look out for the Pogue-ish **Belfast Food**, who sing a memorable version of *Dirty Old Town* ("Šporki stari grad") in coastal dialect.

THE CROATIAN LANGUAGE

Croatian is a difficult language to learn, and the locals rarely expect anyone to bother, making them all the more pleasantly surprised if you make the effort to learn a few phrases. The vast majority of Croatians speak at least one foreign language: most people – especially the young – understand some English, while German and Italian are also widely spoken on the coast.

Croatian, Serbian and Bosnian are usually regarded as dialects of a single Slavonic language described by linguists as **Serbo-Croat** (although native speakers rarely use this description themselves). Croats, Serbs and Bosnians can understand one another perfectly well, although each community has preserved its own linguistic idiosyncracies, even in areas where they have lived side by side for generations.

You'll find additional variations in dialect all over Croatia itself, the principal ones being named after the three different ways of saying "what?" – *kaj?*, *ča?* and *što?* In Zagreb and the Zagorje people speak *kajkavski*, because of their use of the word *kaj* for "what", while on the Adriatic coast people speak *čakavski*, and in Hercegovina and Slavonia *štokavski*. The literary language is based on *štokavski*, and although the other dialects are heard on the streets, they don't feature on the radio, TV or in newspapers – except in a humorous context.

The best of the **self-study courses** available are *Colloquial Croatian and Serbian* by Celia Hawkesworth (Routledge), closely followed by *Teach Yourself Serbo-Croat* by David Norris (Hodder Headline). Both books concentrate on the Croatian variant of the language, although Serbian reading passages are also included.

Pronunciation is not as difficult as it first appears. Every word is spoken exactly as it's written, and each letter represents an individual sound. The only letters you're likely to have problems with are the following consonants, which differ from their English equivalents.

c "ts" as in cats
č "ch" as in church
ć a softer version of č; similar to the "t" in future
đ "d" as in verdure
g always hard, as in get
j "y" as in youth
r always rolled; fulfils the function of a vowel in words like Hrvatska ("Croatia").
š "sh" as in shoe
ž "s" as in pleasure

CROATIAN WORDS AND PHRASES

BASICS

Da	Yes	*Hajde!*	Go on!
Ne	No	*Hajdemo!*	Let's go!
Molim	Please	*Bog!*	Hi!/Bye!
Hvala	Thank you	*Dobar dan*	Hello/Good day
Hvala lijepo	Thank you very much	*Dobro jutro*	Good morning
Gdje?	Where?	*Dobra večer*	Good evening
Kamo? /kuda?	Where to?	*Laku noć*	Good night
Kada?	When?	*Do viđenja*	Goodbye
Zašto?	Why?	*Kako ste?*	How are you? (polite)
Koliko	How much?	*Kako si?*	How are you?
Koliko stoji/koliko košta?	How much does it cost?		(informal)
		Dobro, hvala	Fine, thanks
Ovdje	Here	*Govorite li engleski?*	Do you speak
Tamo	There		English?
Desno	Right	*Ne razumijem*	I don't understand
Lijevo	Left	*Ne znam*	I don't know
Pravo	Straight on	*Kako se kaže na*	
Gdje je/gdje se nalazi..?	Where is..?	*hrvatskom..?*	How do you
Je li to blizu?	Is it nearby?		say in Croatian..?
Koliko je daleko?	How far is it?	*Kako se zove ovo na*	
Veliko	Large	*hrvatskom?*	What is this
Malo	Small		called in Croatian?
Više	More	*Hrvatska*	Croatia
Manje	Less	*Hrvat*	Croatian person (m)
Jeftino	Cheap	*Hrvatica*	Croatian person (f)
Skupo	Expensive	*Hrvatski*	Croatian language
Dobro	Good	*Ja sam iz. . .*	I am from. . .
Loše	Bad	*Velike Britanije*	Great Britain
Toplo	Hot	*Irske*	Ireland
Hladno	Cold	*Amerike*	the US
Sa/Bez	With/Without	*Kanade*	Canada
Izvinite	Excuse me	*Australije*	Australia
Oprostite or *Sorry*	Sorry	*Nove Zelandije*	New Zealand
Izvolite	Here you are		

ACCOMMODATION

Imate li. . .	Do you have. . .	*Noćenje i doručak*	Bed and breakfast
sobu?	a room?	*Pansion/polupansion*	Full board/half board
jednokrevetnu sobu?	a single room?	*Imam rezervaciju*	I have a reservation.
dvokrevetnu sobu?	a double room?	*Mogu li rezervirati sobu?*	Can I book a room?
sa francuskim ležajem	with a double bed	*Slavina/svijetlo/telefon/*	
sa tušem/banjom	with a shower/bath	*televizor ne radi*	The tap/light/
sa pogledom na more	with a sea view		telephone/ TV
To je skupo	That's expensive		doesn't work
Imate li nešto jeftinije?	Do you have anything cheaper?	*Gdje je najbliži*	Where's the nearest
		autokamp?	campsite?
Mogu li pogledati sobu?	Can I see the room?		continues over. . .

NUMBERS

Jedan	1	Devet	9	Sedamnaest	17	Šezdeset	60
Dva	2	Deset	10	Osamnaest	18	Sedamdeset	70
Tri	3	Jedanaest	11	Devetnaest	19	Osamdeset	80
Četiri	4	Dvanaest	12	Dvadeset	20	Devedeset	90
Pet	5	Trinaest	13	Dvadeset i jedan	21	Sto	100
Šest	6	Četrnaest	14	Trideset	30	Dvjesta	200
Sedam	7	Petnaest	15	Četrdeset	40	Trista	300
Osam	8	Šesnaest	16	Pedeset	50	Tisuća	1000

DAYS, MONTHS AND SEASONS

Dan	Day	Uvečer	In the evening	Travanj	April
Tjedan	Week	Ponedjeljak	Monday	Svibanj	May
Mjesec	Month	Utorak	Tuesda	Lipanj	June
Godina	Year	Srijeda	Wednesday	Srpanj	July
Danas	Today	Četvrtak	Thursday	Kolovoz	August
Sutra	Tomorrow	Petak	Friday	Rujan	September
Jučer	Yesterday	Subota	Saturday	Listopad	October
Prekosutra	The day after tomorrow	Nedjelja	Sunday	Studeni	November
		Praznik	Holiday	Prosinac	December
Prekjučer	The day before yesterday	Blagdan	Church holiday, saint's day	Proljeće	Spring
				Ljeto	Summer
		Siječanj	January	Jesen	Autumn
Ujutro	In the morning	Veljača	February	Zima	Winter
Popodne	In the afternoon	Ožujak	March		

SOME SIGNS

Ulaz	Entrance	Zatvoreno	Closed
Izlaz	Exit	Tržnica	Market
Polazak	Arrival	Bolnica	Hospital
Odlazak	Departure	Ljekarna	Pharmacy
Otvoreno	Open	Zabranjeno pušenje	No smoking

TRAVELLING

U koliko sati polazi vlak/autobus/trajekt?	What time does the train/bus/ferry leave?	Jednu kartu za. . .molim u jednom pravcu povratnu kartu	A ticket for. . .please single return
Kada polazi sljedeći autobus/trajekt/ vlak za..?	When does the next bus/ferry/train leave for..?	Mogu li rezervirati sjedište?	Can I reserve a seat?

GLOSSARY

GENERAL TERMS

Autocesta Motorway
Beč Vienna
Beograd Belgrade
Brdo/Brijeg Hill
Buk Waterfall
Centar Centre
Cesta Road
Crkva Church
Dolac Dell (in karst areas, a small cultivable area enclosed by wall)
Dolina Valley
Draga Vale, bay
Dvor Palace, court, courtyard
Dvorac Castle
Dvorište Yard, courtyard
Fortica Fortress
Gaj Grove
Gat Quay
Grad Town
Groblje Graveyard
Haustor Door or passageway leading from the street to the inner courtyard of a house or residential block
Hram Temple, church
Jadran Adriatic Sea
Jama Pit, cave
Jezero Lake
Jugo Southerly wind
Kamenjar Stony, infertile land; used to describe the arid areas of Hercegovina and inland Dalmatia
Kaštel Castle, fortress
Kolo Folk dance
Kolodvor Station: *Autobusni kolodvor* is bus station; *željeznički kolodvor* is train station
Kolosijek Platform in train station
Konoba Inn, tavern, folksy restaurant
Korzo Evening promenade
Krčma Inn, tavern
Kuća House
Lučka kapetanija Harbourmaster's office
Luka Port
Lungomare Shoreline road or promenade

Maestral North wind
Mandrać Inner harbour for small boats
Mleci Venice
More Sea
Most Bridge
Obala Shore, quayside
Oluja Storm
Otok Island
Palača Palace
Perivoj Park, public garden
Peron Platform
Plaža Beach
Poljana/ Polje Field, square
Poluotok Peninsula
Postaja Small station, bus stop
Put Road, way
Rat/Rt Cape
Rijeka River
Riva Seafront
Samostan Monastery
Selo Village
Stajalište Bus stop
Staza Path
Šetalište Walkway, promenade
Školj Small island
Škor/Škver Shipyard or part of fishing village where boats are repaired
Špilja Cave
Šuma Forest, wood
Toranj Tower
Trajekt Ferry
Trg Square
Tržnica Market
Tvrđava Fortress
Ulica Street
Uvala Bay
Varoš Central residential quarter of an old town
Vijećnica Council chamber, town hall
Vikendica Holiday house or cottage
Vodopad Waterfall
Vodoskok Fountain
Vrata Gate, door
Vrh Peak
Vrt Garden
Zaljev Bay, gulf
Zamak Castle, fortress

Zdenac Well
Zidine Walls
Zračna luka Airport
Zvonik Bell-tower, campanile
Žal Beach
Ždrilo Gorge
Županija County

ARTISTIC AND ARCHITECTURAL TERMS

Apse Semicircular recess at the altar (usually eastern) end of a church.

Baldachin Canopy, often resting on columns, above main altar.

Cardo Principal north–south street in a Roman town.

Caryatid Pillars in the form of women, often decorating the facade of a building.

Ciborium See "Baldachin".

Decumanus Principal east–west street in a Roman town.

Incunabula Books printed before 1500.

Lapidarium Collection of sculpture.

Lunette Semicircular niche above a doorway or portal.

Peristyle Colonnade surrounding a courtyard or building.

Polyptych Painting on several joined wooden panels.

Plutej Pleatwork design characteristic of early medieval Croatian stonecarving.

Revelin Bastion; defensive tower.

Secession Movement of artists who split from Vienna's Academy of Arts in 1897. Also used more generally as a term roughly synonymous with Art Nouveau.

POLITICAL AND HISTORICAL TERMS

Austria-Hungary Official name adopted by the Habsburg Empire in 1867, designed to make the Hungarians feel that they were equal partners with the Austrians in the imperial enterprise.

AVNOJ Anti-fascist council of national liberation of Yugoslavia. Provisional parliament established by the Partisans during World War II. First convened in Jajce, Bosnia-Hercegovina, in 1943.

Ban Governor or viceroy. Title given to rulers of Croatia appointed by Hungarian (later Austrian) monarchs.

Blijesak "Flash". Name given to the Croatian Army offensive which drove Serbian forces out of western Slavonia in 1995.

Bošnjak Bosnian Muslim.

Četnik Serbian irregular fighter. The term was first coined during the anti-Turkish struggles of the nineteenth century and subsequently used to describe nationalist anti-communists in World War II, then Serbian forces active in Croatia and Bosnia in 1991–95.

Domovinski rat "Homeland War". Official Croatian name for the 1991–95 conflict.

Dragovoljac Croatian volunteer in the Domovinski rat (see above).

Dual Monarchy Another name for Austria-Hungary (see above).

Glagolitic The script used by the Croatian Church in the early Middle Ages. Survived in some areas of Istria and the Kvarner region until the early nineteenth century, when it was replaced by the Latin script.

Habsburg Empire The central European state ruled by the Habsburg family, who first gained control of parts of Austria in the early thirteenth century, and went on to control an empire comprising – among others – Germans, Italians, Czechs, Slovaks, Hungarians, Slovenes and Croats. The empire was broken up in 1918.

Hajduk Brigand. Romantically associated with popular struggles against the Turks, the term has positive connotations for Croats, Serbs, Bulgarians and other southeast European peoples.

HDZ Croatian Democratic Union. Right-of-centre pro-independence political movement formed in 1989 and led by Franjo Tuđman. The governing party in Croatia from 1990 to 2000.

HRT Croatian Radio and Television. The main state-owned broadcasting network.

Hrvatski narodni preporod Croatian National Renaissance. Name given to the the the mid-nineteenth-century upsurge in Croatian culture, language and consciousness.

HVO Croatian Defence Council. Formed by Croats in Bosnia-Hecegovina to organize themselves militarily against the Serbs (and subsequently Muslims) in the Bosnian war of 1992–95.

Illyria Roman name for the territories which are nowadays roughly covered by the states of Croatia, Bosnia-Hercegovina, Serbia and Albania. The term was resurrected by Napoleon in 1805 with the creation of the Illyrian Provinces, which stretched from Villach in southern Austria to Dubrovnik in Dalmatia. Some Western writers continued to use the term "Illyria" to describe the South Slav lands throughout the nineteenth century.

Illyrianism Early nineteenth-century Croatian cultural movement which stressed the linguistic affinities of Croats and Serbs.

JNA Yugoslav People's Army. Official title of Yugoslavia's army from 1945 to 1991. Generally sided with the Serbs during the 1991–92 conflict.

Knez Prince, duke or (in Dubrovnik and other Dalmatian towns) city governor or rector.

Kralj King.

Military Frontier (Vojna krajina in Croatian; Militärgrenze in German). Belt of territory running along Croatia's border with Ottoman-controlled Bosnia-Hercegovina, created in the early sixteenth century and finally dismantled in the mid-nineteenth. Designed to prevent Ottoman expansion, it was under the direct rule of Habsburg military bodies in Graz or Vienna.

Mletačka Republika Republic of Venice.

NDH Puppet Croatian state established under Nazi auspices 1941–45.

Non-Aligned Movement Created by Tito, Nehru and Nasser to give a voice to countries which existed outside the East–West divisions of the Cold War.

Oluja "Storm". The Croatian offensive of August 1995 which finally defeated secessionist Serb forces and brought an end to the war in Croatia.

Pacta Conventa Agreement of 1102 which recognized the right of the Hungarian king to the Croatian crown.

Partisan Anti-fascist fighter in World War II.

Ragusa Old name for Dubrovnik.

RS Serbian Republic. Name adopted by Serbian-controlled areas of Bosnia after 1992.

RSK Republic of the Serbian Krajina. Serbian name for the territories controlled by Serbian secessionists in Croatia 1991–95.

Sabor Assembly, parliament.

SDP Social Democratic Party. Successor to the SKH. Principal opposition party from 1990 to 2000, and leading partner in the coalition elected to power in January 2000.

Self-management. System whereby factories and businesses were run by workers' councils. Developed in the 1950s to distinguish Yugoslav communism from the Soviet model.

SKH Croatian League of Communists.

SKJ Yugoslav League of Communists.

Uskok see box on p.187.

Ustaša (plural Ustaše). Croatian Nazi movement formed by Ante Pavelić which came to power with German help in 1941, forming the NDH.

INDEX

Stay in touch with us!

ROUGH*NEWS* **is Rough Guides' free newsletter.
In four issues a year we give you news, travel
issues, music reviews, readers' letters and the
latest dispatches from authors on the road.**

ROUGH GUIDES: Travel

AVAILABLE AT ALL GOOD BOOKSHOPS

ROUGH GUIDES: Mini Guides, Travel Specials and Phrasebooks

MINI GUIDES
Antigua
Bangkok
Barbados
Big Island of
 Hawaii
Boston
Brussels
Budapest

Sydney
Tokyo
Toronto

Egyptian Arabic
European
French
German
Greek
Hindi & Urdu
Hungarian
Indonesian
Italian
Japanese

Dublin
Edinburgh
Florence
Honolulu
Jerusalem
Lisbon
London
 Restaurants
Madrid
Maui
Melbourne
New Orleans
Rome
Seattle
St Lucia

TRAVEL SPECIALS
First-Time Asia
First-Time
 Europe
Women Travel

Mandarin
 Chinese
Mexican
 Spanish
Polish
Portuguese
Russian
Spanish
Swahili
Thai
Turkish
Vietnamese

PHRASEBOOKS
Czech
Dutch

ROUGH GUIDES:
Reference and Music CDs

REFERENCE
Classical Music
Classical:
  100 Essential CDs
Drum'n'bass
House Music
Jazz
Music USA

Opera
Opera:
  100 Essential CDs
Reggae
Reggae:
  100 Essential CDs
Rock
Rock:
  100 Essential CDs
Techno
World Music
World Music:
  100 Essential CDs
English Football
European Football

Internet
Millennium

ROUGH GUIDE MUSIC CDs
Music of the
  Andes
Australian
  Aboriginal
Brazilian Music
Cajun & Zydeco

Classic Jazz
Music of
  Colombia
Cuban Music
Eastern Europe

Music of Egypt
English Roots
  Music
Flamenco
India & Pakistan
Irish Music
Music of Japan
Kenya & Tanzania
Native American
North African
Music of Portugal

Reggae
Salsa
Scottish Music
South African
  Music
Music of Spain
Tango
Tex-Mex
West African
  Music
World Music
World Music Vol 2
Music of
  Zimbabwe

AVAILABLE AT ALL GOOD BOOKSHOPS